SAUCES

CLASSICAL AND CONTEMPORARY SAUCE MAKING

SAUCES

CLASSICAL AND CONTEMPORARY SAUCE MAKING

FOURTH EDITION

JAMES PETERSON

Houghton Mifflin Harcourt

BOSTON   NEW YORK   2017

TO MEGAN MOORE

www.hmhco.com

LIBRARY OF CONGRESS CATALOGING-IN-PUBLICATION DATA IS AVAILABLE.
ISBN 978-0-544-81982-5 (hbk); 978-0-544-81983-2 (ebk)

Book design by Vertigo Design NYC

Printed in China

SCP 10 9 8 7 6 5 4 3 2 1

CONTENTS

RECIPE CONTENTS

18 PURÉES AND PURÉE-THICKENED SAUCES

19 PASTA SAUCES

20 ASIAN SAUCES

21 DESSERT SAUCES

ACKNOWLEDGMENTS

When the end of a book project approaches, I'm amazed by how many people are needed to make an idea a reality. I must start by thanking my editor, Stephanie Fletcher, who has been with me since the beginning of this new revision. She not only guided the schedule (such as imposing deadlines on me), but learned along with me the many new concepts presented in this edition.

I'd like to thank production editor Jamie Selzer, art director Melissa Lotfy, and production coordinator Kevin Watt, and designer Alison Lew at Vertigo Design, for their amazing input into the design of the book. Copy editors are essential in my life, as much would slip by otherwise. Thank you, Suzanne Fass, copy editor with relentless attention to detail.

Here, at my studio/office, I've had the pleasure to work with some amazing people, mostly young, who inspire me and help propel me to the next stage. Julia Choi provided the hands in the earlier part of the book and gave me a unique perspective on Korean cooking. Jermaine Haughton was here from the beginning. We used his hands in some of the photos, but more important, he kept the computer and the camera software working. Ricky Dolinsky is one of those crazy people whom I am instantly drawn to. He has a mind grounded in the scientific method. He also happens to know a lot about modernist cuisine. So his hands not only appear in the photos, but he helped me test recipes and provided valuable ideas.

It must be said that artists build upon each other's work. I would have been lost without The Cooking Lab's giant opus, *Modernist Cuisine*. I must also acknowledge the contributions of Hervé This, who was kind enough to interview with me on my last visit to Paris. Thanks also to the team at Modernist Pantry (modernistpantry.com) for answering my many questions.

There are some people without whom my life would be very different. Laurie Knoop has been by my side for well over a decade. She follows my work and provides invaluable help. She introduced me to Jermaine, Julia, and Ricky. I couldn't do what I do without her.

My friend Rhona Poritzky keeps me in one piece by calling every day from Paris. Joel Hoffman has saved me from much of the torture of writing alone when assaulted by uncertainty and doubt. My love for Paul Geltner, whom I've known since we studied together in Paris in the late seventies, sustains me through much. I have other friends, Coletta Perry, Megan Moore, and Sukey Pett, who have always encouraged me, loved me, and pushed me to higher goals.

My agents, Elise and Arnold Goodman, have been with me since the first edition of *Sauces*, over twenty-five years ago, and have fought for me for all that time.

My husband, Zelik Mintz, is not only my spouse, but my best friend. We have been together for twenty-six years.

FOREWORD FROM THE FIRST EDITION

Sauces: Classical and Contemporary Sauce Making, faithful to its title, is a synthesis of the past and present. At nearly a century's remove, James Peterson has done for sauces that which Escoffier did for the cuisine of *La Belle Époque*: simplifying and streamlining methods and techniques and lightening the food to meet the demands of an ever more hurried society, while respecting the architecture of traditional cuisine and stressing the vital importance of fresh produce.

In his introduction to the first edition of *Le Guide Culinaire*, Escoffier wrote, "I wanted to create a tool, rather than a book…a constant companion, always within hand's reach… it is reserved especially for young people; for those who, beginning today, will be leaders in their field twenty years hence." No words could serve as a better introduction to *Sauces*.

Sauces is, above all, a manual for the professional cook and as such, it will rapidly become a classic and indispensable reference in professional kitchens. But it is much more than a manual, it is a romance as well—James Peterson's romance with the kitchen—and it is easily accessible to the home cook, to whom particular explanations and suggestions are addressed throughout. There are important sections on improvisation replete with hints and possible paths to follow, lest the reader forget that cooking is a creative art. But that creativity cannot exist in a vacuum; the cook must have a firm hold on the basic precepts of cooking before spreading his or her wings.

After a couple of decades of anarchy and chaos in the kitchen disguised as *la nouvelle cuisine*, a treatise such as *Sauces*, grounded in common sense, infuses one with renewed faith.

−RICHARD OLNEY

PREFACE TO THE FOURTH EDITION

When *Sauces* was translated into French, the translator proposed the title *L'Art de Bien Cuisiner* (*The Art of Cooking Well*) because she realized that the book is about much more than sauces. To prepare a sauce well, especially an integral sauce made from the juices released by the food being prepared, one must know how to cook. Some of these methods are simple (beurre blanc, despite its reputation, is a snap) while others, such as a perfectly caramelized jus, can be tricky.

In the first edition of *Sauces*, I integrated the techniques of *la nouvelle cuisine*—learned in France in the 1970s—with classic sauces, some dating from centuries past. I brought forth the distinction between "integral" sauces and "non-integral" sauces, two terms I invented to describe foods in which the sauce is either derived from juices released by the food being cooked or, in the case of "non-integral" sauces, from stock and/or other ingredients often designed to emulate integral sauces. I also introduced the notion of unbound sauces, best served in soup plates, containing no thickener and no fat.

The second edition introduced so-called foreign sauces (meaning not French) and included hierarchical systems for cuisines such as Indian and Chinese. While these cuisines don't receive the attention of French classics and their derivatives in this book, I do introduce methods for improvising such sauces. In any case, many of the techniques first presented in earlier editions are applicable to these cuisines.

The third edition further expanded the premises of the earlier editions by adding recipes that illustrate additional nuances.

This fourth edition includes the most radical additions, those of so-called modernist cuisine. The emphasis is on using these techniques and ingredients within the context of more traditional approaches. Modernist techniques and ingredients are given relevance by how they function within the classic/nouvelle cuisine/mother sauce continuum and hierarchy. In my preface to the third edition, I stated that the dining public had become insistent on having a sauce with every dish. Of course, this gave my book a raison d'être, but the public, fickle as it is, has come to look at some traditional sauces as archaic. While much of the premise of my book is based on sauces that reflect and extend the flavors of the food at hand, "modern" sauces have become condiment-like in that they may taste nothing like the food they are saucing—they are designed to offer contrast. Such has been the tectonic shift in the way most Americans dine today.

Sauces exist along a continuum with highly contrasting sauces on one end (such as tartar sauce, mustard, ketchup, chimichurri sauce) and integral sauces on the other end, of which the archetype is a natural jus. While over time our tastes and expectations have shifted toward contrasting sauces, like anything in the culinary world, this will no doubt change.

While *Sauces* does indeed address condiments, my feeling is that they can emerge straight from the imagination and don't require an elaborate, hierarchical, and interlocking system. Some distinctions do exist: Chutneys are different than relishes, and dipping sauces are different than glazes. With these and other simple distinctions, chefs can easily categorize their creations and work within a loose system to invent condiment sauces.

While there are those who question a rigid system that has evolved over centuries, it has long been my feeling that artistic creativity is best accomplished within limits, be they rules, budget, or limited access to ingredients. The unconscious seems to work best when it isn't given absolute free rein.

My goal has been to synthesize the methods, techniques, and ingredients used in Western (and to a lesser degree in Eastern) cooking into a large, well-integrated system. For example, a classic bordelaise sauce is made with demi-glace that itself has been thickened with flour. A nouvelle cuisine version is likely to include *glace de viande* (thickened with reduction alone) and a fair amount of butter. A modernist version might include an emulsifier or emulsion stabilizer, such as liquid lecithin, worked into the butter before it is whisked into the sauce.

This fourth edition provides a quantum leap in that it addresses many of the techniques, equipment, and ingredients used in "modernist" cooking, a term first made popular by Nathan Myhrvold and his team in their magnificent five-volume set *Modernist Cuisine*. While many of us associate modernist cooking with elaborate and meticulously prepared foods served in rarefied settings, its techniques and ingredients can be incorporated into virtually all types of sauces. One characteristic of this new approach is the use of ingredients that may to some sound like suspect chemicals. Most of these ingredients are organic and derived from natural sources like seaweed, algae, various fermented roots, and an immense variety of tapioca flour derivatives. Most revolutionary is the use of hydrocolloids, substances that thicken, emulsify, or stabilize emulsions. These ingredients are usually used in minute quantities and, unless used incorrectly, have little or no flavor of their own. While many modernist preparations border on the bizarre and seem to rely on unconventional juxtapositions, flavors, and surprise, in *Sauces*, they are integrated into a traditional system that includes classic sauces, nouvelle cuisine sauces, unbound sauces, and modernist sauces.

This new edition contains a newly constructed liaison chart that compares the thickening power of various starches, fats, and hydrocolloids. For example, you might want to use xanthan gum to thicken a sauce having the consistency of a beurre blanc. A glance at the chart will show the amount of xanthan gum, or other ingredient, required to make a sauce of similar thickness.

I believe that we needn't be restricted to any single technique, tradition, or system, but that all three approaches—classic, nouvelle, and modernist—can be used by the saucier to create a finished sauce. An example might be a béarnaise in which the egg yolks are stabilized with an emulsifier or hydrocolloid and the finished sauce piped out with a whipping siphon. With all this in mind, the saucier will need to integrate these various ingredients and techniques to make a finished sauce designed depending on budget, formality, and availability of ingredients. For example, a stock can be reduced six times or so (instead of fifteen times for demi-glace and thirty times for glace de viande) and thickened with a delicate hydrocolloid. Depending on its style, the sauce may then be finished with cream and/or butter in varying amounts. Or cream and butter can be dispensed with and the sauce finished with beurre manié or other traditional thickener. Or the sauce may be left unbound.

When you better understand the underlying traditions that underscore our work, you are able to expand and invent, making your own contributions to this complex and varied art.

PREFACE FROM THE FIRST EDITION

Sauce making allows the cook more freedom to work with flavors, textures, and color than any other area of cooking. A carefully constructed sauce is often prepared in several stages. Each stage has rules of its own and requires the close attention of the chef, cook, or saucier. Unlike roasts or cakes, which need only to be checked from time to time, the construction of a sauce requires constant tasting and fine tuning to balance its flavors and perfect its consistency.

A sauce is never eaten alone but exists to complement the food it is designed to accompany. Some sauces function as condiments by contrasting with foods, as mustard balances the richness of pork or the direct flavor of grilled foods. Other sauces—the natural drippings from a roast or the liquid from a stew—extend the intrinsic flavors of foods. Most sauces lie between these two poles: Disparate or contrasting tastes are superimposed over a background of the food's natural flavors.

In the last twenty years, many of the techniques of sauce making have changed. Chefs are not only eager to invent new taste combinations and improve upon older methods but have set out to make sauces healthier and less rich. In the 1970s, chefs in France and the United States began to eliminate flour—a standard ingredient since the eighteenth century—from their sauces and replace it with cream and butter. The latest trend is to eliminate the cream and butter and experiment with even newer methods.

Most of the training available to chefs does little to explain these newer sauce-making techniques, and the typical beginning cook is forced to learn them on the job. No amount of book learning can provide a substitute for hands-on experience, but it is helpful to understand the concepts of sauce making and to have a rudimentary knowledge of how ingredients behave and why.

Sauces presents the basic sauce-making techniques that have been used in the past and that are popular today. Because most discussions of sauce making found in textbooks or books on French cooking for the amateur contain only variations of classic sauces or a cursory treatment of contemporary methods, both approaches are discussed and analyzed herein. With a fundamental knowledge of the variety of sauce-making methods available, the chef can make his or her own decisions based on the needs of the clientele, the budget, and style of the restaurant.

Sauces is meant to encourage the chef or saucier to improvise. Basic sauce-making concepts are emphasized, and recipes that exemplify the techniques are included, but this book is not designed as a collection of sauce recipes. An attempt is made to show how liquids, flavorings, and thickeners work and to explain traditional approaches and combinations that will provide the chief with technical guidelines and underlying aesthetic principles.

Although *Sauces* can be used as a quick reference guide, a useful approach is to read it through for ideas and then to apply the ideas to the ingredients on hand, the guests, the wines, and the seasons. A basic concept is far more powerful for an improvising chef than a recipe, because concepts can be adapted to a far greater variety of ingredients and situations.

The number and kinds of sauces served during a meal must be well thought out. Sauce-making expertise is of little value if the arrangement and juxtaposition of the sauces are not carefully planned and the myriad factors inherent in the design of a meal closely considered. Every meal is an event that happens only once—a kind of reflection or distillation or a grouping of people in a particular setting.

Remember not to serve too many sauces in a single meal; one is often appropriate, and two is usually the maximum. If more than one sauce is served at the same meal, make sure that the flavors, colors, and textures of the sauces contrast while the style remains the same. The time of year and the formality of the meal will significantly affect the kinds of sauces that are best to serve.

Beginning chefs and amateur cooks sometimes include too many contrasting colors or flavors on the same plate. It is better to meld the flavors of a sauce carefully into an integral and seemingly simple whole than to cover the plate with different-flavored garnitures or more than one sauce. Usually sauces (and foods) move from light to dark and from cold to hot in the succession of courses, to avoid fatiguing the palate (or the eye). Avoid strong sauces at the beginning of the meal unless you are planning to follow through with something at least equally robust.

Sauces should be chosen according to the style and formality of a meal. An aioli or a Mexican salsa is more likely to be served at an informal summer lunch than is a sauce poivrade, which is classic, formal, and best for fall or winter.

Sauces is organized around the principles of classic French cooking. This is not because classic French sauces are inherently better than regional sauces or sauces from other countries, but because they are based on a rigid and systematic framework that is easy to remember, build on, and refer to.

Although French cooking also has an elaborate vocabulary for discussing sauce making and general cooking techniques, much of the traditional nomenclature is confusing and contradictory. Many of the cornerstone sauces of French cooking have changed or are made in new ways. Much of this nomenclature is explained in both the text and glossary.

Despite its French orientation, the concepts and techniques explained in this book can be adapted to other cuisines. Once the saucier is familiar with basic sauce-making techniques and understands how various ingredients behave, he or she will be able to invent new combinations, devise new interpretations of classics, and more easily execute unfamiliar recipes.

A SHORT HISTORY OF SAUCE MAKING

Perhaps in no period in history have a nation's eating habits changed so profoundly as during the last three decades. Until twenty or thirty years ago, it seemed that the history of sauce making and cooking was complete. Thirty years ago, if asked about the future of classical cooking, a French chef would likely have replied that all the classical dishes had been invented by the end of the nineteenth century and that there was no place for new combinations or techniques. In spite of this, the previous decades have seen the advent of *nouvelle cuisine*, with its increased experimentation and richer preparations; an increased familiarity with flavorful ingredients from around the globe; and most recently the simultaneous ascendance of two diametrically opposed movements—farm-to-table cooking and modernist cuisine. After a long period of established culinary canon, few would have predicted the sophistication and enthusiasm for cooking that exists today.

Why begin with a history of sauce making? A rule of cooking—and of other creative arts—is that creation must take place in the context of a tradition and set of aesthetic values. At a time when creativity and originality in cooking are considered more important than reliably executing classic dishes, one of the difficulties confronting American chefs is the lack of a rigid traditional system of cooking like the system that France adopted in the middle of the nineteenth century, which went virtually unchallenged for over a hundred years. America has a rich culinary heritage, but its cooking from many different regions has never crystallized into a national cuisine. While the limitations imposed by a rigid traditional system can be stultifying, they also provide structure. This protects the chef who is working out a combination of flavors, an innovative presentation, or a new juxtaposition of textures from eccentricity and excess.

Many chefs have been (and some still are) stifled by the dogmatism of classical French cooking. Until recently, straying from classic tradition was considered heretical and signified only ignorance or audacity on the part of the chef. Creativity was limited to interpretation within the classic structure.

As an American teaching in a French cooking school, I was particularly suspect if I deviated even slightly from classic norms. Any innovation or improvement was dismissed as an American eccentricity. My only defense was to find the idea in the literature of French cooking. By delving far enough back, it became clear that "classical" French cooking was only a stage in the evolution of cooking, rather than the culmination and assimilation of the entire history of French cooking. I also discovered that most seemingly new, even startling, combinations had been used before.

A true history of sauce making is not easy to chart. Research is limited to the written word, which until the nineteenth century described only the eating habits of the rich. Cookbooks, which have been around for thousands of years, describe an era's affinity for certain flavors and ingredients, but early cookbooks rarely give quantities. Left merely with a description of flavors and techniques, it is hard to guess how foods tasted. But a description of how flavors have been used over the centuries is often surprising—dishes that seem new or even eccentric often have a lengthy history. Veal with raspberries, roast meats with saffron and ginger, chicken with oysters—all were written about from 500 to 200 years ago.

Cookbooks also fail to describe the context of foods within a meal. Recipes are presented with little or no description of how they should be served, in what order, or with what wines. When nineteenth-century authors describe meals in a social context (Balzac and Zola are good sources), we begin to get a sense of how rich and poor ate and which foods were reserved for special occasions.

ANCIENT GREEK COOKING

Some historians have theorized that the Greek dietetic system, which was closely linked with Greek medicine, had a powerful influence on both Western European and Middle Eastern cuisine. Unfortunately, no complete copies of Greek cookbooks survive. Much of what we know of Greek gastronomy is found in the writings of Archestrate, which focus on the origin of the products—giving recommendations on how to purchase various foods, especially fish—rather than the techniques used in their preparation. The cooking techniques that are mentioned are simple and direct—usually frying or roasting. (Archestrate's most famous recipe recommends that a hare be roasted rare and simply sprinkled with salt.) Cheese and oil are often used in sauces and are sometimes flavored with cumin. One fish recipe warns against preparation by a Sicilian or an Italian, who will "ruin it with too much cheese, vinegar, and asafetida-infused brine."

ANCIENT ROMAN COOKING

Much of our knowledge of Roman cooking comes from Marcus Gavius Apicius, who lived in the first century AD. Many of the ingredients used in Apicius's recipes are seen again in medieval European cooking. Although reproductions of his manuscripts have been available in Europe since the Middle Ages, it is difficult to know whether the style of medieval European cooking was a direct result of his influence or the natural outcome of preparing food in a particular cultural and geographical climate.

Although many of the ingredients in Apicius's text are familiar and sometimes even appetizing to the modern reader, we have little idea how they tasted because of the almost universal use of *garum*. Garum, a liquid mixture based on fish entrails, was used abundantly in Roman cooking, not only alone as a sauce but in combination with other ingredients such as leeks, onions, a wide variety of spices, wine, honey, and olive oil. Apparently it was not a haphazard conglomeration of ingredients: A note in Apicius's *De re coquinaria* describes a remedy for garum that has taken on an unpleasant odor or too salty a taste, implying that there were criteria for garum. We can only guess how it tasted; the closest modern equivalents are probably the fermented fish sauces used in Southeast Asian cooking (*nampla* in Thailand, *nuoc mam* in Vietnam, *patis* in the Philippines).

Most Roman sauces, in addition to garum, called for honey as well as a variety of spices and herbs. Many of these are still used today but are more common in Asian cooking than in European cuisines: cumin, coriander leaves (cilantro), lovage, asafetida (a stinky spice that turns surprisingly mild when cooked, popular in Indian cooking), rue, dill, bay (laurel) berries, and caraway. Wine and vinegar were often used in Roman cooking, but the wines that were served—and probably used in cooking—were often flavored with spices and combined with honey. The Roman predilection for adding honey to wine probably indicates that naturally fermented sweet wines were not common. There are, however, references to a sweet wine made with raisins (*passo*). Sauces were sometimes colored with wine that had been cooked down (*defritum*) to an intense inky color.

Many Roman recipes tell the reader to "bind" the sauce, often without saying what to use. Some recipes mention starch. Others suggest whole eggs.

Below are several sauces translated from Apicius's *De re coquinaria* (via the French translation by Jacques André; bracketed additions are mine).

CUMIN SAUCE FOR OYSTERS. [Crushed] pepper, [chopped] lovage, parsley, dried mint, malobathre [cassia leaves, related to but not to be confused with cinnamon, which at the time was worth more than its weight in gold], a little more [sic] cumin, honey, vinegar, and garum.

SAUCE FOR GOURDS. Grind together pepper, cumin, and rue. Cover the mixture of spices with vinegar, garum, and a small amount of oil. Cook the sliced gourds in the sauce. Bind the sauce with starch, and sprinkle with pepper.

CELERY PURÉE. Boil the celery in water containing bicarbonate of soda [technique sometimes used today to keep vegetables green]. Drain and chop finely. With a mortar and pestle, grind together pepper, lovage, oregano, onion. Moisten the mixture with wine, garum, and oil. Cook the spice mixture in a pot, and add the chopped celery.

SAUCE FOR CARDOONS. Grind together fresh rue, mint, coriander, and fennel. Add pepper, lovage, honey, garum, and oil.

COOKING IN THE MIDDLE AGES

There is very little literature describing the cuisine of Europe—indeed, there is very little literature of any sort—between the fall of Rome and the late Middle Ages. Most historians agree that the cooking of Europe was influenced by the Saracens, whose cuisine was in turn influenced by the ancient Greeks. The limited number of cookery books of medieval Europe reflect the influence of Middle Eastern ingredients (often originating in India) and the acquired tastes of the returning Crusaders.

Many Crusaders to the Middle East in the eleventh, twelfth, and thirteenth centuries found the lifestyle there more inviting and never returned to Europe. Those who did return brought back ingredients never before tasted in Europe, including sugar (in cane form), almonds, pistachios, pomegranates, citrus fruits, and spinach. Spices had been used in Western Europe since Roman times, but their variety was limited, and they were served only in noble and royal circles. As the Crusaders returned, the use of spices became more common, as they not only provided flavor but probably masked the taste of tainted meat.

Verjuice (the unsweetened juice of unripe grapes and sometimes crabapples) and vinegar are most often called for when a liquid is needed. In later manuscripts influenced by Middle Eastern cooking, orange and lemon juice were sometimes used.

Verjuice and vinegar are distinctly sour ingredients, and the Saracens and Western Europeans juxtaposed them with sweeteners. Honey and dried fruits were used initially but were partially replaced with sugar, which remained quite rare and was treated as a spice. The medieval *brouet* (a kind of liquid stew) was sometimes sweetened with dates, raisins, or sugar.

The modern system of preparing stocks had not yet appeared, but beef bouillon and the cooking liquids of both meats and fish were bound with bread, almonds, and egg yolks to convert them into sauces.

Almost every medieval recipe includes spices such as saffron, ginger, nutmeg, cloves, cinnamon, cardamom, and long pepper. Rarely was the flavor or nuance of one spice emphasized in contrast with a dish. Instead, most dishes contain three or more spices with seemingly little attention to their relationship. Medieval texts (Taillevent's *Le Viandier* and *Le Ménagier de Paris*) are filled with recipes for soups and ragoûts in which the element being prepared—liver, meat, fish—is puréed and used to bind the liquid.

When bread or almonds were used to bind sauces, they were pounded together at the beginning and moistened with verjuice, vinegar, wine, almond milk, and sometimes cow's milk. When used, egg yolks were beaten and added at the end, just as they are today. In some recipes, liver (it is often not clear what kind) is used to thicken the sauce.

Although we do not know what the exact textures of sauces were like in medieval cooking, the eating habits of the times would have made it difficult if not impossible to appreciate a delicately balanced sauce. Most foods were served on thick slices of bread (trenchers) instead of plates and eaten with the fingers instead of with forks. If a sauce were too thin, it would have been absorbed by the bread. More than likely, sauces were thickened so they would cling to the foods and stay on top of the trenchers. Later, as plates came into more widespread use, it became possible to make thinner, more delicately thickened and flavored sauces that would not disappear into the bread. Two recipes from Taillevent's *Le Viandier* follow.

BROUET DE CANELLE. Cook a chicken in water and wine or other liquid. Remove it from the liquid, and cut it into quarters. Cook the quarters in fat. Cook unpeeled almonds and cinnamon in beef broth. Grind them and strain them with beef bouillon, and moisten the chicken pieces with this liquid. Add verjuice, ginger, cloves, grains of paradise [*Aframomum melegueta*]. The sauce should be well bound.

BROUET GORGIÉ. Cut the chicken or meat being prepared into pieces. Cook the pieces in lard with finely chopped parsley and onions. Take livers, lightly toasted bread, wine, and beef broth, and boil everything together [the text is not clear whether these are boiled with the meat or separately]. Simmer the mixture until it thickens, and flavor with ginger, cloves, and saffron. Add verjuice.

SPICE MIXTURE

Here is a spice mixture written about in the middle of the sixteenth century. Long pepper, grains of paradise, and galangal are sold online. Galangal can be found in shops that sell Thai ingredients.

YIELD: ½ CUP (125 MILLILITERS)

ground ginger	3 tablespoons	45 milliliters
freshly ground black pepper	2 teaspoons	10 milliliters
grated nutmeg	1 tablespoon	15 milliliters
grains of paradise, ground in a coffee grinder	1 tablespoon	15 milliliters
ground cinnamon	1 tablespoon	15 milliliters
long pepper, ground in a coffee grinder	1 tablespoon	15 milliliters
ground cloves	2 teaspoons	10 milliliters
ground galangal (also called laos)	1 tablespoon	15 milliliters

Stir together all the ingredients and store in a tightly sealed container in the freezer.

Use to dust chicken and seafood to lend a medieval flavor.

Adapting Medieval Recipes

Adapting historical recipes to modern tastes is an exciting means of designing new dishes that are still grounded in culinary tradition. The flavors, textures, and colors inherent in an old recipe can be adapted to modern tastes without losing sight of the original recipe. References to the aesthetic of the original can be made without compromising the dish's flavor or appeal.

One can only guess at the intensity and balance of the flavors. Most authors assume that the spices were used in large quantities. Some have also assumed that spices were used carelessly because many spices were used in one preparation. Whether or not these assumptions are true is irrelevant to the modern cook, who is free to adapt historical recipes to today's tastes. Obviously the quantities of spices used can be adjusted to taste, and a variety of spices in the same dish—as Indian curries prove—does not necessarily imply a careless hodgepodge of flavors.

The choice of liaison requires liberty on the part of the chef. Although bread is an interesting liaison (see "Bread," page 126), a bread-thickened sauce may not be appealing in a contemporary dish. Binding sauces with nut butters, however, is both authentic and satisfying.

When experimenting with an unknown dish in which a variety of flavors meld—such as a medieval recipe containing three or more spices—infuse the spices individually in small amounts of liquid, such as stock or cream, and then gradually combine the liquids until the flavors of the spices are in balance.

GOLD-PLATED CHICKEN WITH GINGER, SAFFRON, AND ALMONDS

This modern adaptation is not based on any particular recipe but is taken from several recipes in Taillevent's *Le Viandier* (fourteenth- and fifteenth-century manuscripts). Ginger, saffron, and mint are the principal flavorings; ginger and saffron were the spices most often called for in medieval recipes, and mint was one of the most commonly used herbs. The sauce is bound with almond butter, a typical medieval liaison (bread can also be used). Green-colored marzipan almonds and pomegranate seeds are used as the garniture. The almonds are a reference to the medieval cook's tendency to fashion one food from another to surprise and titillate the diner. They are sweet (and surprisingly good with the sauce), recalling the inclination to juxtapose the savory with the sweet in the medieval meal. The gold plating is extravagant and can be eliminated (or silver leaf can be substituted), but it is taken from an authentic recipe. Gold and silver foil are still used in Indian cooking to decorate desserts. Medieval diners were fond of bright colors, hence the gold, pomegranate seeds, saffron, and colored almonds.

YIELD: 4 SERVINGS

chicken, quartered, 1	3 pounds	1.4 kilograms
salt and pepper	to taste	to taste
butter or lard	2 ounces	60 grams
onion, chopped	1 medium	1 medium
white chicken stock	2 cups	500 milliliters
almond paste	2 ounces	55 grams
green food coloring or chlorophyll	several drops	several drops
pomegranate	1	1
saffron threads, soaked in 1 tablespoon hot water	1 pinch	1 pinch
finely grated fresh ginger	2 teaspoons	10 milliliters
mint leaves	1 small bunch	1 small bunch
almond butter (page 442)	2 tablespoons	30 milliliters
gold or silver leaf	as needed	as needed

(continued)

1. Season the chicken pieces with salt and pepper. In a 4-quart (4 liter) straight-sided sauté pan, cook the seasoned chicken pieces over medium heat, skin side down, in the butter or lard. After about 15 minutes, turn and cook until the flesh side is browned and the chicken is firm to the touch, about 10 minutes more. Avoid burning the butter. Remove the chicken and keep warm.

2. Add the onions to the butter in the pan and lightly brown.

3. Add the stock to the pan and reduce it down to a little less than a cup. Skim carefully. Strain and transfer to a 2-quart saucepan.

4. While the chicken is resting, work the almond paste with the food coloring until it is bright green. Shape the colored paste into 12 almonds and set aside.

5. Remove and reserve the seeds from the pomegranate. Discard the flesh.

6. Add the saffron threads and their soaking liquid to the saucepan with the stock.

7. Add the ginger to the liquid in the saucepan and let it infuse for 5 minutes. Chop the mint and add it to the pan.

8. Whisk in the almond butter until the sauce has the desired consistency. Season with salt and pepper. Strain the sauce if desired.

9. Apply the gold or silver leaf: Press the gold side of the foil onto the chicken, then gently peel away the backing **(see photo)**.

10. Serve the chicken with the sauce, pomegranate seeds, and green almonds.

RENAISSANCE COOKING: THE SIXTEENTH CENTURY

Surprisingly little has been written about cooking in the sixteenth century. In France one important book was published, a translation of Bartolomeo Platina's *De Honeste voluptate*. Whereas most other books were based on earlier works and were medieval in character, Platina gives us a deeper understanding of both the cooking and the priorities of Renaissance Italy and France. During the Renaissance and for several centuries thereafter, culinary methods were closely linked to health and medicine. Much of Platina's writing was influenced by medieval medicine, which itself was based on Greek medicine with its elaborate system of humors and emphasis on the use of diet to balance the basic "personalities": sanguine, phlegmatic, choleric, and melancholic.

The ingredient that appears in greater quantities in sixteenth-century recipes is sugar. Although by no means inexpensive, refining methods made it more accessible than it had been during the Middle Ages. Coupled with intense interest in gardening and cultivation, this resulted in new methods of preserving fruit, including jellies and jams as they are known today. Previously, fruits were preserved by drying or by storage in vinegar and honey.

LEEKS WITH ALMOND MILK, CINNAMON, AND ROSES

Almond milk, extracted from almonds using hot water, was popular in medieval and Renaissance cooking as a substitute for dairy products. It can still be used today for its flavor and for vegan cooking. The rosewater is typical of the Renaissance; it and attar of roses are obtainable at Indian groceries.

YIELD: 6 SERVINGS

whole almonds	1 cup	150 grams
sliced almonds	1 small handful	1 small handful
hot water	2 cups	500 milliliters
rosewater _or_ attar of roses	1 teaspoon _or_ 1 drop	5 milliliters _or_ 1 drop
ground cinnamon	1 small pinch	1 small pinch
heavy cream	½ cup	125 milliliters
sugar	1 teaspoon	5 milliliters
salt and pepper	to taste	to taste
leeks, greens removed, whites split lengthwise, rinsed	6 medium	6 medium

1. Preheat the oven to 350°F (175°C). Separately toast the whole almonds and sliced almonds in the oven for 15 minutes. Let cool. Set aside the sliced almonds. Grind the whole almonds in a food processor for 5 minutes or until they have a pasty consistency. Put the mixture in a pot with the hot water. Bring to a simmer and let steep for 15 minutes. Work through a fine-mesh strainer. Reserve the liquid and discard the almonds, or grind them further with a mortar and pestle to use as a sauce thickener.

2. Add the rosewater or attar of roses, cinnamon, cream, and sugar to the almond milk. Season with salt and pepper.

3. Spread the leeks in an oval baking dish just large enough to hold them and pour over the almond milk. Bake until tender, about 35 minutes. Sprinkle over the sliced almonds and serve.

THE SEVENTEENTH CENTURY

In the seventeenth century, French cooking began to distinguish itself from that of the rest of Europe; a new aesthetic developed with criteria that are much the same as those of today.

Particularly important to sauce making was the notion that food should taste of itself. Spices that disguised natural flavors were gradually abandoned. Sauces began to concentrate and emphasize the flavor of a particular dish rather than accent or distort it. Barbara Wheaton, in her book *Savoring the Past*, discusses how cooking over the centuries has gravitated from one pole to another on an aesthetic spectrum:

> Cooks and diners have long argued over whether the best cooking makes food "taste of itself" or transmutes ingredients into something new and unrecognizable. To satisfy its advocates, food that tastes of itself should be locally produced and in season, served at the peak of its natural ripeness; in contrast, transmuted food is a compound of the rare, exotic, and the difficult, made from ingredients belonging to other places and seasons and produced by techniques that require special skills or equipment. From the sixteenth century onward, both points of view have had persuasive supporters; they are the extremes to which the pendulum swings. In the late sixteenth century, the early eighteenth century, and the nineteenth century the transmutationists usually prevailed; at other times the purists have had the upper hand. At present two parts of our society are pursuing separate paths: traditionalist cooks and diners interested in fine cooking emphasize recognizable ingredients; food technologists and the mass market are more interested in the final combination of flavors. Ironically, today the simpler ingredients are likely to be more expensive. Most of us would not recognize many of the ingredients prominent in processed foods. How many of us can differentiate, with eye, nose, or palate, among hydrolyzed vegetable protein, guar gum, and BHA? Food technologists claim that they can synthesize the flavors of our familiar foods, transmuting, for example, textured soy protein into bacon. Analogously, the chefs and confectioners who served the sixteenth-century diner contrived to astonish him by clever deceptions. The plates of sugar "fish" at the reception for Elizabeth of Austria exemplify this point of view. Then, as now, the willing suspension of disbelief on the part of the diner is essential.

The most obvious manifestation of this shift from one end of the aesthetic spectrum to the other was the complete abandonment of certain medieval spices (ginger, saffron, galangal, and others) and a moderate use of modern spices, especially pepper, which were less likely to distort the intrinsic flavor of foods.

As spices were less used, chefs relied more on indigenous herbs and vegetables to supply aromatic interest to their sauces and stews. Although medieval cooks used some herbs (especially mint, parsley, and hyssop), many of the herbs we use today (including tarragon, chervil, basil, and thyme) did not enter into the culinary mainstream until the seventeenth century.

Although onions were often called for in medieval recipes, aromatic ingredients such as shallots, carrots, and celery were little mentioned until the seventeenth century. Wild mushrooms and truffles, so prized in later centuries, were first used in seventeenth-century recipes. Savory ingredients such as anchovies, capers, and cornichons (sour gherkins) also gradually made their way into French cooking and sauce making.

Another noticeable difference between cooking texts of the Middle Ages and those of the seventeenth century is the substitution of butter for lard. In Taillevent's *Le Viandier*, lard is the fat most often used for the preparation of the flavor base, usually sweated onions. In the seventeenth century, butter is used not only to brown or sweat ingredients but also as a component in sauces.

The principal liquid flavorings used in medieval sauces, vinegar and verjuice, are extremely acidic. Remnants of these sauces can be seen in simple green sauces flavored with herbs, especially mint and sorrel (see Mint Sauce for Lamb, page 486). These plain vinegar-based sauces are still sometimes served with cold roasts. Although vinegar and other acidic liquids continued to be used, their acidity was attenuated by combining them with oil (somewhat equivalent to modern cold and hot vinaigrette), coulis (like a modern sauce Robert), and butter.

The following recipe, from *L'Art de bien traiter* by L.S.R. (1674), is for a butter-bound white sauce similar to a beurre blanc. It also contains capers, anchovies, oranges, and lemons, all of which are typical seventeenth-century ingredients. The recipe, which was originally designed to be served with pike, is a fairly exact translation of the original and suggests that all the ingredients be put in the pan at the beginning. A more reliable approach would be to make an infusion with all the ingredients except the butter and then whisk in the butter in the same way as when preparing a beurre blanc.

> In a saucepan combine fresh butter, 1 or 2 spoonfuls of court-bouillon, a pinch of salt and white pepper, capers, several slices of lemon or orange, nutmeg (optional), and one anchovy (desalted and chopped). Stir the sauce with a wooden or silver spoon [over the heat] until the sauce binds and thickens. Serve the sauce immediately so that it does not turn into oil, which is most undesirable and disgusting in a bound sauce.

Medieval sauces would have contained more acidic ingredients and some additional spices, but no butter, making them very strong. This implies that the medieval concept of a sauce was similar to the modern view of condiments such as mustard. The idea of a suave, delicate sauce that gently supported the flavor of a dish had not yet come into being.

Medieval and Roman sauces often contained both sweet and sour ingredients: varying combinations of verjuice and vinegar with honey, dried fruits, cooked wine must (*raisiné*), and later, sugar. Although some of these sweet-and-sour combinations still exist—gastrique (page 193), red currant jelly in a Sauce Grand-Veneur (page 198), mint sauce for roast lamb (page 486), duck with orange sauce (page 194)—their use declined rapidly in the seventeenth century.

The basic mixtures that function as cornerstones in French cooking—the bouillons, stuffings, and liaisons—were first categorized at this time. What later became a cohesive cooking system—expanded in the eighteenth and nineteenth centuries—that still forms the basis for French cooking today started in the seventeenth century.

One of the most important innovations was the introduction of roux (*farine frite*). Before then, toasted bread was the thickener most often used in sauce making. Although bread has certain advantages (a less floury taste), roux provides a smoother-textured sauce and became the thickener of choice well into the twentieth century. When first used, roux was an integral step in the preparation of a *coulis*, the concentrated veal or beef essence that was critical to seventeenth- and eighteenth-century French cooking. The meat was cooked with bouillon and aromatic vegetables until it "attached" to the bottom of the pot and began to caramelize. (The term *pincer* was later used in French cookbooks to describe this process.) Flour was then added to the caramelized juices and cooked until it took on a toasty smell or turned a reddish color (probably the origin of the term *roux*). This method of thickening is still used for making stews and gravies, but in classic sauces, roux is prepared separately and measured before being combined with stock. The older method, pincer, is rarely used because it is very difficult to cook both the meat and the vegetables properly in one vessel: The former burns or the latter remain raw. (In the early twentieth century, Escoffier warned against it and instead recommended careful sweating of the aromatic vegetables and separate browning or searing of meats on the stove or in the oven.)

In the seventeenth century, a system of preparing intensely flavored liquid bases from enormous quantities of meat was used. A *jus* was prepared by browning large pieces of meat, poking the meat with a knife, then putting it in a press to extract the juice. A *restaurant* was prepared by putting meat in a well-sealed bottle and gently cooking until the meat released its natural juices; no liquid was used. Brown sauces were relatively simple and were mostly based on coulis. The coulis was the basis for brown sauces well into the nineteenth century, when it was replaced by sauce espagnole and classic demi-glace. Coulis was prepared by moistening a variety of meats (mutton was often used, along with beef, veal, and chicken) with an already rich bouillon.

Although a version of roux was introduced during the seventeenth century, other liaisons were also used. Puréed almonds, used since medieval times, were often added to thicken coulis. La Varenne's *Cuisinier françois* listed several liaisons, including almonds combined with bouillon, breadcrumbs, and egg yolks, the mixture flavored with lemon juice, onions, mushrooms, and cloves; mushrooms puréed with almonds, onions, parsley, breadcrumbs, egg yolks, and capers, the mixture then worked through a drum sieve; roux made with lard, with onions added after cooking the flour, and the mixture seasoned with bouillon, mushrooms, and vinegar—a kind of primitive velouté that was kept on "hot ashes" to be quickly accessible as a thickener; and truffles puréed along with flour, onions, and mushrooms and used to thicken ragoûts.

Some of the sauces that eventually made their way into the classic French repertoire first appear in seventeenth-century cookbooks. Seventeenth-century sauce poivrade has a distinctly medieval character: It was made with onions or scallions, vinegar, lemon and lime zests, and pepper; no coulis, stock, or butter was used to attenuate the acidity of the vinegar. A modern Sauce Poivrade (page 197) is made with concentrated stock and no lemon or orange. La Varenne's green sauce (*sauce verte*), made from chard and vinegar, also has a distinctly medieval character; no oil, butter, or stock was used and the sauce was thickened with toasted bread.

CHICKEN WITH CAPERS AND OYSTERS

Seventeenth-century cooks, or at least those who wrote about cooking, were excessively fond of capers—they show up in the most unlikely places—and had nothing against pairing fowl and seafood. This dish is particularly good with oysters from northern climes, especially Belons.

YIELD: 4 SERVINGS

chicken, quartered, 1	4 pounds	2 kilograms
butter	1½ ounces	45 grams
chicken broth	2 cups	500 milliliters
heavy cream	½ cup	125 milliliters
capers, drained	2 tablespoons	30 milliliters
finely chopped chives (optional)	1 tablespoon	15 milliliters
oysters, shucked, patted with a kitchen towel to eliminate grit	12	12
salt and pepper	to taste	to taste

1. Cook the chicken over medium heat in the butter, about 5 minutes on each side, until lightly browned, but not yet firm to the touch. Discard the fat and add the broth. Simmer, covered, until the chicken bounces back to the touch, about 10 minutes.

2. Take the chicken out of the pan and boil down the stewing liquid to about ½ cup (125 milliliters). Whisk in the cream and simmer until the sauce has the consistency you like.

3. Add the capers, chives, if using, and oysters and heat just enough to see the oysters curl a little. Season with salt and pepper.

4. Spoon the oysters, capers, and sauce over the pieces of chicken.

THE EIGHTEENTH CENTURY

The eighteenth century brought about greater systemization of the basic components—coulis, jus, and bouillons—introduced during the seventeenth century. This made it easier for professional cooks to work in different kitchens and produce consistent results. Once this system was mastered, individual recipes were easy to remember and integrate into a cook's repertoire.

Although many of the sauce recipes found in seventeenth-century cookbooks were little-changed versions of medieval recipes, by the eighteenth century few of those sauces remained in the literature. Most were replaced by versions containing coulis, butter, and the contemporary flavors such as anchovies, capers, and cornichons.

Cookbooks before the eighteenth century were written primarily for royalty and the aristocracy; they were likely written for the masters of the households rather than the cooks, who were usually illiterate. The eighteenth century saw the first cookbook for the middle class, Menon's *La Cuisinière bourgeoise*, which is filled with accessible and delicious recipes.

Many new sauces were introduced in the eighteenth century. Until then, sauces were usually one of two types. The first were made by slightly modifying a basic coulis, but it was essentially the coulis that gave the character to the sauce. This is by no means a criticism—sauces made from rich coulis are still the best brown sauces—but this approach is distinctly different from a later approach, popular in the nineteenth and twentieth centuries, which placed more emphasis on the final flavoring of the sauce than the coulis or demi-glace base. The second category of sauces, usually based on vinegar, verjuice, or citrus juices flavored with herbs and sometimes spices, was more medieval in character. As sauce making progressed during the eighteenth century, these two sauce styles began to merge. Coulis was added to an acidic sauce base (for example, sauce Robert); oil or butter was added to acidic sauce bases for a softer-flavored sauce with more finesse (for example, vinaigrette, beurre blanc); egg yolks, although used since the Middle Ages as sauce thickeners, were used (or at least described) more carefully; and the first versions of the modern hollandaise began to evolve.

In classic French cooking, roasts are served in their natural, unthickened juices (*jus de rôti*). In eighteenth-century cooking, chefs were far more likely to convert the natural juices from the roasts into an array of flavored sauces. Oranges, chopped shallots, truffles, anchovies, garlic, foie gras, and herbs were all used to give roasting juices a variety of flavors.

Roux became the liaison of choice. Early versions of velouté (*coulis bourgeois*) appeared and were made in much the modern way: preliminary cooking of roux, addition of bouillon flavored with wine, parsley, bay leaf, mushrooms. The only spices used were cloves and nutmeg, in moderation. Flour was used in roux (now prepared with butter instead of lard), and for beurre manié. During the eighteenth century, many classic sauces—espagnole, béchamel, italienne—were developed. Although these sauces have changed over the last 200 years, the ingredients used still sound appealing and appropriate.

CHICKEN WITH ANCHOVIES, OLIVES, CAPERS, AND ORANGE JUICE

This chicken comes from a book by the late-seventeenth- and early-eighteenth-century writer Massailot. This combination of olives, capers, and orange juice was very popular at the time. This recipe is completely authentic except for finishing the sauce with butter.

YIELD: 4 SERVINGS

chicken, quartered, 1	4 pounds	2 kilograms
salt and pepper	to taste	to taste
olive oil	2 teaspoons	10 milliliters
chicken broth	2 cups	500 milliliters
dry white wine	½ cup	125 milliliters
pitted olives	½ cup	125 milliliters
capers, drained	1 tablespoon	15 milliliters
anchovy fillets, rinsed	12	12
minced chives	1 tablespoon	15 milliliters
finely chopped parsley	1 tablespoon	15 milliliters
juice of 1 orange		
butter	2 ounces	60 grams

1. Season the chicken with the salt and pepper and brown it in a sauté pan in the oil for about 5 minutes on each side over high heat.

2. Take the chicken out of the pan, discard the fat, put the chicken back in, and pour over the broth and wine. Simmer the chicken, covered, for about 10 minutes, until firm to the touch.

3. Take the chicken out of the broth and simmer the broth until reduced to a syrupy glaze. Add the olives, capers, anchovy fillets, chives, parsley, and orange juice and stir gently to heat through all the ingredients.

4. Whisk in the butter. Season with salt and pepper. Spoon the sauce over the chicken.

THE NINETEENTH CENTURY

Before the nineteenth century, the greatest cooking in France was done in private homes and palaces for the wealthiest classes. When the French Revolution brought the fall of the aristocracy, a large number of talented chefs found themselves out of work. At the same time, a newly assertive middle class was eager to establish itself and emulate the fallen aristocracy. French cooking moved out of the home and into the restaurant, where the elaborate creations of the chefs were suddenly accessible to anyone who could afford them. An insecure bourgeoisie, eager to compete for social status, brought about an almost obsessive interest in cuisine and gastronomy. The great chefs were treated like stars. Whereas many of the basic preparations of the eighteenth century and before (including Béchamel, Mornay, and Soubise) were named for members of the nobility, many of the dishes and sauces invented in the nineteenth century were named for professional chefs (Dugléré, Véron). During the first half of the nineteenth century, a clear break occurred between what is now called *cuisine à l'ancienne* and the contemporary cooking of the time, now called *la cuisine classique*.

Early-nineteenth-century cookbooks used dishes and techniques popular in the late eighteenth century, but new ingredients and sauces also appeared. In eighteenth-century texts, sauce espagnole was given the same attention as other sauces, but by the early nineteenth century, it began to take on special importance. Velouté (also called *coulis blanc*) first appeared, as did the first versions of tomato sauce, hollandaise sauce (made with hard-boiled egg yolks), and ketchup (spelled *ket-chop* and made with mushrooms and anchovies). An early version of mayonnaise—a kind of vinaigrette with herbs but no egg yolks—also appeared.

Antonin Carême is usually considered the father of classic French cooking. Carême was the most prolific food writer of the nineteenth century—perhaps of all time—but more important, he systematized the fundamental *sauces mères* (mother sauces) and derivative sauces of classic French cooking. Although most of the so-called *grandes sauces* had been in use long before Carême, he was the first to state clearly that the four basic sauces—espagnole, velouté, allemande, and béchamel—were the basis for an infinite variety of *petite sauces*. Before Carême, even the so-called petite sauces were prepared by moistening additional meat (usually ham and veal) with various stocks, jus, and coulis, which made each sauce time consuming to prepare. Carême emphasized the importance of reducing the mother sauces so that only the basic flavors (he used an assortment of fumets and essences) had to be added to prepare last-minute derivative sauces. In addition to his descriptions of the classic mother sauces with their modern names, Carême also described many of the classic derivative sauces that are still used today. The first modern description of mayonnaise (spelled *magnonaise*), made with raw egg yolks, olive oil, and aspic, was also recorded. Carême enabled chefs working throughout the nineteenth century to invent derivative sauces using his foundation as a base. Many sauces invented by the famous Parisian chefs of the time were the same sauces with a single ingredient changed or added.

The first cookbooks with regional recipes were published in the nineteenth century. Parisians had never tasted Provençal cooking until one of the first restaurants of the century (Les Trois Frères Provençaux) began serving it. Later books on regional cooking, with their simple but judiciously prepared recipes, were a welcome relief from the baroque constructions of late-nineteenth-century classic cooking. They often emphasized the quality and origin of ingredients, with dishes prepared in simple, direct ways that enhanced their flavor.

THE TWENTIETH CENTURY

As the nineteenth century drew to a close, the innovations of chefs building on the foundations established by Carême were recorded by Auguste Escoffier in *Le Guide Culinaire*. *Le Guide Culinaire* standardized the cooking of the nineteenth century and for many still remains the ultimate authority on classical French cooking. As complicated as some of the recipes appear to the modern reader, Escoffier clearly pointed out that his recipes were a simplification of late-nineteenth-century cooking. He specifically mentioned eliminating the plinth (*socle*), the base that was widely used for the elaborate presentations of the late nineteenth century.

Escoffier continued to simplify sauce-making methods by eliminating many of the essences and fumets used by Carême and by affirming the importance of four mother sauces—espagnole, velouté, béchamel, and tomato (an addition since Carême)—and to a lesser degree, hollandaise and mayonnaise. His recipes were concise and easy to follow.

Escoffier used the recipes in *Le Guide Culinaire* to standardize the cooking at the Ritz hotels in England and on the continent—one striking difference between the cooking of the late nineteenth and early twentieth centuries and the approach to food today. At the turn of the century, typical wealthy diners in a Ritz hotel would insist on consistency in a particular dish whether they were in Nice or London. Today, sophisticated diners would be more reassured by the appearance of regional dishes using local ingredients than by a menu that seems to exist independently of the location.

Although less widely read than Escoffier, Edouard Nignon, an early-twentieth-century restaurateur, wrote several important books that discuss sauce making. His sauce recipes are particularly interesting because the brown sauces contained no flour; instead of basing his brown sauces on espagnole and demi-glace in the tradition of Carême and Escoffier, his sauces were prepared with concentrated veal stock (*blond de veau*), with veal glaze and concentrated veal and beef stock (*jus brun*). These methods, while resembling those of the eighteenth century, were precursors of the methods now used in contemporary French restaurants.

One of the most admired French chefs of the twentieth century is Ferdinand Point, who owned a restaurant in Vienne (near Lyons) in the late 1940s and early 1950s. He started one of the currently enduring trends of cooking by developing and enhancing the cuisine of his region. Regional cuisine, for years considered the domain of women cooks, has been gradually adopted by professional chefs (both men and women) and prepared with the same technical expertise that had been reserved for classic French cooking. Ferdinand Point was one of the first to pay homage to the cuisine of his region and was an inspiration to many of his apprentices, who later became the influential chefs of the 1960s and 1970s.

The term *nouvelle cuisine* was first used in the late 1960s (so-called nouvelle cuisine had already appeared several times over past centuries). Initially, and perhaps most important, the development of a "new" cooking gave chefs permission to invent. This concept may be difficult for an American chef to understand, because unless European-trained, an American chef has no rigid system from which to break away. But in France the precepts and techniques of classical cooking were questioned, and many of the old dishes were lightened and simplified or completely abandoned.

Of the technical innovations of the 1960s and 1970s, none were more profound or longer lasting than those in the area of sauce making. Chefs began to eliminate flour (used in one way or another since the Middle Ages) from their sauces and to thicken their sauces with cream, butter, and egg yolks. Sauces were served in smaller quantities and were usually lighter textured.

Some chefs and authors question the value of eliminating flour from sauces. Preparing flourless sauces takes skill and experience; many of the sauces used by our current nouvelle cuisine chefs are overly rich and overly reduced. Although many chefs and writers claimed that the new sauces were lighter than the older flour-thickened versions, the reverse is actually true. Some chefs, in an effort to eliminate flour, thickened their sauces almost entirely with cream and butter; the result was far from light. Often the decision to use flour as a thickener is a question of style. In the rarefied atmosphere of a Michelin three-star restaurant, a flour-thickened sauce, unless prepared in the careful tradition of Escoffier and the nineteenth century, may seem incongruous. On the other hand, a regional dish such as a coq au vin or one of the many varieties of country-style stews is best served with its own cooking liquid lightly thickened with flour, preferably added at the beginning, during the browning of the meat.

One of the most innovative chefs of the 1970s was Michel Guérard, whose book *La Grande cuisine minceur* contained recipes for sauces made almost entirely without cream, butter, or egg yolks. He was one of the first to suggest serving dishes surrounded by full-flavored aromatic broths with no liaison. He introduced yogurt and fresh cheese as liaisons and developed a method for using a light sabayon to thicken savory sauces.

Both French and American chefs have borrowed largely from ethnic and regional cuisines to devise new techniques and flavor combinations for sauce making. American chefs are finally beginning to use regional American cooking as a source of inspiration and exciting sauce ideas. Jeremiah Tower, in his book *New American Classics*, has integrated the satisfying, rough-hewn cuisine of California and the American Southwest with the sophistication and technique of traditional French cooking. French chefs are experimenting with the traditional dishes of the provinces instead of automatically following the precepts of a classic cuisine. French chefs working both in France and in the United States have looked to the cuisine of India and their own medieval past, and after centuries of neglect, they are beginning to experiment with spices in sauce making. In the history of cooking and sauce making, there have been periods of both innovation and stagnation. Vincent de la Chapelle wrote during the first half of the eighteenth century that if a nobleman served the same dishes at his table that had been popular twenty years before, his guests would leave dissatisfied. The same is true today—food is fashionable, and the public has grown fickle and eager for innovation. The American public is at times almost fanatically health conscious and concerned with diet—a trend reminiscent of the sixteenth century. While this concern with health sometimes detracts from the pleasure of a good meal, it has forced Americans to be conscious of the foods they eat and more open to experimenting with new dishes. One upside is that sophisticated diners are opting for the pure and simple. The emphasis is on the quality of the ingredients, their seasonality, and where they've been grown.

THE TWENTY-FIRST CENTURY

During the last two decades, there has been a steady movement away from the rich sauces of nouvelle cuisine. Some chefs and sauciers have gone in the direction of making lighter textured broth-like sauces such as those described in many of the chapters of this book.

Thanks largely in part to chefs—especially Spaniards—such as Ferran Adrià, some kitchens have seen a revolution. Much of this is due to the discovery of compounds up until now used only in industry, and how to apply them in the kitchen. Emulsifiers and thickeners such as hydrocolloids allow chefs to perform feats one would never have thought possible a few decades back.

The early period of this century has also witnessed the use of sous vide cooking. In essence, sous vide cooking is cooking in an elaborate bain-marie where the temperature can be closely controlled. Sous vide cookery permits exact temperature control and allows the chef to hold various fragile combinations during a busy restaurant service or an elaborate dinner party at home. Many sauces can be prepared sous vide so the exact temperature can be maintained throughout the evening. This, in combination with tasteless stabilizers, allows the chef to come up with a variety of sauces, all of which will remain stable in the sous vide tank.

While this modernist revolution is one approach to cooking, often executed in rarified environments, simple, ingredient-driven cooking has also come to the forefront. The public has finally realized something that many professional cooks already understand: The quality of a prepared dish reflects the quality of the ingredients. Farm-to-table cooking focuses on fresh, in-season ingredients, and the "locavore" movement encourages one to eat foods grown or raised within a relatively short radius. The resulting dishes tend to be prepared simply in order to highlight the flavors of high-quality ingredients at the peak of freshness.

EQUIPMENT

Much of the equipment essential for traditional sauce making will probably already be on hand in a well-equipped home or restaurant kitchen. However, some of what you need, including fine-mesh strainers, drum sieves, and saucepans with sloping sides, is specialized for sauce making. Tools for modernist cuisine are very specialized and can be expensive, but they are often well worth the investment, especially once you are able to use them for improvisation.

COOKWARE
Materials

There seems to be no perfect material for constructing pots and pans. Copper is heavy and needs to be retinned; stainless steel is expensive and a poor conductor of heat; aluminum stains certain sauces. The list of disadvantages goes on. The best pots and pans—and the most expensive—combine materials to make the optimum use of each.

Whatever the material, the most important consideration in selecting pots, saucepans, and sauté pans is that they be thick. If not, they will heat unevenly and the bottoms will burn or scald and possibly warp.

ALUMINUM

Aluminum cookware is popular in professional kitchens because it is inexpensive. Good-quality heavy-gauge aluminum can be used for roasting pans, sauté pans, and, to a limited degree, saucepans. It is especially practical for large stockpots, which would be prohibitively expensive in copper or stainless steel.

Aluminum is only a moderately efficient conductor of heat. Large sauté pans and roasting pans tend to warp, because their centers expand before the outside does. This problem occurs less often if a flat-top stove is used, rather than burners that concentrate the heat in one area of the pan. Food tends to stick to aluminum pans, so they should be avoided when sautéing fish or fragile meats. When using aluminum pans, be sure to heat them very hot before adding foods—oil should smoke—to prevent sticking.

Aluminum saucepans can discolor pale sauces, especially sauces containing egg yolks. Any kitchen should have at least a couple of lined copper or copper-bottomed stainless-steel saucepans for emulsified egg sauces.

The most important factor when purchasing aluminum pans is gauge (thickness): choose as heavy a gauge as possible. Several types of aluminum cookware are available. Most aluminum has a plain, shiny surface. One brand, Calphalon, anodizes the aluminum, which renders the aluminum less reactive, preventing it from discoloring foods. It is attractive but quite expensive. It also has the disadvantage of being almost black on the inside, making it difficult to see the condition of any caramelized juices before deglazing.

CAST IRON

By far the best bargain in cooking materials, cast-iron cookware can be found in most cooking supply stores and, less expensively, in hardware stores. It is typically very heavy, and because of this cooks evenly. While an excellent material, there are certain drawbacks that make it less than ideal. First, to inhibit sticking and to prevent the iron from reacting with acidic ingredients and from discoloring foods, it must be kept "seasoned" by heating it after each use over high heat with a little oil and salt in it, followed by vigorous rubbing of the surface with a towel. This detaches any food remnants. Iron should not be cleaned with water and abrasives, as these will remove the seasoning. The seasoned surface must be kept intact by avoiding water or other liquids, which could cause the pan to rust; this makes deglazing difficult, but not impossible. Cast iron also has the disadvantage, shared by anodized aluminum, of being dark. It is impossible to see the formation of coagulated juices or to assess burning on the bottom of a dark pan.

Cast-iron pans can also be used as flame tamers (see page 30).

COPPER

Because it is an excellent heat conductor, copper has long been the material of choice for professional cookware. When made of heavy-gauge copper, saucepans and sauté pans distribute heat evenly, decreasing the risk of burning pan drippings or scalding sauces. Because of its conductivity, copper is also less likely to warp.

However, copper pots and pans are expensive. While nowadays, most copper pans are lined on the inside with stainless steel, older ones must be tinned on the inside every few years if used heavily. In principle, copper should not come directly in contact with food, although the occasional exposure is not serious (think of beating egg whites or making caramel in a copper bowl). However, frequent exposure is risky to the liver. Home cooks should be especially vigilant about untinned copper since they are more likely to use the same pot on a regular basis. It is most important that sauces not sit exposed to copper for long periods, as this will leach out a dangerous amount of the metal's ions.

Copper should also be polished each time it is washed. Although tarnish does not affect the efficiency of copper cookware, a kitchen filled with tarnished pots somehow looks sloppy and amiss. One of the advantages of copper is the gleaming professional look it gives to a restaurant kitchen.

When purchasing copper cookware, be sure to select pots and pans with iron rather than brass handles. Because iron is a poor conductor of heat, the handles will not get hot so quickly.

EARTHENWARE

Although many home cooks could never do without earthenware for slow-cooking stews and braises, it is rarely practical in a professional kitchen, where it is unlikely to survive the frenzied pace. It is often used, however, for dishes such as gratins, which are served in the same dish in which they are baked.

ENAMELED CAST IRON

While cast iron is impractical for saucepans and sauté pans because it rusts easily, may discolor foods, and is very heavy, it is excellent for braising because it conducts heat slowly and evenly. An enameled surface is nonreactive, unlike plain cast iron which will rust if not kept perfectly dry and oiled. Enameled cast-iron pots are available in a variety of sizes and shapes, including oval, which makes them convenient for braising when a close-fitting vessel is needed.

Enameled cast iron is not suitable for roasting pans or sauté pans because the juices from meats and fish do not adhere to it, making the separation of the juices from the fat before deglazing difficult.

Over the years, enameled cast-iron cookware can become chipped, so that sections of iron start showing through. Be especially vigilant about keeping these exposed areas clean as they can harbor bacteria. If large amounts of iron are exposed, it may give foods a metallic taste, especially after a long braise.

GLASS

Most cooks and chefs avoid glass because it is easy to break and it's a poor conductor of heat. It does have the advantage, however, of allowing you to see closely what's happening in the pan or pot. It is not recommended for sautéing, because juices will not adhere to the surface, coagulate, and caramelize. Because of this, and because sudden sharp temperature changes can cause glass to shatter, it is impossible to deglaze a hot glass pan. If you're using glass, be sure it's Pyrex or a similar heat-resistant borosilicate brand, which is somewhat less sensitive to temperature changes. Always use a flame tamer (see page 30). Some of the photos in this book show sauces in glass cookware, for the purpose of showcasing the foods' colors and consistencies. But I don't recommend this for everyday use.

Glass is now used in kitchens in the form of beakers and flasks for measuring and for boiling under vacuum. See "Beakers, Measuring Cups, Flasks, Test Tubes, and Other Glassware," page 28, and "Vacuum Pumps," page 36.

NONSTICK SURFACES

Nonstick cookware is excellent for quickly sautéing meats and fish when a minimum of fat or oil needs to be used. However, nonstick pans are not good for making integral sauces, which involve deglazing; none of the meat or fish juices will adhere to the surface.

STAINLESS STEEL

The advantage of stainless-steel cookware is that it is almost completely inert; it will not rust, tarnish, or react with foods. Its disadvantages are that it is a relatively poor conductor of heat, and it is expensive.

The best stainless-steel pots and pans have a thick disk of copper in the base of the pan that helps conduct heat and prevent scalding. Well-made copper-bottomed stainless-steel pots and pans are a good choice for a professional kitchen.

Types of Cookware

BAIN-MARIES AND INSERTS

Traditional bain-marie pans are used to keep sauces warm during a restaurant service. They have a tall, cylindrical shape with a handle near the top, and are designed to be set in a pan of hot water.

Some version of a bain-marie is essential for sauces that are made in advance. Unfortunately, tinned-copper bain-marie pans are expensive, and aluminum reacts with too many sauces. Stainless-steel bain-marie pans are difficult to find.

Good substitutes for bain-marie pans are the cylindrical stainless-steel inserts used in steam tables. When new they tend to be expensive, but they can often be found in good condition secondhand. They can also be filled with hot water and used to hold whisks, tasting spoons, and ladles during the restaurant service.

CASSEROLES

In American usage, a casserole is a heavy lidded pot with relatively low sides (but not as low as a sauté pan) that is used for stewing and braising. This may confuse cooks accustomed to French terms; in French, *casserole* simply means "saucepan," and the term *cocotte* is used to describe the American casserole.

Casseroles are either round or oval. For stews the shape is of little importance, but for braising larger pieces of meat, where the casserole must fit the dimensions of the meat as closely as possible, an oval casserole is indispensable.

Purists insist that the best material for slow, even cooking is earthenware in one of its many regional shapes, and that the best method is to bury the earthenware casserole (carefully sealed with a flour-and-water luting paste) under the ashes in the hearth. The purpose of these conditions is to protect braising meats from sudden increases in temperature, which might cloud the braising liquid. Professional chefs—and indeed most home cooks—are rarely willing to sacrifice efficiency to cook in this way, and usually use heavy copper or enameled cast-iron pots with tight-fitting lids.

Most casseroles have rounded lids that cause condensed moisture to drip down the sides of the pan rather than over the meat. It helps to put the lid on upside down so the condensation bastes the meat.

GRATIN DISHES AND BAKING DISHES

Because food is often served in gratin dishes, the dishes need to be both efficient and attractive. Most gratin dishes are made of porcelain or stoneware that gives the finished dish a comforting, rustic look and also retains heat well. Some restaurants use tinned-copper gratin dishes when serving more elaborate classic gratins such as crayfish or lobster.

Gratin dishes traditionally have an oval shape, but in the United States, individual enameled cast-iron or porcelain gratin dishes are sometimes round with small wing handles on each side.

LIDS

Most pots and saucepans are available with their own exactly fitting lids, but in a busy professional kitchen there is rarely time to rummage through the lids to find the right size. In older kitchens, a series of copper lids with iron handles was always on hand, but these have become almost as expensive as good saucepans. Today's cooks will often haphazardly grab a lid—even if it is too large—and turn it upside down over the pot. If the lid is rounded on top, it will stay in place even if too large.

The most practical lids for the professional kitchen are inexpensive aluminum with rounded tops (the lid will not come in contact with the food).

PRESSURE COOKERS

While cooking under vacuum emulates mountain conditions, causing liquids to boil at lower temperatures than they would at sea level, pressure cookers make use of the opposite effect: Water boils at a higher temperature when under pressure, as when heated in an hermetically sealed vessel. Pressure cookers can cut the time required for many kitchen tasks by half.

While their advantage in fast-paced environments is indisputable, certain caveats apply. First, a pressure cooker can only be used for relatively small amounts of liquid. When a pressure cooker is used to make meat, fish, or poultry stock, the stock must not be allowed to boil or it will become cloudy and greasy. To avoid this, you must keep a close eye on the pressure cooker and modulate the heat so it doesn't release any steam. If steam is shooting out the top or out of a valve, it means that the liquid on the inside is boiling and will easily be ruined.

When buying a pressure cooker, look for one with a meter that shows the internal pressure. This will allow you to better estimate cooking times and help avoid boiling. Pressure cookers used for canning usually have such a meter, but they have thin bottoms, which can cause scalding on the inside.

ROASTING PANS

It is imperative that roasting pans be made of heavy-gauge metal with a clear, shiny surface. If the roasting pan is too thin, it will heat unevenly and the juices from the roast will burn. Aluminum or tinned copper make the best roasting pans because they enable the condition of the meat drippings to be seen. Dark metals, such as cast iron or anodized aluminum, although suitable conductors of heat, make it difficult to see whether the drippings are burning. Enameled cast-iron should be avoided because the drippings tend to float into the fat, making it difficult to separate them to prepare a jus.

Many cooks make the mistake of using a roasting pan that is too large, so the meat drippings burn. A well-equipped kitchen should have several sizes. Since it is sometimes difficult to find roasting pans in a variety of shapes and sizes (most are square or rectangular), heavy-bottomed sauté pans or oval casseroles can be substituted.

SAUCEPANS, SLOPING SIDED

A surprisingly large number of professional kitchens do not have a single saucepan with sloping sides (*sauteuse évasée*). They are essential for making hot emulsified sauces, where constant beating is necessary to emulsify the sauce and incorporate air. The bottom corners of a straight-sided saucepan are too sharply angled to allow access with a whisk, so egg yolk sauces and other delicate mixtures may curdle.

Sloping-sided saucepans must be made with heavy tinned copper or copper-bottomed stainless steel. Each saucepan's characteristics will take a little getting used to when making emulsified sauces; a heavy-bottomed pan retains a lot of heat and will continue to cook the sauce for a short while after being removed from the heat. This is one time in which an extremely thick gauge of copper is disadvantageous.

SAUCEPANS, STRAIGHT SIDED

These saucepans (*casseroles* in French) should be made of heavy tinned copper, aluminum, or copper-bottomed stainless steel with iron or hollow handles. A professional kitchen should have a good collection of different sizes. The size of the saucepan should match the flame under it: If the flame wraps around its sides during reduction, browning and discoloration of the sauce may result.

SAUTÉ PANS, STRAIGHT SIDED

Many cooks, including professionals, confuse straight-sided sauté pans (*plats à sauter* or *rondeaux*) with sloping-sided sauté pans—what Americans call frying pans, and the French, *poêles*. The difference is important. A straight-sided sauté pan is excellent for making integral sauces, because meats, vegetables, and other ingredients can be browned in the pan and the sauce made in the same pan. This is difficult in a pan with sloping sides, where a sauce can scald or burn during reduction.

Straight-sided sauté pans should be constructed of heavy-gauge tinned copper, aluminum, or copper-bottomed stainless steel. Most straight-sided sauté pans have a long iron handle on one side, which makes it easy to move them around on the stove. In certain instances, however, it is useful to finish cooking a dish in the oven, and a sauté pan with two small handles (*rondeau*) is more useful. These pans can also double as small roasting pans.

SOUS VIDE TANK AND RELATED EQUIPMENT

When selecting a tank for sous vide cookery, keep in mind that the tank mustn't be too small or the food will be crowded and instead of circulating, the water will form hot or cold pockets. These will throw off the accuracy of the cooking. If the tank is too large, it will require a lot of time to bring the water up to temperature, and an undue amount of energy to keep it hot. An excellent tank, which can be procured in all sizes, is an aquarium. (A) One tip: When heating the water to the desired temperature, start with hot tap water to cut down on the time required for heating.

Once you have a tank on hand, you will also need a way to immerse whatever it is you're cooking in the water. You can suspend resealable plastic bags with the food from a wire cake rack set on top of the tank. (Paper clips come in handy here.) If the contents of the bag float up in the tank, attach a large clamp to the bottom of the bag to weight it. Alternatively, use a large jar with a tight-fitting lid: Put lead sinkers (which you can buy at a hardware store) or other heavy material in the jar to keep it from bobbing up and turning over. Place the sealed bag of food inside, tightly close the jar, and submerge it in the water bath. For extra assurance, seal the jar in its own bag as well.

An immersion circulator is needed to get the water to move around in the tank and to maintain it at a given temperature. (B) These come in many varieties and range enormously in price, but can be had for relatively little. The circulator clamps onto the side of the tank, and must remain at least half submerged. Most immersion circulators are quite precise and measure to within 0.1°F (0.5°C).

STEAMERS

The most useful steamer—a *couscoussière*—has a large pot with a colander-like insert that fits tightly inside, on top. It is excellent for quickly steaming fish, meats, and vegetables, because any aromatic liquid can be boiled in the bottom pot and used to scent the foods steaming in the basket.

STOCKPOTS

In professional kitchens where stocks are prepared on a regular basis, it may be necessary to have a collection of large pots for stocks in various stages of preparation and reduction. The most important consideration in choosing a stockpot is that it must have a heavy bottom; since the sides do not come in contact with the heat, they are of little importance. Make sure that stockpots have handles riveted onto two sides.

Some stockpots have taps on the bottom to facilitate draining—an especially useful feature when preparing large quantities, which are cumbersome to move.

A variety of smaller pots is also necessary in kitchens where reduced stocks and glazes are prepared regularly. A stockpot that is only one-third full of liquid is difficult to skim and degrease; the liquid should be transferred to a smaller pot.

KITCHEN TOOLS AND UTENSILS

BEAKERS, MEASURING CUPS, FLASKS, TEST TUBES, AND OTHER GLASSWARE

Glass laboratory receptacles are often graduated in both American measurements and metric and are normally heat resistant. Beakers are easy to clean and make it easy to see what's going on inside. They also look great in the kitchen. When it's necessary to see a small amount of liquid at close range, a test tube is perfect. They are handy for checking on emulsions and thickened mixtures, making it easier to judge their stability.

Pyrex measuring cups can do the same job as beakers (although they rarely have metric graduations), but aren't as attractive or scientific looking.

Flasks are an alternative to metal pots and pans for heating liquids. By far the most useful are Erlenmeyer flasks, which have a distinct shape—flat and wide on the bottom, narrow on the top. Erlenmeyer flasks are useful for boiling liquids because they have a large surface area on the bottom, which hastens evaporation. They also will protect liquids from "bumping," in which a bubble forms and pops with a great splash. Erlenmeyer flasks are also the best vessel for setting up a vacuum pump (see page 36). However, they can be hard to clean. Don't boil citrus other juices that contain pulp or the pulp will stick to the insides and be almost impossible to remove.

When using beakers, flasks, or other glass lab equipment, you'll need food-grade rubber corks in a range of sizes to seal them. Have on hand a few corks with holes in them for inserting thermometers, so you can measure the temperature inside flasks, especially when under vacuum or pressure. You'll also need rubber tubing and sections of glass tubing to insert into the corks for vacuums etc.

BLOWTORCH

In traditional cooking, meat is browned at the beginning, before braising or roasting. In the case of sous vide cooking, however, foods are often browned after they are cooked, just before serving. To accomplish this quickly, without overcooking the inside of the food, a blowtorch is used for the final browning and to quickly create a crust. A blowtorch that burns propylene instead of propane burns at a higher temperature, working more efficiently to form a crust and less likely to cook the food further. Don't use a welding torch, which uses acetylene and oxygen and burns with an intensely hot flame.

CLEANING BRUSHES

When working with lab glassware and other hard-to-clean small glassware, it's imperative to have an assortment of cleaning brushes. They are usually sold in sets and are useful for cleaning flasks and test tubes.

CHINOIS

Two types of chinois are essential in the professional kitchen. The first type, a coarse chinois (sometimes called a china cap), has a conical shape with a sturdy stainless-steel or tinned handle. The cone is made from heavy stainless steel, aluminum, or tinned steel, and perforated with small holes. A coarse chinois will stand up to wear and tear that would quickly damage a fine chinois. Stocks containing bones and liquids containing sharp objects (such as lobster or crab shells) that would damage a fine chinois must be strained first through a coarse chinois. However, a coarse chinois will not eliminate small particles from liquids. For smooth sauces, the liquid must be further strained through a fine chinois.

A fine chinois is essential for straining sauces and stocks. Most have a fine-mesh conical screen made of stainless or tinned steel, held in place around a sturdy circular frame. They are expensive and must be treated carefully to help them last. When buying a fine chinois, inspect it carefully for small holes or spaces in the mesh—one small hole will defeat its purpose. When using a fine chinois to strain sauces, always use a small ladle and a gentle up-and-down motion to get the liquid to drain through. Never use a spoon and never use pressure. Do not throw a fine chinois into a sink with dirty dishes, where it might be damaged.

DRUM SIEVES

Drum sieves are necessary for straining relatively stiff mixtures, such as vegetable purées, that would damage a fine chinois. Drum sieves consist of a mesh screen held by a circular wooden or metal frame. A professional kitchen should have a sturdy metal-framed drum sieve for straining hard or coarse purées and a fine-meshed nylon sieve for finishing purées that require a very fine consistency.

When straining mixtures through a drum sieve, place it on a flat surface rather than over a bowl, unless the mixture is very liquid. This makes it easier to hold the sieve in place while applying pressure from the top. Mixtures are traditionally forced through sieves with a wooden pestle-like implement called a *champignon* (because of its mushroom-like shape). A plastic pastry scraper or even the bottom of a small stainless-steel bowl will also work well.

When selecting a drum sieve, look for one that allows for replacement of the screen, usually the first part to wear out.

FAT SEPARATORS

Very few of the gadgets that accumulate on the shelves of home kitchens make it into a professional setting; professionals prefer proven traditional equipment and techniques. A glass or plastic fat separator may become one of the few exceptions. It consists of a pitcher with a tubular spout attached just above the bottom. When roasting juices or other liquids that need to be degreased are placed in the fat separator, the fat floats to the top. The liquid portion is then poured off.

FILTERS

Filtering is common in kitchens and is usually carried out with a chinois or simple strainer. Coffee filters or pieces of muslin work for finer filtration. To filter with muslin or a simple cotton kitchen towel (don't use terrycloth), line the inside of a chinois with the cloth. Moisten the cloth first with water, then pour in the liquid to be filtered. Tap

the side of the chinois with a wooden spoon to facilitate the passage of the liquid through the cloth. Don't push down, especially if you're straining stock, or you may cloud the final filtered liquid. After a few minutes, the cloth will become clogged with particles and the flow will stop. Grip one end of the cloth and pull it gently to one side so that a new section is now lining the chinois. Complete until all the liquid has gone through, replacing the cloth as necessary.

In more recalcitrant situations, you may need to use more force and resort to vacuum filtration, using a vacuum pump with a trap (see page 36), an Erlenmeyer flask with a sidearm, a special filter called a Büchner funnel, an adapter to attach the filter to the top of the flask, and rounds of filter paper that fit the inside of the funnel.

A Büchner funnel is usually made of porcelain or polypropylene and has holes in the top surface through which to draw liquids. Because the holes are large and do little to filter out solids, a moistened round of filter paper is placed on top, the liquid to be filtered is poured in, and the vacuum pump, attached to the side arm of the flask, turned on. The vacuum draws the liquid through the paper and through the holes.

FLAME TAMERS

The asbestos pads used in the past have been replaced with any number of devices meant to act as an interface between the heat source and the cooking vessel, usually a metal plate set over the burner. Flame tamers come in handy when using cookware made from glass, earthenware, or other delicate and heat-sensitive materials. If you don't have one handy, use a large cast-iron or other heavy-duty skillet. Set it over the flame and then set the cooking vessel on top.

FOOD MILLS

These devices are useful for straining purées or thick sauces such as tomato or tomatillo. They are available in different sizes. The smaller sizes are not of much use in a professional kitchen, because it is just as easy to work a small amount of the mixture through a medium-mesh strainer. A large food mill, however, is almost indispensable for straining large amounts of tomato coulis and purée-thickened mixtures. Food mills come with several perforated metal plates that can be switched depending on the desired consistency of the mixture.

FUNNELS

Though often neglected, every kitchen should have an assortment of funnels in different sizes to accommodate transferring liquids to smaller or larger containers. When working with small amounts of hydrocolloid materials, glass funnels are best; for general kitchen use, use plastic.

LADLES

Ladles are constantly used in professional kitchens for skimming stocks, straining liquids, and saucing foods on the plate. There should be a variety of sizes always within easy reach.

Today most ladles are made of stainless steel, which will not tarnish or rust and is easy to clean. Select ladles with handles that are almost perpendicular to the surface of the bowl, which facilitates skimming stocks and removing fat from roasting juices. The best ladles are constructed from a single piece of stainless steel, rather than a separate bowl and handle welded or riveted together. Welded ladles are more difficult to clean because food residue accumulates in the joint.

LARDING NEEDLES

Two types of larding needles are used to insert strips of fatback into large pieces of meat to keep them moist during braising. The larger of the two, a *lardoire*, consists of a tube with an opening along the length on one side. It has a sharp pointed tip and a handle. The strip of fat is put into the tube and the larding needle is pushed through the meat, then withdrawn, so that the fat is left running through the meat. Ideally, the fatback should make an attractive checkerboard pattern when the meat is sliced. The second type, an *aiguille à piquer*, is used for larding the surface of meats. It resembles a small knitting needle and has a toothed hinge on the back end to hold the strip of fat. The needle is used to "sew" the strips through the meat's surface.

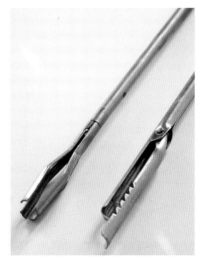

MANDOLINES

This kitchen tool is used for quickly julienning and slicing an array of vegetables. Until recently, the large French stainless-steel mandoline was the only type found in professional kitchens, where it has been used since the nineteenth century. A mandoline-style vegetable slicer, such as the Benriner cutter from Japan, has become more common in recent years. It has a razor-sharp blade that will slice vegetables from ¼ inch (5 mm) thick to almost paper thin. It works especially well for truffles (much better than the expensive Italian truffle slicer, page 32) and has a toothed blade for extremely fine julienne.

MEASURING CUPS AND SPOONS

These utensils are rarely used in professional kitchens, where most sauces are made by eye. In instances where careful measurement is necessary—such as for roux or when standardizing recipes for food costing—a kitchen scale is more reliable and easier to use.

Because they are made of glass, graduated glass pitchers, whether or not they are used for measuring, are useful for degreasing roasting juices.

MILK FROTHER

Some sauces, especially those containing milk, can be beaten into a froth with a small device called a milk frother. The end of the frother spins around and creates a foam like that on top of a cappuccino.

MORTAR AND PESTLE

Although often thought of as anachronistic, a good mortar and pestle are necessary for grinding certain ingredients when the action of a food processor either is too brutal or will not crush the ingredients in the way necessary to release their flavor.

Mortars and pestles are probably not used more often because good ones are difficult to find and can be very expensive. The best are relatively large and made from solid chunks of stone. Marble, granite, and other kinds of stone have the advantage of being very heavy, so that the mortar does not move around during grinding, and it does not absorb odors.

A good second choice is a heavy, glazed-porcelain mortar with an unglazed inner surface that acts as an abrasive and helps along the grinding. Because even porcelain mortars and pestles are expensive, cooks often buy them too small, which makes them very difficult to use efficiently. Shops selling Southeast Asian ingredients sometimes sell relatively inexpensive but efficient stone mortars and pestles from Thailand. A *suribachi*, a wide Japanese mortar with flaring sides and ribbed interior, is especially efficient for grinding sesame seeds.

PIPETTES

A pipette is like a mini turkey baster or large eyedropper. (A) It is designed for distributing or removing small amounts of liquids, usually a drop at a time. It's essential for spherification (see page 182). Since most pipettes only deliver a single stream of drops, making timing difficult, it's useful to have a Finnpipette, which will deliver anywhere from 12 to 96 drops at a time. (B)

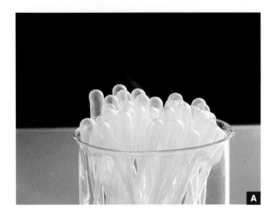
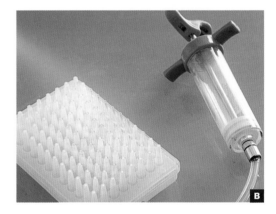

STRAINERS

A selection of inexpensive strainers is useful for quick and easy straining of purées and fruit coulis, getting the peels out of a small amount of tomato coulis, and other coarse straining.

TRUFFLE SLICER

This elegant little gadget is used to slice or shave white truffles at the table. In the kitchen a Japanese mandoline does a more efficient job, but for the dining room, an Italian truffle slicer is far more presentable.

WHIPPING SIPHON

Whipping siphons are mainly used for making whipped cream at the last minute, just before serving. They can also be used to hold liquids in a water bath during a busy restaurant service or a complicated dinner party. They can turn many sauces into foams. They look a bit like insulated coffee pitchers but have a tube with a lever handle sticking out the top at an angle. A small cylinder of nitrous oxide fits into another opening on top. After the siphon is filled half full with liquid, the nitrous oxide cylinder is screwed on. It discharges and the gas becomes distributed and pressurized in the liquid; this is sometimes referred to as "charging the siphon." (Nitrous oxide is chosen as the gas because of its high solubility in fats. For this reason a siphon works well with liquids containing butter, cream, eggs, oils, or other fats.) When the lever is pressed, the gas-charged liquid is released. With the sudden drop in pressure, the gas in the liquid expands and causes the liquid to foam or froth.

Whipping siphons don't have to be limited to making sturdy foams, but can also enhance classic cream- and butter-based sauces by frothing them onto the plate. Whipping siphons are also convenient for storing sauces in a bain-marie during a busy service in order to hold them at a particular temperature.

WHISKS

The best whisks for sauce making are made entirely of stainless steel, and have an elongated shape and a large number of fine wires. Balloon whisks are designed for beating air into mixtures and are less convenient for stirring and reaching into the corners of a saucepan. A sauce whisk is best held like a pencil and rotated in a circular or figure-eight motion.

Many professionals leave a small whisk in a pot of sauce or in an insert on the side so they can quickly give the sauce a stir every few minutes as necessary.

WOODEN SPOONS AND SPATULAS

Although a whisk is usually used in professional kitchens to stir sauces, wooden spoons and spatulas are indispensable for stirring egg yolk–thickened sauces, for which it is essential to reach into the corners of the saucepan. A whisk will also generate too much hard-to-remove froth on the surface of some egg yolk–thickened sauces. For some sauces (such as crème anglaise), a wooden spoon or spatula is essential for verifying the sauce's consistency.

Wooden spoons are also useful for stirring sauces that have not yet been strained and contain chunks of food, such as vegetables, bones, and crustacean shells, that would get caught in the wires of a whisk.

Never leave a wooden spoon or spatula sitting in a sauce, or the flavor of the wood may affect the sauce's flavor. It is also impossible (as well as unsanitary) to taste a sauce from a wooden spoon—the wooden flavor is too pronounced.

MACHINES

BLENDER

Always buy the simplest blender available. Small home-kitchen types with an array of buttons for every conceivable consistency of liquid are usually less powerful and reliable than a simple blender with a heavy base and only two speeds: slow and fast. Companies such as KitchenAid and Vitamix manufacture extra heavy–duty blenders that work well for soups and large amounts of sauce.

Observe three precautions when using blenders for hot liquids: Never fill a blender more than half full; always start the blender on slow speed; and wrap a kitchen towel tightly around the lid of the container. Hot liquids expand quickly in the blender, and can shoot out the top and make a nasty spill. When using a blender for sauces containing a large proportion of cream, remember that the sauce must be 120°F (50°C) or more, or the cream will turn into butter.

When combining a stiff element (such as blanched watercress leaves) with a liquid (such as stock or cream) in a blender, it is always best to add the stiff element first and then slowly pour the liquid through the opening in the center of the lid while the blender is on. If the liquid is added too quickly, the stiff element may escape the blender blades and remain in large pieces.

Often more convenient than a conventional blender is an immersion blender. Essentially a long handle with the blender rotor and blades on one end, immersion blenders are excellent for puréeing and emulsifying sauces directly in the pot in which they are made and don't require dirtying a blender container and lid. They can also be used to aerate mixtures by using the flat blade and holding the blade near the surface of the liquid, which cannot be done in a regular blender. Many immersion blenders come with more than one attachment and may include a shearing attachment, a puréeing attachment, a frothing attachment, and a whisk.

ELECTRIC STAND MIXERS

Electric mixers are essential for preparing compound butters—especially crustacean butters—for which long working of the ingredients is necessary. Large Hobart mixers or the smaller KitchenAids are the most reliable and useful on today's market. They come equipped with a flat paddle blade to work stiff ingredients such as cold butter or very stiff purées. The whisk attachment can be used to whip butters and beat cream and egg whites.

FOOD PROCESSOR

A food processor is especially useful for preparing stiff purées that would be too much of a burden for a blender. It is often used for stiff mixtures and purées that were traditionally prepared with a mortar and pestle or by laborious working the mixture through a drum sieve.

It is better not to use a food processor for starchy purées such as those made with potatoes or celeriac, which will quickly become gluey if overworked. In some instances, especially for vegetable and fruit purées and coulis, it is useful to purée the mixture in a food processor before forcing it through a drum sieve.

PLASTIC BAG VACUUM SEALER

When preparing foods to be cooked sous vide, a plastic bag holding the food must be sealed in a way that removes any air it might contain. The low-tech approach is to use heavy-duty resealable plastic bags and press out excess air by placing the bag on the edge of a counter and gradually moving the bag down to expel the air. This is also a good method for storing sensitive liquids.

The most expensive kind of sealer is a chamber vacuum sealer. To use a vacuum sealer, a bag is placed on its side with its opening running along a sealing bar. The lid is closed, a powerful vacuum is produced, and the seal is made with heat. This has the enormous advantage of being able to seal in liquids, whereas other machines do not.

Other sealers, such as impulse sealers, are much less expensive than vacuum sealers, but cannot handle liquids. In some cases, they fail to eliminate all of the air contained in the bag.

A busy (and profitable) restaurant may well find a vacuum sealer to be a worthwhile investment, but for a small restaurant or for the home cook, this is usually overkill. Keep in mind that perfect vacuum packing is only needed when the food-filled bags need to be stored for any length of time. Food exposed to air is much more likely to attract bacteria, especially if the liquid is warm. If the food is being served right away, a little air in the pouch rarely does any harm.

ROTOR STATOR HOMOGENIZER

This resembles an immersion blender but instead of a propeller-like blade at the end, it has a fixed tube with a rotor that spins within it. With settings up to 30,000 rpm, rotor stator homogenizers can create emulsions mechanically, sometimes without any emulsifier in the recipe. For example, a vinaigrette with no mustard made using a rotor stator homogenizer remains stable for days. The device is invaluable for making emulsified sauces such as mayonnaise, hollandaise, beurre blanc, and other stubborn emulsions.

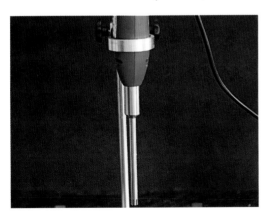 

SCALES

In most restaurant kitchens, a standard kitchen scale measuring to a tenth of a gram is sufficient. For some of the newer compounds being used by modernist cooks, which may be used in minute amounts, a more accurate scale, measuring to a hundredth or even a thousandth of a gram, is necessary. Because such sensitive scales will weigh only modest amounts, most kitchens have two scales: one for measuring relatively large amounts and the other reserved for working with smaller amounts of powerful compounds.

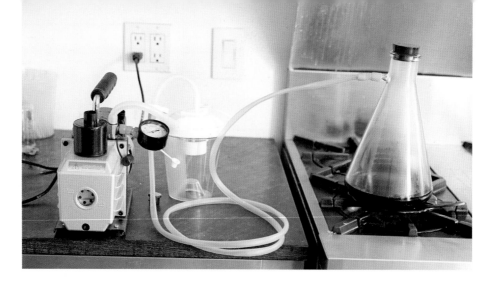

VACUUM PUMPS

Some sauces or sauce components are best boiled or evaporated under vacuum so that the temperature inside the vessel can remain relatively low. This way, the sauce can be reduced and its more delicate and fleeting components remain intact, since they have not been exposed to high heat. This is especially useful when working with fine wines or delicate gelées in which the finesse of the sauce is particularly important.

While there are many kinds of vacuum pumps, some costing many thousands of dollars, two types are most commonly used in the kitchen. A medical vacuum pump is relatively inexpensive, and convenient to use. Most such pumps come with a separate vessel—a trap—that can be used to condense excess water vapor and thus prevent moisture from entering the pump (which would cause damage). A trap is in essence another flask with a two-holed stopper and two lengths of glass tubing (one for each hole) that is set up between the main flask and the pump. The trap is best submerged in ice water (along with any tubing leading to it) so that it condenses any moisture before it can reach the pump.

Least expensive is a vacuum aspirator that connects to the kitchen tap. When the water is run, a vacuum is created in the side arm of the device. While these can be highly effective, they have the disadvantage of using a great deal of water.

To use a vacuum pump, set up an Erlenmeyer flask with a one-hole stopper. Insert a couple of inches of glass tubing into the hole to attach the hose. Attach about 3 feet of rubber tubing to the glass tubing in the cork, then attach the other end of this tubing to the trap. There are several ways to set up a trap (see page 633), but one easy way is to use another Erlenmeyer the same size as the other one. Insert a two-hole stopper and connect the hose from the first flask. Attach another length of rubber tubing from the second hole in the cork to the pump.

Submerge the first flask and the first length of rubber tubing in ice water. Keep the flask from bobbing up by securing it to the bottom of the bowl. In this way, as the vapor comes off the boiling liquid, it is condensed and liquefied in the trap before making it to the pump.

VISCOMETER

Used to measure the viscosity of liquids, a viscometer is rarely essential in a modern kitchen. It measures the absolute thickness of a liquid, so it is extremely useful for standardizing thickeners and thickening mixtures. If, for example, you want to prepare a sauce with the exact thickness of a particular béchamel sauce, but you want to use

xanthan gum instead of flour, a viscometer will allow you to establish the quantities of ingredients you need. (So will the chart in the back of this book on page 637—carefully calculated using a viscometer.)

Viscometers come in many forms. Perhaps the most common kind is a rotary (or rotational) viscometer. This determines the thickness of a liquid by twirling a probe of given dimensions within the liquid and calculating the amount of resistance the liquid exerts on the probe as it spins. Another viscometer uses a small sphere that is allowed to fall through the liquid. By timing its fall, the viscosity can be determined. Avoid glass viscometers, called Ubbelhode viscometers, because they require a toxic solution for cleaning.

SERVING UTENSILS

PLATES

Plates for serving foods with sauces must have a distinct rim, to prevent the sauce from running up onto the plate's border. The depth of the inner section of the plate will depend on the style of sauce and the presentation. For light-style sauces, a relatively deep well is appropriate. For denser sauces served in smaller amounts, the plate's inner well should be smaller, so the sauce does not spread too thinly and congeal.

SAUCE SPOONS

While they've been around since the nineteenth century, sauce spoons had fallen out of favor until the 1960s, when they became popular as an aspect of nouvelle cuisine. They allow the diner to sip the sauce without resorting to mopping it up with bread, which dulls the sauce's flavor and adds unwanted bulk to the meal. Sauce spoons are oval shaped and are almost perfectly flat so that they can be easily slid against the bottom of the plate.

WIDE BOWLS

Unbound, brothy sauces are often too pale and too liquid to be served on regular plates. Many chefs now present dishes in wide soup bowls, from which the sauce can be sipped with a spoon. Some companies are taking this concept further and producing "plates" with a deep circular center well and a wide rim. These give elegance to small portions of food that might look ridiculous on a regular plate.

INGREDIENTS

Because sauces are often more intensely flavored than the foods they accompany, they must be prepared with the best available ingredients. The foods described in the following pages comprise both the liquid medium for a sauce—ingredients such as dairy products and wine—and flavorings, such as herbs, spices, anchovies, and vinegar. Some of these ingredients also function as sauce thickeners.

ASIAN SAUCES, CONDIMENTS, AND OTHER INGREDIENTS

Condiments and Sauces

CHILE OIL

Because commercially available chile oils are often of questionable quality, most serious cooks of Chinese foods make their own by infusing dried chiles or chile flakes and sometimes other aromatic ingredients such as ginger into vegetable oil (usually peanut oil) combined with dark Asian sesame oil (see page 601). It is used for flavoring dipping sauces or to give heat and flavor to stir-fries.

CHINESE CHILE PASTE

Bottled Chinese chile paste provides a convenient method of quickly incorporating heat and flavor into last-minute sauces and stir-fries. Chinese chile paste also has a particular flavor of its own because it has been fermented.

FERMENTED SOY BEAN PASTES

While Japanese miso (see page 41) is the best known, Korea has its own version (*twoenjang*, page 42) and China has its sauce-like *jiang*. Soy bean pastes are fermented with differing amounts of various grains, spices, and salt. The beans themselves may be left whole, chunky, or ground to a smooth paste. Any of these versions can be added to Asian sauces (Japanese or Korean broth-like sauces or sauces based on Chinese stir-fries) to give the sauces a distinctive and easily recognized regional or national character. Most fermented soy beans and pastes are first combined with a small amount of liquid, such as dashi or broth, and worked to a smooth paste before being combined with the rest of the ingredients.

FISH SAUCE

This bottled sauce is as fundamental to Southeast Asian cooking as soy sauce is to the cuisine of China. Fish sauce is made by allowing anchovies, other small fish, and occasionally squid to ferment in barrels for months at a time. The liquid released becomes fish sauce. Just as olive oil comes in different grades and potencies, so too does fish sauce (although the best quality will cost only a dollar or two more than the cheapest). Fish sauce keeps for at least a year in the refrigerator, although it may grow dark. Although much of the best fish sauce is from Vietnam, Thai brands are easier to find and are perfectly suitable.

HOISIN SAUCE

This popular Chinese sauce is rather sweet and has a jam-like consistency. Hoisin sauce, like so many Asian sauces and condiments, is based on fermented soy beans. Used alone, hoisin sauce is overly sweet and thick, but it can be used in combination with other Chinese sauce ingredients (rice vinegar, soy sauce, sesame oil, and so on) to provide a note of sweetness, or as a glaze for grilled meats. Small amounts of these mixtures are also welcome additions to simple stir-fries.

KOCHUJANG

This Korean chile paste, made from red chiles, Korean soy bean paste (twoenjang), and rice flour, is used as a spicy flavoring in Korean sauces, soups, and stews. It's almost essential in some recipes for contributing a characteristically Korean flavor.

MIRIN

A very sweet, sake-like cooking wine, mirin is often used in Japanese sauces. It provides a perfect balance to the smokiness of dashi and the saltiness of soy sauce. Mirin is found in small bottles in Japanese specialty stores. It's inexpensive and keeps indefinitely in the refrigerator. Kikkoman brand is excellent and available almost everywhere.

MISO

This is the best known of Japanese fermented soy bean pastes (China and Korea have their own styles). There are subtle differences between every brand of miso. The most commonly found miso in the United States is the pale tan *shinshu-miso*. It is relatively inexpensive, and makes a good all-purpose miso. *Shiro miso*, which contains a large proportion of rice, is very pale yellow and relatively sweet. It is excellent in delicate sauces such as cold dipping sauces or salad sauces. It can also be combined with stronger red miso to balance the shiro miso's sweetness and the red miso's saltiness. Of the darker, more savory misos, *inaka miso*, or "red" miso, and *hatcho miso* (the more expensive of the two) are the best for full-flavored broth-like sauces.

OYSTER SAUCE

Often used as a condiment and flavoring to give a sea-like note to Chinese sauces and stir-fries, oyster sauce, however, has none of the delicacy of fresh oysters. Brands vary in quality; if in doubt, buy the most expensive.

SESAME PASTE

The better-known version of sesame paste, tahini, sold in Middle Eastern groceries, is made from raw sesame seeds and has a rather delicate flavor. In Asian cooking, it is preferable to use sesame paste made from toasted seeds. Toasting and grinding sesame seeds is not terribly difficult (see page 585), but Chinese sesame paste (on some bottles called "sesame butter") is made from roasted seeds and makes a good substitute for homemade.

SHRIMP PASTE

A popular condiment in Southeast Asian cooking, shrimp paste, made by fermenting shrimp in the sun, has a strong fishy smell that can easily stink up a kitchen. When used discreetly it gives an essential depth of flavor to Southeast Asian sauces and stews. To avoid the strong smell, wrap the shrimp paste in aluminum foil and toast it in a skillet. Let it cool before stirring it into sauces and stews.

SOY SAUCE

When working with soy sauce, there are a few things to look out for. Most important, avoid cheap synthetic supermarket brands and look for an authentic sauce that has been naturally brewed. Naturally brewed soy sauces will mention only water, soy beans, wheat, salt, and occasionally sodium benzoate, a preservative. Authentic soy sauce is made by fermenting roasted soy beans with wheat for at least four months and up to two years.

Japanese soy sauces are less salty than Chinese versions, and although Chinese cooking purists would disagree, in a pinch good quality Japanese sauce can be substituted for Chinese. Japanese soy sauce comes in both dark and light. Light soy sauce contains more salt and is used in sauces where the deep color of dark soy sauce would discolor the dish in an unpleasant way.

Indonesia has its own soy sauces, called *kecap* (pronounced like "ketchup"). *Kecap asin* is dark and salty, while *kecap manis*, also dark, is very sweet.

TWOENJANG

The Korean equivalent of miso, twoenjang has a distinctive—and stronger—flavor, essential in a number of Korean sauces. While Japanese miso can be used as a substitute, it will not give a sauce an essential Korean character.

Herbs and Spices

ASAFETIDA

Usually sold as a powder or in chunks (which are preferable, but need grinding), asafetida is used in Indian cooking as a replacement for onion. Asafetida has a peculiar pungent odor when heated. It is one of the flavorings in Sambaar Powder (page 609).

CURRY LEAVES

These leaves look somewhat like bay leaves but have a milder and distinctly different flavor; they are used in larger amounts. Curry leaves are widely used in India (especially Southern India) as a flavoring for vegetarian bean and lentil dishes. Curry leaves can be found dried, frozen, and occasionally fresh in Indian groceries.

FENUGREEK SEEDS AND LEAVES

Ground or whole, fenugreek seeds are rarely used alone. They are primarily a component in curry powders whose flavor they soften. Ground fenugreek harmonizes will with other spices. Fenugreek seeds taste a lot like maple and are used as a flavoring in artificial maple syrup. Fenugreek leaves are used in Indian cooking, primarily as a flavoring for starchy vegetables such as potatoes.

GALANGAL

Similar in appearance to ginger, galangal is most often used in Indonesian and Thai cooking as a flavoring for soups, curries, and sauces. It has a distinct and exotic pine-resin flavor. The best place to find galangal is in Thai or Indonesian specialty food stores, where it is called *kha* or *laos*. Galangal can sometimes be found fresh but is usually sold frozen, either whole or in slices. Powdered dried galangal is also available, but it is much less aromatic than fresh or frozen.

LEMONGRASS

Lemongrass comes in long stalks. The tough outermost sheath is peeled off and discarded and only the relatively soft white root end is used. Traditionally, sliced lemongrass is infused in Southeast Asian sauces, stews, and soups or ground up with other ingredients in Thai curries. Western chefs have caught on to lemongrass and infuse it in delicate broth-like sauces. Finely julienned lemon zest of one lemon, quickly blanched to eliminate its bitterness, will replace a 3-inch (8 cm) section of lemongrass stalk. Lemongrass can be kept for several months, tightly wrapped, in the freezer.

MAKRUT LIME LEAVES AND FRUIT

Makrut (sometimes called kaffir) lime leaves, rind, and juice are all used in Southeast Asian cooking. Makrut lime (*Citrus hystix*) is closely related to our common lime (*Citrus aurantifolia*), but the flavor of makrut lime is more subtle and more lemony. Makrut lime leaves are simmered whole in Southeast Asian sauces and stews in much the same way as bay leaves enter into their Western equivalents.

Makrut lime rind, sold frozen in Asian markets, is usually ground to a paste as a component of Thai curries (pages 590 to 596) and makrut lime juice (difficult to find) is used to provide acidity. The zest of the common lime (blanched and julienned or chopped) can be used as a substitute for makrut lime leaves and rind, and regular lime juice can be used to provide acidic tang. Makrut leaves are sold fresh or frozen in Asian markets. Both the leaves and rind will keep frozen for several months.

Other Ingredients

BONITO

A fish closely related to tuna, bonito is dried and smoked, and sold in what look like very ripe bananas called *katsuo-bushi*. In the best kitchens, katsuo-bushi is shaved into flakes almost immediately before being used, but more commonly bonito is sold already shaved in flakes called *hana-katsuo* or *kezuri-bushi*. Typically, bonito flakes are infused in hot water that has already been infused with a strip of konbu, to make the broth called dashi (see page 576), which is almost universal in Japanese cooking.

COCONUT MILK

This is almost essential for making Southeast Asian curries and curries from Southern India, where it is used in much the same way Western cooks would use cream.

Many cooks who think that coconut milk is the liquid trapped inside a fresh coconut are surprised to discover that coconut milk is made by soaking ground or grated pulp in hot water and then squeezing out the liquid (method follows). Coconut cream is the rich, congealed coconut fat that floats to the top of both homemade and good canned coconut milk. The cream should be added along with the milk. Fortunately, excellent coconut milk is available inexpensively in cans (Thai brands are best). Avoid coconut milk containing stabilizers (even the best brands, however, contain sodium benzoate as a preservative), and "cream of coconut" containing sugar, which is designed for making piña coladas.

To make about 2 cups (500 milliliters) fresh coconut milk, shake the coconut to hear whether there's liquid sloshing around inside. If there's no liquid, the coconut may have been punctured and could be rancid inside; do not use it. Use a hammer and a screwdriver to puncture holes in two of the coconut "eyes" (the dark oval spots near the top). Drain out the liquid, which is perfectly drinkable but too thin to use in a sauce. Bake the coconut in a 375°F (190°C) oven for 20 minutes to get the pulp to separate from the shell. Wrap the coconut in a towel and hit it with a hammer to crack it open. Pull out the pulp.

Peel the thin, dark peel off the sections of pulp with a vegetable peeler. Grind the pulp in a food processor for about 1 minute or grate it with a hand grater.

Put the grated pulp in a mixing bowl and add 1 cup (250 milliliters) boiling water. Let the mixture sit for 10 minutes, then drain through a medium-mesh strainer into another bowl, reserving the liquid. Wrap the drained pulp in a kitchen towel and wring out any remaining liquid over the bowl. Put the wrung-out pulp back in the original mixing bowl and add another cup (250 milliliters) boiling water. Repeat the draining and wringing process.

Fresh coconut milk and opened canned coconut milk can be kept in the refrigerator for 1 week or frozen for several months.

FERMENTED BLACK BEANS

These salted and partially dried beans look like dark raisins but have an intense salty flavor that makes them particularly delicious in Chinese stir-fries and sauces. Black beans are often used in conjunction with dried chiles or chile paste, garlic, ginger, and sesame oil. Black beans should be rinsed; if they're not rinsed or they'll make the sauce too salty. When buying fermented black beans, look for brands that have been flavored with ginger but not with Chinese five-spices.

GHEE

A favorite cooking fat and flavoring in India, ghee is the same as beurre noisette (see page 438).

SEAWEED

There are many kinds of seaweed (also somewhat euphemistically called "sea greens" or "sea vegetables"), but only one, konbu, is used with any regularity for sauce making.

Konbu is a dried seaweed sold in 18-inch to 3-foot-long (45 to 90 cm) strips that have been folded over themselves for easy packaging. The best konbu comes from the northern Japanese island of Hokkaido and is usually covered with a white, delicate, salt-like dust. Along with dried bonito, konbu is the basis for the basic broth dashi (page 576), common to most Japanese broth-like sauces.

TAMARIND

Tamarind in the husk looks vaguely like a withered and dried brown fava bean. The husk is removed to reveal a series of beans surrounded with a sticky brown pulp. The pulp, not the beans, is used in Southeast Asian cooking to give sourness to sauces, soups, and stews. Since fresh tamarind isn't always available, it's fortunate that packages of tamarind paste (which looks like brown tar) are inexpensive and easy to find. Add tamarind paste to taste to Southeast Asian and Southern Asian broth-like sauces. The pulp should be strained out of the liquid before serving. Lime or lemon juice makes an adequate substitute.

CONDIMENTS

Mustard

Mustard comes in three forms: dried powdered; crushed and macerated in flavorful liquid; and whole-grain. The mustard's flavor is controlled by the liquid used to macerate the mustard seeds or by adding herbs or other flavorings at the end.

RED WINE MUSTARD

This mustard sometimes tastes bitter when first made. The bitterness disappears after a few hours.

YIELD: 2 CUPS (500 MILLILITERS)

black mustard seeds	4 ounces	125 grams
distinctly flavored red wine	¾ cup	185 milliliters
red wine vinegar	¾ cup	185 milliliters
shallot, finely chopped	1	1
salt	1 teaspoon	5 milliliters
freshly ground black pepper	to taste	to taste
chopped herbs (thyme, marjoram, tarragon)	to taste	to taste

1. Combine all the ingredients in a ceramic or stainless-steel bowl, cover with plastic wrap, and refrigerate overnight.

2. Purée the mixture in a blender until it attains the desired thickness and texture. Store in the refrigerator in a jar with a tight-fitting lid.

Oils

Derived from a variety of natural sources—grains, seeds, nuts, and fruits—oils offer the cook their own particular flavors. Oils are used for sautéing and deep-frying, and are the predominant ingredient in mayonnaises, vinaigrettes, flavored oils, and even some hot emulsified egg sauces.

Oils vary widely in quality and cost, and the cook must use them judiciously so as not to waste an expensive oil needlessly or spoil a dish using a cheap one. Delicately flavored oils, for example, should not be used for sautéing, as the high heat would destroy their flavor.

The most common problem with oil is rancidity. Rancid oil tastes and smells like stale nuts; in fact so many cooks are accustomed to using rancid oil that they no longer recognize it. A good-quality oil should be completely tasteless (when it will be used to sauté, to dilute the flavor of more assertive oils, or when needed to provide substance but no flavor such as in mayonnaise or vinaigrette) or have the clear taste of the plant from which it is derived. Oils are best stored well covered in a cool place or in the refrigerator.

Because oils contain no protein or other emulsifiers, as do butter, egg yolks, and cream, they are usually not added to a sauce unless some kind of emulsifier is used with them (see Chapter 16, "Salad Sauces, Vinaigrettes, Salsas, and Relishes," page 463).

AVOCADO OIL

Perhaps the most inert of all the oils, avocado oil makes it easier to emulate the ubiquitous *huile d'arachide* (peanut oil) found in France. It makes perfect mayonnaise and vinaigrette and doesn't, like extra-virgin olive oil, turn bitter when it is beaten. Its only disadvantage is its expense.

GRAPESEED OIL

Grapeseed oil is sometimes used for browning meats and fish because of its high smoking temperature. Since it is virtually tasteless, it can be used to dilute the flavor of olive or nut oils or be used on its own in vinaigrette and mayonnaise.

NUT OILS

In addition to flavoring vinaigrettes and mayonnaise, nut oils are excellent with assertive or bitter greens, fennel, and artichokes.

Remember that oils made from roasted nuts have a deeper color and fuller flavor than oils made from raw nuts; they also hold up better against rancidity. Avoid raw nut oils, as they are *extremely* perishable. Raw nut oil will probably be rancid when you open it; nut oils made from roasted nuts will last about a year if kept in a cool spot.

OLIVE OIL

Of all oils, olive oil is the most versatile and essential for sauce making and general cooking. It is available in different grades that are based on how the oil is extracted from the olive, and the amount of oleic acid it contains. Oleic acid gives olive oil a harsh, biting feel in the mouth. The best-quality olive oil, extra-virgin (*vierge extra* in French, *extra vergine* in Italian), contains 1 percent or less oleic acid and usually has the words "first cold pressed" or "*première pression à froid*" on the label. This means that cold pressure alone, rather than heat or chemicals, has been used to extract the oil from the olives. Extra-virgin olive oil is a completely natural product of often startling delicacy and complexity, which are influenced by climate, soil, the age of the trees, the vintage, and other factors. There are no reliable rules as to which oils—Italian, Spanish, French, Greek—are the best; like wine, each oil needs to be judged on its own.

Although there are several grades of olive oil, the most common grades seen in America are extra-virgin olive oil and oil designated "pure." Pure olive oil may contain up to 4 percent oleic acid, can come from second or later pressings, and need not be cold pressed. It is useful for sautéing and deep-frying, when the delicacy of extra-virgin olive oil would be destroyed. Pure olive oil is considerably less expensive. Many professional chefs keep both oils in the kitchen: extra-virgin for sauces and flavorings, and pure for sautéing, deep-frying, and to use in conjunction with extra-virgin to soften its flavor in certain sauces. Extra-virgin olive oil will keep a year or two if kept cool and shielded from light.

This intensely flavored, deep brown oil is used sparingly in many Asian sauces and, nowadays, in Western-style sauces as well. Use only dark sesame oil, made from roasted seeds, and preferably a brand from Japan. Avoid pale and clear sesame oil sold in health food stores (it has little flavor).

VEGETABLE OILS

Although raw cold-pressed oils made from grains can be found in health food stores, a tasteless commercial variety is most useful to the saucier. In addition to their use for browning meats and fish (they smoke at a very high temperature), these oils are sometimes used by sauciers in conjunction with olive oil or a flavorful nut oil for vinaigrettes and mayonnaises.

In France an inexpensive, commercially available peanut oil (huile d'arachide) is used whenever a tasteless oil is needed. In the United States, the situation is somewhat more difficult because many of the widely available brands of peanut oil, corn oil, vegetable oil, and safflower oil have a peculiar and unpleasant taste. When heated, these oils often smell like fish. Relatively tasteless and odorless brands of these oils can be found (avocado oil is great but expensive), but a little searching and comparative tasting may be needed. It is also possible to buy French huile d'arachide, but it is almost as expensive as olive oil. A good-quality pure olive oil (see page 46) will often work better than vegetable oil when a relatively tasteless oil is needed.

Use vegetable oils sparingly in mayonnaises and vinaigrettes; they not only can adversely affect the taste, but will often leave an unpleasant greasy feeling in the mouth.

Verjuice

Verjuice (*verjus*) is the juice of underripe grapes. It was widely used as a sauce flavoring and condiment in medieval and Renaissance French and Italian cooking. Very acidic, its function in a sauce is somewhat like that of vinegar or lemon juice but not exactly like either one. It is the latest darling of French chefs and is beginning to show up in sauces, usually for fish. It seems to go particularly well with fennel and coriander seeds. Try experimenting with verjuice as a replacement for lemon juice in fish sauces.

Vinegar

Vinegar is an indispensable ingredient for sauce making. A few drops added to a sauce along with the final seasoning will awaken the flavor of the sauce without making it overwhelmingly acidic. Vinegar can also be used in surprisingly large amounts for stewing and braising meats—the result is full-flavored and mild. It is also, of course, a primary ingredient in vinaigrette.

Many types of vinegar are available and, as with most ingredients, the way to determine which is best is to taste and compare them. Essentially, vinegar consists of a mixture of acetic acid and water; additional flavor components derived from the source of the vinegar (such as wine, cider, beer) and developed during aging give the vinegar its finesse and make it useful in the kitchen.

Commercial vinegars range in strength from 5 to 7 percent acetic acid. Wine vinegar is the type most often used for sauce making. Distilled white vinegar should be avoided, as it contains none of the by-products that soften the flavor of vinegar and make it palatable.

Select a wine vinegar that has a high acid content but is not harsh. Sherry vinegar has a rich, complex flavor and full acidity that make it excellent for finishing brown sauces. Champagne vinegar is much less complex in flavor than sherry vinegar but has a clean, sharp taste that makes it useful in preparations where sherry vinegar would be too assertive, such as beurre blanc and sauce béarnaise.

Authentic balsamic vinegar is a specialty of Modena, Italy, made by aging in a series of wooden barrels for years or even decades. Most of the so-called balsamic vinegar is factory made, but even these mass-produced substitutes have an appealing sweetness and complexity that makes them useful for sauce making. Keep in mind that balsamic vinegar will make vinaigrette and pale sauces turn dark.

In Asia, vinegars are typically made from grains such as rice, wheat, millet, and sorghum. The mildest of these vinegars is Japanese rice vinegar, which has been diluted down to a manageable 4.3 percent acetic acid. Chinese rice vinegars (don't buy rice "flavored" vinegars) are far tastier and are better in dishes with stronger, more competitive flavors. The most flavorful Chinese vinegar is black vinegar, made mostly of fermented wheat but also other grains, and aged in much the same way as balsamic vinegar.

Vinegar is used for storing herbs—particularly tarragon, whose flavor is far less altered by vinegar than by drying. There are many types of herb vinegars on the market, but the herb flavor in these vinegars is often not assertive enough to make them useful for sauce making. If you have a garden, or fresh herbs are available, it is more practical to prepare these vinegars yourself (see Infused Vinegars, page 474). An assortment of full-flavored herb vinegars will enable you to adjust the sauce's final flavor without having to chop the herb, add it to the sauce, give it time to infuse, and perhaps strain it out.

Fruit-flavored vinegars can be prepared by steeping a particular fruit in wine vinegar for a week or two and then straining the mixture through a chinois or a fine-meshed drum sieve. Commercially available fruit vinegars seem to contain cooked or concentrated fruits that give them an excessively sweet, candy-like flavor. (For a discussion of herb-infused vinegars for vinaigrette, see page 467.)

DAIRY PRODUCTS

Butter

The subtle flavor and satiny texture of butter make it one of the most important ingredients in sauce making. It contributes its own nuances to a sauce while gently amplifying and bringing into perspective the sauce's primary flavors. Butter, if used in moderation, can be added to a sauce without diluting the sauce's flavor or distorting its character.

Any wholesome salt-free butter can be used in sauce making with good if not excellent results, but some butters have different flavors and behave differently. As you use one kind of butter, its behavior will become familiar and you can more closely predict how it will act in specific preparations.

French butter tastes and behaves differently from American butter. French butter is made from crème fraîche—cream that is thickened by inoculation or natural fermentation (see page 465) with beneficial and lactic-acid producing bacteria. When cream that has been fermented in this way is churned into butter, the butter will have a complex, slightly nutty taste. Butter made from fresh cream or from cream that has been pasteurized (such as American butter) soon after being separated from the milk will have a milder flavor than butter made from crème fraîche. If you are trying to imitate the flavor of sauces tasted in France, be sure to use French butter.

The terms "wet" and "dry" sometimes refer to the actual water content, which can vary from 15 to 25 percent. Moisture content is important in sauce making because it helps determine how much butter will be needed to give the desired consistency to a liquid. If the butter contains a lot of water, more will be required to thicken a sauce. More often, "wet" and "dry" refer to the types of fat that constitute the butter. Wet butter will leave an oily film on the hands, while a dry butter will leave the hands relatively dry. This difference is caused by the varying proportions of naturally hydrogenated fats contained in each. Dry butters (which contain more hydrogenated fats) work more effectively as liaisons in sauce making.

Because the flavor of milk, and thus butter, depends on an almost infinite variety of conditions, butter can be an extremely individual product. Butter is affected by the time of year and by the species of cows and their grazing conditions. Cows that feed in fresh pastures will produce fuller-tasting milk than cows fed on hay. Traditional farm butter will taste different from one farm to the next.

In France, and more recently in America, cooks are beginning to appreciate traditionally-made farmhouse butter. Such butter develops individual nuances in part because of the microbial action that is allowed to take place before the butter is churned. Strains of bacteria differ from region to region and even from farm to farm. Each batch of butter results from the activity of an individual ecosystem on the components in the cream. Each of these bacterial "societies" leaves traces of flavor components in the butter, giving the butter its character.

In mass-produced French-style butter, the cream is pasteurized before it is inoculated with laboratory cultured bacteria to give it the gentle acidic tang to which the French have grown accustomed. These bacteria contribute to the cream's complexity— and ultimately, the butter's—but because the butter is always prepared from the same bacterial strain, individuality is lost.

Because butter is a natural emulsion containing fat, water, and a complex collection of proteins, it must be handled carefully so that this emulsion stays intact. Once butter has been melted, the water and proteins separate from the fats, which become clarified butter.

Cheese

Made by separating curds from whey and then fermenting, cooking, and/or aging the curds, cheese comes in hundreds of varieties.

BLUE CHEESES
Some blue cheeses give a complex yet forthright flavor to sauces, especially white sauces such as mornay sauce (see page 137). Many cooks do not realize that there are many types of blue cheese; some are delicious, while others border on the inedible. Always buy the best available. The best-known blue cheese is Roquefort. Authentic Roquefort comes from a closely delineated area in France and is made entirely of sheep's milk. When sufficiently aged, it is one of the world's finest cheeses.

France alone produces over thirty varieties of blue cheese, with each stamping its character onto a sauce. Apart from Roquefort, Fourme d'Ambert, Bleu d'Auvergne, and Bleu de Bresse are especially good. Two other deservedly famous blue cheeses are British Stilton and Italian Gorgonzola. Danish blue and industrial blue cheeses manufactured in the United States are not recommended, as they have an aggressive and unpleasant odor and taste.

DRY CHEESES

Although Parmesan and Gruyère are the cheeses most often used for making traditional cheese sauces, almost any well-aged, honest dry cheese will do. If a cheese has too high a moisture content or is insufficiently aged, it will lack flavor and make the sauce stringy. It may even ruin the sauce by bunching up into a solid mass. Always use authentic cheeses rather than substitutes. Buy only Italian Parmesan cheese labeled Parmigiano-Reggiano. Never buy grated Parmesan.

"Swiss cheese" is a generic term that denotes a certain style but in no way guarantees the quality or flavor of the cheese. Authentic Emmentaler cheese is sometimes labeled "Imported from Switzerland." Although this is an honest cheese, it is usually too young to be suitable for sauce making because it contains too much moisture and will turn stringy. Gruyère and Fribourg have less moisture and are excellent in sauces. The French often use Comté instead of Gruyère. Raclette is a bit strong but also especially good.

American and British recipes often call for Cheddar cheese. Authentic well-aged Cheddar from England, as well as good American Cheddar-style cheese, is excellent in sauces. Avoid Cheddar-style cheeses that have been colored with orange dye; it has no effect on flavor but will make the sauce look weird.

FRESH CHEESE

Fresh cheese (*fromage blanc*) is manufactured in two ways. One method relies on rennet to coagulate the milk, while the other uses a lactic acid–producing bacterial culture. Fresh cows' milk cheese is difficult to obtain in the United States (young goat cheese, on the other hand, is easy to find). Fresh cheese is not difficult to make, but check your local health regulations before serving a homemade version to the public.

Fresh cheese is sometimes used as a thickener for low-fat white sauces. Because it often has a rough texture in the mouth, it is best combined with at least a small amount of heavy cream or crème fraîche.

Cream

Heavy cream is indispensable for many traditional white sauces as well as nouvelle cuisine sauces thickened with reduced cream. It is an extremely stable emulsion that can be boiled and reduced to almost any consistency. Unlike milk, which must be stabilized with emulsifiers such as flour, hydrocolloids, or egg yolks, heavy cream will not break unless it is boiled without stirring or is overreduced. Heavy cream contains about 58 percent water, 35 to 37 percent fat, 3 percent carbohydrates, and a small percentage of ash and various minerals. Don't substitute milk, half and half, or light cream for heavy cream.

SOUR CREAM

Manufactured sour cream is prepared by mixing milk fat and skim milk with nonfat solids and other ingredients. The mixture is then pasteurized, inoculated with lactic acid–producing bacteria, and allowed to set. Because of the texture, many beginning cooks assume that sour cream is as rich as heavy cream and can be used in the same way. Sour cream contains less butterfat than heavy cream (about 18 percent versus 35 percent) and is a much less stable emulsion. For this reason sour cream cannot be reduced or even boiled, or it will curdle. A large number of recipes—of mostly Eastern European origin—finish stews and sauces with sour cream (such as beef Stroganoff). When finishing a sauce with sour cream, make sure the sauce base is overly thick before adding the sour cream, which will thin it. A too-thick sauce can easily be thinned, but once the sour cream has been added, no further reduction is possible.

Yogurt

Yogurt is manufactured by inoculating whole or skim milk with a culture containing two types of bacteria, *Lactobacillus bulgaricus* and *Streptococcus thermophilus*. The ratio between the two organisms has much to do with the flavor of the yogurt. When *L. bulgaricus* dominates, the yogurt will have more acidity and tang. A greater percentage of *S. thermophilus*, on the other hand, will give the yogurt a deeper flavor with more finesse. In food establishments where yogurt is used on a regular basis, it may be worth obtaining cultures of both microorganisms so that the flavor of the yogurt used in sauce making can be closely controlled.

Some sauces (primarily fish sauces) benefit from the acidity of a tangy yogurt, while a less-acidic yogurt is useful for lightening mayonnaises, emulsified egg yolk sauces, and similar preparations (see "Yogurt and Fresh Cheese," page 124). Don't allow sauces containing yogurt to boil.

HERBS

In culinary usage spices are usually roots, seeds, berries, bark, and other fruits (see page 61), while herbs are leaves or flowers. The aromatic vegetables, such as garlic and shallots, comprise a third group of flavorings.

An experienced saucier uses herbs at several stages of the sauce-making process. The decision as to when to use a certain herb depends on the herb's flavor and its reaction to heat. Some herbs contribute to the background flavor of a sauce, while others are added at the last minute to add finesse and freshness or a character of their own.

Some herbs, such as thyme and bay leaf, release their flavor slowly into the surrounding liquid. When added discreetly at the beginning of the sauce's preparation, their flavor is subtle enough to blend with the sauce's savory constituents, giving the sauce complexity without distracting from its primary flavor. Used in this way, herbs meld with the other ingredients in the sauce so their presence, though not immediately recognizable, gives a sauce mystery and depth of flavor. While thyme, for example, is usually added to a bouquet garni and long simmered, it can also become the sauce's predominant flavor by chopping it and adding it near the end.

Certain herbs, primarily parsley, chervil, tarragon and chives (the four herbs that constitute *fines herbes*), can be finely chopped and added to give the sauce finesse and freshness. The flavor of these herbs, except that of the tarragon, dissipates quickly, so they should be chopped and added during the last few minutes of cooking to give the sauce freshness and vitality without altering its predominant flavor. If using fresh herbs in a sauce finished with butter, turn the herbs into a compound butter and use that to finish the sauce. In this way the herbs won't turn black or dry out.

SMALL BOUQUET GARNI. Tie in a bundle with kitchen twine, or in a sachet if using dried thyme: 1 bay leaf, 3 sprigs parsley, 1 sprig thyme (or ½ teaspoon/ 3 milliliters dried leaves).

MEDIUM BOUQUET GARNI. Tie in a bundle with kitchen twine, or in a sachet if using dried thyme: 1½ bay leaves, 6 sprigs parsley, 2 sprigs thyme (or ¾ teaspoon/4 milliliters dried leaves).

LARGE BOUQUET GARNI. Tie in a bundle with kitchen twine, or in a sachet if using dried thyme: 2 bay leaves, 1 large bunch parsley, 5 sprigs thyme (or 1 teaspoon/5 milliliters dried leaves).

Dried Versus Fresh Herbs

Some dried herbs retain their flavor better than others. Thyme, marjoram, oregano, lavender, savory, and rosemary can be dried without altering or seriously attenuating their flavor. It is always preferable, however, to start with the fresh herb and dry it on the branch. Bottles of dried thyme or savory never have the same flavor as leaves that have been dried and left on the branch.

The flavor of some herbs is either lost or irreversibly distorted once dried. Basil, chervil, tarragon, parsley, and chives do not dry well and should not be used. If confronted with an abundance of fresh tarragon, it is better to pack it tightly in jars with white wine vinegar than to dry it. The flavors of basil, chervil, chives, and parsley, however, are unpleasantly altered when the herbs are stored in vinegar.

Chopping Herbs

Many chefs and amateur cooks, in an attempt to be well prepared, chop their herbs in advance and have them on hand to be used as last-minute flavorings. Some chopped herbs immediately begin to lose flavor, or worse, their flavor is unpleasantly changed.

When chopping herbs, make sure they are perfectly dry. If an herb is chopped while wet, the flavors dissipate into the surrounding liquid. The chopped herb will also form clumps and become impossible to chop finely and evenly. Many cooks wring chopped parsley out in a towel after it is chopped to eliminate excess moisture and make the parsley easy to sprinkle in sauces or over foods. Such parsley may be easier to handle, but most of its flavor and finesse will be lost.

Always use an extremely sharp knife. If herbs are chopped with a dull knife, they are crushed, prematurely releasing most of their flavor into the surrounding air or into the cutting board.

Certain herbs, such as basil and tarragon, almost immediately turn black when chopped. The best way to prevent this discoloration is to protect the herb from oxygen by first coating the leaves with a thin layer of olive oil or by chopping the herbs with a small chunk of butter. In either case, chop the herbs as close to the last minute as possible.

Fines Herbes

The term "fines herbes" refers to a mixture of equal parts of four herbs: tarragon, chervil, parsley, and chives. While traditional recipes insist that tarragon be used in the same amounts as the other herbs, it can easily overwhelm the sauce; many chefs use it in smaller amounts or leave it out. Fines herbes are added to a sauce near the end to wake it up and give it finesse and freshness.

BASIL

Basil's vibrant sunny smell and bright flavor make it a natural component of intense, full-flavored sauces. It is not a subtle herb, but works beautifully with other assertively flavored ingredients such as saffron, garlic, and olive oil. It is irresistible when used in Mediterranean fish sauces.

Basil works best when added to a sauce at the very end of the sauce's cooking. Its flavor is so volatile that it will rapidly dissipate if cooked for more than a minute or two. Like tarragon, basil quickly turns black when chopped, so it is best to dribble a little extra-virgin olive oil over the leaves before beginning or incorporate the basil into a compound butter.

Basil does not dry well but can be frozen if chopped finely with olive oil and stored in a tightly sealed plastic container.

BAY LEAF

One of the basic components of a bouquet garni, bay leaf, if cooked for an hour or more, lends a gentle complexity to stews and to red wine and game sauces. The amount to use must be gauged carefully, or the flavor will either be too dominating or disappear altogether. Dried bay leaf is acceptable, but the leaves should be broken in two and sniffed to ensure they are not stale. California bay leaves have an aggressive eucalyptus flavor and should not be used.

CHERVIL

Chervil may be the most delicate of all herbs. Fresh chervil (dried chervil has no value) has a delicate anise flavor, vaguely reminiscent of tarragon but far more subtle and fleeting. Because of its delicacy, chervil should be used only in the last minutes or two of cooking.

CHIVES

Chopped chives can be used near the end of cooking to impart their delicate onion-like flavor to a sauce. When cooked for only a minute or two, their flavor melds with the other components and gives the sauce renewed vitality. Unlike onions or shallots, chives are never overly assertive.

Be careful when chopping chives. Hold a small bunch firmly between the thumb and first three fingers of the left hand (or right hand if you are left-handed), and carefully slice with a very sharp knife. If chives are chopped haphazardly, the pieces will be uneven and the excitement of seeing the tiny cubes in the sauce will be lost. Chives should always be chopped finely. Longish pieces of chives floating in a sauce may be appealing to the eye, but they are unpleasant in the mouth and will release their flavor suddenly and aggressively rather than gently caressing the sauce's basic flavors.

CILANTRO

The leaves of the plant that produces the spice coriander are known as cilantro. Freshly chopped cilantro leaves have a natural affinity for tomatoes, garlic, and hot peppers. The flavor is especially delicious in Mexican salsas and Indian curries. This herb is also discussed in conjunction with coriander in the "Spices" section, page 61.

DILL

The flavor of dill is so distinctive that it doesn't meld well with other herbs. It is delicious with seafood such as scallops and salmon, and works particularly well with sauces containing cream, which attenuates its domineering character. Some chefs confuse it with fennel—it looks vaguely like fennel greens—but the taste is entirely different.

LAVENDER

There are several varieties of lavender, but the most aromatic, and the best for cooking, is French lavender, *Lavandula spica*. Chefs rarely use lavender as the only herb in a dish, but may use it unknowingly in French *herbes de Provence* mixtures, of which it is a component. Lavender gives foods a distinctive aromatic flavor. It is wonderful with garlic; the two can be crushed together to a paste in a mortar and sprinkled over sautéed mushrooms or zucchini about a minute before they are removed from the heat—the flavor is irresistible. Be sure to use culinary (food-grade) lavender that hasn't been treated with pesticides.

LEMON THYME

Although lemon thyme looks much like regular thyme, it has a delicate, lemony flavor that makes it delightful in fish sauces and delicate court-bouillons served *à la nage*. It should not be thought of as a replacement for regular thyme, however, because it does not meld with other flavors in the same way.

MARJORAM

Although its flavor is completely different, marjoram is sometimes confused with oregano, its botanical cousin. Fresh marjoram (or recently dried) has an unmistakable aroma and flavor all its own. It is difficult to imagine a food that would not be complemented by fresh chopped marjoram (dried will do in a pinch), but it seems to work best with Mediterranean foods and flavors and is excellent with grilled meats and fish (often used combined with olive oil or worked into a compound butter). It can be sprinkled or brushed on and all sorts of vegetables, especially tomatoes, mushrooms, and squash. It can be added to sauce early or late depending on the desired effect.

MINT

Mint is used in Middle Eastern and Mediterranean cooking, and is popular with Americans and the English (think mint jelly). There are many varieties, with a wide spectrum of flavors; best known are spearmint and peppermint. Mint is an excellent flavoring in salad vinaigrettes, where it is best ground with a pinch of coarse salt using a mortar and pestle and then combined with lemon juice and oil just before serving. It is also excellent for scenting heavy cream served as a sauce for cucumbers and figs.

OREGANO

Oregano is one herb that improves and becomes fuller flavored when it is dried. There is considerable confusion as to the flavor of oregano, which seems to be influenced by the climate where it is grown. The fresh cultivated oregano available in the United States is surprisingly delicate. It is lovely with grilled rabbit. Don't confuse it with marjoram.

PARSLEY

Freshly chopped parsley can be added to a sauce during the last minute of cooking to contribute freshness and flavor without taking over. In larger amounts, it can be used as a primary flavor. Parsley should never be kept for more than 15 minutes after it has been chopped or its fresh, pungent vitality will rapidly dissipate. Stale parsley has a sour, grassy smell and taste and should be thrown out.

ROSEMARY

Although rosemary occasionally makes its way into a bouquet garni in Italian and southern French stews, it is best when used sparingly to scent grilled and roasted meats. It can be used in a marinade so that its flavor will be softened by the time it is captured in the roast's natural jus. If used carelessly or in excess, rosemary easily dominates the surrounding flavors. One use of rosemary is to throw a handful of the twigs on the hot coals near the end of grilling. The smoke lightly scents the grilled foods.

SAGE

When fresh, sage is wonderfully aromatic but can be frightfully strong. It is usually too aggressive to be used as a flavor finish for sauces but can be used for scenting veal and pork roasts or grilled meats and poultry. It is beautiful when cooked in frothy butter and poured over sautéed foods such as meats or fish. Be careful with dried sage—it sometimes smells and tastes like dust.

SAVORY

Two types of savory are used: summer (*Satureia hortensis*) and winter (*Satureia montana*). Both have a pungent yet malleable perfume reminiscent of thyme, which they sometimes replace in a bouquet garni. Winter savory seems to be the more useful of the two in sauces because its flavor is more subtle and melds more easily with other ingredients.

SORREL

Sorrel has a faint perfume but an intense, sour flavor. It is best used in fish sauces, where its sharp tang is a welcome alternative to the ubiquitous lemon wedge. Sorrel should be used in sauces containing at least a small amount of cream or butter, which soften its acidity.

TARRAGON

Tarragon is an assertive, full-flavored herb with an intense anise-like flavor. Unlike chervil and parsley, which willingly sacrifice their individuality to the whole, tarragon retains its character and always makes its presence felt. For this reason, it is usually used as the focal point of a sauce. It is a beautiful accent to the flavor of chicken, veal, and crustaceans such as lobster and crayfish. Tarragon is usually added near the end of sauce preparation, as the flavor is only weakened by lengthy cooking.

Tarragon turns black when exposed to air and thus should be chopped with a small chunk of butter or a tablespoon or more of oil to protect it. Tarragon does not dry well; drying not only attenuates but distorts its flavor. If fresh tarragon is not available, tarragon in vinegar is an excellent substitute (see page 474).

THYME

Thyme is one of the most subtle and versatile herbs used in sauce making. The saucier can control the directness of its flavor by using it at different stages during a sauce's preparation. Thyme added at earlier stages (such as in a bouquet garni in a stock) will meld into the background flavors of the sauce. When used in this way, it not only contributes its own subtle flavor but unifies the sometimes disparate flavors of vegetables, wine, meat, or fish. Owing to these characteristics, thyme is one of the three components of a traditional bouquet garni (the others are bay leaf and parsley; see page 52).

Thyme can also be used (cautiously) at a later stage. It is often sweated with mirepoix vegetables, which are in turn moistened with wine, stock, or other flavored liquids to give the sauce its final character.

MUSHROOMS AND TRUFFLES

Mushrooms

Not so long ago, most Americans were suspicious of anything other than the standard white mushroom, *Agaricus bisporus*. Nowadays, cremini mushrooms, which look like basic white mushrooms but are brown, are popular. They contain less water than white mushrooms and have more flavor. Wild mushrooms have become almost standard ingredients in upscale shops and with fancy wholesalers. Wild mushrooms, especially morels and cèpes (porcini), lend a magnificent complexity to sauces. When dried, a mushroom or two will flavor a large amount of soup or stock. They are magnificent, reconstituted in a duxelles (see page 179) or when used to make mushroom cooking liquid.

If wild mushrooms are clean or if bits of sand and soil can easily be brushed free, it is best to avoid washing them. To wash mushrooms, rinse them under rapidly running cold water in a colander while tossing them between your fingers rather than letting them soak in a bowl or sink.

Mushrooms, which contain a large amount of water, benefit from first being sautéed in very hot fat or oil, which lightly caramelizes their juices and concentrates their flavor. Don't sauté too many mushrooms at once or they will release liquid and stew in their own juices. Wait for each batch to brown before adding more.

CHANTERELLES

Chanterelles (*Cantharellus cibarius*) are often called *girolles* in French. These golden horn-shaped mushrooms range from 2 to 3 inches (5 to 8 cm) long and 1 to 2 inches (2.5 to 5 cm) wide. They are very popular. They are pretty, plentiful, and easy to cook and unlike some mushroom varieties, they do not release much water during cooking.

The French name for these mushrooms (species name, *Craterellus cornucopioides*) is *trompettes de la mort* (trumpets of death) because of their shape and black color. Fortunately, they are delicious, and their jet-black color is striking on the plate. They should be sautéed before they are infused in sauces or other preparations.

MORELS

Morels (*Morchella esculenta*) have a distinctive shape, a kind of sponge-like cone. Their flavor is delicate but, once brought out by a preliminary sautéing, is complex and irresistible.

Dried morels should be quickly rinsed under cold running water to eliminate sand and other particles. After they have been rinsed, put them in a bowl and sprinkle them with Madeira. They usually require about 10 minutes to soften and absorb the Madeira. Save any liquid left in the bottom of the bowl as an additional flavoring for sauces. Be sure they are thoroughly cooked to rid the sauce of any residual alcohol.

Gyromitra mushrooms, sometimes called "false morels" or "brain mushrooms," are sometimes sold as morels. They are less flavorful and have gnarled and irregular caps. While some say they are poisonous, they are frequently served (knowingly or not) in fine restaurants both in the U.S. and abroad.

Truffles

The most famous and aromatic truffles, black winter truffles (*Tuber melanosporum*), are in season from November to March. The less-flavorful but not-to-be-ignored summer truffle (*Tuber aestivum*) is in season—as the name implies—during the summer. If you want truffles at any other time, you will have to use truffles that have been preserved in some way. These are pale reflections of the real thing.

While there are many varieties, the most famous are the French black *truffe du Périgord* and the white Italian truffle (*Tuber magnatum*).

Italian white truffles are harvested starting in November and usually show up in the United States two or three weeks before the black French variety. The flavor and odor of these truffles is almost impossible to describe, but those who have made an attempt usually agree that the white Italian variety has a pungent, garlic-like aroma. The Italians use white truffles raw, shaved over fresh pasta or on a risotto. They can, however, be cooked. Chicken with white truffles slid under the skin, the whole bird wrapped in aluminum foil, and roasted before being presented and unwrapped at the table is a magnificent thing and will smell up a whole dining room.

Black truffles start appearing in the United States in December, a fortunate time of year, because some of the expense can be justified for holiday feasting.

BUYING TRUFFLES

A fresh truffle, whether white or black, should be firm to the touch and fill a room with its aroma almost immediately once the container is opened. If the scent is barely detectable, the truffle is probably stale or of inferior quality.

The best preserved truffles are frozen, but these are sometimes hard to find and must be obtained from a reliable source that has frozen them soon after they have been harvested. Preserved truffles in jars and cans can also be found at most fancy food shops.

The best-quality black truffles usually come in jars rather than cans and are often labeled "*première cuisson*" and either "*surchoix*" or "*1er choix.*" Première cuisson indicates that the truffles have been cooked only once during the preservation process. Inferior brands of canned truffles have been cooked twice and, as expensive as they are, have little flavor. Surchoix guarantees that the truffles are of a certain size and have a regular shape; 1er choix truffles are likely to be slightly smaller and a bit more irregular than those labeled surchoix. In any case, none of these are comparable to a fresh or frozen truffle and are rarely worth the money.

Black truffle juice is not actually the juice of the truffle but the cooking liquid from the preserving process. This "juice" can be used to give sauces a subtle hint of truffle (perhaps unrecognizable, but still giving the sauce a mysterious complexity). It works especially well in cold sauces such as mayonnaise- and vinaigrette-based sauces. Brands of truffle juice vary considerably in quality—some have little flavor and are too salty, so a bit of comparative tasting is worthwhile.

STORING FRESH TRUFFLES

Fresh truffles should be used as quickly as possible but can be kept for a day or two in a tightly sealed jar. Many chefs recommend keeping the truffles embedded in a jar of raw rice. This does no harm to the truffle but not much good either. Because the aroma of truffles clings to foods containing fats, such as eggs, butter, and cream, it makes more sense to store truffles in a jar with butter or with whole eggs in their shells. Butter that has been stored with truffles can then be used to finish sauces. It will keep for a year, tightly sealed, in the freezer. The aroma of truffles penetrates eggshells and perfumes the egg inside. The eggs can then be used for omelets, or the yolks used for egg yolk–based emulsified sauces.

Black truffles are best preserved raw and wrapped in plastic wrap, sealed again in a plastic bag, then frozen. They can also be placed in jars and covered with goose fat, which preserves them for two to three months.

CHOPPING AND SLICING TRUFFLES

Truffles are more easily sliced if the peels, which are somewhat hard, are first removed with a paring knife. The peelings can be chopped and used in sauces or omelets. The best method for slicing truffles is to use a Japanese mandoline (see page 31), which can cut them paper thin. An Italian truffle slicer can also be used—especially if the slicing is being done at the table—but it will not slice as thinly as a Japanese mandoline.

USING TRUFFLES IN SAUCE MAKING

The flavor and aroma of truffles are extremely volatile and will be attenuated or completely lost if the truffles are cooked for long periods. Consequently, most recipes recommend infusing chopped or sliced truffles in a sauce in a covered saucepan during the last 10 minutes of cooking.

What chefs often ignore when cooking with truffles is that the aroma is far easier to infuse in fat than in liquids such as stock or fortified wines. The flavor of fortified wines such as Madeira works well with truffles, but does little to draw the truffle flavor into the sauce. If a truffle sauce contains fat such as butter, cream, or egg yolks, the best way to flavor the sauce is to infuse the chopped or sliced raw truffles into the butter, cream, or egg for an hour or two before making the sauce. Frozen truffle butter can also be used to mount the sauce shortly before it is served.

When finishing sauces with cream, cover the sliced or chopped raw truffles with the heavy cream before using it in the sauce. If the cream is to be reduced, reduce it first, add the truffles, cover the pan, and let the truffles infuse for 5 minutes before finishing the sauce with the reduced cream.

NUTS, SEEDS, AND NUT AND SEED MILKS AND BUTTERS

ALMONDS

Slivered almonds add a much-needed crunch to stir-fries and curries. Almond milk is used as a substitute for dairy products. Almond butter is used as a thickener in Indian cooking, although nowadays it has largely been replaced by cashews, which are less expensive. Bitter almonds, which are much more intensely flavored than regular almonds, are used in the proportion of one bitter almond to one hundred sweet almonds. This mixture is often used as a flavoring for marzipan or in other sweets where an intense almond flavor is desirable. Bitter almonds cannot be sold in the United States because of their high natural cyanide content. Regular almonds can be toasted in the oven to enhance their flavor and help preserve them. Almond extract can be used (very sparingly) to emulate the flavor of bitter almonds.

CASHEWS

In addition to their role in Chinese stir-fries, Thai curries (in the finished dishes, not as the paste), and in other Asian dishes, cashews are ground into cashew butter that is then used as a thickener and flavoring in Indian curries.

PEANUTS

Ground into peanut butter, peanuts are used throughout the world (in Africa, Asia, and South America) as a thickener and flavoring in sauces and stews. They are delicious when combined with coconut milk, tomatoes, cilantro, and curries.

SESAME SEEDS

Sesame seeds come in white and black. White sesame seeds, more popular than the black variety, are lightly toasted and ground into a coarse flaky paste. Unlike classic mortars with smooth walls, a Japanese mortar and pestle called a *suribachi* has grooves along the inside of the mortar that make it perfect for grinding small seeds. Lacking a suribachi, grind toasted sesame seeds in a coffee grinder. Freshly made sesame seed paste is used as a thickener and flavoring in dipping sauces and salad sauces. Commercially made sesame paste is not an adequate substitute for freshly ground seeds.

Nut Milks and Nut Butters

When nuts or seeds (ideally toasted) are ground, soaked in hot water, and the liquid strained, the result is nut or seed milk such as almond milk. These milks are useful in sauce making (especially for Indian sauces), but usually require a hydrocolloid or emulsifier to keep them from breaking apart when heated.

Nut or seed butters are made by grinding the nuts or seeds to a smooth paste. Lacking a suribachi (see page 32), a coffee grinder is best for this. Nut butters are whisked into sauces as thickeners and flavorings, but in most cases must be stabilized with thickeners such as starch or hydrocolloids.

PORK PRODUCTS

Raw pork and various cured pork products such as ham, pancetta, and bacon are often used to contribute savor to a sauce's flavor base. Because some of these products have a delicate flavor while others are smoked or cured with strong spices, the saucier should know how to select them.

BACON

In the United States, bacon is smoked pork breast. It should not be used as an all-purpose component of a flavor base or to contribute savor and natural gelatin to a braise because of its strong smoky taste. It can, however, be used as a substitute for salt pork and cut into small strips (lardons) and used as a garniture for a variety of dishes. The lardons should be blanched for 10 minutes in boiling water to eliminate some of the smoky taste.

FATBACK

Fatback has no lean. It is used as a source of fat in charcuterie and for larding large pieces of meat for braising or the individual pieces of meat in a stew. Sheets of fatback called "bards" are also wrapped around roasts or braises to prevent the meat from drying out while cooking.

HAM

In sauce making, ham is used primarily to contribute savor and depth of flavor. Most ham has been cured in one of a variety of ways and is available either raw or cooked.

The most versatile ham for sauce making is an unsmoked, raw, salt-cured prosciutto such as Parma prosciutto from Italy or Bayonne ham from France. Because prosciutto is expensive, use the end pieces, which can be had for much less money.

Many of the raw cured and cooked hams available in the United States have been smoked and must be used carefully if used at all. When used sparingly, pieces of these hams can add distinction and a delicate smoky taste to red wine sauces. These hams are also very salty and should be used only in tiny amounts for heavily reduced sauces.

Commercially produced cooked hams—especially the canned variety—have no place in sauce making. They are either too aggressive or have no flavor at all. There do exist good-quality cooked hams—from York, England, and a few from New England and the American South—but these are best eaten for what they are. They are usually smoked and would overwhelm a sauce.

PANCETTA

Essentially unsmoked bacon, pancetta is usually rolled rather than left in slabs. It has a deep pork flavor that makes it excellent for sauce making. When unrolled and cut into strips, it can be used in stews and braises. It is best cooked along with a mirepoix or other sweated ingredients.

PORK RIND

The rinds from unsalted fatback, unsmoked bacon, and fresh or unsmoked ham can be saved and used to provide natural gelatin to brown stocks, stews, and braised dishes.

SPICES

Spices were the main flavoring used in medieval European cooking and up until the seventeenth century, when they were largely replaced by herbs. They have always been important in Middle Eastern and Indian cooking but only in the last few decades have been rediscovered in European-style cooking. Contemporary chefs are experimenting more and more with delicate infusions of spices in both white and brown sauces.

ALLSPICE

These small dried berries have a smell and flavor much like cloves. In European cooking, allspice is most often used in combination with other spices such as ginger, nutmeg, and curry mixtures. It is also used in marinades, sometimes with juniper berries.

CARDAMOM

One of the principal ingredients in curry, both green and black cardamom have an intense piney aroma and flavor. Cardamom is sometimes used to flavor white sauces or crème anglaise. It is sold in small green pods that must be peeled (rock over them first with a heavy pot) before they are used. The tiny granules found inside the pods are also sometimes found for sale, but the most common commercial form is powdered. Cardamom is almost always combined with other spices and aromatics such as coriander seeds, cumin, or ginger.

CAYENNE PEPPER AND GROUND CHILES

Cayenne pepper is made by grinding cayenne chiles, hot little red chiles. Excellent for adding zest to sauces where large amounts of black or white pepper would be inappropriate, cayenne works especially well with sauces containing tomatoes, sweet peppers, and cilantro. It can also be used in almost imperceptible amounts to wake up the flavor of fish sauces. Other chile powders are made by grinding other dried chiles such as anchos, guajillos, mulatos, or pasillas in a food processor or blender and then working the powder through a strainer (see also "Chiles," page 70).

CINNAMON

While today cinnamon is used almost exclusively to accompany sweets, it was used in medieval cooking, often in conjunction with ginger, saffron, and cloves, for both meat and fish sauces. Vestiges of these flavor combinations can still be found in English and Eastern European recipes (for example, mincemeat pie). Cinnamon is also an important ingredient in Indian curries, where it is often combined with other sweet spices such as cloves and cardamom.

The ground or whole cinnamon sold on supermarket spice shelves in the United States is actually cassia. Cassia comes in many different grades and may come from China, Indonesia, or Vietnam. In supermarkets, cinnamon is sold ground or in hard, tightly wound woody sticks; specialty spice shops and Asian groceries sometimes sell Chinese or Indonesian cinnamon in chunks. Like cassia, true cinnamon comes in tightly wound sticks, but cinnamon sticks are softer and easier to break. True cinnamon is from Ceylon and has a less aggressive flavor than cassia.

CLOVES

The most common use of cloves in European cooking is in meat broths, when a clove is stuck into an onion. By the time the sauce is reduced and used in sauce making, the clove flavor is almost imperceptible. Cloves are also a common ingredient in Indian cooking, where they are used—often in conjunction with cinnamon or cardamom—to flavor rice and meats. They are added to classic Indian spice mixtures including Garam Masala (page 607).

CORIANDER

Coriander seeds are small and round with a thin husk and vaguely resemble white peppercorns. They are only rarely called for in classic French cooking (in salade grecque, for example). Their flavor merges amazingly well with fennel. Coriander seeds are also used as an ingredient in Indian curries, to which they add an aromatic, almost floral aroma, and soften the more aggressive flavors of other curry spices. Coriander seeds should be roasted in a hot oven for 5 to 10 minutes or gently tossed in a hot skillet on top of the stove until they release their aroma. Coriander seeds are also easy to grind in a blender or coffee grinder, and the ground mixture can be gently toasted in a dry sauté pan on the stove.

CUMIN

Available in small, slightly curved seeds (the same shape as fennel seeds) or in powder form, cumin has a distinctive flavor that can easily overwhelm the flavor of a sauce, especially when used alone. Cumin is rarely used in French cooking but is commonly used in India, the Middle East, and Mexico. In India, cumin is roasted, ground, and sprinkled over appetizers and salads as well as used often in spice mixtures. Black cumin, which has little resemblance to the familiar common variety (called "white" cumin in India), can sometimes be found in Indian groceries. Black cumin seeds are smaller than regular cumin seeds and have a pungent pine-like aroma and taste, and are usually used whole.

CURRY POWDER

Curry powder is a mixture of up to twenty different spices and varies from brand to brand. In India, it would be unthinkable to resort to a commercial curry powder for cooking instead of roasting and grinding the individual spices. For Western chefs eager to expand their vocabulary of flavors, blending curries is an educational project. Roast each of the spices and grind them separately in a coffee grinder.

In classic French cooking, curry powder is cooked in a small amount of butter for a minute or two before it is added to a sauce.

FENNEL SEEDS

Fennel seeds are often confused with anise seeds, which come from a different plant. While the flavors are somewhat different, the two can be used interchangeably, although the amounts will need to be tweaked. Fennel seeds, like anise seeds, are used in Mediterranean cooking to impart an anise-like note to fish stews and soups. In sauce making it is often preferable to use fresh fennel (infused in a court-bouillon, chopped in a marinade, stalks used in stocks, dried and smoked on the grill) or a small amount of anise liqueur such as Pernod or Ricard. Fennel has a marvelous affinity for other Mediterranean flavors, such as tomatoes, garlic, olives, basil, and fresh seafood. Fennel seeds are also used, whole or ground, in Indian spice mixtures and curries.

GINGER

In Asian cooking ginger is used almost as universally as onions and garlic in the West. In Indian cooking it enters into an almost ubiquitous flavor base in the same way that carrots, onions, and celery compose French mirepoix. It is an excellent flavoring for crème anglaise but also works well in savory sauces. Medieval sauce recipes (see chapter 1) are a good source of ideas for how to combine ginger with other spices. Ginger works especially well with saffron and fennel, but medieval recipes also use it with cinnamon, cloves, mace, and other spices. Ginger is available candied, powdered, and fresh.

HORSERADISH

Grated horseradish root gives an exciting, dissonant note to a variety of sauces. It is marvelous in Sauce Suédoise (mayonnaise with apples and horseradish, page 421), and it works beautifully with mustard. It can also be used with dill.

JUNIPER BERRIES

Because juniper is the principal flavoring in gin, many people are familiar with its smell and flavor. It has a piney aroma and in European cooking is usually used with full-flavored meats, especially game. Juniper berries are most often used in marinades, but they can be finely ground and sprinkled into sauces as needed. They can be used in sauces along with marc or grappa to impart a distinct gamy flavor.

MACE

The outer lace-like coating of the nutmeg, mace is close to nutmeg in flavor. In French cooking its use is restricted to sauce béchamel, gratins, and cheese soufflés. Mace is often encountered in Northern Indian cooking. Mace is stronger and more pungent than nutmeg, with a slightly different flavor.

MUSTARD SEEDS

Rarely used whole in European cooking, mustard seeds are popular in Indian cooking. Indian mustard seeds are dark brown (they are often called "black" or "brown" interchangeably), and in Southern Indian cooking are often cooked whole in hot oil for a few seconds until they pop and spatter. Brown mustard seeds are also used as a pickling spice and in some parts of India they are ground into a paste.

NUTMEG

Although used in spice mixtures such as the French mixture of four spices called *quatre épices*, nutmeg is very domineering and should be used in only minute quantities. It is available whole (a small grater is needed) or powdered. In sauce making, nutmeg is most often used in white sauces, especially traditional flour-thickened white sauces containing cheese. Nutmeg is also used in Northern Indian cooking.

PAPRIKA

A member of the same genus of peppers (*Capsicum*) that provides cayenne and fresh peppers, paprika is made by finely grinding sweet red peppers. In Hungary and Spain, there are different versions, some as hot as cayenne pepper, but in the United States, most paprika is so mild that it has almost no taste at all. Use Spanish *pimentón*, which is smoked and has a complex subtle flavor. Good paprika is used in fish stews and the traditional Hungarian goulash.

PEPPER

Pepper, *Piper nigrum*, is unrelated to *Capsicum* peppers, which include sweet bell and hot peppers. It is the most useful and indispensable of all the spices. Black, white, and green peppercorns are all berries of the same plant picked at different degrees of maturity.

Peppercorns that have been allowed to fully mature are black. They come in various sizes, the largest being the most aromatic and expensive. Malabar peppercorns, and the even larger Tellicherry peppercorns from India, are considered the best.

White peppercorns are black peppercorns that have been allowed to mature even further and are then soaked in water until the black outer husk can be removed. Some chefs put both black and white peppercorns together in a pepper mill. Freshly ground white pepper is especially useful for white sauces in which black flecks would be distracting.

Pepper should always be ground as it is needed, never in advance. The flavor of pepper is aromatic and volatile, so pepper should be added or infused into sauces only at the last minute. Pepper added to stocks or sauces too early loses its aromatic, piney scent and leaves an unpleasant, harsh quality that is hard to eliminate.

Green peppercorns are picked before the berries are completely mature. They have a fresh, pungent, pine-like aroma and are sold dried or packed in brine. Dried green peppercorns can be ground like black or white peppercorns or reconstituted in water. Green peppercorns soaked in brine should be crushed with the side of a knife before being added to sauce so there's no danger of biting into a whole one. Green peppercorns in brine or vinegar should be used within a few weeks of opening, or they will take on an unpleasant gray color that stains sauces. They also lose some of their aroma.

Pink peppercorns are not related to black, white, or green peppercorns but come from a common shrub, *Schinus terebinthifolius*. All the rage in the early 1980s, pink peppercorns inspired some debate as to their toxicity, but nevertheless enforcement of the ban seems to be lax, and they still appear—rarely—on menus.

QUATRE ÉPICES

One of the few spice mixtures used regularly by the French, quatre épices ("four-spice mixture") is rarely used in sauce making but mostly for forcemeats and terrine and sausage fillings. A typical mixture includes ground cloves, ginger, nutmeg, and pepper.

SAFFRON

Taken from the flowers of the autumn crocus, saffron is expensive. Fortunately a little goes a long way. Saffron has been used in Italian and French regional cooking for centuries and is popular in Mediterranean-style fish dishes. It has a natural affinity for tomatoes, basil, coriander seeds, cardamom, and fennel. Saffron is also used in Indian cooking in curries and even desserts.

Saffron is available in little threads (the whole dried stigma) or in a powder; the threads, which can be decorative when left in the sauce and are harder to adulterate. Saffron threads should be soaked for 20 minutes in 1 tablespoon (15 milliliters) of warm water before they are incorporated with the water into the sauce.

SICHUAN PEPPERCORNS

These berry-like peppercorns are brown rather than black and have a pleasant spicy and pine-like aroma. Unlike black peppercorns, Sichuan peppercorns should be roasted before they are used, to bring out their perfume. They can be ground over foods in the same way as black pepper, or they can be infused in oil destined for stir-frying, used for Chinese smoking, and added to a variety of Chinese sauces.

STAR ANISE

The dried fruit of a variety of magnolia, star anise pods contains small star-shaped seeds that have a pungent anise flavor. The ground seeds, known as *ba jiao*, have long been used in Chinese cooking (most often as an ingredient in Chinese five-spice mixture) and in Malaysian curry mixtures. Star anise has recently been discovered by French chefs, who have been experimenting with infusing it in meat broths and natural aspics.

TURMERIC

A root with a distinctive, pungent flavor, turmeric is available fresh but unfortunately is most commonly found in powdered form, which usually has little if any flavor. It is used primarily as an inexpensive coloring (often to mimic the costly saffron) and as a component of curries, chutneys, and commercial mustard. Turmeric is handy to have around for coloring curries that standard spice mixtures may have turned a dull gray or brown.

SPIRITS

Spirits are prepared by distilling fermented liquids to concentrate the alcohol and some of the flavor components. They are often used to flavor and give complexity to sauces. Spirits usually contain both volatile and nonvolatile components. Volatile components are those that come off the still during distillation and develop to some degree while the spirit is aging. These components cook off rapidly when spirits are heated. Nonvolatile components comprise mostly wood extracts that work their way into the spirit during aging. These tend to remain during cooking and may even be concentrated.

Spirits are used primarily at the end of cooking since their flavor is mostly volatile and cooks off in seconds. Most common is Cognac, which, when used in small amounts, gives an ineffable complexity to a finished brown sauce or the braising liquid from a braise or stew. It is essential that they be cooked in the sauce for at least 20 to 30 seconds for their alcohol to evaporate.

BRANDY

Applied loosely, the term *brandy* describes distilled wine made from any fruit, coming from any part of the world. More typically, the term describes distilled grape wine.

The best brandy for use in sauce making is a less-expensive Cognac or Armagnac, which are natural pot-distilled products that contain the natural flavors useful for sauce making. When selecting a Cognac or Armagnac for the kitchen, look for a full, fruity flavor with a background of oak (the oak will be more predominant in Armagnac than in Cognac). Do not judge the quality of the brandy by the subtlety or finesse of the bouquet. These traits, although important to the brandy drinker, will be lost once the brandy is heated. Fullness, roundness, fruit, and purity of flavor are much more important in the kitchen.

Many chefs and restaurateurs substitute a generic brandy chosen blindly off the shelf or recommended by the liquor wholesaler. Such brandies often have meaningless designations such as "Fine French Brandy" or "Napoleon Brandy." These brandies may be half the price of a better Cognac or Armagnac but usually have little flavor. What flavor they do have is harsh and biting.

When preparing sauces with brandy, the brandy should be added near the end of the cooking. If it is added too early, practically all its flavor will be lost. If, however, it is added at the very end, alcohol will remain in the sauce.

Although traditional sauces seem to use brandy infrequently, it can be used to shape the final flavor of brown sauces and to wake up and add subtlety to brown sauces and red wine sauces.

FRUIT BRANDIES

Fruit brandies are of two types: fruit-flavored grape brandy and genuine fruit brandy made by distilling fruit wines. Fruit-flavored grape brandies are usually made by adding a concentrated fruit flavoring to the brandy. The result is syrupy and often sickeningly sweet and cloying.

Genuine fruit brandies are clear and perfectly dry. They do not have the characteristic amber hue of grape brandies because they have not been aged in oak casks. In France, Germany, and Switzerland, there are hundreds of varieties of these brandies (called eaux-de-vie). Fruit brandies are useful in sauce making to underline the character of a fruit-based or fruit-flavored sauce. For example, the sauce for a roast duck with cherries can be finished with Kirsch (cherry brandy), or a roast or braise garnished with plums could be finished with mirabelle (plum brandy).

Practically all the flavor contained in fruit brandies is volatile, so it is especially important to use fruit brandies in the very last stages of a sauce's preparation. A few drops of the brandy should be added to the sauce at the end, and the sauce should then be removed immediately from the heat. There's so little that the alcohol shouldn't be a problem.

MARC AND GRAPPA

Marc and grappa are the French and Italian names for the same thing: brandy distilled from the grape pomace—the pits, stems, and skins that remain after the juice has been run off for wine making. The quality varies enormously from raw, clear brandy served in the villages near the distillery to deep-colored, long-aged products from famous vineyards. Genuine marc or grappa has a characteristic earthy flavor that makes it useful and interesting in sauces. It is often possible to substitute marc or grappa in a recipe that calls for Cognac, Armagnac, or brandy to give a more rustic, regional flavor to the finished sauce. Marc and grappa are splendid in game sauces and with chocolate.

In recent decades, "grappa" is used in Italy to describe brandy made from wine rather than pits and stems. Such "grappa" has more of the fruity flavor of an eau-de-vie like framboise or Kirsch than it does traditional grappa. However, many of these eaux-de-vie are fascinating because they are made from different wines.

VODKA, GIN, AND RUM

Occasionally a recipe will call for one of these spirits. Vodka is useless in sauce making because it is a completely neutral-tasting product containing only alcohol and water. Gin is sometimes useful to reinforce the flavor of juniper in certain game sauces. Rum is useful in dessert sauces but must be chosen correctly. Martinique rum is the best for cooking because it is pot-distilled and full flavored. The color of rum has little to do with its depth of flavor.

WHISKEY

Whiskey is made by fermenting grain that has first been treated with malt enzymes to convert the starch into sugar. The fermented mash is then distilled. The types of grain used, the method of distillation, and the aging process determine the type of whiskey. Irish and bourbon whiskeys can each be used to give their characteristic nuances to a sauce. Scotch whisky, with its classic smoky flavor, is rarely appropriate for sauce making. Whiskey can be used as a substitute for Cognac. The result is different but can be very satisfying.

Whiskeys are often blended with neutral spirits to make them more palatable for drinking. The most flavorful whiskeys, which are best for sauce making, are unblended pot-distilled products. When using bourbon whiskey, select one labeled "straight bourbon" rather than blended whiskey, which contains a high percentage of neutral spirits. Canadian whiskey is blended and too light for sauce making.

WINE

It is hard to imagine food without wine, not only as an integral component of the cooking process itself but also as the perfect accompaniment. It not only accents food at the table but also enhances and brings out the natural flavor of meats, fish, and vegetables.

Many cooks assume that wine chosen for drinking is also the best for cooking. Because wine is radically transformed by heat and other aspects of the cooking process, the criteria for selecting cooking wines depend on the type of wine and the preparations in which it is to be used. The finesse and complexity of great wines is destroyed by heat, which makes their use in the kitchen impractical. Meat jellies, which are sometimes finished with fine wines, are an exception to this axiom because the wine is never heated. Choose white wine with plenty of acidity such as Muscadet (inexpensive, dry, and perfect for beurre blanc). Unlike red wine for drinking, red wine for cooking should be low in acidity and tannins. California wines, often too alcoholic, are perfect for this because their alcohol will be cooked off. Wines from Chile and Argentina work well and are often good values.

CHAMPAGNE

Authentic Champagne comes from a closely delineated region of northern France whose soil imparts a characteristic steely/chalky flavor to the wine. Still Champagne is converted to the sparkling variety using an involved traditional process (*méthode champenoise*). Don't bother using other sparkling wines such as prosecco or most cavas because they leave little character in the sauce.

Those who write recipes using Champagne often naively assume that the flavor and elegance of Champagne are somehow going to work their way into a cooked preparation. Cooking will immediately destroy the natural carbonation that has required so much time and expense, and it will destroy much of the natural finesse of the wine as well. Many chefs, when confronted with one of these recipes, are horrified at the idea of opening an expensive bottle of Champagne and will substitute a less-expensive sparkling wine. This makes no sense, because the bubbles will be lost and only the basic flavors of the wine will remain. It is far more logical to substitute a still Champagne (*Coteaux Champenois*), which will have the same basic flavors as sparkling Champagne minus the yeastiness and some complexity. Although these wines are never cheap, they are usually half the price of the sparkling variety.

Recipes that call for Champagne should be examined closely to determine if Champagne is truly needed. Both the sparkling and still varieties contain a great deal of natural acid, which is often desirable, such as in a beurre blanc or white wine stew (the meat clarifies out much of the acid). If the recipe calls for long or radical reduction of the wine, most of the subtlety will be lost, so that using even a still Champagne would be a needless expense. In this case it would be practical to substitute a less-expensive wine with a similar structure (dryness, high acidity) such as Muscadet or a French Sauvignon Blanc.

When a preparation calls for very gentle cooking or no cooking at all—dessert sabayons, cold fruit sauces, for example—the added expense of Champagne may be justified. Perhaps most magnificent is to sweeten it and freeze it into a granita. The granita won't taste cloyingly sweet and the subtle identity of the wine will shine through.

MADEIRA

True vintage Madeira, even 100-year old Malmsey Madeira, has a surprising amount of acidity. Genuine Madeira is produced on the island of Madeira; imitations made in other places lack the depth of flavor and balance of genuine Madeira.

There are several kinds of Madeira. Sercial is completely dry and, because of its acidity and lack of sugar, is little used in the kitchen. Verdelho is sweeter and softer than Sercial, which makes it useful for sauce making. Bual and Malmsey are the richest and sweetest types of Madeira. They can be used in sauces calling for Madeira—they are often the best—but use them carefully, because they can be aggressive; they are also expensive.

The most common variety found in America is a medium-sweet blend called Rainwater. It has a good balance of complexity, sweetness, and acidity, making it a good standby for sauce making. It is also easy to find.

PORT

Port is often used to impart a subtle, caramel-like sweetness to sauces. Genuine port comes from Portugal. Wine makers in other countries have attempted to make port-like wines, some of which are very good, but it is best to use a genuine Portuguese port.

Port is made by adding alcohol or brandy to the wine must before fermentation is completed. This stops the fermentation prematurely and leaves natural grape sugar in the wine. There are four styles of port. Vintage port is made from grapes of a single year and is left in wood casks for a relatively short time before being bottled. Vintage port may last 100 years in the bottle and should have at least ten to fifteen years in the bottle. It is the most expensive of the four types. Late-bottled vintage port (wood port) is left longer in wooden casks, so it matures more quickly. It is lighter in style and less expensive than vintage port.

Tawny port is traditionally manufactured by blending ports from different vintages and allowing them to age for many years in oak, which causes the color to turn from deep red to a characteristic brick-like hue. Some less-expensive tawny ports are simple blends of red and white port. Ruby port is a young, blended port. It is the lightest and least expensive.

Because of the price of good port, ruby port is usually used in the kitchen. Select a ruby port with a deep red color, full flavor, and a complex caramel or butterscotch background in the mouth. Some brands of ruby port are so light (visible in the glass) and at the same time so sweet that they will impart little to the sauce. If you're finishing a delicate sauce (perhaps one with truffles), use a good tawny port (added at the very end) to give more sophistication to the sauce.

RED WINE

The behavior of red wine in cooking is complex. When cooked with foods that contain protein, such as fish or meat, the tannins and pigments in the wine combine with the proteins that are released during cooking. This clarifies out much of the color and acidity, and any astringency due to the tannins will disappear. Specks of pigment are often visible in the sauce and, if need be, can be strained out.

Red wine reduced alone or with flavor components that contain no protein, such as onions, garlic, or a bouquet garni, will be entirely different from wine that is cooked with meat, fish, or stock. Protein "clarifies" the wine's acids and tannins; red wine reduced in the absence of protein will retain harsh tannins and acids Hence, when making a red wine sauce containing meat or fish stock, simmer them together, not separately.

Lightly colored, fruity wines such as Beaujolais or California Gamay should not be used for sauce making. The delicate fruitiness that makes these wines charming to drink will be lost and the sauce will be pallid and acidic.

The best red wines for sauce making are deeply colored, low-acid wines. Wines from hot climates or those made from early-ripening grapes, such as Merlot, which are often considered too "soft" or "flabby" by wine connoisseurs, are the best red wines for sauce making. Choose red wines with several years of bottle age, so that the flavors are well developed and most of the tannins have fallen out. A certain amount of oakiness is also welcome in a red wine sauce. California Zinfandel and Merlot work especially well, as do Spanish wines such as Rioja.

It is sometimes possible to find red wines that have passed their peak and are no longer agreeable to drink. The volatile acids contained in these wines will be attenuated by cooking, if not eliminated entirely. Save bottle ends—it's okay to combine them—for cooking. If they turn a little to vinegary, use them anyway.

RICE WINE

Japanese rice wine, sake, is the best known of Asian rice wines and is often added to mixtures of dashi, mirin, soy sauce, and sometimes miso to flavor broth-like Japanese sauces. Unless the sake is being cooked, it's a good idea to simmer it for a minute in a saucepan to burn off the alcohol. Sake imparts freshness to sauces and functions in much the same way as white wine, except that it doesn't have the acidity of white wine.

Chinese Shaoxing wine is made with rice but using a different process from that used for making sake. Shaoxing wine is quite strong, with a deep amber color that makes it more like sherry than sake or white wine. Sherry can be used as a substitute in recipes calling for Chinese rice wine.

SHERRY

Sherry can be used for sauce making in the same way as Madeira, but unlike some styles of Madeira, authentic sherry is almost never naturally sweet. Authentic Spanish sherry is available in several different styles. Amontillado, which is aged longer than other types and has a full-bodied, nutty flavor, is best for sauce making. If using sherry in a consommé, add the sherry *before* clarification. When added at the end, it clouds the consommé.

WHITE WINE

When selecting a white wine for the kitchen, remember that the alcohol will evaporate when exposed to heat, leaving the nonvolatile acids contained in the wine. If the wine is reduced, the tartaric, malic, and other nonvolatile acids in the wine will be concentrated. White wine is best cooked or reduced with proteins—meat or fish—to attenuate its acidity. Sometimes, concentrated acidity is useful. An acidic wine should always be used in the preliminary reduction for a beurre blanc; Muscadet is traditional. Because beurre blanc contains such a high proportion of butter, the nervous tang of a wine's natural acids is necessary to balance the richness of the sauce. French wines typically contain more acid than most New World wines.

OTHER INGREDIENTS

ANCHOVIES

Anchovies packed in salt are more often used in Europe while canned anchovy fillets packed in oil (ideally, extra-virgin olive oil) are popular in the United States.

Canned oil-packed anchovy fillets may benefit from a 5-minute soak in cold water to rid them of some of their salt and oil, but this depends on the particular anchovy.

Salted anchovies, which usually come whole and clinging together like a solid mass, should be soaked in cold water for several minutes and the anchovies pulled away from the clump as they loosen. To preserve them and make them more convenient to use, take the fillets away from the backbones starting from the head and working down toward the tail. Pack the fillets in jars and add enough extra-virgin olive oil to completely cover by at least 1 inch (2.5 cm). Store in a cool place or in the refrigerator for up to several months. These anchovies don't need to be soaked again before they are used.

CHILES

Sometimes erroneously called "peppers" (chiles have no relation to peppercorns), chiles come in many shapes, sizes, colors, and, most important, flavors. They come fresh, dried, smoked, ground, and occasionally canned. Because of their diversity, chiles, especially dried chiles, can be used in sauces to add not only heat but an array of subtle flavors, variously described as smoky, leathery, fruity, and earthy. To explore the flavor of dried chiles, lightly toast them and reconstitute them in water (discard the water when done) and chop them rather fine. Infuse each one, separately, in a small amount of cream. This will reveal the subtle difference between chiles and offers an exciting angle for sauce making.

Fresh chiles are best when they have been grilled and the skin peeled off. This releases their flavor and makes them more complex. Peeled chiles (this includes bell peppers) can be infused into liquids such as meat broths, tomato broth, or cream.

DRIED CHILE CREAM SAUCE

This is the simplest of all chile sauces, and it allows the flavor of the chiles to come through unaltered by other ingredients such as onions or garlic (or in the case of mole, chocolate). Not only is this sauce delicious, but because each chile surrenders its own identity to the sauce, it provides excellent training for cooks wanting to familiarize themselves with the nuances of individual dried chiles. This sauce requires little reduction because the chiles act as thickeners.

YIELD: 1 CUP (250 MILLILITERS), ENOUGH FOR 4 MAIN-COURSE SERVINGS

large dried chiles, such as ancho, guajillo, mulato, pasilla, pasilla de Oaxaca, or chihuacle negro	2	2
heavy cream	1 cup	250 milliliters
salt	to taste	to taste
cayenne pepper (optional)	to taste	to taste

1. Cut the stems off the chiles. Cut the chiles in half lengthwise, and shake out their seeds. Toss the chiles in a hot skillet for a minute or two, until they smell fragrant. Put them in a bowl and add enough boiling water to barely cover. Soak the chiles for about 30 minutes, until they feel soft and leathery. Drain; discard the soaking liquid. Chop the chiles very fine, until they have a paste-like consistency. Combine them with the cream in a small saucepan.

2. Bring the cream to a slow simmer over medium heat while whisking; cook for about a minute, until the sauce thickens. Take the pan off the stove and let it sit for 5 minutes to give the flavor of the chiles time to infuse the cream. Season with salt and, if you want more heat, cayenne.

CHOCOLATE

The flavor and consistency of chocolate desserts is determined almost entirely by the chocolate itself. While at one time American chocolate was distinctly inferior to European chocolate, there are now very high-quality producers in the United States. The best method for determining the quality of a brand of chocolate is simply to taste it.

Most chocolate sauces call for bittersweet or semisweet chocolate. One is not necessarily more bitter than the other—the names simply differ depending on the brand. Chocolate labeled bittersweet or semisweet contains cocoa liquor, cocoa butter, and sugar. The cocoa liquor is responsible for the color, bitterness, and depth of flavor of chocolate, while the cocoa butter gives it finesse and a smooth texture. In Europe the manufacturer is required to put the percentage of cocoa liquor on the label, and high-quality manufacturers in other places have continued this tradition.

Milk chocolate is only rarely used in sauce making. Unsweetened or baking chocolate is more often used by American cooks than by Europeans. This is fine; it's simply necessary to adjust the sugar needed.

White chocolate contains no cocoa solids; it is simply a mixture of cocoa butter, milk solids, and sugar. Because of the milk solids it contains, it is very sensitive to temperature and should never be heated to higher than 120°F (50°C).

ESSENTIAL OILS

Most essential oils are prepared by distillation, in which the volatile components come off the still. Unlike essential oils, an absolute is prepared by extracting aromatic compounds with hexane (essentially gasoline) and then removing the hexane either through simple evaporation or vacuum evaporation. Since there's no hexane left, it doesn't pose a problem.

Some essential oils are prepared with simple extraction. Lemon zest, for example, can simply be pressed to extract its oil.

The ne plus ultra of aroma extraction is enfleurage. Flower petals are arranged on trays of hard fat, traditionally tallow but nowadays usually hydrogenated palm oil. After several hours or overnight, the petals are replaced with fresh ones. The process continues until the fat is completely saturated with the aroma of the flowers. The aroma is then extracted from the fat with ethanol (drinkable alcohol) and the ethanol evaporated to leave only the exquisite enfleurage.

FOIE GRAS

Foie gras is the liver taken from a specially fattened goose or duck. In France the animals are force fed, but in the United States, foie gras is now being produced with an especially ravenous species of duck (mulard) that needs no inducement to overeat.

Foie gras behaves differently, according to the water content of the livers. Because American foie gras tends to contain a larger amount of water than French varieties, it is better to use foie gras that has been precooked into a terrine so that any excess liquid will have been released. Goose or duck foie gras work equally well in sauce making, but duck foie gras is usually fuller flavored and less subtle.

If you are using whole raw livers for terrines or other foie gras preparations, the veins running along the inside of each lobe should first be removed with a small paring knife. Bits and pieces that are left over from this process can be puréed by gently pressing them through a fine-mesh drum sieve and saved for use in sauces.

When a small amount of puréed foie gras is whisked into cooking liquids or stocks, it provides a rich, creamy texture and a full, complex flavor. If adding puréed foie gras to a hot cooking liquid or flavor base, first combine the foie gras with an equal quantity of butter or the foie gras may coagulate on contact with the hot liquid. The resulting sauce will have a grainy consistency. Once the foie gras has been added, never allow the sauce to approach a simmer.

When raw foie gras is baked in a terrine, sautéed, roasted, or poached, it renders a deeply flavored yellow fat. If the fat has not been exposed to too high a temperature, it can be saved for other uses. Because of its intense, full flavor, a small amount can be used to give character to a sauce. When using foie gras fat, remember that it cannot be stirred directly into a sauce unless the sauce is already emulsified or the fat will just melt and float to the top. Whisk the fat (melted or not) only into sauces that have been finished with cream, butter, egg yolks, or some other stable emulsion such as vegetable purée. Foie gras fat is magnificent in a hollandaise sauce.

The flavor of foie gras fat can also be introduced into a sauce by using it to gently sweat preliminary flavor components, such as onions, mirepoix, or bits of meat, before they are moistened with liquid.

MARROW

Beef marrow is sometimes used in sauce making, especially for traditional Sauce Bordelaise (page 186). Some wholesalers sell perfect cylinders of marrow already removed from the bone but if these are unavailable, buy marrow bones cut into 2-inch (5 cm) lengths. Press firmly on one end with both thumbs to push out the marrow. When this method does not work, set the bone, end up, on a butcher block and crack the outer bone (try to avoid hitting the marrow) with a cleaver in two places and removing the marrow.

Once extracted from the bone, marrow should be soaked overnight in heavily salted ice water. The salt draws out the blood, which turns an unsightly gray when cooked.

Marrow added to sauces as a garniture should be added just long enough before serving to heat it through; any longer and it will melt to nothing.

THICKENERS AND EMULSIFIERS

While flavor is doubtlessly the primary quality by which sauces are judged, one should not underestimate appearance, mouthfeel, consistency, and thickness. In old-fashioned classic cuisine, starches were used as thickeners. When nouvelle cuisine was at its height in the '60s and '70s, butter and cream were the fallback thickeners. When handled judiciously, these result in sauces with irresistible mouthfeel that, despite their richness, give the impression of lightness.

In recent decades, there has been much discussion of "modernist" cuisine. Modernist chefs have made valuable discoveries that allow us to manipulate food (and sauces) in new and unexpected ways. The modernist adaptation of compounds and techniques used in industrial cooking is particularly enlightening. Research by chefs and writers such as Ferran Adrià, Heston Blumenthal, Wylie Dufresne, and Nathan Myhrvold has highlighted exciting new techniques, equipment, and compounds.

Most important for the saucier are highly efficient emulsifiers, stabilizers, and thickeners. Each of these has its own mouthfeel and appearance. Many take the guesswork out of making such delicate creations as sabayons and other egg yolk-thickened sauces. While almost thirty years ago, when *Sauces* first went to press, there were few options other than starch, cream, or butter, today there is a whole panoply of thickeners and stabilizers to choose from.

Hydrocolloids

A colloid is a solution with solids dispersed within it. A soup is a colloid, as is a consommé, assuming it contains gelatin, natural or otherwise. A hydrocolloid (A, page 74) is a compound such as xanthan gum that is used as a thickening agent, emulsifier, or stabilizer.

Most hydrocolloids are similar to more traditional thickeners such as flour or cornstarch in that they are composed of a chain of linked-together sugar molecules. When added to liquids such as water, the long chains unravel, tangle up, and, sometimes with

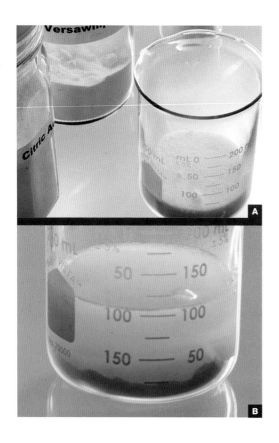

the aid of heat, thicken the liquid. Some hydrocolloids are proteins and function in a similar way as sugar-linked chains except that a protein hydrocolloid will form long chains of amino acids instead of sugars. Each hydrocolloid has its own characteristics and needs to be handled in its own specific way. A hydrocolloid must first be dispersed in water. Usually, but not always, this involves agitating the hydrocolloid (usually a powder) by hand or with an immersion blender or rotor-stator homogenizer (see page 35). **(B, C)** Once the hydrocolloid has absorbed enough water to have softened and enlarged its particles, it can be combined with the mixture to be thickened. **(D)** Hydrocolloids each have a temperature in which they dissolve. Some can be stirred with water or other liquids at any temperature while others may require heating, sometimes for as long as 15 minutes with nonstop agitation.

AGAR

While agar **(A, page 76)** was used for centuries, it fell into disuse and has only recently been discovered to have many characteristics that make it useful for modernist cooking. It is used to stabilize foams and emulsions and to give a silky mouthfeel to sauces and broths. It can also be used to prepare fluid gels (see chapter 13), which in turn function as sauces. Agar is often combined with a very small amount of xanthan gum, a powerful emulsifier. The agar and xanthan gum are dissolved, allowed to set, and puréed into a fluid gel. Agar should be used in percentages ranging from 0.01% and 0.9% by weight to the liquid being set.

ALGINATES

Propylene glycol alginate (no relation to the propylene glycol found in antifreeze) (A, page 76) and sodium alginate are both derived from seaweed. Like low-acyl gellan (see page 76), both require calcium ions to thicken or set. These ions can be supplied by hard tap water or by calcium in the form of calcium lactate and other compounds.

Propylene glycol alginate acts as a thickener, stabilizes emulsions and foams, lends a creamy mouthfeel to sauces, and forms clear gels. It forms an even stronger gel when used with sugar. Like many hydrocolloids, it resists syneresis—the weeping out of liquid from colloids such as vegetable purées. It hydrates at any temperature, with stirring, in about 5 minutes. It is typically used in concentrations of 0.4% to 1%.

Sodium alginate will tolerate alcohol (something to think about when making dessert sauces), but needs another hydrocolloid to gel. It is mostly used for spherification (see page 182).

CALCIUM CHLORIDE/CALCIUM GLUCONATE/CALCIUM GLUCONOLACTATE

Each of these is used to provide calcium ions to hydrocolloids and emulsifiers that require them to gel. If calcium chloride seems bitter, try replacing it with calcium gluconate or calcium gluconolactate. These are also used in spherification (see page 182).

CARRAGEENANS

Extracted from seaweed, carrageenans (B, page 76) come in three forms: lambda, iota, and kappa. The lambda form is the one most often used in sauce making. Named after the town in Ireland where it was first used, carrageenan is used widely as a thickener and stabilizer. Lambda carrageenan is clear and will thicken and stabilize but will not, on its own, form a gel. It gives a creamy mouthfeel to sauces. Carrageenans are powerful emulsion stabilizers and thickeners. They are best used for thickening nondairy milks such as almond, soy, or coconut milk and giving them a dairy-like mouthfeel. Lambda carrageenan is typically used in concentrations of 0.03% to 2%. It hydrates in cold water.

GELATIN

Well known for its ability to form gels—when done well, delightful gelées that melt as soon as they hit the tongue—gelatin comes in both powdered and sheet form. The sheet form is easier to work with, but given that it's harder to find, it's certainly permissible to use the powdered variety.

Derived from animal sources, gelatin sets (and melts) at around body temperature, making it the perfect substance for gels. Gels that melt at a higher temperature (such as those made with agar) may seem sticky and perhaps out of place, but a gelatin gel melts in the mouth. Gelatin should be soaked in cold water and be allowed to bloom before it is added to the hot liquid in which it dissolves. It is used in a wide range of concentrations, but in most cases gelatin solutions should be tested by chilling in the refrigerator to judge their consistency. The gel or, at this point, gelée, should be barely set so it melts in the mouth; it should not be the slightest rubbery.

Gelatin makes great foams, often as simple as combining it with a fatty material and piping it out with a whipping siphon. When stabilizing emulsions, it's usually used in concentrations from 0.2% to 1.5%.

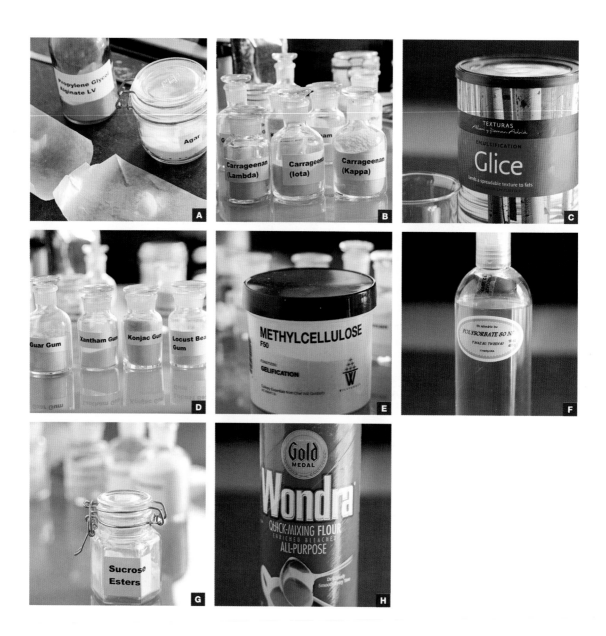

GELLAN

Gellan is a fermented product that comes in two forms: low-acyl gellan (sometimes sold under the name Kelcogel F) and high-acyl gellan (sometimes sold under the name Kelcogel T100). Don't equate the two simply because they are both gellans, but keep in mind they're as different as any one hydrocolloid from another.

What the two gellans do have in common is the ability to thicken sauces and form emulsions with a creamy mouthfeel. Low-acyl gellan, which is clear when in a gel, is sometimes used to give body to consommé.

While high-acyl gellan has no sensitivity to calcium ions or alcohol (at least up to 50%), low-acyl gellan is among those hydrocolloids that require ions, especially calcium, to work. Often, if tap water is used there's enough calcium present, but if the water is particularly soft or you've used distilled or de-ionized water, you'll need to add a trace of calcium using calcium chloride, calcium lactate, or calcium gluconate.

Keep in mind, however, a problem with including calcium in the liquid medium for low-acyl gellan: It raises the hydration temperature to close to the boiling point and can even make complete hydration impossible.

Low-acyl gellan gives sauces a lovely mouthfeel and yields a perfectly clear gel, but because it can be a nuisance to hydrate, cooks sometimes hesitate to use it during a busy service.

Low-acyl gellan is also a good foam stabilizer. When heated and puréed into a fluid gel, it can be used for hot or cold foams. The style of the foam—its frothiness, ideal temperature, and bubble size—is controlled by altering the amount of the gellan.

High-acyl gellan requires no calcium or other ions to thicken, set, or stabilize it. It creates sauces and gels that are opaque, but works beautifully for dairy-like sauces.

Sometimes high- and low-acyl gellan are used together. This combination is sometimes used for hot gels or eggless custards. Perhaps most dramatic, this combination stabilizes emulsions so efficiently that it can be used to pull together such divergent ingredients as beef suet or duck fat and aqueous liquids.

GLICE

A brand name for a mixture of mono- and diglycerides, Glice (C, opposite) is dissolved in the fat that's to be used in an emulsion. It is used in concentrations ranging from 2% to 5%. Oils and fats containing Glice must be heated to 140°F (60°C). Glice is used in fats destined for emulsions because it stabilizes them and makes it easier (or possible) to form emulsions with water or other aqueous liquids. While technically not a hydrocolloid (because no water is involved), Glice is usually lumped together with hydrocolloids proper.

GUAR GUM

A powerful thickener, guar gum (D, opposite) is best used in combination with other thickeners; if not, at higher concentrations it tends to develop a slick mouthfeel. It can be dissolved in either hot or cold water. It makes a stronger gel when combined with agar, but in sauce making this is largely irrelevant. When used as a thickener, it typically is used in concentrations of 0.4% to 0.9%. When being used as an emulsion stabilizer, the percentage is lower (0.1% to 0.6%). Guar gum hydrates in both cold and hot water.

GUM ARABIC

A natural resin formed by acacia trees, gum arabic is a powerful emulsifier. Uniquely, it can be used in surprisingly high concentrations and will emulsify essential oils into liquids. It has a high tolerance for alcohol, which makes it useful in certain liqueurs. It is an extremely powerful and reliable emulsifier that is often incorporated into foams and classic emulsified sauces. A vinaigrette made with gum arabic will not separate.

LECITHIN

Found in egg yolks, lecithin is a type of emulsifier called a surfactant. One end of a surfactant molecule dissolves in fat and the other end in water such that the two are held together into an emulsion. Lecithin comes in both liquid and powdered forms. The liquid is best dissolved into fats that are later to be emulsified, while the powder is best for making foams. Both forms are used in concentrations of 0.5% to 3% of the fat they are emulsifying.

LOCUST BEAN GUM

A powerful thickener, locust bean gum is derived from carob tree pods. Because of proteins it contains, it also acts as an emulsifier and an emulsion stabilizer. It is usually used with other hydrocolloids such as xanthan gum (see page 79). It is used in very small quantities, from 0.05% to 0.20%. It hydrates at a rather high temperature, over 195°F (92°C). Locust bean gum prevents the formation of ice crystals in frozen desserts, such as ice cream.

METHYLCELLULOSE

Cellulose gums, of which there are several, have an unusual characteristic: They set when hot and turn liquid when cold. They are sometimes used in baked goods, such as pies, to prevent hot liquid released by fruit from running out the sides. Once the pie cools, the firm fruit gel formed by the cellulose returns to a liquid. This strange characteristic of turning liquid when cold has led chefs to invent any number of (sometimes bizarre) dishes.

Methylcellulose (E, page 76) is the cellulose gum most important to the saucier. When combined with xanthan gum and piped through a whipping siphon, it yields a foam much like meringue or royal icing with air in it. When the mixture is hot, it is used to make hot marshmallows. The methylcellulose and xanthan gum are dissolved in cool to slightly warm water. The water is heated until the gel sets and the gel then chilled until it returns to liquid form.

PECTIN

Used for making jams and jellies, natural pectin's usefulness has been somewhat limited by its need for a sugary and acidic medium. This is fine for sweet and sour preparations such as those made with fruit, but is severely limiting for savory preparations that don't share these characteristics. However, there are now available both high-methoxyl pectin and low-methoxyl pectin. High-methoxyl pectin is used at a very low concentration for thickening or gelling preparations under acidic conditions (low pH). It can be used for sweet or savory preparations, provided they have the requisite acidity. Low-methoxyl pectin, which also can be used in very small concentrations, doesn't require the acidic ingredients or sugar needed by traditional pectin, and can be used for making low-sugar jams and jellies as well as savory gels.

POLYSORBATES

There are a number of these powerful emulsifiers on the market, each with a different number, but Polysorbate 80 (F, page 76) takes care of most sauce-making jobs. It is valuable because it makes sauces containing fat seem particularly creamy. One must exercise caution, however, not to use too much, as it has an unpleasant taste. It is typically used in concentrations from 1% to 5%.

SUCROSE ESTERS

Related to sugar but not sweet and related to alcohol but not alcoholic, sucrose esters (G, page 76) are powerful emulsifiers and thickeners. They have the unusual characteristic of being soluble in both fats and water, which means that an emulsion such as hollandaise can be reinforced by adding sucrose esters to both the oil and any aqueous liquid.

TAPIOCA STARCH

An extremely useful thickener, tapioca starch comes in numerous forms. Each one of these exhibits its own special characteristics. Tapioca starch can be cooked sous vide with water for an hour or more to create a translucent colloid that itself can be used as a thickener or emulsifier. Brands such as Ultra-Tex 3 or 8 or Ultra-Sperse 3 are tapioca starches that have been hydrated or gelatinized to make them easier to use. They are effective thickeners and emulsifiers and are used in rather large concentrations, up to 6%. Ultra-Tex 3 and Ultra-Sperse 3 are so similar that they can be used interchangeably.

WONDRA

A popular brand of pre-hydrated and pre-gelatinized flour (H, page 76) that can be stirred into a jus to convert it into a gravy, without first making a roux. It is first whisked until smooth with some liquid to make a slurry, then whisked into the jus.

XANTHAN GUM

For both its convenience and consistency, xanthan gum has been used in industry for decades. It is only recently being used in restaurants and home kitchens. It has relatively little taste, and a small amount goes a long way. It is easily hydrated in either cold or hot water, which means it can be added to the sauce regardless of the temperature.

Like most hydrocolloids, xanthan gum functions as a thickener, requiring less than 0.5% to thicken a solution. It has a creamy mouthfeel if not used in too large an amount; if too much is used, it turns slimy.

Xanthan gum is also used to stabilize emulsions. If you're worried about your beurre blanc breaking during a long and hectic service, a pinch of xanthan gum, hydrated first and whisked in at the beginning (into the shallot-vinegar reduction is best), will go far in keeping the sauce whole. The stabilization provided by the xanthan gum will also allow you to keep a sauce overnight, then "remount" it the next day by whisking the congealed cold sauce into a little heavy cream or lightly acidulated water. This also applies to mayonnaise, especially if it's going to be held in the refrigerator overnight.

Xanthan gum also inhibits syneresis, the tendency of particle-thickened liquids to separate on the plate. This is especially useful for vegetable and tomato purées where the sauce separates from the solids along the edges of the plate.

Xanthan gum is also whisked with lecithin and/or other ingredients to form large-bubble froths and foams. It can be combined with Versawhip to make cold small-bubble foams or with albumin for hot small-bubble foams. It can also stabilize other foam combinations.

STOCKS, GLAZES, AND ESSENCES

A *stock* is a flavorful extract made by cooking meat, fish, or vegetables in water or broth. The purpose of stocks in sauce making is to supply or augment the nutritive and savory components that are released by meats, vegetables, and fish during cooking. Glazes such as *demi-glace* or *glace de viande* are made from stocks that have been slowly cooked down (reduced) to a thick syrup. These are convenient to have on hand in professional kitchens because they keep well and can be added to sauces at the last minute to give a richer flavor, a deeper color, and a smoother texture. Some chefs rely almost entirely on glace de viande for preparing brown sauces (see Chapter 7, "Brown Sauces").

Classic demi-glace is a stock that has been bound with starch and reduced until it has the consistency of a very light syrup or glaze; it is the basis for classic brown sauces. Natural demi-glace is thickened by reduction or continual remoistening with additional meat; no starch or other thickener is used in its preparation.

The term *jus* traditionally describes the light, natural liquid derived from the drippings of a roast. Because a natural jus is perhaps the most satisfying and flavorful of all sauces, chefs use a variety of techniques to simulate the flavor of a natural jus using meat trimmings and bones. To prepare a stock with some of the full, natural flavor of a jus, meat trimmings are browned and cooked for a short time before being deglazed with a small amount of stock. The stock is then caramelized on the bottom of the pan with the meat still in it. This process can be repeated indefinitely, deglazing with more stock each time. Each time the pan is deglazed and the stock evaporated until it caramelizes, the stock will become more like a jus.

Essences are extracts made from vegetables, meats, or seafood. While rarely used today, in classic sauce making essences are usually used as a final flavoring for more complex stock-based sauces. Most of the time essences can be dispensed with and the ingredient itself simply infused in the sauce and strained out at the last minute.

STOCKS

Stocks were originally invented to facilitate kitchen organization and to augment integral sauces. *Integral sauces* are those prepared directly from the juices released by meats and fish during cooking. There are two major difficulties in preparing sauces with only the natural savory elements released in cooking. First, meats and fish, especially when roasted, rarely supply enough of their own flavorful elements to make enough savory sauce to go around. Second, in a restaurant setting, it is difficult and impractical to prepare an integral sauce for each dish. Because of these problems, chefs developed stocks, which can be made from less-expensive cuts of meat, inexpensive meat trimmings, and bones.

The first stocks were simple broths, by-products of poached meat and fish dishes. Before the method of preparing stocks was refined and systematized, meat was often braised or roasted with a thick slice of ham or veal on the bottom of the pot or roasting pan to give extra body to the sauce.

The challenge to the chef is to get the maximum flavor into a stock with a minimum of expense. A stock made with a large proportion of meat, carefully reduced to a light glaze, will have a magnificent flavor but will be too expensive for most restaurants. For this reason, many chefs have replaced much of the meat in older stock recipes with bones. Although bones can supply gelatin and a certain amount of savor to a stock, a stock made with bones will never have the depth and flavor of one made with meat.

Much of the expense of using meat in a stock can be defrayed by saving the cooked meat for another use, to serve either in the restaurant or to the staff. Boiled beef (actually poached beef) can, for instance, be made into excellent salads (with capers, pickles, and vinaigrette), into a *salade bouchère* (with hard-boiled eggs, potatoes, tomatoes, and chopped parsley), and into ravioli filling (seasoned and chopped with a little beef marrow). It can also be reheated in tomato sauce, cooked in a *miroton* (a kind of gratin with stewed onions, breadcrumbs, and a little vinegar), or used with potatoes as *hachis Parmentier* (the meat is minced, covered with mashed potatoes, and baked).

Traditional stock recipes are divided into white and brown. White stocks are usually prepared by first blanching meat and bones (don't skip this step or the stock will look gray and taste muddy) and then moistening them with cold water. Brown stocks are prepared by first browning the meats or bones, either in the oven or on top of the stove.

Improving a Stock's Flavor

PREPARE DOUBLE AND TRIPLE STOCKS

Stocks can always be improved by using an already prepared stock to moisten meats for a new batch. When the moistening liquid for a stock is an already prepared stock, the result is called a "double stock." If a double stock is in turn used to moisten more meat, the result is a triple stock. The elaborate stocks of the eighteenth and nineteenth centuries were made using this method of continuous remoistening with progressively richer and richer stock.

Making double and triple stocks is expensive. Most methods for making stock are designed to imitate double and triple stocks without the expense. If, however, the chef can defray the cost of the ingredients so that double and triple stocks made with meat can be used for sauce making, the resulting sauces will have an inimitable depth, complexity, and savor.

CARAMELIZE THE INGREDIENTS

Stocks can be given heightened color and flavor by first caramelizing the meat juices on the bottom of the pan before the final moistening with water or stock. Precooking the ingredients in this way will also result in a clearer stock. For a detailed description of this method, see "Jus" and "Essences" later in this chapter.

ADD GELATINOUS CUTS

Some recipes call for the addition of a veal foot (split and blanched, starting in cold water) or strips of pork rind to stocks. These ingredients contribute gelatin and give the stock a smoother, richer texture. However, when stocks are made with knuckle bones (not marrow bones), the bones provide enough of their own gelatin.

BALANCE THE INGREDIENTS

The final decision as to how stocks will be prepared depends on the kitchen's cooking style and budget. The chef will have to rely on experience and expertise to balance the components in the stock to derive the best flavor from the ingredients.

If a stock is to be radically reduced for sauce making or if double or triple stocks are being prepared, the chef must determine whether additional vegetables and a second or third bouquet garni are needed. If too many vegetables are added to the preliminary stock or if additional vegetables are added at each stage in the preparation of a double or triple stock, the natural sugars in the vegetables may become too concentrated, and the stock will be too sweet. You may find that, as the stock nears completion, one of the vegetables or one of the herbs in the bouquet garni is too assertive; decrease the amount of that ingredient the next time you make the stock.

If a finished stock tastes flat, improve its flavor by adding a fresh bouquet garni and some freshly sweated mirepoix vegetables. Whether or not this is necessary depends on how the stock will be used.

Dos and Don'ts

1. Always moisten stock with cold liquid. If hot water is added to meat, it causes the meat to release soluble proteins (albumin) quickly into the surrounding liquid. These proteins immediately coagulate into very fine particles and cloud the stock. When cold liquid is used and slowly heated, the proteins contained in the meat or fish coagulate in larger clumps and float to the top, where they can be skimmed off. When adding liquid to an already simmering stock to compensate for evaporation, make sure it is cold.

2. Never allow a stock to boil. As meat and bones cook, they release proteins and fats into the surrounding liquid. Stock should be heated slowly to only a simmer. At a slow simmer, these components appear as scum and grease on top of the stock and can be skimmed. If the stock is boiling, these substances are churned back into the stock and become emulsified. The resulting stock is cloudy and has a dull, muddy, greasy flavor, which will only worsen if the stock is reduced—or bound—for a sauce. When the stock comes to a simmer, keep it to one side of the heat source so any grease or scum is pushed to one side, where it can be more easily skimmed. Skim the stock with a ladle every 5 to 10 minutes for the first hour to prevent fat and scum from working their way back into the stock. As the stock cooks further, it needs to be skimmed only every 30 minutes to an hour. Keep the ladle in a container of cold water next to the pot so it is convenient for skimming and does not become caked with fat and scum.

3. Do not use too much liquid. The higher the proportion of solid ingredients to liquid, the more flavorful the stock will be. Many beginning cooks cover the solid ingredients with too much liquid at the beginning of cooking. Because the solid ingredients in a stock settle during cooking, the cook often finds that he or she has added more liquid than necessary and the resulting stock is thin. It is best to use only enough liquid or stock to cover the ingredients. The only exceptions to this rule are stocks with extremely long cooking times, where any excess liquid will evaporate anyway.

4. Do not move the contents of the stock during cooking and straining. As stock cooks, albumin and other solids settle along the bottom and sides of the pot. If the stock is disturbed, these solids will break up and cloud the stock. When straining the finished stock, do not press on the ingredients in the strainer; allow enough time for the liquid to drain naturally. Work slowly and deliberately.

5. Do not overreduce. Stocks are often reduced to concentrate their flavor and give them an appetizing, light, syrupy texture. Although reduction is an almost essential technique for converting stocks into sauces, much of the delicacy and flavor of meats is lost if reduced for too long. Many of the flavors contained in stock are aromatic and evaporate when simmered over a prolonged period, leaving a flat taste. Highly reduced stocks often contain a large concentration of gelatin, which gives them a sticky feeling and texture in the mouth. (See "Jus," page 98.)

6. Do not add the liaison until all the fat and scum have been carefully skimmed. Recipes often suggest adding a thickener such as roux, starches such as cornstarch or arrowroot,

or hydrocolloid thickeners to stock to thicken it lightly and give it texture. Once a liaison is added to a stock, any fat emulsified in the liquid will be held in solution by the liaison and will become difficult to skim off and remove.

7. Store stocks carefully. Warm stock is a perfect medium for bacteria (beef broth was originally used to line petri dishes in laboratories). Avoid keeping stocks between 40° and 140°F (4° and 60°C) for long periods. The danger of spoilage increases in hot weather and when larger amounts of stock are being prepared. A quart or two (1 to 2 liters) of stock can be allowed to cool at room temperature before it is refrigerated with little danger of spoilage. Larger amounts of stock are best cooled by floating a container of ice (make sure the outside of the container is well scrubbed) in the stock to chill it before refrigerating. Large amounts of stock may require several batches of ice. If ice is limited, don't bother using it while the stock is hotter than 140°F (60°C). Once the temperature drops into the danger zone—below 140°F—start using ice.

BROWN CHICKEN STOCK

Brown chicken stock is especially useful in kitchens where it is not practical to prepare beef and/or veal glazes and stocks. If the kitchen does not generate enough chicken carcasses for the stock, most wholesale butchers will deliver chicken carcasses at a nominal cost. Chicken wings and drumsticks are inexpensive and more flavorful than carcasses or backs.

Brown chicken stock can be used for deglazing sauté pans and roasting pans and as a base for more concentrated, specialized stocks such as game or pigeon. It is good to have brown chicken stock on hand to use as a thinner for sauces that may have become too reduced.

YIELD: 8 QUARTS (8 LITERS)

chicken carcasses, drumsticks, or wings	12 pounds	6 kilograms
onions, 2 medium, coarsely chopped	1 pound	500 grams
carrots, 2 medium, coarsely chopped	8 ounces	250 grams
celery, 1 stalk, sectioned	3 ounces	100 grams
cold chicken stock or water	1 quart	1 liter
cold water	8 quarts	8 liters
bouquet garni (1 bay leaf, 1 large bunch fresh thyme, 1 handful tarragon stems, 1 bunch parsley, preferably with roots)	1	1

(continued)

1. Preheat the oven to 400°F (200°C).

2. Thoroughly rinse the chicken carcasses with cold water. Give them a sniff to make sure they are fresh. Drain them well. Trim any excess fat off the carcasses. Cut off the tails, which are attached to the backs, and break up the carcasses. Spread the carcasses, onions, carrots, and celery over the bottom of a large roasting pan in a single layer. (If the chicken is heaped up in the pan, it will not brown. Conversely, if sections of the roasting pan remain exposed, the juices are liable to burn.)

3. Roast the chicken and vegetables. (A) Check after about 30 minutes. The chicken should be golden brown on top. Stir with a wooden spoon and continue roasting.

4. After 30 to 90 minutes of roasting, when the pieces of chicken are completely browned and any juices have caramelized on the bottom of the roasting pan, remove the pan from the oven and remove the chicken and vegetables from the pan. Place the pan on top of the stove. (B)

5. If there is a large amount of rendered chicken fat in the bottom of the roasting pan, ladle it off. Add 1 quart (1 liter) cold stock or water to the roasting pan and turn the heat under it to high. Scrape the bottom of the roasting pan with a wooden spoon to dissolve the caramelized juices.

6. Carefully transfer the browned chicken parts and vegetables to a 25-quart (22 liter) stockpot, along with the deglazing liquid. Add the remaining cold water and the bouquet garni to the pot. (C) Push the bouquet garni down into the pot with the back of a ladle so it does not keep floating to the top.

7. Gently bring the stock to a slow simmer. Do not let it boil. Keep the pot to one side of the heat source so any scum or froth is pushed to one side and is easier to skim; skim the stock regularly with a ladle to remove fat and scum. (D) After about 40 minutes, most of the excess fat should be gone.

8. Cook the stock for a total of 3 hours. Do not cover the pot at any point.

9. Strain the finished stock first through a coarse chinois, then through a fine chinois. Do not press on the solids while they are draining, or the stock may cloud. Let the stock cool at room temperature and then in an ice bath before refrigerating.

10. After the stock has completely cooled, any remaining fat will have congealed on its surface. Carefully scrape it off with a metal spoon. (E) Brown chicken stock will keep for 5 days in the refrigerator. If it needs to be kept longer, bring it to a simmer for 10 minutes, skim, and quickly cool. It will keep for another 5 days.

Red Wine Chicken Stock

Sauces that call for red wine are typically made by reducing the wine and then adding meat glaze or demi-glace. The mixture is then reduced to the right consistency and finished with butter. The problem with this method is that the tannins and acid in the wine are concentrated in a way that makes the sauce harsh. This can be alleviated somewhat by reducing the wine simultaneously with the demi-glace, whose proteins clarify out some of the tannins. But the best method is to make a red wine stock by moistening meat or bones with red wine, cooking the stock in the usual way, and reducing it to a sauce-like consistency. This method is also useful when making braised dishes that call for red wine—chicken with red wine sauce, for example—for which the braising time is relatively short, too short to soften the tannins in the wine. It is also useful when wine is being used to deglaze a pan.

Prepare brown chicken stock (opposite) but replace the water with red wine. Simmer in the same way.

WHITE CHICKEN STOCK

White chicken stock is less flavorful but more subtle than brown chicken stock. It is useful for sauces where a pure white appearance is important and as a poaching liquid for white stews (*blanquettes*).

Because the chicken carcasses are not browned in the oven before being moistened, it is important that they be well trimmed of fat before being put into the stockpot. White chicken stock will render more fat than brown once it is simmering in the pot, so be especially careful to keep the stock from boiling, and be sure to skim frequently.

If white chicken stock is prepared with only carcasses—without meaty chicken parts such as drumsticks—it will be cloudy unless the carcasses are thoroughly sweated or blanched before the water is added. Clouding is not a problem if the stock is to be used in an opaque sauce containing cream, but if the clarity of the stock is important, be sure to include drumsticks or wings, as in this recipe.

YIELD: 8 QUARTS (8 LITERS)

chicken carcasses, drumsticks, or wings	8 pounds	4 kilograms
onions, 2 medium	1 pound	500 grams
carrots, 2 medium	8 ounces	250 grams
celery, 1 stalk	3 ounces	100 grams
bouquet garni (1 bay leaf, 1 large bunch fresh thyme, 1 handful tarragon stems, 1 bunch parsley, preferably with roots)	1	1
cold water	8 quarts	8 liters

1. Smell the carcasses to make sure they are fresh. Rinse and drain them well in a colander. Carefully trim the carcasses of excess fat. Cut off any tails left attached to the backs. Coarsely chop the carcasses with a cleaver. If you're using drumsticks or wings, leave them whole.

2. Coarsely chop the onions, carrots, and celery.

3. Place the chopped vegetables and the bouquet garni in a 20-quart (18 liter) stockpot and cover them with the chicken pieces. Add the water, just enough to come three-quarters of the way up the sides of the chicken. (The chicken and vegetables will settle as the stock cooks.)

4. Slowly bring the stock to a simmer; this should take about 40 minutes. Carefully skim with a ladle any fat and scum that float to the top of the pot. (Because the bones and meat for white stock have not been browned first in the oven, there will be more fat and scum than for a brown stock.) Keep the stock to one side of the heat source so grease and froth are easier to skim off. Continue slowly simmering the stock for 3 hours.

5. Strain and cool in the same way as brown chicken stock.

CHICKEN DEMI-GLACE

While demi-glace is usually made with beef and/or veal stock, it can also be made with chicken by reducing chicken stock by about 15 times. If you want to make a glaze equivalent to glace de viande, reduce by 30 times.

YIELD: 2 CUPS (500 ML)

brown chicken stock (page 85)	8 quarts	8 liters

Reduce the stock down to 2 cups (500 ml), skimming regularly; it should have a lightly syrupy consistency. Strain the stock into a very small saucepan and continue reducing until only about ½ cup (125 ml) remains. Strain a final time through the finest possible strainer. Store in tight-fitting jars.

BROWN BEEF STOCK

In this beef stock, meat and vegetables are browned together in the oven and then simmered in water or broth. While the meat and vegetables are roasting, be sure to turn them over from time to time to ensure that they are thoroughly and evenly browned. If the bottom of the roasting pan begins to darken and burn, add a couple cups of water. Don't add too much liquid or the bones will steam instead of brown.

YIELD: 8 QUARTS (8 LITERS)

onions, 2 medium	1 pound	500 grams
carrots, 2 medium	8 ounces	250 grams
celery, 1 stalk	3 ounces	100 grams
beef knuckle bones	12 pounds	6 kilograms
garlic head, cut crosswise in half	1	1
cold water or stock (optional)	1 cup	250 milliliters
cold water or stock	9 quarts	9 liters
large bouquet garni (page 52)	1	1

1. Preheat the oven to 450°F (230°C). Coarsely chop the onions (see Note), carrots, and celery. The vegetables need not be peeled if they are thoroughly washed.

(continued)

2. Spread the bones, garlic, and vegetables in a heavy roasting pan. (A) Roast the bones and vegetables for 30 to 90 minutes, until browned. (B)

3. After the bones have been browned on both sides, transfer the vegetables to a 25-quart (22-liter) pot, cover with the bones, add the bouquet garni, and cover with the water or stock.

4. Slowly simmer the stock for 12 hours, skimming every 10 to 15 minutes for the first few hours (C). As the bones cook, they will fall into the liquid and release fat, which floats to the top. (D) As the stock reduces, the bones will then protrude above and are best removed with tongs or even by hand. (E)

5. Gently strain the stock through a chinois. Do not push on the pieces of meat or vegetables to force out the liquid, or the stock may cloud.

Knocking the side of the chinois with a wooden spoon helps the stock flow through without clouding it.

6. Brown beef stock can be cooled and stored in the same way as brown chicken stock. If you're in a hurry, you can skim off the fat before the stock has cooled. (F) Alternatively, after the stock has completely cooled, any remaining fat will have congealed on its surface. Carefully scrape it off with a metal spoon.

Note: In professional kitchens where a flat-top stove is used, onions are often cut in half crosswise, and the exposed surfaces are burned by turning them face down on the stove surface. Onions blackened in this way contribute color to brown stocks. If the meat and vegetables have been adequately browned, this method should not be necessary.

WHITE VEAL STOCK

Veal stock is an excellent base for both white and brown sauces because it has a deep, subtle flavor that makes it especially adaptable to a variety of preparations. Veal stock—both white and brown—was the basic stock used in professional kitchens during the nineteenth and into the twentieth centuries. Because of its expense, it has largely been replaced with beef stock, chicken stock, or stocks made with veal bones alone. However, there is one cut that remains inexpensive—breast. If you're using the meat (say, for a blanquette de veau), cut it away from the bones. Simmer the bones (after blanching) for 12 hours. Blanch the meat, cut to the appropriate size and shape, and simmer it very gently in the bone broth for 2 to 3 hours.

The ingredients below can be used for either white or brown veal stock; the initial procedure is for white stock, with the variation for brown stock following. When preparing white veal stock, the meat and bones must first be blanched—placed in a pot of cold water and brought to a simmer—then drained and rinsed before being used in the final stock. If this step is ignored, the stock will be cloudy and gray and taste muddy.

YIELD: 5 QUARTS (5 LITERS)

breast of veal	15 pounds	6.7 kilograms
onions, 2 medium, peeled and halved	1 pound	500 grams
carrots, 2 medium, halved	8 ounces	250 grams
celery, 1 stalk	3 ounces	100 grams
large bouquet garni (page 52)	1	1
cold water	5 quarts	5 liters

(continued)

1. Separate the meat from the bones and set it aside for later. Cut away and discard excess fat—there will be a lot. Break the breast down into manageable pieces by slicing between the ribs.

2. Put the bones in a pot with enough cold water to cover and bring to a simmer. Blanch the bones for about 5 minutes, then drain in a colander. Rinse them thoroughly with cold water.

3. Place the onions, carrots, celery, bouquet garni, and bones in a 15-quart (14 liter) stockpot.

4. Cover the ingredients with the cold water. Add enough water to come about 4 inches (10 cm) above the top of the bones.

5. Bring the stock slowly to a simmer; this should take at least 30 minutes. Skim off any froth, fat, and scum that float to the surface.

Cook the stock at a very low simmer for 11 hours more, skimming every 30 minutes.

6. Carefully strain the stock, first through a coarse chinois, then through a fine chinois. Discard the bones and vegetables.

7. Cut the meat into the shape you need (cubes for stew, for example) and blanch it in the same way as the bones. Drain, rinse, and cover with the bone stock. Simmer gently, while skimming, for 2 to 3 hours.

8. Strain the stock through a fine chinois and set aside the meat for whatever preparation you're using it for.

9. Clarify the stock somewhat by reducing it by one-quarter or so, skimming off scum as you go.

Brown Veal Stock

Roast all the ingredients for white veal stock, except the bouquet garni, in a 450°F (230°C) oven. Turn the meat, bones, and vegetables from time to time until they are evenly browned. Avoid burning any of the ingredients or letting the juices burn onto the bottom of the roasting pan. Transfer the bones and vegetables to a stockpot and add the bouquet garni. Set the meat aside for later. Deglaze the roasting pan with water. When all the juices have dissolved, add the deglazing liquid to the stockpot. Add the bouquet garni. Moisten and simmer gently for 12 hours. Strain the stock, discard the bones and vegetables, and use the stock to simmer the meat for 2 to 3 hours, skimming all the while. Strain the stock through a coarse chinois—pick out the cooked meat—and again through a fine chinois. Reduce by about one-fourth, being sure to skim, to clarify somewhat.

Fish Stock

FISH FUMET

Fish stock, also called fish fumet, is normally prepared with bones and trimmings of lean flatfish such as sole and flounder. Oily varieties of fish, such as salmon and mackerel, should be avoided except when preparing red wine sauces. In areas where fresh fish is abundant (an increasingly rare occurrence), fish stock can be made with fresh baby whole fish rather than bones. Whether fish or fish bones are being used, it is essential they be impeccably fresh and that the fish stock be prepared within an hour or two from the time the fish is filleted. If the bones have a fishy or strong iodine smell, throw them out.

Fish skeletons should be thoroughly gutted (fishmongers do not bother gutting fish for fillets), and the gills should be removed. The bones should be soaked for a couple of hours in cold water to remove any traces of blood, which would discolor the stock. Never add the skin from fillets to a fish stock; the stock will turn gray. The vegetables used for the stock, as well as the bouquet garni, can be varied depending on the final use of the stock. Fennel branches add a lightness and freshness and are too often ignored in recipes for fish stock. In any case, since the cooking time is so short, the vegetables should be chopped fine.

If impeccably fresh ingredients are not available, it is often better to substitute court-bouillon or the cooking liquid from mussels or clams in sauces that call for fish stock. Remember that fish stock and fish sauces should smell and taste of the sea and should not be fishy.

YIELD: 3 QUARTS (3 LITERS)

assorted fish or fish bones	5 pounds	2.5 kilograms
onion, 1 medium	8 ounces	250 grams
carrot, 1 medium	4 ounces	125 grams
celery, ½ stalk	2 ounces	50 grams
leeks, green parts only	1 bunch	1 bunch
butter	1 ounce	30 grams
fennel branches, sectioned	4 ounces	125 grams
garlic head, cut crosswise in half	1	1
cold water	3 quarts	3 liters
dry white wine	2 cups	500 milliliters
bouquet garni (1 bay leaf, 1 small bunch fresh thyme, 1 small bunch tarragon sprigs, 1 bunch parsley, preferably with roots)	1	1

(continued)

1. Carefully smell and examine the fish or fish bones, checking for freshness. Remove the gills and pull out any roe or viscera from inside. There is often a vein containing blood running along the spinal column where the ribs join. This should be scraped with the tip of a paring knife so the blood can be washed away during soaking. Snap the bones over themselves so each skeleton is broken in two or three places. Soak the bones in cold water for an hour or two and transfer to a colander to drain.

2. Peel and roughly dice the onion, carrot, and celery into ¼-inch (5 mm) cubes (they are cut small to cook quickly). Cut the leek greens into 1-inch (2.5 cm) lengths.

3. Melt the butter in an 8-quart (8 liter) pot. Sweat the diced vegetables, leek greens, fennel, and garlic in the butter for 5 minutes, and then add the fish or bones. Stir the ingredients over medium heat for about 5 minutes more, until the bones turn white and start to smell appetizing.

4. Add the water, just enough to come three-quarters up the sides of the bones. Pour in the wine. Gently bring the stock to a slow simmer.

5. When the stock simmers, carefully skim off any fat and scum that float to the top. Add the bouquet garni. Continue gently simmering the stock for 20 minutes. **(see photo)**

6. Strain the stock through a fine chinois and let it cool in a plastic or stainless-steel container. If a perfectly clear fish stock is required, leave the stock undisturbed for an hour or two, then carefully draw the stock off the top with a ladle. The particles of fish, which are harmless, will have settled to the bottom. The remaining cloudy stock is perfectly acceptable and can be used for sauce finished with cream or for poaching liquid.

Note: The recipe for fish stock given here differs somewhat from the classic version. A classic fish stock contains no carrots, celery, or fennel and the bones are not cooked before water is added.

Vegetable Stock

COURT-BOUILLON OR NAGE

Vegetable stock can be used to impart a lightness and a delicate aromatic flavor to sauces. In traditional cooking it was primarily used as a poaching liquid for fish and sometimes calves' brains. Contemporary chefs are using it more frequently in sauce making because of its delicacy, freshness, and ease of preparation. Vegetable stock is often an excellent substitute for fish stock when good-quality fresh fish or fish bones are unavailable.

Although the terms *court-bouillon* and *nage* are often used interchangeably, court-bouillon describes a broth from which the vegetables have been strained, whereas a nage is used for serving fish and shellfish *à la nage*—a style of presentation in which the fish is served surrounded by the poaching liquid containing the vegetables used in the court-bouillon cut into decorative shapes.

The technique for preparing court-bouillon depends on whether the chef wants the vegetables to release all their flavor into the surrounding liquid or prefers them to retain some of their flavor and texture (as in the preparation à la nage). To get the vegetables to release the most flavor into the surrounding liquid, they are best sweated in a small amount of butter or oil before being moistened. When preparing à la nage, where the vegetables will be served as an accompaniment, simmer them for 10 minutes in water before adding the wine and/or vinegar. (Acids slow the softening of vegetables in liquid.)

There are no hard and fast rules for which and how many vegetables should go into the stock; this decision depends largely on the final use of the stock. It is practically impossible to add too many leek greens or fennel branches, whereas too many carrots or onions (never use sweet onions for making stock) can make the stock too sweet, especially if it is going to be reduced for a sauce. Although traditional recipes call for a standard combination of vegetables to arrive at an anonymously flavored vegetable stock, contemporary chefs often prepare court-bouillon using only one or two vegetables to give a sauce a particular, subtle flavor. Court-bouillon made with leeks or fennel alone will give a delicate yet pronounced character to a sauce. Salt should be added to a vegetable stock only if the stock is to be used as is, without reduction.

The following recipe suggests the usual bouquet garni ingredients, but these too can be altered to give the stock a personal or regional character. Full-flavored herbs, such as oregano, marjoram, or lavender, should generally be avoided except under special circumstances—for example, for grilled fish surrounded by a court-bouillon-based sauce or for steamed crustaceans.

(continued)

This recipe emphasizes the flavor of the stock rather than the integrity of the vegetables. If using vegetable stock as an accompaniment to fish or meats cooked à la nage, the vegetables should be cut carefully and evenly. Vegetable stock is best used the day it is made.

YIELD: 3 QUARTS (3 LITERS)

red or yellow onions, 2 large	1½ pounds	750 grams
carrots, 2 medium	8 ounces	250 grams
celery, 1 stalk	3 ounces	100 grams
garlic cloves, peeled	4	4
fennel branches, sectioned	4 ounces	125 grams
olive oil *or* butter	2 tablespoons *or* 1 ounce	30 milliliters *or* 30 grams
large bouquet garni (page 52)	1	1
cold water	3 quarts	3 liters
dry white wine	2 cups	500 milliliters
good-quality white wine vinegar	½ cup	125 milliliters

1. Peel and coarsely dice the onions, carrots, and celery or, if you're serving à la nage, cut them into decorative shapes such as julienne.

2. In an 8-quart (8 liter) pot, sweat the diced vegetables, garlic, and fennel in the olive oil or butter for about 10 minutes. Do not allow them to brown.

3. Add the bouquet garni and cold water and bring to a simmer. Simmer gently for 10 minutes.

4. Add the white wine and vinegar and continue simmering for 15 to 20 minutes more.

5. Let the court-bouillon cool before straining out the vegetables.

Glace de Viande

MEAT GLAZE

Meat glaze, usually called *glace de viande*, takes 8 to 15 hours to prepare from already made stock. If it is difficult to work in a single stretch, the glaze can be reduced for several hours, allowed to cool, and then continued the next day. It is best to begin reduction of the bone stock in a wide-mouthed pot to encourage evaporation and rapid reduction. As the stock reduces, it should be transferred into clean pots of decreasing size. Usually three pots are required to reduce 10 quarts (10 liters) of stock.

Meat glazes can be prepared from any kind of stock, but the technique works best for stocks that already contain a fair amount of gelatin and a certain amount of meaty savor. For this reason, meat glaze is most often prepared with a stock made from beef knuckle bones, which release a large amount of gelatin into the surrounding liquid. Stocks containing little gelatin require too much reduction to become glazes, and by the time the reduction is complete, much of their savor has been compromised.

YIELD: 1¼ CUPS (330 MILLILITERS) OF 30X GLAZE

brown beef stock (page 89), made from knuckle bones	10 quarts	10 liters

1. Transfer the beef stock into a wide-mouthed 12-quart (12 liter) stockpot. If the stock is cold and jelled, use a ladle. (Do not try to pour jelled stock from one pot into another—it will bounce out onto the floor.) Gently bring the stock to a simmer over about 40 minutes. Keep the pot to the side of the heat source to make skimming easier.

2. Keep a ladle in a container of cold water next to the pot during reduction. (The water rinses the ladle after each use and prevents it from becoming caked with scum and gelatin.) Skim the stock every 10 to 15 minutes during the first 2 hours of reduction. After this, occasional skimming should suffice.

3. When the stock has reduced by half, strain it through a fine chinois into a 5-quart (5-liter) pot.

4. Continue simmering. As the glaze becomes increasingly concentrated, transfer it to a 2-quart (2 liter) pot and use a smaller ladle for skimming.

5. The glaze is ready when it has the consistency of honey and coats the back of the ladle. The stock should have reduced to one-thirtieth of its original volume (for example, 10 quarts/10 liters of stock should yield 1¼ cups/330 milliliters glaze). Strain the glaze through a fine chinois into a nonaluminum container with a tight-fitting lid.

6. After the meat glaze cools, it will have the texture of hard rubber. It will keep, tightly sealed, in the refrigerator for a month or longer and in the freezer indefinitely.

Fish Glaze

Glace de Poisson

Fish glaze is prepared in the same way as meat glaze except that fish stock is used instead of meat stock. Fish glaze has a strong fishy taste that it can impart to sauces if used in more than tiny amounts. It is better to substitute reduced mussel or clam cooking liquid or reduced court-bouillon. If concentrated fish stock is required, prepare a double fish stock by moistening fish or fish bones with a previously made fish stock.

JUS

Long, slow cooking is not always the best way to prepare a stock or jus with the flavor of a specific meat. Although slow simmering will extract much of the gelatin and nutritive elements from meat and bones, much of the character, individuality, and freshness of the meat will be lost. Many chefs mistakenly assume that the best method of extracting and intensifying the character of a particular meat such as game, duck, pigeon, or lamb is through long cooking and subsequent reduction of the simmering liquid. Actually, the best method for extracting the natural flavor from meats is to brown them in a heavy-bottomed pot or saucepan with a small proportion of mirepoix vegetables until their juices are released and caramelize on the bottom of the pot. This process of caramelization is essential to extracting and amplifying the natural savors and should be repeated several times by deglazing the pan with a small amount of stock, wine, or water. These successive deglazings create steam that further cooks the meat and causes it to release juices, which are again caramelized on the bottom of the pot.

After several deglazings, the meat trimmings and bones should have released most of their savor, which will in turn have caramelized on the bottom of the pot. At this point, any fat will have separated and can be easily removed. The caramelized trimmings are moistened with a small amount of water or stock and cooked only long enough to dissolve the juices that have already been released. If the trimmings are moistened with a full-bodied stock, the jus should not require any reduction. If a thicker texture is desired, it is better to add meat glaze to the jus rather than reducing it.

In the recipe that follows, a small amount of jus is prepared in a pot. To master the technique of caramelizing the meat trimmings in stages, it is easier to see and control the process in a pot on top of the stove. For larger quantities, however, it is often easier to brown the ingredients in a roasting pan in the oven.

MEAT JUS

YIELD: 1 CUP (250 MILLILITERS)

meat trimmings or bones	1 pound	500 grams
onion, 1 small	3 ounces	100 grams
carrot, 1 small	3 ounces	100 grams
pure olive oil	2 tablespoons	30 milliliters
freshly chopped thyme leaves	1 pinch	1 pinch
white wine	½ cup	125 milliliters
brown chicken stock (page 85), brown beef stock (page 89), or water	3 cups	750 milliliters

1. Remove as much fat as possible from the meat trimmings or bones.

2. Peel the onion and carrot and and dice into ¼-inch (5 mm) cubes.

3. Heat the olive oil in a 4-quart (4 liter) heavy-bottomed pot or saucepan. Add the meat trimmings or bones and vegetables.

4. Brown the meat trimmings and vegetables over medium heat for 10 to 20 minutes. (If the pot is too crowded for the meat and vegetables to brown, do not worry; the juices are the concern here, and they will brown on the bottom of the pot.) As the mixture browns, keep checking the bottom of the pot to see whether the juices are beginning to adhere and caramelize. There may be an initial stage when the trimmings have released juices that have not yet browned.

5. When the juices have browned (the fat will also separate out at this point, so you can pour or ladle it off), add the thyme leaves. Stir for a minute or two, then add the wine. Scrape the bottom of the pot with a wooden spoon so that the caramelized juices dissolve in the wine. Continue cooking until the juices caramelize a second time.

6. Add 1½ cups (375 milliliters) of the stock to the pot, scrape up the juices, and let the stock reduce until the juices caramelize a third time. If there is a large amount of fat, carefully drain or ladle it off.

7. Turn down the heat and add the rest of the stock to the pot. Gently bring the stock to a simmer and cook the mixture for 3 minutes. Skim off any scum or fat that floats to the surface.

8. Strain the jus through a fine chinois.

ESSENCES

Before the twentieth century, cookbooks made frequent reference to essences, especially essences of specific game birds. Most cooks assume that the best way to extract the essence of flavor from a pigeon carcass, for example, is to roast it with a little mirepoix (correct) and then simply simmer it for a couple of hours (incorrect). Truth be told, long simmering does little to extract the essential flavor of a carcass or meat trimmings; it will, however, produce a stock that is always useful in the kitchen as a base for essences. In short, if you're making a pigeon essence and you're fortunate enough to roast pigeons on a regular basis, proceed as follows: Brown broken-up carcasses (cooked or not; it's fine to use leftover carcasses from a roast) in a pot with onion and carrot. Add a bouquet garni and just enough stock to cover. Simmer for 2 hours, and strain. This is the stock. Take another batch of carcasses, brown them thoroughly with onion, carrot, and perhaps a little thyme, and deglaze the pan with the stock you made. Scrape up the caramelized juices and stir the carcasses around in the stock over the heat for about 5 minutes. Strain; this is the essence. Use these barely cooked carcasses to make stock for the next batch. By using this method—quick deglazing with very little cooking—you capture the essence of a thing. The stock provides body and a backdrop, but it's the final 5 minutes of simmering that capture the essence.

Mushroom Essence

Mushroom essence is made by reducing mushroom cooking liquid to one-fourth its original volume. Mushroom cooking liquid is prepared by cooking mushrooms for 15 minutes in a covered pot with just enough water to come halfway up the sides of the mushrooms. Although most recipes calling for mushroom essence assume that ordinary cultivated mushrooms are used, the essence is far better when prepared from wild types such as morels, cèpes (porcini), or chanterelles. If you use cultivated mushrooms, use cremini, which are much tastier than the relatively tasteless white variety.

100

JAPANESE-STYLE MUSHROOM SAUCE

This sauce is broth-like and should surround the food it sauces, such as fish or chicken, in a wide bowl. Substitute whatever mushrooms are available.

YIELD: ENOUGH FOR 6 SERVINGS

dashi (page 576)	2 cups	500 milliliters
mirin	1 tablespoon	15 milliliters
soy sauce	1 tablespoon	15 milliliters
dried porcini mushrooms (cèpes), soaked until soft in just enough water to cover	½ cup	125 milliliters
dried morel mushrooms, soaked until soft in just enough water to cover	½ cup	125 milliliters
dried shiitake mushrooms, soaked overnight in enough water to cover, stems removed	8	8

1. Bring the dashi to a simmer, and add the mirin and soy sauce.

2. Slice the porcini, morel, and shiitake mushrooms and add them to the simmering dashi. Add the mushroom soaking liquids to the dashi, leaving any grit behind in the soaking containers.

3. Simmer the mushrooms for 10 minutes. Serve over and around chicken or fish.

Truffle Essence

Older recipes for classic sauces often call for truffle essence. Truffle essence is prepared by infusing sliced truffles in a small proportion of brown stock in a covered saucepan. Today, truffles are so scarce that it is unlikely a restaurant would make truffle essence to have on hand to use in sauces. It is more likely that sliced truffles would be infused in the sauce itself or that the sauce would be finished with Truffle Butter (page 446) or commercially available truffle juice (see page 58).

Vegetable Essences

Almost any vegetable can be chopped and cooked in a small amount of stock, water, or wine. The method is almost the same as preparing a court-bouillon, except that the flavor of one vegetable, rather than a combination, is accentuated. These flavorful essences can then be served as accompaniments to delicately flavored foods such as fish, or can be combined with other ingredients for more complex sauces.

LIAISONS:
AN OVERVIEW

A *liaison* is an ingredient used to thicken liquids, transforming them into sauces. Until recently it was often consistency alone that distinguished a sauce from a broth; poaching liquids, stocks, and other flavorful liquids became sauces as soon as they were thickened, usually with starch. Today, the difference between a sauce and a broth is less clear, especially in contemporary kitchens where unbound but intensely flavored liquids are served with meats, fish, and vegetables.

Sauces are distinguished from broths and soups not only because they are thicker, but because they are more intensely flavored. Liaisons were used in ancient and medieval cooking as thickeners so that the sauces would cling to the foods they accompanied, making the food easier to eat with the fingers. These liaison-thickened sauces were further developed in the seventeenth century as an economical alternative to earlier sauces, which were essentially concentrated extracts made with enormous quantities of meat. For centuries since, sauces have been thickened not only to help them cling to food but to give them the look of highly concentrated and flavorful meat juices or cooking liquids.

Sauces can be thickened by suspending solids in liquids (such as starch- and vegetable purée–thickened sauces), liquids in liquids (emulsions, such as hollandaise and mayonnaise), and, in some cases, air in liquids ("foams"—such as sabayons and hollandaise—and modernist foams; see Chapter 16, Foams). A well-made Sauce Béarnaise is both a foam and an emulsion: Minute fat globules and microscopic bubbles of air are surrounded by a liquid medium.

Nowadays, chefs and diners have become skeptical of sauces that are thickened only to give them a richer appearance. Today's diner is more impressed by a light-appearing sauce than one that is thick or seems overly rich. Modern sauces are often less thick than traditional ones and may have been thickened with reduction alone or by the light-handed use of modernist thickeners such as hydrocolloids (see page 73).

HOW LIAISONS THICKEN

Liaisons usually cause thickening by dispersing solids or insoluble liquids in a water-based medium; on a molecular level, these fine components prevent the water from moving freely and thus increase the sauce's viscosity.

Thickeners can be divided into eight categories:

REDUCTION. Most often used with heavy cream. Heavy cream alone or sauces containing heavy cream are reduced until much of the water is driven out of the emulsion and the sauce thickens. Stocks can also be reduced to demi-glace or glace de viande.

STARCH. The classic starches used in traditional cooking are flour, cornstarch, arrowroot, potato starch, and tapioca starch. These thicken sauces because their molecules unravel in the liquid medium and bond into larger groupings with the water molecules.

PARTICLES. Some sauces are thickened by containing a large number of tiny particles that keep the sauce from flowing as it would if it had no thickener. Typical of these thickeners are vegetable and fruit purées, ground nuts, spices, and other ingredients that break down into minute insoluble particles. These thickeners are especially useful when making vinaigrettes or other sauces in which the solid matter also functions as the emulsifier. A rotor stator homogenizer (see page 35) comes in very handy for this because you can purée on almost a molecular level; for home cooks, a powerful immersion blender is almost as good. Particle-based sauces should be stabilized with xanthan gum and other ingredients (see page 79) to prevent syneresis, which is when sauces and purees separate.

PROTEIN. Thickeners such as eggs, gelatin, lecithin, condensed and evaporated milk, liver and foie gras, and blood are examples of proteins that thicken when heated. Many proteins are heat sensitive and will break down in boiling mixtures. Because of this, they should be gently heated while stirring. Hot liquids should be gently whisked into blood or mixtures containing it, not the other way around. The sauce should be removed from the heat as soon as it thickens. Giblets, especially the liver, can also be puréed with an equal amount—by volume, but there's no need to be precise—of butter and be whisked into the warm (not too hot) sauce as thickeners.

COAGULANTS. When acid is added to heavy cream, the cream thickens. The source of this acid can be lactic acid simply stirred into cream. It can also be the result of natural fermentation (the cream must start out raw) or inoculation. Similar reactions happen when rennet and other coagulants are added to milk to make cheese.

PECTIN. A starch-like compound usually used to thicken fruit mixtures. It works best in the presence of acid and sugar.

EMULSIONS. A hollandaise is an example of an emulsion thickened with butter; mayonnaise with oil; vinaigrette with oil. These sauces are examples of true emulsions. Such an emulsion is created when one phase of the mixture (either the fat or liquid components) is dispersed in the other by proteins that act as emulsifiers. In water and oil emulsions, for example, the water forms tiny droplets that remain suspended in fat. New hydrocolloid emulsifiers make emulsions possible that would have been unheard of a decade or two ago (see page 73).

PURÉES. Vegetable and fruit purées can also be used as thickeners; they function in different ways depending on how they are used and what natural thickeners and emulsifiers they contain. Some vegetable purées contain sufficient starch that helps them emulsify, but most purées contain insoluble components that give purée-thickened sauces a relatively rough texture and matte appearance. They also contribute flavor, whereas plain starch does not (at least not an agreeable one). Some purées, such as those made with tomato or green vegetables, contain so little starch that they thicken a sauce simply by adding a large bulk of fine solid particles to a liquid medium. Sauces thickened with these purées alone will separate into liquid and solid (syneresis)—think of the way liquid separates from carrot or tomato purée near the edge of the plate when left to sit—unless another liaison is used along with the purée. Vegetable purées are also used in vinaigrettes, where they prevent the vinegar (or other acid) and the oil from coalescing (joining up into larger globules). In most cases, when using vegetable purées as thickeners, it is a good idea to add an emulsifier such as propylene glycol alginate to the water phase (including the purée) and liquid lecithin to the oil or fat.

GELATIN

As meats and fish cook, they release juices that contain gelatin, a water-soluble protein. Depending on the cooking method, these juices end up in the roasting pan or the sauté pan or, in the case of poaching and braising, they are released into the surrounding liquid. When the gelatin is sufficiently concentrated, it gives the cooking liquid a natural, lightly syrupy consistency.

The natural gelatinous consistency that is so appealing in sauces and braising liquids can be achieved in several ways. The most obvious and expensive is to continually reuse meat or fish stocks as moisteners for more meat or fish until the gelatin (and flavor) is so concentrated that the stock has a natural consistency of its own. The resulting liquid is a natural, unthickened demi-glace. Home cooks and professionals have long added strips of pork skin, veal feet, veal knuckles, or chicken or turkey wing tips to stews and stocks to contribute additional natural gelatin. Restaurant chefs often combine these methods with careful reduction to eliminate liquid and concentrate the natural gelatin. In a restaurant setting, natural gelatin is most often added to sauces at the last minute in the form of meat glaze (glace de viande) or fish glaze (glace de poisson). These glazes not only give a finished sauce the natural texture that results from careful reduction but also provide a complex flavor backdrop to offset more assertive components, such as wine or herbs, that are added to give the sauce its final character.

In recent decades, sauces made by natural reduction and concentration of meat and fish flavors have gradually replaced the more traditional flour-thickened sauces. Although these sauces are almost always better than a carelessly made roux-based sauce, there are disadvantages to relying on reduction alone to give a sauce a syrupy or "sauce-like" consistency. If a sauce has been overly reduced, it will feel gluey in the mouth; it will also quickly congeal on hot plates. Stocks and sauces that have been overly reduced often have a flat, cooked taste that must be offset with more assertive flavors. For this reason, natural gelatin alone is rarely relied on to thicken a sauce. Sauces containing a high concentration of natural gelatin are often finished with butter, which attenuates the gelatin's stickiness.

STARCHES

Starches derived from roots and grains are among the oldest and most versatile thickeners for sauces. They are inexpensive and efficient in small amounts, so they can be used without imparting a flavor of their own.

Starch thickens sauces because its large molecules (made up of bush-like rows of sugar molecules) unravel in the liquid medium and bond into larger groupings with the water molecules. The efficiency of a particular starch as a thickener depends on the shape and size of its molecules and how they disperse in the liquid medium.

Starches must be combined with liquid and heated to be effective. Some starches are purer than others. Cornstarch, arrowroot, tapioca starch (which comes in various forms), and potato starch are almost pure starches and produce shiny sauces, whereas wheat flour contains protein, which gives flour-thickened sauces a slightly matte appearance.

Flour

In Western cooking, flour has long been the most popular sauce thickener. Although flour has largely been replaced in recent years by other thickeners, it is still the appropriate choice for many country-style and regional dishes. Chefs are also learning to use flour in limited amounts in conjunction with other thickeners.

One precaution to take when using flour for sauce making is to always make sure that liquids to be thickened have been thoroughly degreased before the flour is incorporated. Flour binds with fat and holds it in suspension throughout the liquid, making it difficult to skim. The result is a greasy, indigestible sauce with a muddy texture and flavor. One trick is to whisk in Wondra flour, which has been pretreated so it dissolves straight into a liquid without a preliminary cooking with butter. It should, however, be stirred with water to make a slurry before it is whisked into the jus or other liquid.

ROUX

The most common method for thickening liquids with flour is to prepare a roux by cooking the flour with an equal volume of butter. This attenuates the flavor of the flour and eliminates lumps. Hot liquids are then added to the cooked roux, and the mixture is brought to a simmer until it thickens. Because flour contains proteins and other compounds that impart flavor, sauces thickened with roux are usually skimmed for at least 30 minutes once they have been brought to a simmer to eliminate impurities. Although stock that is used for sauce making should be carefully skimmed and degreased before it is combined with roux, further skimming is necessary once the roux has been added, to eliminate the butter and to remove impurities in the flour.

One excellent method for using flour is to cut the amount called for in classic sauces by half and then reduce the thickened sauce carefully to the desired thickness. This method allows more time for skimming and degreasing and will attenuate any floury taste.

Both white and brown roux are used in classic French cooking. White roux is used for white sauces, brown roux for espagnole, the traditional base for the classic brown sauces. To prepare brown roux, the flour is either cooked for 15 to 20 minutes in clarified butter or browned first in the oven and cooked with butter in the same way as white roux. Brown roux is rarely seen in modern restaurant kitchens.

To prepare roux, use a whisk to stir together equal volumes of butter and flour in a saucepan over medium heat. Bring the liquid to be thickened (such as stock or milk, for velouté or béchamel, respectively) to a simmer in another pot. Cook the roux for about 5 minutes, until it has a pleasant toasty smell, and then remove the saucepan from the heat for a minute to let the roux cool. Return the pan to the heat and pour in the hot liquid while whisking. Continue whisking until the sauce comes to a simmer. Turn down the heat and slowly simmer the sauce for 30 minutes. Skim any froth and impurities from the sauce's surface with a ladle. It is also possible to thicken liquids with roux by simply adding the cold liquid to the hot roux, thus saving time and a pot. When using this method, however, be careful to whisk thoroughly to prevent lumps.

BEURRE MANIÉ

Like roux, beurre manié contains equal parts by volume of butter and flour. It differs from roux, however, in that it is not cooked and is usually added at the end of a sauce's cooking rather than at the beginning. It is most often used to thicken stews at the end of cooking when the braising liquid is too thin.

To prepare beurre manié, simply work together equal parts by volume of flour and butter with the back of a dinner fork until they form a smooth paste (see photos). To thicken a liquid, simply whisk in the beurre manié a bit at a time, and wait for the liquid to come to a simmer after each addition (the thickening effect does not occur and cannot be gauged until the mixture comes to approaches a boil). Continue in this way until the liquid has the right thickness. Unlike roux, beurre manié should not be cooked any longer once the mixture thickens or the sauce will develop a strong floury taste. (One of the peculiarities of flour is that it develops a strong floury taste after 2 minutes of cooking that begins to disappear as the cooking progresses, usually after 30 minutes.)

FLOURING INGREDIENTS FOR A STEW

In home-style and country cooking, stew meat is often floured (in French, *singer*) before it is browned in hot fat. This is an excellent technique because the flour is thoroughly browned, eliminating any starchy flavor; moreover, the browning of the meat is made easier because the flour helps form a crust. The total amount of flour added to the stew is relatively small so that, if necessary, the cook can add more thickener (beurre manié) or reduce the stewing liquid at the end of cooking.

Some cooks add flour to stews by cooking it in the pan along with chopped aromatic vegetables after the meat has been removed. This method is effective as long as the caramelized meat juices on the bottom of the pan are not allowed to burn and too much flour is not used. Be sure to discard any burned fat and replace it with fresh butter or olive oil before stirring in the flour.

USING FLOUR TO MAKE GRAVY

A gravy is a jus (the natural juices from a roast) that has been thickened with flour. Depending on the amount of cooking liquid remaining in the roasting pan, gravies can be prepared using one of two similar techniques. If a small amount of jus remains in the pan, it should be boiled down on top of the stove until it caramelizes; all but a tablespoon or two (15 to 30 milliliters) of fat should be removed and discarded. The flour is added and cooked for 2 to 3 minutes in the roasting pan on top of the stove; the mixture is then moistened with a small amount of stock, water, or other liquid. If a large amount of roasting jus remains in the pan, it should be transferred to a saucepan or glass container and the fat skimmed off with a ladle. You can also use a fat separator and pour the stock out from the bottom, leaving the fat behind. A roux is then prepared in the roasting pan with a little of the fat or some fresh butter. The jus is returned to the roasting pan, brought to a simmer, and whisked until smooth and thickened.

Because flour used as a last-minute thickener for gravies has little time to cook, an alternative is to use a previously thickened velouté- or espagnole-style flour-thickened sauce instead of plain stock to deglaze the pan; the roux is then omitted.

One trick, long underappreciated in professional kitchens, is to use Wondra flour. It can be whisked into liquids (after a preliminary mixing with water to form a slurry) to thicken them without preliminary cooking into a roux.

Other Starches

In the first edition of *Le Guide Culinaire*, published at the turn of the twentieth century, Escoffier predicted that the traditional roux-thickened sauces would be replaced with sauces thickened with purer forms of starch such as arrowroot, potato starch, cornstarch, and especially tapioca starch. Using these starches would eliminate the need for the careful skimming necessary to rid flour-thickened sauces of impurities. He was correct in predicting the demise of flour-thickened sauces, but incorrect in assuming that other starches would be used to fill the gap.

Perhaps the glossy look of sauces thickened with these pure forms of starch explains why Western chefs and diners have never grown accustomed to cornstarch- or arrowroot-thickened sauces. The look of these sauces is almost too perfect, like costume jewelry that glitters just a bit too garishly.

Almost any thickener has drawbacks that can be lessened by using the thickener in tandem with other methods or ingredients. A small amount of starch added to an already well-reduced stock or cooking liquid will hardly be noticed.

One method occasionally used in contemporary kitchens is to prepare a basic brown stock, reducing and degreasing it to concentrate flavor and eliminate impurities, then thickening the stock with arrowroot. This lightly thickened brown sauce base—a kind of arrowroot espagnole—is then used as a base for made-to-order derivative sauces. When preparing a base in this way, starch must be used judiciously: There is nothing more irksome than a deeply colored, glistening sauce with no taste.

Purified starches should be worked to a thin paste with cold water before being added to hot liquids. If added directly, they will form insoluble lumps that must be strained out. Purified starches are approximately twice as efficient as flour is in thickening.

ARROWROOT

Although not as easy to find as cornstarch, arrowroot is the best of the purified starches for thickening sauces because it remains stable even after prolonged exposure to heat. It is used in the same way as cornstarch: Combine the arrowroot with four times its volume of cold water. After letting it sit for 5 minutes, whisk it into liquids.

CORNSTARCH

Of the purified starches, cornstarch is the most familiar. It should be used only as a last-minute thickener for sauces and cooking liquids that are being served immediately. When it is cooked for long periods, it begins to break down and lose its thickening power. Blend cornstarch with four times its volume of cold water. After 5 minutes, the slurry is ready to be used.

LAMBDA CARRAGEENAN

Carrageenans, of which there are a number, are particularly well suited to dairy preparations or preparations designed to emulate dairy. It also works to emulate dairy because of its synergistic effects with dairy and its solubility in water.

POTATO STARCH

Although potato starch was one of the first starches to be used in French cooking, it has never been popular as a sauce thickener in the United States. It is used in the same way as cornstarch and arrowroot. Like cornstarch, it tends to break down after prolonged exposure to heat.

TAPIOCA STARCH

Modernist chefs have adopted tapioca starch, which comes in various more or less modified forms, because of its neutral flavor and unobtrusive mouthfeel. Often marketed under the names Ultra-Sperse 3 or Ultra-Tex 3 and 8, each of these has slightly different thickening characteristics. Ultra-Sperse 3 is usually used in concentration from 0.2% to 5%, while Ultra-Tex 8 is usually used from 1% to 6%. Plain tapioca starch, sometimes labeled tapioca flour, is commonly available at grocery stores, but it is inconsistent and thickens less effectively then pretreated starches such as Ultra Sperse and Ultra-Tex.

EGG YOLKS

Because they thicken sauces in several ways, egg yolks are versatile liaisons. They provide the base for emulsified sauces such as mayonnaise and hollandaise, and are used in conjunction with cream to finish the cooking liquid of poached meats and fish. They not only form emulsions of fat and liquids but also combine with air, so they can be used for sabayon sauces. They are also used to give richness and texture to crème anglaise.

Egg yolks contain several emulsifiers, among them cholesterol and lecithin, which accounts for their versatility. Many scientific studies have been done to explain the behavior of egg yolks, and a few tips and precautions are especially useful to the saucier. Sauces containing egg yolks should not be allowed to boil (lest they coagulate) unless they contain a large proportion of flour, which stabilizes them. Pastry cream is an example of a sauce made with flour that is boiled after the yolks are added. Egg yolks are also stabilized to some degree by sugar and acids such as lemon and vinegar, but not so much that the yolks can be boiled without curdling. Only flour and hydrocolloid thickeners and emulsifiers can prevent this. If a crème anglaise contains a sufficient proportion of alcohol, the alcohol will boil off before the crème anglaise gets to the temperature needed to set the egg yolks. So if the sauce is bubbling but not thickening, it's the alcohol.

When combining egg yolks with hot liquids, be sure to whisk some of the hot liquid into the yolks before returning the mixture to the saucepan. If the yolks are added directly to a hot liquid, they are liable to coagulate as soon as they come in contact with the heat.

Never cook sauces containing egg yolks in aluminum pots or the sauce will turn gray.

If you want to use more stable egg yolks, cook the beaten yolks sous vide for 30 minutes at 140°F (60°C). Whisk the liquid into the yolks in the normal way.

Finishing Poaching Liquids: Egg Yolk and Cream Liaisons

Egg yolks are rarely used alone as a thickener for sauces, but are usually combined with cream and added to a liquid that has already been lightly thickened with flour. Blanquette de veau, a white veal stew finished with cream and egg yolks—one of the cornerstones of French home cooking—illustrates the use of egg yolks as a final liaison for poached meats. The blanched pieces of veal are poached in water or white veal stock along with aromatic vegetables and a bouquet garni. When the veal is tender, after 2 to 3 hours, the liquid is strained, thickened into a classic velouté with flour—about 3½ ounces (100 grams) roux to 1 quart (1 liter) poaching liquid—and then finished with the cream and egg yolk liaison. Recipes vary, but an egg yolk liaison is usually made by combining each yolk with 3 to 4 tablespoons (45 to 60 milliliters) heavy cream, then using 3 to 4 egg yolks' worth of this mixture to thicken 1 quart (1 liter) velouté. After the liaison has been added to the velouté, the sauce is gently stirred until it naps the back of a spoon. The stability of the egg yolks will depend on the proportion of flour in the velouté, but most recipes do not risk curdling and warn against letting the sauce boil.

A mixture of egg yolks and cream is also used to finish a traditional chicken fricassée and for fish cooked *en sauce* (see "Braising," page 301 in Chapter 10). Contemporary chefs sometimes use cream and egg yolks as the only finish for flourless sauces, creating a kind of savory crème anglaise (see Flourless Sauce Allemande, page 143).

Another approach is to stabilize the egg yolks by cooking them sous vide to 140°F (60°C). Liquid lecithin (1% to 2%) can also be added to the egg yolks or egg yolk–cream mixture and 0.5% propylene glycol alginate to the stock or milk base. These two compounds will stabilize the yolks and make it much harder for them to curdle. However, take the usual precautions when cooking egg yolks.

See also Chapter 13, "Hot Emulsified Sauces," and Chapter 14, "Mayonnaise-Based Sauces," for additional information on egg yolks as liaisons.

CREAM

During the height of nouvelle cuisine, reduced cream largely replaced roux as a thickener, becoming an almost universal base for white sauces. Because of its richness, today's chefs are beginning to use cream more judiciously, and many of the reduced-cream-thickened sauces of decades past are being abandoned for lighter versions, in which only enough cream is used to contribute a smooth texture.

Heavy cream can be used to finish a sauce, to give it a smooth consistency and a more subtle flavor, but it becomes effective as a thickener per se only when it is reduced. Heavy cream or crème fraîche can be reduced and used in two ways: It can be reduced alone and used as needed as thickener for last-minute sauces; one of the most commonly used methods is to finish pan sauces with cream. Or the cream can be combined with the sauce base or cooking liquid and the two reduced together. This second method is best used for sauces made in advance.

Whichever method is used, several precautions should be followed when reducing cream. Always reduce cream in a saucepan three to four times its volume; if cream is allowed to boil for even a few seconds, it will boil over. Although it is not necessary to stir or whisk simmering cream continually, give the cream a quick whisking at least every 2 minutes while it is reducing. Cream that is allowed to sit unheeded over even a low flame will become granular and may break.

Always use a saucepan with a large enough diameter to accommodate a medium to high flame. If the pan is too small, the flame will wrap around the outside of it and cause the cream to brown along the pan's side, discoloring the finished sauce. This is less of a problem on an electric range.

Never cook cream covered. Water will condense on the bottom of the lid and drip down into the cream, causing it to become granular and eventually to break.

When using reduced cream as a thickener for wine sauces, be sure to reduce the wine thoroughly before adding the cream. Not only can the raw wine's acidity cause the cream to break, but an unpleasant flavor of uncooked wine will remain in the sauce.

The degree that heavy cream should be reduced can vary, from one-third to two-thirds its original volume, depending on its butterfat content and the desired thickness of the finished sauce. For example, if 1½ cups (375 milliliters) heavy cream were added to ½ cup (125 milliliters) flavor base, the mixture could be reduced to ½ cup (125 milliliters) for a very thick sauce or to 1 cup (250 milliliters) for a lighter sauce (see chart, page 637).

When used alone, reduced cream is very rich and sometimes has a slightly chalky texture in the mouth. Thus it is rarely used as the only thickener for sauces but is usually used in conjunction with butter, egg yolks, flour, or modernist ingredients. Butter is often used to finish reduced-cream sauces to give them an appealing sheen and a smoother texture; it of course does nothing to attenuate the sauce's richness. Some chefs use roux as a preliminary thickener for the sauce base or add beurre manié at the end so that the sauce requires less reduction and hence is less rich (and expensive).

Double Cream

European recipes often call for double cream, or *crème double*. Double cream has an especially high butterfat content and is particularly useful as a sauce thickener because it requires less reduction. It is not marketed in the United States but can be prepared using homemade crème fraîche. To prepare double cream, line a large strainer with a wet napkin or a triple layer of cheesecloth, fill it with crème fraîche, tie it at the top, and suspend it overnight in the refrigerator over a bowl. The whey drains from the cream, leaving the remaining cream with a higher butterfat percentage. The approximate butterfat content of the finished cream can be calculated by measuring the amount of liquid (whey) that drained off the cream. For example, if 1 quart (1 liter) of cream released 2 cups (500 milliliters) of whey—that is, half its volume—then the butterfat content has been doubled to 70 percent, given that heavy cream is 35 percent butterfat.

Pan Sauces Finished with Cream

Heavy cream is a handy thickener for both brown and white pan sauces that are made to order. Most sauces that are finished with cream also include a small amount of butter to smooth the texture and give the sauce an appealing sheen.

In a restaurant setting, where sauces are made to order in small quantities, it is best to pre-reduce certain ingredients, such as the stock, the cream, and sometimes even the deglazing liquid. This, of course, saves time but also improves the flavor of the sauce by avoiding long reduction in the sauté pan. The character of a well-made pan sauce is imparted by the caramelized juices that adhere to the bottom of the pan after sautéing meats or fish. This flavor is lost if it is cooked for more than a minute or two while the sauce is being reduced. Ideally, liquids used for making the sauce should remain in the pan only long enough to dissolve the caramelized juices.

WHITE WINE SAUCE WITH THREE LIAISONS

YIELD: APPROXIMATELY 3 CUPS (750 MILLILITERS)

white wine	1 cup	250 milliliters
shallots, minced	2	2
heavy cream or crème fraîche	1 quart	1 liter
flour	2 tablespoons	30 milliliters
butter	5 ounces	150 grams
lemon juice	to taste	to taste
salt and pepper	to taste	to taste

1. Combine the white wine and shallots in a 2-quart (2 liter) saucepan and reduce the mixture by three-fourths.

2. Add the cream to the reduced white wine–shallot base and bring the mixture to a simmer.

3. Work together the flour and 1 ounce (30 grams) of the butter to make a beurre manié; whisk it into the cream sauce. Continue reducing the cream mixture until it has the desired consistency.

4. Cut the remaining butter (4 ounces/120 grams) into chunks and whisk it all at once into the sauce.

5. Add lemon juice. Season with salt and pepper. If desired, thin the sauce with cream or water, and adjust the seasoning. (Do not ever thin a finished sauce with raw wine.)

BUTTER

Butter has long been used in classic French cooking to finish sauces thickened with flour and for certain pan-deglazed sauces. When nouvelle cuisine was at its peak, it became popular as a liaison for flourless sauces and in fact became the thickener of choice for made-to-order brown sauces. Some such sauces were (and are) made almost entirely with butter.

When butter is whisked into a hot liquid, it forms an emulsion, similar to the action of egg yolks. The milk solids and proteins contained in the butter act as emulsifiers that keep microscopic globules of fat in suspension and give butter sauces their characteristic sheen and consistency. Because the milk solids contained in the butter are what maintain the emulsion, sauces and cooking liquids cannot be thickened with clarified butter unless another emulsifier is used. In fact, cold butter, itself an emulsion, is preferable to warm butter, which may have begun to turn oily.

Emulsions based on butter alone are less stable than reduced-cream sauces, egg yolk sauces, or sauces that contain flour. Until nouvelle cuisine, butter was almost always used in conjunction with other thickeners. Even today, many emulsified butter sauces are made to order only so they do not sit around and break.

To stabilize these sauces, you can dissolve 2% liquid lecithin in the butter and blend 0.5% propylene glycol alginate into the stock or flavor base.

Enriching Sauces with Butter (*Monter au Beurre*)

Finishing sauces with butter has become one of the most important and widely used techniques in contemporary sauce making. The technique consists of swirling chunks of cold butter into a hot flavor base, usually just before serving. Essentially the technique is the same as that used for making beurre blanc or other emulsified butter sauces, except that the technique is most often used today for last-minute made-to-order sauces.

Certain precautions should always be followed when using butter as a thickener. If too large or too small a proportion of butter is used for a given amount of liquid, the sauce will break. The proportion of butter used to thicken a given amount of liquid can vary from about 20 percent butter to almost ten times as much butter as flavor base (for example, Beurre Blanc, page 434). If too small a proportion of butter is used, it tends to separate and float to the surface of the sauce unless the sauce is already an emulsion based on cream or egg yolks, or contains flour or modernist emulsifiers or stabilizers. Large proportions of butter are used to finish intensely flavored liquids—beurre blanc is again an example—but if too much butter is used, the taste of the flavor base is lost and the sauce takes on a thick, waxy appearance and may break.

Most chefs finish made-to-order sauces by eye and can quickly judge the correct amount of butter to add based on the sauce's look and flavor. Even though many well-reduced flavor bases do not require a liaison because of the natural gelatin they contain, butter is often added to soften the sauce's flavor and also to eliminate the sticky consistency of highly reduced meat and fish sauces. When using butter to finish a flavor base, it is better to risk overreducing the flavor base before adding the butter; a butter sauce can easily be thinned, but thickening a sauce already containing butter would require reduction, and boiling a butter-enriched sauce for any length of time will cause it to break and become oily.

As a general rule, a made-to-order butter sauce should contain about one-third butter. In other words, 4 ounces (125 grams) of butter should be used to finish 1 cup (250 milliliters) of liquid sauce base. These proportions will vary widely, depending on the thickness of the sauce base, the intensity of its flavor, the water content of the butter, and the desired consistency of the finished sauce.

Because of the richness of butter-enriched sauces, many chefs are starting to use butter in combination with vegetable purées. Tomato and mushroom purées (which can be combined with propylene glycol alginate) work especially well as preliminary thickeners for brown sauces. Much less butter is then required to give subtlety and a brilliant sheen to the sauce.

BUTTER-THICKENED MADE-TO-ORDER RED WINE SAUCE

YIELD: 4 TO 6 TABLESPOONS (60 TO 90 MILLILITERS), ENOUGH SAUCE
TO ACCOMPANY 2 SERVINGS OF MEAT

steak, lamb chops, pork chops, or the like	2 servings	2 servings
vegetable oil or rendered fat (for sautéing)	as needed	as needed
red wine	½ cup	125 milliliters
brown stock (pages 85 and 89) or glace de viande (page 97)	½ cup or 1 tablespoon	125 milliliters or 15 milliliters
butter, cut into cubes	1½ ounces	45 grams
salt and pepper	to taste	to taste

1. Sauté the meat in the oil or fat in a heavy-bottomed sauté pan. When the meat is done, transfer it to a plate and discard the fat in the sauté pan.

2. Pour the wine into the sauté pan and reduce it by half.

3. Add the stock and reduce until it takes on a syrupy consistency, or simply stir in the glace de viande.

4. Whisk in the butter and bring the sauce to a simmer for about 10 seconds.

5. If desired, adjust the thickness of the sauce by thinning with stock or thickening with more butter. Season with salt and pepper.

GIBLETS AND FOIE GRAS

Americans have long been familiar with the traditional giblet gravy served with the holiday turkey. Most home cooks precook the gizzards, liver, and heart by simmering them in water. The giblet broth is then used along with the roasting juices to make the gravy; the giblets are chopped and added to the gravy at the end. Giblets cooked and chopped in this way, while contributing a delightful texture and contrast, do not actually thicken.

The French—both professionals and home cooks—have long used raw giblets, often in conjunction with blood, to finish sauces. Giblets used in this way thicken the sauce; contribute a full, often gamy, flavor; and give the sauce a characteristic muddy appearance, sometimes unappealing to the uninitiated but delicious once tasted.

The most straightforward technique is to purée the raw giblets (liver, gizzard, heart, and lungs) of a bird to be roasted or braised with about half their volume in butter (the butter prevents the mixture from clumping when it is combined with the sauce) in a food processor. Appropriate herbs, a few drops of marc or Cognac, port, or crushed juniper berries can also be added to the giblet mixture to enhance its flavor. The roasting or braising juices are then prepared in the usual way and finished by whisking half the juices into the giblet-butter mixture. In restaurant settings, the technique can also be used for made-to-order pan sauces.

Because raw giblet sauces are inherently unstable, emulsifiers such as liquid lecithin (2%), dissolved in the liver mixture, can be used to stabilize them. Propylene glycol alginate (0.5%) can be blended into the liquid base.

SAUTÉED PIGEON BREASTS WITH GIBLET SAUCE

t is best to obtain pigeons that have been eviscerated but contain all the giblets—heart, liver, gizzard, and lungs. If these are unavailable, the pigeon livers can be used alone. This dish is particularly good with fresh boiled and buttered fava beans.

YIELD: 4 SERVINGS

pigeons	4	4
onion, chopped	3 ounces	100 grams
carrot, chopped	3 ounces	100 grams
garlic cloves, peeled	2	2
oil	as needed	as needed
brown chicken stock (page 85) or other stock (or more as needed)	2 cups	500 milliliters
small bouquet garni (page 52)	1	1

butter	3 ounces	90 grams
juniper berries, crushed and chopped	5	5
marc or grappa	1 tablespoon	15 milliliters
salt and pepper	to taste	to taste
wine vinegar	a few drops	a few drops

1. Remove the giblets from the pigeons and set them aside. Carefully remove from the carcasses the pigeon breasts (with skin attached) and the thighs, which can be left attached to the breasts. Coarsely chop the pigeon carcasses.

2. Brown the chopped carcasses in a pan with the onion, carrot, and garlic, in a very small amount of oil.

3. Deglaze the pan with ½ cup (125 milliliters) stock; reduce it rapidly until it forms a glaze and caramelizes. Add the rest of the stock and the bouquet garni and simmer for 20 minutes. Strain this base and reserve. Skim off any fat that floats to the top.

4. Purée the butter, giblets, juniper berries, and marc in a food processor. Work the mixture through a strainer. Cover this mixture with plastic wrap and keep refrigerated until needed.

5. When ready to serve, sauté the pigeon breasts and thighs in a small amount of oil. Transfer them to a plate, discard the fat in the pan, and deglaze the pan with the pigeon stock.

6. Finish the sauce with about 1 tablespoon (15 milliliters) of the giblet mixture per serving. Pour the liquid into the giblet mixture, not the other way around.

7. Season with salt and pepper and add vinegar, drop by drop, to taste.

8. If you like, slice the breasts lengthwise and arrange them over a vegetable such as fava beans. Nap or surround the sautéed breasts and thighs with the sauce.

VARIATIONS

Stabilize the sauce with 2 grams liquid lecithin worked into the butter. Stabilize the stock part of the sauce with about 0.5 grams propylene glycol alginate per ½ cup (100 milliliters) stock base.

Foie gras can also be worked into the butter (see below).

Foie Gras

Foie gras can be used in the same way as giblets: combined with one-third to one-half its weight in butter and whisked into sauces at the end. The finished sauce is smoother and paler, with a more delicate flavor. Foie gras can be used for finishing roasting and braising juices and pan juices, and even as a finishing touch in Red Wine Beef Stew (page 273). See "Variations" above.

ROAST CHICKEN WITH GARLIC AND FOIE GRAS EMULSION

The roasting method used here is the same as for Oven-Roasted Chicken (page 248), except that garlic cloves replace the standard aromatic vegetables and the finished roasting juices are flavored and thickened with garlic purée and foie gras.

When using foie gras as a thickener, it is better to use foie gras that has been cooked first—foie gras terrine—so that excess water is released in advance. While this sauce can be prepared without any stabilizers, it becomes a very delicate operation to avoid curdling the mixture. Adding liquid lecithin to the fat and propylene glycol alginate to the stock helps prevent the sauce from separating.

YIELD: 4 SERVINGS

roasting chicken (4 pounds/2 kilograms)	1	1
garlic heads, broken into cloves, unpeeled	2	2
foie gras mousse or bloc	2 ounces	50 grams
butter	1 ounce	30 grams
liquid lecithin (optional)		2 grams
brown chicken stock (page 85)	1 cup	250 milliliters
propylene glycol alginate (optional)		1.8 grams
salt and pepper	to taste	to taste

1. Surround the chicken with the garlic cloves and roast it. If the garlic cloves or roasting juices start to burn on the bottom of the pan, add ½ cup (125 milliliters) water or stock every time they threaten to burn.

2. Purée the foie gras with the butter and lecithin, if using, in a food processor. If your food processor cannot handle such a small quantity, work the butter, lecithin, and foie gras together in a bowl with a wooden spoon, then force the mixture through a drum sieve.

3. Remove the chicken from the roasting pan. Deglaze the pan, which still contains the garlic cloves, with the stock. Strain the roasting juices, reserving the garlic cloves and skimming off excess fat. Blend the propylene glycol alginate, if using, into the roasting juices.

4. Force the garlic cloves through a coarse chinois or drum sieve.

5. Whisk half the foie gras mixture and half the garlic purée into the roasting juices.

6. Adjust the texture and flavor of the finished sauce by adding more garlic purée and/or foie gras mixture. Season with salt and pepper.

Note: In restaurants or fast-paced situations, it is sometimes impractical to prepare the garlic purée along with the chicken jus as described here. The garlic purée may be prepared in advance and used as needed (see Baked Garlic Purée, page 515). If you're using the liquid lecithin and propylene glycol alginate, the whole sauce can be prepared ahead of time and held in a bain-marie at 140°F (60°C). You could also hold it in a whipping siphon, which would give it a frothy consistency.

ROAST TURKEY WITH JUS, GRAVY, OR GIBLET GRAVY

A gravy is made by thickening juices from a roast with flour. Making a generous amount of well-flavored turkey jus or gravy involves a paradox: If the turkey is properly cooked or if it is stuffed, it will release little in the way of juices. When over-cooked, as most turkeys are, it will provide plenty of juices for your gravy. If the turkey has released an abundance of juices—a couple of cups (500 milliliters) or more—serving the jus is a simple matter of skimming off the fat and serving the juices as they are, as a jus. If the juices taste insipid, they can be reduced by half or more. To convert them to gravy, make a roux and add the juices to that. To make giblet gravy, roast the giblets in the pan along with the turkey, chop them fine, and add them to the finished gravy.

If you've cooked your turkey just right, you won't see much in the bottom of the pan and what there is won't have a whole lot of flavor. To get the most flavor out of a small amount of juices, boil down the juices until they caramelize on the bottom of the pan, pour out the fat (or leave a few tablespoons in the pan if you're making a roux), and deglaze the pan with stock. Use only as much stock as you need to serve the guests at hand—about 3 tablespoons (45 milliliters) per person—because the more stock you add, the less flavorful the juice will be. If you're a fanatic, you can bring up the flavor of the jus by adding a little stock at a time and caramelizing after each addition. To stretch a small amount of jus without diluting its flavor, consider swirling in ½ ounce (15 grams) butter per serving.

Generally, when preparing a jus, you want to eliminate as much fat and grease as possible so the jus is clean and not oily. The trick for this is to caramelize all the juices on the bottom of the pan so the liquid fat ends up floating on top. Once the fat has been removed, an emulsifier can be used to thicken or add texture to the jus. An emulsifier should never be added too early or it will emulsify in the grease.

Sometimes, however, you may want to incorporate particularly delicious fats (foie gras comes to mind) into a jus. Incorporating clarified butter, beurre noisette, or ghee has long been thought impossible, since, unlike whole butter, they contain no emulsifiers and just sit on top of the sauce like an oil slick. However, there are a couple of approaches to emulsify in the clarified butter. One is to add a small amount of liquid lecithin (2% of the weight of the fat) to the fat along with a small amount of propylene glycol alginate (0.5% the weight of the liquid) to the liquid base.

YIELD: 6 SERVINGS GRAVY OR JUS (ABOUT 1¼ CUPS/300 MILLILITERS)

(continued)

roast turkey, giblets roasted in the pan with the turkey	1	1
flour or wondra (for gravy)	3 tablespoons	45 milliliters
turkey or chicken stock (page 85) or water (if there are insufficient juices)	up to 2 cups	up to 500 milliliters
cold butter, sliced (optional)	3 ounces	90 grams
liquid lecithin (optional)		2 grams
beurre noisette, melted (see page 438; optional)	3 ounces	90 grams
propylene glycol alginate (optional)		1.5 grams
salt and pepper	to taste	to taste

1. Transfer the turkey to a platter and pour any juices that have accumulated in the cavity into the roasting pan.

2. Chop the giblets, if using, until quite fine but not into a purée. Set aside.

3. If the pan is swimming in juices and fat, pour everything into a glass measuring cup. Skim off the fat with a ladle. Discard the fat if you're making jus or using Wondra to make gravy. If you're making gravy with regular flour, put 3 tablespoons (45 milliliters) of the fat back in the roasting pan and discard the rest. If necessary, add stock to the skimmed juices to make 2 cups (500 milliliters). Proceed to step 5 (jus) or step 6 (gravy).

4. If there are less than 2 cups (500 milliliters) juices and fat in the roasting pan, put the pan on the stove over high heat. Move the pan around every couple of minutes so it heats evenly. Continue in this way until the juices evaporate, a brown crust forms on the bottom of the pan, and the only liquid in the pan is a layer of shiny liquid fat. If you're making gravy with flour, leave 3 tablespoons (45 milliliters) of the fat in the pan; otherwise pour out the fat.

5. **TO MAKE JUS:** Deglaze the roasting pan with the stock, scraping the bottom of the roasting pan with a wooden spoon to dissolve the juices, or put the combined skimmed jus and stock in a saucepan. Proceed to step 7.

6. **TO MAKE GRAVY:** If using flour, add it to the fat in the pan and stir over medium heat until it smells toasty, about 3 minutes; return the juices plus stock to the pan, or add the stock. Scrape the pan, if necessary. If you're using Wondra, first stir it into a slurry. Deglaze the pan with the stock, if necessary, or add the stock to the pan. Stir in the slurry.

7. Simmer the jus or gravy until reduced to 1¼ cups (300 milliliters). Strain. If using the giblets, stir them into the gravy.

8. Whisk in the cold butter, if using. Alternatively, if using the beurre noisette, dissolve the lecithin into the warm beurre noisette, and the propylene glycol alginate into the jus, then whisk the beurre noisette into the jus. Season with salt and pepper.

BLOOD

Blood has long been used in European cooking to finish sauces for braised or roasted game, poultry, or rabbit. A sauce finished with blood has a characteristic matte appearance. Blood not only deepens a sauce's flavor but also acts as a thickener.

Whereas European recipes often substitute pork blood for the blood of the animal being cooked, fresh pork blood is not easy to obtain in the United States, so it is necessary to use live or at least recently killed game or poultry. (In some states, serving foods cooked with blood is illegal, so be sure to check with local health authorities before serving a blood-based sauce to the public.) Many American cities have live-poultry markets that kill birds to order and are willing to save the blood. Be sure to bring a jar containing a teaspoon (5 milliliters) of Cognac and a teaspoon (5 milliliters) of wine vinegar as a receptacle for the blood. The Cognac and vinegar will prevent the blood from coagulating. Be sure to strain the blood to eliminate feathers, animal hairs, and other debris.

When finishing a sauce with blood, the blood must never be allowed to boil; the hot sauce should be whisked into the blood and the mixture returned to the saucepan, not the other way around. Blood is very perishable and should not be used after 24 hours.

CIVET DE LAPIN
BRAISED RABBIT STEW

A *civet* is a stew that has been finished at the last minute with blood. In this recipe, large rabbits are first carefully larded and then braised. The braising liquid is used to heat the rabbit pieces and is then finished to order with the reserved blood. Large rabbits (5 pounds/2.25 kilograms after cleaning) are best for braising.

YIELD: 8 SERVINGS

large older rabbits	2	2
cognac	1 teaspoon	5 milliliters
wine vinegar	1 teaspoon	5 milliliters
fatback	12 or 14 ounces	350 or 400 grams
garlic cloves, peeled	2	2
parsley	½ bunch	½ bunch
lard (optional)	¼ cup	50 grams
onion, coarsely chopped	1 medium	1 medium
carrot, coarsely chopped	1 medium	1 medium
garlic cloves, unpeeled	2	2
brown veal or chicken stock (page 92 or 85)	1 quart	1 liter
medium bouquet garni (page 52)	1	1

(*continued*)

1. Have the rabbits killed and skinned, and the blood saved in a jar containing the cognac and vinegar.

2. Cut 12 ounces (350 grams) of the fatback into strips (lardons) about 6 × ⅜ × ⅜ inches (15 cm × 5 mm × 5 mm). Finely chop the peeled garlic and parsley and toss with the fatback lardons. Let this mixture sit for several hours or overnight.

3. Remove the thighs and saddles from the rabbits. The saddles should be cut away from the front quarters so that three ribs remain attached to each side of the saddle. Remove the forelegs and cut the rib cages into three sections. Cut the heads in half. The saddles can be halved crosswise or boned.

4. Thoroughly lard the saddles and thighs with the fatback lardons.

5. Preheat the oven to 350°F (175°C). Cube and render the remaining 2 ounces (50 grams) fatback in a heavy-bottomed rondeau, or use already rendered lard. Brown the pieces of rabbit, including the forelegs, heads, and rib cages. Add the onion and carrot and unpeeled garlic cloves midway through the browning.

6. When the rabbit is thoroughly browned, pour off any excess fat and add enough stock to come two-thirds of the way up the sides of the rabbit. Add the bouquet garni. Bring the stock to a slow simmer on the stove.

7. Cover the rondeau with aluminum foil and a tight-fitting lid. Braise the rabbit in the oven until the pieces are easily pierced with a skewer, usually about 2 hours. Check from time to time to make sure the braising liquid is not boiling. After about an hour of braising, turn over the rabbit sections in the liquid so that what was above the liquid is now below.

8. Remove the rabbit thighs and saddles and keep covered on a plate. Leave the oven on. Strain the braising liquid into a saucepan; discard the heads, bones, vegetables, and bouquet garni. (The forelegs can be eaten by the kitchen staff but should not be served.)

9. Bring the braising liquid to a slow simmer and skim off any fat or froth that floats to the surface. Simmer and skim for at least 30 minutes.

10. Place the rabbit thighs and saddles in a clean rondeau and add the braising liquid. Put the rondeau, uncovered, in the oven. Baste the rabbit with the braising liquid for 30 to 45 minutes, until the rabbit looks shiny and glazed.

11. Strain the braising liquid and reserve. Keep the rabbit pieces covered until needed.

12. If reheating the rabbit, which does it no harm, place the appropriate number of rabbit pieces per order in a saucepan with sloping sides or in a straight-sided sauté pan with a tight-fitting lid. Add about ¼ cup (60 milliliters) of braising liquid per order, cover the pan, and heat over low heat for 15 minutes.

13. Just before serving, put 1 tablespoon (15 milliliters) blood per order in a stainless-steel bowl. Whisk in the hot braising liquid. Transfer the rabbit pieces to serving plates and return the braising liquid to the saucepan or sauté pan.

14. Gently heat the sauce while whisking or blending with an immersion blender until it thickens. Don't let the sauce boil. Serve over the rabbit.

Note: Although this sauce is already deeply flavored, many chefs add a few drops of vinegar and a tiny bit of Cognac to bring its flavors into focus. Parsley, finely chopped at the last minute, will also enhance the sauce, giving it a note of freshness. The civet can be garnished with mushrooms, pearl onions, or glazed root vegetables.

Finishing Sauces with Giblets and Blood

Many roasts, especially poultry and game, are often finished with a mixture of chopped giblets and blood, rather than either alone. In the case of wild game, the blood, liver, lungs, and heart are combined with a little Cognac and vinegar. The mixture is then puréed in a food processor and used to finish the braising or roasting juices.

Blood and giblets are also used to finish a special type of roast, called a *salmis*. To prepare a bird *en salmis*, the bird is first partially roasted, and the meat and giblets are removed from the carcass. The partially cooked giblets are then finely chopped and seasoned, the carcass is pressed in a duck press, and the resulting jus thickened with the chopped giblets. The meat is then gently stewed in the finished sauce. In France, salmis are prepared with special ducks and sometimes pigeons that have been strangled so that their blood remains in the meat. Since these are unavailable in the United States, the process can be circumvented by saving the blood when the animal is killed and adding it to the chopped giblets just before finishing the sauce.

SAUCE ROUENNAISE I

Nineteenth-century food writers simplified sauce rouennaise by defining it as derived from a red wine sauce base—Sauce Bordelaise (page 186)—finished with livers puréed with butter. Named for the Norman city Rouen, it is unlikely that sauce rouennaise has its roots in Bordeaux.

A more elaborate and probably more authentic version (except for the foie gras, which can be omitted anyway) can be prepared with duck stock, duck blood and liver, and foie gras.

YIELD: 1½ CUPS (375 MILLILITERS)

red wine	½ cup	125 milliliters
small bouquet garni (page 52)	1	1
brown duck stock	1 cup	250 milliliters
duck liver (not foie gras)	1	1
foie gras	1 ounce	25 grams
butter	1 ounce	30 grams
liquid lecithin (optional)		1 gram
heavy cream or crème fraîche	¼ cup	60 milliliters
duck blood	¼ cup	60 milliliters
cognac	a few drops	a few drops
wine vinegar	a few drops	a few drops
salt and pepper	to taste	to taste

(continued)

1. Reduce the red wine by half in a saucepan with the bouquet garni.

2. Add the duck stock and reduce the mixture again by half. Skim off any froth that floats to the surface.

3. Purée the duck liver, foie gras, butter, and lecithin, if using, in a food processor. Work the mixture through a fine-mesh strainer. Keep the purée covered with plastic wrap until needed.

4. Add the cream to the reduced red wine–stock mixture. Bring to a simmer for 1 minute.

5. Off the heat, whisk the liver mixture into the reduced stock mixture.

6. Whisk the hot sauce into the blood in a stainless-steel bowl. Return the sauce to the sauce-pan.

7. Add a few drops each Cognac and vinegar to the sauce. The sauce can be thinned if necessary by adding stock or cream. Season with salt and pepper.

Note: This sauce can be kept in a whipping siphon held in a water bath at 140°F (60°C) and piped out to order.

YOGURT AND FRESH CHEESE

Both yogurt and fresh cheese (*fromage blanc*) can be used to finish and thicken sauces. In European cooking they are mainly used as dietetic substitutes for heavy cream or butter.

Because yogurt and fresh cheese contain lactic acid, which is responsible for their tangy flavor, they must be used in small quantities or in combination with cream or butter, which attenuates their acidity. They can also be emulsified with a small amount of lambda carrageenan to keep them from turning grainy in the sauce, but this isn't essential.

The best yogurt for sauce making is the thick Middle Eastern type called *leben*, or Greek yogurt. Because it is so thick, a relatively small amount is needed to thicken a sauce. If Greek or leben yogurt is unavailable, lighter plain yogurt (preferably without stabilizers) can be thickened by draining overnight in a colander lined with a kitchen towel.

Fresh cheese is widely available in France, where it is flavored in a variety of ways and used as a snack or breakfast food in the same way yogurt is eaten in the United States. The closest equivalent available in the United States is ricotta, which is far too rough-textured for use in sauce making. Most fresh cheese is made with skim milk and contains very little fat, but there are richer varieties available made from whole milk or even cream. Although fresh cheese contains less lactic acid than yogurt (some of the acid is drained off in the whey or, if the cheese is made with rennet, it never develops in the first place), it still must be used sparingly or it will give the sauce a rough, chalky texture.

Fresh cheese should be used as soon after it is made as possible. As it sits, the curd becomes coarser and the texture rougher. Although fresh cheese is available in fancy food shops, it is rarely as fresh as it should be for sauce making and is rarely consistent. If fresh cheese is used on a regular basis, a bit of experimentation with in-house fabrication might be worthwhile (see "Fresh Cheese," page 50). Some hydrocolloid thickeners such as carrageenan work particularly well for stabilizing fresh cheese and yogurt.

Finishing Sauces with Yogurt

Yogurt is an excellent thickener for fish sauces, which benefit from its natural acidity. It is best used with a small amount of heavy cream, which smooths out the sauce's texture. Yogurt can partially replace the cream or butter used to finish braised fish sauces, such as that used in Fillets of Dover Sole Bercy and its variations (page 302). The exact amount of yogurt to use depends on the desired consistency of the finished sauce. This recipe contains a small amount of optional lambda carrageenan, which will help keep the yogurt from separating, but the sauce is good without it.

YOGURT-FINISHED SAUCE

YIELD: 1½ CUPS (375 MILLILITERS)

heavy cream	¼ cup	60 milliliters
sauce base (such as stock, braising liquid/nage, or court-bouillon), cold	1 cup	250 milliliters
lambda carrageenan (optional)		5 grams
leben yogurt or drained yogurt	¾ cup	180 milliliters
minced fines herbes (chives, parsley, chervil, and tarragon)	1 tablespoon	3 grams
salt and pepper	to taste	to taste

1. Add the cream to the cold sauce base. Bring the mixture to a simmer. At the same time, blend the lambda carrageenan, if using, into the yogurt with an immersion blender, adding a little of the sauce base if needed to help blend.

2. Blend the hot cream mixture into the yogurt in a saucepan, preferably one with sloping sides.

3. Gently heat the sauce, but do not allow it to boil.

4. Add the fines herbes. Season with salt and pepper.

Finishing Sauces with Fresh Cheese

Fresh cheese can be used to thicken sauces traditionally finished with heavy cream or crème fraîche. It is used in the same way as yogurt, but since it contains less acid, it is more appropriate than yogurt for meat sauces. The amount of fresh cheese needed to thicken a given amount of liquid will vary according to the style and freshness of the cheese. Because fresh cheese sometimes has a grainy texture, finish these sauces in a powerful blender or with a rotor stator homogenizer (see page 35) to smooth them. Hydrocolloids such as lambda carrageenan are excellent emulsifiers for sauces made with fresh cheese or yogurt.

WINE LEES

French chefs occasionally refer to using the sediment at the bottom of the oak casks used to age wine as a thickener for red wine sauces. Reliable recipes are difficult to track down, but for someone living in a vineyard area, it would be a worthwhile experiment to whisk a few tablespoons of these lees into an unbound brown sauce or red wine sauce base. Lees from Pinot Noir would be best in keeping with the Burgundian tradition.

CORAL AND ROE

Coral is actually the ovary, often containing eggs (roe), of female shellfish. A variety of shellfish corals can be used as last-minute flavorful sauce thickeners. Sea urchin roe and scallop coral are among the most popular. To use either of these, purée them in a food processor with about an equal amount (by volume) of butter, then work the mixture through a drum sieve. The mixture can then be whisked into a sauce as a final flavorful finish. Lobster coral is excellent for finishing crustacean sauces (see "Special Flavors and Finishes for Fish Sauces," page 404).

BREAD

Before the development of roux in the seventeenth century, bread was an almost universal thickener for sauces and cooking liquids. It is still used today as a thickener for a rather bland béchamel-like sauce that the English like to serve with game. It is also used in thick and strongly flavored sauces, such as the Spanish romesco, sauce rouille, and in some versions of the French garlic mayonnaise aïoli, where it attenuates the flavor, gives the sauce body, and makes the sauce less rich, so it can be eaten in larger amounts.

The majority of medieval sauces were thickened with bread that was lightly toasted in front of the fire. The technique is still a valid one for making rustic, rough-hewn sauces without resorting to flour, with its predictable, sometimes monotonous consistency. Bread, especially when it has been toasted, gives a satisfying nutty flavor to sauces and has a comforting, homey flavor and texture. Many Mediterranean sauces that today contain puréed potatoes (which originated in the New World) were originally made with breadcrumbs.

Some recipes from Taillevent's *Le Viandier*, written in the late fourteenth century, also follow. None of the recipes contain quantities, so we can only guess whether the sauces had a pomade-like texture similar to a modern romesco or were thinner and used to nap meats and fish. Most medieval sauce recipes contain a combination of several spices. However, some of the simpler recipes found in fourteenth-century French cookbooks closely resemble regional sauces still found in Mediterranean cooking. The main difference seems to be that medieval cooks had a liking for acidic ingredients, either vinegar or verjuice.

SAUCE ROUILLE

Traditionally, sauce rouille is served as an accompaniment to Provençal fish soups, including bouillabaisse. It can be whisked into the soup just before serving or presented at the table in a mortar. It is also delicious served on slices of toasted French bread.

YIELD: 1 CUP (250 MILLILITERS)

sweet red pepper, grilled, peeled, and chopped	½	½
garlic cloves, coarsely chopped	3	3
cayenne pepper	½ teaspoon	2 milliliters
powdered saffron	1 small pinch	1 small pinch
slightly stale white bread, crusts removed	2 slices	2 slices
fish or chicken stock (page 93 or 88)	¼ cup	60 milliliters
extra-virgin olive oil	½ cup	125 milliliters
salt	to taste	to taste

1. Work the chopped red pepper, garlic, cayenne, and saffron into a paste with a mortar and pestle or in a food processor.

2. Soak the bread in the stock. Combine the moistened bread with the pepper mixture and work until smooth with a mortar and pestle or in a food processor. If you're using a food processor, don't overdo it or the sauce will turn gluey.

3. Slowly add the oil in the same way as when preparing mayonnaise. Season with salt.

BREAD-THICKENED RAW SAUCES (SAULCES NON BOULLUES) FROM TAILLEVENT'S *LE VIANDIER*

SAULCE AULX BLANS. Work together garlic and bread. Thin the mixture with verjuice.

SAULCE AULX CAMELINS. Grind cinnamon and bread with a mortar and pestle. Thin the mixture with vinegar.

SAULCE VERTE. Grind together bread, parsley, and ginger with a mortar and pestle. Thin the mixture with vinegar and verjuice.

POIVRE JAUNET. Grind together ginger, saffron, and lightly toasted bread (*pain hallé*). Thin the mixture with vinegar, and boil.

POIVRE NOIR. Grind together ginger and dark toasted bread with a mortar and pestle. Thin the mixture with vinegar and verjuice, and boil.

HYDROCOLLOIDS

In recent years, chefs have been exploring products that provide an amazing variety of textures, thicknesses, and consistencies. Some of these are used much like starch, but often in far smaller amounts—helpful when the thickener at hand has a strong taste.

Perhaps the most important family of these new (and not so new) thickeners consists of hydrocolloids. Technically, a hydrocolloid is anything that disperses particles in water. Even though some hydrocolloids are starches or very similar to starches, when chefs refer to hydrocolloids, they're talking about substances that form long chains of polymers (usually of simple sugars, but sometimes amino acids). These polymers interfere with the fluidity of water and render a sauce thicker. Many hydrocolloids also act as emulsifiers and hence thicken—or at least keep from breaking—sauces such as hollandaise or mayonnaise. Hydrocolloids can also cause liquids to gel, a useful characteristic when making chauds-froids and gelées. For a list of hydrocolloids, see page 73.

EMULSIFIERS AND STABILIZERS

Whereas the viscosity of starch-thickened sauces can be attributed to solids suspended in a liquid (the scientific term for this kind of system is *sol*), emulsified sauces consist of two mutually insoluble liquids—usually fat and water—suspended one within the other. Emulsions rely on various additional ingredients to prevent the tiny particles from running into one another, joining up into larger particles, and eventually separating into two distinct layers—the usual course of events when combining water and oil alone.

Emulsifiers usually work in one of two ways. In the first, the emulsifier is made up of long molecules that float between the microscopic globules of fat (or water, depending on what is suspended in what), preventing the globules from touching one another; the stability of butter sauces containing flour is an example of this. In the second system, the emulsifier molecules are asymmetrical: Half of the molecule is soluble in fat, the other half in water. The result is that half of the molecule embeds itself in the suspended globule while the other half protrudes into the liquid medium. The protruding ends of these molecules prevent the globules from touching and forming larger aggregates. Egg yolks and lecithin emulsify in this way.

There is a difference between true emulsifiers, sometimes called "surfactant emulsifiers," and emulsion stabilizers. A true emulsifier is made of molecules in which one end is soluble in fat and the other in water. In this way, microscopic globules of one or the other end up surrounded, with the jutting-out ends of the emulsifier to prevent coalescing.

Some emulsifiers are soluble in fats—they must be added to the fat (such as butter or oil) before the sauce is emulsified. Mono- and diglycerides, sometimes marketed under the name Glice, are dissolved in fat in concentrations ranging from 1% to 5% of the fat. Polysorbate 80 is a powerful emulsifier that gives a creamy consistency to sauces. It is usually used in concentrations ranging from 1% to 6% of the fat. Perhaps most important is liquid lecithin, which is dissolved in fat at a concentration ranging from 1% to 2%.

Other emulsifiers are dissolved in the aqueous, or liquid, phase of the emulsion, usually water or stock. Propylene glycol alginate, used in concentrations ranging from 0.3% to 0.9% of the liquid, is an excellent emulsifier and is often used in conjunction with fat-soluble emulsifiers such as lecithin. Ultra Tex 3 and Ultra Tex 8, derived from tapioca, are excellent liquid-soluble stabilizers because they form very smooth- and creamy-textured sauces.

Stabilizers are usually thickeners but thickeners are not necessarily stabilizers. Thickeners make it difficult for microscopic globules of fat and water to move about and eventually coalesce. Agar, which sets up like gelatin but has a much higher melting point, is used for solid mixtures such as creams that aren't going to be heated above 140°F (60°C).

Some ingredients' thickening power comes from their ability to form emulsions. Egg yolks, reduced cream, mustard, and lecithin, to name a few, are all stabilizers and emulsifiers. (In other words, fats and water/stock can be held together in a sauce that is thicker than either of the parts.) Think hollandaise or a reduced cream sauce to which clarified butter can be added, causing the mixture to thicken.

WHITE SAUCES FOR MEAT AND VEGETABLES

Traditional white sauces are prepared with milk or white stock, thickened with white roux, and finished with heavy cream, egg yolks, or butter. Sauce béchamel is essentially milk thickened with roux; sauce velouté is identical to sauce béchamel except that the milk is replaced with white stock. When sauce béchamel is finished with cheese, it becomes a mornay sauce; when finished with cream, a cream sauce; finished with onions, a sauce soubise; finished with crustacean butters, a sauce nantua (crayfish) or sauce cardinal (lobster). When sauce velouté is enriched with cream, it becomes a sauce suprême; when finished with egg yolks, it becomes a sauce allemande.

In nouvelle cuisine, velouté sauces were often replaced with butter-enriched sauces, reduced-cream sauces (which contain no roux), or reduced stock. Modernist chefs thicken the milk slightly with hydrocolloids, specifically lambda carrageenan (0.03% to 2%).

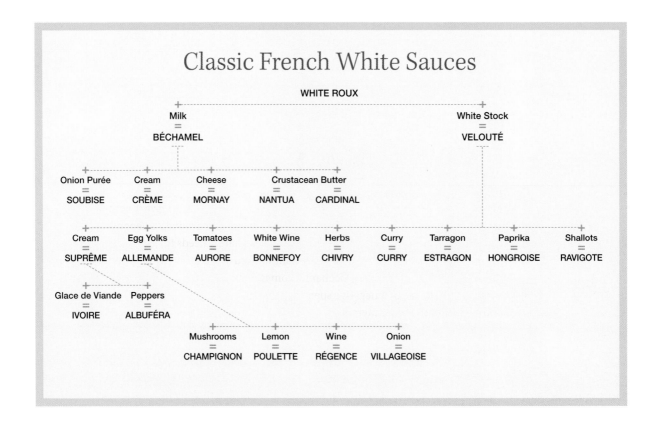

Classic French White Sauces

WHITE ROUX

- + Milk = **BÉCHAMEL**
- + White Stock = **VELOUTÉ**

Under BÉCHAMEL:
- + Onion Purée = **SOUBISE**
- + Cream = **CRÈME**
- + Cheese = **MORNAY**
- + Crustacean Butter = **NANTUA**
- **CARDINAL**

Next row:
- + Cream = **SUPRÊME**
- + Egg Yolks = **ALLEMANDE**
- + Tomatoes = **AURORE**
- + White Wine = **BONNEFOY**
- + Herbs = **CHIVRY**
- + Curry = **CURRY**
- + Tarragon = **ESTRAGON**
- + Paprika = **HONGROISE**
- + Shallots = **RAVIGOTE**

Next row:
- + Glace de Viande = **IVOIRE**
- + Peppers = **ALBUFÉRA**

Bottom row:
- + Mushrooms = **CHAMPIGNON**
- + Lemon = **POULETTE**
- + Wine = **RÉGENCE**
- + Onion = **VILLAGEOISE**

SAUCE BÉCHAMEL

Sauce béchamel has long been a mainstay in both professional and home kitchens. In the 1970s and '80s, however, the reaction against flour-thickened sauces became so vehement that this one-time cornerstone of classic French cooking was almost completely abandoned and replaced with sauces based on reduced cream. While these cream-based versions have their merits, the straightforward appearance and flavor of a béchamel-covered gratin will often satisfy a deeper need than a refined and intricate cream sauce.

One of the best uses for sauce béchamel is in a gratin. It is prepared by blanching or sweating vegetables, spreading them in a flat (usually oval) baking dish, pouring over a layer of béchamel, sprinkling with grated cheese or breadcrumbs, and baking until a flavorful, lightly browned crust forms on the surface. Some chefs have replaced the béchamel in vegetable gratins with heavy cream or crème fraîche. For gratins of starchy foods such as pasta or potatoes, cream is a welcome replacement. Many vegetable gratins, however, become too rich when the béchamel is replaced with cream. Béchamel also allows the brown crust—so characteristic of gratins—to form on the surface, whereas cream will overreduce and get oily.

Like recipes for practically any sauce, béchamel recipes have changed dramatically over the centuries. Early recipes have little relation to modern versions, and were based on velouté sauces to which heavy cream was added (now called sauce suprême).

The simplest and most modern version of sauce béchamel prescribes thickening milk with hydrocolloids or pretreated flour such as Wondra. When using Wondra, mix with cold water until smooth and simply whisk into the hot milk—no roux, no fuss. The same amount of Wondra as flour in a roux should be used. The more traditional approach uses white roux and cooks the mixture long enough to eliminate the flour taste. Some recipes suggest onion (either first sweated in butter and then sprinkled with flour to become an integral part of the roux, or left whole or in large pieces, poked with a clove, and simmered with the milk), a piece of bay leaf, and a tiny pinch of nutmeg. Nineteenth-century recipes often begin by sweating mirepoix, ham, and veal as components of the roux before moistening with milk or a mixture of milk and stock.

Whether to prepare the simplest form of béchamel (given below) or to give it complexity and additional flavor with ham, veal, mirepoix, onion, or other aromatics depends largely on common sense. Béchamel used for a gratin of leeks hardly needs to be flavored with onions, but a few trimmings from a cured ham cooked with the roux will work beautifully. Much of the appeal of sauce béchamel comes, paradoxically, from its lack of flavor, and like a rest in music or a negative space on a canvas, it provides a backdrop for the flavor and texture of the other ingredients.

SAUCE BÉCHAMEL

The amount of roux per given amount of milk depends on the use of the sauce. Thick versions, used as the base thickener in traditional soufflé recipes, often call for as much as 8 ounces (250 grams) of roux per quart (liter) of milk, whereas béchamel-based soups use approximately 2 ounces (60 grams) per quart (liter) of milk. This recipe produces a medium-thick sauce, appropriate for vegetable gratins.

YIELD: 1 QUART (1 LITER)

milk	1 quart	1 liter
butter	3 ounces	90 grams
flour	⅓ cup	80 milliliters
seasonings (salt, pepper, nutmeg; optional)	to taste	to taste

1. Bring the milk to a simmer in a 2-quart (2 liter) saucepan. Whisk it from time to time to prevent a skin from forming on its surface (see Note).

2. In a second 2-quart (2 liter) saucepan, gently melt the butter and add the flour. Stir the butter and flour over medium heat for about 2 minutes, until the flour has a pleasant, toasty smell. (A, page 134) Remove from the heat for about 30 seconds to cool slightly.

(*continued*)

3. Whisk the simmering milk into the roux. Return the sauce to the stove and bring it back to a simmer while whisking. **(B)**

4. Once the sauce has returned to a slow simmer, turn down the heat and move the saucepan so that only one side is over the flame. (This will cause a skin to form on only one side of the sauce's surface, making it easy to skim.) Cook the sauce gently for 30 minutes to 1 hour, skimming off the skin. It is a good idea also to occasionally rub around the bottom and corners of the saucepan with a wooden spoon to prevent the sauce from scalding.

5. When the starchy taste has cooked out of the sauce, it can be seasoned and strained, depending on its final use. Béchamel should be stirred while it is cooling to prevent a skin from forming on its surface. Putting the pan over a tray of ice will, of course, speed cooling.

Note: Some chefs do not first bring the milk to a simmer and instead pour cold milk, all at once, over the roux. This method saves time—and a pot—but be sure to whisk the sauce vigorously to prevent lumps and skin from forming.

VARIATIONS

Use a pretreated flour such as Wondra. Simply mix the Wondra (the same amount as flour called for in the traditional recipe) in cold water until smooth (make a slurry). Bring the milk to a simmer. Whisk in the slurry. Simmer until the sauce thickens. It should be smooth, but just in case, work it through a chinois.

While béchamel is a fairly stable sauce, there are times (especially if the flour is old) when it will break. To avoid this, blend hydrocolloids into the finished sauce. Lambda carrageenan lends an authentic dairy-like mouthfeel to the sauce and is easy to use. Start by adding 1% lambda carrageenan to the sauce and build up as needed to get the thickness you want.

MODERNIST BÉCHAMEL

Any number of hydrocolloids and emulsifiers can be used to thicken milk and create a béchamel sauce. Lambda carrageenan goes especially well with dairy products so it makes sense to use it here.

YIELD: 1 QUART (1 LITER)

milk	1 quart	1 liter
medium bouquet garni (page 52)	1	1
lambda carrageenan (or more as needed)		10 grams
salt and pepper	to taste	to taste
grated nutmeg	to taste	to taste

Bring the milk to a simmer with the bouquet garni. Simmer for 5 minutes, then take out the bouquet garni. Sprinkle the lambda carrageenan over the milk and blend with an immersion blender. Bring back to a simmer while continuing to blend. Strain through a chinois and season with salt, pepper, and nutmeg.

COCONUT "BÉCHAMEL"

When making béchamel, any liquid can be used as a substitute for the milk provided that the mixture is stabilized enough that whatever the liquid is—almond milk, soy milk, coconut milk, etc.—it doesn't curdle or separate.

Unless it has emulsifiers, coconut milk out of the can is going to separate into solid cream and a light liquid (the milk). Unlike classic béchamel made with milk, one made with coconut milk needs emulsifying. Emulsifiers must be added not only to the liquid phase (the milk)—in this case propylene glycol alginate, a very efficient emulsifier—but to the fat phase (the cream), so the two bind up together into an emulsion.

Your approach will depend on the coconut milk. If it comes out of the can with solid lumps of cream clearly visible and separate from the milk, then the cream can be used to absorb the emulsifiers that dissolve in fat (here, liquid lecithin and a combination of mono- and diglycerides sold as Glice). If, however, the coconut fat is dispersed in the milk and difficult to separate, then another source of fat—here, butter—must be used to get the emulsion going.

(continued)

This "béchamel" starts with a thick emulsified base to which the rest of the coconut milk is then added. If no coconut cream is available, butter can be used to hold the fat-soluble emulsifiers. Once the sauce is soundly emulsified (the butter mixture works up with the liquid phase), it is thickened with Ultra-Tex 3 (2% to 4%), a modified tapioca starch with a natural mouthfeel.

YIELD: 4 CUPS (1 LITER)

unsweetened coconut milk, homemade or canned	1 quart	1 liter
propylene glycol alginate		5 grams
liquid lecithin		4 grams
mono- and diglycerides (glice)		1 gram
polysorbate 80		2 grams
butter or coconut cream, melted	2 ounces	60 grams
ultra-tex 3		3 grams
ultra-sperse 3 (for medium viscosity; optional)		20 grams

1. Bring the coconut milk to a simmer. Use an immersion blender to blend in the propylene glycol alginate.

2. Stir the lecithin, Glice, and the polysorbate 80 into the melted butter or coconut cream (it must be at least 140°F [60°C] to dissolve the Glice) until they dissolve. Use an immersion blender to work 1 cup (250 milliliters) of the coconut milk into the butter mixture. Once you have an emulsion, add the Ultra-Tex 3 and purée with an immersion blender.

3. This initial mixture will be quite thick. With the emulsion on the stove, whisk in the rest of the coconut milk and bring to a simmer. Blend in the Ultra-Sperse 3, if using, and return to a simmer while stirring gently with a whisk. Continue to stir for a couple of minutes.

Traditional Derivatives of Béchamel Sauce

Three traditional derivatives of Sauce Béchamel are Sauce Mornay, which contains cheese; Sauce Soubise, which contains blanched and puréed onions; and Sauce Crème (traditional cream sauce), made by finishing sauce béchamel with heavy cream. All of these sauces are excellent for gratins. Sauce Nantua (crayfish sauce) is also a derivative of béchamel, but today it is usually prepared using a base of cream (page 339) or a base of stock or milk thickened with hydrocolloids.

SAUCE MORNAY

Sauce Mornay is usually used as the base for cheese soufflés or for gratins. When it is used for gratins, additional cheese and sometimes breadcrumbs and butter are added to its surface to encourage the formation of a crust. Sauce Mornay is made by adding grated cheese to sauce béchamel. Be sure to choose a full-flavored, well-aged cheese for this sauce. If the cheese is too young, the sauce will not only lack flavor but will be stringy.

Classic recipes use half grated Gruyère and half grated Parmesan (at least three-year-old Parmigiano-Reggiano), but the sauce can be made with other well-aged, honest cheese. English farmhouse Cheddar and Vermont Cheddar (not the commercial kind that has been dyed orange) both work well. Blue cheeses can also be incorporated into Mornay sauces, but be sure to taste and select them carefully to avoid some of the poor-quality versions that have a coarse, sour-milk smell and flavor. Select genuine Roquefort, Stilton, Gorgonzola, Fourme d'Ambert, or Bleu d'Auvergne. Keep in mind that blue cheeses tend to make sauces a bit gray.

To prepare Sauce Mornay, add approximately 4 ounces (115 to 125 grams) cheese per quart (liter) of béchamel. Stir the sauce just long enough for the cheese to melt; overcooking the cheese can cause it to turn stringy. Some recipes call for finishing Mornay with egg yolks (about 2 per quart/liter of sauce). This is useful if the sauce is being used as a base for cheese soufflé, but otherwise the yolks contribute little to the sauce except unnecessary richness.

At times, if the cheese is too young, a Sauce Mornay may break. To avoid this, you can blend hydrocolloid stabilizers (0.15% percent xanthan gum and 1% lambda carrageenan) into the béchamel before adding the cheese.

CAULIFLOWER GRATIN

Béchamel derivatives, especially Mornay sauce, make excellent toppings for gratins because they brown and become extremely aromatic. Practically any vegetable can be pre-cooked slightly and then baked while covered with sauce.

YIELD: 6 SERVINGS

cauliflower, 1 large bunch or 2 small bunches		
mornay sauce	1 quart	1 liter
grated gruyère or similar cheese	1½ cups	180 grams

(continued)

137

1. Preheat the oven to 350°F (180°C). Cut the cauliflower into florets. Boil for about 5 minutes. Drain and transfer to a gratin dish just large enough to hold the cauliflower in a single layer.

2. Ladle the Mornay sauce in an even layer over the cauliflower. (A)

3. Sprinkle the cheese over the gratin. (B) Bake until a golden crust forms on top, about 30 minutes.

SAUCE SOUBISE I

Sauce Soubise is prepared by combining onion purée with béchamel sauce. Modern versions sometimes replace the béchamel with cream, but when the sauce is being used for gratinéed dishes—the most famous is veal Orloff, a veal chop covered with a layer of duxelles, napped with soubise, then Mornay, and gratinéed under the broiler—the béchamel is essential; a cream-based soubise would break.

Traditional recipes for sauce soubise call for blanching sliced onions before sweating them in butter and combining them with the béchamel. The key is to not allow the onions to brown. Sweat 1 pound (500 grams) sliced white onions (blanched or not) until they are soft, and combine them with 2 cups (500 milliliters) sauce béchamel. Cover the sauce and cook it slowly, either in the oven or on top of the stove, for approximately 30 minutes. Blend with an immersion blender (A) and strain through a fine chinois (B). (For a flourless version, see Stewed Onion Purée, page 520; for a sous vide version, see Sauce Soubise III, page 520.)

SAUCE SOUBISE II

Peel and slice 2 medium onions (1 pound/500 grams), and blanch them for 10 minutes in boiling salted water. Drain the onion slices and gently cook them in butter until they are completely soft, usually about 20 minutes. Do not allow them to brown. Add 2 cups (500 milliliters) sauce béchamel to the onions, and season with salt, white pepper, and a pinch of sugar. Cover the pot or saucepan and put it in a 300°F (150°C) oven for 1 hour. Strain the sauce and finish it with ½ cup (125 milliliters) heavy cream and 1 ounce (30 grams) butter.

SAUCE CRÈME (CREAM SAUCE)

Traditional cream sauce is prepared by finishing 1 quart (1 liter) béchamel with 7 fluid ounces (210 milliliters) heavy cream or crème fraîche, reducing the mixture down to three-quarters the original volume of the béchamel (in this case 3 cups/750 milliliters), then adding 5 fluid ounces (150 milliliters) more cream to enrich it and provide the correct consistency. The sauce is then seasoned and finished with the juice of half a lemon. In most modern kitchens, unless the surface of the sauce will be glazed under the broiler, cream sauce is usually replaced with lightly reduced cream.

SAUCE VELOUTÉ

In classical cooking, most white sauces are based on sauce velouté, which is white stock that has been thickened with white roux. This basic sauce is then flavored and used as the foundation for a myriad of derivative sauces. The two most important derivatives of basic velouté are sauce allemande (literally, "German sauce") and sauce suprême. Sauce allemande is prepared by finishing sauce velouté with egg yolks and mushroom cooking liquid (see page 142). Sauce suprême is prepared by finishing a velouté with mushroom cooking liquid, heavy cream, and butter. Sauce allemande and sauce suprême are themselves usually flavored to make additional derivative sauces.

While velouté sauces are unlikely to break, they can be stabilized with a small amount of lambda carrageenan (1.5%) and Ultra-Sperse 3 (2% to 3%).

SAUCE VELOUTÉ

YIELD: 1 QUART (1 LITER)

white stock (veal, page 91; chicken, page 88; or other)	5 cups	1.2 liters
butter	2 ounces	60 grams
flour	¼ cup	60 milliliters

1. Bring the stock to a simmer in a 2-quart (2 liter) saucepan. Whisk it from time to time to prevent a skin from forming on its surface.

2. In a second 2-quart (2 liter) saucepan, gently melt the butter and add the flour. (A, B) Stir the butter and flour over medium heat for about 2 minutes, until the flour has a pleasant, toasty smell. (C) Remove from the heat for about 30 seconds to cool slightly.

3. Whisk the simmering stock into the roux. (D) Return the sauce to the stove and bring it back to a simmer while whisking. (E)

4. Once the sauce has returned to a slow simmer, turn down the heat and move the saucepan so that only one side is over the flame. (F) (This will cause a skin to form on only one side of the sauce's surface, making it easier to skim.) Cook the sauce gently for 1 hour while skimming off the skin that forms. (G) It is also a good idea to occasionally rub around the bottom and corners of the saucepan with a wooden spoon or spatula to prevent the sauce from scalding.

5. Strain the velouté through a fine chinois and stir it until it cools, to prevent a skin from forming.

MODERNIST VELOUTÉ

While a classic velouté contains approximately 3 tablespoons (20 grams) flour per quart (liter), giving it a distinct floury quality, a modern velouté is made with less roux or no roux at all. Instead, modern thickeners give the sauce a more subtle quality without contributing a strong flavor.

YIELD: 1 QUART (1 LITER)

veal, chicken, or fish stock (pages 91, 88, or 93)	1½ quarts	1.5 liters
ultra-sperse 3		75 milliliters
lambda carrageenan		3 grams

Reduce the stock by one-third, until 1 quart (1 liter) remains. Keep the saucepan to one side of the burner and skim off froth and scum. Blend the Ultra-Sperse 3 and lambda carrageenan into the stock with an immersion blender. For a thicker sauce, add more Ultra-Sperse 3, a little at a time. Bring to a simmer. Strain through a fine chinois.

Primary Derivatives of Sauce Velouté

SAUCE SUPRÊME
Combine 1 quart (1 liter) sauce velouté with 1 quart (1 liter) white veal, chicken, or other white stock; 1 cup (250 milliliters) mushroom cooking liquid (see page 100); and 1 cup (250 milliliters) heavy cream or crème fraîche. Reduce the mixture by about two-thirds until only 1 quart (1 liter) is left. Be sure to skim off any fat or scum that forms on the surface during reduction. Finish the sauce by swirling in ½ cup (125 milliliters) heavy cream and 3 ounces (90 grams) butter. Yield: 1 quart (1 liter)

SAUCE ALLEMANDE
Combine 2 cups (500 milliliters) white veal, chicken, or other white stock; 1 cup (250 milliliters) mushroom cooking liquid; and 1 tablespoon (15 milliliters) lemon juice. In a medium saucepan, reduce this mixture to 1 cup (250 milliliters). Combine with 1 quart (1 liter) sauce velouté and reduce back to 1 quart (1 liter) or, better, until the sauce takes on the desired consistency. Whisk together 5 egg yolks and pour half the velouté mixture into the yolks while whisking. Return the egg yolk mixture to the saucepan, place over low to medium heat, and stir constantly with a wooden spoon until the liquid takes on a silky consistency in much the same way as a crème anglaise. By no means let the sauce boil. Whisk 4 ounces (120 grams) cold butter into the sauce. Yield: 1 quart (1 liter)

Notice that, contrary to what's often called for in traditional recipes, the components to this sauce are reduced before adding the egg yolks. Sauces containing egg yolks can only be boiled if they contain a large percentage of flour. The flour stabilizes the sauce so the yolks don't break. Pastry cream is an example of this principle. When translating traditional sauce recipes containing flour into flourless versions, the egg yolks should be added only at the end; the sauce should never be allowed to boil.

FLOURLESS SAUCE ALLEMANDE

A flourless sauce allemande is exactly analogous to a savory crème anglaise. Because crème anglaise can be tricky—the yolks can curdle in a second—and savory crème anglaise even more so than the sweet variety (sugar helps stabilize the yolks), for large amounts, it may be worth cooking the egg yolks sous vide at 140°F (60°C) to stabilize them before using them in the sauce.

YIELD: 2¼ CUPS (550 MILLILITERS)

white chicken stock (page 88)	¾ cup	180 milliliters
mushroom cooking liquid (page 100)	6 tablespoons	75 milliliters
egg yolks, lightly beaten, stabilized (see page 111)	5	5
liquid lecithin		1.2 grams
melted butter	4 tablespoons	60 grams

Combine the stock and mushroom cooking liquid and bring them to a simmer. Whisk half the hot mixture into the egg yolks. Return the mixture to the pan and continue cooking, stirring constantly, until the sauce thickens in the manner of a crème anglaise. Work the lecithin into the butter, then whisk the butter into the sauce.

Modern Techniques for Velouté Sauces

In nouvelle cuisine kitchens, traditional veloutés, sauce allemande, sauce suprême, and their derivatives were largely replaced by reduced stocks finished with heavy cream, butter, and occasionally egg yolks. The flavors used in these nouvelle cuisine–style sauces often relied on the same ingredients as the classic French derivative sauces, but because no flour was used, the sauces were left comparatively thin, were reduced to the desired consistency, were finished with butter, and sometimes all three.

Despite the fact that velouté sauces contain flour, which stabilizes the egg yolks, the flour doesn't do a complete job; the sauce has to be as thick as pastry cream to allow you to boil it. All of this is to say that the saucier is left cooking the sauce gently, keeping a close eye, until the egg yolks thicken the sauce to the right consistency (see photo). The sauce must then be kept in a bain-marie so it doesn't get too hot and curdle.

Modernist cooks have reacted to this conundrum by cooking the egg yolks sous vide to a temperature of 140°F (60°C) for 40 minutes to stabilize them before blending them into the sauce.

SOUS VIDE COOKERY: ITS USES IN SAUCE MAKING

Much has been made about cooking in sealed plastic bags under water at precise temperatures (see page 27). Sous vide cookery allows for such precise temperature control that it's now possible to cook and stabilize liquid egg yolks. Sous vide cooking is also used to pregelatinize starch, which can be used as a thickener or emulsion stabilizer. The method is also handy for infusing herbs in vinegar or water and hence can save considerable time.

In any case, having an immersion bath set to an exact temperature can be a boon in a kitchen where careful control of bain-marie temperatures is imperative. You can hold a sauce at 140°F/60°C until needed. For a finished sauce with a frothy consistency, you can keep the sauce in a whipping siphon pressurized with nitrous oxide in the bain-marie or sous vide immersion tank.

BUTTER-ENRICHED WHITE SAUCES

These sauces are prepared by finishing reduced white stock—sometimes combined with aromatic ingredients such as wine or herbs—with butter. They have a more intense flavor and more velvety texture than traditional flour-thickened veloutés. They are, however, extremely rich and require concentrated stock.

The stock used should be approximately six times as concentrated as a simple stock, lightly syrupy and similar in consistency to the desired sauce. The amount of butter needed to give the sauce the desired consistency depends on the water content of the butter; the lower the water content, the less butter is needed to thicken the concentrated stock. French butter, because of its low water content, works especially well in butter-enriched sauces. It also has a distinct and superlative flavor.

When preparing butter-enriched sauces, the stock should be reduced until it has the consistency desired for the finished sauce. Once the butter is added, the sauce will be somewhat thick and can be thinned by adding additional stock, which is preferable to thickening the stock once the butter has been added.

This sauce is somewhat unstable and should be prepared shortly before serving. During service, it should be stirred every few minutes to keep it from breaking. If it starts to thicken, immediately thin it by adding a tablespoon or two (15 to 30 milliliters) cold water.

BROTH-AND-BUTTER SAUCE

YIELD: 2 CUPS (500 MILLILITERS)

concentrated white stock (6 times reduction)	2 cups	500 milliliters
cold butter, cut into 1-inch cubes	7 ounces	200 grams
salt and white pepper	to taste	to taste

1. Melt the stock in a 1-quart (1 liter) saucepan. Reduce it, if necessary, until it has a lightly syrupy consistency. Add the butter all at once—as though making a beurre blanc—and whisk constantly until the butter is absorbed.

2. Bring the sauce quickly to a boil and allow it to boil for only about 5 seconds; any longer may cause it to break. (This short boil gives the sauce an agreeable sheen. If a more opaque, matte look is wanted, do not allow the sauce to boil at all.) Season with salt and pepper. The sauce can be kept warm for an hour or two in the saucepan in a pot of hot water. Check the temperature of the sauce and whisk it lightly every 10 minutes to prevent it from breaking. If it starts to thicken, whisk in a tablespoon or two (15 to 30 milliliters) water or stock to keep it fluid. Letting it get too thick will cause the butter to coalesce and the sauce to break.

VARIATION

Regardless of one's efforts, butter sauces have a propensity for breaking, especially when held for any length of time in a bain-marie. The usual way around this is to add a tablespoon of liquid every 15 minutes or so to thin the sauce, but as an alternative, they can be stabilized by working 2% liquid lecithin (as a percentage of the butter; in this case, 4 grams) into the butter before it used to finish the sauce. An emulsifier such as propylene glycol alginate (0.5% as a percentage of liquid, in this case 0.25 gram) can be added to liquids such a béarnaise reduction to further reinforce the emulsion. Use an immersion blender to work these emulsifiers into the butter and stock before whisking the two together in a sauce.

WHITE SAUCE BASED ON REDUCED CREAM

Starting in the 1950s, sauces in France began to be thickened with reduced cream. By the 1980s, they had become almost universal and in most cases completely replaced roux-thickened white sauces. Because they are given body by reduction instead of roux, they are usually more intensely flavored than their roux-thickened predecessors. The main disadvantages to using reduced-cream-thickened sauces are the large amount of stock required and the time needed to reduce them to give them body and full flavor. Despite their light appearance, these sauces have an extremely high fat content, more than roux-thickened versions.

(continued)

One error beginning sauciers sometimes make is trying to make cream-finished sauces too thick. If a reduced-cream sauce is boiled down until it is as thick as a traditional flour-thickened sauce, the resulting sauce is heavy and cloyingly rich, and much of the intense flavor of the meat stock will be lost. One method of avoiding this is to think of the sauce as more a creamy broth than a sauce that must adhere to the surface of the meat, and serve meats in deep plates or shallow bowls.

When reduced cream is combined with concentrated stock, the resulting sauce is roughly analogous to a traditional sauce suprême. The only differences are that roux-thickened stock (sauce velouté) is replaced with concentrated, unbound stock, and a higher proportion of cream is used.

Concentrated (reduced) stock is often used for making flourless sauces, not only because of its intense flavor but because it contains natural gelatin that, along with the reduced cream, contributes to the consistency of the finished sauce.

YIELD: 1 QUART (1 LITER)

heavy cream	1 quart	1 liter
concentrated white stock (6 times reduction)	2½ cups	625 milliliters
salt and pepper	to taste	to taste

1. Reduce the cream in a 4-quart (4 liter) saucepan over medium to high heat until it is reduced by about a third and starts to thicken. **(see photo)** (The saucepan should be especially large to prevent the cream from boiling over.) If the cream threatens to boil over, whisk it or reduce the heat. In any case, the cream should be whisked for a few seconds every minute or so to prevent it from breaking or becoming grainy. Never cook cream covered or it will break.

2. Heat the stock in a 2-quart (2 liter) saucepan. Simmer if necessary until the stock has a syrupy consistency.

3. Whisk the reduced cream into the stock. The sauce will have a light texture. The consistency can be adjusted by reducing if the sauce is too thin or by adding cream or stock if it is too thick.

4. Season with salt and pepper. Strain the sauce through a fine chinois.

LOW-FAT "CREAM"

Most of us respond to cream based on its consistency. Its extra viscosity gives the impression of richness. Cream also has a luxurious mouthfeel. By thickening milk (or even skim milk) with the appropriate thickeners, we can emulate cream. Lambda carrageenan is especially appropriate because it gives liquids a dairy-like finish. Whey powder is derived from milk during cheese making. Keep in mind, though, that this mixture doesn't behave exactly like cream. If you want to thicken it, simply add more of the hydrocolloids, rather than simmering to reduce.

YIELD: 1 QUART (1 LITER)

methylcellulose		0.7 gram
whey powder		25 grams
lambda carrageenan		2 grams
milk or skim milk, cold	1 quart	1 liter

Stir together the dry ingredients. Use an immersion blender or rotor stator homogenizer (see page 35) to blend them into the milk. Refrigerate until needed.

EGG YOLK–THICKENED WHITE SAUCE

A traditional sauce allemande is prepared by finishing a sauce velouté with egg yolks. Egg yolks can also be used to thicken reduced stocks for lighter-textured modern sauces. One method of using egg yolks as thickeners is discussed in Chapter 13, "Hot Emulsified Sauces," page 389. The other method is given here. Remember that egg yolk–thickened sauces must never be allowed to boil unless they contain a large amount of flour.

YIELD: 1 QUART (1 LITER)

full-flavored white stock (see page 91)	3 cups	750 milliliters
egg yolks	10	10
butter, cold	4 ounces	120 grams
salt and white pepper	to taste	to taste

(continued)

1. Bring the stock to a simmer in a 2-quart (2 liter) saucepan. Be sure to skim off any scum or froth that floats to the surface.

2. Whisk the egg yolks for about a minute in a 2-quart (2 liter) mixing bowl, until they turn from orange to pale yellow. If you're working with a large number of egg yolks, you may want to stabilize the yolks by cooking them sous vide at 140°F (60°C) for 30 minutes before you use them.

3. Pour half of the hot stock over the egg yolks, whisking quickly until thoroughly combined. Remove the saucepan containing the remaining half of the hot stock from the stove. Whisk the egg yolk–stock mixture into the rest of the stock.

4. Heat the sauce over a medium flame and stir gently with a wooden spatula or spoon, being especially careful to reach into the corners of the saucepan to prevent the egg yolks from overheating and congealing. Continue stirring until the sauce begins to thicken. Egg yolk–thickened sauces do not thicken as dramatically as starch-thickened sauces do. The best way to check the sauce's consistency is to lift the spatula out of the sauce, hold it sideways, and draw a horizontal line with the tip of a finger. If the sauce clinging to the spatula runs together, immediately obscuring the line, the sauce is not ready. If the line remains, the sauce should be removed immediately from the heat.

5. Whisk in the butter. Continue stirring the sauce after removing it from the heat to keep it from setting and to prevent a skin from forming on its surface.

6. Season with salt and pepper. Strain the sauce through a fine chinois.

Other Derivatives of Sauce Velouté

Nowadays, traditional velouté-based sauces are prepared using an array of alternative methods. The following recipes describe the traditional methods using sauce velouté as a base, as well as using reduced stock enriched with butter, reduced cream, and modernist cuisine methods.

SAUCE AURORE (TOMATO-FLAVORED VELOUTÉ)

This sauce works well with veal, chicken, or eggs. Veloutés based on veal, chicken, fish, or other white stocks can all be used. Traditional sauce aurore is always strained so that it is pale pink (*aurore* means "dawn") and perfectly smooth. Some chefs like to finish the sauce with small cubes of chopped tomato for contrast of both color and texture, although purists would argue that it is then no longer a sauce aurore. One or two teaspoons (5 to 10 milliliters) of wine vinegar enhance all versions of this sauce.

CLASSIC METHOD. Combine 3 cups (750 milliliters) of sauce velouté with 1 cup (250 milliliters) of tomato purée. Adjust the sauce's consistency by reducing it (to thicken) or by adding a small amount of stock (to thin). Complete the sauce by whisking in 4 ounces (125 grams) of butter. Adjust the seasonings. Yield: 1 quart (1 liter)

BUTTER-ENRICHED METHOD. Combine 1 cup (250 milliliters) of concentrated (four to six times) stock with ¼ cup (60 milliliters) of tomato coulis that has been cooked down until it is completely dry. Reduce the mixture slightly if necessary to give it a lightly syrupy consistency. Whisk in 4 ounces (125 grams) of butter and adjust the seasonings. Yield: 1½ cups (350 milliliters)

REDUCED-CREAM METHOD. Combine 1 cup (250 milliliters) of reduced-cream white sauce with ¼ cup (60 milliliters) of cooked tomato coulis. Adjust the consistency by further reducing the sauce (to thicken) or adding stock or heavy cream (to thin). Finish the sauce with 1½ ounces (45 grams) of butter to give it a smooth texture.

MODERNIST METHOD. A modernist approach is likely to use a combination of methods including thickening (Ultra-Sperse 3 and xanthan gum come to mind) and emulsifying. Modernist versions of velouté or béchamel, which contain these ingredients, can be used as the base for virtually any derivative sauce. Once the sauce base is made, it can be finished with cream and/or butter and should be finished with the flavors at hand, in this case, tomato purée.

SAUCE BONNEFOY (WHITE WINE BORDELAISE)

This sauce is similar to an early-nineteenth-century version of a sauce bordelaise made with garlic, tarragon, and Sauternes.

CLASSIC METHOD. Combine 2 cups (500 milliliters) of white wine with ¼ cup (60 milliliters) of finely chopped shallots, 1 teaspoon (5 milliliters) of cracked pepper, 1 sprig of fresh thyme, and 1 small bay leaf. Reduce the mixture until only ½ cup (125 milliliters) remains. Add 1 cup (250 milliliters) of full-flavored sauce velouté to the reduction and simmer slowly for 15 minutes, skimming off any scum that floats to the surface. Strain the sauce through a fine chinois and stir in 1 tablespoon (15 milliliters) of chopped tarragon and 1 to 2 teaspoons (5 to 10 milliliters) of lemon juice to bring out the sauce's flavor. Yield: 1½ cups (375 milliliters)

BUTTER-ENRICHED METHOD. Prepare and reduce the white wine infusion as described for the classic method. Add 2 cups (500 milliliters) of concentrated (three to four times) white stock and reduce the mixture until it has the consistency desired for the finished sauce. Whisk in approximately 4 ounces (125 grams) of butter. Taste the sauce before adding all the butter to avoid adding too much and obscuring the flavor of the sauce. Finish with 1 tablespoon (15 milliliters) of blanched tarragon leaves, chopped or left whole. Yield: 2 cups (500 milliliters)

REDUCED-CREAM METHOD. Prepare and reduce the white wine infusion as described for the classic method. Add 1 cup (250 milliliters) of reduced-cream white sauce to the infusion. Reduce the sauce slightly if necessary. Finish the sauce with 1 ounce (30 grams) of butter and 1 tablespoon (15 milliliters) of blanched tarragon leaves, chopped or left whole. Adjust the seasonings. Yield: 2 cups (500 milliliters)

MODERNIST METHOD. Replace the concentrated white stock with a stock (perhaps a lighter one) thickened with any number of hydrocolloids (xanthan gum, Ultra-Sperse 3), emulsifiers (propylene glycol alginate), and/or emulsion stabilizers (gelatin, agar). This interpretation of the sauce can then be finished with small amounts of cream and butter.

SAUCE CHIVRY (HERB SAUCE)

Traditionally, sauce chivry is made by straining an infusion of herbs and white wine through a kitchen towel before combining it with the other ingredients. Another approach is to combine all the ingredients and strain the sauce at the end. Strictly speaking, sauce chivry should always be prepared with the herbs listed, but the methods presented here can be used for sauces based on other herbs.

CLASSIC METHOD. Bring ½ cup (125 milliliters) of white wine to a simmer and simmer long enough to cook off the alcohol. While the wine is still hot, add 1 teaspoon (5 milliliters) each of chervil, parsley, tarragon, chives, and salad burnet (if available). Cover the pan and let the mixture infuse for approximately 5 minutes. Add this infusion to 3 cups (750 milliliters) of sauce velouté and finish the sauce by whisking in 4 ounces (125 grams) of Chivry Butter (page 443). Strain the sauce through a fine chinois. Yield: 1 quart (1 liter)

BUTTER-ENRICHED METHOD. When sauce chivry is prepared following the classic method given above, a flavored velouté is finished with chivry butter (herb butter). The only difference when preparing a strictly butter-enriched version is that the flour-thickened velouté is replaced with concentrated white stock and a higher proportion of butter is used. Prepare the infusion as described for the classic method. To ½ cup (125 milliliters) of infusion, add 1 cup (250 milliliters) of concentrated (six times) white stock. Reduce the mixture until 1 cup (250 milliliters) remains, and whisk in 4 ounces (125 grams) of Chivry Butter (page 443). Yield: 1½ cups (375 milliliters)

REDUCED-CREAM METHOD. Prepare the herb infusion as described for the classic method and combine it with 1 cup (250 milliliters) of reduced-cream white sauce. Reduce the sauce if it seems too thin. Finish it with 1 ounce (30 grams) of butter. If it seems too thick, it can be thinned at the end with a little stock or cream. Yield: 1 ½ cups (375 milliliters)

MODERNIST METHOD. Use the butter-enriched method, but replace the classic sauce velouté with a modernist version such as those on page 142 and page 143.

CURRY SAUCE

There are many methods for preparing curry sauce, some of which use completely different sauce bases, such as hollandaise, mayonnaise, and sabayon. The traditional white sauce version of curry sauce is prepared using a mixture of sauce velouté and coconut milk.

Commercial curry powders vary enormously in hotness and flavor. It is also possible to prepare your own curry powder, balancing the spices according to taste (see Basic Curry Powder, page 614). When preparing butter-enriched or reduced-cream versions of curry sauce, coconut milk can be reduced and added, or coconut can be infused directly into the sauce. Almost any curry sauce is enhanced by adding 1 tablespoon (15 milliliters) chopped fresh cilantro per 1 cup (250 milliliters) sauce at the end.

CLASSIC METHOD. Finely chop 1 medium onion and sweat it in butter, being careful not to let it color. Sprinkle the onion with 2 tablespoons (30 milliliters) of curry powder and sweat the mixture for a minute or two more, to bring out the flavor of the curry. Add 2 cups (500 milliliters) of canned or fresh coconut milk (see page 43) and 2 cups (500 milliliters) of sauce velouté to the onion-curry mixture, and let the sauce simmer for 15 minutes. Skim off any scum that floats to the top of the sauce. Finish the sauce with ½ cup (125 milliliters) of heavy cream and the juice of half a lemon. Yield: 1 quart (1 liter)

BUTTER-ENRICHED METHOD. Prepare the mixture of onion, curry, and coconut as described for the classic method. Add 2 cups (500 milliliters) of concentrated white stock (6 times) and 4 ounces (125 grams) of chopped coconut to the mixture. Simmer the sauce for 10 to 15 minutes. Strain out the coconut. Reduce the mixture slightly if necessary to give it the desired final consistency. Finish the sauce with 5 ounces (150 grams) of butter and 2 teaspoons (10 milliliters) of lemon juice. Yield: 2 cups (500 milliliters)

REDUCED-CREAM METHOD. Prepare the mixture of onion and curry as described for the classic method. Add 2 cups (500 milliliters) of reduced-cream white sauce and 4 ounces (125 grams) of chopped coconut. Gently simmer the sauce for 15 minutes to infuse the coconut before straining it through a fine chinois. Yield: 2 cups (500 milliliters)

MODERNIST METHOD. In most cases, a modernist sauce is designed much like a classic sauce, but instead of relying on reduction of such ingredients as stock or cream, one or more of these bases is thickened with a hydrocolloid. Such sauces are also designed to be stable, making them more reliable, especially in fast-paced situations.

SAUCE ESTRAGON (TARRAGON SAUCE)

Older recipes for this sauce suggest blanching tarragon leaves, working them to a paste with a mortar and pestle, then combining them with sauce velouté. An easier method is to infuse a small bunch of tarragon, stems and all, into the velouté or concentrated stock, and then strain the sauce before finishing it with tarragon butter. The methods described below can also be used to prepare sauces flavored with other herbs.

> **CLASSIC METHOD.** Blanch 2 tablespoons (30 milliliters) of fresh tarragon leaves in simmering water for 5 seconds. Quickly rinse them and dry them on a towel. Crush the leaves in a mortar and gradually add ¼ cup (60 milliliters) of sauce velouté to form a paste. Add the paste to 1 quart (1 liter) of hot velouté, strain the sauce, and finish with 1 tablespoon (15 milliliters) of freshly chopped tarragon. Yield: 1 quart (1 liter)

> **BUTTER-ENRICHED METHOD.** Combine 2 cups (500 milliliters) of concentrated white stock with 1 bunch of tarragon and bring the mixture to a simmer. Reduce if necessary until it is lightly syrupy. Turn off the heat and cover the pan. Let the tarragon infuse in the stock for 10 minutes. Strain the sauce and finish it with 4 ounces (125 grams) of Tarragon Butter (page 446) and 5 ounces (150 grams) of plain butter. Adjust the seasonings. Yield: 2 cups (500 milliliters)

> **REDUCED-CREAM METHOD.** Chop 1 small bunch of tarragon and infuse it in 2 cups (500 milliliters) of reduced-cream white sauce for 10 minutes. Strain the sauce through a fine chinois and finish it with 4 ounces (125 grams) of Tarragon Butter (page 446). It may be necessary to thin the finished sauce slightly by adding white stock. Yield: 2 ½ cups (625 milliliters)

> **MODERNIST METHOD.** To stabilize the sauce, work 2% liquid lecithin (0.25 gram for 4 ounces/125 grams butter) into the tarragon butter before whisking it into the sauce.

SAUCE HONGROISE (PAPRIKA SAUCE)

Most commercially available paprika has a stale, dusty taste and contributes little flavor to a sauce. Consequently, it makes better culinary sense to prepare a Sauce Albuféra (page 156), which is finished with Sweet Red Pepper Butter (page 446). The following recipes can be used if good-quality paprika is available. They are also excellent models for other spice-flavored sauces.

> **CLASSIC METHOD.** Finely chop 1 large onion and sweat it in butter without letting it brown. When the onion is completely cooked, sprinkle over 2 table-spoons (30 milliliters) of paprika. Add 1 quart (1 liter) of sauce velouté to the mixture and gently simmer the sauce for 10 to 15 minutes. Thin the sauce to the desired consistency with white stock, milk, heavy cream, or a mixture. Strain the sauce through a fine chinois and finish it by whisking in 4 ounces (125 grams) of butter. Yield: 1 quart (1 liter)

BUTTER-ENRICHED METHOD. Sweat 1 medium onion in butter and add 2 tablespoons (30 milliliters) of paprika. Add 2 cups (500 milliliters) of reduced white stock (6 times) to the paprika-onion mixture. Add ½ cup (125 milliliters) of heavy cream, reduce again to the same syrupy consistency, and finish the sauce with 10 ounces (300 grams) of butter or Paprika Butter (page 444). Yield: 2 cups (500 milliliters)

REDUCED-CREAM METHOD. Sweat 1 medium onion in butter and add 2 tablespoons (30 milliliters) of paprika. Add 2 cups (500 milliliters) of reduced-cream white sauce and simmer the mixture for 10 minutes. Strain the sauce and finish with 2 ounces (60 grams) of butter or Paprika Butter (page 444). Yield: 2 cups (500 milliliters)

MODERNIST METHOD. Following the butter-enriched method, combine the 2 cups (500 milliliters) white stock (which may or may not be reduced) and the half cup (125 milliliters) cream. Use an immersion blender to work 0.4% lambda carrageenan (0.25 gram) into the stock-cream mixture. Do not reduce the sauce. Whisk in the butter or Paprika Butter if desired. For futher stability, combine 2% liquid lecithin (6 grams) with the butter used to finish the sauce.

SAUCE RAVIGOTE (SHALLOT AND HERB SAUCE)

Older recipes for this sauce (those by Escoffier and others) flavor it by finishing it with shallot butter. A simpler method is to infuse chopped shallots in the white wine and vinegar reduction before adding the sauce velouté or concentrated white stock. A butter-enriched method for making this sauce is not given below because it would be virtually identical to a beurre blanc.

CLASSIC METHOD. Combine ½ cup (125 milliliters) of white wine vinegar with ½ cup (125 milliliters) of white wine and reduce the mixture by half. Add 3 cups (750 milliliters) of sauce velouté to the reduction and bring the mixture to a simmer. Remove the sauce from the heat and finish it with 3 ounces (75 grams) of shallot butter. This sauce will probably need to be thinned with stock, heavy cream, or milk. Yield: 1 quart (1 liter)

REDUCED-CREAM METHOD. Infuse ¼ cup (60 grams) of finely chopped shallots in a mixture of ½ cup (125 milliliters) of white wine and ½ cup (125 milliliters) of white wine vinegar. Reduce the mixture by three-quarters. Add 2 cups (500 milliliters) of reduced-cream white sauce to the infusion, reduce if necessary, and finish the sauce with 3 ounces (90 grams) of butter or shallot butter. Adjust the seasonings. Straining is optional. Yield: 2 ½ cups (500 milliliters)

MODERNIST METHOD. Given that this sauce is almost identical to a beurre blanc, see the stabilized beurre blanc recipe on page 436.

Derivatives of Sauce Allemande

These sauces are based on a traditional sauce allemande (sauce velouté thickened with egg yolks). They can be adapted to flourless sauce-making techniques by thickening the flavor base with egg yolks, reduced cream, or butter. When egg yolks are the only thickener, 8 to 10 yolks per quart (liter) of liquid should be used, depending on the desired thickness of the sauce.

When thickening liquids with egg yolks, remember that they must not boil. Bring the liquid to be thickened to a simmer on top of the stove and whisk the egg yolks together in a bowl. Pour half of the simmering liquid over the yolks while whisking. Return the mixture to the pot containing the rest of the simmering liquid. Turn the flame down low and stir the sauce with a wooden spoon or spatula. Be sure to reach into the corners of the saucepan, where the sauce is most likely to congeal. Keep checking the thickness of the sauce by lifting the wooden spatula out of the sauce, holding it so the flat side is facing sideways, and making a horizontal line with the tip of a finger. When the line remains—that is, when the sauce does not run over and obscure it—the sauce is thick enough and should be removed from the heat. Be sure to remove the sauce from the heat while checking the spoon or it may curdle while you're trying to figure it out. With experience, the spoon technique is no longer needed—it's easy to tell when the egg yolks have done their job by the consistency of the sauce.

If any of these techniques is particularly intimidating—working with egg yolks can be tricky—stabilize the yolks by beating them together and cooking sous vide at 140°F (60°C) for 30 minutes.

Classic sauce allemande is finished with about 10 percent its volume of butter. When the allemande is being used as a base for derivative sauces, the butter should be added to the derivative sauce at the end. Butter is also recommended for flourless versions, which otherwise taste too eggy.

SAUCE POULETTE (MUSHROOM AND LEMON SAUCE)

Sauce Poulette is best prepared with either fresh or dried wild mushrooms, but be forewarned that some wild mushrooms will discolor the sauce. It goes particularly well with hot vegetables and seafood.

> **CLASSIC METHOD.** Reduce 1½ cups (375 milliliters) of mushroom cooking liquid by two-thirds and add it to 3 cups (750 milliliters) of sauce allemande (without the butter). Reduce the sauce if necessary until it has the appropriate thickness. Finish with 3 ounces (90 grams) of butter, 2 teaspoons (10 milliliters) of lemon juice, and 2 tablespoons (30 milliliters) of chopped parsley. Yield: 1 quart (1 liter)

> **EGG YOLK–THICKENED METHOD.** Combine 1½ cups (375 milliliters) of mushroom cooking liquid with 1½ cups (375 milliliters) of concentrated white stock. Reduce this mixture slightly if necessary to concentrate the flavor of the mushrooms. Combine the mushroom-stock mixture with 10 to 12 beaten egg yolks, as described for Egg Yolk–Thickened White Sauce (page 147), and gently cook over low heat while stirring until the sauce turns silky and thickens.

Remove from the heat and continue stirring for a couple of minutes to let the sauce cool and to prevent it from curdling. Finish the sauce with 3 ounces (90 grams) of butter, 2 teaspoons (10 milliliters) of lemon juice, and 2 tablespoons (30 milliliters) of finely chopped parsley. Yield: 1 quart (1 liter)

TARRAGON SAUCE

Although there is no classic version of this sauce, an allemande-based tarragon sauce can be prepared by swirling tarragon butter and lemon juice into a sauce allemande. This tarragon sauce should not be confused with a classic sauce estragon that is based on sauce velouté.

> **MODERN METHOD.** Thicken 2 cups (500 milliliters) of full-flavored white chicken stock with 6 egg yolks, as described for Egg Yolk–Thickened White Sauce (page 147), and gently cook until the sauce thickens and turns silky. Do not let it boil. Finish the sauce with 3 ounces (75 grams) of Tarragon Butter (page 446) and 2 teaspoons (10 milliliters) of lemon juice. Blanched tarragon leaves can be added as a garniture and for additional flavor. Yield: 3 cups (750 milliliters)

SAUCE RÉGENCE BLANCHE (RHINE WINE, MUSHROOM, AND TRUFFLE SAUCE)

> **CLASSIC METHOD.** Combine 1 cup (250 milliliters) of Rhine wine, 1 cup (250 milliliters) of mushroom cooking liquid, and 2 ounces (60 grams) of chopped black truffles or truffle peelings. Reduce the mixture by half and add 3 cups (750 milliliters) of sauce allemande (without the butter). Strain the sauce through cheesecloth or a fine chinois. Finish the sauce with 2 tablespoons (30 milliliters) of truffle juice and 4 ounces (125 grams) of Truffle Butter (page 446). Yield: 1 quart (1 liter)

> **MODERNIST METHOD.** Combine the Rhine wine, mushroom cooking liquid, and the chopped black truffles as described for the classic method, and reduce the mixture only by about a quarter. Blend 1.5 grams (0.5%) xanthan gum into 2 cups (500 milliliters) concentrated white stock to thicken it, and reduce slightly if necessary to concentrate its flavors. Thicken the sauce with 8 egg yolks. Finish with 2 ounces (60 grams) of Truffle Butter (page 446). Yield: 3 cups (750 milliliters)

SAUCE VILLAGEOISE (MUSHROOM AND ONION SAUCE)

This sauce can be prepared by adding mushroom cooking liquid to white stock as suggested in the classic method, or sliced mushrooms can be infused directly in the stock before it is finished with velouté, butter, or reduced cream. Either traditional béchamel-based soubise (page 139) or the Stewed Onion Purée (page 520) can be used to finish any of the versions.

Because the sauce is traditionally finished with egg yolks, it is included as a derivative of sauce allemande.

CLASSIC METHOD. Add ½ cup (125 milliliters) of white veal stock and ½ cup (125 milliliters) of mushroom cooking liquid to 3 cups (750 milliliters) of sauce velouté. Reduce the sauce to 3 cups (750 milliliters) and strain it through a fine chinois. Add 1 cup (250 milliliters) of Sauce Soubise I (page 139), and finish the sauce with 4 egg yolks and 4 ounces (125 grams) of butter. The sauce may need to be thinned with stock or heavy cream. Yield: 1 quart (1 liter)

BUTTER-ENRICHED METHOD. Combine 1 cup (250 milliliters) of mushroom cooking liquid with 2 cups (500 milliliters) of concentrated white stock, and reduce the mixture until it has the desired consistency of the finished sauce. Add 1 cup (250 milliliters) of Sauce Soubise I (page 139), and finish the sauce with 8 ounces (250 grams) of butter. Yield: 3 cups (750 milliliters)

REDUCED-CREAM METHOD. Combine 1 cup (250 milliliters) of mushroom cooking liquid with 2 cups (500 milliliters) of reduced-cream white sauce. Reduce the mixture until it has the desired final consistency; add 1 cup (250 milliliters) of Sauce Soubise I (page 139). Thin the sauce with stock or reduce it slightly if necessary to adjust its consistency, and finish with 1½ ounces (45 grams) of butter. Yield: 3 cups (750 milliliters)

MODERNIST METHOD. Prepare the butter-enriched method, but don't reduce any of the ingredients. Instead, blend 0.75 gram xanthan gum (0.25%) and 1.2 grams sodium alginate (0.4%) into the mushroom cooking liquid–stock mixture. Bring the mixture to a simmer and finish with Sauce Soubise I and butter as described in the butter-enriched method.

Derivatives of Sauce Suprême

Sauce Suprême is a sauce velouté that has been enriched with heavy cream or crème fraîche. In classical sauce making, it can be finished with additional ingredients to produce derivative sauces. The nouvelle cuisine equivalents of classic suprême-based sauces are based on reduced white stock and reduced cream or on butter.

SAUCE ALBUFÉRA (RED PEPPER SAUCE)

A classic Sauce Albuféra is prepared by adding glace de viande to a sauce suprême and finishing the sauce with Sweet Red Pepper Butter (page 446). A more up-to-date version involves grilling and seeding fresh bell peppers and infusing them in the sauce before it is strained.

CLASSIC METHOD. To 3 cups (750 milliliters) of sauce suprême, add ½ cup (125 milliliters) of meat glaze. When the glaze has completely dissolved, finish the sauce by whisking in 2 ounces (50 grams) of Sweet Red Pepper Butter (page 446). Yield: 1 quart (1 liter)

BUTTER-ENRICHED METHOD. Peel 1 large sweet red pepper by burning off the skin on a grill, in the flame of a gas stove, or under a broiler. Remove the seeds from the pepper, coarsely chop the pulp, and put it into a saucepan with 2 cups (500 milliliters) of concentrated white stock. Slowly simmer the chopped red pepper in the stock for 10 minutes. Add ½ cup (125 milliliters) of heavy cream to the mixture and reduce the mixture if necessary to the desired consistency. Finish the sauce with 8 ounces (250 grams) of butter. Season the sauce and strain it through a fine chinois. A small pinch of cayenne pepper or a few drops of hot pepper sauce will help wake up the flavor of this sauce. Some chefs prefer making this sauce with Sweet Pepper Purée (page 516), which gives it more color and a more assertive taste. Yield: 3 cups (750 milliliters)

REDUCED-CREAM METHOD. Prepare the infusion of white stock and sweet red pepper as described for the butter-enriched method. Add 2 cups (500 milliliters) of reduced cream to the infusion, reduce if necessary, and finish the sauce with 2 ounces (60 grams) of butter or Sweet Red Pepper Butter (page 446). Yield: 3 cups (750 milliliters)

MODERNIST METHOD. Add 2% liquid lecithin to the butter used to finish the sauce to stabilize it. Instead of reducing the cream, add 0.25% lambda carrageenan, which is especially well suited for use with dairy products, and/or 0.4% xanthan gum.

SAUCE IVOIRE (IVORY SAUCE)

This sauce is given an ivory color by adding 4.5% glace de viande (page 97) to Sauce Suprême (page 142)—for example, 3 tablespoons (45 milliliters) glaze to 1 quart (1 liter) sauce.

IMPROVISING WHITE SAUCES

In real-life situations, a saucier is likely to use a combination of methods to prepare a particular sauce, rather than adhering rigidly to one technique at a time. The methods presented in this chapter represent extremes within a range of possibilities. Each technique has its advantages and disadvantages and must often be adapted to a particular situation. Classic sauces made with flour are relatively inexpensive to prepare, but often have a muted quality that modern diners (and chefs) eschew. Butter-enriched white sauces are delicious but require an enormous amount of stock because the stock must be reduced anywhere from six to fifteen times, to a demi-glace, for it to have the natural consistency that these sauces require. This time-consuming reduction is often impractical in all but the most expensive restaurants. Reduced-cream sauces are also delicious, but they are extremely rich and, like butter-enriched sauces, require large amounts of reduced stock. Classic versions are less expensive to prepare but will often taste flat to diners accustomed to flourless sauces.

Some chefs prepare butter-enriched and reduced-cream sauces with stock that has been only partially reduced (for example, by six instead of by fifteen), or not reduced at all, and then thickened with arrowroot or hydrocolloids before it is finished with cream and butter. Except when using hydrocolloids, which require exact amounts, the degree of reduction of a stock is largely a question of its beginning concentration and depends on time and money. Keep in mind that stock, more or less reduced, can be thickened with traditional or modernist thickeners, such that there is a continuum between stock that has been thickened and stock that gains its consistency from reduction alone. When time and money are tight, you might reduce a stock less and thicken it more. Conversely, if your aim is flavor regardless of cost, you should rely more on reduction. Most recipes given here suggest reducing stock by six times (or by fifteen for demi-glace; by thirty for glace de viade), but they can be adjusted according to the whims of the chef. Excellent sauces can also be prepared by making traditional roux-thickened stocks with half as much roux as the classic recipes stipulate and then reducing them to the necessary consistency before using them in sauces finished with cream, butter, or egg yolks. The resulting sauce will have a smoother texture and a lighter consistency than its traditional counterpart but will not be as rich as a completely flourless sauce.

Modernist chefs like to prepare sauces using the classic methods, but instead of flour or another starch as a thickener, they use hydrocolloids such as xanthan gum, lambda carrageenan, or Ultra-Sperse 3. Wondra flour, which is pretreated for easy dissolution, is convenient because it doesn't require making a roux; it is just combined with water in a slurry and whisked in. Because these liaisons have little taste of their own, they let the direct flavors of the sauce shine through without the muting often found in starch-based sauces.

In a contemporary setting, chefs are likely to combine modernist methods and ingredients with those used in nouvelle cuisine. For example, the chef may decide on a certain degree of reduction instead of using straight stock as in the classic version. He or she may then whisk in cream, reduce a tad more if necessary, and do the final thickening with a hydrocolloid. The sauce can be finished with butter.

To stabilize an emulsion, work 2% liquid lecithin into the butter or dissolve it in the cream.

Light-textured flourless sauces can also be left thinner than the classic versions. Although these sauces will appear lighter, they will have a more intense flavor than the classic versions, will be less expensive to prepare because less reduction is required, and will be less rich.

To improvise a new sauce or to improve one that is already familiar, gather together the necessary ingredients: reduced stocks, glace de viande, heavy cream, butter, the liaison, emulsifiers, and the necessary aromatics (such as chopped herbs, wild mushrooms), any wines that might work, vinegars, spirits, and the like. Once you decide on the basic flavor of the sauce, the first step is to decide how best to extract and accent it. Three methods can be used: Ingredients can be (1) infused in an appropriate liquid such as wine or stock, either on top of the stove or sous vide; (2) worked with butter to prepare a compound butter that is whisked into the sauce at the end; or (3) puréed and used both as thickeners and flavorings for the sauce. The next step is to decide on the final consistency of the sauce and determine how the sauce will be thickened—with reduced cream, starch, egg yolks, hydrocolloids, emulsifiers, butter, or a combination.

Once you have an idea of what the consistency of the finished sauce should be, prepare your flavor base, reduce it if it needs to be more intense, and start working with the liaisons. You may want to start with an initial thickening with a hydrocolloid and then finish with cream and/or butter. Cream is the easiest to experiment with because it can be reduced; remember when working with butter, egg yolks, and some hydrocolloids, once they are added you will not be able to reduce the sauce. When the basic sauce is complete—that is, has attained the desired consistency—start tasting and thinking about how to enhance its flavor. This is the most creative part of the sauce-making process. You can experiment with adding herbs, spices, chiles, compound butters, or spirits to impart different nuances. The last step is to bring the flavors into focus with salt and pepper.

BROWN SAUCES

Until the seventeenth century, most brown sauces for meat were derived from the natural cooking juices of roasted and braised meats. In the homes of the wealthy, these natural integral sauces were often supplemented by adding a large slice of veal or ham to the bottom of the pot if the meat was braised, the idea being that these would caramelize and release syrupy, sapid juices. Roast meats were sometimes coated with a layer of *matignon* containing ham and aromatic vegetables and wrapped with fat before being put on the spit.

In large kitchens, this method of preparing an individual integral sauce for each dish was inconvenient and difficult to organize. In the seventeenth century, a system was developed for streamlining the preparation of many sauces. Instead of adding additional meat to each preparation, the extra meat was poached and the resulting broth was then used to moisten a particular preparation. In wealthy homes, these broths were enriched several times by using a previously made broth to moisten more meat. In France, each stage of the preparation had a name of its own. A simple brown stock was called an *estouffade* (nowadays "estouffade" has a different meaning; see the Glossary, page 639). The estouffade was in turn used to moisten more meat, the resulting liquid was called a *fond de braisage* ("braising stock"). When the fond de braisage was used to moisten the last batch of meat, the result was a coulis.

Over the course of the eighteenth century and into the nineteenth, the system of preparing stocks, glazes, demi-glaces, and essences was perfected and systematized. The most basic brown sauces or mother sauces were prepared and used as the basis for a wide variety of derivative sauces.

After the method of making stocks was perfected, it became possible to make meat sauces independent of a particular preparation. When the chef or saucier had at hand the necessary stocks and glazes, he could quickly manipulate their character and produce an almost infinite number of sauce preparations. These sauces are traditionally called *petite sauces*, derivative sauces, or compound sauces. Once the basic sauces were standardized at the beginning of the nineteenth century (credit is usually given to Carême), chefs went about inventing new compound sauces. A "new" sauce would often consist of a slight variation of an already known sauce—maybe onions would replace shallots, or vice versa—and be given a new, dramatic name.

By the end of the nineteenth century, although chefs did not always agree on the exact method of their preparation, these derivative sauces had become familiar classics. The recipes for these classic sauces were standardized in Escoffier's *Le Guide Culinaire* in 1902.

All of this is to say nothing of the adventures of modernist chefs who continue to experiment with thickeners and emulsifiers that Escoffier would have swooned over. Each of these compounds (many of which are hydrocolloids; see page 73) has a slightly different mouthfeel and effect on a sauce.

DEMI-GLACE

Traditional *demi-glace* ("half-glaze") is brown stock that has been thickened with roux and reduced until it has the consistency of a light syrup. By the beginning of the twentieth century, demi-glace had become the standard sauce base (mother sauce) in professional kitchens and replaced many of the elaborate preparations that had been used up to that time. Nowadays, demi-glace is a simple reduction of stock, typically about fifteen times. Glace de viande is made in the same way except that it is reduced more, typically by about thirty times (see page 97). When "concentrated stock" is called for here, it usually means four to six times.

A natural demi-glace is made without roux or any other thickener. It is prepared by poaching meat in stock and using the resulting broth to remoisten more meat. The process is repeated until a natural, lightly syrupy liquid is obtained. This method may require up to four batches of meat. The resulting natural demi-glace (in old books referred to as a "coulis") was the basis for brown sauces into the seventeenth and eighteenth centuries, when it was replaced with a more economical roux-thickened interpretation. Although a concentrated stock with the consistency of natural demi-glace can be prepared by reducing brown stock to one-fourth or one-fifth its original volume, concentrated stock prepared by reduction is not as flavorful as one prepared by successive moistenings, because much of the aromatic flavors are lost during long cooking.

Needless to say, these unbound and very concentrated stocks are extremely expensive to prepare, especially if the traditional meats (veal and beef) are used. The need for an economical sauce base has led chefs to use thickeners, usually roux (see page 107) to give the basic mother sauces the necessary light syrupy consistency without using as much meat. Escoffier's 1902 demi-glace, although a far cry from the extravagant preparations of the eighteenth and nineteenth centuries, requires more expense and labor than most modern chefs and restaurants can afford.

ESCOFFIER'S DEMI-GLACE OR SAUCE ESPAGNOLE

Escoffier's demi-glace is prepared by reducing sauce espagnole to a lightly syrupy consistency. Escoffier described demi-glace as sauce espagnole "taken to the extreme limit of perfection." Sauce espagnole is simply reduced brown stock containing roux and fresh tomatoes or tomato purée. The tomatoes give a deeper color to the sauce. Because tomatoes are not always desirable in a brown sauce, they are listed as optional.

Notice that 12 quarts (12 liters) brown stock are used to prepare 5 quarts (5 liters) of demi-glace (a reduction of about two-thirds). This is made possible by the use of roux. This recipe uses approximately 4½ ounces (150 grams) of roux per quart (liter) of finished sauce, which sounds like a very large amount of roux. But much of the roux is eliminated by long, slow cooking and continuous skimming. A natural demi-glace, reduced with no thickener, will yield substantially less.

If you wish, eliminate the roux and thicken the sauce with a combination of lambda carrageenan and Ultra-Sperse 3. Use 15 grams of Ultra-Sperse 3 per quart (liter) and 1.4 grams lambda carrageenan per quart (liter) of sauce. Unlike roux, these hydrocolloid thickeners can be added near the end of cooking.

YIELD: 5 QUARTS (5 LITERS)

(continued)

butter (optional)	11 ounces	330 grams
flour (optional)	1 cup plus 6 tablespoons	170 grams
brown stock (see note)	12 quarts	12 liters
lean, unsalted pork breast or blanched bacon	5 ounces	150 grams
carrots, 2 medium	8 ounces	250 grams
onion, 1 small	5 ounces	150 grams
thyme	1 small bunch	1 small bunch
bay leaves	2	2
white wine	6 tablespoons	90 milliliters
tomato purée (optional) or fresh tomatoes, chopped (optional)	1 quart or 2 pounds	1 liter or 1 kilogram
ultra-sperse 3 (optional)		75 to 100 grams
lambda carrageenan (optional)		6.5 grams

1. If you're using a roux, prepare a brown roux with the butter and flour (see "Roux," page 107). If you're not using roux, simply eliminate it and reduce the stock as described.

2. Bring 8 quarts (8 liters) of the brown stock to a simmer. Whisk the brown roux into the stock. Make sure the roux is slightly warm before adding it to the stock; otherwise it will poach before it has a chance to dissolve into the stock and may form lumps. If it does form lumps, puree it with an immersion blender.

3. Place the pot of hot stock containing the roux on the stove so that the flame is to one side of the bottom of the pot. (This causes the stock to simmer on one side only. The scum that floats to the top of the pot will therefore be forced to one side and will be easier to skim.) If using a flat-top range, wedge a spoon or wooden spatula under one side of the pot so there is more heat on one side. Skim the stock regularly. Be sure to keep the stock from boiling.

4. Chop the pork breast or bacon, carrots, and onion into approximately ¼-inch (5 mm) cubes. Gently sweat the pork in a sauté pan until they start to render fat. Add the vegetables, thyme, and bay leaves to the pork. Gently cook until the vegetables soften. Pour off the excess fat, deglaze the pan with the white wine, and reduce the wine by half.

5. Add the vegetable-pork mixture to the simmering stock. Continue to skim the stock to eliminate any fat released by the mixture.

6. After about 1 hour of simmering the stock with the vegetables and pork, strain the mixture into a new pot and add 2 quarts (2 liters) more of the brown stock. Simmer for 2 hours more while skimming. (At this point, the stock may be strained and allowed to cool, so the process can be finished the next day if desired.)

7. Add the final 2 quarts (2 liters) of the brown stock and, if desired, the tomato purée or the

chopped fresh tomatoes. If you did not use roux and are using Ultra-Sperse 3 and lambda carrageenan, blend these, together, into 2 cups (500 milliliters) of the hot sauce 30 minutes before serving. Strain the thickened stock through a fine chinois into the rest of the simmering stock. If using roux, simmer the sauce for 30 minutes more, being careful to skim. If using the hydrocolloids, you can stop cooking and skimming as soon as the stock stops throwing off froth, usually in a manner of minutes.

8. Strain the sauce through a coarse chinois lined with two thicknesses of cheesecloth.

Note: The brown stock for this sauce should be made with equal parts of veal and beef shanks. (Use the recipe for Brown Beef Stock on page 89, replacing half of the beef shanks with veal shanks.) However, the use of veal makes the stock very expensive, so it may make sense to opt for the turkey and pork Alternative Demi-Glace on page 168.

Alternative Liaisons for Demi-Glace

Many chefs do not like the texture and floury taste that roux gives to sauces. Because flour is an impure form of starch (it contains a fairly high percentage of protein), it must be simmered in the stock and carefully skimmed for several hours to eliminate insoluble components that could cloud the finished demi-glace. It also has a distinct smell and taste that only long cooking can eliminate. And because roux contains butter, it is also necessary to cook it long enough in the stock to release the butterfat so it can be skimmed from the surface of the stock.

For these reasons, other types of starch, such as arrowroot, cornstarch, tapioca starch, or potato starch among others, can also be used to bind stocks and give them a demi-glace consistency. Because these are purer forms of starch, they can be added nearer the end of cooking. If too much of any of these starches is used, the sauce may develop an unnatural, glossy sheen and an unpleasant, slippery texture. Cornstarch also has the disadvantage of breaking down after long cooking. You may find it preferable to use hydrocolloid thickeners such as Ultra-Sperse 3 (a modified starch) or lambda carrageenan (derived from seaweed). Xanthan gum thickens in minute quantities and has little taste, but if you're thickening to a relatively high viscosity, it can leave a weird slippery feeling on the tongue. For this reason, xanthan gum shouldn't be relied on as the only thickener in a sauce but rather one that augments other hydrocolloid thickeners such as Ultra-Sperse 3 and lambda carrageenan.

MODERN DEMI-GLACE AND GLACE DE VIANDE

To make modern demi-glace, simply take a good gelatinous stock and reduce it to about one-sixth its original volume; to make glace de viande (meat glaze), reduce the stock to a thirtieth its original volume.

MODERN METHODS FOR MAKING BROWN SAUCES

The long-evolved method of making sauces with demi-glace is easy to abuse. The time and money required to prepare classic or unthickened demi-glace can be daunting, and many chefs have not resisted the temptation to use the stockpot indiscriminately for kitchen refuse, including poorly defatted meat trimmings, stale carcasses, and vegetable ends. Indeed, many chefs have gradually replaced the meat in their stocks with bones.

Although bones can contribute body and natural gelatin to a stock and the resulting sauce, they do not supply the necessary savor to a demi-glace thickened with roux. Remember that roux was originally added to stocks as an economy measure; roux-thickened meat stocks were seen as a compromise and replacement for the concentrated sauces of the seventeenth and eighteenth centuries. To make stock with bones and then thicken it with roux is thus a double economy with far from satisfying results. This method has caused chefs to react, often unjustifiably, against demi-glace and sauce espagnole, usually because they have never tasted a correctly made version of either one.

It is perhaps in part because of these abuses that nouvelle cuisine chefs reacted against the use of starches as liaisons in sauces. Butter- and cream-thickened sauces, or sauces with no thickener at all, became de rigueur. Most chefs preferred brown sauces prepared with glace de viande (meat glaze) or very light, unbound sauces. Both of these methods are not only delicious but also economy measures; most glace de viande is prepared with bones, but sauces made with carefully made glace de viande are far superior to those made with carelessly or cheaply made demi-glace. Although unbound sauces can be made from intensely flavored meat stock, they are usually made from a light broth or jus.

WHAT IS "NATURAL" DEMI-GLACE?

Escoffier's demi-glace, which required a frightful amount of meat, was thickened with flour (roux) so that it didn't have to be reduced so much to have the right consistency. Essentially the roux was used as a way to cut costs and end up with more demi-glace with less reduction. The demi-glace recipes given here are all for "natural" demi-glace: demi-glace that has thickened naturally by concentrating the gelatin in the stock by extreme reduction. While these demi-glace recipes will make sauces as good as any anywhere, they too are frightfully expensive. To obtain more demi-glace from one of these recipes, the stock can be thickened with roux. Keep in mind that 1 tablespoon (15 milliliters) flour thickens 2 cups (500 milliliters) liquid, so if you wanted a demi-glace recipe to provide you with 2 quarts (2 liters) instead of 1 quart (1 liter) unthickened demi-glace, whisk in a roux made with ¼ cup (60 milliliters) flour and 2 ounces (60 grams) butter at the beginning of reduction.

Today's chefs continue to eschew flour, but instead of reflexively adding cream and/or butter, they often rely on hydrocolloids such as xanthan gum, which can thicken in minute amounts. These hydrocolloids are used in percentages as low as 0.02% and rarely more than 1% so they do little to inhibit or interfere with flavor. Many of these hydrocolloids, depending on how and in what they are used, provide the same mouthfeel as cream and butter.

Some hydrocolloids also function as emulsifiers. Because of this, they shouldn't be added to the broth until the end of reduction; otherwise they will emulsify free-floating fat into the reduction. Once added, however, they're great for stabilizing monté au beurre sauces (see page 114).

Preparing Brown Sauces with Glace de Viande

Classic brown sauces are made by first preparing a basic flavor element. Usually some type of wine is used to extract the flavor of a particular ingredient such as onions, shallots, mirepoix, herbs, or mushrooms. Once this flavor element is ready, demi-glace is added to give the sauce body, a meaty flavor, and a lightly syrupy consistency. The sauce is then often reduced to thicken it slightly or, conversely, stock is added to thin it. At this point, glace de viande may be added to give the sauce additional body. After straining, butter, compound butters, essences, mustard, herbs, truffles, ham, or other ingredients are added to give the sauce its final character.

Sauces prepared exclusively with glace de viande instead of demi-glace are approached somewhat differently. The preliminary flavor base is prepared in the same way, but instead of adding demi-glace to the base, a proportionately smaller amount of glace de viande is added. Because glace de viande is highly reduced (usually by about thirty times), the resulting sauce base may become extremely thick and syrupy. The chef will often thin the mixture by adding a small amount of stock or appropriately flavored liquid (wines or liquors can be used in small amounts, depending on the type of sauce). The sauce is then finished by swirling in butter or adding heavy cream. If cream is used, the sauce is then reduced to the desired consistency.

Sauces prepared with glace de viande are often thickened with a relatively large proportion of butter or cream. Using butter or cream as a thickener gives the resulting sauce a velvety texture and a delicate flavor. The disadvantage to these sauces is that they are extremely rich and can break if held too long. If the sauces are made to order (ideal), this tendency to break is not a problem since the sauce doesn't have time; it's sent out immediately on the plate. But if the sauce is meant to sit in a bain-marie for the evening's service, it should be stabilized to keep it from breaking.

Stabilized Butter Emulsions: Keeping Brown Sauces in a Bain-Marie

To ensure that brown sauces don't break, use an immersion blender to work in 0.5% propylene glycol alginate with the glace de viande–flavor base mixture. Use the paddle blade of a stand mixer to work together butter with 2% liquid lecithin (2 grams per 100 grams butter). (Butter with lecithin added can be made in large amounts and used as needed.) Whisk the butter into the base just before the beginning of service and hold the sauce in a bain-marie, whipping siphon (which will allow you to pipe out the sauce and make it frothy), or immersion bath at 140°F (60°C). If you're making sauces to order, this method isn't essential but will ensure that the sauce doesn't separate on a hot plate.

Using Alternative Demi-Glace

For many years, the basic stocks used to prepare brown sauces have been based on veal and beef. This is partly because these meats were abundant (at least for the wealthy) when brown sauces were first being invented. These meats, especially veal, are relatively neutral in flavor and thus will not overwhelm a sauce's flavor. Unfortunately, their cost has become prohibitive, necessitating a variety of compromises: the use of roux- and starch-thickened mother sauces, stocks prepared from bones alone, and the exclusive use of glace de viande for preparing brown sauces.

Other meats, especially pork and turkey, can be used to prepare brown stocks that are much less expensive than versions made with beef and veal. A brown stock made with pork shoulder or shanks and turkey wings will cost one-fourth as much as a stock made with beef and veal. Because these stocks are cooked for long periods and carefully skimmed, the character of the meats is softened and blended into the whole.

ALTERNATIVE DEMI-GLACE

This concentrated stock has a fairly neutral taste because it is concentrated by reduction, which makes it an excellent backdrop for brown sauces. A more savory version can be prepared by repeating the recipe four times, omitting the vegetables for the last two, and moistening the meat with the stock from the previous batch. This may sound extravagant, but the cost is actually the same because the yield is four times greater.

YIELD: 5 QUARTS (5 LITERS)

onions, 6 medium	3 pounds	1.4 kilograms
carrots, 6 medium	1½ pounds	750 grams
celery, 3 stalks	9 ounces	250 grams
pork shoulder	20 pounds	9 kilograms
turkey wings	20 pounds	9 kilograms
large bouquet garni (page 52)	1	1
cold water	12 quarts	10 liters

1. Preheat the oven to 450°F (220°C). Thoroughly rinse the vegetables, but don't bother peeling them. Cut the onions into quarters and the carrots and celery into 1-inch (2.5 cm) pieces. Trim any large chunks of fat off the pork shoulder and cut the pork into 2-inch (5 cm) cubes.

2. Roast the turkey wings with half the vegetables in the oven until they are well browned, 45 minutes to 1 hour.

3. Roast the pork cubes with the remaining vegetables in a separate roasting pan until they are well browned and any juices they have released caramelize on the bottom of the pan, 45 minutes to 1 hour.

4. Combine the vegetables, bouquet garni, turkey wings, and pork cubes in a 40-quart (36 liter) stockpot. Deglaze the roasting pans with water and pour this liquid into the stockpot. Add enough cold water to the stockpot to cover the meat.

5. Slowly bring the stock to a simmer. Skim off any froth and fat that float to the top. Allow the stock to simmer slowly for 5 to 6 hours.

6. Strain the stock through a coarse chinois into a 20-quart (18 liter) stockpot.

7. Reduce the stock by half while skimming carefully. Strain it through a fine chinois into a 12-quart (12 liter) pot. Reduce again by half.

Brown Sauces Without Liaisons

Most liaisons add little if any flavor to a finished brown sauce, affecting only its consistency and appearance. Until very recently, diners expected sauces to have an ability to cling to meats or other foods. The flavor of a thick, deeply colored sauce is often a disappointment if too much thickener has been used or if the sauce has been overly reduced. Chefs often compromise the flavor of a sauce in an attempt to make the sauce thicker.

Chefs are, however, beginning to serve light, flavorful broth or consommé and natural jus instead of artificially thickened sauces. Sophisticated diners are no longer impressed by thick, clinging sauces, and usually prefer a light, natural broth to the same broth bound with too much butter or flour.

When serving light, unthickened sauces, the choice of china and silverware is important. Be sure to use fairly deep plates or even wide, flat bowls so the sauce is contained and does not run up on the rim of the dish. Spoons—either very flat sauce spoons or European-style oval soup spoons—should be included at each setting.

Classic brown sauces can be prepared in a modern light style simply by using stock that's not as radically reduced (usually only six times instead of fifteen) where demi-glace or glace de viande would normally be used. The consistency of a sauce can also be controlled by reducing the stock to varying degrees.

Some of the sauces described in this chapter are rarely served today but are included as sources of ideas and as examples of sauce-making technique. The recipes include classic methods, and a slightly updated method based on unthickened demi-glace. Also include are those sauces based on methods that use glace de viande. The recipes using glace de viande are finished with cream or butter. Other sauces, such as natural "jus," are left unbound. Last are brown sauces made with so-called modernist techniques and ingredients.

NAMING BROWN SAUCES

Most derivative brown sauces were "invented" in the nineteenth century and compiled by Escoffier in his famous *Guide Culinaire* at the beginning of the twentieth century. Whereas today chefs tend to give sauces descriptive names (such as red wine duck sauce or shallot butter sauce), nineteenth-century chefs named their sauces more whimsically. When preparing a variation on a classic sauce, the chef may decide to retain the original classic name or give the sauce an entirely new name.

It is sometimes difficult to determine when a traditional French sauce, modified by an individual chef's whim and style, steps out of the classic definition and becomes another sauce entirely. To the conservative, the slightest alteration in the sauce's flavor or texture means that the sauce can no longer be called by its classic name, whereas others will allow for more flexibility.

In much the same way as the classical musician shapes the rhythm and dynamics of a piece of music within the bounds of the written score, making each rendition an individual creation, the chef can create and improvise flavors within the context of a classic recipe. The chef can also choose to step out of the boundaries of a classic recipe and use it as a reference point, in the same way the jazz musician improvises but continually returns to the theme.

In America, where the name of a classic French sauce is less likely to conjure up associations and expectations, the acceptable boundaries of the sauce's definition are less important than in France. But the way a sauce is named will still influence how it will be experienced by the diner. When the chef has worked out a variation, he or she may decide to alert the diner to what might otherwise go unnoticed, or he may prefer understatement and surprise. Understatement can, of course, be taken too far. To make a "chicken chasseur" with cèpes (porcini mushrooms) sautéed in goose fat and deglazed with Sauternes will produce a dish so different from the classic that naming it as the classic may confuse the diner.

When a chef decides how to name a sauce, he or she should consider the intended dining audience. There is usually no point in using an obscure classic sauce name for a dining public unlikely to have ever heard it, to whom it is meaningless. Perhaps it is in reaction to snobbishness and pseudosophistication that both French and American chefs have taken to naming their dishes in a clear, descriptive way. This is certainly a healthy trend, but there may be times when a little mystery and even obscurity will intrigue diners and set their appetites on edge.

INTEGRAL VERSUS STOCK-BASED BROWN SAUCES

The brown sauces presented in this chapter are based on stocks and are prepared independently of a specific dish such as roasted, braised, or sautéed meat. In modern kitchens, integral sauces made from the juices released during the cooking of meats are often enhanced with the addition of a savory element such as glace de viande. In a professional kitchen, the saucier will combine methods, using both stock-based brown sauce and integral sauce techniques. For example, the chef may sauté a steak and deglaze the pan with a premade sauce bordelaise base, or the drippings from a roast chicken may be incorporated into a tarragon sauce. Whenever stocks and glazes are used in integral sauce making, they are used to reinforce, not determine, the sauce's identity (see Chapter 9, "Integral Meat Sauces," page 233).

WHITE WINE–BASED DERIVATIVE BROWN SAUCES

Sauce Chasseur (*Mushroom Sauce for Chicken*)

Because Sauce Chasseur is most often used for chicken sautés, it is best prepared in the pan used to brown the chicken so the caramelized juices from the chicken contribute their flavor to the sauce.

CLASSIC METHOD. Sauté 3 ounces (75 grams) sliced mushrooms in butter until lightly brown. Sprinkle the mushrooms with 1 heaping tablespoon (20 milliliters) finely chopped shallots about 2 minutes before they are done. When the mushrooms are lightly browned and no liquid remains in the bottom of the sauté pan, deglaze the pan with 6 tablespoons (90 milliliters) white wine and 2 tablespoons (30 milliliters) Cognac. Quickly reduce the wine-Cognac mixture by half. Add 6 tablespoons (90 milliliters) tomato sauce (page 506; optional) and 6 tablespoons (90 milliliters) demi-glace. (If the tomato sauce is omitted, use ¾ cup/185 milliliters demi-glace.) Bring the sauce to a simmer and skim off any fat or scum that floats to the top. Whisk in 1½ ounces (45 grams) butter. Finish the sauce with 1 teaspoon (5 milliliters) chopped chervil and 1 teaspoon (5 milliliters) chopped tarragon. Yield: 1 cup (250 milliliters)

GLACE DE VIANDE METHOD. Prepare the flavor base used in the classic method (that is, sauté the mushrooms, add the shallots, deglaze with Cognac and white wine, and reduce by half). Dissolve 3 tablespoons (45 milliliters) glace de viande (page 97) in the flavor base. Thin the mixture to a light syrup by adding from ½ to ¾ cup (125 to 185 milliliters) concentrated (about six times) brown chicken stock. The base should have approximately the same consistency as the finished sauce. If you add too much stock and the base seems too thin, reduce it for a minute or two to bring it to the right consistency. It is preferable that the base be slightly thick rather than too thin; the sauce can be easily thinned at the end but cannot be reduced after the butter has been added.

Once the mixture has the right consistency, whisk in 1½ ounces (45 grams) cold butter and add 1 tablespoon (15 milliliters) chopped chervil and 2 teaspoons (10 milliliters) chopped tarragon. Bring the sauce to a simmer for about 20 seconds to give it sheen. Season with salt and pepper and correct the consistency by adding a small amount of chicken stock if necessary. Yield: 1 cup (250 milliliters)

UNTHICKENED METHOD. Sauce chasseur can be presented as a light, almost fat-free broth by replacing the demi-glace called for in the classic version with a well-reduced flavorful stock or jus and omitting the butter. Yield: 1 cup (250 milliliters)

MODERNIST METHOD. A modernist sauce does not rely on reduction alone to create body and thicken the sauce, but rather incorporates natural hydrocolloid thickeners that can have much the same mouthfeel as butter or cream. To give body to a sauce with xanthan gum, blend in about 0.2 gram per ¾ cup (190 milliliters) liquid. Xanthan gum is convenient because it disperses in both hot and cold water and thickens immediately. But there are some who find the mouthfeel of xanthan-thickened sauces to be "slippery" or "slick." To avoid this, use half the amount of xanthan gum (0.1 gram per ¾ cup/190 milliliters liquid) and blend in 0.5 gram propylene glycol alginate per ¾ cup (190 milliliters). If you're creating an emulsion and wish to stabilize it, add 1.5% lecithin and perhaps 2% to 4% Glice (mono- and diglycerides) to the butter.

ALTERNATIVES AND VARIATIONS. Because sauce chasseur is used almost exclusively for chicken, it should expand the flavors of the chicken and bring them into focus. For this reason, it is better to use brown chicken stock demi-glace rather than demi-glace or glace de viande based on other meats.

A LARGE NUMBER OF SAUCE CHASSEUR VARIATIONS IS POSSIBLE. Practically any variety of edible wild mushroom can replace the cultivated mushrooms, and olive oil or goose fat can replace the butter used for sautéing the sliced mushrooms. As the mushrooms are sautéed, they can be sprinkled with fresh chopped thyme, chopped hyssop leaves, marjoram, lavender, or winter savory; eliminate the tarragon and chervil added at the end. A white wine with a distinct character, such as Sauternes, or one with a lightly madeirized character, such as Madeira or sherry, can be used to give the sauce individuality and distinction. The Cognac can be replaced with marc, grappa, Armagnac, or a local brandy (if making the sauce in California, a good pot-distilled brandy will give the sauce a bit of regional character). The herbs used at the end can be replaced—the tarragon and chervil should be replaced if any of the strong Provençal herbs mentioned above are used—if the flavors clash. If a special brandy or wine is used in the sauce, herbs should be chosen and used carefully, so the nuances imparted by the wine or brandy are not lost. It would be best to finish the sauce with fines herbes without tarragon, or with any of the three individual herbs (chives, parsley, chervil).

CONSIDER, ALSO, INTERPRETING SAUCE CHASSEUR AS A COLD SAUCE. Infuse the various components (herbs, mushrooms, etc.) in a clear broth or consommé and allow the broth to set in a thin layer in chilled soup plates. Arrange cold chicken on top and garnish with the mushrooms; if you have broth remaining, chop it and use it to decorate the plate. You can also coat the chicken with the clear broth.

Derivative Brown Sauces

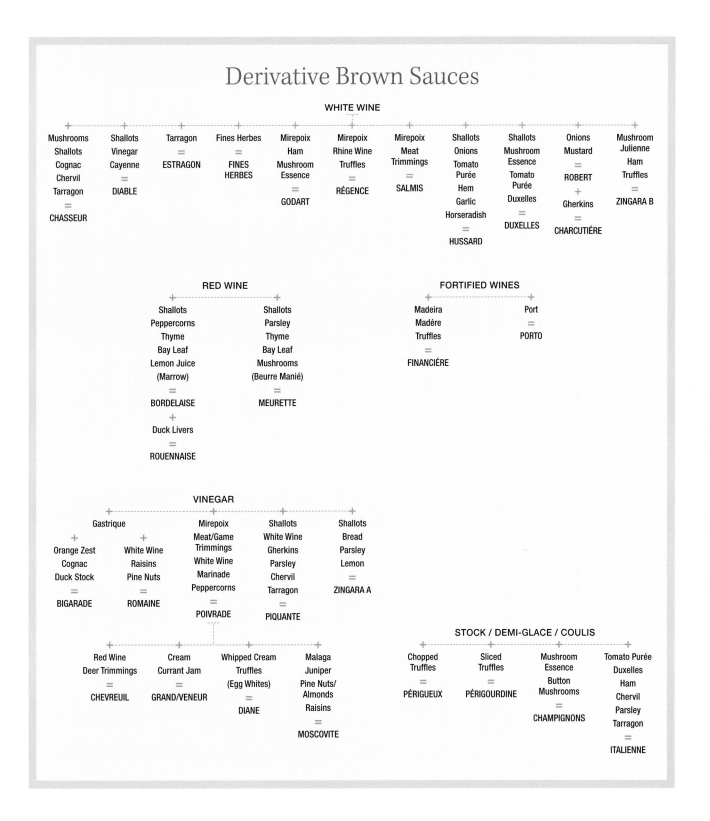

WHITE WINE

Mushrooms / Shallots / Cognac / Chervil / Tarragon = CHASSEUR

Shallots / Vinegar / Cayenne = DIABLE

Tarragon = ESTRAGON

Fines Herbes = FINES HERBES

Mirepoix / Ham / Mushroom Essence = GODART

Mirepoix / Rhine Wine / Truffles = RÉGENCE

Mirepoix / Meat Trimmings = SALMIS

Shallots / Onions / Tomato Purée / Hem / Garlic / Horseradish = HUSSARD

Shallots / Mushroom Essence / Tomato Purée / Duxelles = DUXELLES

Onions / Mustard = ROBERT **+** Gherkins **=** CHARCUTIÉRE

Mushroom Julienne / Ham / Truffles = ZINGARA B

RED WINE

Shallots / Peppercorns / Thyme / Bay Leaf / Lemon Juice / (Marrow) = BORDELAISE **+** Duck Livers **=** ROUENNAISE

Shallots / Parsley / Thyme / Bay Leaf / Mushrooms / (Beurre Manié) = MEURETTE

FORTIFIED WINES

Madeira / Madére / Truffles = FINANCIÉRE

Port = PORTO

VINEGAR

Gastrique + Orange Zest / Cognac / Duck Stock = BIGARADE

White Wine / Raisins / Pine Nuts = ROMAINE

Mirepoix / Meat/Game Trimmings / White Wine / Marinade / Peppercorns = POIVRADE

Shallots / White Wine / Gherkins / Parsley / Chervil / Tarragon = PIQUANTE

Shallots / Bread / Parsley / Lemon = ZINGARA A

Red Wine / Deer Trimmings = CHEVREUIL

Cream / Currant Jam = GRAND/VENEUR

Whipped Cream / Truffles / (Egg Whites) = DIANE

Malaga / Juniper / Pine Nuts/Almonds / Raisins = MOSCOVITE

STOCK / DEMI-GLACE / COULIS

Chopped Truffles = PÉRIGUEUX

Sliced Truffles = PÉRIGOURDINE

Mushroom Essence / Button Mushrooms = CHAMPIGNONS

Tomato Purée / Duxelles / Ham / Chervil / Parsley / Tarragon = ITALIENNE

Sauce Diable

This sauce is best served with grilled chicken or other poultry. Its flavor should be straightforward and fairly acidic to balance the grilled flavor. Some traditional recipes use only white wine, while others insist on vinegar. The following recipes use a combination. The sauce is finished with cayenne pepper and should be quite spicy.

CLASSIC METHOD. Finely chop 3 shallots (2 ounces/60 grams) and combine them with 5 fluid ounces (150 milliliters) white wine and 5 fluid ounces (150 milliliters) white wine vinegar. Reduce the mixture by two-thirds, until about 6 tablespoons (90 milliliters) of flavor base remain. Add 7 fluid ounces (200 milliliters) demi-glace and reduce slightly until the sauce has a very lightly syrupy consistency. Season with salt and pepper and add cayenne to taste. Yield: 1 cup (250 milliliters)

GLACE DE VIANDE METHOD. Prepare the same flavor base as described for the classic method. There should be approximately 5 tablespoons (75 milliliters) flavor base remaining after reduction. Add 2 tablespoons (30 milliliters) glace de viande (page 97) to the reduction. Adjust the consistency of the sauce by either thinning with stock or reducing slightly. Whisk 1 ounce (30 grams) butter into the sauce. Season with salt and pepper and add cayenne to taste. Yield: ½ cup (125 milliliters)

UNTHICKENED METHOD. Replace the demi-glace or called for in the classic method with a full-flavored brown chicken stock or jus. Taste the sauce before adding all the stock or jus so as not to completely muffle the taste of the flavor base. The flavor of the finished sauce can be enhanced with freshly chopped thyme, savory, or marjoram. Yield: 1 cup (250 milliliters)

ALTERNATIVES AND VARIATIONS. Although purists would insist that it is no longer a sauce diable, the sauce will have a more complex flavor if the shallots are gently caramelized in a small amount of butter before being moistened with the white wine and vinegar. This will also give a darker, richer color to the sauce.

If the sauce is being used for grilled poultry such as chicken, pigeon, or pheasant, some of the trimmings, such as the wing tips or necks, can be caramelized with the shallots before being moistened with the vinegar and white wine. It is also possible to impart some of the grilled flavor to the sauce by lightly grilling the trimmings before adding them to the sauce. Strain the sauce before serving.

The flavor of all three versions of the sauce is enhanced by finishing the sauce with 1 tablespoon (15 milliliters) chopped chives followed by a minute of simmering.

Sauce Estragon (*Tarragon Sauce*)

This sauce is best served with veal or chicken.

CLASSIC METHOD. Bring ¾ cup (185 milliliters) white wine to a simmer. Let it simmer just long enough to evaporate the alcohol, then add a small handful (about 4 teaspoons/20 milliliters) coarsely chopped tarragon stems. Cover the pan and let the stems infuse in the hot wine for 10 to 15 minutes. Add 1 cup (250 milliliters) demi-glace to the infusion, and reduce the mixture by one-third. Strain through a fine chinois. Finish the sauce with 2 teaspoons (10 milliliters) tarragon leaves that have been chopped at the last minute. Yield: 1 cup (250 milliliters)

GLACE DE VIANDE METHOD. Prepare the tarragon infusion as described for the classic method. Add 3 tablespoons (45 milliliters) glace de viande (page 97) to the infusion, and reduce slightly until the mixture has a lightly syrupy consistency. Strain the mixture and whisk in 1½ ounces (45 grams) butter or tarragon butter (page 446). Finish with 2 teaspoons (10 milliliters) freshly chopped tarragon leaves. Yield: 1 cup (250 milliliters)

UNTHICKENED METHOD. Prepare the infusion as described for the classic method, but replace the demi-glace with jus, clear stock, or consommé. This mixture will be considerably more acidic than the same sauce made with demi-glace. In some cases, this acidity is desirable, and the mixture can be left as is. Otherwise, additional stock or jus can be added to taste. Decorate the sauce with blanched whole tarragon leaves. Yield: 1 cup (250 milliliters)

ALTERNATIVES AND VARIATIONS. This sauce can be used as a model for almost any herb sauce: a preliminary infusion in white wine; reduction with demi-glace or glace de viande; and a final finishing with the chopped herb leaves either added directly or first worked into a compound butter. The method without thickener can also be used as a model.

Sauce Fines Herbes

Most recipes for this sauce contain the traditional fines herbes mixture: equal parts chervil, tarragon, parsley, and chives. Of these four herbs, tarragon is by far the most assertive. The sauce will be better balanced if the amount of tarragon is reduced by three-fourths or even eliminated. The technique and quantities are identical to those used for sauce estragon (above) except that tarragon is replaced by the fines herbes mixture.

SAUCE GODART (PROSCIUTTO AND MUSHROOM SAUCE)

CLASSIC METHOD. Prepare 2 ounces (50 grams) finely chopped mirepoix, which should include one-quarter unsmoked cured ham, such as Prosciutto di Parma (use the ends to save money). Combine the mirepoix with 7 fluid ounces (200 milliliters) Champagne or white wine. Reduce the mixture by half. Add 6 tablespoons (90 milliliters) mushroom essence (see page 100). Add 2 cups (500 milliliters) demi-glace. Simmer the sauce gently for 10 minutes, skimming any froth that floats to the surface. Strain through a fine chinois. Put the strained sauce in a clean saucepan and reduce it to the desired consistency. Strain through a fine chinois. Yield: 2 cups (500 milliliters)

GLACE DE VIANDE METHOD. Prepare the white wine–mirepoix mixture and reduce it by half as described for the classic method. Add 6 tablespoons (90 milliliters) mushroom essence and reduce the mixture again by half. About 6 tablespoons (90 milliliters) liquid should remain. Dissolve 3 tablespoons (45 milliliters) glace de viande (page 97) in the hot flavor base. Check the consistency of the base; it should be lightly syrupy. If it is too thin, reduce it or add a bit more glace de viande. If it is too thick, thin it with stock. Whisk in 1½ ounces (45 grams) butter. Strain the sauce through a fine chinois. Yield: ¾ cup (185 milliliters)

UNTHICKENED METHOD. Prepare the white wine–mirepoix mixture as described for the classic method. Replace the demi-glace with the same amount of jus, clear stock, or consommé. Mushrooms can be poached directly in the stock if mushroom cooking liquid is not on hand. Yield: 1 cup (250 milliliters)

ALTERNATIVES AND VARIATIONS. Champagne is not necessary for this sauce, but be careful to select a fairly austere white wine with relatively high acidity (such as Coteaux Champenois, Muscadet, Chablis, or Sancerre). If the ham used in the mirepoix is too salty, soak the slices in cold water for 30 minutes. The flavor of the sauce can be made more assertive by sweating the ham and mirepoix in ½ ounce (15 grams) butter until they lightly caramelize, before moistening with the wine.

Much of the character of this sauce comes from the mushroom cooking liquid or mushroom essence, so avoid trying to alter it by finishing the sauce with strongly flavored ingredients. The sauce is enhanced by wild mushrooms. A slice or two of dried cèpes (porcini) or a few reconstituted dried morels will work wonders. Wild or cultivated mushrooms, whole, chopped, or cut into julienne, make an attractive garniture for the finished sauce.

Sauce Hussarde (*Prosciutto-Scented Horseradish Sauce*)

This sauce traditionally accompanies grilled red meats.

CLASSIC METHOD. Gently sweat 1 finely chopped shallot (1 ounce/25 grams) and 1 finely chopped medium onion (6 ounces/150 grams) in ½ ounce (15 grams) butter until they are translucent but not browned. Add 7 fluid ounces (200 milliliters) white wine and reduce by half. Add 7 fluid ounces (200 milliliters) demi-glace, 1 tablespoon (15 milliliters) tomato purée, 6 tablespoons (90 milliliters) concentrated white veal or chicken stock (four to six times), 1 ounce (25 grams) chopped unsmoked cured ham (such as prosciutto), ½ garlic clove (crushed), and 1 small bouquet garni (page 52). Slowly simmer for 30 minutes. Strain through a fine chinois. Finish the sauce with 1 ounce (25 grams) ham cut into brunoise, 1 teaspoon (5 milliliters) freshly grated horseradish, and 1 tablespoon (15 milliliters) finely chopped parsley. Yield: 2 cups (500 milliliters)

GLACE DE VIANDE METHOD. Prepare the shallot-onion–white wine reduction as described for the classic method, which should produce about 5 tablespoons (75 milliliters) flavor base. Add 3 tablespoons (45 milliliters) glace de viande (page 97) to the reduction, along with 1 tablespoon (15 milliliters) tomato coulis (page 507), 1 ounce (25 grams) chopped unsmoked cured ham, ½ garlic clove (crushed), and 1 small bouquet garni (page 52). Simmer, covered, for 30 minutes. Strain the sauce and finish it with the ham, horseradish, and parsley as described for the classic method. Thin if necessary with stock. Whisk in 1½ ounces (45 grams) butter. Yield: 1 cup (250 milliliters)

UNTHICKENED METHOD. Like many of the derivative brown sauces, unthickened sauce hussarde can be presented as a bouillon or consommé, hot or cold, underneath, surrounding, or atop the meat. When presenting the sauce in this way, the horseradish should be julienned instead of grated and should be allowed to infuse in the bouillon for about 15 minutes. The ham should be carefully cut into brunoise and lightly poached; otherwise it may cloud the bouillon. If the sauce has been carefully skimmed and strained, it will have the clarity of a consommé without needing clarification with egg whites. Yield: 1 cup (250 milliliters)

ALTERNATIVES AND VARIATIONS. The classic recipe for sauce hussarde is based on an infusion of shallots and onions in white wine. The flavor of onions and shallots can be intensified by lightly caramelizing them in a small amount of butter with a pinch of sugar before moistening them with the white wine. This method will also give a deeper color to the sauce. If the sauce is being presented unbound in a bowl, the butter should be carefully skimmed off after the liquid has been moistened with stock.

Sauce Régence (*Rhine Wine and Truffle Sauce*)

Rhine wine, which lends a subtle sweetness, is traditionally called for in the flavor base for this sauce. The term *Rhine wine* encompasses a variety of wines that include dry Alsatian-style Rieslings and Sylvaners as well as German Rheingau, Rheinhessen, or Rheinpfalz wines, which usually contain some residual sugar. Opt for the German wines, which contribute a light sweetness to the sauce. They also work well with the truffles, so if you want to be traditional, a German spätlese or auslese Riesling would work best. These wines also have an intense varietal character that is more likely to hold up after the addition of the other ingredients. Beware when buying German kabinett, spätlese, and auslese wines. Many of these wines are now vinified dry and will be labeled accordingly. *Troken* is dry and *halbtrocken* is off-dry. If you don't see one of these terms, you can be reasonably sure the wine is made in the traditional style and will contain the residual sugar necessary for this sauce. Late-harvest California Riesling can also be used.

CLASSIC METHOD. Prepare 2 ounces (50 grams) mirepoix and gently cook it in butter until it softens. Moisten with 5 fluid ounces (150 milliliters) Rhine wine. Reduce the mixture by half, and add 1 tablespoon (15 milliliters) chopped truffle peelings or ¼ cup (60 milliliters) truffle juice or essence. Add 1¾ cups (450 milliliters) demi-glace to the infusion and bring to a simmer. Skim off any scum that floats to the top. Strain through a fine chinois. Yield: 2 cups (500 milliliters)

GLACE DE VIANDE METHOD. Prepare the mirepoix–Rhine wine infusion as described for the classic method. Add the truffle peelings or essence, and replace the demi-glace with ¼ cup (60 milliliters) glace de viande (page 97). Adjust the consistency to a light syrup by reducing slightly or thinning with stock. Finish the sauce with 2 ounces (60 grams) butter or truffle butter (page 446) before straining. Yield: 1 cup (250 milliliters)

UNTHICKENED METHOD. Gently simmer 5 fluid ounces (150 milliliters) Rhine wine with an equal amount of full-flavored stock or jus until the mixture reduces by half. Finish the sauce with 6 tablespoons truffle juice or simply add fresh julienned or sliced truffles. If you're using truffles, cover the sauce and cook the truffles for 5 to 10 minutes. Serve immediately in deep plates or bowls. Yield: 1 cup (250 milliliters)

ALTERNATIVES AND VARIATIONS. Traditional recipes stipulate straining out the chopped truffle peelings used to flavor the sauce. Truffles have become such a rarity, and most diners are so unaccustomed to seeing truffles on their plates, that the sauce will probably be more appreciated if they are retained. In fact, the sauce can be made more dramatic by adding thinly sliced black truffles to it at the end.

To impart a more intense truffle flavor, the sauce can be finished with truffle butter (page 446).

Sauce Robert (*White Wine–Mustard Sauce*)

This brightly flavored sauce is excellent with grilled meats and pork dishes. Use a fairly acidic white wine—Muscadet and French versions of Sauvignon Blanc both work well.

CLASSIC METHOD. Sweat 1 medium onion (6 ounces/150 grams), chopped, in ½ ounce (15 grams) butter until translucent. Add 7 fluid ounces (200 milliliters) white wine and reduce by two-thirds. Moisten the onion–white wine infusion with 1¼ cups (300 milliliters) demi-glace. Cook for 10 minutes to infuse the flavor of the onions thoroughly. The sauce may either be strained or the onions may be retained. Finish the sauce with a pinch of sugar (to bring out the flavor of the onions) and 1 tablespoon (15 milliliters) Dijon mustard. Do not allow the sauce to come to a boil after adding the mustard. Yield: 1½ cups (375 milliliters)

GLACE DE VIANDE METHOD. Sweat the onion and add the wine as described for the classic method, but reduce by only half. Add 3 tablespoons (45 milliliters) glace de viande (page 97) to the infusion in place of demi-glace. Adjust the consistency of the sauce, add the mustard and sugar, and finish with 1½ ounces (45 grams) butter. Yield: 1 cup (250 milliliters)

UNTHICKENED METHOD. Sauce Robert works particularly well when no flour or butter is used. Prepare Sauce Robert in the same way as for the classic method, but replace the demi-glace with unthickened full-flavored stock or jus (pork jus is especially good). An unthickened, almost medieval version can also be prepared with no stock at all, but it is too sharp and acidic for most modern tastes. Yield: 2 cups (500 milliliters)

ALTERNATIVES AND VARIATIONS. Sauce Robert is traditionally finished with Dijon mustard. Other mustards, such as whole-grain Meaux-style or home-made mustard, can be used instead to give the sauce a personal touch. Herb-flavored mustards can also be used, but if you want the flavor of a particular herb, it is usually better to finish the sauce with an unflavored mustard and add the chopped fresh herb separately.

Sauce Charcutière (*White Wine and Gherkin Sauce*)

To 2 cups (500 milliliters) Sauce Robert, add 2 ounces (50 grams) sour gherkins (cornichons), cut into julienne.

Sauce Duxelles (*Chopped Mushroom Sauce*)

This sauce is based on duxelles, a standard mushroom preparation used in classic French cooking. Duxelles is prepared by slowly cooking chopped mushrooms in butter until all their moisture has evaporated. It is best when prepared with wild mushrooms (even a few added cèpe/porcini stems or reconstituted dried cèpe/porcini slices are magnificent) but is most often made with cultivated mushrooms. To prepare 1 cup (250 milliliters) duxelles, finely chop 1 pound (500 grams) mushrooms or mushroom stems and 3 shallots. Sweat the shallots for 5 minutes in 1 ounce (30 grams) butter and add the mushrooms. Sprinkle the mushrooms with the juice of half a lemon (to prevent the duxelles from turning black) and gently cook the mushrooms until no moisture is left in the bottom of the pan. Keep them covered in a bowl until needed.

CLASSIC METHOD. Combine 1 tablespoon (15 milliliters) finely chopped shallots with 6 tablespoons (90 milliliters) white wine and 6 tablespoons (90 milliliters) mushroom cooking liquid (see page 100). Add 1 cup (250 milliliters) demi-glace, ¼ cup (60 milliliters) tomato purée, and 2 tablespoons (30 milliliters) fine, dry duxelles to the sauce. Simmer the sauce for 5 minutes, and finish it with 2 teaspoons (10 milliliters) finely chopped parsley. Yield: 2 cups (500 milliliters)

GLACE DE VIANDE METHOD. Use the same ingredients and procedure as for the classic method, but replace the demi-glace with ¼ cup (60 milliliters) glace de viande (page 97). Finish the sauce with 1½ ounces (45 grams) butter. Yield: 1½ cups (375 milliliters)

UNTHICKENED METHOD. Duxelles will usually disperse when mixed with a full-bodied broth, creating a sauce that looks somewhat like mushroom soup. It is better to cut the mushrooms into julienne and add them directly to the broth. This method is even more impressive if a combination of different-colored wild mushrooms is used, such as black trumpets, white oyster mushrooms, chanterelles, morels, porcini (cèpes), and the like. To prepare an unthickened version, follow the directions for the classic method but replace the duxelles with julienned mushrooms and the demi-glace with a lighter stock or jus. Yield: 2 cups (500 milliliters)

Sauce Salmis

This excellent sauce is usually made to accompany game and small birds, but the same method can be used for almost any kind of meat. Because the trimmings from the game enter into the preparation, the sauce has much of the wholesomeness and character of an integral sauce or natural jus. Whatever kind of trimmings you use, be sure that all skin and fat are removed. If they are left on, they may make the sauce greasy.

CLASSIC METHOD. Sweat 3 ounces (75 grams) mirepoix in butter until it starts to soften. Break up 1 pound (500 grams) game meat or fowl trimmings into ½-inch (1 cm) pieces with a cleaver or heavy knife and add them to the mirepoix. When the trimmings begin to brown, add 5 fluid ounces (150 milliliters) white wine and reduce by two-thirds. Add 1¾ cups (450 milliliters) demi-glace. Cook for about 45 minutes to extract the flavor from the trimmings and mirepoix. Strain the sauce, first through a coarse chinois, then through a fine chinois. Add 7 fluid ounces (200 milliliters) appropriately flavored stock to the strained flavor base. Reduce if necessary to thicken. Finish the sauce by whisking in 2 ounces (60 grams) butter. Season with salt and pepper. Yield: 2½ cups (625 milliliters)

GLACE DE VIANDE METHOD. Sweat the mirepoix and add the trimmings as described for the classic method. Gently cook the mirepoix with the trimmings until the juices on the bottom of the pan begin to caramelize. Add 6 tablespoons (90 milliliters) white wine to the pan and continue reducing until all the liquid evaporates, leaving a brown layer of caramelized juices on the bottom of the pan. (The steam generated by the reducing wine causes the trimmings to release their juices, which should then caramelize on the bottom of the pan.) When the wine has been completely reduced, add ½ cup (125 milliliters) brown beef or chicken stock (page 89 or 85), and again reduce until no liquid remains, gently scraping the bottom of the pot with a wooden spoon or spatula while the stock is reducing, so that the caramelized juices dissolve. When the stock has reduced and formed a thick caramelized glaze on the bottom of the pot, add 6 tablespoons (90 milliliters) white wine and cook it just long enough to scrape up and dissolve the caramelized juices. Add 1¾ cups (450 milliliters) brown beef or chicken stock (or game stock, if available), and simmer for 45 minutes. Strain into a clean saucepan through a coarse chinois. Stir enough glace de viande (page 97) into the sauce to give it the consistency of a light syrup and to reinforce its color—usually about ¼ cup (60 milliliters) glace de viande is needed. Whisk 2 ounces (60 grams) butter into the sauce. Strain through a fine chinois. Yield: 2 cups (500 milliliters)

Sauce Zingara B

Sauce Zingara has such a convoluted history and so many variations that, by the time the classic sauces were categorized at the end of the nineteenth century, two types of it—imaginatively named Zingara A and Zingara B—had to be listed. Zingara A is one of the few sauces in the classic repertoire that is thickened with breadcrumbs, a technique used since the Middle Ages. Because it is based on vinegar, its recipe is included in the section on vinegar-based derivative brown sauces (see page 193). Zingara B is white wine based and finished with an elaborate garniture of ham, mushrooms, and truffles.

CLASSIC METHOD. Prepare 2 ounces (50 grams) julienned mushrooms. Simmer the julienne for 5 minutes in 5 fluid ounces (150 milliliters) white wine. Strain the wine and save the mushroom julienne to add to the sauce at the end. Return the white wine to the saucepan and reduce it by half. Add 7 fluid ounces (200 milliliters) demi-glace, 1 cup (250 milliliters) tomato sauce (page 506), and ¼ cup (60 milliliters) white chicken or veal stock (page 88 or 91). Gently simmer and skim for 5 or 10 minutes, until it has a lightly syrupy consistency. Strain the sauce through a fine chinois, and finish it with the julienned mushrooms as well as 2 tablespoons (30 milliliters) unsmoked cured ham cut into fine julienne and 1 tablespoon (15 milliliters) black truffles, also cut into julienne. Yield: 2½ cups (625 milliliters)

GLACE DE VIANDE METHOD. Prepare the sauce exactly as for the classic method, but replace the demi-glace with 3 tablespoons (45 milliliters) glace de viande (page 97). Finish the sauce by whisking in 2 ounces (60 grams) butter just before adding the julienned mushrooms, ham, and truffles. Yield: 2 cups (500 milliliters)

UNTHICKENED METHOD. Prepare the sauce as for the classic method, but substitute a lighter stock for the demi-glace. Yield: 2½ cups (625 milliliters)

SPHERIFICATION

Much has been made of Ferran Adrià's adaptation of the industrial technique of making spheres that, much like caviar, have a thin skin and liquid or soft center. The spheres can be made virtually any size, from olives down to the smallest sevruga caviar.

At first glance, this technique hardly seems to be relevant to sauce making. True, the little spheres can be stirred into a sauce and in essence function as a garniture much as capers might, but the real fascination begins when these spheres become an integral part of the sauce. A sauce can be deconstructed, with one or more essential flavor elements left out, and instead of being stirred into the sauce, encapsulated in spheres. Such an application might, for example, be used to ensure that the taste of truffles makes it through the complex array of ingredients in the sauce. If, for example, you take a sauce financière, leave out the truffle essence or juice, and instead seal the essence up in spheres, the spheres will pop in the mouth as the sauce is pressed against the tongue and the roof of the mouth, releasing a burst of truffle flavor.

This same concept can be applied to any number of sauces. Tiny spheres containing vinegar can be stirred into a sauce so that they break up under the tongue and wake up the sauce—and the diner. Essences of herbs (made by heating the herbs sous vide for several hours or steeping them for several days) can be sealed in spheres and used in such sauces as béarnaise or in any sauce that calls for herbs to be added near the end. Fortified wines (alcohol first burned off) can be used in spheres that call for such wine. The impression of "something missing" will be replaced with awe and surprise.

There's nothing particularly difficult about making spheres, except for the formation of the spheres, which in a traditional kitchen have to be prepared one by one. This makes it impossible to time the spheres since those added to the solution at the beginning will obviously spend more time in the bath and will have a different consistency from those added near the end. The solution is a Finnpipette with twelve to ninety-six openings, the kind used by biochemists for dispensing small amounts of liquids into vials (see page 32), which can make more than a drop at a time.

Spheres are made using alginates (usually sodium alginate). Alginates, which are made from seaweed, lend themselves to the technique because they harden in the presence of calcium ions (see "Ions" in the Glossary). Hence, a flavorful liquid is combined with sodium alginate and the mixture is added, 12 drops or more at a time, to a solution of calcium chloride. When the drops come in contact with the calcium, the outside hardens. Depending on the length of time the spheres are steeped in the calcium solution, the inside will be liquid, semi-liquid, or even gummy. This process can also be done in reverse, with the calcium ions worked into the base mixture and the alginate in the steeping solution; as the drops of the calcium-containing liquid fall through the alginate solution, the outsides harden in the same way.

SAUCE FINANCIÈRE WITH TRUFFLE SPHERES

Sauce Financière is essentially a Madeira sauce flavored with truffles. Everything is done to preserve the truffle aroma and flavor. The sauce contains truffle juice that hasn't been reduced, so that none of the precious perfume has evaporated. Truffle butter is sometimes used to mount the sauce with butter. Truffle spheres offer an entirely new way of delivering the truffle flavor without concern that it will evaporate or volatilize. Here, this luxurious sauce is served atop a tasty steak.

YIELD: 6 SERVINGS

(continued)

SPHERE LIQUID (MAKES ABOUT 300 THE SIZE OF SMALL CAVIAR EGGS)		
calcium lactate		1.5 grams
xanthan gum		0.1 gram
truffle essence or commercial truffle juice	½ cup	125 milliliters
ALGINATE SOLUTION		
sodium alginate		2.5 grams
water	2 cups	500 milliliters
BASE SAUCE		
rainwater madeira	¼ cup	60 milliliters
mushroom essence (see page 100)	¼ cup	60 milliliters
glace de viande (page 97)	2 tablespoons	30 milliliters
butter	1 ounce	30 grams
salt and pepper	to taste	to taste

1. Make the sphere liquid: Whisk together the calcium lactate, xanthan gum, and truffle juice and reserve.

2. Make the alginate solution: Dissolve the sodium alginate in the water.

3. To load the Finipipette, fill the large syringe attached to the Finipipette with the sphere liquid. Reattach the syringe to the Finipipette and push down the plunger until you see drops form at the end of each nozzle. (A, B, C, D)

4. To make the spheres, let 12 or more drops form on the Finnipipette and fall into the alginate solution at a time. (E) You should be able to make several additions without throwing the timing too far off. Wait about 3 minutes for the spheres to set (the longer you wait, the firmer the sphere wall will be). Spoon out the spheres—a small strainer or fine-slotted spoon is good for this—and transfer them to a bowl of cold water. (F) Reserve until you make the sauce.

5. Make the sauce: Combine the Madeira, mushroom essence, and glace de viande in a small saucepan. Simmer gently until the sauce reaches the desired consistency. Whisk in the butter and season with salt and pepper. Stir in the spheres just before serving.

RED WINE–BASED DERIVATIVE BROWN SAUCES

Red wines used for sauce making must be chosen carefully (see "Red Wine," page 69). A red wine sauce will always be improved if the wine is cooked with meat trimmings or stock rather than being reduced by itself or with aromatic vegetables alone; the proteins in the meat or stock help eliminate undesirable tannin from the wine. Most classic recipes take this into consideration and call for reducing the red wine a second time with demi-glace or meat stock.

Do not make glace de viande–based sauces by simply reducing red wine, adding the glaze, and finishing with butter. The resulting sauce will be sour or even bitter because of the concentration of the wine's tannin and acids during reduction. Keep meat trimmings and stock on hand when preparing these sauces.

When preparing red wine sauces, it is best that the red wine be cooked for at least 30 minutes with stock or meat trimmings or that red wine stock made with beef or chicken (page 87) be used instead of the usual red wine reduction combined with glace de viande. This is especially important in unthickened sauces because butter, which would help attenuate the wine's acidity, is not used. If the resulting sauce is nonetheless sharp or even astringent, you will have to relent and swirl in a little butter or lightly thicken the sauce with a vegetable purée, such as mushroom, lentil, or tomato. If neither stock nor meat trimmings are available, excellent red wine sauces can be prepared using a base of mirepoix with unsmoked cured ham (see Meurette Sauce, page 189).

Sauce Bordelaise

In the first half of the nineteenth century, recipes for Sauce Bordelaise called for white wine. A similar sauce, Sauce Bonnefoy (page 149), is still made with white wine.

CLASSIC METHOD. Combine 1¼ cups (300 milliliters) red wine with 2 tablespoons (30 milliliters) finely chopped shallots, 1 teaspoon (5 milliliters) crushed black pepper, a sprig of fresh thyme, and half a bay leaf. Reduce the mixture by three-fourths. Add 6 tablespoons (90 milliliters) demi-glace or 2 tablespoons (30 milliliters) glace de viande (page 97) to the reduction. Gently simmer for 15 minutes, being sure to skim off any scum that floats to the surface. Add water or stock as necessary if the sauce becomes too thick. Strain the sauce through a fine chinois into a clean saucepan. If the sauce is too thin, adjust its consistency by stirring in 1 tablespoon (15 milliliters) glace de viande. Add 1 teaspoon (5 milliliters) lemon juice and 2 ounces (60 grams) beef marrow cut into dice or rounds or butter cut into cubes. Season with salt and pepper. Yield: 1 cup (250 milliliters)

GLACE DE VIANDE METHOD. A good-tasting Sauce Bordelaise is difficult to make using glace de viande as the only form of meat protein; meat stock, meat trimmings, or both are essential. Sweat 5 ounces (150 grams) beef or veal trimmings with 2 tablespoons (30 milliliters) finely chopped shallots in ½ ounce (15 grams) butter. When the meat trimmings and shallots begin to brown lightly, pour 6 tablespoons (90 milliliters) red wine into the pan. Reduce the red wine until it evaporates completely, but do not let the bottom of the pan burn. Add 6 tablespoons (90 milliliters) brown beef or chicken stock (page 89 or 85), and again reduce until the stock evaporates and lightly caramelizes on the bottom of the saucepan. Add 1¼ cups (300 milliliters) red wine, 6 tablespoons (90 milliliters) brown beef or chicken stock, half a bay leaf, a sprig of fresh thyme, and 1 teaspoon (5 milliliters) freshly crushed black pepper.

Gently simmer for 15 to 20 minutes. Strain through a fine chinois into a clean saucepan. Dissolve 2 tablespoons (30 milliliters) glace de viande (page 97) into the hot sauce to give it a thicker, lightly syrupy consistency. Finish with 1 teaspoon (5 milliliters) lemon juice and 2 ounces (60 grams) beef marrow cut into dice or rounds, or 1½ ounces (45 grams) butter. Yield: 1½ cups (375 milliliters)

UNTHICKENED METHOD. Sauce Bordelaise can be presented under meats in deep plates or wide plate-like soup bowls. To prepare an unthickened version, follow the procedure given for the glace de viande, but omit the glace de viande and butter. Yield: 2 cups (500 milliliters)

ALTERNATIVES AND VARIATIONS. Purists would argue that a sauce without marrow cannot be called a Bordelaise, but the sauce is perfectly good tasting without it. Finely chopped parsley or chervil added along with the butter to finish the sauce will give it a freshness that is otherwise missing, and the green flecks against the deep red background are pleasing to the eye. A teaspoon (5 milliliters) Cognac or Armagnac added just long enough before the end to cook off the alcohol will give the sauce a bit more depth and mystery, as will a drop or two of Kirsch. The finished sauce can be made less rich by adding 2 tablespoons (30 milliliters) tomato coulis (page 507), which acts as a thickener, and by cutting the butter in half.

Keep in mind that broth-like versions of this sauce can be set into delicate gels. Here, there's no need to add a gelling agent since there's plenty of gelatin from the concentrated stock. If the gel is too hard or gummy, thin it with some clear broth or consommé so it sets into a delicate, barely trembling gelée. Consider encapsulating a trace of diluted thyme-infused sherry vinegar (instead of the lemon juice) or flambéed Cognac in tiny spheres (see page 182) and serving them with the hot sauce.

BORDELAISE SAUCE MADE WITH RED WINE STOCK

This classic sauce, once made with white wine, is made in a classic kitchen by adding demi-glace or glace de viande to a red wine reduction and finishing the sauce with cubes of beef marrow. The marrow can be replaced with a swirl of butter. The red wine is best reduced along with the demi-glace or glace de viande so the proteins take out some of the tannin. Best of all is a Bordelaise sauce made starting with red wine stock (simply make a veal stock or other stock using red wine instead of water). As for all brown sauces, the thickness of the sauce is largely a matter of taste. If red wine stock is used, very little reduction will be required to cook off the acid and tannin in the wine and the sauce can be left almost like a rich broth, served around a good steak in a soup plate, or it can be reduced and thickened with butter, perhaps in conjunction with hydrocolloids, emulsifiers, and emulsion stabilizers.

YIELD: 1 CUP (250 MILLILITERS), ABOUT 6 SERVINGS

red wine stock	2 cups	500 milliliters
or	or	or
red wine	1 cup	250 milliliters
and	and	and
veal, beef, or chicken demi-glace	¾ cup	185 milliliters
or	or	or
glace de viande (page 97)	¼ cup	60 milliliters
minced shallots (about 1 shallot)	2 tablespoons	30 milliliters
black pepper, crushed	1 teaspoon	5 milliliters
fresh or dried thyme	1 sprig	1 sprig
or	or	or
dried thyme leaves	1 pinch	1 pinch
imported bay leaf	½ leaf	½ leaf
red wine vinegar (or to taste)	2 teaspoons	10 milliliters
cognac	2 teaspoons	10 milliliters
beef marrow cubes or cold butter	1½ ounces	45 grams
salt	to taste	to taste

1. Combine the red wine stock, or the red wine and the demi-glace or glace de viande, with the shallots, pepper, thyme, and bay leaf and simmer gently until reduced by slightly more than half, or until the sauce has a lightly syrupy consistency. Strain into a clean saucepan.

2. Whisk in the vinegar and Cognac, simmer for 30 seconds, and whisk in the marrow or butter. Season with salt.

MEURETTE SAUCE
BURGUNDIAN RED WINE SAUCE

The classic version of this sauce contains no meat stock, so it can be quickly prepared by home cooks. Meurette sauce is popular in Burgundy, where it is served over poached eggs as shown here, but it is a versatile sauce that can also be used over meat or even fish. This sauce is made by sweating aromatic vegetables (mirepoix) with unsmoked cured ham (prosciutto), then moistening with red wine. It can be improved by sweating fresh meat trimmings with the ham-mirepoix base and by using some concentrated stock (four to six times) along with the red wine. Add a bouquet garni (page 52) and 3 cups (750 milliliters) red wine, and gently simmer the mixture for 30 minutes. The sauce base can be reduced to a very small amount and the sauce finished with butter alone, or the base can be reduced less dramatically and the sauce then finished with beurre manié (see page 108).

YIELD: 1 CUP (250 MILLILITERS), ABOUT 6 SERVINGS

onion, peeled, minced	1 small	1 small
carrot, minced	1 medium	1 medium
celery, minced	½ stalk	½ stalk
garlic cloves, crushed	2	2
prosciutto, chopped (see Note)	3 tablespoons	45 milliliters
meat trimmings, diced (optional)	1 cup	250 milliliters
butter (for the mirepoix)	1 ounce	30 grams
glace de viande (page 97; optional)	2 tablespoons	30 milliliters
red wine	3 cups	750 milliliters
medium bouquet garni (page 52)	1	1
cold butter (if using beurre manié)	1 tablespoon	15 grams
flour (if using beurre manié)	1 tablespoon	15 grams
cold butter (if using butter alone)	4 ounces	100 grams
red wine vinegar	2 teaspoons	10 milliliters
salt and pepper	to taste	to taste

1. Cook the onions, carrot, celery, garlic, prosciutto, and meat trimmings, if using, in butter in a saucepan over medium heat until well browned and any juices released by the meat have caramelized on the bottom of the pan. Stir in the glace de viande, if using, and stir over medium heat for about 2 minutes to caramelize the glaze slightly. (A, page 191)

(continued)

2. Pour over the red wine (B) and add the bouquet garni (C). Simmer gently for 30 minutes. Strain into a clean saucepan and simmer down to 1 cup (125 milliliters) if you're using beurre manié, or ½ cup (125 milliliters) if you're using only butter.

3. If using beurre manié, work the tablespoon of butter and the flour into a paste. Whisk half the beurre manié or all the butter into the sauce (D) and bring back to a simmer for just a second (E).

If you're using beurre manié and the sauce is too thin, whisk in the remaining beurre manié and return to a simmer. Whisk in the vinegar and season with salt and pepper.

Note: When buying prosciutto for sauce making, ask for the ends. Often they are available at very little cost.

ALTERNATIVES AND VARIATIONS

If wild mushrooms are available, by all means use them. They can be infused in the simmering red wine for 5 to 10 minutes, removed, and added whole to the sauce at the end, or they can be simply sautéed, sprinkled with herbs and chopped shallots, and used as a garniture. Infusions of wild mushrooms such as cèpes (porcini) can be put into spheres (see page 182).

As concerns alternative thickeners, the classic and traditional thickeners, beurre manié or pure butter, are best left alone.

Sauce Rouennaise II

This sauce is prepared by thickening Sauce Bordelaise (page 186) without the marrow, with a purée of raw duck livers (not foie gras, just plain livers). Purée 1 duck liver with an equal volume of butter and, if desired for greater stability, 2% liquid lecithin in a food processor for about 3 minutes. Force this mixture through a drum sieve. Gently whisk 1 cup (250 milliliters) of hot Sauce Bordelaise into the liver mixture and return the sauce to the pan. Be careful not to let the sauce boil once the liver has been added, or it will break and turn grainy. If using glace de viande–based Bordelaise, replace the butter called for with the liver-butter purée. Yield: 1 cup (250 milliliters)

For a different, and perhaps more authentic, version of Sauce Rouennaise that is thickened with blood and liver, see page 123.

DERIVATIVE BROWN SAUCES BASED ON FORTIFIED WINES

Most fortified wines used in sauce making have a large amount of residual sugar that remains in the wine after fermentation. Whereas red wines will become acidic if overly reduced, fortified wines, if used carelessly, are liable to make a sauce too sweet. Because different styles and brands of Madeira and port have different amounts of natural sugar, do not blindly follow a recipe for these sauces, because each wine will behave slightly differently.

Sauce Madère (*Madeira Sauce*)

For the choice of Madeira, see page 68.

CLASSIC METHOD. Combine 2 cups (500 milliliters) demi-glace with ¼ cup (60 milliliters) Madeira. Gently reduce the mixture back down to 2 cups (500 milliliters). Skim off any froth or scum that floats to the surface. Yield: 2 cups (500 milliliters)

GLACE DE VIANDE METHOD. Reduce 1 cup (250 milliliters) Madeira by half. Add 3 tablespoons (45 milliliters) glace de viande (page 97) to the reduction, and finish with 2 ounces (60 grams) butter. Season with salt and pepper. Yield: 1 cup (250 milliliters)

UNTHICKENED METHOD. Reduce ½ cup (125 milliliters) Madeira by half. Add ¾ cup (185 milliliters) concentrated clear brown stock (four times) to the reduction. Reduce or thin the sauce as necessary to adjust its consistency. Yield: 1 cup (250 milliliters)

ALTERNATIVES AND VARIATIONS. Adding 2 tablespoons (30 milliliters) mushroom essence to 1 cup (250 milliliters) of sauce will greatly improve glace de viande–based Madeira sauce; or wild or cultivated mushroom stems can be simmered for 5 minutes in the Madeira.

Sauce Porto (*Port Sauce*)

The methods for making port sauce are the same as for Madeira sauce except that the Madeira is replaced with a full-bodied port. Don't waste a vintage or wood port on a sauce but, instead, use a ruby or tawny port. A tawny is going to lend more complexity but is far from necessary.

Port and Mushroom Sauce

This unbound sauce is similar to Sauce Duxelles (page 179) except that port is used in the sauce base and the mushrooms are cut into julienne. Reduce ½ cup (125 milliliters) port by half. Add 1 cup (250 milliliters) concentrated brown stock (four times) and 2 ounces (50 grams) mushrooms cut into julienne. Reduce or thin the sauce as necessary to adjust its consistency. Finish with 1 tablespoon (15 milliliters) chopped parsley. Adding 1 to 2 teaspoons (5 to 10 milliliters) balsamic vinegar to the sauce at the end will bring up the flavor of the mushrooms. Yield: 1 cup (250 milliliters)

Sauce Financière

This sauce is prepared by flavoring Madeira sauce with truffles. Classic recipes reduce the Madeira sauce by one-tenth and then add enough truffle essence to return the sauce to its original volume. In this way, the truffle essence is never cooked in the sauce, which would cause much of its aroma to evaporate.

An alternative to using truffle essence is to finish the sauce with butter that has been stored with fresh truffles (see "Storing Fresh Truffles," page 58). The sauce can also be finished with chopped truffle peelings, truffle slices, or truffle spheres (see page 182).

VINEGAR-BASED DERIVATIVE BROWN SAUCES

There are two kinds of vinegar-based classic brown sauces. The first includes sweet-and-sour sauces, such as the sauce used for duck à l'orange. These sauces are usually prepared with a mixture of vinegar and caramelized sugar called a *gastrique*. The second type of vinegar-based classic brown sauce is the poivrade family (see page 196). These sauces, which are traditionally used for red meats and game, are prepared by cooking mirepoix vegetables and meat trimmings with vinegar and the marinade used for the meat.

Sweet-and-Sour Sauces: Gastrique

A gastrique is prepared with approximately one part sugar to two parts wine vinegar by volume. Usually about 2 tablespoons (30 milliliters) gastrique are used per quart (liter) of sauce, but the amount may vary depending on the type of sauce and the strength of the vinegar.

Heat ½ cup (100 grams) sugar in a heavy-bottomed saucepan or in an untinned copper poêlon (used specifically for making caramel). When the sugar has melted and turned a deep red, pour ½ cup (125 milliliters) wine vinegar into the saucepan to dissolve the caramel and stop the cooking. Stand back in case the mixture spatters. Heat and stir the gastrique to make sure the caramelized sugar is completely dissolved in the vinegar. Even though this may seem like a large amount of gastrique, it is hard to prepare in smaller amounts. In any case, it will keep indefinitely in the refrigerator.

Most classic recipes for gastrique suggest caramelizing the sugar by moistening it with the wine vinegar. Because of the high heat required to caramelize sugar, little if any vinegar remains in the gastrique when this method is used.

To use the gastrique in a sauce, pour small amounts into the sauce, not the other way around. Be careful to taste as you go; gastrique is powerful, and a few drops too many can spoil a sauce.

In classic French cooking, gastrique is used only in sweet-and-sour sauces or sauces containing fruit. When used discreetly, gastrique can enhance the flavor of other brown sauces as well (see "Using Gastrique," page 205).

Sauce Bigarade (*Orange Sauce for Duck*)

Sauce Bigarade is named after the bitter Seville oranges that were first used to flavor duck à l'orange. Most recipes for this are integral sauces prepared from the braising liquid or pan drippings from a roasted duck. The sauce can also be prepared from reduced duck stock, gastrique, and orange zests.

Prepare a concentrated duck stock without liaison by reducing the stock to a lightly syrupy consistency. Alternatively, bind partially reduced stock with a starch liaison such as roux, cornstarch, or arrowroot, or with a hydrocolloid such as xanthan gum and/or Ultra-Sperse 3.

Reduce the juice of 4 oranges (1¼ cups/300 milliliters) by half. Add 1 cup (250 milliliters) of the concentrated duck stock and reduce the sauce until it has a lightly syrupy consistency. Add 4 teaspoons (20 milliliters) gastrique to the sauce. Add the gastrique gradually, while tasting, to avoid adding too much. Strain the sauce through a fine chinois. Finish the sauce with 2 ounces (60 grams) butter and 1½ teaspoons (8 milliliters) julienned and blanched orange zest. The flavor of the sauce can be improved by adding 1 to 2 teaspoons (5 to 10 milliliters) Cognac. (A couple of drops of Grand Marnier do no harm either.) Yield: 2 cups (500 milliliters)

UNTHICKENED METHOD. A deeply flavored yet light duck broth can be prepared by lightly browning duck trimmings with aromatic vegetables and then moistening them with a previously made duck, chicken, or veal stock and simmering for 20 minutes. This method combines the advantages of long-simmered and short-simmered stocks: Long-simmered stocks provide body, whereas short-simmered ones provide flavor, character, and vitality. The finished duck broth should then be infused with the orange zest for 5 to 10 minutes and flavored with gastrique.

VARIATION. Make an infusion of orange by soaking some grated orange zests in Grand Marnier for a day or two. (To hurry things up, cook sous vide.) Strain out the zests and burn the alcohol off the Grand Marnier. Seal this orange infusion into spheres (see page 182) and stir the spheres into the Sauce Bigarade so the orange bursts in the mouth.

Sauce Romaine (*Raisin and Pine Nut Sauce for Game*)

This gastrique-based sauce is finished with both white and dark raisins and toasted pine nuts. Traditionally it is served with game. Although this delicious sauce is undeservedly ignored today, it is an excellent model for fruit-flavored brown sauces.

CLASSIC METHOD. Add 1 tablespoon (15 milliliters) gastrique to 1¼ cups (300 milliliters) demi-glace and 5 fluid ounces (150 milliliters) game stock. Reduce the sauce by one-fourth or until syrupy, and strain it through a fine chinois. Finish with 1 tablespoon (15 milliliters) dark raisins, plumped, and 1 tablespoon (15 milliliters) white raisins, plumped. (Soak each type of raisin in 1 tablespoon [15 milliliters] warm water for 20 minutes to plump and soften them before adding to the sauce.) Lightly toast 1 tablespoon (15 milliliters) pine nuts in the oven and add them to the sauce. Yield: 1½ cups (375 milliliters)

GLACE DE VIANDE METHOD. Soak 2 tablespoons (30 milliliters) each white and dark raisins in ¼ cup (60 milliliters) port. Heat the mixture on the stove for 5 minutes to soften the raisins—do not let it boil. Add 5 fluid ounces (150 milliliters) game or other brown stock to the port-raisin base. Instead of adding demi-glace, add ¼ cup (60 milliliters) glace de viande (page 97) and 2 teaspoons (10 milliliters) gastrique (page 193). Reduce the sauce slightly, until it has a lightly syrupy consistency. Finish it by whisking in 2 ounces (60 grams) butter and 2 tablespoons (30 milliliters) toasted pine nuts. Yield: 1 cup (250 milliliters)

UNTHICKENED METHOD. Soak 2 tablespoons (30 milliliters) each white and dark raisins in ¼ cup (60 milliliters) port. Heat the mixture on the stove for 5 minutes to soften the raisins—do not let it boil. Add ¼ cup (60 milliliters) concentrated (four to six times) brown stock to the port-raisin base. Flavor the sauce with 2 teaspoons (10 milliliters) gastrique, and finish with 2 tablespoons (30 milliliters) toasted pine nuts. Yield: 1 cup (250 milliliters)

Barbecue Sauces

Sauces basted on meats and fish during barbecuing are unique because they end up being scented with smoke. By stoking the fire with wood chips or sawdust, there is a constant source of smoke to flavor whatever is under the lid of the grill.

SWEET-AND-SOUR SAUCE FOR RIBS OR BRISKET

The basic flavors, sugar and vinegar, give this sauce a sweet-and-sour tang, while beer provides flavor and moisture. This sauce is very spicy. To make it more mild, eliminate one of the chipotle chiles, or eliminate both and substitute one finely minced jalapeño chile.

YIELD: 5 CUPS (1350 MILLILITERS), ENOUGH FOR 4 STRIPS RIBS OR 1 BRISKET

onion, minced	1 medium	1 medium
garlic cloves, minced	3	3
chipotle chiles, reconstituted dried or rinsed canned, chopped fine	2	2
cider vinegar	1 cup	250 milliliters
sugar	½ cup	100 grams
beer, 2 bottles	3 cups	750 milliliters
white wine	1 cup	250 milliliters
minced cilantro	2 tablespoons	60 milliliters

Combine all the ingredients in a saucepan and simmer gently for about 10 minutes to dissolve the sugar and cook the alcohol off the wine and beer. Use the mixture to brush on barbecuing ribs or brisket.

The Poivrade Family of Sauces

These deeply flavored sauces are prepared by moistening caramelized mirepoix with vinegar and the marinade used for red meats and game. The marinade itself is prepared with herbs, mirepoix vegetables, and white wine. Traditional recipes moisten this intensely flavored infusion with demi-glace. The sauces are then flavored by infusing cracked black pepper for 10 minutes before the sauce is strained. Pepper should never be cooked longer than that in the sauce or its delicate pine-like perfume will be lost—only a grating harshness will remain.

Nowadays many chefs feel that strong marinades distort the natural flavor of meats. For this reason, you may wish to prepare the marinade simply to use in the sauce. If you do not have marinade on hand, replace the amount called for in the recipe with white wine.

MARINADE FOR POIVRADE SAUCES
Finely slice 1 small onion (3 ounces/100 grams), half a medium carrot (3 ounces/100 grams), and 1 shallot (1 ounce/25 grams). Crush and peel 1 garlic clove. Cover the aromatic vegetables with 3 cups (750 milliliters) white wine and 1 cup (250 milliliters) white wine vinegar. Add 1 small handful of parsley stems, 2 or 3 sprigs of fresh thyme, half a

bay leaf, and 1 crushed clove. If the meat is to be marinated, add ½ cup (125 milliliters) extra-virgin olive oil. Store the marinade in a plastic or stainless-steel container (not aluminum, which will react with the acidity in the wine and vinegar) overnight in the refrigerator. Yield: 1 quart (1 liter)

SAUCE POIVRADE (PEPPER-FLAVORED GAME SAUCE)

CLASSIC METHOD. Coarsely chop 1 small onion (3 ounces/100 grams) and half a medium carrot (3 ounces/100 grams); you can also strain out the vegetables from the marinade and use those. Brown the vegetables in 1½ ounces (45 grams) butter with 1 pound (500 grams) trimmings from red meat or game. As the meat begins to brown, add 3 sprigs of fresh thyme, half a bay leaf, and 1 small handful of parsley stems. Cook the mixture for several minutes more. When the vegetables and meat trimmings are well browned, tilt the pan and drain off the butter.

Moisten the browned trimmings and vegetables with 5 fluid ounces (150 milliliters) white wine vinegar and 6 tablespoons (90 milliliters) white wine. Reduce the liquids until they evaporate completely, leaving a caramelized glaze on the bottom of the pan.

Add 2 cups (500 milliliters) demi-glace or concentrated brown stock (four to six times), 1 quart (1 liter) brown game, beef, or chicken stock, and 2 cups (500 milliliters) of the strained marinade or white wine. Bring the liquids slowly to a simmer and skim off any froth or scum that floats to the top. Reduce by half. Cover the pot and cook over a very low flame for 3 hours.

Skim off any fat or scum that has floated to the top of the sauce during simmering. Crush 10 whole peppercorns and add them to the hot sauce. Let them infuse for 10 minutes and then strain the mixture through a fine chinois into a fresh saucepan.

Add ½ cup (125 milliliters) strained marinade and ½ cup (125 milliliters) brown beef, game, or chicken stock to the strained sauce. Gently bring the sauce back to a simmer. Skim the sauce and reduce it until it has a lightly syrupy consistency. Strain through a fine chinois and finish with 2 ounces (60 grams) butter. Yield: approximately 2 cups (500 milliliters)

GLACE DE VIANDE METHOD. Follow the steps for the classic method, but replace the demi-glace with an appropriately flavored brown stock. During the last stage, when the sauce has been strained into a clean saucepan, dissolve 5 tablespoons (75 milliliters) glace de viande (page 97) in the reducing sauce. Finish the sauce with slightly more butter than is called for in the classic method (3 ounces/90 grams). Yield: 2 cups (500 milliliters)

UNTHICKENED METHOD. Prepare the sauce base in the same way as for the classic method: Brown the trimmings with the aromatic vegetables, deglaze with the vinegar and white wine, and reduce the liquids completely until they form a glaze on the bottom of the pan. Add 1 cup (250 milliliters) full-flavored brown stock to the pan and reduce a second time, until the liquids evaporate and caramelize on the bottom.

Moisten the mixture with 2 cups (500 milliliters) more stock and 1 cup (250 milliliters) marinade. Gently simmer the sauce for 30 minutes, skimming off any froth that floats to the surface. Add 10 crushed peppercorns to the sauce, and let them infuse for 10 minutes. Strain through cheesecloth. Yield: 2 cups (500 milliliters)

ALTERNATIVES AND VARIATIONS. If the sauce poivrade is being served with game, a teaspoon or two (5 to 10 milliliters) of good marc added near the end will give the sauce a pleasant gamy flavor. Adding 10 crushed juniper berries at the same time as the peppercorns or 1 teaspoon (5 milliliters) good gin will also contribute gamy nuances to the sauce. (Purists may argue that such a sauce is now a Moscovite, page 199, just without the raisins.) Unthickened versions can be presented as gels served on the bottom of the plate and, chopped, around the food.

SAUCE CHEVREUIL (RED WINE SAUCE FOR GAME)

Sauce Chevreuil (literally "deer sauce") is almost identical to Sauce Poivrade except that ½ cup (125 milliliters) red wine replaces the marinade during the final reduction. Classic recipes also suggest adding ham to the mirepoix and meat trimmings during caramelization of the flavor base.

SAUCE GRAND-VENEUR (CREAM-FINISHED SAUCE POIVRADE)

Sauce Grand-Veneur is a poivrade finished with cream and lightly sweetened with red currant jelly. It is delicious when served with game. To 2 cups (500 milliliters) sauce poivrade that has not been finished with butter, add 1 tablespoon (15 milliliters) red currant jelly and ½ cup (125 milliliters) of heavy cream. If necessary, the sauce can be lightly reduced. Yield: 2½ cups (625 milliliters)

SAUCE DIANE (WHIPPED CREAM AND TRUFFLE–FINISHED GAME SAUCE)

Sauce Diane is simply a sauce poivrade that is folded with whipped cream just before serving. It has a light, airy texture along with incredible depth of flavor. Classic authors call for truffle slices cut into crescent shapes (use a small cookie cutter) and cubes of hard-boiled egg white to be added at the end. The sauce is improved by eliminating the egg white. It is not essential to finish the sauce with truffles, though when used they will add a whole new dimension to the sauce. Cutting them into crescent shapes is a nineteenth-century affectation, and their flavor will certainly not suffer if they are julienned, sliced, or chopped. It is also possible to impart the flavor of truffles by whisking Truffle Butter (page 446) into the sauce before folding in the whipped cream, or by storing the sliced truffles overnight in the refrigerator in the cream to be whipped.

Make sure that the sauce poivrade is well reduced and quite thick before folding it with the whipped cream. Otherwise, the mixture will separate into a layer of runny sauce covered with a layer of whipped cream. Do not try to serve this sauce too hot, or the whipped cream will fall and the sauce will turn runny.

Combine 5 fluid ounces (150 milliliters) sauce poivrade (either classic or glace de viande based) with ¼ cup (60 milliliters) heavy cream that has been beaten until medium-stiff. Do not overbeat the cream, or it will leave tiny globules of fat on the surface of the finished sauce. Finish the sauce with 1 tablespoon (15 milliliters) chopped truffles. Yield: 1 cup (250 milliliters)

Keep in mind that truffle juice can be enclosed in spheres (see page 182), which can be used to garnish the sauce.

SAUCE MOSCOVITE (JUNIPER-INFUSED SAUCE POIVRADE)

This obscure poivrade-based sauce is flavored with juniper berries and Malaga, a fortified wine that is difficult to obtain in the United States. Other fortified wines, such as Madeira or port, can also be used. Juniper berries are excellent for reinforcing—even mimicking—the flavor of game. In classic recipes, the sauce is finished with white raisins and toasted almonds or pine nuts.

Add ½ cup (125 milliliters) Malaga wine and 10 crushed juniper berries to 2 cups (500 milliliters) sauce poivrade. Gently simmer the sauce for 15 to 20 minutes to reduce the wine and infuse the juniper. Strain through a fine chinois. Add 1 ounce (25 grams) white raisins, plumped, and 1 ounce (25 grams) toasted almonds or pine nuts. Yield: 2 cups (500 milliliters)

Other Vinegar-Based Sauces

SAUCE PIQUANTE

Sauce Piquante is most often used for grilled meats or pork. Sauces for grilled meats and pork (such as Robert and Charcutière) should always be fairly acidic, to cut through the richness of pork and the assertive, smoky flavor of barbecued and grilled meats. When preparing these sauces with glace de viande, be careful not to use too much butter in the end or the sauce will be too rich and its directness will be lost.

> **CLASSIC METHOD.** Combine 5 fluid ounces (150 milliliters) white wine and 5 fluid ounces (150 milliliters) white wine vinegar with 2 tablespoons (30 milliliters) finely chopped shallots. Reduce the mixture by half, and add 1¼ cups (300 milliliters) demi-glace. Simmer for 10 minutes more, being careful to skim off any scum that floats to the surface. Remove the saucepan from the heat and add 1 tablespoon (15 milliliters) sliced cornichons (sour gherkins) and 1 teaspoon (5 milliliters) each chopped parsley, chervil, and tarragon. Yield: 2 cups (500 milliliters)

> **GLACE DE VIANDE METHOD.** Follow the procedure for the classic method, but add 3 tablespoons (45 milliliters) glace de viande (page 97) to the white wine–vinegar reduction instead of the demi-glace. Finish with the chopped herbs, a tablespoon or two (15 to 30 milliliters) of coarsely chopped cornichons, and 1 ounce (30 grams) butter. Yield: 2 cups (500 milliliters)

> **UNTHICKENED METHOD.** Combine the white wine, vinegar, and shallots as for the classic method, but reduce the infusion by three-quarters instead of by half. Add 1¼ cups (300 milliliters) full-bodied brown stock to the reduction, and simmer the mixture slowly for 20 minutes. Strain through a fine chinois. Finish with a tablespoon or two (15 to 30 milliliters) of coarsely chopped (or julienned) cornichons and a pinch each of chopped parsley, chervil, and chives. Yield: 1 cup (250 milliliters)

There are two types of sauce zingara. Zingara A, based on a very acidic reduction of vinegar and shallots, is one of the few breadcrumb-thickened sauces that survive in the classic repertoire. (Zingara B, page 181, is based on white wine.)

Combine ½ cup (125 milliliters) white wine vinegar with 1 tablespoon (15 milliliters) finely chopped shallots. Infuse the flavor of the shallots in the vinegar by reducing by half. While the vinegar is reducing, gently cook 3 ounces (75 grams) breadcrumbs in 2 ounces (60 grams) butter. Cook the breadcrumbs until they begin to smell toasty, but do not let them brown. Add ¾ cup (185 milliliters) brown chicken or beef stock to the vinegar reduction, then add the breadcrumbs. Simmer the sauce for 5 to 10 minutes. Finish the sauce with 1 tablespoon (15 milliliters) finely chopped parsley. (Some recipes suggest finishing the sauce with lemon juice, but taste the sauce first; it is probably already acidic enough.) Yield: 1 cup (250 milliliters)

DERIVATIVE BROWN SAUCES WITHOUT WINE OR VINEGAR

Most derivative brown sauces are prepared by infusing flavorful ingredients, such as mirepoix, shallots, ham, or onions, in wine or vinegar. For delicately flavored sauces, the acidity of wine and vinegar can be troublesome. This is especially true of sauces containing truffles or mushrooms. And sauces that contain other acidic ingredients such as tomatoes or sorrel do not usually benefit from the additional acid derived from wine and vinegar.

Sauce Périgueux and Sauce Périgourdine

Both of these sauces are traditionally prepared by adding truffle essence to demi-glace. The only difference between the two is that périgueux sauce is finished with chopped truffles whereas périgourdine sauce is finished with truffles turned in miniature olive shapes or with whole truffle slices. If you are using whole truffles, it is certainly far more dramatic to slice them than it is to chop them. If you have a Japanese mandoline (see page 31), a single truffle will supply fifty to sixty slices. Both of these sauces will benefit by finishing with Truffle Butter (page 446).

Truffle Essence (page 101) is used in these sauces to reinforce the flavor of the truffles. If none is available, it can be replaced with a full-bodied brown stock.

CLASSIC METHOD. Bring 1½ cups (375 milliliters) demi-glace to a slow simmer. Skim off any froth that rises to the surface. Add 5 tablespoons (75 milliliters) truffle juice and 2 ounces (50 grams) chopped or sliced truffles. Remove the saucepan from the stove and cover with a tight-fitting lid, allowing the truffles to infuse into the sauce for at least 5 minutes. Yield: 2 cups (500 milliliters)

GLACE DE VIANDE METHOD. Bring 5 tablespoons (75 milliliters) of appropriately flavored brown stock (that is, beef stock for beef, duck stock for duck, and so forth) to a slow simmer. Skim off any froth that rises to the top and add 5 tablespoons (75 milliliters) truffle juice and 3 tablespoons (45 milliliters) glace de viande (page 97). As soon as the glace de viande dissolves in the hot stock, whisk in 2 ounces (50 grams) butter or truffle butter (page 446), and add 2 ounces (50 grams) chopped or sliced truffles. Cover the saucepan and put the sauce back on the stove just long enough for it to come to a simmer and gain a sheen. Remove the pan from direct heat (the sauce should not boil). Let the truffles infuse for at least 10 minutes in the covered saucepan before serving. Yield: 1 cup (250 milliliters)

UNTHICKENED METHOD. A consommé-like version of Sauce Périgourdine looks striking when served on a deep white plate or wide bowl. The easiest way to prepare an unbound version is to simply infuse truffle slices into a deeply flavored beef or appropriately flavored clear brown stock for 10 minutes over low heat.

TOURNEDOS ROSSINI
FILETS OF BEEF WITH SAUCE PÉRIGUEUX

A tournedo is a perfect center-cut filet mignon from the tenderloin. Tournedos should always have the chain muscle that runs along one side of the filet removed. The classic Rossini garniture consists of a slice of terrine of foie gras and Sauce Périgueux made with chopped and sliced truffles. Terrine of foie gras is used rather than raw foie gras because it contains less water and holds up better when it is heated.

YIELD: 4 SERVINGS

center-cut filets mignons, chain muscle removed, 6 ounces (175 grams) each	4	4
salt and pepper	to taste	to taste
clarified butter or vegetable oil	2 tablespoons	30 milliliters
foie gras terrine slices, 2 ounces (60 grams) each, warmed in a low oven	4	4
sauce périgueux (page 200)	¾ cup	185 milliliters

1. Season the tournedos with salt and pepper and allow them to come to room temperature.

2. In a 2-quart (2 liter) straight-sided sauté pan, sauté the tournedos in the butter or oil on both sides to the desired doneness, preferably rare.

Pat off the cooking fat with paper towels and place on heated plates.

3. Place a slice of warm foie gras terrine on each tournedo. Pour the sauce over and serve.

Sauce aux Champignons (*Mushroom Sauce*)

Mushroom Sauce is simply a combination of reduced mushroom essence and demi-glace or glace de viande and butter.

CLASSIC METHOD. Reduce 5 fluid ounces (150 milliliters) mushroom essence (page 100) by half. Add 1¾ cups (450 milliliters) demi-glace to the reduction. Bring the mixture to a simmer and skim off any froth that rises to the surface. Strain through a fine chinois and whisk in 1 ounce (30 grams) butter. Finish with 2 ounces (60 grams) button mushrooms that have been simmered in a covered saucepan in ¼ cup (60 milliliters) water or light stock and drained. The cooking liquid from the mushrooms can be used to supply or augment the mushroom essence. Yield: 2 cups (500 milliliters)

GLACE DE VIANDE METHOD. Add ¼ cup (60 milliliters) glace de viande (page 97) to 5 fluid ounces (150 milliliters) mushroom essence (page 100). Gently simmer the mixture long enough for the glace de viande to dissolve. Finish with 2 ounces (60 grams) butter and 1 ounce (30 grams) button mushrooms, cooked. Yield: 1 cup (250 milliliters)

UNTHICKENED METHOD. Full-flavored brown stock can be infused with mushrooms by bringing equal parts mushrooms and stock by weight to a simmer and letting the mixture infuse for 10 minutes in a covered pot. That is, use ½ pound (250 grams) mushrooms per cup (250 milliliters) stock.

ALTERNATIVES AND VARIATIONS. This sauce can be used as a model for sauces based on a wide variety of wild mushrooms. The mushrooms are first cooked in a small amount of water or stock, which then becomes the basis for the sauce. The cooked mushrooms are reserved and added at the end. Although the foregoing recipes call for whole button mushrooms, leaving the mushrooms whole is impractical with large wild mushrooms such as *Boletus edulis* (cèpes/porcini). It is, of course, acceptable to slice or cube the mushrooms.

The flavor of mushrooms can be made more assertive by first sautéing them in hot olive oil, goose fat, or butter until they brown. Some recipes call for sprinkling the mushrooms with chopped shallots, chopped garlic, or persillade.

Sauce Italienne

This sauce is almost identical to Sauce Duxelles (page 179) except that traditionally Sauce Italienne contains ham.

CLASSIC METHOD. Add 5 tablespoons (75 milliliters) tomato purée to 1½ cups (375 milliliters) demi-glace. Simmer the sauce gently for 10 minutes. Skim off any scum or froth that floats to the surface. Add 2 tablespoons (30 milliliters) duxelles and 2 ounces (50 grams) ham cut into small cubes (brunoise). Finish the sauce with 1 teaspoon (5 milliliters) each chopped parsley, chervil, and tarragon. Yield: 2 cups (500 milliliters)

GLACE DE VIANDE METHOD. Combine 5 fluid ounces (150 milliliters) brown chicken or beef stock with ¼ cup (60 milliliters) tomato purée. Dissolve ¼ cup (60 milliliters) glace de viande (page 97) into the mixture. Finish the sauce with 1 tablespoon (15 milliliters) duxelles, 1 ounce (25 grams) ham cut into cubes, 1 ounce (30 grams) butter, and 1 teaspoon (5 milliliters) each chopped parsley, chervil, and tarragon. Yield: 1½ cups (375 milliliters)

UNTHICKENED METHOD. Sauce Italienne can be reinterpreted by finishing a full-flavored brown stock with cubes of fresh tomatoes, a mushroom julienne or tiny chanterelles, and the cubes of ham and herbs called for in the classic sauce.

TIPS ON IMPROVING THE FLAVOR OF BROWN SAUCES

Using Meat Trimmings

In a well-organized kitchen, a brown sauce is always improved if meat is first sweated and its juices caramelized along with the aromatic vegetables used to prepare the flavor base. Early French recipes almost invariably called for lining the bottom of the pot with a slice of ham or veal as a preliminary step in sauce preparation.

Unsmoked cured ham (prosciutto) will also contribute enormously to the flavor and complexity of a sauce. Cut the ham (use the ends; they're cheaper) into cubes and sweat it along with the aromatic vegetables used to make the flavor base.

Virtually all brown sauces are based on reduced stock that provides a meaty flavor and sauce-like consistency from the gelatin in the reduced stock. But many of meat's most direct and vital flavors are cooked off during the long simmering of the stock. To restore these flavors, follow the same principles as when making a jus: Augment the meat flavors with caramelized meat juices. For example, if you're making a filet with a Bordelaise sauce and the sauce calls for glace de viande, try cooking some meat trimmings in a little butter with a little onion until the trimmings brown. Add some stock or sauce, 1 cup (250 milliliters) or so, and boil it down until it caramelizes on the bottom of the pan. Deglaze with another cup (250 milliliters) stock and repeat as many times as you wish or can afford. Add the final deglazing to your sauce and reduce to the desired consistency. Or add glace de viande before adding any enrichment such as butter.

Successive Caramelization

The majority of classic brown sauce recipes combine raw or gently sweated aromatic vegetables with wine or stock before adding demi-glace. The flavor of these sauces can be greatly improved if the aromatic vegetables are cooked long enough with meat trimmings or ham so that their juices fall to the bottom of the saucepan and lightly caramelize. This process can be repeated by moistening the ingredients with stock, wine, or water and reducing the liquid until it forms a glaze and caramelizes a second or third time on the bottom of the pot. When the vegetables and meats used for the sauce base have been caramelized in this way, they are ready for the final moistening with demi-glace. After the final moistening, the glazed vegetables and meat trimmings should not be simmered for more than 45 minutes, or the deep, meaty flavor brought out by successive caramelization will be lost. In classic French sauce making, this technique is called *faire tomber à glace* (literally, "to cause to fall to a glaze").

This procedure is time-consuming because the pot has to be closely watched so the juices do not overreduce and burn, but the technique will give a fresh, jus-like character to the sauce.

Increasing Acidity

Long-simmered brown sauces, even when carefully prepared with the best ingredients, often taste flat, usually because during the long reduction, the volatile flavor components in the meats, herbs, and vegetables have been cooked off. A small amount of good-quality wine vinegar (anywhere from a few drops to a few teaspoons per cup/250 milliliters sauce) added to the sauce near the end will awaken the flavor.

Reducing Acidity

Even experienced professional chefs are perplexed about correcting a sauce that has become too acidic as a result of using a poorly chosen wine for cooking or because of the reduction of acidic ingredients such as tomatoes. The obvious solution is to add sugar. Some sauces, such as long-simmered tomato sauces, benefit from a little sugar, which when used carefully will compensate for the lack of natural sugar that would have been present if the tomatoes were ripe.

In brown sauces, sugar rarely melds successfully with the other flavors and often tastes out of place even when used discreetly. For this reason, chefs usually prefer to introduce sweetness into a sauce by adding a small amount of fortified wine such as port or Madeira.

Although sweetness seems the obvious counterbalance to excess acidity in a sauce, there are instances when a particular kind of tartness refuses to be attenuated or balanced by sweetness alone. Although it sounds like a contradiction, a sauce's tartness is often softened and brought into perspective by adding vinegar. The best method for dealing with stubborn, excess acidity is to work with the sauce before the addition of butter so that, if necessary, its consistency can be adjusted by reduction. By continuously increasing a sweet element and a sour one, the inner tension of the sauce is increased and the flavor made more dynamic. Add a small amount of port and reduce the sauce slightly to evaporate the alcohol. Keep doing this bit by bit until the sweetness begins to be barely perceptible. Then add a small amount of wine vinegar, just enough so that you can no longer taste the sweetness of the port. Add a bit more port, then a bit more vinegar. Keep repeating this process, going back and forth between port and vinegar, until the sauce's acidity is in balance with the other flavors.

Adding Cognac, Armagnac, or Kirsch

A teaspoon or two (5 to 10 milliliters) of Cognac or Armagnac added to 1 cup (250 milliliters) sauce at the very end of cooking will give complexity and depth to a sauce's flavor. Once the Cognac or Armagnac has been added, a sauce should be held at a simmer for 10 to 15 seconds to evaporate the alcohol.

Kirsch is particularly useful for bringing out the natural fruitiness of red wine– and fortified wine–based sauces. Use only a few drops at a time, tasting all the while. Be careful in your choice of Kirsch (see "Fruit Brandies," page 66).

Using Gastrique

The use of gastrique has traditionally been limited to specific sweet-and-sour sauces, which nowadays are most often served with duck. The delicate balance of bitterness, tartness, and sweetness characteristic of a carefully prepared gastrique will often enhance a variety of other brown sauces as well.

Finishing with Fresh Herbs

As noted previously, sauces that have been greatly reduced or cooked for long periods will often end up tasting flat. A small bouquet garni containing a sprig of thyme, a piece of bay leaf, and a small bunch of parsley can be simmered with the reduced stock for about an hour before the stock is strained and added to the sauce's flavor base. The aromatic flavor of the herbs will help restore the stock's flavor.

A quick way of refreshing the flavor of almost any sauce is to finish it with freshly chopped parsley, chervil, or chives. None of these herbs will overpower the sauce, either when used alone or in a fines herbes mixture without tarragon.

IMPROVISING BROWN SAUCES

When preparing a classic French sauce, the skillful saucier constantly adjusts the sauce's flavor, consistency, and color. Several brown sauce methods have been presented in this chapter, including classic demi-glace, glace de viande, and unbound versions. Experienced sauciers rarely adhere to one method alone when constructing a sauce and will usually prepare a sauce using a combination of methods, sometimes inventing and improvising as they go along.

As an example, consider a sauce hussarde. The flavor base is prepared by gently sweating onions and shallots in butter and then adding white wine, which is reduced by half. If, at this point, the chef has on hand a full-flavored brown stock but no demi-glace, he or she could add flour to the sweating onion-shallot mixture to ensure that the sauce quickly develops a lightly thickened consistency. If the chef wants to avoid flour, and if time and budget permit, he or she may decide to reduce the brown stock until it has the consistency of a demi-glace. Or he or she might decide, after adding the stock, to thicken the sauce with a little starch such as arrowroot, combined first with cold water, or with a hydrocolloid or two, blended in while hot or cold, depending on the hydrocolloid(s).

A chef may use any number of hydrocolloid thickeners—xanthan gum and Ultra-Sperse 3 come to mind—as well as emulsifiers such as lecithin (which can be worked into cold butter or dissolved in hot) or propylene glycol alginate (blended into the liquid base). Each of these ingredients is helpful for keeping butter sauces emulsified during a long service when they are not made to order.

If demi-glace is on hand, the chef may decide to combine techniques and use demi-glace along with a full-flavored brown stock or jus and then adjust the consistency of the sauce with glace de viande. He or she may then decide to finish the sauce with butter or cream or thicken it with hydrocolloids or stabilize it with modernist emulsifiers such as lecithin. Or the chef may decide to keep the sauce unbound except for a small amount of butter added at the end. (Keep in mind that unless such sauces are served immediately, they risk breaking and should be stabilized.) The saucier's ability to shift among techniques and methods allows the creation of the best possible sauce given the limits of time, cost, and clientele.

When the chef wants to design a sauce to accompany meats, he or she must first decide whether the purpose of the sauce is to concentrate and extend the natural flavors of the meat or to function as a condiment or accent. If the sauce's role is to concentrate or extend, the chef should combine classic brown sauce techniques with integral sauce methods (see Chapter 9, "Integral Meat Sauces") and should take care that flavor elements used to finish the sauce do not mask the meat's natural flavors. If, however, the primary function of the sauce is to accent and juxtapose with the flavors of the meat, then all the saucier must consider is how the sauce will be presented (which will help decide its texture) and what its flavor will be.

While the methods for constructing a sauce can be categorized and illustrated using classic French sauces as examples, the final choice of how to flavor a sauce will depend on whim, setting, availability of ingredients, and a variety of circumstances. The ethnic or regional character of the food will usually provide a set of ingredients for the saucier to use as a source of flavor ideas. For example, in a restaurant serving Mexican food, the chef may decide to use a purée of tomatillos instead of tomato purée, or to sweat garlic and chiles instead of shallots for the flavor base. Instead of using parsley and chervil to finish the sauce, he or she may choose cilantro. In a restaurant serving Thai food, the saucier might replace the vinegar called for in a flavor base with tamarind, and finish the sauce with coconut cream instead of butter. (Coconut cream, when added in this way, is best emulsified into the sauce with lecithin, Glice, or polysorbate 80. The relatively thin milky part of the coconut milk can be stabilized with propylene glycol alginate.)

Sometimes the chef will want to design a sauce around a special ingredient, perhaps a newly found, locally grown herb, a basket of fresh morels, or a particularly fat and stinky truffle. The emphasis is then on how best to extract and concentrate the ingredient's individual flavor. In a sense, the meat then becomes the backdrop for the sauce.

Because of their potential for subtlety, brown sauces are usually enhanced when served with wine. At times a chef will need to design sauces around a menu highlighting a special bottle or type of wine. This task is often very difficult. Many chefs mistakenly assume that the sauce should share as many flavors with the wine as possible, whereas, in fact, a wine's nuances are better showcased when they contrast gently with but are not overpowered by the flavors of food. Considering the origin of the wine will be helpful in deciding on appropriate flavors for the sauce.

PORTERHOUSE WITH IMPROVISED RED WINE AND MUSHROOM SAUCE

ere is an example of a sauce made by first sautéing meat—any steak cut will work for this—and then deglazing the pan with shallots (which are allowed to toast a few seconds) and red wine. Glace de viande is added and the sauce finished with parsley.

YIELD: 2 SERVINGS

porterhouse, 1	about 2 pounds	1 kilogram
salt and pepper	to taste	to taste
clarified butter or oil	2 tablespoons	30 milliliters
shallot, 1 small, minced	2 ounces	50 grams
red wine	¾ cup	180 milliliters
glace de viande (page 97)	2 tablespoons	60 milliliters
brown beef stock (page 89; optional)	as needed	as needed
butter	2 to 3 tablespoons	30 to 45 grams
finely chopped parsley	1 tablespoon	15 milliliters
mushrooms, quartered or sliced	6 ounces	175 grams

(continued)

1. Season the porterhouse with salt and pepper and sauté it in very hot butter or oil. (A, B) When sautéed to the desired degree, remove the porterhouse and let it rest, lightly covered with foil.

2. Pour the fat out of the pan and stir in the shallots. (C) Sauté until any liquid released caramelizes on the bottom of the pan. Add the wine (D) and glace de viande (E) and adjust the consistency by reducing or thinning with stock. Be sure to simmer long enough to cook off the alcohol in the wine.

3. Whisk in the butter (F) and then the parsley (G). Carve the steak (H) and serve with the sauce and mushrooms.

Note: Remember when carving a porterhouse that the steak contains two muscles that form a cross section, one small round and one larger and vaguely elliptical. These are the tenderloin (filet) and the shell steak if the bone is left attached or strip steak, if the bone is removed. When carving, you want to make sure that each guest gets a little of each muscle. To this end, carve along both sides of the T-bone so you can remove each of the muscles and carve them separately.

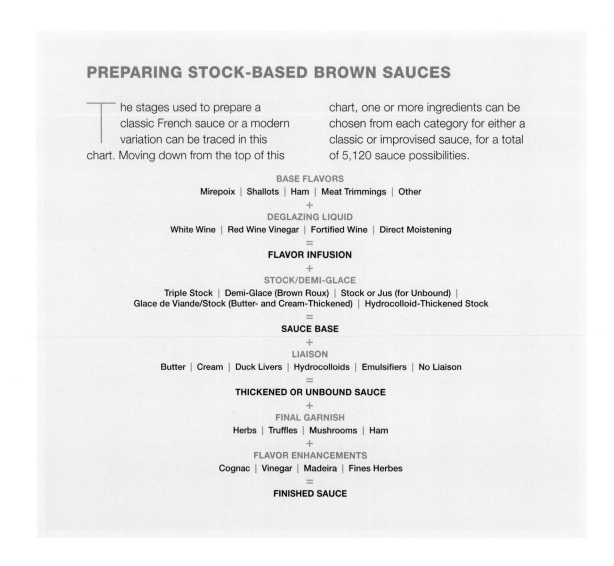

PREPARING STOCK-BASED BROWN SAUCES

The stages used to prepare a classic French sauce or a modern variation can be traced in this chart. Moving down from the top of this chart, one or more ingredients can be chosen from each category for either a classic or improvised sauce, for a total of 5,120 sauce possibilities.

BASE FLAVORS
Mirepoix | Shallots | Ham | Meat Trimmings | Other
+
DEGLAZING LIQUID
White Wine | Red Wine Vinegar | Fortified Wine | Direct Moistening
=
FLAVOR INFUSION
+
STOCK/DEMI-GLACE
Triple Stock | Demi-Glace (Brown Roux) | Stock or Jus (for Unbound) |
Glace de Viande/Stock (Butter- and Cream-Thickened) | Hydrocolloid-Thickened Stock
=
SAUCE BASE
+
LIAISON
Butter | Cream | Duck Livers | Hydrocolloids | Emulsifiers | No Liaison
=
THICKENED OR UNBOUND SAUCE
+
FINAL GARNISH
Herbs | Truffles | Mushrooms | Ham
+
FLAVOR ENHANCEMENTS
Cognac | Vinegar | Madeira | Fines Herbes
=
FINISHED SAUCE

209

Troubleshooting Brown Sauces

PROBLEM	PROBABLE CAUSES	SOLUTION
Too thin; watery consistency and flavor	Stock too thin Insufficient reduction	Check stock method Reduce to correct consistency before finishing sauce Bind with starch or hydrocolloids Finish with emulsifiers (if butter emulsion has broken down)
Too thick; sticky when tasted	Overly reduced Too much glace de viande added Too much liaison	Thin with stock or wine if appropriate
Pale color	Vegetables and meats for stock insufficiently browned	Add vegetables caramelized with stock to sauce Infuse blackened onion halves in stock
Threatening to break	Overreduction Sitting too long	Continue to stir in small amounts of water to restore the sauce to its original consistency
Flat taste	Long cooking or reduction Lack of acidity	Add vinegar Add freshly chopped parsley, chives, or chervil Add fortified wines, gastrique, Cognac Successive caramelization of stock Add improvised jus made from meat trimmings
Too sweet	Too many vegetables used to prepare stock Too much fortified wine Excessive reduction	Add small amount of vinegar and Cognac
Too salty	Overly reduced stock (this is more common with stocks made with meat only)	Lengthen with butter, cream, or light stock; serve as sauce with thinner consistency
Too acidic	Improperly chosen cooking wine Wine reduced without stock or trimmings Too much vinegar added	Balance with fortified wine or gastrique and vinegar

Brown sauces were originally designed to streamline the organization of professional kitchens. A modern kitchen, where stocks and glazes are made as part of the daily routine, will always have on hand the necessary bases for preparing classic and improvised sauces. Because the sauce bases are prepared in advance, cooks are freed from last-minute preparations and reductions and can put together complicated, time-consuming sauces in a matter of minutes.

The advantages of having standard sauce bases on hand in the professional kitchen are obvious. Unfortunately, the long-simmered stocks and glazes of the classic French kitchen can sometimes detract from the character and individuality of different types of dishes. It is perhaps for this reason that home-cooked meals are often satisfying in a way that restaurant meals are not. Consequently, many contemporary chefs have at least partially abandoned many of the traditional techniques used in classic sauce making and kitchen organization and are instead preparing integral sauces to order, keeping little in reserve beyond some freshly made stocks.

Some restaurants may use only chicken stock as an all-purpose moistening and deglazing liquid for made-to-order sauces. It can be prepared in various versions—reduced, as a twice-moistened jus, and so on. Preparing glace de viande is time-consuming, but once the glaze is finished, it is easy to store and always useful for last-minute sauces.

STOCK-BASED AND NONINTEGRAL FISH SAUCES

The best fish sauces are integral sauces prepared using the methods in Chapter 10, in which a sauce is made at the same time as or immediately after the fish is cooked. In many restaurant or catering situations, however, it is impractical to prepare a sauce at the last minute. Over the centuries, chefs have designed sauce-making methods to deal with the constraints imposed when limited personnel are available to prepare dishes for a large number of people. The development of fish stock was the natural outcome of preparing integral-like sauces in advance. In one sense, stock-based sauces for fish are integral sauces made ahead of time with fish heads and bones.

In classic French cooking, fish sauces usually capture the flavor of the fish itself. For hundreds of years, fish velouté has been the basis for the majority of stock-based fish sauces. Traditional fish velouté is fish stock thickened with roux, then flavored with a variety of infusions, herbs, compound butters, cream, and wines, to produce the whole range of classic derivative fish sauces. Modern versions of fish velouté are thickened with thickeners other than flour or are not thickened at all.

Starting in the 1950s and '60s, roux-thickened sauces were gradually eliminated, the idea being that flour makes a sauce needlessly rich and detracts from its finesse and clear flavor. (Actually, the nouvelle cuisine sauces that replaced the old flour-thickened sauces are far richer.) Traditional fish velouté was replaced with sauces based on reduced fish stock (fish glaze, glace de poisson) and reduced cream, butter, or a combination of both. Egg yolk–thickened hollandaise-type sauces containing reduced fish stock, sabayon sauces, sauces thickened with vegetable purées, and allemande-type sauces (thickened with egg yolk like a crème anglaise but containing no flour) are other attempts to eliminate flour from the kitchen.

Most of the sauce-making methods that were developed during la nouvelle cuisine to replace the classic roux-thickened sauce techniques were designed to duplicate the thick consistency of the classic sauces. For this reason, many of these sauces can be extremely heavy and rich—most of the cream and butter is used not to improve the flavor of the sauce but to give it a supposedly appropriate texture and consistency.

Today, many of the butter- and cream-thickened sauces popular in the 1960s and '70s have given way to lighter, broth-like versions or versions, still with a light consistency, that have been thickened with modern hydrocolloids, emulsion stabilizers, and emulsifiers (such as the formula on page 216). These light but intensely flavored sauces were made possible by three innovations in the dining room: For the first time in centuries, food was plated in the kitchen instead of the dining room, giving chefs far greater latitude; deep plates with rims (*assiettes creuses*) hold a sauce almost like a soup; and sauce spoons (*cuillères à sauce*) enable the diner to sip the sauce without having to rely on the sauce clinging to the fish to get it from plate to mouth. Instead of serving the fish coated with a sauce, it is surrounded by the sauce, like a fish stew or even a soup. In addition, compounds only recently arrived in the kitchen allow the saucier to produce much the same effect as a cream-finished sauce with less cream and/or butter.

CLASSIC FRENCH FISH SAUCES

Although today's chefs have abandoned many of these classic sauces, the sauces still provide valuable models and flavor combinations. Most of these sauces begin with an infusion of flavor components, such as white wine, shallots, various herbs, and mushroom essence. Fish velouté is added to the infusion, and the sauce is then enriched with any number of elements, such as egg yolks, cream, butter, compound butters, and crustacean butters.

In nouvelle cuisine versions of these classics, the fish velouté is replaced with a much smaller quantity of fish glaze and the sauce finished with butter or cream.

Contemporary broth-textured versions of classic fish sauces use a small amount of freshly prepared fish stock, or may even replace the fish stock with a light vegetable stock (court-bouillon). At no point is the fish stock—if it is used—or the finished sauce reduced, the feeling being that reduced fish stock and fish sauces develop a strong, flat, fishy flavor. Contemporary fish sauces often include acidic elements such as vinegar, lemon or lime juice, or verjuice, which give them a brighter, more assertive flavor than their classic counterparts. Contemporary sauces and nouvelle cuisine interpretations of classic sauces need to be more intensely flavored than the traditional versions because in most cases, less of the sauce is served: 2 to 3 tablespoons (30 to 45 milliliters) is typical.

Classic French Fish Sauces

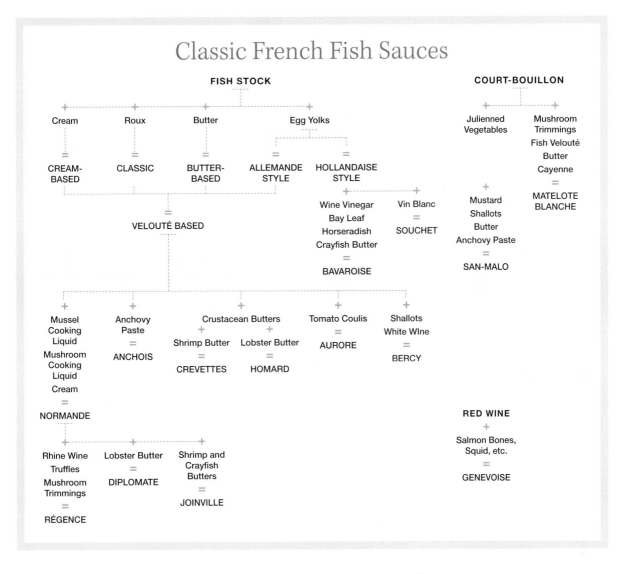

FISH STOCK

Cream — CREAM-BASED

Roux — CLASSIC

Butter — BUTTER-BASED

Egg Yolks — ALLEMANDE STYLE / HOLLANDAISE STYLE

CLASSIC → VELOUTÉ BASED

HOLLANDAISE STYLE + Wine Vinegar, Bay Leaf, Horseradish, Crayfish Butter = BAVAROISE

Vin Blanc = SOUCHET

COURT-BOUILLON

Julienned Vegetables

Mushroom Trimmings, Fish Velouté, Butter, Cayenne = MATELOTE BLANCHE

+ Mustard, Shallots, Butter, Anchovy Paste = SAN-MALO

VELOUTÉ BASED:

Mussel Cooking Liquid, Mushroom Cooking Liquid, Cream = NORMANDE

Anchovy Paste = ANCHOIS

Crustacean Butters + Shrimp Butter = CREVETTES / Lobster Butter = HOMARD

Tomato Coulis = AURORE

Shallots, White Wine = BERCY

NORMANDE:

Rhine Wine, Truffles, Mushroom Trimmings = RÉGENCE

Lobster Butter = DIPLOMATE

Shrimp and Crayfish Butters = JOINVILLE

RED WINE
+ Salmon Bones, Squid, etc. = GENEVOISE

CLASSIC FISH VELOUTÉ

YIELD: 1 QUART (1 LITER)

fish stock (page 93)	1½ quarts	1.5 liters
butter	1 ounce	30 grams
flour	3 tablespoons	15 grams

1. Bring the fish stock to a simmer in a 2-quart (2 liter) saucepan. Skim off any froth that floats to the surface.

2. Prepare a white roux with the butter and flour in a heavy-bottomed 2-quart (2 liter) saucepan over low heat. Cook for 5 to 10 minutes.

(continued)

3. Remove the roux from the heat and pour in the simmering fish stock. Whisk to dissolve the roux.

4. Return the mixture to the heat and allow it to come to a slow simmer. Make sure that the saucepan is placed slightly to one side of the flame; this encourages a film to form to one side of the sauce, where it can be more easily skimmed.

5. Skim the velouté for approximately 30 minutes, until it has reduced down to 1 quart (1 liter). Strain through a fine chinois. Stir the velouté while it is cooling to prevent a skin from forming on its surface.

MODERN FISH VELOUTÉ

While a classic fish velouté contains approximately 3 tablespoons (45 milliliters) roux per quart (liter), which gives it a distinct floury quality, a more modern velouté is made with less roux or no roux at all and can be thickened instead with a wide range of thickeners—in this version, Ultra-Sperse 3 (a modified starch) and lambda carrageenan. These modern thickeners give the sauce a more subtle quality than flour without adding their own tastes.

YIELD: 1 QUART (1 LITER)

fish stock (page 93)	1½ quarts	1.5 liters
ultra-sperse 3		30 grams
lambda carrageenan		2 grams

Reduce the fish stock by one-third, until 1 quart (1 liter) remains. Keep the saucepan to one side of the burner and skim off any froth and scum. Blend the Ultra-Sperse 3 and the lambda carrageenan into the hot fish stock with an immersion blender. Bring to a simmer. Strain through a fine chinois.

Sauce Normande

Sauce Normande is one of the most important of the classic fish sauces because it is full flavored, making it good as is as well as adaptable to variation. The classic version uses mussel cooking liquid, but other shellfish cooking liquids, such as those from clams or cockles (but not that from oysters), can be used with excellent results.

Because Sauce Normande contains so many of the elements of modern fish sauces, it is useful to examine the sauce in detail, with an eye to possible variations and modifications.

CLASSIC SAUCE NORMANDE

A classic sauce Normande is based on fish velouté to which mushroom cooking liquid, mussel cooking liquid, and additional fish stock are added, giving the sauce deeper flavor and more complex character. The sauce is finished with heavy cream (in the manner of Sauce Suprême, page 142), lemon juice, and egg yolks (in the manner of Sauce Allemande, page 142). Classic recipes call for reducing the sauce after the addition of the egg yolks (the idea being that the egg yolks are stabilized by the flour), but this is risky, as the yolks may curdle. A more reliable system is to complete reduction before adding the egg yolks, then gently cook the sauce—without boiling—just long enough for the egg yolks to contribute their characteristic satiny texture.

YIELD: 1 QUART (1 LITER)

fish velouté, classic or modern, (page 215 or 216)	3 cups	750 milliliters
mushroom cooking liquid (see page 100) *or* mushroom essence (see page 100)	½ cup *or* 2 tablespoons	125 milliliters *or* 30 milliliters
mussel cooking liquid	½ cup	125 milliliters
fish stock (page 93)	1 cup	250 milliliters
heavy cream	1½ cups	375 milliliters
egg yolks	5	5
lemon juice	2 tablespoons	30 milliliters
butter	4 ounces	125 grams
salt and pepper	to taste	to taste

(continued)

1. Combine the fish velouté, mushroom cooking liquid or essence, mussel cooking liquid, fish stock, and cream in a 2-quart (2 liter) saucepan and bring to a simmer.

2. Reduce the sauce by about one-third over medium to high heat, until it takes on the desired consistency of the finished sauce. (This is to ensure that no further reduction will be required once the egg yolks are incorporated; the sauce can always easily be thinned.)

3. Whisk 1 cup (250 milliliters) of the hot sauce into the egg yolks in a small mixing bowl. Stir this mixture into the rest of the sauce off the heat. Heat the sauce over low to medium heat, while stirring, until it thickens slightly and becomes satiny. Do not allow it to boil.

4. Stir the lemon juice and butter into the sauce and strain through a fine chinois. Season with salt and pepper.

VARIATIONS OF SAUCE NORMANDE

Although classic sauce Normande is rarely prepared in restaurants today, many contemporary fish sauces contain similar elements. Nouvelle cuisine fish sauces are normally based on fish velouté that has been thickened with reduced cream and/or finished with butter. Modern fish sauces contain no flour and use considerably less of the three classic rich liaisons—cream, butter, and egg yolks.

Some contemporary Normande-style sauces contain only a few of the traditional flavor elements. Mussel or clam cooking liquid finished with a small amount of heavy cream is in itself an excellent sauce, as is mushroom cooking liquid, especially if made with morels or other wild mushrooms.

When preparing a nouvelle cuisine sauce Normande, it is important to decide how the completed dish will be presented. If a thick sauce is needed to coat the fish or fish fillets, the basic flavor elements (fish stock, mussel cooking liquid, and mushroom cooking liquid) will have to be reduced until they are almost dry, and a relatively large amount of cream, butter, or some combination will be required to give the sauce the necessary consistency. Egg yolks, which are also rich, are sometimes but not always used as a final thickener. A fish sauce made in this way will have a smoother, more unctuous consistency than a traditional sauce Normande but will be extremely rich because its consistency is derived almost entirely from fats. A less dense sauce will require far less cream or butter and very little, if any, reduction.

CREAM-BASED SAUCE NORMANDE. Reduce 2 parts fish stock (1 cup/250 milliliters), 1 part mushroom cooking liquid (½ cup/125 milliliters), and 1 part mussel or clam cooking liquid (½ cup/125 milliliters) to the desired thickness. Add 4 parts (2 cups/500 milliliters) heavy cream and reduce again to the desired thickness. Finish with ¼ part (2 tablespoons/30 milliliters) butter. Season with salt and pepper.

BUTTER-BASED SAUCE NORMANDE. Reduce 2 parts fish velouté, 1 part clam or mussel cooking liquid, 1 part mushroom cooking liquid, and 1 part heavy cream until the mixture has the consistency you want for the finished sauce. Whisk in 2 parts butter. Season with salt and pepper.

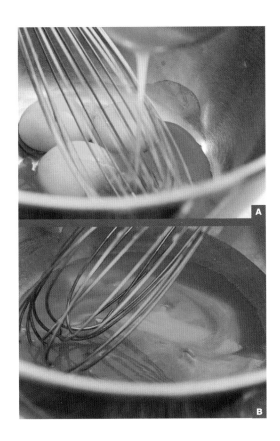

EGG YOLK–BASED SAUCE NORMANDE (CRÈME ANGLAISE METHOD). There are two approaches to preparing sauce Normande with egg yolks. The first is to combine the ingredients and cook gently over the stove, as when making a crème anglaise or sauce allemande, until the sauce thickens: Bring to a simmer 2 parts fish stock, 1 part mushroom cooking liquid, 1 part mussel or clam cooking liquid, and ½ part heavy cream. Whisk into 8 egg yolks per quart (liter) stock mixture **(A, B)**, return the mixture to the pan, and cook gently while stirring until the sauce thickens **(C)**. Whisk in ½ part butter or herb butter. **(D)** Season with salt and pepper.

EGG YOLK–BASED SAUCE NORMANDE (HOLLANDAISE METHOD). This approach is analogous to a sauce vin blanc made in the style of a hollandaise by reducing flavorful liquids (mushroom, mussel, white wine etc.) and whisking them up into a sabayon (see page 404) before whisking in clarified or whole butter (whole butter results in a looser sauce). Reduce 1 quart (1 liter) of a combination of fish stock, mushroom cooking liquid, and clam or mussel cooking liquid to ½ cup (125 milliliters). Whisk into a sabayon with 8 egg yolks and finish with 8 ounces (250 grams) clarified or whole butter. Season with salt and pepper.

When using egg yolks to thicken or stabilize sauces, it is best to stabilize the egg yolks by cooking them sous vide for 30 minutes at 140°F (60°C).

MODERN SAUCE NORMANDE

A modern sauce Normande is based on modern fish velouté, fish stock that has been thickened with hydrocolloids such as xanthan gum, guar gum, and/or lambda carrageenan. Cream is added to the sauce and it is thickened in the classic way, with egg yolks.

YIELD: 5 CUPS (1.25 LITERS)

modern fish velouté (page 216)	2 cups	500 milliliters
mussel or clam cooking liquid (see page 294)	1 cup	250 milliliters
mushroom cooking liquid (see page 100)	1 cup	250 milliliters
heavy cream	½ cup	125 milliliters
egg yolks (preferably stabilized; see page 219)	4	4
butter	4 ounces	125 grams
salt and pepper	to taste	to taste

Combine the velouté, mussel cooking liquid, mushroom cooking liquid, and cream and bring to a simmer. Whisk together the egg yolks and whisk in half the hot liquid. Whisk thoroughly and return to the stove over low heat. Stir until thickened in the manner of a crème anglaise. Whisk in the butter. Season with salt and pepper.

COMBINING METHODS

Each of the methods for flavoring and thickening fish sauces has certain disadvantages. Cream and butter sauces are rich and expensive to prepare, egg yolk–thickened sauces sometimes have an eggy taste or a chalky texture, and flour-thickened sauces often taste starchy. Modern versions, if made with too much of certain hydrocolloids or emulsifiers, can have a slimy or mucilaginous finish. To avoid this, start by adding small amounts of these substances—even a little less than called for in the recipe—and building up, tasting all the while. It is also very helpful to combine different thickeners and emulsifiers so that no particular one dominates. You may want to include traditional thickeners such as cream, egg yolks, and butter in at least small amounts so that they lend their natural characteristics to the sauce.

Preparing a successful fish sauce sometimes requires using several techniques. One method is to prepare a very light classic velouté with one-quarter as much roux as the classic recipe calls for, carefully reducing the velouté by half (skimming carefully and removing any skin that forms on its surface), and then finishing this lightly thickened base with cream, butter, egg yolks, or a combination of the three. Because of the consistency of the velouté base, it is possible to use much less of these classic thickeners.

Derivatives of Fish Velouté and Sauce Normande

Many of the classic fish sauces are based on either fish velouté or sauce Normande. Most of these variations are prepared by making an infusion of basic flavors, adding fish velouté or sauce Normande as a sauce base and thickener, sometimes reducing the mixture (unless an egg yolk–thickened version is used), and then enriching it with cream, butter, or egg yolks or combinations of two or three.

These derivative sauces are often a simple matter of finishing a sauce Normande with additional flavorings.

SAUCE ANCHOIS is a sauce Normande finished with anchovy butter (page 442) and diced anchovy filets.

SAUCE AURORE is a velouté (fish or otherwise) finished with reduced tomato purée; one part tomato purée to three parts fish velouté is traditional.

SAUCE BERCY is based on a reduction of white wine, shallots, and fish velouté; the reduction is finished with butter and parsley.

SAUCE MATELOTE BLANCHE is prepared by combining reduced court-bouillon with fish velouté (either modern or classic) and then flavoring the mixture with mushroom trimmings. It is in some ways a precursor of contemporary sauces because of its use of court-bouillon. Many contemporary chefs replace fish stock entirely with court-bouillon. The sauce is finished with butter and cayenne pepper.

SAUCE RÉGENCE FOR FISH is prepared by adding reduced Rhine wine (which lends a subtle sweetness) and fish stock to a sauce normande and infusing the sauce with mushrooms and truffles. A somewhat more practical approach, since mushrooms release a lot of liquid, is to use mushroom cooking liquid or essence instead. Or, for truffles, store the truffles overnight with a stick of butter and then use the resulting truffle-scented butter (see page 446) to finish the sauce.

Hollandaise-Style Fish Sauces (*Sauces Vin Blanc*)

SAUCE VIN BLANC (WHITE WINE FISH SAUCE)
Classic white wine fish sauce is prepared using one of two methods, both of which use egg yolks. The first method is based on a sabayon prepared with reduced fish stock and egg yolks, then finished with butter in the same way as a sauce hollandaise. The second method consists of finishing fish velouté with egg yolks and butter as in preparing a sauce allemande.

SAUCE VIN BLANC (HOLLANDAISE METHOD). Reduce 1 cup (250 milliliters) fish stock (which includes the white wine; page 93) by two-thirds. Let the reduction cool and combine it with 5 egg yolks. Whisk the mixture over the heat until it becomes airy and thickens. Finish with butter in the same way as preparing Sauce Hollandaise (page 398). Classic recipes call for almost 4 ounces (125 grams) butter per egg yolk, but the sauce can be made lighter by using half as much. Yield: 2 to 3½ cups (500 to 875 milliliters), depending on the amount of butter used

SAUCE VIN BLANC (ALLEMANDE METHOD). Finish 3 cups (750 milliliters) modern or classic fish velouté with 4 egg yolks and 4 ounces (125 grams) butter, or prepare a nouvelle cuisine flourless version by finishing 3 cups (750 milliliters) fish stock with 8 egg yolks and 4 ounces (125 grams) butter. The sauce should first be thickened with the egg yolks, with the butter whisked in at the end. Remember, do not let the sauce boil. Yield: 3½ cups (875 milliliters)

SAUCE VIN BLANC VARIATIONS

The two best-known classic variations are Sauce Saint-Malo, which is Sauce Vin Blanc (Hollandaise Method) finished with mustard, shallot butter, and anchovy paste; and Sauce Souchet, a very contemporary sauce based on court-bouillon. The elements in the court-bouillon are julienned and used to garnish the fish. The fish is poached in the court-bouillon and then the court-bouillon reduced before being used as the base for a classic Sauce Vin Blanc (Hollandaise Method).

Fish Sauces Flavored with Crustacean and Coral Butters

Crustacean butters are often used to finish fish sauces to give them additional complexity and an appealing red or orange hue. Many of the classic fish sauces that are finished with crustacean butter have a similar taste because it is hard to distinguish among the different butters. To capture the full complexity of a crustacean's flavor, it is essential to start with the whole living animal (see Chapter 11, "Crustacean Sauces"). The sauces listed below should be thought of as fish sauces nuanced with crustacean butters, rather than the full-flavored crustacean sauces that can be found in that chapter. A sauce can also be finished with coral or roe from scallops (provided it has clean, orange coloring) or sea urchins. Generally these ingredients are best worked with an equal amount of butter before being added to the sauce; this makes them less likely to curdle.

Classic approaches include Sauce Bavaroise, which is prepared like a hollandaise-style sauce vin blanc except that the reduction is made with wine vinegar, bay leaf, thyme, parsley, and grated horseradish. The sauce is finished with clarified butter, crustacean butter, and a small amount of whipped cream.

Other classic sauces are clearly derivative: Sauce Crevettes is Sauce Vin Blanc (either method) finished with shrimp butter or other crustacean butter.

When the shrimp butter is replaced with lobster butter, the sauce becomes Sauce Homard.

Sauce Diplomate is Sauce Normande finished with lobster butter and cubed truffles and lobster tails.

When made with shrimp and crayfish butters, it is known as Sauce Joinville.

Other classic variations call for crustacean butters made from crustacean flesh (rather than shells).

SEA URCHIN SAUCE

Sea urchin butter (about equal parts roe and butter by volume) gives a delicate, sea-like flavor to a variety of sauce bases. This sauce combines cream with fish velouté and has a very light, soup-like consistency. If a thicker sauce is needed, the shellfish cooking liquid should be reduced with half the cream before the egg yolk–roe mixture is incorporated. Sea urchin sauces are best served with delicate fish dishes such as poached sole, turbot, or other flat fish. Don't let the sauce get hotter than 158°F (70°C).

YIELD: 2 CUPS (500 MILLILITERS)

sea urchin roe	4 ounces	125 grams
butter	4 ounces	125 grams
fish velouté, modern or classic (page 216 or 215)	1½ cups	375 grams
heavy cream	½ cup	125 milliliters

1. Work the sea urchin roe with the butter through a drum sieve two times.

2. Bring the fish velouté to a simmer, add the cream, and reduce to the desired consistency.

3. Just before serving, whisk in the sea urchin butter.

SAUCES USING SCALLOP CORAL

Because most American scallops are marketed without the coral, there is little opportunity to use it in sauce making. If fresh scallops with the coral are available, the coral can be incorporated into a sauce. The most direct method is to purée the coral in a food processor (it's firmer than sea urchin roe and thus has to be pureed before straining), strain it through a drum sieve, and combine it with butter, heavy cream, or egg yolks (as for the Sea Urchin Sauce, page 223) before using it to finish a fish sauce base. Make sure the base is slightly thicker than you want the final sauce, especially if adding heavy cream, which will lighten the consistency. If you need the sauce to be particularly stable, work 1% liquid lecithin into the scallop butter (as a percentage of the butter, not the whole sauce) and blend 1% propylene glycol alginate (as a percentage of the liquid base) into the hot liquid base.

Red Wine Fish Sauces

Red wine sauces are excellent when served with full-flavored fish such as salmon, mackerel, squid, and tuna. Most recipes for fish sauces discourage using salmon bones for making fish stock because of their strong, sometimes aggressive flavor. Red wine sauces are an exception; a sauce made with a full-bodied red wine and salmon bones makes an assertive yet complex and subtle sauce.

The following recipe can also be prepared with squid. Replace the salmon bones with 2 pounds (1 kilogram) fresh squid that has been cleaned, well rinsed, and finely sliced.

Red wine fish sauces prepared in this way are similar to the classic Sauce Genevoise that was made with reduced fish stock bound with roux and finished with anchovy butter.

RED WINE SAUCE FOR SALMON

YIELD: 2 CUPS (500 MILLILITERS)

salmon head(s)	1 large or 2 or 3 small	
butter	1½ ounces	45 grams
carrot, coarsely chopped	1 medium	1 medium
onion, coarsely chopped	1 medium	1 medium
garlic cloves, coarsely chopped	3	3
red wine	5 cups	1.2 liters
medium bouquet garni (page 52)	1	1
butter (optional)	as needed	as needed
flour (optional)	as needed	as needed
red wine vinegar or sherry vinegar (or to taste)	1 tablespoon	15 milliliters
salt and pepper	to taste	to taste

1. Ideally, the salmon heads should be split in half. Given that this is difficult, it is best to have it done by the fish supplier. If you just have the whole heads, use them as described here. Remove the gills from the salmon head(s). Rinse with cold water, or, better, soak the head(s) in a bowl of cold water for a couple of hours or overnight (in the refrigerator), changing the water every hour or so.

2. Melt 1½ ounces (45 grams) butter in a saucepan and add the carrots, onions, garlic, and salmon head(s). (A) Add 1 cup (250 milliliters) of the red wine and stir over medium heat until the vegetables soften and a brown layer of caramelized juices begins to form on the bottom of the pan. This may take as long as 15 minutes. The salmon should completely fall apart (B) and the liquid should completely evaporate until it

(continued)

forms a caramelized layer on the bottom of the pan. There will also be plenty of fat, which can be spooned off, if practical. (C, page 225)

3. Deglaze the pan with the remaining red wine (D, page 225) and add the bouquet garni. Simmer the sauce gently, stirring occasionally, while scraping with a wooden spoon against the bottom of the pan. (E, page 225) After about 45 minutes, strain the sauce through a fine chinois into a 2-quart saucepan, using a rolling pin to force through the sauce. (F, G, page 225)

4. Place the saucepan on the heat, keeping it to one side of the heat source. Skim off any froth and scum. (H, page 225) Simmer until about 2 cups (500 milliliters) liquid remain, skimming until the sauce is free of fat.

5. You can either finish the sauce with butter alone (such a sauce will be more intense and richer, and there will be less of it) or finish it with beurre manié. If you want to finish the sauce with butter alone, reduce the liquid to ¾ cup (180 milliliters), or until it has the consistency you like, and then whisk in enough butter to get the right effect. You could also omit the butter; keep in mind, however, that the red wine sauce base can take on an acrid quality that is best softened with butter.

6. If finishing the sauce with beurre manié, work together about 1 ounce (30 grams) butter with 2 tablespoons (15 grams) flour. Whisk in 2 tablespoons (30 grams) of the beurre manié to start, bring to a boil, and judge the consistency. If you want the sauce thicker, add more beurre manié and return to a boil again to assess its thickening power.

7. Add the vinegar and season with salt and pepper.

RAÏTO

The Provençaux have their own methods of finishing red wine sauces; *Raïto* is one of the best known. The sauce is garnished in various ways—sometimes with olives, sometimes capers, and sometimes a combination of the two—but tomato purée is always used to thicken a full-flavored red wine base like the one described above. Walnuts are also occasionally used as an additional liaison. Fish served *en raïto* is usually lightly sautéed before being finished in the sauce.

To make Raïto, combine 1 cup (250 milliliters) of the reduction described for Red Wine Sauce for Salmon (page 224) with ½ cup (125 milliliters) of the very reduced tomato coulis shown on page 507. You can also reduce red wine by first boiling it down (A) and then thickening it with beurre manié (B) to the consistency you like. Add about the same amount of tomato coulis as the sauce base. (C) Reduce if needed to get the consistency you're looking for, and balance the amounts of wine reduction and tomato to your taste. Finish the sauce by adding 2 to 4 tablespoons (30 to 60 milliliters) capers, pitted black olives, or both. Although traditional recipes do not suggest it, mussel, cockle, or clam cooking liquid can be added to the red wine base (creating the need for a little further reduction). (D) The shellfish can then be used to surround the fish (in this case, tuna).

A

C

B

D

CONTEMPORARY FISH SAUCES

Today the best restaurants prepare either integral fish sauces or lightened versions that contain only a small amount of cream and butter—or even none at all. Although many of the ingredients and techniques called for in classic French fish sauces are still used by chefs, roux, large amounts of cream and butter, and even fish stock are giving way to more contemporary methods. Contemporary fish sauces differ from older versions in several important ways:

1. Fish stock and fish glaze have largely been replaced by court-bouillon or the cooking liquid from bivalves such as mussels, clams, or cockles. Many chefs feel that fish stock and especially fish glaze are too aggressive and fishy tasting.

2. The consistency of fish sauces is often much thinner than in the past. Contemporary sauces often have a consistency similar to unreduced heavy cream.

3. Much less sauce is given per serving. Today, a small amount of fish sauce is often served around the fish. Two to 3 tablespoons (30 to 45 milliliters) of sauce per serving is typical.

4. Vegetable purées such as tomato concassée, sorrel purée, and mushroom purée often constitute both the base and liaison of the sauce. They are sometimes combined with xanthan gum and Ultra-Sperse 3 to prevent syneresis (see page 298).

5. Sauces are more direct and intensely flavored than in the past. Because much less sauce is used, an intensely flavored sauce will not overwhelm the fish.

6. Acidic ingredients, such as lime juice, lemon juice, assorted vinegars, and most recently verjuice, are used in higher proportions.

7. Court-bouillon is no longer prepared using a single standard set of ingredients. Chefs are eager to emphasize the character of specific vegetables, such as fennel or leeks, and will often prepare a court-bouillon with only one or two ingredients. Some chefs are even experimenting with vegetable juices as sauce bases and flavorings.

8. Vinaigrette-like emulsions of oils and acidic ingredients are newly popular.

9. Combinations of already prepared sauces such as beurre blanc, hollandaise-type sauces, vinaigrettes, and vegetable purées are often combined with fish sauces at the last minute.

10. Spices are more widely used. Chefs are looking toward the cooking of India and the Far East as well as the European cooking of the Middle Ages to devise new flavor combinations.

11. Chefs are experimenting with thickeners such as hydrocolloids (see page 73). They are also using emulsifiers and emulsion stabilizers once relegated to industrial food production. Such emulsifiers allow the chef to build a hollandaise-style sauce vin blanc without egg yolks (the flavorful reduction is thickened with hydrocolloids instead) or to incorporate nonemulsified fatty liquids such as oils into an emulsion that would otherwise not hold them.

TOMATO-BASED VINAIGRETTE/HOLLANDAISE SAUCE FOR FISH

|n classic French cooking, a tomato sauce for fish would be based on fish velouté, which would then be flavored with tomato purée (see Sauce Aurore, page 148). In the following sauce, the tomato purée becomes the base of the sauce by contributing not only flavor but body. It also functions, along with modern emulsifiers such as liquid lecithin, as an emulsifier for vinegar and oil. This sauce can, when oil is used, be described as an elaborate vinaigrette. When hollandaise sauce replaces all or some of the oil called for in the recipe, the sauce veers from elaborate vinaigrette to an emulsified butter sauce.

This sauce can be modified by using different vegetable purées as the base, by altering the ingredients in the court-bouillon (or replacing the court-bouillon with shellfish cooking liquids), and by using emulsified or butter sauces other than hollandaise (sauces finished with crustacean and coral butters work well).

YIELD: 2 CUPS (500 MILLILITERS), ABOUT 10 SERVINGS

court-bouillon (page 366)	2 cups	500 milliliters
thick tomato coulis (page 507)	1 cup	250 milliliters
dijon mustard	2 teaspoons	10 milliliters
sherry vinegar	4 tablespoons	60 milliliters
xanthan gum		0.4 gram
extra-virgin olive oil or hollandaise sauce (page 398), or a combination	¾ cup	200 milliliters
mono- and diglycerides (glice) (optional)		2 grams
liquid lecithin (optional)		2 grams
salt and pepper	to taste	to taste

1. Reduce the court-bouillon to ½ cup (125 milliliters).

2. Use an immersion blender to blend together the tomato coulis, reduced court-bouillon, mustard, vinegar, and xanthan gum. This is the liquid base for the vinaigrette.

3. If using only olive oil, heat it to 140°F (60°C). Add the Glice and liquid lecithin. Stir until they dissolve. Immediately remove from the heat and let cool to room temperature.

4. Blend the olive oil into the tomato mixture in a steady stream as though making mayonnaise. If you're using hollandaise, simply fold the base and hollandaise together. If you're using both oil and hollandaise, stir in the hollandaise first (being an emulsion, it helps stabilize the sauce), and then work the oil into the sauce in a steady stream.

5. Season with salt and pepper.

VINAIGRETTE- AND COURT-BOUILLON–BASED CHIVE SAUCE

This sauce is based on court-bouillon that is lightly thickened with butter, acidulated with vinaigrette, and flavored at the end with chives. The flavor of the sauce can be varied by modifying the court-bouillon and the components in the vinaigrette. The chives may be replaced or augmented with other herbs or spices.

Because vinaigrette in itself is unstable, you will attain better results using the stabilized vinaigrette on page 479. If you've not stabilized the vinaigrette, the court-bouillon, emulsified butter, and the vinaigrette itself should be combined at the last minute.

YIELD: 1 CUP (250 MILLILITERS), ABOUT 8 SERVINGS

court-bouillon (page 366)	2 cups	500 milliliters
lemon juice	1 tablespoon	15 milliliters
water	2 tablespoons	30 milliliters
butter, in chunks	2 ounces	60 grams
stabilized vinaigrette (page 479) or basic vinaigrette (page 478)	¼ cup	60 milliliters
finely chopped chives	2 tablespoons	30 milliliters
salt and pepper	to taste	to taste

1. In a 2-quart (2 liter) saucepan, reduce the court-bouillon to 6 tablespoons (90 milliliters).

2. In a 1-quart (1 liter) saucepan, combine the lemon juice and water and bring the mixture to a simmer. Whisk in the butter. Keep this sauce warm.

3. Remove the reduced court-bouillon from the stove and whisk in the emulsified butter.

4. Whisk in the vinaigrette and the chives.

5. Season with salt and pepper and, if necessary, adjust the flavor by adding more vinaigrette. Serve immediately.

IMPROVISING FISH SAUCES

When improvising any sauce, it is always helpful to have the actual foods that are available within view. Foods that are fresh and in season are almost always inspiring. Some of the best ideas for new dishes or fresh interpretations of old dishes happen while shopping in a large market. Many chefs miss this opportunity because hectic schedules compel them to order food by telephone and have it delivered unseen.

Sometimes a single ingredient will be impossible to pass by because of its beauty, freshness, or rarity and will become the focal point of the sauce. As a rule, the more perfect or inspiring the ingredient, the simpler the preparation need be. Some example approaches follow.

Tomatoes

Perfectly ripe late-summer tomatoes can be lightly stewed into a soup-like base, which is then used as a simple sauce for fish. On those few occasions when perfect tomatoes can be found, little needs to be done to amplify or alter their flavor, but variations might include stewing them with the trimmings from the fish; augmenting their flavor with garlic, fennel, or onions; or finishing the sauce with mayonnaise (aïoli, saffron, or another full-flavored type), cream, butter (either directly or after the butter has first been worked into a beurre blanc–like emulsion), compound butters, or vinaigrettes. The tomato can also be cooked down to a thick sauce and used as the base for a vinaigrette. Tomato coulis- or concassée-thickened sauces may need to contain a small amount of xanthan gum and Ultra-Sperse 3 to prevent syneresis (see page 298).

A tomato sauce for fish can also be approached from the other direction, by preparing a sauce base such as a cream- or butter-based sauce aurore and then finishing it with tomato purée or other purées such as sorrel purée.

Mushrooms

The cooking liquid from mushrooms gives almost any sauce an ineffable finesse and is sometimes used in contemporary kitchens as a replacement for fish stock. When wild mushrooms are available, they can be used to give a deep, mysterious flavor to sauces. Their shapes also provide interesting contrasts for the presentation of the finished plate. Don't, however, use portobello mushrooms—they will turn your sauce a deep gray.

Depending on the types available, mushrooms can be gently stewed in a small amount of butter, water, or court-bouillon to provide a liquid sauce base; the stems can then be puréed and used as a liaison and to contribute flavor or serve as the base for a vinaigrette, while the caps can be used to garnish the plate.

Other Vegetables

1. Vegetables are stewed until almost dry, puréed, and strained to convert them into a coulis, and then worked into butter. This compound butter is then served with grilled fish.

2. Finely diced vegetables such as bell peppers are used to coat the surface of grilled or sautéed fish fillets. Diced or puréed vegetables are sometimes combined with other diced vegetables or vegetable purées, or lightly bound with other sauces, such as beurre blanc or vinaigrettes.

3. Vegetables are stewed until soft, moistened with court-bouillon, and worked through a drum sieve. This coulis is then converted into a sabayon, which can be served as is or finished with butter (plain, compound, or crustacean) or olive oil and flavored with herbs.

4. Reduced vegetable coulis can be used as the base for a hot vinaigrette.

5. Chopped and stewed vegetables can be used to flavor a mayonnaise. The mayonnaise can then be served as accompaniment to cold or deep-fried fish or whisked with hot fish stock or court-bouillon just before serving and used as a hot sauce.

6. Bell peppers can be grilled, peeled, and then infused in a small amount of court-bouillon; the infusion is then enriched with butter for a beurre blanc–style butter sauce.

INTEGRAL
MEAT SAUCES

Integral sauces are made from the natural juices released by meats, fish, and vegetables during cooking. The methods used to prepare these sauces depend on whether the food is sautéed, poached, braised, roasted, or grilled. A well-made integral sauce is an extract of a food's natural flavors and should capture and heighten the flavor of the food being prepared. Many contemporary chefs have at least partially abandoned some traditional stock-based sauce-making methods in favor of integral sauces, which often have a fuller, more direct, more spontaneous, home-cooked flavor.

INTEGRAL SAUCES FOR SAUTÉED MEATS

Meats are sautéed by rapid cooking in a small amount of hot fat. The technique should not be confused with frying, in which meat is cooked by being partially or entirely submerged in hot fat, or stewing, in which meats are often first browned in hot fat but then finish cooking in liquid. Even experienced cooks are sometimes confused by careless nomenclature that confuses stews and sautés. In strict culinary parlance, a *sauté* is composed of pieces of meat (including poultry) that have been browned in hot fat and finished cooking, without added liquid, either on top of the stove or in the oven. The sauce for a sauté is then prepared in the pan used to brown the meat and combined with the cooked meat just before serving—not sooner. When pieces of meat are browned but then cooked in liquid, the preparation is an authentic stew.

When meats are sautéed, they should fit neatly into the sauté pan with no extra room. If the pan is too large so that part of its surface is exposed during sautéing, the meat juices, which are essential to pan-deglazed sauces, will burn. An overcrowded pan, on the other hand, will prevent the meat from browning evenly and may even cause it to release its juices too quickly, so that it simmers in its own juices rather than browns. Meat should always be thoroughly dried with a towel before sautéing, as any moisture left on the surface will create steam and prevent browning.

Meats should always be sautéed in a heavy-bottomed pan, which distributes heat evenly. If the pan is too thin, it will be too hot in the area directly over the flame and in any section not in contact with the meat. This uneven heating in turn results in uneven browning and may cause the meat juices to burn in areas where the pan is too hot. Heavy-gauge copper, stainless-steel, or aluminum sauté pans are best for sautéing. Iron skillets conduct heat well, but because of their black surface, it is difficult to see the juices that adhere to the bottom and determine whether they are burning. Nonstick and enameled pans should be avoided because the juices released by the meat will not adhere to their surfaces.

When meats are sautéed, they release juices that caramelize and attach to the bottom of the sauté pan. These caramelized juices are intensely flavorful and are the basis for pan-deglazed integral sauces. Once the meat is removed from the pan, the first step in preparing a sauce is to remove the fat used for sautéing. If the meat has been sautéed properly, the juices will have formed a sticky, caramelized glaze adhering to the bottom of the pan; the fat remaining in the sauté pan is then simply poured off and discarded.

Once the fat has been removed from the sauté pan, the caramelized juices are dissolved in liquid by deglazing the pan with water or a flavorful liquid such as wine or stock. The bottom of the pan is then scraped with a wooden spoon to dissolve the juices into the deglazing liquid. The wide range of possible deglazing liquids makes this technique extremely versatile.

Although an acceptable sauce can be made by simply deglazing a sauté pan with wine, water, or stock, most professionals add other ingredients to give the sauce greater depth of flavor and a richer consistency. Using meat stocks either alone or in conjunction with wine will give a more complex flavor to a pan-deglazed sauce. Most stocks, however, require considerable reduction to concentrate their flavors and give them the consistency needed for a sauce. For this reason, glace de viande or demi-glace is often used by professionals to give consistency, body, and flavor to a sauce without requiring time-consuming last-minute reduction. In lighter sauces, the glace de viande can be replaced by veal or chicken stock that has been well reduced in advance. The sauce or stock used to make the sauce can also be thickened with hydrocolloids such as xanthan gum (not more than 0.2% or it can make the sauce slimy). Emulsifiers such as propylene glycol alginate or liquid lecithin and emulsion stabilizers such as agar can also be added so that oils and other ingredients can be added and the sauce will stay emulsified.

Once the sauté pan has been deglazed and the body of the sauce rounded out with stock, demi-glace, or concentrated stock, the sauce can be served as is or be lightly bound. Most nouvelle cuisine–style pan-deglazed sauces are finished with cream or butter, which gives them a rich texture and flavor. When used in moderation, cream and butter also lengthen a sauce without diluting or weakening its taste. Pan-deglazed sauces can also be lightly thickened with vegetable purées (see Chapter 17, "Purées and Purée-Thickened Sauces"), yogurt, fresh cheese (see "Yogurt and Fresh Cheese," page 124), or hydrocolloids (see page 73).

Some chefs prefer unbound versions of pan-deglazed sauces, which contain no butter or cream. Excellent sauces can be prepared by simply deglazing the pan and adding glace de viande or reduced stock until the sauce has the desired consistency. The one danger with this method is that too much glace de viande or stock will give the sauce a sticky, gluey consistency. Light-textured versions of pan-deglazed sauces prepared with very little or no cream or butter are often presented *under* the meat in a deep plate or wide bowl.

When a pan-deglazed sauce has the desired consistency (through reduction or adding liaisons such as cream, butter, or vegetable purées), it can be finished with an almost infinite variety of additional flavorings. Vinegar, Cognac, freshly chopped herbs, tomato purée, mustard, and chopped truffles are just a few examples.

Sautéed meats are usually accompanied by vegetables or other garnitures. Depending on the style and presentation of the sautéed meat, vegetables and other accompaniments are either served separately or combined with the sauce used to cover or surround the meat. Most sautéed dishes are completed by heating a garniture, such as mushrooms, small strips of bacon (lardons), turned vegetables, baby vegetables, or pearl onions, in the sauce before it is poured over or placed under the sautéed meats.

MODEL FOR A PAN-DEGLAZED SAUCE

Meats for Sautéing

Lamb (chops, medallions, noisettes)

Pork (chops, medallions, noisettes)

Veal (loin and rib chops, scallops, medallions)

Chicken parts (quarters or smaller)

Steaks (tenderloin, strip, club, other tender parts)

Calves' liver

Kidneys

Game (boneless breasts from wild ducks, partridges, pheasants, or other game birds; whole small birds such as quail; venison steaks)

Fats for Browning

Oil (pure olive, safflower, grapeseed)

Rendered poultry fat (goose, duck, chicken)

Clarified butter

Whole butter (at lower temperatures)

Deglazing Liquids
(Alone or in combination)

Water

Wine (red, white, fortified)

Vinegar (good-quality wine or cider)

Stocks (white or brown, depending on the desired sauce color and flavor intensity)

Cider

Beer

Brandies (Cognac, Calvados)

Additional Stock or Glaze
(Alone or in combination)

Reduced chicken, veal, or beef stock

Pork and turkey stock (Alternative Demi-Glace) (page 168)

Glace de viande

Demi-glace (classic or natural)

Roasting juices

Liaisons
(Alone or in combination)

Butter

Cream

Starches

Vegetable purées

Mayonnaise-based sauces

Béarnaise-based sauces

Foie gras

Yogurt

Fresh cheese

Hydrocolloids

   Xanthan gum

   Ultra-Sperse 3

   Guar gum

   Carrageenan (lambda, iota, kappa)

   Gum arabic

   Konjac gum

   Methylcellulose

   Alginates

EMULSIFIERS

Sucrose esters

Propylene glycol alginate

Lecithin

EMULSION STABILIZERS

Agar

Gelatin

Gellan

Final Flavorings

Spirits (Cognac, Calvados, eau-de-vie, marc, whiskey)

Freshly chopped herbs

Vinegar

Mustard

Truffles

Salt and pepper

Spices (saffron, curry, juniper berries, green peppercorns)

Garnitures

Mushrooms

Assorted vegetables (baby or turned)

Lardons

Pearl onions

Fruits

Shellfish

Quenelles

MAKING A PAN-DEGLAZED SAUCE

To make a pan-deglazed sauce from the juices left over in a sauté pan, add any aromatic ingredients (here, shallots, but garlic or ginger would also work) to the still-hot pan and stir until you can smell a toasted aroma, about a minute. At this point, you can add flavorful liquids such as wine. **(A)** Wine especially should be simmered a minute or two to dissolve the caramelized juices and to evaporate the alcohol. Add concentrated stock to contribute body and savor to the sauce. **(B)** Stir in some cream, which will smooth out the flavors of the sauce and give it an attractive consistency. **(C)** Boil down the cream until the sauce reaches the consistency you are looking for. **(D)** Whisk in butter (*monter au beurre*) to finish the sauce and give it sheen. **(E)** Wake up the flavor of the sauce with a few drops of Cognac **(F)**; bring to a simmer for a second to evaporate the alcohol.

CHICKEN WITH FINES HERBES

One of simplest and most delicious flavorings in saucemaking is a combination of fresh herbs—chervil, parsley, chives, and tarragon—called *fines herbes*. It is best to use about one-quarter as much tarragon relative to the other herbs, or else its flavor will overpower the others. In this recipe, chicken breasts are sautéed and then a sauce is made by deglazing the caramelized juices in the pan and adding the herbs.

YIELD: 2 SERVINGS

unsalted butter	2 ounces	60 grams
bone-in chicken breasts	2	2
salt and pepper	to taste	to taste
white wine	⅓ cup	75 milliliters
heavy cream	½ cup	125 milliliters
chopped chives	2 teaspoons	10 milliliters
chopped parsley	2 teaspoons	10 milliliters
chopped chervil	2 teaspoons	10 milliliters
chopped tarragon	½ teaspoon	3 milliliters

1. Heat the butter in a heavy-bottomed sauté pan just large enough to hold the breasts in a single layer. Season the breasts with salt and pepper and sauté them on both sides until they are golden brown and firm to the touch, 15 to 20 minutes **(see photo)**.

2. Transfer the chicken to a clean surface and pull away the bones sticking out the side of the breast. It is not necessary to remove the breastbone. Keep warm.

3. Pour out and discard the cooked fat in the pan and add the wine. Simmer until the wine evaporates by three-quarters. Add the cream and herbs and simmer gently for about 2 minutes, until the cream thickens slightly and the herbs have a chance to infuse.

4. Serve the chicken topped with the sauce.

POULET SAUTÉ À LA MARENGO
CHICKEN WITH TOMATOES, OLIVES, AND MUSHROOMS

Although chicken sautés can be varied almost infinitely by changing the garniture, the cooking method for the chicken sauté remains the same. Chicken Marengo was originally served with deep-fried eggs and crayfish, but most restaurants and home cooks usually serve this version.

YIELD: 8 SERVINGS

chickens, 2, total weight	6 to 8 pounds	3 to 4 kilograms
salt and pepper	to taste	to taste
olive oil	¼ cup	60 milliliters
small mushrooms	8 ounces	250 grams
chicken stock (page 85 or 88)	1 cup	250 milliliters
garlic cloves, crushed, peeled	2	2
tomatoes, peeled, seeded, chopped	4 to 6 medium	4 to 6 medium
white wine	1 cup	250 milliliters
green olives, pitted	24	24
chopped parsley	1 tablespoon	15 milliliters

1. Cut the chickens into quarters. Pat the pieces dry with paper towels and season with salt and pepper.

2. Heat the olive oil in a 10- to 12-inch straight-sided sauté pan and brown the chicken, skin side first. If the pieces stick when turning them, they probably are not brown enough; wait a few minutes and try again. The pieces usually require about 10 minutes of cooking on each side. When the chicken is cooked, transfer it to a plate and keep it warm while preparing the sauce.

3. While the chicken is browning, cook the mushrooms in ½ cup (125 milliliters) of the stock in a covered 2-quart (2 liter) saucepan for 5 minutes.

4. After removing the chicken, pour off the fat from the sauté pan and add the garlic, tomatoes, wine, mushroom cooking liquid, and the remaining stock. Reduce until about 2 cups (500 milliliters) remain. (Some recipes suggest thickening the sauce at this point with beurre manié, but this step is not necessary.) Remove the garlic.

5. Heat the olives and cooked mushrooms in the sauce for 1 to 2 minutes.

6. Serve the chicken napped with the sauce. Sprinkle with parsley.

STEAK WITH GREEN PEPPERCORN SAUCE

Any good cut of steak, such as beef tenderloin (filet), sirloin strip, or rib steak, can be lightly cooked in a straight-sided sauté pan, with the drippings used as the sauce base. This recipe calls for glace de viande and a reduction of cream as a liaison. It can also be made as a butter-enriched version by replacing the cream with 1½ ounces (45 grams) butter, or as a classic version by leaving out both cream and butter and finishing with demi-glace.

YIELD: 4 SERVINGS

steaks	4	4
clarified butter (see note)	3 tablespoons	45 milliliters
shallot, finely chopped	1	1
port	2 tablespoons	30 milliliters
cognac	¼ cup	60 milliliters
glace de viande (page 97)	3 tablespoons	45 grams
heavy cream	6 tablespoons	90 milliliters
green peppercorns in brine, drained	1 tablespoon	15 milliliters
butter	1 ounce	30 grams
salt and pepper	to taste	to taste
red wine vinegar	a few drops	a few drops

1. Dry the steaks thoroughly. In a straight-sided 2-quart (2 liter) sauté pan, sauté the steaks in the clarified butter. When they are cooked to the desired doneness, remove them from the pan and keep warm.

2. Pour off the fat from the sauté pan. Whisk in the shallot. Let the pan cool slightly, then add the port and Cognac to deglaze the pan. Tilt the pan and ignite the fumes. Reduce the liquids until the flames die out.

3. Add the glace de viande, cream, and green peppercorns. Reduce the sauce to the desired consistency and swirl in the butter.

4. Season with salt and pepper and add a few drops of vinegar.

Note: The clarified butter used to brown the steaks may be replaced by ½ ounce (15 grams) whole butter and 2 tablespoons (30 milliliters) oil. Keep in mind, however, that you'll have to keep an eye on things to make sure the butter doesn't burn.

PORK CHOPS WITH ONION PURÉE–THICKENED SAUCE (SOUBISE)

This sauce demonstrates a method of finishing an integral pan sauce with vegetable purée—in this case onions, a modern version of the classic soubise.

YIELD: 2 TO 4 SERVINGS

rib or loin pork chops	4	4
clarified butter (see note)	3 tablespoons	45 milliliters
brown pork or chicken stock	½ cup	125 milliliters
stewed onion purée (page 520)	6 tablespoons	90 milliliters
additional stock or heavy cream	as needed	as needed
salt and pepper	to taste	to taste

1. Dry the pork chops. In a 2-quart (2 liter) straight-sided sauté pan, sauté the chops in the clarified butter until well browned and cooked through. Transfer them to a plate and keep warm.

2. Pour off the fat from the pan and deglaze with the stock.

3. Reduce the stock by about one-fourth and whisk in the onion purée. Adjust the thickness by reducing the sauce slightly (to thicken) or adding stock or cream (to thin). Season with salt and pepper.

Note: The clarified butter may be replaced by ½ ounce (15 grams) whole butter and 2 tablespoons (30 milliliters) oil. Keep in mind, however, that you'll have to keep an eye on things to make sure the butter doesn't burn.

INTEGRAL SAUCES FOR ROASTS: THE JUS

Unlike pan-deglazed sauces for sautéed meats, which can be flavored and bound in many different ways, sauces for roasts are best kept simple and should capture the flavor of the meat. Additions that distort or weaken the natural flavor of the roast should be kept to a minimum.

The best method for roasting meats is on a spit in front of a wood fire. When this method is used, a dripping pan (*lèchefrite*) placed in front of the fire directly under the roasting meat is used to capture the drippings. Most of the fat is removed from the drippings, and the remaining jus is served as is. If the jus is pale, it can be rapidly cooked down on top of the stove until it caramelizes; the fat is then poured off and the caramelized juices are deglazed with an appropriately flavored or neutral stock.

When oven-roasting meats, be sure to select a heavy-bottomed roasting pan (a sauté pan will work in a pinch) that closely fits the size of the roast. If the roasting pan is too large, the juices will spread out over its surface and burn. If the pan is too thin, any surface that is not in direct contact with the meat will overheat, also causing the drippings to burn. Many recipes, especially in the United States, recommend setting roasts on top of special racks, presumably to expose them to the heat of the oven and help them brown evenly. Unfortunately, when the roast is suspended over the pan on a rack, the drippings fall into an overheated roasting pan and burn. A better method is to set the roast on a layer of meat trimmings and vegetables. These contribute flavor to the finished jus and keep the meat from sticking to the pan.

When the roast is done, the flavor and color of the drippings can be improved by heating the roasting pan on top of the stove so that the drippings caramelize. The fat is then easily poured off and the pan deglazed with water or stock. When dealing with large roasts that release large amounts of natural juices, it is usually impractical and unnecessary to caramelize the juices. The fat is simply skimmed off and the jus served as is.

The flavor of natural roasting juices, when skimmed of fat, cannot be surpassed. The problem that most often confronts professional chefs is that most roasts do not provide enough full-flavored jus to go around. This problem can be resolved in several ways. In classic French cooking, roasting pans are often deglazed with *jus de veau lié* (brown veal stock that has been reduced and lightly bound with arrowroot). Arrowroot, when used sparingly, gives a light sheen to the jus and looks more like a natural, unthickened jus than stock thickened with roux. Contemporary chefs, who are usually less compelled to use thickeners, are more likely to stretch a natural jus with unthickened, full-flavored stock. A stock with a natural jus-like flavor can also be prepared in advance with meat trimmings and used to deglaze the roasting pan.

The flavor of a jus can be reinforced with additional meat trimmings and aromatic vegetables. Some chefs surround roast meats with chopped onions, carrots, and meat trimmings that cook along with the roast and contribute to the flavor of the meat juices. This method requires a certain amount of skill and judgment to determine when to add the vegetables and trimmings and how finely they should be chopped. If they are chopped too finely or added too soon, they are liable to burn; if chopped too coarsely or added too late, they will remain undercooked and not contribute any flavor. Finely chopped vegetables can also be added to the roasting pan and caramelized on top of the stove along with the juices. In general, moisture should never be introduced into the oven during roasting (which by definition is cooking with dry heat), but if the meat juices or chopped vegetables start to overcook during the roasting, a small amount of water or stock can be added to the bottom of the roasting pan to prevent burning.

Any number of thickeners, hydrocolloids or not, can be used to give body to a jus. Most traditional is cornstarch, worked into a slurry and added until the proper thickness is achieved. Nowadays, chefs often use Wondra, which can be worked into a slurry and added in the same way as cornstarch.

Cooks are often baffled as to whether or not roasts should be basted. The purpose of basting is to prevent the surface of the roast from drying out and to give the roast an even color and sheen. In true roasting, meats are basted with fat. Basting meats with liquid such as wine or stock may prevent browning and cause the meat to braise rather than roast. For poultry and game birds, a dry, crispy skin may be desirable and basting should be avoided. However, a chicken or game bird may benefit from basting with reduced stock or glace de viande near the end of roasting, which will give it sheen, moist skin, and a full-bodied jus. The choice of basting liquids depends to a large extent on intuition and skill. Keep in mind, however, that constant basting will lower the oven temperature and may interfere with browning.

Gravies and Thickened Jus

In classic French restaurants, a natural jus or one that has been only lightly thickened with arrowroot is traditionally served in a sauceboat, either offered by the waiter or placed on the table where guests usually help themselves. This is both a simple and elegant method for serving roasts. In less formal cooking or in people's homes, a gravy is likely to be served instead of a jus. A gravy is simply a jus that has been thickened with flour in the roasting pan.

Although there are more refined and sophisticated methods for dealing with meat drippings, one of the most reassuring is a simple flour-thickened gravy. Most gravy recipes suggest removing most but not all of the fat from the roasting pan, stirring in flour with a wooden spoon, cooking the mixture for 4 to 5 minutes, and then adding water or stock.

To avoid lumpy gravy, you can use Wondra, a pretreated flour, instead of making a roux. Stir Wondra flour with a small amount of water until smooth. Pour an appropriate amount of this mixture into the jus, bring to a simmer, and whisk until the jus thickens; do not blend, which can make the sauce gluey.

244

WONDRA-THICKENED GRAVY

YIELD: 1½ CUPS (375 MILLILITERS)

wondra flour	1 to 2 tablespoons	15 to 30 milliliters
water	¼ cup	65 milliliters
jus	1¼ cups	300 milliliters

Stir together the flour and water until the mixture is smooth and contains no lumps. (A) Don't use a blender or immersion blender for this or the flour may become gummy. Heat the jus to a bare simmer and whisk in the water-flour mixture. (B) Bring back to a boil and boil until the jus thickens. If the gravy seems lumpy, go ahead and strain it. (C) The finished gravy (D) should be passed at the table in a sauceboat.

CHICKEN JUS WITH BEURRE NOISETTE

n most cases, a jus should be well degreased, although Escoffier says that it shouldn't look like consommé and that a trace of fat can actually improve it. In general, when adding ingredients to a jus, they must be emulsions or thickeners or they'll simply separate. Butter is an example of an ingredient that works well for finishing a jus, but if you want the flavor of beurre noisette, you'll have to emulsify the oily butter into the jus using different emulsifiers. Here, a small proportion of propylene glycol alginate and xanthan gum are blended into the jus before the beurre noisette, combined with lecithin and Glice, is added.

YIELD: ABOUT ¾ CUP (185 MILLILITERS)

propylene glycol alginate		0.4 gram
xanthan gum		0.2 gram
chicken jus, warmed	½ cup	125 milliliters
liquid lecithin		1.2 grams
mono- and diglycerides (glice)		1.2 grams
beurre noisette (see page 438), warmed	4 tablespoons	60 milliliters
salt and pepper	to taste	to taste

Use an immersion blender to blend the propylene glycol alginate and xanthan gum into the jus. Stir the liquid lecithin and Glice into the beurre noisette until well dissolved. Add the beurre noisette to the jus in a slow, steady stream while blending with an immersion blender. Season with salt and pepper.

A natural jus can also be thickened with puréed vegetables. The easiest and most flavorful method is to roast the meat with chopped aromatic vegetables such as carrots, turnips, onions, or garlic, degrease and deglaze the pan, and force the vegetables and cooking jus through a food mill or strainer. In restaurants or other professional settings where this is impractical, vegetable purées can be prepared on the side and used as thickeners for the jus (see Chapter 18, "Purées and Purée-Thickened Sauces"), but the vegetables will not have benefited from being cooked with the fat and drippings from the roast.

Most Americans are familiar with giblet gravy, which is finished with the precooked and chopped heart, liver, and gizzard of turkeys or chickens. Although this is an excellent method—the chopped meats provide textural contrast and flavor—a different and somewhat more flavorful jus is obtained by puréeing the giblets (a food processor works well) while still raw with an equal amount of butter. The purée is then beaten into the jus at the last minute. Another refinement is to replace the giblet mixture with a purée of foie gras (see page 72).

The natural cooking liquid from game, rabbits, and poultry is sometimes thickened with blood, usually used in combination with the puréed liver and a few drops of Cognac or marc and vinegar (see page 121). Sauces for roast game also benefit from a few crushed juniper berries infused in the jus before the addition of the blood.

Sauces thickened with foie gras or blood will benefit from an added emulsifier. A small amount of propylene glycol alginate can be dissolved in the sauce base, while liquid lecithin and mono- and diglycerides (Glice) are blended into the foie gras, blood, or giblet butter.

MODEL FOR PREPARING A JUS

Main Ingredient
Meat to be roasted

Aromatics
(Alone or in combination, added to the roasting pan with the meat)

Carrots

Celery

Onions

Garlic

Fennel

Meat Trimmings
Ham

Bones or carcasses

Deglazing Liquids
(Alone or in combination)

Water

Stock (neutral or the same kind as the meat being roasted)

Wine (in combination with stock or water)

Liaisons
(Alone or in combination)

Jus de veau lié (see page 243)

Flour

Vegetable purée (made from the vegetables roasted with the meat or separately)

Mushrooms

Sorrel

Tomatoes

Butter

Cream

Puréed livers (from poultry or game)

Foie gras

Hydrocolloids
Xanthan gum

Guar gum

Gum arabic

Ultra-Sperse 3

Carrageenan

EMULSIFIERS
Propylene glycol alginate

Lecithin

Sucrose esters

EMULSION STABILIZERS
Agar

Gelatin

Gellan

Final Flavorings
Chopped fines herbes (chervil, parsley, chives, tarragon)

Other herbs (marjoram, savory, thyme, alone or in combination)

Spices (curry, juniper berries, saffron)

OVEN-ROASTED CHICKEN WITH NATURAL JUS

n kitchens with professional-quality stoves and hot ovens, it is rarely necessary to brown the chicken on top of the stove before roasting. However, the smaller the bird being roasted, the more likely will be the necessity for prebrowning; by the time a quail browns in the oven, it will have dried out and overcooked. Chicken can go either way. The oven should be piping-hot so as to brown the chicken before it ends up completely cooked. If the oven isn't hot enough, the chicken should be browned on the stove before roasting.

Older recipes suggest covering the breast of a roast chicken with a sheet of fatback (barding) for the first stage of roasting so the thighs and breasts will be done at the same time. This is still a good idea but a bit of a nuisance when sheets of fatback are not on hand. An easy alternative is to double up a small sheet of aluminum foil and place it over the breast, leaving the thighs exposed, while the chicken is roasting. The foil is removed at least 30 minutes before the end of roasting to allow the breast to brown.

YIELD: 4 SERVINGS

chicken, 1	3 to 4 pounds	1.5 to 2 kilograms
onion, quartered	1	1
carrots, peeled, cut into 3-inch (7-cm) lengths	2	2
enough meat trimmings or chicken bones to cover roasting pan (optional)		
chicken stock (page 85 or 88) or water	2 cups	500 milliliters
salt and pepper	to taste	to taste

1. Remove the giblets from the chicken. Truss the chicken with string.

2. Spread the meat trimmings or chicken bones in a single layer in a roasting pan that fits the chicken. It's important that none of the roasting pan is exposed. Place the chicken in the roasting pan, breast side up. Cover the breasts with folded sheets of aluminum foil. **(A)** Surround the chicken with its giblets, except the liver, which may give the jus a strong taste. Roast for 30 minutes.

3. Remove the foil and roast for 15 to 20 minutes more, until the juices from a thigh run clear when it is poked with a trussing needle or sauté fork. **(B)**

4. Transfer the chicken to a plate or platter. Lift it out of the roasting pan in such a way that any juices contained in the cavity run out into the pan.

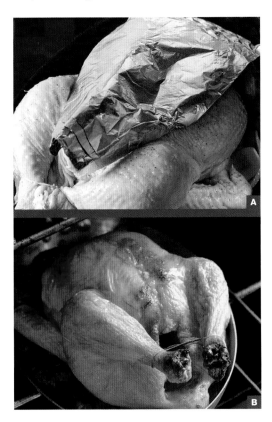

(continued)

5. Heat the roasting pan on the stovetop until the juices caramelize on the bottom of the pan and the fat separates. Do not stir. (C, page 249)

6. Remove the fat from the roasting pan with a ladle, or pour it off. (D, page 249, E)

7. Add 1 cup (250 milliliters) of stock or water to the roasting pan and reduce until the stock caramelizes. (F)

8. Add the remaining stock. Gently heat the stock, while scraping the bottom of the pan with a wooden spoon, until all the caramelized juices dissolve in the stock. (G)

9. Strain the jus through a fine chinois. (H)

10. Season with salt and pepper. While not necessary, the jus can then be thickened and flavored in a variety of ways, as described earlier in this chapter.

ROAST RACK OF LAMB WITH NATURAL JUS

A rack of lamb, being a red meat, is roasted to a lower internal temperature than chicken, veal, or pork, meaning that it releases little in the way of juices during the roasting process. To supplement the jus, spread the roasting pan with the trimmings from the rack (with the fat trimmed off) or a pound (500 grams) or so of lamb stew meat cut into small pieces, and brown these in a hot oven before setting the rack on top. (This base of trimmings is called a *fonçage*.)

YIELD: 4 MAIN-COURSE SERVINGS

american 8-rib rack of lamb	1	1
or	*or*	*or*
new zealand 8-rib racks of lamb	2	2
salt and pepper	to taste	to taste
trimmings from the rack(s)		
or		
lamb stew meat cut into ½-inch (1 cm) pieces	1 pound	450 grams
stock or water	as needed	as needed

1. Season the lamb with salt and pepper and allow it to come to room temperature. Preheat the oven to 450°F (230°C).

2. Spread the lamb trimmings or stew meat over the bottom of a roasting pan just large enough to hold the rack(s) and roast until lightly browned, about 20 minutes.

3. Place the rack(s) on top of the trimmings and return the pan to the oven. Roast until springy to the touch, about 25 minutes. Transfer the rack(s) to a plate or platter. Let rest, loosely covered with aluminum foil, for 15 minutes.

4. Put the roasting pan on top of the stove and pour over 1 cup (250 milliliters) stock or water. Bring to a boil and boil until a brown crust of caramelized juices forms on the bottom of the roasting pan. Pour out any liquid fat floating on top. Deglaze again with another cup (250 milliliters) stock or water and scrape up the juices. If you're using stock, repeat the caramelization as many times as practical before deglazing a final time. Strain the jus through a fine chinois. Pass the jus in a sauceboat at the table.

INTEGRAL SAUCES DERIVED FROM POACHED MEATS

Poaching is one of the most fundamental and straightforward techniques for cooking meat. In English-speaking countries, we have the habit of speaking of boiled dishes, but when prepared correctly, so-called boiled dishes are actually poached—the poaching liquid is never allowed to reach a full boil. In France, dishes such as *pot au feu* ("boiled" beef with vegetables), *poule au pot* (poached hen with vegetables), and innumerable *potées* (poached meats, usually pork with beans or potatoes and vegetables, almost always including cabbage) have long been the mainstay of the rural diet. More refined poached dishes, such as *blanquette de veau* (poached veal stew with cream; see below), *boeuf à la ficelle* (tender cuts barely poached in broth), and *petite marmite* (a rich consommé with vegetables and marrow), have made their way into middle-class homes and elegant restaurants. The age-old technique of serving poached meats surrounded with flavorful broth instead of a thickened sauce is popular with contemporary chefs because the dish is light and digestible.

The difference between poaching and stewing or braising is largely a question of the amount of liquid used for cooking the meat. Stewed and braised meats are cooked with a small amount of liquid and thus produce a small amount of concentrated cooking liquid, whereas poaches, because the meat is completely submerged in liquid, provide a relatively dilute, soup-like broth. Consequently, most sauces derived from poached meats require reduction or the addition of reduced stock, demi-glace, or glace de viande to intensify their flavor.

For some poached meats—the French pot au feu is a prime example—the poaching liquid is left alone and served either as a separate course or around the meat (here the distinction between soup and sauce is a bit cloudy). In a potée, the meat (often pork) is gently simmered with starchy foods such as beans or potatoes, which give substance to the dish; if they do not completely absorb the surrounding liquid, at least they lightly thicken and contribute body to the broth.

There have been many so-called refinements (refinements, yes; improvements, not necessarily) of fundamental poached dishes such as potées and pot au feu. Boeuf à la ficelle consists of poaching beef tenderloin (or another tender cut) in the pot au feu broth and serving the still-rare beef with the pot au feu vegetables and broth. Contemporary chefs have taken this refinement several steps further, often serving game, pigeon, or even lobster and crayfish in a carefully reduced and clarified poaching liquid.

Poaching liquids can also be thickened and finished with a wide variety of flavorful ingredients. The traditional French blanquette de veau is composed of chunks of veal poached in water or stock flavored with aromatic vegetables and a bouquet garni. Once the meat is cooked, the broth is thickened with roux and finished with heavy cream combined with egg yolks. While today the term *blanquette* is often applied to any meat or fish that has been poached and surrounded by a sauce derived from the poaching liquid and finished with cream, this is an example in which the traditional thickener—flour—is appropriate because it has deep associations with the dish. A blanquette thickened with cornstarch or hydrocolloids would seem oddly out of place.

Poached chicken also provides a flavorful broth that can be reduced and finished with cream, or more traditionally, converted into a velouté and finished with cream or vegetable purées and a variety of flavorful ingredients. If vegetables purées are being used, they are better when stabilized with 0.2% xanthan gum and 0.6% Ultra-Sperse 3 (each as a percentage of the whole sauce).

Poaching liquids thickened with vegetable purées are analogous—and sometimes almost identical—to puréed soups. This is one area in which the distinction between soup and sauce is sometimes difficult to discern. The usual difference, however, is that a sauce is more intensely flavored and can be richer, simply because there is less of it.

MODEL FOR PREPARING SAUCES FOR POACHED MEATS

Basic Ingredients
(Alone or in combination)

Stewing hens or roosters (potées, poule au pot)

Pork shoulder, loin, sausage (potées)

Beef shank, rump, short ribs (pot au feu)

Beef tenderloin, sirloin strip (boeuf à la ficelle, petite marmite)

Veal stewing meat (blanquette de veau)

Game, duck, pigeon (potées, contemporary pot au feu derivatives)

Aromatics

Onions

Celery

Carrots

Turnips

Garlic

Cabbage (for potées; blanched separately first)

Fennel

Bouquet garni (classic [page 52] or with regional herbs such as marjoram or rosemary)

Starchy Ingredients
(For Liaison and Body)

Potatoes

Beans (such as white beans, fava beans, lentils)

Moistening Liquids

Water

Stock

Wine (in combination with stock or water)

Cider

Liaisons

Cream

Egg yolks (in combination with cream)

Roux

Vegetable purées (derived from aromatic vegetables poached with the meat or cooked separately)

HYDROCOLLOIDS
Xanthan gum

Ultra-Sperse 3

EMULSIFIERS
Propylene glycol alginate

Lecithin

Sucrose esters

EMULSION STABILIZERS, CONVERTED TO FLUID GELS OR WORKED INTO FATS

Agar

Gelatin

Final Flavorings and Garnitures

Chopped herbs

Mushrooms

Vegetables (cut or turned into appropriate sizes or small to begin with, such as pearl onions and button mushrooms)

Truffles

POT AU FEU

A pot au feu is an example of poached meats par excellence. There was a day when every farmhouse had a pot of broth simmering on the stove or in the hearth to which various meats could be added and gently simmered. Traditionally a pot au feu is served in two courses: the broth, followed by the meat. In this version, the meat is served surrounded with the broth. Traditional accompaniments are mustard, cornichons (sour gherkins), and coarse salt, but the Mostarda di Cremona and Green Sauce on pages 497 and 423 are delicious with the various meats. When buying short ribs, be sure to buy them cut crosswise so the ribs themselves are only a couple of inches (5 cm) long.

YIELD: 12 SERVINGS

clove	1	1
onion, peeled	1 medium	1 medium
large bouquet garni (page 52)	1	1
oxtail	4 pounds	2 kilograms
beef or veal stock or water, as needed to cover	8 quarts	8 liters
beef or veal shanks	4 rounds	4 rounds
chuck roast, 1, tied in two directions	4 pounds	2 kilograms
beef short ribs	4 pounds	2 kilograms
carrots, halved lengthwise, cut into 2-inch (5 cm) pieces	4 medium	4 medium
leeks, greens removed, whites halved lengthwise, rinsed	6 medium	6 medium
turnips, peeled, each cut into 6 wedges	3 large	3 large
2-inch (5 cm) marrow bones (optional)	12	12
mustard		
cornichons		
coarse salt		

1. Stick the clove into the onion and put the onion in a large pot with the bouquet garni.

2. Arrange the oxtails on top and pour in enough stock or water to cover **(see photo)**.

3. Put the pot over medium to high heat. When it reaches a gentle simmer, turn the heat down so the top of the liquid barely vibrates. Simmer for 2 hours. Skim off any fat and froth as they rise to the top of the liquid. Add the shanks, roast,

and ribs. Add more liquid if needed to cover. As the meats heat up, they will release froth and scum that will need to be skimmed. Simmer for 90 minutes.

4. Add the carrots, leeks, and turnips and simmer about 1 hour more, again while skimming, until a knife slices easily in and out of the shanks, short ribs, and chuck roast. Add the marrow bones, if using, and simmer for 10 to 15 minutes more.

5. Slice the chuck roast and arrange the slices on a large platter with the rest of the meats, the marrow bones, and the vegetables, and march triumphantly into the dining room. Serve in wide, deep soup plates. Ladle broth over each serving. Pass the condiments at the table.

VARIATION

The meats in a pot au feu are cooked in the manner of stew meat; once cooked, they should offer

(*continued*)

little resistance to the tooth. The French, in their need to add luxurious touches, also sometimes briefly poach a lean, tender cut of meat (such as a beef tenderloin) or duck breast in the broth so that they can serve elegant slices of the rare or medium-rare meat along with the vegetables and pot au feu meat. Such dishes are called *à la ficelle*, which means "with string." The string refers to the string tied around the meat so that it can be easily retrieved once cooked.

POACHED CHICKEN

If you're repeating this dish with any frequency, save the poaching liquid from the previous batch for poaching each new chicken. The poaching liquid's flavor will continue to improve. By serving the poaching liquid around the chicken, you have a dish that's perfectly lean, but you can also enrich it with a little cream and flavor it with herbs, especially chopped tarragon. You can also thicken the poaching liquid with egg yolks as described in the variation that follows.

This simple and satisfying version can be presented by simply serving the sliced chicken in wide soup bowls with the reduced broth, a sort of chicken à la ficelle. The broth can be scented with whole leaves of basil, chopped herbs, truffles, cubes of ham, and the like.

YIELD: 4 SERVINGS

chicken, 1	4 pounds	2 kilograms
carrots, sectioned, turned (turning optional)	2 large	2 large
turnip, cut into wedges, turned (turning optional)	1 large	1 large
cold chicken stock (page 88) or water, to cover	6 quarts	6 liters
bouquet garni (about 7 sprigs fresh tarragon, 1 bay leaf, 1 bunch parsley)	1	1
string beans, ends snapped off	8 ounces	225 grams
peas, fresh or frozen (optional)	½ cup	125 milliliters
salt and pepper	to taste	to taste

1. Truss the chicken and put it in a pot surrounded with the carrots and turnips.

2. Add enough stock to cover and nestle in the bouquet garni. Bring to a gentle simmer and simmer until the juices are clear when you poke the joint between the thigh and the drumstick.

During the poaching, skim off any fat and scum that float to the surface.

3. Add the string beans to the poaching liquid and simmer until they lose their crunch, about 5 minutes. Add the peas, if using, and simmer for 1 minute.

4. Season the broth with salt and pepper and ladle it around the quartered chicken in soup plates. Distribute the vegetables among the servings.

VARIATION
The poaching liquid can be finished with a variety of thickeners. The best known is to finish the sauce as you would a Sauce Allemande (page 142), with cream and egg yolks. This classic method for poaching chicken and finishing the poaching liquid with roux and a liaison of cream and egg yolks is the same as preparing a white veal stew (blanquette). It is also similar to a fricassée, except that a fricassée is made with cut-up chicken that is usually partially cooked gently in butter before being moistened with stock. Use about 1 egg yolk and about 2 tablespoons (30 milliliters) cream per serving.

POACHED CHICKEN WITH GARLIC EMULSION

This recipe provides an example of thickening a poaching liquid with a purée made from roast garlic. Because roast garlic and vegetable purées in general have a hard time staying emulsified and even more so acting as emulsifiers, the garlic purée called for in this recipe is augmented with xanthan gum (about 0.2%) and a specially treated starch, Ultra-Sperse 3 (about 3%).

YIELD: 4 SERVINGS

chicken, 1, trussed	4 pounds	2 kilograms
cold chicken stock (page 88), to cover	about 2 quarts	2 liters
medium bouquet garni (page 52)	1 medium	1
onion, quartered	1	1
carrot, cut into 1-inch (2.5 cm) sections	1	1
garlic purée, squeezed out of about 3 heads roasted garlic	½ cup	125 ml
ultra-sperse 3		15 grams
salt and pepper	to taste	to taste

1. Place the chicken in a pot and pour over stock to cover. Add the bouquet garni, onion, and carrot and bring slowly to a simmer. Poach for approximately 40 minutes, until the juices run clear after poking a thigh.

2. Transfer the chicken to a platter or cutting board and keep warm. Strain the broth into a large clean pot or sauté pan and reduce rapidly, with the pan on the side of the heat, ideally without letting the chicken get cold, skimming off fat all the while, down to about 2 cups (500 milliliters).

3. Blend the garlic purée and Ultra-Sperse 3 into the reduced broth. Bring to a simmer. Season with salt and pepper. Serve the chicken quarters in soup plates and ladle the emulsion around.

INTEGRAL SAUCES MADE FROM BRAISED MEATS

Meat is braised by slow cooking in a small amount of liquid. The main difference between braising and poaching is that braising is accomplished in a minimum amount of liquid, whereas poaching requires a relatively large amount, enough to cover the meat completely. Usually herbs and aromatic vegetables are braised along with the meat for extra flavor and complexity. As meat cooks, it releases juices into the surrounding liquid, which becomes intensely concentrated and flavorful. If the braising has been done carefully, little if anything needs to be done to improve the flavor and consistency of the braising liquid.

Braising Terminology

There are many different techniques and approaches to braising, as well as an elaborate and contradictory terminology that often confuses even experienced cooks.

Stews are simply braises in which the meat has been cut up into small pieces, browned or not depending on recipe or whim, and covered with water, stock, or aromatic liquids such as wine, cider, beer, or vinegar. Stews are infinitely varied and are subcategorized into an endless variety of daubes, estouffades, coq au vin variations, and fricassées.

Until the middle of the nineteenth century, braising and stewing always implied that the meat was cooked for long periods—until the muscle tissue had completely broken down and the meat was tender. This technique is called "long braising." Since then, many chefs also use a technique known as "short white braising" for tender cuts of white meats such as veal or pork. Meats that are white braised are not browned, and are cooked in a small amount of liquid only long enough to reach a relatively low internal temperature, like a roast. Keep in mind that there are four combinations of braising techniques: long brown, short brown, long white, short white. When a piece of meat or fish is browned before braising, it is a brown braise. When foods are braised without browning, the braise is said to be a white braise. When a piece of meat or stew is simmered long enough to break down the muscle and yield something tender out of something tough, it is a long braise. When foods, more likely seafood, are cooked in a small amount of liquid (braised) just long enough to cook them through, they are said to be short braised. Hence, the two techniques—long braising and short braising—can be coupled with brown or white to yield the four combinations.

An *étouffée* (sometimes *étuvé*) is a type of braise in which the meat is cooked in a covered pot, with no or only a small amount of liquid. When meat is cooked, covered, with no liquid—only butter—the technique is called *poêlage*.

Brown braising—browning the meat before it is braised—is a more traditional technique than short white braising, and is best used for relatively tough cuts, either white meat or red meat. There are several ways that large pieces of meat (3 to 7 pounds/1.5 to 3.25 kilograms) can be brown braised, but the oldest and most sophisticated uses a two-stage process that works well for both red and white meats. In long brown braising, the meat is carefully larded to prevent it from drying out, browned in fat along with aromatic vegetables, placed in a close-fitting casserole, and covered halfway with water or stock. The casserole is then covered (with the lid inverted so that moisture accumulates, drips down over the meat, and bastes it inside the pot), and the pot is placed in the oven for 2 to 3 hours, depending on the weight of the meat. Some recipes call for slow cooking of meat for much longer periods, even to the point where the meat can be served with a spoon (*à la cuillère*).

When the meat is easily pierced with a skewer, it is gently transferred to a clean smaller casserole and the braising liquid is strained into a saucepan, where it is reduced slightly and carefully degreased. The braising liquid is then placed in the new casserole with the meat, and the whole thing is returned to the oven. The braising continues, uncovered, and the meat is basted with the reduced liquid until a shiny glaze forms on its surface.

A quicker, more straightforward technique for braising meats is to tie the meat, brown it in butter, and bake it slowly in a tightly covered pot with aromatic vegetables. From time to time the pot should be checked so that a few tablespoons of water can be added if needed to prevent the juices on the bottom of the pot from drying up and burning. This is the method most often used for American pot roasts and French étuvés. Meats braised in this way can be cooked to a relatively low internal temperature (as for roasts and white braises), or the process can be continued until the meat fibers soften in the same way as long brown braises, in which case the meat should be larded to prevent it from drying out.

When meat is cooked with butter and no additional liquid, the technique is called *poêlage*, sometimes translated as "pot roasting." Because this technique provides little liquid from which to prepare a sauce, the bottom of the pot or casserole is deglazed with water, stock, or wine after the meat is removed, and the liquid is then gently simmered to extract the flavor of the juices and aromatic ingredients left in the bottom of the pot. Poêlage is very similar to oven roasting, the only difference being that a covered pot is smaller than an oven.

In white braising, the meat is moistened with water, stock, wine, or a combination. The simplest approach is to place the meat in a casserole or close-fitting pot along with aromatic vegetables, a bouquet garni, and enough liquid to come halfway up the sides of the meat. The pot is then set on top of the stove until the liquid comes to a boil. The whole thing is then baked in the oven, with or without a lid, and basted regularly. The meat is cooked to the same degree of doneness as a roast.

Methods and Ingredients for Braises and Stews

PRELIMINARY BROWNING

Classic French cookbooks claim that preliminary browning of braised meats is necessary to create a seal to retain the meat's natural juices during the first stage of braising. The reasoning behind this theory is that as the internal juices are released within the meat, pressure is generated that separates the meat fibers and aids in the cooking. All theory aside, perfectly acceptable braises and stews can be prepared without preliminary browning.

Preliminary browning does, however, improve the color of the braising liquid and, especially if the aromatic vegetables are browned as well, will give the braised meat or stew a somewhat more complex flavor. Initial browning also offers the chef the opportunity to flour the meat, which will help bind the finished liquid without giving it a floury taste. Browning cubes of meat for stews requires a certain amount of care and attention. If the meat is cold or added to the hot pan all at once, or the pan or pot used for browning is not hot enough to begin with, the meat will not brown properly and may even release liquid and begin to boil in its own juices. This has a disastrous effect on the meat, so it is best to add the meat to the pan in increments, about a quarter at a time, to prevent sudden cooling of the pan. Care should also be taken when turning the meat. If it is turned haphazardly or all at once, it may cool the pan too quickly, causing the juices to release. When browning large amounts of meat, it may be necessary to change pans during browning so that the caramelized juices do not overheat and burn.

MOISTENING LIQUIDS AND AROMATIC VEGETABLES

Moistening liquids for stews and braised meats have traditionally evolved out of necessity. Germans have long used vinegar; the French, wine (or cider in Normandy); the Irish have had to rely on water (with potatoes to contribute body); and Caribbean cooks sometimes use rum. Some recipes augment these liquids with various types of tomatoes; purées of capers, pickles or olives; and, of course, stock. Standard aromatic vegetables—onions (often studded with a clove or two), celery, and carrots—are sometimes replaced or augmented with garlic, turnips, or chiles, depending on nation or region. The combinations of moistening liquids and aromatic vegetables used in stews and braised meats are almost limitless, which is probably why no braise or stew tastes exactly like another.

BOUQUET GARNI

The bouquet garni has become so standardized that chefs often add it to a stew with little thought as to how the herbs meld with the stew's other components. (See page 52 for a basic version in different sizes.) Rarely will parsley, thyme, and bay leaf—the standard components of a bouquet garni—clash with the other aromatic ingredients in a stew, but often a bouquet garni can be used to give a stew individuality and distinction, with the addition of other herbs. Early French recipes often called for basil and hyssop in a bouquet garni; Italian and southern French cooks will often add marjoram, wild thyme, or oregano. In Mexico, a piece of cinnamon stick will sometimes make its way into the bouquet garni. Medieval cooks, more attuned to spices than herbs, often simmered their meats in elaborate combinations of saffron, ginger, cinnamon, and other spices.

MARINADES

Meat for stews and braises is often given added flavor by being first marinated in various mixtures, usually containing aromatic vegetables, wine or vinegar, herbs, a small amount of oil, and sometimes spices such as cloves, juniper berries, and crushed peppercorns. Although some contemporary chefs feel that marinades sometimes distort the natural flavor of meats, when used discreetly they give aromatic support and character to stews and larger pieces of braised meat as well. Marinades are usually composed of the liquids, aromatic vegetables, herbs, and spices that will be braised along with the meat. If strong liquors such as Cognac, grappa, or whiskey are being used in the braise, they should not be added to the marinade—they will give the meat an odd, unnatural taste.

When the meat is finished braising or stewing, the chef should be left with an intensely aromatic, flavorful liquid. Often this liquid, after an initial degreasing, is complete—it is simply served with the stew or atop slices or spoonfuls of the braised meat.

LIAISONS FOR BRAISING LIQUIDS

At times, especially when no flour has been used to brown the meat and no pork trotters or rinds have been added during braising, the braising liquid may be too thin or not flavorful enough. The most straightforward approach is simply to reduce it until it has the proper flavor and texture. If this is impractical, there are several methods that can be used to thicken the liquid. In classic French cooking, beurre manié is the thickener most often used for red wine–moistened stews and braises. This solution has the advantage of being quick and, if carried out properly, of not giving the stew a starchy taste. For veal and pork that has not been cooked with red wine, the resulting clear, jus-like braising liquid can be thickened with cornstarch or arrowroot (first worked to a thin paste with a little water or stock), which if used carefully will contribute a natural jus-like sheen and consistency. In some recipes, such as a classic chicken fricassée, the thickener—in this case, cream and egg yolks—is inherent in the definition of the dish. Well-reduced stocks or glace de viande can also be added to braising liquids to give them body and lengthen them if not enough is available to moisten the meat. If using modernist techniques and ingredients, try various hydrocolloid thickeners such as 0.2% xanthan gum or 3% Ultra-Sperse 3. If you want to emulsify clarified butter or other nonemulsified fat such as oil into the sauce, work 1% or 2% liquid lecithin into the fat component and blend 0.5% propylene glycol alginate into the liquid base.

The modern aversion to flour and other starch-based thickeners has led chefs to experiment with new and sometimes very old methods of thickening braising liquids. An obvious and wholesome approach is to purée the aromatic vegetables that have cooked with the stew, then whisk this purée into the strained braising liquid until it has the desired thickness. Irish stew, in which potatoes give body to the liquid, exemplifies how a vegetable can give body to the surrounding liquid as an integral part of the braising process.

Some chefs reduce braising liquids or add glace de viande to give them a thicker consistency, almost like demi-glace. The liquid is then finished with butter. These sauces have great depth of flavor and considerable finesse, but many chefs find them too rich and think their refinement detracts from the satisfying earthiness of a hearty stew. Red wine stews can also be finished with a small amount of foie gras puréed with butter. If you're going to be holding the stew for any length of time, you may want to add an optional 1% to 2% liquid lecithin to the butter.

Braises and stews prepared from rabbit, game, and rooster (an authentic coq au vin) are sometimes thickened with the animal's blood, either alone or combined with the puréed liver of the animal. The French call such dishes *civets* (see "Blood" and Civet de Lapin, page 121).

Adjusting the Flavor of Braising Liquid

Although a properly made stew or braise will always produce a full-flavored liquid, the chef may wish to enhance the flavor of the liquid by underlining one or more of its elements or by finishing it with distinct and assertively flavored ingredients to give it an individual or regional character. Many of the techniques suitable for brown sauces (see Chapter 7, "Brown Sauces") can be used to improve the flavor of braising and stewing liquids. Careful additions of vinegar, Cognac, or marc will often bring up the flavors inherent in the stew without distorting them. The most common and useful final flavorings for stews and braises are freshly chopped herbs. Chopped fines herbes—without tarragon— either alone or in combination, or tarragon alone, are best for flavoring delicate braises of chicken, pork, or veal cooked with water or stock. More assertive meats, such as beef, lamb, or venison, especially if they have been braised with red wine or vinegar, can do with more assertive treatment. Freshly chopped marjoram or oregano will give the dish a southern French or Italian character, and chopped cilantro will give final distinction to a Mexican-style stew.

A skilled saucier is likely to use a combination of methods to adjust the consistency and flavor of a finished braising liquid. He or she may reduce the liquid slightly, thicken it with aromatic vegetable purée or one or more hydrocolloids, and finish it with a final touch of butter; or he or she may prefer to leave the braising liquid alone and serve the stew or braise in the style of a hearty red wine soup.

Garnitures

The term *garniture* is somewhat confusing because it is used in so many different ways. In America, a garniture often means a bit of decoration, usually not meant to be eaten, that is put on the side of the plate to give added color—most commonly, a sprig of parsley. In French terminology, a garniture is usually a vegetable or vegetables served as an accompaniment to meat or fish.

Garnitures for braised meats and stews are often served over the sliced meat or along with the pieces of meat in the stew, to give the impression that the garniture has been cooked with, and is an intrinsic component of, the braise or stew.

In some cases, especially in home cooking, stews and braised meats are served along with the aromatic vegetables used in the cooking. In most professional settings, however, the aromatic vegetables are separated from the meat at the end of cooking and either discarded or puréed as a sauce thickener. New garnishing vegetables are then either cooked along with the meat near the end of the braising, simmered in some of the braising liquid, or cooked entirely separately, to be added to the meat as it is served.

Garnitures for stews and braises are almost endless. For many home-cooked stews, aromatic vegetables are cut into same-size shapes and added to the stew during the last 45 minutes of cooking. A somewhat more sophisticated approach, more often used in restaurants, is to cook aromatic vegetables (sometimes turned or cut into decorative shapes) on top of the stove in some of the cooking liquid drawn off the stew or braise. Certain garnitures, such as wild mushrooms, are sautéed on top of the stove and added to the stew or over the braised meat just before serving. This method is useful for accenting and giving character to the finished stew without altering the flavor of the braising liquid. A beef daube, for example, covered at the last minute with wild mushrooms sautéed with lavender flowers and garlic will benefit from the heady aroma of the mushrooms while the delicate suavity of the braising liquid is left intact.

CLASSIC GARNITURES FOR STEWS AND POT ROASTS

The classic French literature is filled with garnitures for stews and pot roasts. Remember that the basic stewing or braising method stays the same and the aromatic vegetables (the onions, carrots, etc.) cooked with the meat are strained out before the final garniture is added. While many of these garnitures are dated, they provide plenty of ideas for more contemporary interpretations. Garnitures are always expressed in the feminine because the "à la" is short for *à la façon de*, which is feminine. Here are a few of the classics.

ALGÉRIENNE. Potatoes croquette made with sweet potatoes, rolled into cork shapes and fried; baked tomato halves

ALSACIENNE. Surrounded with tartlets filled with braised cabbage

ANDALOUSE. Surrounded with grilled peppers, rice, and rounds of eggplant sautéed in olive oil; topped with sautéed tomatoes

BERRICHONNE. Braised cabbage in little rounds the size of an egg, bacon, pearl onions, and glazed chestnuts

BOUQUETIÈRE. Turned carrots and turnips, château potatoes, peas, diced string beans, cauliflower florets

BOURGEOISE. Turned carrots, glazed onions, diced bacon

BRÉHAN. Artichoke bottoms filled with fava bean purée, cauliflower, fingerling potatoes

CHÂTELAINE. Artichoke bottoms filled with thick soubise (onion purée bound with béchamel), noisette potatoes (sautéed potatoes cut out with a melon baller)

DUBARRY. Cauliflower coated with Mornay sauce and gratinéed

FINANCIÈRE. Quenelles made from chicken or veal, button mushrooms, cockscombs, kidneys, truffles, olives

JARDINIÈRE. Carrots, turnips, string beans, flageolet beans, peas, cauliflower

JUDIC. Stuffed tomatoes, baby lettuces, château potatoes

MACÉDOINE. Like jardinière, but the vegetables are arranged in artichoke bottoms

PRINTANIÈRE. Like jardinière, but noisette potatoes also included

RENAISSANCE. Baby artichokes filled with miniature turned carrots and turnips, string beans, peas, asparagus tips, and cauliflower, everything coated with hollandaise sauce

SARLADAISE. Sautéed sliced potatoes and truffles

Braised Veal, Beef, and Pork Recipes

There are so many methods of braising, each with its own nuances that cause variations in the texture of the meat and the flavor of the sauce, that it is sometimes difficult to sort out the various techniques. The first few of the following recipes are all for a tied shoulder clod of veal to make comparison easy, but veal round will work well for white braising and pot roasting (poêlage) when the meat is not cooked long enough to dry it out.

American chefs usually use the meatiest section of the shoulder, called the *clod* (#310 by the National Association of Meat Purveyors), which is tied up for roasts and braises. Smaller pieces of the shoulder are cut into chunks and used as stew meat. The shoulder clod is tender enough to be used for roasting, but it can also be braised.

MODEL FOR PREPARING BRAISES AND STEWS

Meat

BEEF
Braising: bottom round, rump (well larded), shanks

Stewing: shank, short ribs, chuck, round (well larded)

LAMB
Braising: whole shoulder (NAMP #207 whole or #208 boneless)

Stewing: shoulder, leg (well larded), shanks

VEAL
Braising: shoulder clod, round (well larded), breast

Stewing: shoulder, shank

PORK
Braising: shoulder

Stewing: shoulder, shank

POULTRY
Stewing: older hens or roosters, duck legs, goose (larding of breasts is suggested)

GAME
Braising and stewing: older animals or tougher cuts from large animals such as deer or boar

Marinade Ingredients
(Optional)

LIQUIDS
Red or white wine

Vinegar (good-quality wine or cider)

OILS
Olive

Grapeseed

Inert-tasting oil, such as peanut or safflower

AROMATIC VEGETABLES
Onions

Garlic

Carrots

Celery

Turnips

Fennel

HERBS
Parsley

Bay leaf

Thyme

Tarragon

Hyssop

Basil

Marjoram

SPICES
Juniper berries

Cloves (usually stuck into onions)

Peppercorns

Moistening Ingredients

Water

Wine (white, red, and fortified wines, alone or in combination)

Stock (neutral, such as veal or chicken, or the same type as the meat being braised)

Spirits (brandy, whiskey, marc), flamed

Beer

Cider

Aromatic Vegetables

Same as those used in the marinade

Herbs

Same as those used in the marinade

Spices

Same as those used in the marinade

Liaisons

Optional

Flour (used to coat meat before browning or sprinkled over during browning; beurre manié used at the end to finish the braising liquid)

Arrowroot or cornstarch (combined with water, used to finish the braising liquid; produces a glossy appearance)

Vegetable purée (puréed aromatic vegetables taken from the braise or stew, or vegetable purées prepared on the side from garlic, beans, mushrooms, potatoes, turnips, celeriac root, and the like)

Liver (usually for poultry, game, or rabbits), can be emulsified with 0.2% xanthan gum and 0.5% propylene glycol alginate

Blood (usually for game and rabbit civets, but also coq au vin), worked with butter, can be emulsified with liquid lecithin

Butter

Foie gras (puréed with butter; can be stabilized with 2% liquid lecithin worked into the foie gras)

Hydrocolloids (such as xanthan gum, carrageenan, Ultra-Sperse 3, gellan, assorted gums, propylene glycol alginate)

Emulsifiers (liquid and powdered lecithin, propylene glycol alginate, Glice [mono- and diglycerides], polysorbates, sucrose esters, gum arabic)

Emulsion stabilizers (gelatin, agar)

Final Flavorings

Fines herbs (without tarragon, or tarragon alone, usually for chicken, pork, or veal)

Assertive herbs (thyme, marjoram, oregano, basil, usually for red meats or game)

Spirits (Cognac, Armagnac, marc or grappa, eau-de-vie, whiskey)

Garnitures

(Heated in the braising liquid)

Carrots (cylinders with core removed; turned; julienned; cut into bâtonnets)

Turnips (turned, julienne)

Pearl onions

Garlic cloves (peeled)

Mushrooms

Truffles

(Sautéed or heated separately and added at the end of cooking)

Wild mushrooms (with herbs, garlic, shallots)

Artichoke hearts

Poultry or rabbit livers

Olives

Croutons (heart-shaped, gently cooked in clarified butter, ends dipped in chopped parsley are classic)

Bacon lardons

The shoulder clod is the meatiest part of the shoulder, and is easy to tie up into an ovoid or round shape. It can be cooked using virtually every braising method.

Most recipes for white braising (braising without preliminary browning) suggest moistening the braise with enough stock to come halfway up the meat and then cooking, uncovered, with frequent basting. In an étouffée, the stock is added a bit at a time so that it can gently and repeatedly caramelize during the braising. If too much stock is added at the beginning, the finished jus will have the flavor of a poaching liquid and may require reduction. If too little stock is added, the juices will caramelize and burn. This method of repeated caramelizations is best if the clod is being long braised. If it is short braised, it won't release enough juices to caramelize. If it is cooked to the point that it releases juices, it will be overcooked. The jus for an étuvé is best when the cooking liquid is kept constantly on the verge of caramelizing. The amount of stock that must be added during the last stage of cooking will depend on the oven temperature and the amount of liquid released by the veal.

It is also a good idea, when long braising, to carefully and thoroughly lard the meat (see page 31).

In an authentic poêlage, usually performed as a short braise, no moisture comes in contact with the meat during cooking; the meat is cooked in a covered casserole with mirepoix vegetables and butter alone. At the end of cooking, it is transferred to a platter while a jus is prepared by moistening the mirepoix with stock. The oven temperature must be carefully controlled: If it is too hot, the juices released by the veal will burn; if it is not hot enough, the juices will not caramelize and the veal will stew in its own juices. If you look in the casserole and see liquid, remove the lid to dry it out; if there's no liquid and the aromatic vegetables are starting to brown, add ½ cup (125 milliliters) stock or water.

LONG BROWN-BRAISED VEAL SHOULDER CLOD

Long brown-braised meats are browned and cooked until the muscle fibers break down, leaving the meat tender. This method shows off the veal shoulder clod at its best. Remember to lard it thoroughly, a process that may take as long as 40 minutes.

YIELD: 8 TO 10 SERVINGS

fatback	1 pound	500 grams
garlic cloves, chopped	2	2
veal shoulder clod	4 to 5 pounds	1.8 to 2.3 kilograms
onion, chopped	1 medium	1 medium
carrot, chopped	1 medium	1 medium
celery, chopped	½ stalk	½ stalk
veal or pork trimmings, pancetta, or prosciutto, chopped	5 ounces	150 grams

clarified butter	¼ cup	60 milliliters
white or brown meat stock	2 quarts	2 liters
large bouquet garni (page 52)	1	1

1. Cut the fatback into 6 × ⅜-inch (15 cm × 5 mm) strips. Toss the strips in a stainless-steel bowl with the garlic. Cover and refrigerate for 2 to 3 hours.

2. Open the shoulder clod and lay it out on a cutting board. Insert the strips of fatback into the various inside muscles with a larding needle (an *aiguille à piquer*, not a *lardoir*; see page 31). Turn the meat over and lard the outside. Tie the shoulder clod into an even shape. Preheat the oven to 350°F (175°C).

3. Select an oval casserole that will just hold the shoulder clod. Put the onion, carrot, celery, meat trimmings, and clarified butter in the casserole. Set the shoulder clod on top.

4. Roast the shoulder, uncovered, for approximately 40 minutes, until it is golden brown and there are caramelized meat drippings on the bottom of the casserole; don't worry if the juices haven't caramelized. When the top of the clod is browned, usually in about 20 minutes, turn it over and brown the second side. Once browned, turn down the oven to 300°F (150°C).

5. Place the casserole, with the meat in it, on top of the stove over high heat and add 1 cup (250 milliliters) of the stock. Cook until the stock reduces to a glaze and caramelizes on the bottom of the casserole.

6. Add the bouquet garni and enough of the remaining stock to come halfway up the sides of the meat. Bring it to a slow simmer on top of the stove. Cover the casserole with a sheet of aluminum foil that is pressed down in the middle (which causes liquid to condense and drip down over the meat, so it is basted from the inside), and put on the lid. Return the casserole to the oven.

7. As the veal braises, check the casserole every 20 minutes to make sure the liquid is not boiling. After 90 minutes of braising, turn the roast over so what was above the liquid is now in it. Continue cooking the veal, checking it every 20 minutes, for 2 to 3 hours, until a skewer inserted in the veal slides in and out with no resistance.

8. Carefully remove the meat (at this stage it is very fragile) from the braising liquid, and place it in a clean and, ideally, smaller oval casserole. Turn the oven back up to 350°F (175°C) and slide the casserole with the meat back into the oven. Add about ½ cup (125 ml) of braising liquid to the casserole to prevent the bottom of the casserole from burning. While you're reducing the braising liquid, check on the meat every 10 minutes or so to make sure it isn't burning. If it threatens to run dry, add more braising liquid.

9. Strain the remaining braising liquid and place it in a saucepan on top of the stove. Bring it to a simmer and skim off any froth and fat that float to the surface. Continue skimming and reducing for 20 minutes.

10. Pour the reduced and degreased braising liquid over the veal, and return the casserole, uncovered, to the oven. Baste the veal every 5 minutes with the surrounding liquid. Continue until the braising liquid has a lightly syrupy consistency and the veal is shiny and reddish brown.

11. Transfer the veal to a plate or platter and strain the braising liquid to serve alongside.

Note: Unlike roasts, short white braises, and pot roasts (poêlage), which cannot be reheated without causing them to overcook, slices of braised meats can be reheated to order in a small amount of braising liquid in a covered sauté pan.

OTHER BRAISED VEAL TECHNIQUES

One particularly excellent technique for cooking veal is to cook it as an étuvé, a method that combines roasting and braising. *Étuver* (sometimes called "étouffer") refers to roasting/braising in the oven or, sometimes, in a closed vessel. Initially, the only thing added to the meat being treated in this way is butter, preferably clarified butter that poses no risk of burning. As the meat cooks, a small amount of stock is added as needed to keep any liquid on the bottom of the pan from burning.

The secret to success requires understanding what happens to a roast such as a veal round when it gets hot. Essentially, it releases juices that should caramelize as soon as they reach the hot outer surface of the meat. If the oven isn't hot enough, the juices accumulate in the bottom of the pan and cause the roast to steam. If the oven is too hot, the juices burn. It is necessary to maintain a kind of homeostasis in which the juices are constantly caramelizing on the surface of the meat. If you see liquid in the pan, turn up the oven. If, on the other hand, you see any signs of excessive darkening, add a little stock to the roast to stop the caramelization. Keep in mind that if you're cooking veal à l'étuver, that lean cuts can dry out if you keep waiting for them to release more juices. For this reason, it is sometimes better to prepare a jus using meat trimmings that have been repeatedly caramelized and deglazed.

Almost all braised dishes include aromatic vegetables, particularly onions, carrots, celery, and often garlic. In traditional French cooking, these vegetables are taken out of the dish before serving or left in depending on whether the style is *ménagère* (meaning "housewife"), *bourgeoise* (as in *cuisine bourgeoise*), or *classique*. In cuisine ménagère, the

INTEGRAL MEAT SAUCES

aromatic vegetables are left in and served with the braised or stewed meat. In cuisine bourgeoise, the vegetables are strained out and discarded and new vegetables are added to the braise during the last hour or so of cooking. In cuisine classique, the vegetables are cooked separately on the stove, and added to the dish at the very end.

Osso buco is especially good when braised. The meat is first browned (A, B), then braising liquid is added, and aromatic vegetables added halfway through the braising (C, D). The vegetables can be left in the braise, in the tradition of la cuisine ménagère, or discarded and replaced with new vegetables as in cuisine bourgeoise.

BRAISED SWEETBREADS

Regardless of how sweetbreads are cooked—they're usually braised or sautéed—they first undergo a blanching and weighting process to compact them. Sweetbreads come in two forms. One, long and a bit ragged, is called in French the *gorge*, meaning "throat," while the other, compact and spheroid, is called the *noix*, meaning "nut." Always choose the noix, which will look neater on the plate and braise more evenly.

The most frequently made mistake when preparing this dish is adding too much liquid for braising. Keep in mind that the liquid released from the sweetbreads should be allowed to caramelize. It has a flavor of its own that shouldn't be compromised with the addition of large amounts of stock or other liquids.

YIELD: 6 SERVINGS

sweetbreads, preferably noix pieces	2½ pounds	1.25 kilograms
carrot, cut into small dice	1 large	1 large
onion, minced	1 medium	1 medium
garlic clove, minced	1	1
butter	1 ounce	30 grams
white wine	½ cup	125 milliliters
glace de viande (page 97; optional)	2 tablespoons	30 milliliters
heavy cream	1 cup	250 milliliters
salt and pepper	to taste	to taste

1. Put the sweetbreads in a pot with enough cold water to cover and bring to a boil over high heat. As soon as the water comes to a boil, take out the sweetbreads and put them on a sheet pan. Put a cutting board on top with some cans or pots on top of that to weight the sweetbreads. Store in the refrigerator for 6 hours or overnight. Trim off loose pieces of fat and tissue.

(continued)

2. In a pan just large enough to hold the sweetbreads in a single layer, sweat the carrots, onions, and garlic in the butter over medium heat until the onion is translucent but not brown, about 10 minutes. Preheat the oven to 400°F (200°C).

3. Arrange the sweetbreads over the vegetables in the pan. Place a round of parchment paper or aluminum foil loosely on top of the sweetbreads and slide the pan into the oven. Check every 10 minutes to make sure the juices are caramelizing but not burning. If the juices are threatening to burn, add half the wine.

4. Bake for about 25 minutes, or until firm to the touch. Take the sweetbreads out of the pan and keep them warm. Add the wine to the pan and boil it for about 10 seconds to cook off the alcohol. Add the glace de viande and cream and bring to a simmer. Reduce the sauce if it needs thickening, but be careful not to overdo it or the sauce may end up gloppy. Season with salt and pepper. Slice the sweetbreads and top with the sauce. Here the vegetables are left in the sauce, but they may also be strained out.

VARIATIONS

This technique for braising sweetbreads and building a sauce is almost universal, but various ingredients can be added to the sauce minutes before serving to give it a different character. Chiffonade of sorrel, chopped fines herbes, sautéed fresh or reconstituted dried cèpes (porcini mushrooms), morels, and truffles are just a few possibilities. In the early twentieth century, sweetbreads were often served à la financière with truffles, chicken quenelles, and cockscombs. It's also possible to use a brunoise of carrots and turnips along with the minced onions to braise the sweetbreads and then use this as part of the garniture. Michel Guérard serves a dish of sweetbreads in which the sweetbreads are separated into pieces—virtually all the connective membrane is removed—and the braised pieces served in a sauce made with morels and truffles. Wedges of artichoke bottoms are served with the sweetbreads to provide a subtly contrasting texture.

RED WINE POT ROAST

The most important step in making a pot roast is to choose the right cut of meat. A blade roast from the shoulder is best.

In French cooking there are all sorts of ways to finish a pot roast, including the classic Burgundian garniture of mushrooms, pearl onions, and bacon lardons. Other variations include braising the beef with a substantial number of sliced carrots and leaving them in as the garniture. The aromatic garniture (the vegetables braised with the meat) can be left in or strained out. Here we strain it out.

YIELD: 6 SERVINGS

beef blade roast (from the shoulder), 1	5 pounds	2.25 kilograms
onion, chopped fine	1 large	1 large
carrots, sliced	2 large	2 large
red wine	3 cups	750 milliliters
glace de viande (page 97; optional)	¼ cup	60 milliliters

large bouquet garni (page 52)	1	1
salt and pepper	to taste	to taste
red wine vinegar (or to taste)	2 tablespoons	30 milliliters

1. Preheat the oven to 450°F (230°C).

2. Tie up the roast. Spread the onions and carrots in a pot just large enough to hold the roast. Place the roast on top.

3. Roast the meat until it browns and any juices it releases caramelize on the bottom of the pot, about an hour. Be careful at the end of this stage not to burn the juices. If the juices threaten to burn before the roast is browned, add stock or water—about ½ cup (125 milliliters)—as needed.

4. Turn the oven down to 300°F (150°C). Put the pot on the stove and pour over the wine. Add the glace de viande, if using, and the bouquet garni; bring to a simmer. Cover the pot with aluminum foil and braise gently in the oven or on the stove until the meat is easily penetrated with a skewer, about 3 hours. Check on the meat every 20 minutes or so to make sure the braising liquid isn't boiling. If it is, turn down the oven or the stove.

5. Take out the meat and strain the juices into a saucepan. Discard the vegetables or save them to serve with the roast. Discard the bouquet garni. Fit the roast into a smaller pan or clean out the pan just used and put the roast back in. Turn the oven to 400°F (200°C).

6. Simmer the braising liquid on the stove and skim off the fat. Pour the liquid over the roast, and return the roast, uncovered, to the oven. Baste every 5 minutes for about an hour or until the roast becomes shiny and the braising liquid syrupy. Season the braising liquid to taste with salt, pepper, and vinegar.

7. Gently slice the roast. If it's extremely tender, it can even be served with a spoon. Because the braising liquid is not thickened with any kind of starch or hydrocolloid, the roast is best served in soup plates with the braising liquid spooned over.

VARIATION

By garnishing this stew with lardons, heart-shaped croutons dipped in chopped parsley, sautéed mushrooms, and pearl onions, it becomes boeuf à la bourguignonne. Don't confuse this dish with boeuf bourguignon (see page 273), which is a stew.

PORK SHOULDER CHOPS WITH WHITE WINE AND PRUNES

This French country dish demonstrates an excellent method for braising. Here we use shoulder chops, which require long braising; if you're using loin chops, short braise them by cooking them only long enough for the heat to penetrate them. Here the garniture is simple, prunes steeped in water, then simmered in white wine (traditionally Vouvray), but this dish is a model for braising shoulder chops and can be garnished with virtually anything.

YIELD: 6 SERVINGS

(continued)

shoulder pork chops	6 large	6 large
salt and pepper	to taste	to taste
oil	3 tablespoons	45 milliliters
butter	1½ ounces	45 grams
carrot, chopped	1 medium	1 medium
onion, chopped	1 medium	1 medium
dry or semi-dry white wine such as vouvray	1 cup	250 milliliters
chicken stock, preferably concentrated (about 4 times), or water	2 cups	500 milliliters
large bouquet garni (page 52)	1	1
prunes, pitted	1 cup	250 milliliters
heavy cream	1 cup	250 milliliters

1. Season the chops with salt and pepper. Brown them in the oil in a heavy-bottomed pan over high heat. Put the chops on a plate and pour the oil out of the pan. Add the butter, carrots, and onions to the pan and cook gently for about 10 minutes.

2. Add the chops back to the pan and pour in the wine and stock. Bring to a gentle simmer. Nestle in the bouquet garni. Cover the chops with a sheet of aluminum foil almost touching their surface. Cover with the lid. Simmer gently for about 2 hours, until a knife stuck into one of the chops goes in and out with no resistance.

3. Meanwhile, soak the prunes in just enough water to cover for 30 minutes.

4. Gently transfer the chops to a plate and keep them warm in a low oven while you make the sauce. Take out the bouquet garni and strain the braising liquid into a saucepan. Simmer gently, skimming off any fat and scum that float to the surface, until the sauce cooks down by about three-quarters or takes on a lightly syrupy con-sistency. Add the cream and simmer again until the sauce thickens just slightly—it should be kept light. Drain the prunes and add them to the sauce.

5. Simmer the prunes in the sauce for a minute to soften them, and season the sauce with salt and pepper. Arrange the chops on heated plates and spoon over the prunes and sauce.

Stews

Stews are braises made with pieces of meat or poultry instead of whole birds or large cuts. The best meat stews are made from gelatinous and relatively fatty cuts. When leaner, more tender cuts are used, the stew is greatly improved by inserting a strip of fatback into each piece so that the meat is moistened from the inside while cooking.

The character of a finished stew is also determined by whether or not it is browned before being moistened; the type of moistening liquid; the types of aromatic vegetables used; the herbs used in the bouquet garni; the final liaison, if any; and the final garniture. Strips of pork rind, split and blanched pork, or veal trotters are also sometimes added to stews and braises to support the texture of the finished liquid.

Stews can be divided into two categories: brown stews, for which the meat or poultry is cooked in fat before moistening, and white stews, for which the meat or poultry is directly moistened without preliminary cooking. In brown stews, the meat or poultry is often dredged in or sprinkled with flour before being cooked in fat. The terms *white* braise or stew and *brown* braise or stew refer only to whether the meat has been browned, not to the final color of the sauce. Thus, a beef stew made with red wine but without browning the meat is still a white stew, even though the final color of the sauce is dark. There is very little difference between a white stew and pieces of meat that have been poached—the only distinction is the amount of liquid used.

RED WINE BEEF STEW

This is a basic recipe for a red wine stew without any garniture. Again, "garniture," in French, refers to anything that's added to a dish at the end and that isn't necessarily a component of the braise itself. Hence, virtually any vegetable can be prepared and added to the stew at the end. Garnished with heart-shaped croutons (dipped in chopped parsley), sautéed mushrooms, pearl onions braised à brun (until lightly browned), and strips of bacon—lardons—this dish becomes boeuf bourguignon.

YIELD: 8 TO 10 SERVINGS

fatback, rind removed	8 ounces	250 grams
garlic cloves, chopped	2	2
cognac	2 tablespoons	30 milliliters
beef shank (4 pounds/1.8 kilograms when cut from the bone)	6 pounds	3 kilograms
carrots, chopped	2 medium	2 medium
onions, chopped	2 medium	2 medium
garlic cloves, crushed	2	2
red wine	3 cups	750 milliliters
large bouquet garni (page 52)	1	1
olive oil	6 tablespoons	90 milliliters
butter	1½ ounces	45 grams
flour (optional)	¼ cup	40 grams
brown beef or veal stock	3 cups	750 milliliters
liaison, such as beurre manié, arrowroot, vegetable purée, or hydrocolloid (optional)		

(continued)

1. Cut the fatback into 2 × ⅜-inch (5 cm × 5 mm) strips. Marinate the fatback strips in the chopped garlic and Cognac for at least 3 hours.

2. Cut the beef into 3-ounce (90 gram) cubes. Insert a strip of fatback into each beef cube using a larding needle or paring knife. Marinate the meat cubes for several hours with the carrots, onions, crushed garlic, red wine, and bouquet garni.

3. Preheat the oven to 300°F (150°C). Drain the meat in a colander set over a bowl and separately reserve the marinade liquid, vegetables, and bouquet garni. Thoroughly dry the meat. Heat the olive oil in a straight-sided sauté pan and brown the meat.

4. Transfer the meat to a clean bowl and discard the oil. Sweat the reserved vegetables and garlic in the butter. Sprinkle the vegetables with flour, if using, and cook gently for 5 minutes more.

5. Add the reserved marinade liquid, stock, and the reserved bouquet garni to the vegetables and bring the mixture to a simmer while scraping the bottom of the pan with a wooden spoon.

6. Transfer the contents of the sauté pan to a 4-quart (4 liter) pot. Add the meat. Cover and cook in the oven for 2 to 3 hours, until the meat cubes are easily pierced with a fork.

7. Strain the stewing liquid into a 2-quart (2 liter) saucepan, reserving the solids. Spread the meat and vegetables on a baking sheet. Separate the meat from the chopped vegetables, which should be discarded or can be puréed for use as the liaison. Bring the liquid to a slow simmer and skim off any froth and fat that float to the surface. The stewing liquid can be reduced to the desired thickness or bound with beurre manié (the most traditional method), arrowroot, vegetable purées, or hydrocolloid liaisons. Remember that beurre manié is simply whisked into the hot sauce and the sauce allowed to boil. Arrowroot, cornstarch, and some hydrocolloids should be whisked up with an equal amount of water into a slurry. Most hydrocolloids will need to be sheared in with a blender. Work the hydrocolloid into a small amount of the stewing liquid. When it is thoroughly combined, whisk it into the rest of the liquid.

8. Reheat the meat cubes in the stewing liquid. Serve with an appropriate garniture.

BEEF IRISH STEW

Not surprisingly, Irish stew is all about potatoes. The secret is to use two kinds: Yukon Golds, which dissolve and give a silky body to the stew, and waxy potatoes, which keep their shape and give a contrasting texture to the stew. Most recipes say to slice the potatoes, but you can also shape them into miniature eggs. As for a daube, the meat for Irish stew isn't browned. Usually Irish stew is made with lamb, but it's delicious with beef.

YIELD: 6 SERVINGS

beef stew meat, cut into 1-inch (2.5 cm) cubes	4 pounds	2 kilograms
onions, minced	2 medium	2 medium
beef stock, chicken stock, or water, to cover	3 cups	750 milliliters
large bouquet garni (page 52)	1	1

yukon gold potato, peeled, sliced as thin as possible, and kept in water to prevent darkening	1 large	1 large
white or red waxy potatoes, peeled	3 large	3 large
pearl onions or walnut-size boiling onions, peeled (optional)	2 cups	500 milliliters
heavy cream (optional)	½ cup	125 milliliters
salt and pepper	to taste	to taste

1. If you'll be cooking the stew in the oven, preheat the oven to 300°F (149°C).

2. Place the meat, minced onions, and enough stock to cover in a tall pot and nestle in the bouquet garni. Bring to a simmer on the stove and skim off any froth that floats to the surface. Add the Yukon Gold potato, cover, and maintain at a gentle simmer on the stove or in the oven.

3. After an hour, stir with a wooden spoon to dissolve the sliced potato.

4. Slice the waxy potatoes into ¼-inch-thick (5 mm) rounds or shape the potatoes into elongated football shapes, 4 to 8 out of each one. When the stew has been simmering for 2 hours, add the waxy potatoes and the pearl onions, if using.

5. Simmer until the meat and potatoes are both easily penetrated with a skewer. Stir in the cream, if using, and bring back to a simmer. Simmer a minute or two if needed to thicken the sauce, and season with salt and pepper. Serve in heated soup plates.

Poultry Braises and Stews

The techniques for stewing poultry and rabbit are essentially the same as for veal and red meats. The term *fricassée* traditionally refers to a chicken dish in which the chicken has been cut up, gently cooked in butter without being browned, and stewed with water or stock. The cooking liquid is then finished with heavy cream and egg yolks. The term is sometimes used more loosely to define any chicken or white meat that has been cooked in a small amount of liquid after a gentle preliminary cooking in fat.

Fricassées differ from sautés in that the chicken finishes cooking in liquid, whereas sautés are cooked entirely with a small amount of fat either on top of the stove or in the oven.

Older poultry can be braised, either cut into pieces as for a coq au vin or left whole.

An excellent method for cooking a whole chicken or other small- to medium-size poultry is to cook it covered in a close-fitting casserole. When poultry is prepared in this way—the French call it *en cocotte*—it is cooked to the same doneness as roasts and white braises.

Keep in mind that long-braised poultry white meat tends to dry out. The only way to prevent this is to lard the meat thoroughly with strips of fatback—a laborious task that few restaurants are willing to undertake. Most of what is served as coq au vin (rooster braised in red wine) in American restaurants is really a red wine chicken sauté.

POULET EN COCOTTE
WHOLE CHICKEN IN A CASSEROLE

Chicken cooked in this way is first browned either in the oven or on top of the stove before it is placed into an oval casserole, covered, and baked. Some recipes suggest cooking the chicken with butter alone (poêlage), whereas others suggest adding a small amount of liquid, such as water or wine.

YIELD: 4 SERVINGS

bacon	3 ounces	75 grams
chicken, 1	3 to 3½ pounds	1.4 to 1.6 kilograms
pearl onions, peeled	20	20
potatoes, turned to the size of large olives	12	12
concentrated chicken or veal stock	as needed	as needed

1. Preheat the oven to 500°F (260°C). Cut the bacon into 1 × ⅜-inch (2.5 cm × 5 mm) lardons and blanch them in boiling water for 5 minutes. Gently brown the lardons in a straight-sided sauté pan large enough to hold the chicken. Remove them with a slotted spoon.

2. Truss the chicken and brown it in the fat rendered by the bacon.

3. Remove the chicken from the sauté pan and brown the pearl onions and potatoes.

4. Place the chicken, lardons, onions, and potatoes in a close-fitting casserole and cover. Bake for approximately 1 hour. Check periodically to make sure the casserole hasn't run dry. If it has, add ½ cup (125 milliliters) concentrated stock. You may also want to turn down the oven. If juices are accumulating without caramelizing, remove the lid. Watch carefully so the jus doesn't burn on the bottom of the pot.

5. Transfer the chicken and garniture to a plate or platter and strain the liquid in the casserole into a small bowl, pitcher, or fat separator. Skim off most of the fat and serve the sauce in a sauceboat.

COQ AU VIN
ROOSTER BRAISED IN RED WINE

Traditional recipes for coq au vin finish the sauce with the rooster's blood, which is still a good idea if starting with a live bird (see "Blood," page 121). Coq au vin is usually thought of as Burgundian, and some cooks underline this fact by using a good marc de Bourgogne to deglaze the pan after browning and again to finish the braising liquid. Another approach is to give the dish local character by using the appropriate wine and herbs, and finishing with the appropriate spirit (such as California Zinfandel or Napa Valley brandy). However, if you're in Burgundy, don't be crazy and use red

Burgundy, traditional or not. It doesn't have the necessary structure, to say nothing of its expense.

In this recipe, the pieces of rooster are coated with flour, browned, and moistened with red wine. The consistency of the braising liquid is adjusted at the end by reduction and with beurre manié. For flourless versions, the flour and beurre manié can be omitted and the braising liquid lent natural body by including blanched pork rinds in the braise. The finished braising liquid can also be combined with concentrated chicken stock, or glace de viande can be added to give it body. With either version, the braising liquid is then reduced to the desired consistency.

YIELD: 4 TO 6 SERVINGS

lean salt pork	5 ounces	150 grams
rooster, 1, cut into serving pieces	5 to 6 pounds	2.3 to 2.7 kilograms
salt and pepper	to taste	to taste
flour	1 cup	150 grams
carrot, chopped	1 medium	1 medium
onion, chopped	1 medium	1 medium
red wine	3 cups	750 milliliters
large bouquet garni (page 52)	1	1
brandy or marc	½ cup	125 milliliters
button mushrooms	8 ounces	250 grams
butter	2 ounces	60 grams
pearl onions, peeled	8 ounces	250 grams
heart-shaped croutons	4 to 6	4 to 6
clarified butter	¼ cup	60 milliliters
beurre manié	¼ cup	60 grams
chopped parsley	2 tablespoons	30 milliliters

1. If you'll be cooking the coq au vin in the oven, preheat it to 300°F (150°C).

2. Cut the salt pork into thick lardons and blanch them in boiling water for 5 minutes. Render the lardons in a 4-quart (4 liter) heavy-bottomed pot large enough to hold the rooster pieces. Remove the lardons with a slotted spoon and reserve.

3. Season the rooster pieces with salt and pepper and dredge them in the flour.

4. Brown the carrot and onion in the rendered pork fat. Remove them with a slotted spoon and brown the pieces of rooster. When the rooster pieces are well browned, remove them and discard the fat in the pot.

(continued)

5. Place the sautéed vegetables, browned rooster pieces, wine, bouquet garni, and brandy or marc in the pot. Cover and bring to a simmer on top of the stove. Cook either in the oven or on top of the stove for 1½ hours or until the pieces of rooster are easily penetrated with a skewer. Check periodically to make sure the liquid isn't boiling. Adjust temperatures accordingly.

6. Sauté the mushrooms in 1 ounce (30 grams) of the butter for about 5 minutes, until lightly browned; set aside. Gently cook the pearl onions in the remaining 1 ounce (30 grams) butter for about 20 minutes, until they soften; set aside. Lightly brown the croutons in the clarified butter and set aside.

7. Carefully remove the cooked pieces of rooster from the pot with a slotted spoon. Strain the braising liquid into a saucepan large enough to hold the rooster and vegetables.

8. Slowly reduce the braising liquid, skimming off any fat or froth that floats to the surface. Continue reducing until the braising liquid has a deep, full flavor.

9. Whisk the beurre manié 1 tablespoon (15 milliliters) at a time into the liquid until the braising liquid has the desired consistency. Season with salt and pepper. (The flavor of the braising liquid can usually be improved by adding a tablespoon or two [15 to 30 milliliters] good vinegar and Cognac.) Gently heat the rooster with the mushroom and pearl onion garniture and the lardons in the sauce. Dip the tips of the croutons in the sauce and then in the parsley. Arrange the croutons around the serving platter.

CHICKEN WITH RED WINE SAUCE
SOMETIMES CALLED COQ AU VIN

An authentic coq au vin is almost unheard of nowadays, since roosters aren't easy to come by and are of questionable quality when they can be found. The traditional blood finish for the sauce is illegal for restaurants in most states.

What we usually eat instead of coq au vin is chicken with red wine sauce. But the inherent problem with cooking chicken in red wine is that a regular chicken cooks too fast for the wine's tannins to soften and for the flavors of the braising liquid to meld into something tasty and complex. The secret is to make a stock with chicken parts and red wine, and then use this liquid to cook the chicken.

YIELD: 4 SERVINGS

red wine chicken stock (page 87)	2 quarts	2 liters
chicken, 1, quartered	4 pounds	2 kilograms
butter	2 ounces	60 grams
mushrooms, quartered if large	10 ounces	300 grams
pearl onions, peeled	1 cup	250 milliliters
water or chicken stock	as needed	as needed
thickly sliced bacon, cut crosswise into 1 × ¼-inch (2.5 cm × 5 mm) strips	6 ounces	170 grams

butter (for bound sauce; optional)	2 ounces	60 grams
parsley, finely chopped at the last minute	2 tablespoons	30 milliliters
salt and pepper	to taste	to taste

1. Simmer the stock, skimming any froth or scum that floats to the surface, until only 2 cups (500 milliliters) remain.

2. Brown the chicken on both sides in 1 ounce (30 grams) of the butter for about 10 minutes on each side in a large sauté pan over medium to high heat. Take out the chicken, discard the fat in the pan, and put the chicken back in along with the reduced stock. Cover the pot and bring to a gentle simmer for about 15 minutes.

3. Sauté the mushrooms in the remaining 1 ounce (30 grams) butter. Set aside.

4. Glaze the onions with enough water or stock to come halfway up their sides. Set aside.

5. Render the bacon until crisp. Drain; set aside.

6. Take the chicken out of the braising liquid as soon as it's firm to the touch and keep it warm while cooking down the liquid in the pan to about 1 cup (250 milliliters).

7. You can serve the chicken in heated soup plates (this allows for the sauce to remain unbound) and spoon over sauce, mushrooms, bacon, and onions, or you can reduce the braising liquid to ½ cup (125 milliliters) and whisk in the butter, if using. Sprinkle with parsley and season with salt and pepper.

Note: To bind the sauce in Step 7, you can also use hydrocolloid thickeners such as xanthan gum and Ultra-Sperse 3. In any case, finish the sauce with the butter to give it the right mouthfeel.

COLD RED WINE–CHICKEN DAUBE

You can skip the nineteenth-century touch of larding the chicken with prosciutto, but it does make the dish special. The secret to the gelée is to make a red wine stock as you would regular brown stock but replace the water with red wine.

YIELD: 4 MAIN-COURSE SERVINGS

prosciutto slice, about ⅛ inch (3 mm) thick, cut into strips (optional)	1	1
chicken, 1, quartered	4 pounds	2 kilograms
red wine chicken stock (page 87)	2 quarts	2 liters
butter	1½ ounces	45 grams
salt and pepper	to taste	to taste
parsley, finely chopped at the last minute	2 tablespoons	30 milliliters

(continued)

1. Insert the strips of prosciutto into the flesh of the chicken on both the skin and flesh sides with a hinged larding needle (see page 31).

2. Simmer the stock, while skimming off any froth or scum that floats to the surface, until 3 cups (750 milliliters) remain.

3. Cook the chicken in the butter in a nonstick sauté pan until well browned and firm to the touch. Remove from the pan and drain on paper towels.

4. Season the hot stock with salt and pepper and add the parsley. Let cool.

5. Arrange the chicken in a baking dish just large enough to hold it in a single layer and pour over the stock. Chill until the gelée sets. Serve the chicken with the gelée.

CHICKEN FRICASSÉE

Although some contemporary recipes have stretched the traditional definition of a fricassée—browning the chicken and using a variety of moistening liquids and garnitures—a classic fricassée should be almost perfectly white and the braising liquid always finished with heavy cream and egg yolks.

In this recipe, flour is cooked with onions sweated in the butter used for the chicken to form a roux. But a more intensely flavored sauce can be prepared by eliminating the flour, moistening the chicken with a well-concentrated white stock, and reducing the braising liquid to an almost demi-glace consistency before finishing with the cream and egg yolks. It is also possible to eliminate the egg yolks, reduce the cream alone, and finish the sauce with 1 to 1½ ounces (30 to 45 grams) butter. Hydrocolloids can also be incorporated as thickeners. One percent lecithin in the butter and 0.5% propylene glycol alginate in the braising liquid will stabilize the sauce. In any case, however, the sauce should not be allowed to boil.

YIELD: 8 SERVINGS

chickens, 3 pounds (1.4 kilograms) each, cut in serving pieces	2	2
salt and pepper	to taste	to taste
butter	3 ounces	90 grams
onions, chopped	2 medium	2 medium
flour	2 tablespoons	30 milliliters
white chicken stock (page 88), hot	5 cups	1.25 liters
button mushrooms	8 ounces	250 grams
pearl onions, peeled	8 ounces	250 grams
heavy cream	¾ cup	185 milliliters

egg yolks	4	4
lemon juice (optional)	1 teaspoon	5 milliliters

1. If you'll be cooking the chicken in the oven, preheat it to 300°F (149°C).

2. Season the chicken with salt and pepper. In a straight-sided sauté pan, gently cook the seasoned chicken pieces, skin side down, in 2 ounces (60 grams) of the butter. After about 10 minutes, turn them over and cook the flesh side. Cook gently to avoid browning the chicken or burning the butter. Remove the chicken from the pan.

3. Add the chopped onions to the butter in the pan and sweat them, without browning, until translucent. Add the flour and cook gently for 5 minutes.

4. Add 1 quart (1 liter) of the stock to the roux and bring to a simmer. Arrange the chicken pieces in the liquid. Cover. Cook the chicken in the oven or over low heat on the stove for 15 to 20 minutes.

5. Cook the mushrooms in ½ cup (125 milliliters) of the remaining stock for 5 minutes.

6. Simmer the pearl onions in the remaining ½ cup (125 milliliters) stock for about 15 minutes, until they soften.

7. Strain the cooking liquid from both the mushrooms and onions and pour it into the cooking chicken. Keep the mushrooms and onions warm.

8. Strain the braising liquid from the chickens into a 2-quart (2 liter) saucepan. (Keep the chicken pieces warm.) Reduce the liquid, while skimming, until approximately 2 cups (500 milliliters) remain.

9. Whisk together the cream and egg yolks in a bowl. Whisk in half the reduced braising liquid. Return this mixture to the saucepan.

10. Gently heat the cream–braising liquid mixture, while stirring, until the egg yolks thicken it slightly and give it a silky texture. Don't let the mixture boil or the egg yolks will curdle. (There's not enough flour to stabilize them.)

11. Season with salt and pepper. (The lemon juice, if used, will enhance the finished sauce.) Serve the chicken coated with the sauce and topped with the mushrooms and pearl onions.

Note: If desired, you can stabilize the egg yolks in this recipe by cooking them sous vide for 30 minutes at 140°F (60°C) before using them in step 9.

CHICKEN MOLE

The same techniques are used to make a mole as are used to make a classic fricassée; just the flavors are different. Feel free to experiment with different chiles. The heart of a mole sauce is not, as some people assume, chocolate, but rather combinations of chiles with cinnamon and cloves. Raisins and almonds also enter into most moles. This mole makes enough for two chickens.

YIELD: 8 MAIN-COURSE SERVINGS

(continued)

dried mulato chiles	5	5
dried ancho chiles	3	3
dried pasilla chiles	3	3
chipotle chile, dried or canned in adobo sauce	1	1
sesame seeds	2 tablespoons	30 milliliters
coriander seeds	½ teaspoon	2 milliliters
chickens, quartered, 2	8 pounds	4 kilograms
salt and pepper	to taste	to taste
butter	1 ounce	30 grams
onion, chopped	1 medium	1 medium
garlic clove, chopped	1	1
ground cloves	¼ teaspoon	1 milliliter
ground cinnamon	½ teaspoon	2 milliliters
tomatoes, peeled, seeded, chopped	2 large	2 large
almonds with their skin, toasted in a 350°F (175°C) oven for 15 minutes	¼ cup	60 milliliters
sugar (or to taste)	1 tablespoon	15 milliliters
chicken broth	2 cups	500 milliliters
white raisins	3 tablespoons	45 milliliters
sherry vinegar (or to taste)	3 tablespoons	45 milliliters

1. Put the chiles, except the canned chipotle if that's what you're using, in a skillet over medium heat and toast them, about 5 minutes. Soak them in a bowl of warm water for 30 minutes, until pliable. Discard the soaking water.

2. Toast the sesame seeds and coriander seeds in a skillet until fragrant. Grind in a coffee grinder. Reserve.

3. If you're using a canned chipotle chile, rinse the sauce off. Stem and seed all of the chiles.

4. Season the chicken with salt and pepper and cook in the butter in a large rondeau or in two sauté pans for about 5 minutes on each side over medium to high heat. Take out the chicken and

pour out all but about 2 tablespoons (30 milliliters) of fat in the pan. Cook the onion and garlic in the fat for about 10 minutes. Stir in the cloves and cinnamon and cook for about 1 minute.

5. Combine the reserved spices, the chiles, the tomatoes, cooked onion mixture, almonds, sugar, and broth in a blender and purée for 1 minute.

6. Put the chicken back in the pan and pour over the sauce. Simmer, covered, for about 10 minutes or until firm to the touch. Take out the chicken and cook down the sauce, uncovered, until it starts to thicken to the consistency of a thick gravy. Sprinkle over the raisins. Season to taste with vinegar, salt, and pepper.

CHICKEN WITH VERJUICE, SAFFRON, MEDIEVAL SPICES, AND MINT

Verjuice (see page 47) was popular in medieval cooking as a source of acidity and is used more and more in modern cooking. The saffron, of course, is typically medieval, while the mint and sugar are typical of the Renaissance. This dish is quite sour, also typically medieval, but you can attenuate it by adding cream.

YIELD: 4 SERVINGS

chicken, quartered	1	1
salt and pepper	to taste	to taste
spice mixture (page 5)	1 teaspoon	5 milliliters
butter	1½ ounces	45 grams
verjuice	1 cup	250 milliliters
glace de viande (page 97; optional)	3 tablespoons	45 milliliters
saffron, soaked in 1 tablespoon (15 milliliters) water	1 pinch	1 pinch
grated fresh ginger	1 tablespoon	15 milliliters
sugar	1 teaspoon	5 milliliters
fresh mint, chopped at the last minute	2 tablespoons	30 milliliters
heavy cream (optional)	½ cup	125 milliliters

1. Season the chicken with salt, pepper, and the spice mixture. Brown the chicken on both sides in the butter, remove the chicken from the pan, and discard the fat.

2. Put the chicken back in the pan with the verjuice, glace de viande, if using, the saffron with its soaking liquid, ginger, and sugar and simmer gently, covered, for 10 to 15 minutes or until firm to the touch.

3. Whisk the mint into the sauce. Add the cream, if using, and season with salt and pepper. Spoon the braising liquid over the chicken in heated soup plates.

VARIATIONS

When trying to emulate medieval dishes, it's easy to see their resemblance to Moroccan cuisine. Moroccan cooks use spices, herbs, and garnitures, but in moderation (it's always been assumed that medieval cooks used strong ingredients in excess, an unproven summation). They include ingredients like cumin, cinnamon, turmeric, ginger, cloves, saffron, cilantro, slivered almonds, raisins, preserved lemon, and pomegranate seeds. Tagines, which are stews cooked in a traditional cone-shaped vessel, are typically served with harissa sauce, which contains more spices (coriander, cumin), reconstituted dried chiles, cilantro, tomatoes, and olive oil.

(continued)

While the techniques used to make Moroccan food differ from those of the West, the flavor combinations are good imspirations and can be incorporated into any number of dishes, especially those containing chicken. Fricassées and sautés can both be used as the base upon which flavors are built.

CHICKEN WITH TOMATILLO AND ASSORTED CHILE SAUCES

n this dish, the chicken is sautéed until completely done (there's no subsequent simmering in liquid, which makes this dish a classic sauté and not a fricassée. The sauces are prepared separately and then poured over. This plate, which presents an opportunity to experiment with different chiles, actually comprises five sauces: the base tomatillo sauce and the four individual chile sauces.

YIELD: 4 SERVINGS

4 different kinds of dried chiles	4 each	4 each
heavy cream	1 cup	250 milliliters
chicken stock, preferably concentrated (4 to 6 times)	1 cup	250 milliliters
salt and pepper	to taste	to taste
chicken, 1, quartered	4 pounds	2 kilograms
butter	1 ounce	30 grams
onion, chopped	1 medium	1 medium
tomatillos, sheaths removed, halved *or* canned, drained tomatillos	1 pound 2 (15-ounce)	450 grams (425 gram) cans
sour cream	as needed	as needed

1. Prepare the individual chile sauces by toasting each type of chile until fragrant in a dry iron skillet over high heat—don't use any oil. Turn the chiles with tongs. Soak each type of chile separately for 30 minutes in warm water. Remove the stems and rinse out the seeds. Chop the chiles to a paste, keeping each type separate.

2. Put each type of chile in a separate small saucepan with ¼ cup (60 milliliters) cream and ¼ cup (60 milliliters) stock and simmer gently, about 3 minutes. Strain each sauce, season with salt and pepper, and reserve.

3. Cook the chicken on both sides in the butter in a large sauté pan for about 10 minutes per side, until firm to the touch. Take the chicken out of the pan and keep warm.

4. Pour out all but 2 tablespoons (30 milliliters) fat from the pan and add the onion. Cook the onion for about 5 minutes over medium heat. Add the tomatillos. Cover the pan and cook gently for 20 minutes. Strain the sauce through a strainer or pass through a food mill. Season with salt and pepper.

5. Serve the chicken with the tomatillo sauce poured over. Either pass the chile sauces or spoon them over each serving. Pass the sour cream.

DUCK

Ducks available in the United States—the widely sold Pekin duck (not to be confused with Peking duck) and the moulard duck, used to produce foie gras—are covered with a thick layer of fat that has to be rendered in some way before the duck is served. Such ducks cannot be roasted in the same way as a chicken because in order to get the fat to render, the duck has to be overcooked, resulting in a "crispy" duck that's more like confit or braised duck than it is typical of a roast. Duck must be sectioned and the breasts cooked differently than the thighs. Usually, the breasts are sautéed over low to medium heat, skin side down for the most part, to render the fat without overcooking the meat, and served rare to medium rare. The thighs are best braised or slow roasted. Slow roasting is really a kind of braising in which the only liquid is the liquid naturally released by the meat.

The best approach is to braise the thighs and use the braising liquid as the base for a sauce for both the breasts and the thighs.

BRAISED DUCK THIGHS

Restaurants are often stuck with leftover thighs. In fact, the thighs can make an even more impressive dish than the breasts; they just take a little more time. This recipe offers two approaches. The thighs can be gently roasted, skin side up, until they tenderize in their own juices. Alternatively, the roasted thighs can be moistened with liquid, covered, and slowly braised in the oven or on the stove.

YIELD: 6 SERVINGS

moulard duck thighs *or* pekin duck thighs	6 *or* 12	6 *or* 12
salt and pepper	to taste	to taste
onion, sliced	1 large	1 large
carrot, sliced	1 large	1 large
garlic cloves, crushed	2	2
red wine (optional)	1 cup	250 milliliters
unsalted chicken stock, preferably brown chicken stock (page 85; optional)	1 quart	1 liter
large bouquet garni (page 52; optional)	1	1

(continued)

1. Preheat the oven to 400°F (200°C). Season the thighs with salt and pepper and arrange them, skin side up, in a heavy-bottomed sauté pan on top of the onions, carrots, and garlic. Roast until the skin is golden brown and the thighs are easily penetrated with a skewer, about 60 minutes for Pekin thighs or 90 minutes for moulard thighs. The thighs can be served immediately (in essence they've braised in their own juices) or braised, continuing with step 2.

2. To continue braising, turn the oven down to 300°F (150°C). Transfer the thighs to a plate and strain the liquid into a narrow container, leaving the vegetables behind in the strainer. Skim off any fat that floats to the surface and discard. Arrange the cooked vegetables in the pan and place the thighs, skin side up, on top.

3. Add the wine and stock, nestle in the bouquet garni, and bring to a gentle simmer on top of the stove. Cover the pan with a sheet of aluminum foil and press the foil down so it almost touches the tops of the thighs.

4. Cover the pan and simmer very gently, on top of the stove or in the oven, for 1 hour for Pekin thighs or 90 minutes for moulard thighs. Check the oven every 20 minutes or so to make sure the braising liquid isn't boiling.

5. Transfer the thighs, still skin up, into a clean pan that fits them in a single layer as closely as possible. Turn the oven to 400°F (200°C). Strain the braising liquid into a saucepan and bring to a gentle simmer with the pan to one side of the heat source. Skim off the fat with a ladle while you simmer the liquid for about 15 minutes.

6. Pour the degreased braising liquid over the thighs and slide them back in the oven. Baste every 10 minutes until the thighs are covered with a shiny glaze and the braising liquid is syrupy. Serve in heated soup plates surrounded with the braising liquid. The duck thighs can be garnished with vegetables.

DUCK BREASTS WITH PEACHES OR OTHER FRUITS

Because duck breasts are best sautéed rare to medium rare, they release little liquid with which to make a sauce. By braising duck thighs (see page 285), however, you'll have a rich and savory braising liquid that can be used to deglaze the pan used for sautéing the duck breasts. If you don't have braising liquid, it's also possible to make a duck stock with the duck carcass. (A good trick is to make duck stock with half the duck carcasses and then make a jus by roasting the remaining carcasses and deglazing the pan with the duck stock.)

The usual approach when making fruit sauces is to put the fruit in hot reduced demi-glace just long enough for the fruit to release liquid of its own. The fruit is then taken out of the sauce; the sauce reduced to compensate for the liquid released by the fruit and to concentrate its flavor; and the fruit returned to the sauce just before serving. Fruit sauces almost always benefit from a sweet-and-sour element provided by a gastrique or, if you're in a hurry, just a little sugar and vinegar.

YIELD: 6 SERVINGS

pekin duck breasts	6	6
or	*or*	*or*
moulard duck breasts	3	3
duck stock or duck braising liquid	1 cup	250 milliliters
peaches, peeled, pitted, cut into wedges	3	3
glace de viande (page 97; optional)	2 tablespoons	30 milliliters
gastrique (see page 193; or to taste)	2 tablespoons	30 milliliters
butter	1½ ounces	45 grams
salt and pepper	to taste	to taste

1. Make a series of about 20 slashes into the duck skin, penetrating as deeply into the skin as possible without going all the way to the meat. Keep the knife leaning on an angle so you're cutting into the skin sideways, which allows for a deeper cut without cutting through. Make a second series of slashes at a 90-degree angle from the first.

2. Put the duck breasts, skin side down, in a cold sauté pan. Cook over low-to-medium heat for about 12 minutes for Pekin duck breasts and about 20 minutes for moulard breasts. Turn the breasts over and cook them on the meat side for about 2 minutes over high heat. Take them out of the pan and keep warm while preparing the sauce.

3. Pour the fat out of the pan and deglaze the pan with the stock or braising liquid. Add the peaches and bring to a simmer. Simmer for 3 minutes. Remove the peaches with a skimmer, and reserve. Boil down the sauce base, add the glace de viande, if using, and when the sauce has a lightly syrupy consistency, add gastrique to taste. Whisk in the butter, reheat the peaches in the sauce, and season with salt and pepper. Slice the duck breasts and spoon over the sauce.

STEAMED POULTRY

Although recipes for steamed poultry are less common than those for roasting, poaching, or braising, the technique has several advantages over these other methods. Chicken can be steamed in a *couscoussière*, which has a wide-mouthed pot for the steaming liquid and a second pot with a perforated base that fits on top of the pot of boiling liquid and holds the meat. Poultry, however, should not be steamed in an industrial steamer, which uses pressure and temperatures above the boiling point. These steamers generate too much liquid of their own and make it impossible to capture any juices released by the steaming meats.

By adding aromatic ingredients, such as herbs, aromatic vegetables, wines, truffles, and spices, to the steaming liquid, steaming can be used to impart delicate flavors to meat. Restaurant chefs often prefer steaming to poaching (which produces similar results) because it is quick, neat, and easy to organize.

In most settings a relatively large amount of liquid is used to generate steam in the base of the steamer. As the meats cook in the basket above the boiling liquid, they release juices that in most cases are not used because they are diluted in the steaming liquid.

If a small amount of liquid is used in the bottom of the steamer, it will simultaneously reduce and capture the juices being released by the steaming meats. This liquid can then be served as a broth around the steamed meats or converted into a sauce in the same way as a poaching or braising liquid. When a small amount of liquid is used for steaming meats, the steamer has to be watched carefully so the liquid does not run dry and burn.

Another useful method for steaming meats, especially chicken, is to seal the meats in a plastic roasting bag (or a pig's bladder) along with reduced stock or aromatic liquids. The wrapped meat is then baked or poached in simmering water, and steam is generated within the bag. In this way none of the flavorful liquid is lost.

POULARDE À LA VAPEUR
STEAMED FATTENED CHICKEN

In Lucien Tendret's original 1892 recipe for this dish, a stuffing is prepared with cubed truffles and the chicken's liver. In the following modification, truffle slices are slipped under the chicken's skin and added to the steaming liquid. French chefs are predisposed to using black truffles, but the method is at least equally exciting with fresh white truffles. The method can be adapted and the truffles replaced with herbs such as tarragon (again, slipped under the skin) or with chopped wild mushrooms cooked down to a duxelles (see page 179) and placed under the skin.

The original recipe finishes the steaming liquid like a fricassée with roux, cream, and egg yolks, but in this modification, the chicken is served surrounded with the well-truffled steaming bouillon.

YIELD: 16 SERVINGS

fresh black or white truffles	2, as large as you can afford	
chickens, 2½ to 3 pounds (1.25 to 1.75 kilograms) each	4	4
excellent brown chicken stock	1 quart	1 liter

1. Peel the truffles; chop and save the peelings. Slice the truffles about 1/16 inch (1.5 millimeters) thick with a Japanese mandoline.

2. Slip three-quarters of the truffle slices under the skin of the thighs and breasts of the chickens.

3. Truss the chickens, cover well with plastic wrap, and store overnight in the refrigerator (to permeate the meat with the truffle flavor).

4. Pour the chicken stock, the remaining truffle slices, and the peelings into the bottom of a steamer and bring to a simmer. Unwrap the chickens and arrange them in the basket of the steamer. Cover with a sheet of crumpled aluminum foil (this makes a tighter seal) and the lid. It is imperative that the lid fit tightly. (The original recipe sealed the lid on with a luting paste of flour and water.)

5. Steam the chickens over low to medium heat for 1½ hours. If any steam starts to escape from under the lid, turn down the heat. Do not remove the lid during the cooking except to check that the liquid isn't running dry and burning. If it is, add more stock or water.

6. Carve the chickens and serve in deep plates or wide soup bowls surrounded with the steaming liquid, with soup spoons.

GRILLED MEATS

Grilled meats are traditionally served with stock-based sauces such as Sauce Diable (page 174), simple sauces that function as condiments, or compound butters. These sauces are used because the juices released by grilled meats normally fall into the grill and are lost, making it impossible to prepare an integral sauce.

To prepare sauces that capture the flavor of the grill, partially grill the meat and then finish it in stock or other aromatic liquids. The method is somewhat analogous to braising (where meats are first browned on top of the stove and then moistened) or to a salmis, a technique in which meat, usually game or poultry, is partially roasted, a jus is prepared with the trimmings, and the cooking of the meat is completed by gentle reheating in the flavorful jus.

GRILLED GAME BIRDS IN SMOKE-SCENTED BROTH

YIELD: 4 SERVINGS

quails, about 6 ounces (150 grams) each	2	2
squabs, about 1 pound (450 grams) each	2	2
excellent brown stock (as needed to cover carcasses)	2 cups	500 milliliters
large bouquet garni (page 52), with several sprigs of fresh marjoram	1	1
moulard duck breast (see note)	1	1
pheasant or partridge breast, about 6 ounces (150 grams)	1	1
salt and pepper	to taste	to taste
mushrooms	4 ounces	125 grams
extra-virgin olive oil	2 tablespoons	30 milliliters

(continued)

1. Remove the breasts and thighs from the quails and squabs and grill the carcasses over wood coals. When the carcasses are nicely browned, transfer them to a 4-quart (4 liter) saucepan. Break the carcasses up and compress them with the end of a European-style rolling pin. Add just enough brown stock to cover. Add the bouquet garni.

2. Gently simmer the carcasses for 20 minutes. Skim off any froth or fat that floats to the surface.

3. Strain the broth through a fine chinois and then through a strainer lined with a cloth napkin.

4. Season the breasts from the quails, squabs, duck, and pheasant with salt and pepper and grill them, skin side down first, over high heat. Leave the meat rare in the center. The quail breasts will take about 1 minute, the squab breasts about 2 minutes, and the duck and pheasant or partridge breasts about 4 minutes.

5. Slide the mushrooms onto skewers, roll them in olive oil, and grill until they brown and smell fragrant, about 5 minutes.

6. Pour the reserved broth into a 4-quart (4 liter) straight-sided sauté pan and poach the grilled breasts for 30 seconds to 2 minutes, depending on their size. Remove the breasts and season the broth with salt and pepper.

7. Present the breasts (slice the duck and pheasant breasts) and mushrooms (removed from the skewers) in deep plates surrounded by the smoke-scented broth.

Note: Foods surrounded by hot broth may overcook in the bowls. To prevent this, make a small mound of something appropriate (blanched spinach, perhaps) in the bowl and place the meat up against it or on top to keep it out of the hot poaching liquid.

TIPS FOR THE RESTAURANT CHEF

In fast-paced professional kitchens, many chefs find that integral sauces require too much last-minute preparation. Roasting a chicken and preparing a jus to order is impractical in all but the most-well-staffed restaurants. Stock-based sauces were originally invented to free the cook from the last-minute difficulties inherent in preparing integral sauces. Unfortunately, stock-based sauces, especially the way they are prepared in today's economy-oriented kitchens, rarely have the satisfying direct flavor of a well-made integral sauce. It is, however, possible to organize a kitchen so that some of the elements necessary to an integral sauce can be accomplished in advance.

Sautés

Preparing integral sauces for sautéed meats is a quick and straightforward process, provided that any necessary stocks and glazes are on hand. Any necessary stocks should be reduced to the proper degree ahead of time to avoid time-consuming last-minute reduction. If, on the other hand, the stocks are very reduced, the saucier will be constantly thinning the sauce with stock to adjust its consistency.

One problem with pan-deglazed sauces is that they are usually speckled with particles of coagulated meat that have adhered to the bottom of the pan. The obvious solution is to strain the sauce into a bowl or saucepan, but in a busy professional kitchen, this task is a nuisance. In some cases, especially if the sauce is garnished with chopped ingredients such as shallots, herbs, or mushrooms, straining is not necessary.

Roasts

Large roasts, such as turkeys or large cuts of beef, veal, or game, present little problem in a professional kitchen because they are roasted ahead of time, giving the chef ample time to prepare a jus. For smaller roasts, especially chicken and small game birds, which are often roasted to order, last-minute preparation of an individual jus is cumbersome and impractical. For this reason, chefs often prepare a jus with appropriate trimmings just before the restaurant service (see "Jus," page 98).

Poached Meats

It is rarely practical to prepare sauces to order from poached meats, because the liquid is usually so diluted that too much last-minute reduction is required to make a flavorful sauce. Usually integral sauces for poached meats are prepared from the poaching liquid used the day before. In any case, meats are usually poached in advance; pot au feu, blanquettes, and potées are not last-minute affairs.

Poached meats should be reheated in the same way as stews and braises are: gently, in a covered pan, with a little stock.

Braises

Braised meats present little problem in a professional kitchen because they rarely suffer from—and are often improved by—advance preparation and reheating to order. The braising or stewing liquid can be stretched if necessary by adding well-flavored stock. Extra body can be given to the liquid with glace de viande.

Certain liaisons, such as foie gras or butter, can be used only at the last minute, whereas others, such as arrowroot or flour, can be incorporated into the sauce ahead of time. Hydrocolloids and emulsifiers come in handy here, especially when dealing with fragile emulsions such as those created from foie gras and vegetable purées.

When reheating a stew or a piece of braised meat, place it in a tight-fitting covered pan with a little of the braising liquid. Heat it very gently so the surrounding liquid never comes to a boil. If a last-minute liaison is required, simply transfer the meat to a plate and finish the sauce in the pan. If the stewed or braised meat is particularly fragile, wrap each piece carefully in a sheet of caul fat after the initial braising and after it has thoroughly cooled.

INTEGRAL FISH AND SHELLFISH SAUCES

ntegral fish and shellfish sauces are usually made at the last minute from the natural juices released during cooking. Fish and shellfish are especially suited to last-minute integral sauces because they cook quickly and release flavorful liquid as soon as they are heated. Because the best method for preparing an integral sauce depends on how the fish is cooked, this chapter is organized around the various cooking techniques. Although shellfish comprise crustaceans as well as mollusks and cephalopods, because the techniques for cooking crustaceans are so specific, they are treated separately, in Chapter 11.

BASIC PREPARATIONS AND INGREDIENTS

Fish Stock

To prepare fish stock, sometimes called fish fumet, see page 93. Traditional recipes often call for fish stock as the cooking medium for fish and shellfish. If the fish stock is not overcooked and is prepared from impeccably fresh fish, it will help reinforce the sea-like flavor of an integral sauce.

Unfortunately, fish stock is often prepared from stale fish and allowed to sit for too long before use. Such a stock will give any sauce a strong, fishy taste.

Fish Glaze

To prepare fish glaze (glace de poisson), see page 98. Fish glaze is often used to reinforce the flavor of fish sauces. The advantage of fish glaze is that it can be prepared ahead of time and refrigerated until needed. Unlike fish stock, it requires no last-minute reduction. Fish glaze should be used very sparingly or it will give the sauce a strong, fishy taste.

Many contemporary chefs feel that fish glaze, even when correctly prepared and used, detracts from the character of a sauce by giving it a nondescript fish flavor. The trend in the finest restaurants is to try to capture the individuality of a specific fish, which often means sacrificing convenience.

Shellfish Cooking Liquids

The liquid released by mussels, cockles, or clams during steaming has a delicious, forthright flavor, and is excellent as a base for fish sauces. To prepare 1 cup (250 milliliters) cooking liquid, place 1 pound (500 grams) mussels, cockles, or clams and ½ cup (125 milliliters) white wine in a pot and cover with a tight-fitting lid. Heat on the stove over a high flame, shaking the pot from time to time to redistribute the shellfish. After about 5 minutes for mussels and cockles or 12 minutes for clams, open the lid. When the mussels, cockles, or clams have all opened, scoop them out, and the carefully decant the cooking liquid, leaving any grit behind. If the liquid is still gritty, strain it through a fine chinois or through a kitchen towel.

When using shellfish cooking liquids, remember that they are very salty, so avoid too much reduction and be careful if adding additional salt.

Court-Bouillon

Court-bouillon is popular with contemporary chefs because of its lightness and the subtle fresh flavor it gives to sauces. A traditional recipe is given on page 366, but as noted there, different herbs and vegetables can be used, depending on the type of fish being prepared, the region, and the whim of the chef. Court-bouillon can also be reduced and used as a flavor base when thicker sauces are needed.

Wines

White wine almost always works well in fish sauces, which are accented by its natural acidity. Red wine sauces for fish are a bit trickier—the tannin and acids can create an aggressive effect—but when prepared carefully are delicious with stronger-flavored fish such as salmon or mackerel.

Roe and Coral

The roe and coral from sea urchins, sea scallops, and lobsters are sometimes used as a flavorful finish for shellfish sauces.

Although sea urchin roe can be bought already removed from the shells, it is best to remove it just before cooking from perfectly fresh, living urchins. Using a pair of heavy scissors, cut halfway down the side of the sea urchin starting from the hole on the top, and then cut all around the spiny shell and remove the top half. The roe, which is pale orange or brown, can then be easily removed with a spoon. Some sea urchins have a strong and aggressive iodine flavor, so be sure to taste the roe before incorporating it into a sauce.

Sea scallop coral can be simply cut off from the side of the meaty white part of the scallop.

Both sea urchin roe and scallop coral should be combined with an equal amount of butter (usually by volume because it's done by eye) and pushed through a drum sieve before they are used to finish a sauce. These butters can then be used as a final flavoring and light liaison for flavorful sauce bases. To prepare and use lobster coral, see page 338. When preparing sea scallop coral butter, avoid gray coral; use only bright orange coral.

POACHING

Fish is poached by keeping it completely submerged in simmering liquid. As the fish cooks, it releases juices into the surrounding liquid. Integral sauces are then prepared from all or a portion of the poaching liquid. Some recipes suggest starting the poaching in cold liquid, whereas others suggest that the liquid should be at a simmer before adding the fish. Larger fish should be started in cold liquid so the heat will penetrate them slowly and they will cook evenly. Small fish, sections of fish, and shellfish should be started in hot liquid to ensure rapid and even cooking.

The simplest, most direct method of serving poached fish is to place the fish in a bowl and pour over a ladleful of the poaching liquid, which can then be sipped with a spoon as though it were a soup or, in less formal settings, mopped up with chunks of crusty bread. Court-bouillon is the liquid most often used for poaching fish. When the vegetables used to make the court-bouillon are left in the broth and served along with the fish, the term *à la nage* (loosely translated "in the swim") is used. When fish is to be served à la nage, the vegetables should be chopped carefully so they create a decorative effect in the bowl. Some chefs like to cut grooves in the sides of the carrots with a channel knife so that the sliced carrots have a distinct cog-like look. A more contemporary effect can be obtained by cutting the court-bouillon vegetables into julienne. The flavor and color of the poaching liquid can also be improved by adding finely chopped or whole leaves of herbs such as chervil, parsley, or chives just before serving.

Poaching does not lend itself well to making sauces with the traditional consistency—thick enough to coat the fish—because these sauces require long reduction to concentrate the flavor of the poaching liquid or an excessive amount of starch or other thickener. Either of these methods requires keeping the fish warm for too long a period while the sauce is being prepared. For this reason, it is best to serve poached fish with light broth-like sauces. If a thicker sauce is needed, a stock-based sauce should be used (see Chapter 8, "Stock-Based and Nonintegral Fish Sauces"). Some chefs save the poaching liquid to use as a base for a sauce for the next service.

When converting the poaching liquid for fish into a sauce, it is best to combine the poaching liquid with a sauce that has been made in advance. Older recipes sometimes suggest combining some of the poaching liquid with a fish velouté made in advance and then reducing the mixture until it has the correct consistency. A similar method can be used for butter- or cream-based sauces. If the poaching liquid is to be finished with butter, it is best to prepare a butter-enriched sauce (such as a beurre blanc or one of its derivatives) and to combine the sauce with the poaching liquid after the fish is cooked, just before it is served. In this way, last-minute swirling of butter into the poaching liquid is avoided. This is especially practical in fast-paced professional settings and in situations where the proportion of butter to liquid is quite small, making it more susceptible to breaking.

To stabilize butter before it goes into a sauce, you can heat the butter to 140°F (60°C) and work in 2% liquid lecithin and/or 3% to 5% mono- and diglycerides (Glice). The butter is then less likely to separate out of solution. The liquid (aqueous) component, water or stock, can also be emulsified or stabilized with 0.5% propylene glycol alginate, sucrose esters at 1% of the water component, and Polysorbate 80 at 1% of the fat component. Standard thickeners such as guar gum or xanthan gum (0.02% to 0.5% of the liquid component) can also be used to stabilize the emulsion.

Fish poaching liquid can be combined at the last minute with emulsified egg yolk–and-butter sauces, such as hollandaise and its derivatives. The resulting sauce is light and broth-like but still full flavored with just enough richness (see page 427). Usually, equal parts fish poaching liquid and emulsified sauce are used. The richness can be adjusted by varying the ratio of butter to egg yolk, from a classic butter-rich hollandaise-style sauce to a sabayon containing no butter at all. Keep in mind, also, that egg yolks can be stabilized by cooking them sous vide at 140°F (60°C) for 30 minutes. It can be useful to make a big batch and save them in the refrigerator for making egg yolk–based sauces.

TARRAGON-INFUSED HOT EMULSIFIED EGG YOLK SAUCE FOR FISH

This sauce is particularly convenient because the egg yolks are cooked ahead of time and then blended with flavorful liquid just before the restaurant service or the dinner party. The egg yolks can be kept, sealed in their sous vide bag, in the refrigerator for up to five days, and used as needed. The proportions given here contain a rather large percentage of egg yolks, creating a thick and unctuous sauce, but the sauce can be thinned with additional liquid to arrive at the desired consistency.

YIELD: 2 CUPS (500 MILLILITERS)

egg yolks	7	7
sprigs fresh tarragon	5	5
court-bouillon (page 366), fish stock (page 93), or fish poaching or braising liquid	1½ cups	375 milliliters

1. Whisk together the egg yolks. If you want to stabilize them, cook the yolks in a well-sealed sous vide bag at 140°F (60°C) for 30 minutes (this step is optional).

2. Simmer the tarragon in the liquid long enough to infuse the flavor. Scoop out the tarragon. Let the liquid cool for a minute.

3. Use an immersion blender to blend the egg yolks with the tarragon-infused liquid. Gently and attentively cook the sauce, stirring with a wooden spoon, in the same way as a crème anglaise (see page 618). Don't let the sauce boil. Remove from the heat as soon as it takes on a silky consistency.

Another method for preparing sauces with fish poaching liquid is to combine the liquid with mayonnaise. This method has long been used in Provence to prepare the traditional bourride, which combines a full-flavored fish poaching liquid with a Sauce Rouille (page 127) or Saffron-Flavored Aïoli (page 419). Almost any flavored mayonnaise can be used, as long as it does not completely overpower the flavor of the fish or the poaching liquid (see Chapter 14, "Mayonnaise-Based Sauces"). Because sauces made with mayonnaise tend to be unstable, the poaching liquid should be combined with the mayonnaise just before serving. When combining hot poaching liquid with mayonnaise, put the mayonnaise in a stainless-steel bowl and whisk in the hot poaching liquid. The ratio of poaching liquid to mayonnaise can be adjusted according to whether a thin broth-like sauce or a thicker version that will coat the fish is desired.

To render the mayonnaise more stable, purée it with a small amount of liquid (such as fish poaching liquid) using a rotor stator homogenizer (see page 35) or immersion blender on high speed. Another approach is to mix both 2% lecithin and 4% mono- and diglycerides (Glice) into the oil when making the mayonnaise. Propylene glycol alginate can be added to the liquid base (such as the lemon juice) in a concentration of 0.5% of the amount of base. Xanthan gum (0.2%), whisked up with the liquid base and perhaps a little water, will thicken the mayonnaise and render it much more stable. Be careful, though, as xanthan gum gives a slimy feel in the mouth if used in too high a concentration.

The hot poaching liquid from a fish or shellfish can also be combined with a small amount of vinaigrette just before serving. The vinaigrette will give the fish an agreeable tang and will limit the richness of the sauce. Unless you're serving such sauces immediately, they should be stabilized or the vinaigrette will just break apart. A rotor stator homogenizer will do the trick, but given that not every kitchen is so equipped, it's best to use a stabilized vinaigrette such as the one on page 479.

Poaching liquid can also be combined with heavy cream, reduced cream, or reduced cream–based white sauces. For example, a sauce consisting of reduced cream and flavorful ingredients such as sorrel or tomato purée can be prepared ahead of time and then combined as needed with the poaching liquid.

Vegetable and fruit purées make excellent and innovative thickeners for any number of sauces, but given that most of them have no emulsifying properties, they must be stabilized. The same ingredients are used as those used to prevent syneresis: 0.25% xanthan gum and 0.6% Ultra-Sperse 3 (a modified starch), relative to the purée itself, not the whole sauce.

STABILIZED BUTTER SAUCE FOR À LA NAGE

Whenever small amounts of butter are combined with large amounts of liquids such as vinegar or court-bouillon, the butter tends to separate and the whole sauce falls apart. If the sauce is being served immediately, this is rarely a problem. But if the sauce is made ahead of time it will separate and have a thick layer of melted butter floating on top. Shearing with a rotor stator homogenizer (see page 35) will bring the sauce together and render it stable for several hours, eliminating the need for additional emulsifiers and stabilizers, but given that not everyone has a rotor stator homogenizer, adding modern hydrocolloids and emulsifiers allows you to stabilize the sauce using only an immersion blender.

For example, in this recipe for a lightly buttered nage, 2% liquid lecithin and 2% Glice are added to the butter (the butter must be heated to at least 140°F (60°C) to dissolve Glice) and 0.5% propylene glycol alginate to the court-bouillon or other liquid base. The resulting emulsion is so stable that the butter can be blended into the liquid while melted. In any case, work the butter into the court-bouillon within an hour of serving.

YIELD: 3 CUPS (750 MILLILITERS

court-bouillon (page 366) or other flavorful liquid, such as fish stock	2 cups	500 milliliters
propylene glycol alginate		2.5 grams
melted butter	1 cup	250 milliliters
mono- and diglycerides (glice)		5 grams
liquid lecithin		5 grams

1. Heat the court-bouillon until it is hot but not too hot to touch the side of the pan, about 150°F (66°C). Blend in the propylene glycol alginate.

2. The butter should be about the same temperature as the hot court-bouillon. Add the Glice and lecithin and stir to dissolve.

3. Shortly before serving the sauce (it lasts a while, but not forever), use an immersion blender or rotor stator homogenizer to purée the butter into the court-bouillon.

SEA SCALLOPS À LA NAGE

Almost any fish or shellfish can be prepared à la nage in a court-bouillon made from practically any kind of vegetable or herb. The vegetables in this version are those most commonly used, but many chefs add sliced lemons or limes (zest and pith removed), cayenne pepper, or a variety of spices, such as coriander and fennel. Because the vegetables used to prepare the court-bouillon are served with the seafood, so they should be cut in a decorative way and cooked perfectly.

YIELD: 6 SERVINGS

sea scallops (shucked weight) *or*	2 pounds	1 kilogram
large scallops, preferably in the shell	24	24
butter	4 ounces	120 grams
carrot, julienned	3 ounces	75 grams
leek, white part, julienned	2 ounces	50 grams
celeriac, julienned	2 ounces	50 grams
turnip, julienned	3 ounces	75 grams
large bouquet garni (page 52)	1	1
water	1½ cups	375 milliliters
white wine	1½ cups	375 milliliters
sea salt (or to taste)	1 teaspoon	5 milliliters
chopped parsley	1 tablespoon	15 milliliters
whole chervil leaves	1 tablespoon	15 milliliters

(continued)

1. Prepare the scallops **(A)** by shucking them (if they are still in the shell) and removing the small muscle running up the side of each one. (If they have attractive coral, prepare scallop coral butter by puréeing equal parts butter and coral (you can eye it) and working it through a strainer or drum

sieve. (Keep in mind that coral is very perishable, so keep it refrigerated until you're ready to use it, no longer than 24 hours.) If you're using plain butter, work it through the drum sieve to make it easier to work with.

2. Place the carrot, leek, celery, turnip, and bouquet garni in a 2-quart (2 liter) saucepan and moisten them with the water and white wine. **(B)** Add the salt. Bring the liquids to a simmer and cook the vegetables for approximately 15 minutes.

3. Drain the vegetables, reserving the court-bouillon. Spread the vegetables on a tray to cool them quickly and prevent them from overcooking.

4. Taste the court-bouillon and adjust the seasoning if necessary. If it seems to lack flavor, reduce it.

5. Poach the scallops in the court-bouillon, to order or all at once. **(C)** Heat portions of the julienned vegetables with a small amount of the court-bouillon, parsley, and chervil. Whisk the court-bouillon into the reserved scallop roe butter or plain butter. Spoon the scallops into bowls or deep plates and pour over the buttered court-bouillon until it reaches halfway up the sides of the scallops. Place the julienned vegetables and herbs atop and around the scallops.

Note: Combining butter with a large proportion of liquid is likely to cause the butter to break if held too long. To avoid this, you can work in hydrocolloid emulsifiers and stabilizers—2% liquid lecithin into the butter and 0.5% propylene glycol alginate into the court-bouillon.

VARIATIONS AND RESTAURANT TIPS

The cooking liquid for sea scallops à la nage can be converted into a rich broth-like sauce by reducing it and finishing it with butter.

To finish a court-bouillon or other poaching liquid with butter, two approaches can be used. If the dish is being prepared all at once and served right away, simply add the butter, cut into chunks, into the hot liquid. If the dish is being served over an extended period (more than 15 minutes), as during a restaurant service, it is best to whisk the amount of butter anticipated for the service into a small amount of the nage, as though making a beurre blanc, and keep it warm. The nage is then combined with the necessary amount of emulsified butter-nage mixture when the order is placed. This method is preferable because the butter is more stable in a less liquid mixture. It also avoids last-minute whisking of butter into the nage.

If making the nage to order is impractical, you can stabilize it by working 2% liquid lecithin and 2% mono- and diglycerides (Glice) into 8 ounces (225 grams) melted butter (at 140°F/60°C). Blend 0.5% propylene glycol alginate into the nage. Blend the butter, working it in in a slow, steady stream, into the nage using an immersion blender or rotor stator homogenizer (see page 35).

Vegetable and fruit purees (see Chapter 18, "Purées and Purée-Thickened Sauces") can also be added to emulsified nage liquids to add body, color, and flavor. Tomato is especially well adapted to combining with buttered nage. A small amount (0.2%) of xanthan gum and 0.5% Ultra-Sperse 3 (a modified starch) can be added to the vegetable purée to prevent syneresis, the natural tendency of such mixtures to separate.

BRAISING

The essential difference between poaching and braising is the amount of liquid used. When fish is poached, it is completely submerged in hot liquid. When it is braised, the liquid should come only halfway up the sides of the whole fish or fish fillets. Typically, fish to be braised is placed in a flat container that fits its shape as closely as possible; oval-shaped fish pans work especially well for this. Liquid such as fish stock, court-bouillon, white or red wine, or shellfish cooking liquid is added and then brought to a simmer. As soon as the liquid is simmering, the fish is loosely covered with a sheet of aluminum foil or parchment paper and placed in a low oven. Once the fish is cooked, it should be quickly transferred to a plate or platter while a sauce is prepared with the braising liquid.

The advantage of braising over poaching is that the flavorful juices released by the fish are released into a relatively small amount of liquid. Because braising liquid is more concentrated and flavorful than poaching liquid, it can quickly be reduced (although that is not always necessary) and used as the base for a wide variety of integral fish sauces.

The most common methods for converting the braising liquid for fish into a sauce are by adding heavy cream and reducing the mixture to the desired consistency or by reducing the braising liquid as necessary and whisking in butter. It is also possible to finish the braising liquid for fish with mayonnaise-based sauces, sabayons, and hollandaise-based sauces. Each of these sauces can be stabilized with emulsifiers such as lecithin (in the fat component) and propylene glycol alginate (in the broth component). Hydrocolloids can also function as thickeners and stabilizers.

Most of the classic sauces for braised fish are based on the Sole Bercy recipe that follows. Variations usually consist of adding to or changing some of the ingredients in the braising liquid and using cream, whipped cream, butter, or egg yolks, either alone or in combination.

In traditional French recipes, fish is more often cooked and served whole. Nowadays many chefs prefer to use fillets, which are easy for the customer to eat. Many diners, especially in the United States, do not know how to bone fish, and it is often not economically practical to have a waiter bone the fish tableside. In the traditional parlance of French classic cooking, the term *braising* (*braisage*) is used only for whole fish, whereas the expression *en sauce* refers to the braising of fillets. To add to the confusion, American chefs often call the *en sauce* technique "shallow poaching."

FILLETS OF DOVER SOLE BERCY

This recipe uses Dover sole fillets, but any flatfish fillets will work, although they will be more fragile and difficult to handle.

YIELD: 4 FISH-COURSE SERVINGS (FOR MAIN-COURSE SERVINGS, DOUBLE THESE AMOUNTS)

shallot, finely chopped	1 medium	1 medium
chives, finely chopped	1 tablespoon	15 milliliters
dover sole fillets	8 medium	8 medium
salt and pepper	to taste	to taste
white wine	½ cup	125 milliliters
fish stock (page 93)	½ cup	125 milliliters
cold butter	2 ounces	60 grams

1. Preheat the oven to 400°F (200°C). Sprinkle the chopped shallot and chives over the bottom of a straight-sided sauté pan. Add the fillets, with the attractive white bone side up. (The fillets should completely cover the surface of the sauté pan without overlapping.) Season the fillets with salt and pepper and pour over the white wine and fish stock. The liquid should come halfway up the fillets.

2. Cover the fillets loosely with a piece of aluminum foil or parchment paper.

3. Heat over a high flame until the liquid comes to a simmer.

4. Immediately place the pan in the oven. As soon as the fillets are cooked (this will take from 2 to 7 minutes, depending on their size), carefully remove them from the pan and keep them warm.

5. Put the pan on the stove and reduce the braising liquid to a lightly syrupy consistency.

6. Whisk the cold butter into the reduced braising liquid and season with salt and pepper.

7. Place the fillets on plates or a platter and nap them with the sauce.

Sole Bercy Derivatives

The classic French repertoire includes long lists of Sole Bercy derivatives, most of which are rarely served today, at least under their original names. A few of the more important classic derivatives follow.

BRAISED FILLETS OF WILD STRIPED BASS WITH COCKLES AND NORMAN BUTTER

The briny liquid released by cockles or clams as they cook is one of the divine substances of the kitchen. Use it as the base for fish sauces and no one will fail to be seduced by their intense sea-like flavor. To gild the lily, as it were, whisk French butter into the shellfish cooking liquid, grind in a little pepper, and serve. Don't ever use bottled clam juice, which has a coarse, aggressive flavor nothing like the fresh version.

In France, you're more likely to see this treatment used to prepare Dover sole. In America, however, Dover sole is so expensive that it's rare to encounter; chefs are more likely to use whatever fresh fish is nearby.

YIELD: 4 FISH-COURSE OR 2 MAIN-COURSE SERVINGS

sea bass, striped bass, or other white fish fillet	1 pound	0.5 kilogram
salt and pepper	to taste	to taste
white wine	1 cup	250 milliliters
shallots, very finely minced	2	2
new zealand cockles *or* littleneck or cherrystone clams	2 pounds *or* 2 dozen	1 kilogram *or* 2 dozen
cold unsalted butter, preferably french, such as beurre d'isigny or beurre de charentes	3 ounces	90 grams

1. Preheat the oven to 400°F (200°C). Remove the skin if it is still attached to the fillet. Cut the fillet into 4 equal parts. Season with salt and pepper and keep chilled.

2. Place the wine and shallots in a pot large enough to hold the shellfish. Rinse the cockles or scrub the clams and add them to the pot. Cover the pot and cook over medium to high heat until steam shoots out the sides of the lid. Turn the heat down to low. Cook a total of 3 minutes for cockles and 7 to 9 minutes for clams.

3. When all the shellfish have opened (use a knife to coax open any unopened cockles or clams; but if they smell like anything other than the sea, throw them out), use a slotted spoon to transfer them to a bowl to keep warm. Strain the cooking liquid through a fine chinois.

4. Take the meats out of the shells, leaving a few in the shells for decoration. Cover the meats with a little of the cooking liquid and keep warm until needed.

5. Arrange the fish in a straight-sided metal pan in which they fit as snugly as possible. (This minimizes the need for cooking liquid and puts the emphasis on the juices released by the fish). Pour over enough shellfish cooking liquid to come halfway up the sides of the filets. Cook over high heat until the shellfish cooking liquid comes to a simmer.

6. Cover loosely with aluminum foil and slide the pan into the oven.

7. Bake for about 9 minutes per inch (2.5 cm) of thickness at the thickest point of the fish. Check the doneness by feeling the fish; the instant it feels firm, it is ready. If you're not comfortable using this method, slide an instant-read thermometer into one of the pieces. The center of the fillet should be about 130°F (54°C).

8. Transfer the fish to a heated platter. Whisk the butter into the braising liquid over high heat. Serve over the fish, garnished with the cockles. You can instead use the cockles to garnish the plate and serve the sauce in a sauceboat.

SOLE MARGUERY

Made famous by the nineteenth-century Parisian Restaurant Marguery, this sauce is essentially a hollandaise made with the braising liquid from fillets of Dover sole or other flatfish (or, for that matter, roundfish). If you have filleted whole sole, make a fish stock with the bones and use that. If you have no bones with which to make a stock, use the wine alone.

YIELD: 4 SERVINGS

fillets of dover sole or other firm-fleshed fish, 2 to 3 ounces (60 to 90 grams) each	8	8
salt and pepper	to taste	to taste
shallots, minced	2	2
white wine or fish stock (page 93) made from the fish bones	½ cup	125 milliliters
egg yolks (stabilized; see page 111)	2	2
clarified butter	6 tablespoons	90 milliliters

1. Preheat the oven to 375°F (190°C). Season the sole with salt and pepper. Sprinkle an oval pan just the size of the fillets with the shallots and place the fish on top. Pour over the white wine or fish stock. Cover loosely with aluminum foil and slide the pan into the oven.

2. Bake until the fish is white and firm to the touch, about 5 minutes. Transfer the fillets to a heated platter or plates.

3. Strain the braising liquid and then whisk it with the egg yolks in a saucepan with sloping sides over medium heat until the mixture turns fluffy and stiffens. Remove from the heat and whisk in the butter. Season with salt and pepper and pass the sauce at the table.

FILLETS OF SOLE BONNE FEMME

Spread a thin layer of shallots on the bottom of the sauté pan and add 3 sliced medium-sized mushrooms. (In a restaurant, these can be cooked in advance and the liquid added to the braising liquid to save time.) Some recipes finish the sauce with butter in the same way as a traditional Sole Bercy, whereas others add heavy cream and then reduce the sauce to the desired consistency. The fish is napped and glazed in the same way as Sole Bercy.

FILLETS OF SOLE BORDELAISE

Replace the white wine in the Sole Bercy recipe with a full-bodied red wine.

FILLETS OF SOLE CRÉCY

In today's kitchens, this dish is rarely served, but it provides one of the few examples of a classic French recipe for braised fish in which the braising liquid is thickened with a vegetable purée. Traditionally, Sole Crécy is served surrounded with braised artichoke hearts that have been filled with glazed carrots cut into little balls.

Braise the fish in the same way as for Sole Bercy. Reduce the braising liquid slightly and finish it with carrot purée until it has the desired thickness. The sauce can then be finished with butter. When serving sauces thickened by dense particle content, the fiber part of the vegetable or fruit separates from the clear liquid (syneresis). This is easiest to see where the sauce accumulates on the edge of a plate. To prevent this, blend in 0.2% xanthan gum and 6% Ultra-Sperse 3, a modified starch.

FILLETS OF SOLE DUGLÉRÉ

Sprinkle the bottom of the sauté pan with 1 minced shallot; 3 peeled, seeded, and chopped tomatoes; and 1 tablespoon (15 milliliters) finely chopped onions. Finish the sauce with butter in the same way as for Sole Bercy.

FILLETS OF SOLE FOYOT

Prepare the sole in the same way as for Sole Bercy, but add 1 tablespoon (15 milliliters) glace de viande to the braising liquid after removing the fish.

FILLETS OF SOLE THERMIDOR

Prepare Sole Bercy, but finish the sauce with 1 to 2 teaspoons (5 to 10 milliliters) Dijon mustard.

FILLETS OF SOLE VÉRONIQUE

Prepare the sole in the same way as for Sole Bercy, but replace the white wine with an equal amount of additional fish stock and 1 teaspoon (5 milliliters) Grand Marnier. After the fillets have been removed from the pan, add 4 ounces (125 grams) peeled seedless grapes. Reduce the liquid and finish with butter.

Modern Methods for Preparing Braised-Fish Sauces

The traditional system for braising whole fish and fish fillets is excellent because it provides a small amount of concentrated cooking liquid that can be rapidly converted into a variety of sauces. The juices released by freshly cooked fish will inevitably have a better flavor than a sauce made in advance from fish stock. The cooking liquid from braised fish can be finished in the same way as the court-bouillon (nage) used for poached fish. Finishing the cooking liquid from braised fish is even easier because the liquid is more concentrated and does not require as much reduction. The methods and ingredients used for braising fish can be broken down into several stages, as follows.

1. **INGREDIENTS ADDED TO THE PAN BEFORE THE BRAISING LIQUID IS ADDED.** These are most commonly shallots, mushrooms, and chopped parsley, but the inventive cook should feel free to add whatever ingredients seem appropriate. A few examples are garlic, grilled and peeled peppers, almost any chopped herb, wild mushrooms (chopped, sliced, or left whole), truffles (sliced or chopped), tomatillos, and sweated mirepoix.

2. **THE BRAISING LIQUIDS.** In classic recipes, these often include fish stock, white wine, and mushroom cooking liquid, but almost any liquid can be used to give the sauce individuality and excitement. The cooking liquids from mussels or clams can replace fish stock (but be careful of the salt). Other alcoholic beverages, such as hard cider, beer, red wine, flamed whiskey, or Cognac can replace the white wine. Flavorful liquids such as verjuice or lemon juice can also be added at this stage. Reduced meat stocks or glace de viande can be used to give flavor and texture to the sauce.

3. **THE LIAISONS.** Until recently, the liquid from braised fish was almost exclusively finished with either butter or heavy cream. Although these are both excellent additions, the resulting sauce is quite rich and sometimes heavy. In some instances it is possible to serve the braising liquid directly over the fish without thickening or enriching it with a liaison. Some chefs like to finish the braising liquid with yogurt, fresh cheese, or a vegetable purée, but these fragile emulsions are better when stabilized with xanthan gum, liquid lecithin, lambda carrageenan, or propylene glycol alginate.

4. **FINAL FLAVORINGS.** As is true with any sauce, certain ingredients whose flavor rapidly dissipates are best added near the end of a sauce's preparation. This is true of delicate herbs such as chervil and chives, as well as delicately perfumed spirits such as fruit brandies, old Cognacs and Armagnacs, and delicately flavored wines. Some ingredients, such as lemon juice, vinegar, and salt and pepper, may also have to be added near the end, after the sauce has been tasted, to balance the sauce's flavors.

Braised Fish Fillets with Crustacean Sauces

The technique of cooking fish fillets in a small amount of liquid can be adapted to making crustacean-flavored fish sauces. The fish fillets are cooked with the aromatic liquid extracted from lobster as one of the steps in preparing Sauce Américaine (page 335) or one of its variations. The crustacean-flavored braising liquid is then finished using any of the methods appropriate for cooking en sauce—one excellent method is to finish the

sauce with crustacean butter. Keep in mind, however, that crustacean butter is not an emulsion and will not go into the sauce without turning oily. To prevent this, work in whole butter or heavy cream first to create an emulsion. If you're using egg yolks, the crustacean butter won't present any problem, as it will immediately emulsify. Hydrocolloids and modernist emulsifiers and stabilizers can also be used. Liquid lecithin (2%) and 4% mono- and diglycerides (Glice) should be added to the hot (140°F/60°C) crustacean butter to emulsify it. Any type of crustacean cooking liquid can be used and the finished dish served with the appropriate crustacean garniture.

ROASTING

Both whole fish and fish fillets can be roasted, and the juices that are released (there shouldn't be much) during the process can be converted to a sauce. Traditional roasting is done on a spit in front of a roaring fire, but more typically, fish is roasted in a hot oven.

The techniques for oven roasting fish are similar to those for roasting meats. The roasting pan should be heavy and closely fit the size of the fish being roasted, so that no

307

part of the pan's surface overheats and burns the juices released during cooking. The main difference between roasting fish and meat is that fish cooks more quickly. Consequently, any flavorful ingredients placed in the roasting pan with the fish to flavor the sauce must release their flavor almost immediately. These ingredients also keep the fish from sticking to the pan. For this reason, ingredients such as mirepoix or garlic must be chopped very fine or slightly precooked ahead of time. Roasting works best with whole fish, probably because the skin helps contain the juices. Some chefs recommend using unscaled fish, but others like to serve the crispy skin. When roasting large fish, be sure to keep an eye on any aromatic vegetables on the bottom of the roasting pan to make sure they do not burn. If they start to burn, add a small amount of liquid to the bottom of the roasting pan. Once the fish is done, you can remove it from the pan and deglaze the roasting pan in the same way as for roasted meat. The pan can be deglazed with fish stock, court-bouillon, or white wine. Because roasted fish—unless it is overcooked—releases little in the way of juices, the juices can be augmented with a brown fish stock (in which the bones are first cooked until any liquid they release caramelizes and the bones turn pale brown). The pot is then deglazed and the bones simmered for the requisite 20 minutes.

The deglazing liquid, or jus, from the roasted fish should be kept light and relatively simple, like a jus for roast meats, so the natural flavor of the fish stays intact. Some chefs simply finish the jus with freshly chopped herbs, such as parsley, chives, and chervil, and perhaps a small chunk of butter to give it a velvety consistency and a richer flavor. Others may convert it into a sauce by reducing it with cream or finishing it with vegetable purée (remember, you can prevent syneresis by adding xanthan gum and Ultra-Sperse 3), sea urchin roe, or scallop coral. Keep in mind when using roe or coral that these are eggs and, as such, curdle when they get too hot. Always whisk hot liquids into them rather than the other way around, and never allow the sauce to boil.

In some cases a roasted fish releases so little liquid that it is impractical to prepare an integral sauce from the drippings. In this case the fish must be served with a sauce prepared independently, such as a butter or hot emulsified sauce. Some chefs "roast" fish in heat-resistant plastic bags. This is an excellent method but is more akin to braising or steaming than roasting (see "Steaming," page 313).

SAUTÉING

Whole fish, fish steaks, and fish fillets can all be sautéed in the same way as meats. The main difference between sautéing meat and fish is that fish cooks much more quickly, tends to stick to the sauté pan, and becomes extremely fragile once cooked. The best pans for sautéing fish are iron sauté pans that have been carefully seasoned with salt and oil so they have developed a nonstick surface. It is also convenient to have oval pans, which will easily hold whole fish and fillets. Nonstick pans also work well for sautéing fish and can be used with very little fat. The disadvantage to using a nonstick pan is that the juices released by the fish do not adhere to the bottom of the pan. Because of this there is no layer of savory crust to provide the beginnings of a sauce.

Whichever type of sauté pan you use, make sure the butter or oil is hot before adding the fish. Move the pan back and forth for a few seconds after adding the fish so that its surface cooks slightly, making it less likely to stick. Once the fish is cooked, transfer it to a plate and keep it warm while preparing the sauce. The stages in preparing a pan-deglazed sauce for fish are almost identical to those used for preparing meat sauces, but there is a logical succession that should be followed when adding ingredients.

If the fish provides little in the way of juices, a non-integral sauce can be used. The red wine salmon sauce, modelled after a classic meurette sauce, on page 224 is good for full-flavored seafood.

1. **SOLID INGREDIENTS.** Any ingredients that need relatively high heat to release their flavor quickly should be added while the pan is still hot, before any liquid is added. The most common example is finely chopped shallots, but other ingredients such as garlic and mirepoix should also be added at this stage. Watch them carefully to make sure they don't burn.

2. **WINES AND SPIRITS.** Because of the alcohol and natural acidity in wine (and tannin in red wine), it should be quickly and rapidly reduced before other liquids are added. If it is added at a later stage, it may give the sauce an aggressive flavor of raw wine.

Some recipes suggest deglazing a pan with Cognac, whiskey, or some other spirit. If the flavor of a particular spirit forms the predominant flavor of the sauce, then a relatively large amount of that spirit should be used to deglaze the pan. Be careful when deglazing a hot pan with brandy or whiskey. Pull the pan away from the flame, move the bottle away, and stand back when returning the pan to the stove. If the spirit does not ignite immediately, tilt the pan slightly to ignite the alcohol. Flaming the alcohol does not affect the flavor of the sauce, but it prevents unexpected flare-ups in the kitchen.

3. **STOCKS AND GLAZES.** If stocks or glazes are being used, they should be added after the wine has been heated for a few seconds to cook off its alcohol. The stocks should be reduced along with the wine and any solid ingredients until the liquid in the bottom of the pan has the desired consistency for the finished sauce.

4. **LIAISONS.** Liaisons should be added to the sauce at the end, only after the aromatic liquids in the pan have been reduced as much as necessary. This is especially true of butter, lobster coral, sea urchin roe, and egg yolks, which would break if the sauce were heated after they were added. Hydrocolloids and emulsion stabilizers can also be used, but since deglazed-pan sauces are made to order rather than held over long periods, they aren't needed.

5. **FINAL FLAVORINGS.** The flavor of some ingredients is so fleeting that they are best added at the very end. This is true of very delicate herbs such as finely chopped chervil and parsley, and also of certain delicate and expensive spirits such as brandies (eaux-de-vie), Calvados, old Cognac, Armagnac, etc. Once these ingredients are added, the sauce should be heated for only a few seconds to evaporate the alcohol or give the flavor of the herbs a chance to infuse.

The methods for sautéing described here are for sautéing in its strictest sense. Many chefs will use the word in a less rigid way to mean a kind of made-to-order stew. This is especially common with small shellfish, such as shrimp, sea scallops, and bay scallops, for which deglazing the pan, adding flavorful ingredients, and the final liaison all take place while the seafood is still in the pan. This can be an excellent method, provided that excess fat is discarded before the pan is deglazed and cooking times are closely watched.

SAUTÉED SEA SCALLOPS WITH CORAL-THICKENED COURT-BOUILLON

This is an example of a court-bouillon or other appropriate liquid thickened with the coral taken from the scallops. The coral has to be combined with an equal amount of butter (by volume; you can just eyeball it) before it is whisked into the sauce base, the deglazing liquid.

YIELD: 4 SERVINGS

sea scallops, in the shell	12	12
butter	8 ounces	250 grams
olive oil or clarified butter	2 tablespoons	30 milliliters
court-bouillon (page 366), fish stock (page 93), or other flavorful liquid	1 cup	250 milliliters
salt and pepper	to taste	to taste

1. Shuck the sea scallops and remove the coral. (A) Combine the coral with the butter and purée in a food processor. Work the butter through a drum sieve. Reserve in the refrigerator. Cut a crosshatch pattern on both sides of the scallops so the heat can more easily penetrate the center.

2. Heat the oil or clarified butter in a small sauté pan until it ripples and is almost ready to smoke and arrange the scallops on top, adding only a few at a time so they don't release liquid and stew in their own juices. (B) Sauté for at most a minute on each side. The center should be shiny and essentially raw, even though it should be warm. (C)

3. Whisk the hot, but not piping-hot, court-bouillon into the coral butter. Season with salt and pepper. Serve it around the scallops in wide soup plates.

311

SAUTÉED SALMON FILLET WITH SORREL CREAM SAUCE

This dish was first presented at the Troisgros brothers' restaurant in Roanne in the early 1970s, and at the time was considered extremely innovative. The following recipe differs somewhat from the original in that it is prepared in the pan used to sauté the fish, and the sorrel is added without a preliminary blanching. Obviously, each of the components—moistening liquid, butter and cream liaison, and sorrel garniture—can be varied.

YIELD: 6 SERVINGS

salmon fillet	2½ pounds	1.1 kilograms
salt and white pepper	to taste	to taste
butter	3 ounces	90 grams
dry white vermouth	¼ cup	60 milliliters
dry white wine	¼ cup	60 milliliters
heavy cream	½ cup	125 milliliters
sorrel leaves, cut into chiffonade	18	18

1. Slice the salmon fillet on a bias into 6 even portions. Sprinkle with salt and white pepper.

2. Gently sauté the salmon in 1½ ounces (45 grams) of the butter in a large sauté pan. Traditionally, fish is cooked for a total of 9 minutes per inch (2.5 cm) of thickness (4½ minutes per side), but nowadays chefs often cook it less so that it remains shiny and moist inside. Transfer the salmon to a plate covered with a towel (to absorb excess butter).

3. Pour the fat out of the sauté pan. Gently mop out any remaining fat with a paper towel.

4. Deglaze the pan with the vermouth and white wine and reduce by two-thirds.

5. Add the cream and reduce to the desired consistency. If the sauce contains unsightly specks from the bottom of the pan, strain it through a fine chinois into a small saucepan.

6. Add the sorrel chiffonade to the sauce and cook for 30 seconds, until the sorrel melts. Finish the sauce by whisking in the remaining 1½ ounces (45 grams) butter. Season with salt and pepper and serve over or around the salmon.

STEAMING

In most situations, steamed fish cannot be served with an integral sauce because a steamer is usually filled with a relatively large amount of water or aromatic liquid such as court-bouillon. The natural juices from the fish drip into this liquid and can never be retrieved. There are, however, methods that can be used to steam fish and at the same time capture the liquid released by the fish during cooking for an integral sauce. The first and most obvious method is simply to put a very small amount of liquid in the steamer and then convert the liquid into a sauce at the end of cooking. This is the method used for steaming mussels marinière. One disadvantage to this method is that it is easy to let the steamer run dry, ruining both the steaming liquid and the fish.

A more practical method is to cook the fish in a covered sauté pan (with straight sides) with a tight-fitting lid. A small amount of liquid is poured into the sauté pan and brought to a rapid boil over high heat. The fish is then placed in the pan and the lid sealed tightly. The pan can then be left on the stove on low heat or transferred to a hot oven. When the fish is cooked, a small amount of flavorful liquid should remain in the bottom of the pan, which can be quickly converted to a sauce with little or no reduction.

Almost any liquid can be used to steam fish, but it is practical to use something that will contribute a desirable flavor to the finished sauce. Some common steaming liquids are fish stock, court-bouillon, red or white wine, spirits (flamed ahead of time), cider, shellfish cooking liquid, and beer.

Another method used to steam fish is called *en papillote*. A fish fillet is sealed in a parchment paper or aluminum foil sack with lightly precooked aromatic vegetables and a small amount of liquid. The sack is quickly baked in the oven and usually opened in front of the diner. The fish is served surrounded with its own cooking liquid. A similar method, used for whole fish, is to wrap the fish in a heat-resistant plastic roasting bag before it is roasted in the oven. The bag is then opened in the kitchen, and the juices are served unadorned or are converted into a sauce.

STEAMED BASS FILLETS WITH YOGURT CURRY SAUCE

This recipe illustrates how a steaming liquid can be converted into a sauce with yogurt and flavored with curry. Because yogurt can separate when heated, it is better when combined with a hydrocolloid stabilizer. Lambda carrageenan (about 2%) works especially well with dairy products and can be blended into the yogurt.

Here, it's essential to keep an eye on the steaming liquid to make sure it doesn't run dry, burn, and leave nothing with which to make a sauce. As the fish approaches doneness, the steaming liquid should have boiled down by about half. If it has boiled down more than that, add more court-bouillon or water (enough to restore the steaming liquid to its original volume). This technique can be used for practically any steamed fish.

YIELD: 6 SERVINGS

(continued)

313

court-bouillon (page 366)	1 cup, or more as needed	250 milliliters
melted butter	1 tablespoon	15 milliliters
bass fillets, 6 ounces (175 grams) each	6	6
curry powder	1 to 2 teaspoons	5 to 10 milliliters
whole butter	½ ounce	15 grams
lambda carrageenan (optional)		0.9 grams
leben yogurt	3 tablespoons	45 milliliters
finely chopped cilantro	2 tablespoons	30 milliliters
salt and pepper	to taste	to taste
lime juice and hot pepper sauce (optional)	to taste	to taste

1. Pour the court-bouillon into the bottom of a steamer and bring it to a simmer.

2. Brush the inside of the steamer basket with melted butter. Set the fish fillets in it; make sure none of them overlap. Place the basket on the steamer.

3. Cover the steamer and cook the fillets for about 9 minutes per inch (2.5 cm) of thickness, but check them before this much time has elapsed in case they are done sooner. (In fact, it is a good idea to leave them slightly underdone, because they will continue cooking while the sauce is being prepared.) Transfer the fish to a plate to keep warm while preparing the sauce.

4. Strain the court-bouillon from the bottom of the steamer into a 2-quart (2 liter) saucepan with sloping sides. There should be about 5 fluid ounces (150 milliliters) remaining. If there is more, reduce it; if less, thin with additional court-bouillon.

5. Cook the curry powder in the whole butter for about 30 seconds and reserve. Blend the lambda carrageenan, if using, into the yogurt and stir in the curry powder–butter mixture. In a saucepan with sloping sides, slowly whisk the hot court-bouillon into the yogurt mixture until the sauce has the desired flavor and consistency. Don't make the sauce too thin; once combined with the yogurt it can't be reduced.

6. Add the cilantro and season with salt and pepper. This sauce is good when it is quite spicy hot and sour—lime juice and hot pepper sauce, such as Tabasco, are welcome additions. It may be necessary to heat the sauce slightly before it is served, but be careful not to let it boil. Serve the sauce over or around the fish fillets.

COMBINING METHODS: FISH STEWS

The difference between a fish stew and a soup is often difficult to define; the most important difference is that soups usually have a higher proportion of liquid to solid than do stews. Because stews contain less liquid, they can be more boldly flavored than soups.

The table on pages 316 to 317 provides a sense of the diversity of fish stew recipes. There exist almost as many varieties of fish stews as there are combinations of fish, most of which are the natural outcome of combining ingredients available in a particular region, even though many of the stages of preparation are the same. The simplest fish stews are made by first preparing an aromatic liquid with vegetables such as onion, garlic, and fennel, the trimmings from the fish, and wine. When the flavors of the vegetables and trimmings have infused in the wine, the liquid is then strained into a straight-sided saucepan and the pieces of fish are poached in the liquid. When the fish is finished poaching, it is removed with a skimmer and kept warm while the poaching liquid is converted into a sauce. In traditional French recipes where red wine is used, beurre manié is most often used, but more modern nouvelle cuisine versions will often simply reduce the cooking liquid and finish it with butter. White wine–based fish stews are most often finished with cream or a mixture of cream and egg yolks.

Although traditional recipes for fish stews usually suggest poaching the fish in a pre-made aromatic liquid, this method is often impractical in a professional setting because reducing the poaching liquid takes too long. It is more practical to prepare fish stews to order by cooking them in a tightly covered pan with a small amount of aromatic liquid that has been reduced in advance. In this way the pieces of fish release flavorful liquids into the surrounding aromatic base, and little if any reduction is necessary before converting the liquid into a sauce. To prepare a fish stew to order, it is best to cook the precut pieces of fish in a covered pan with a small amount of appropriate liquid (see the discussion on page 313 under "Steaming"). In some cases, as for Red Wine Matelotes (page 318), preparing an aromatic red wine reduction in advance and using it to cook the fish is an excellent method. When the pieces of fish are cooked, they should be quickly transferred to hot plates or bowls; the liquid remaining in the pan is then converted into a sauce.

Some recipes for fish stews suggest browning the fish first in a small amount of butter or oil and then deglazing the pan with liquid and returning the pieces of fish to the pan. The method, roughly analogous to a chicken fricassée (the only difference being that in a fricassee the food isn't browned), is best reserved for relatively large pieces of fish; cooking thin fish fillets and other small pieces in two stages will usually cause overcooking. When prebrowning fish on the stove, it is a good idea to coat the pieces lightly with flour (any excess carefully shaken off) so that they brown quickly.

Traditional Fish Stews and Soups

	ORIGIN	AROMATIC BASE/ FLAVORINGS	MOISTENING LIQUIDS(S)	FISH AND SHELLFISH	LIAISON	GARNITURE
Anguille au Vert	Belgium	Butter, onions	White wine	Eel	Egg yolks	Herbs
Bouillabaisse	Provence (France)	Onions, leeks, fennel, garlic, tomatoes, saffron, bouquet garni with Provençal herbs, dried orange rind	Fish stock made with trimmings, pastis	Mediterranean	Aïoli	Croutons, aïoli
Bourride	Provence (France)	Onions, fennel, thyme, bay leaf, orange zest	Fish stock made with trimmings	Mediterranean	Aïoli	Aïoli
Bourride Sètoise	Languedoc (France)	Leeks, onions, chard, bouquet garni	Fish stock, white wine	Monkfish, monkfish liver	Aïoli	Aïoli
Calderada	Portugal	Onions, sweet green peppers, garlic, tomatoes, thyme	Fish stock made with trimmings and white wine	Saltwater fish, scallops, squid	None	Basil cut in strips (chiffonade)
Caldereta Asturiana	Spain	Olive oil, onions, sweet red peppers, nutmeg	Sherry, water	Cod, sea bass, monkfish and other saltwater fish	None	None
Caudière	Flanders (Belgium)	Onions, cloves, bouquet garni, garlic	Fish stock made with trimmings and water, white wine, mussel cooking liquid	Small Atlantic fish, baby sole, flounder, conger eel, mussels	Cream	Mussels
Chaudrée	Charente (France)	Bouquet garni, pepper	White wine, water	Squid or cuttlefish, baby skate, eel, mullet	Butter	Buttered croutons
Clam Chowder	New England (United States)	Pork, onions	Milk	Clams	Potatoes	None
Cotriade	Brittany (France), Cornwall (England)	Onions, sorrel, potatoes	Water, vinegar	Conger, eel, cod, mackerel	Butter	Stale bread
Matelote Alsacienne	Alsace (France)	Leeks, carrots, onions, bouquet garni	Fish stock made with vegetables and fish trimmings, Riesling	Freshwater fish: carp, eel, perch, etc.	Cream, egg yolks, beurre manié	Buttered croutons

	ORIGIN	AROMATIC BASE/ FLAVORINGS	MOISTENING LIQUIDS(S)	FISH AND SHELLFISH	LIAISON	GARNITURE
Matelote à la Canotière	Alsace (France)	Leeks, carrots, onions, bouquet garni	Fish stock made with vegetables and fish trimmings, Riesling or Sylvaner	Carp and eel only	Butter	Mushrooms, crayfish
Matelote Normande	Normandy (France)	Onions, garlic, bouquet garni	Cider, Calvados	Saltwater fish: sole, flounder, conger eel	Beurre manié, cream	Croutons, mussels
Meurette	Burgundy (France)	Onions, garlic, bouquet garni	Red wine, marc de Bourgogne	Freshwater fish: trout, eel, perch, etc.	Beurre manié, butter	Garlic-rubbed croutons
Pauchouse	Burgundy (France)	Onions, garlic, cloves, bouquet garni	White wine (Bourgogne Aligoté)	Freshwater fish: trout, perch, eel, pike, etc.	Beurre manié, cream	Pearl onions, bacon, mushrooms, croutons
Shchi	Russia	Butter, onions, carrots	Water	White fish	Flour	Sour cream, green onions, cabbage
Ttorro	Basque country (Spain)	Olive oil, onions, garlic, sweet red pepper, hot peppers, saffron, bouquet garni	Stock made with fish trimmings and vegetables	Saltwater fish and shellfish: mussels, langoustines, monkfish, conger eel, shrimps, lobster, etc.	None	Croutons cooked with olive oil, chopped parsley
Vatapá	Brazil	Onions, hot peppers, tomatoes, ginger	Coconut milk, water	Small ocean fish, shrimps	Coconut purée, peanut purée, rice	Chopped cilantro
Waterzooï	Flanders (Belgium)	Butter, onions, bouquet garni, sage	Stock made with fish trimmings and vegetables	Freshwater fish such as trout, eel, perch, walleye, and pike	Butter or heavy cream	Chopped parsley, croutons
Zarzuela	Catalane (Spain)	Onions, sweet red peppers, sweet green peppers, garlic, ham, tomatoes, saffron, bouquet garni	White wine	Lobster, large shrimps, mussels, bay scallops, sea scallops	None	Almonds, chopped parsley
Zuppa di Pesce	Italy	Olive oil, garlic	Water, wine vinegar	Firm fish, mussels, shrimps		

RED WINE MATELOTES

Traditional red wine matelotes have always been made from freshwater fish. The same methods, however, can be adapted to saltwater fish or even a combination of the two. Traditional matelote recipes almost invariably call for poaching the fish in a large amount of red wine, usually flavored with onions, a bouquet garni, and maybe some garlic. The poaching liquid is then thickened with beurre manié. In this version, the red wine is cooked with the trimmings and bones from salmon, aromatic vegetables, and herbs and reduced ahead of time. (Some chefs like to give further body to the aromatic red wine stock by browning squid, chunks of fish, pork, or ham along with the vegetables and fish trimmings). The salmon is then cooked to order with a small amount of the flavored and reduced red wine stock. The base mixture is finished with butter or beurre manié and used to sauce the fish.

YIELD: 6 MAIN-COURSE OR 8 FIRST-COURSE SERVINGS

whole fish (such as trout, salmon, perch, pike, grouper, walleye, or eel)	6 pounds	3 kilograms
butter	5 ounces	150 grams
onion, coarsely chopped	1 large	1 large
garlic cloves, coarsely chopped	4	4
cleaned squid or extra fish (optional)	3 pounds	1.5 kilograms
red wine	6 cups	1.5 liters
large bouquet garni (page 52)	1	1
pearl onions, peeled	18 to 30	18 to 30
small mushrooms	6 ounces	175 grams
liquid lecithin (optional)		0.9 gram
heart-shaped croutons, browned in clarified butter	6 or 8	6 or 8
chopped parsley	2 tablespoons	30 milliliters
cognac, armagnac, or marc	a few drops	a few drops
salt and pepper	to taste	to taste

1. Scale (unless fillets are to be skinned), fillet, and gut the fish. Reserve the heads and bones.

2. Make shallow slits on the skin side of the fillets in two directions to prevent them from curling. Cut the fillets into appropriate-size pieces (size depends on the number of fish being used and whether it is being served as a main course or

first course). Keep the fillets covered and refrigerated until needed.

3. Remove the gills from the fish heads. Rinse the fish bones and heads under cold running water for 15 minutes. Make sure that any remaining organs or bits of coagulated blood are removed.

4. Melt 1 ounce (30 grams) of the butter in a 2-quart (2 liter) saucepan and add the chopped onion, garlic, and fish bones. If using squid or extra pieces of fish, add them. Gently cook for about 15 minutes, until they brown slightly.

5. Add 1 cup (250 milliliters) of the red wine to the browned bones and vegetables. Cook the bones and vegetables with the wine, stirring with a wooden spoon until all the wine has evaporated.

6. Add the rest of the wine and the bouquet garni. Simmer for 30 minutes.

7. Strain the red wine stock through a fine chinois into a 1-quart (1 liter) saucepan. Reduce the wine until 1½ cups (375 milliliters) remain. Skim off any froth that floats to the surface.

8. Glaze the pearl onions in ½ ounce (15 grams) of the butter and enough water to come halfway up their sides until they soften slightly, usually about 15 minutes. Keep warm.

9. Sauté the mushrooms in ½ ounce (15 grams) of the butter until they are well browned, usually 5 to 10 minutes. Keep warm.

10. If you will be cooking the fish in the oven, preheat the oven to 400°F (200°C).

11. Ladle the reduced wine mixture into a straight-sided sauté pan. Bring to a simmer.

12. Place the fish in the simmering wine. If the pieces of fish are of different thicknesses, add the thickest pieces first. Cover the pan. Place the pan over a low flame or in the oven. Add thinner pieces of fish as necessary. Cook for about 9 minutes per inch (2.5 cm) of thickness. Once the fish is done, quickly transfer it to plates or bowls.

13. Check the consistency of the sauce in the sauté pan. If it is overly reduced, thin with court-bouillon, fish stock, or water.

14. If you will be holding the matelote or its sauce for any length of time, work the liquid lecithin into the remaining 3 ounces (90 grams) butter. Whisk ½ ounce (15 grams) of the butter per serving (use all the butter for all the fish) into the sauce.

15. Dip the pointed ends of the croutons into the chopped parsley. Finish the sauce with the remaining parsley and a few drops of Cognac. Season with salt and pepper, and pour it over the fish. Arrange the onions, mushrooms, and croutons over and around the fish.

SQUID WITH RED WINE–INK SAUCE

Squid is best cooked either very quickly, such as when it is fried, or slowly, by braising. It is delicious braised in red wine and served in soup plates with plenty of French bread and a tub of aïoli.

Much is made about squid ink, but the fact is that a typical squid contains so little ink that extracting enough to make a sauce can be mind numbing at best. Fortunately, squid ink is now sold in most fish stores. In Europe, chefs use cuttlefish, which provide more ink. Cuttlefish ink comes in a relatively large sac, is thick and black, and will color and flavor a lot of broth or sauce. Cuttlefish can be found frozen in the United States and are worthwhile as long as they contain the ink sac.

YIELD: 4 MAIN-COURSE OR 6 FIRST-COURSE SERVINGS

(continued)

olive oil	2 tablespoons	30 milliliters
carrot, chopped	1 medium	1 medium
onion, chopped	1 medium	1 medium
garlic cloves, minced	4	4
squid, cleaned, hoods cut into ½-inch (1 cm) rings	3 pounds	1.5 kilograms
red wine	2 cups	500 milliliters
large bouquet garni (page 52)	1	1
flour	1 tablespoon	15 milliliters
butter, at room temperature	½ ounce	15 grams
ink sac from cuttlefish, thick ink reserved, or 1 fluid ounce squid ink	1	1
salt and pepper	to taste	to taste
aïoli (page 418)	as needed	as needed

1. Heat the oil in a saucepan large enough to hold the squid and add the carrot, onion, and garlic. Over medium heat, cook the vegetables until they soften and lightly brown, about 10 minutes.

2. Add the squid and turn the heat to high. Stir the squid as they release liquid. Cook until all the liquid evaporates and caramelizes on the bottom and sides of the pan. Don't let it burn.

3. Add the red wine and nestle in the bouquet garni. Simmer for about 45 minutes, uncovered, so the wine reduces a little.

4. Work the flour, butter, and cuttlefish ink together into a smooth paste (beurre manié) and whisk into the simmering sauce a bit at a time until the sauce has the consistency you like. Season with salt and pepper. Pass the aïoli.

OCTOPUS DAUBE

Octopus takes to slow, long cooking in the same way as tough cuts of meat. It releases so much natural gelatin that it always gives the sauce a lovely consistency. After about 60 minutes of cooking, it becomes melt-in-your-mouth tender.

YIELD: 4 SERVINGS

octopus, 2 to 3 pounds, cleaned	1	1
onion, peeled, chopped	1 medium	1 medium
carrot, chopped	1 medium	1 medium
garlic cloves, chopped	3	3

olive oil	2 tablespoons	30 milliliters
full-bodied red wine	3 cups	750 milliliters
medium bouquet garni (page 52)	1	1
finely chopped parsley	2 tablespoons	10 milliliters
baguette toasts	as needed	as needed
aïoli (page 418)	as needed	as needed

1. Cut the octopus into 1-inch (2.5 cm) sections.

2. In a pot large enough to hold the octopus sections in a single layer, cook the onion, carrot, and garlic in the oil over medium heat for about 12 minutes, or until the onion is softened but not browned.

3. Add the octopus pieces, pour in the red wine, and nestle the bouquet garni in the center of the pot. Bring to a gentle simmer and simmer, covered, for about 1 hour, or until a skewer slides easily in and out of a large piece of the octopus. If some of the octopus is above the liquid, turn the octopus over after 45 minutes of cooking to submerge what was protruding above.

4. Strain the octopus stew and discard the vegetables, sorting out the octopus. Simmer the braising liquid down to about 1 cup (250 milliliters), add the parsley, and serve with the octopus in heated soup plates. Pass the toasts and aïoli.

White Wine Fish Stews

These are prepared in almost the same way as red wine matelotes. In French regional cooking, the poaching liquid is usually thickened with roux rather than with beurre manié, and the stews are often finished with heavy cream or sometimes a mixture of cream and egg yolks. Garnitures vary almost endlessly. Recently chefs have taken to naming these stews "blanquettes," after the traditional veal stew finished with cream and egg yolks. White wine fish stews can also be flavored and thickened using a variety of techniques.

MOISTENING OPTIONS

COURT-BOUILLON (flavored with different wines, herbs, spices, or vegetables)

FISH STOCK (made from the fish carcasses)

SHELLFISH COOKING LIQUIDS

LIAISON OPTIONS

EGG YOLKS AND CREAM (may be stabilized with 2% liquid lecithin or 1% Polysorbate 80)

VEGETABLE PURÉES such as potato, garlic, tomato

COCONUT MILK

BEURRE MANIÉ

MAYONNAISES such as aïoli or rouille

BUTTER, whole or worked into a butter sauce such as beurre blanc or hollandaise

VINAIGRETTE (see the stabilized version on page 479)

YOGURT (may be stabilized with 1% to 2% liquid lecithin)

MUSTARD

LIQUID LECITHIN	MONO- AND DIGLYCERIDES (Glice)
PROPYLENE GLYCOL ALGINATE	ULTRA-SPERSE 3
LAMBDA CARRAGEENAN	WONDRA

GARNITURE OPTIONS

PEARL ONIONS (glazed)	GARLIC (whole cloves, blanched)
MUSHROOMS (cooking liquid added to fish poaching liquid)	FRESH FAVA BEANS (peeled twice, blanched)
FENNEL (cut into wedges, braised)	ARTICHOKES (turned, precooked, cut into wedges)
TOMATOES (peeled, seeded, diced)	

FINAL FLAVORING OPTIONS

CHOPPED HERBS OR COMPOUND BUTTERS	SPIRITS such as Calvados, marc or grappa, eau-de-vie
VEGETABLE PURÉES such as tomato, sorrel, or sweet pepper	

COOKING MOLLUSKS

Once a particular fish or shellfish has released flavorful liquid during cooking, the methods used for manipulating the liquid are the same. Some shellfish, however, lend themselves better to certain techniques.

Oysters

The flavor of oysters varies considerably, depending on the variety and the region where they were harvested. Often the smallest oysters, such as Belons from Maine and Pigeon Points from California, will contribute a more intensely flavored cooking liquid than fatter, more impressive-looking varieties. Recipes and chefs often disagree as to whether the liquor contained in the oyster when it is first shucked should be used for sauce making. Since it often has only a salty taste with little of the sea-like character of the oyster, it is usually discarded. The best guide is to taste the liquor first. The most flavorful component of the oyster is released when it is very gently stewed in almost no liquid. Oysters should never be allowed to boil, only to warm.

OYSTERS WITH CHAMPAGNE SAUCE

These oysters can be served individually as hors d'oeuvres or in larger groupings as a fish course. A still Champagne is excellent for this sauce (see page 67), but if this is unavailable, a dry white wine with high acidity, such as a French Chablis, Sancerre, or Muscadet, can be substituted and the dish renamed accordingly.

YIELD: 3 OR 4 SERVINGS

oysters	12	12
heavy cream	1 cup	250 milliliters
spinach, blanched, excess water squeezed out	1 bunch	1 bunch
sorrel leaves, stems removed (not blanched)	1 handful	1 handful
salt and pepper	to taste	to taste
still champagne or dry white wine	½ cup	125 milliliters
finely chopped parsley or chives	1 tablespoon	15 milliliters

1. Shuck the oysters into a bowl. Refrigerate until needed. Discard the top shells and scrub the bottom shells under running water with a brush. Turn them upside down on a sheet pan to drain and dry.

2. Reduce ⅓ cup (80 milliliters) of the cream in a saucepan until it is on the verge of breaking. Heat the spinach and the sorrel leaves in the cream until the sorrel turns a rather sullen green, about a minute. Season with pepper and a little salt (the sauce will be salty from later additions). Keep warm.

3. Heat the oyster shells in a 250°F (120°C) oven.

4. Poach the oysters in their own liquor in a small saucepan for about 1 minute. Do not let them boil, even for a second.

5. Remove the oysters from their liquor with a slotted spoon. Put them on a clean cloth napkin on a plate to remove specks of shell, and fold the napkin over them to keep them warm.

6. Strain the oyster liquor through a fine chinois into a saucepan and add the wine. Reduce by two-thirds.

7. Add the remaining ⅔ cup (170 milliliters) cream to the oyster liquor–wine reduction and reduce the sauce until it has the consistency of a beurre blanc. Add the chopped parsley and season with salt and pepper.

8. Spoon the spinach-sorrel mixture into the bottom of each oyster shell. Place an oyster on top and nap with the sauce.

Sea Scallops

It is a sad fact that truly fresh sea scallops are rarely, if ever, sold in the United States. The only way to be assured of their freshness is to buy them in their shells and shuck them to order. The amount of cooking they require is inversely proportionate to their freshness.

A popular method for preparing scallops is to sauté them in hot fat, usually butter. Unfortunately, when scallops are sautéed, their flavor is often altered—they take on a vaguely cloying sweet taste—and much of their delicate sea-like flavor is lost. When truly fresh scallops are available, they are best when lightly poached or braised and served immediately. Avoid methods that require holding the scallops for long periods while the poaching liquid is being reduced.

Because sea scallops are often thick, many chefs make the mistake of trying to submerge them completely in poaching liquid. This technique will work only if the scallops are nestled into a perfectly fitting sauté pan with straight sides. A better method is to cook them in a covered pan with a small amount of aromatic liquid. Another excellent method is to slice the scallops into ⅜-inch (5 mm) disks and poach them for no more than 30 seconds. They can then be served on a wide, shallow plate with a few tablespoons of their poaching liquid, which may be finished with the usual sauce-finishing options such as fresh herbs, tomato concassée, vinaigrette, cream, or butter.

If you shuck your own scallops, you'll see that they come with the coral attached, a tongue-like protrusion that wraps halfway around the scallop abductor muscle (the part we eat). In France, every scallop seems to have bright orange coral, whereas in the United States the coral is often a sad-looking gray. But if you find attractive coral, purée it with an equal amount (by volume) of butter, work it through a drum sieve, and whisk it into the sauce at the end. Don't let it boil even for a second.

SCALLOPS ÉTUVÉS WITH CHIVES

YIELD: 6 SERVINGS

sea scallops, preferably with coral	24	24
butter (if using coral)	3 tablespoons	45 milliliters
mussel or clam cooking liquid	6 tablespoons	90 milliliters
freshly chopped chives	2 tablespoons	30 milliliters
salt and pepper	to taste	to taste

1. Cut the scallops crosswise into ⅜-inch (5 mm) disks. If you're using the coral, purée it with the butter and strain through a drum sieve.

2. Put the mussel or clam cooking liquid in a 2-quart (2 liter) straight-sided sauté pan, and distribute the scallops in a single even layer.

3. Cover the pan and place it over high heat for approximately 45 seconds, until the liquid comes to a simmer.

4. Remove the lid and transfer the scallops to hot plates.

5. Whisk the chives and the coral butter, if using, into the hot cooking liquid. Season with salt and pepper. Pour over the scallops.

Bay Scallops

Bay scallops should be bought in their shells and shucked just before cooking. Once shucked, they quickly lose their delicacy and ocean-breeze flavor. When available, they are beautiful when served individually in their shells. Making a sauce to order can be impractical, so a good method is to poach them in a limited amount of liquid and, from time to time, remove enough of the poaching liquid to make enough sauce for several orders.

Mussels

Mussels should be checked carefully to eliminate dead ones before they are cooked; one bad one can spoil an entire dish. The best way to check them is to scrub them thoroughly with a brush under cold running water and press firmly on the two shells in opposing directions—any dead ones will immediately break apart. Many recipes insist that mussels that have opened slightly cannot be used. This is rarely true, as most mussels will close again if the two shells are squeezed together. If in doubt, give the mussel a sniff—it should smell like a clean beach. If it smells like anything else, throw it out.

Occasionally a recipe will insist that mussels be shucked while still raw. Considering the difficulty of the task, it is rarely worth it, especially since mussels are so easily steamed open and their delicious essence so easily captured. It is, of course, best to steam them to order, but if a somewhat complicated dish is being prepared, this is not practical. They can be steamed open an hour or two before serving, the top shell removed, and the bottom shells containing the mussels covered with plastic wrap and refrigerated until needed. Remove any pieces of beard once they have been steamed open.

It's another common misconception that mussels should be steamed only until they open. In fact, it's important to give them another minute or two to ensure that the mussel pulls away from one of the shells and holds together in one piece. If the mussels aren't cooked enough, they'll grip onto both shells and tear apart when you try to get them out.

In some areas, sand-free cultivated mussels, which are small, flavorful, and of uniform size, are available.

Clams

Depending on their size, clams are adaptable to the methods used to cook oysters (shucking and poaching lightly out of their shells) or mussels (steaming open and capturing their cooking liquid à la marinière).

Snails

Although there are hundreds of varieties of land snails, most require careful cleaning and a long preliminary cooking in court-bouillon. Rarely is their cooking liquid converted into a sauce; instead, they are almost always served with a nonintegral sauce, such as garlic-and-parsley butter or a lightly creamed mushroom duxelles. The miniature sea snails (periwinkles) popular in Europe are rarely eaten in the United States, although they are beginning to catch on. Periwinkles cook in about 10 minutes. A popular method for preparing an integral sauce is to simmer the snails in a nage and serve them with the cooking liquid with lots of crusty bread. Any of the methods used to finish court-bouillon—with butter, vinaigrette, mustard, herbs—can also be used.

Sea Urchins

Used for their roe, sea urchins should be cut open with scissors and the pale orange or brown roe removed shortly before it is to be used. Usually the roe is puréed and used as a flavorful liaison to finish and enrich fish sauces. Occasionally, whole pieces of the roe will appear in fish stews or as garniture for sauced fish fillets. Sauces containing sea urchin roe should never be allowed to boil.

CRUSTACEAN SAUCES

Crustaceans are members of the subphylum *Crustacea*, a Latin word that means "shell." Crustaceans have jointed bodies, appendages (which may be legs), and antennae. Mollusks, including clams, mussels, scallops, oysters, snails, squid, and octopus, have unsegmented bodies and thus are classified differently from crustaceans, though both groups are considered shellfish.

Crustaceans are treated separately from fish and other shellfish because they have certain characteristics that require special treatment by the sauce maker. A wide variety of techniques are used to extract the natural flavors from crustaceans and to convert them into sauces.

Flavor can be extracted from three major parts of the crustacean: the flesh itself; the shell; and the organs, including the tomalley and coral. The techniques used for extracting flavor from each of these parts are different and will be analyzed separately.

Flavor is extracted from the fleshy parts of crustaceans in the same way that natural flavors are derived from cooking fish and meat: Juices are released during cooking into the surrounding cooking liquid. (Most traditional recipes call for browning or gently sautéing the cut-up crustaceans with flavor components such as mirepoix or chopped onions and shallots before any liquid is added.) The cooking liquid is then reduced (or deglazed) to concentrate its flavor and usually thickened with some type of liaison. The thickened sauce can then be flavored with additional ingredients such as herbs, Cognac, or tomatoes.

The shells of crustaceans contain components that can be used to provide color and flavor to a finished sauce. The techniques for extracting these components differ from most sauce-making methods because the components are soluble in oil and fat rather than water. The traditional technique for extracting flavor and color from crustacean shells is to prepare a crustacean butter (page 331). Crustacean butters can be prepared in advance and used to finish sauces.

The most flavorful parts of crustaceans are the tomalley (liver) and coral (the ovary, with eggs or roe). In many types of crustaceans, it is impractical to try to remove the coral for use in the sauce. Lobster, however, has coral that is accessible and easy to remove. Lobster coral and tomalley must be handled carefully, as they are extremely perishable and sensitive to heat. Coral and tomalley have a pronounced sea-like flavor that is lost when cooked. Consequently, these components should be used at the very end of the sauce-making process.

Fortunately, crustacean recipes are largely interchangeable. For example, recipes for lobster can be prepared using crabs. Some of the techniques, such as the use of the tomalley and cleaning, vary depending on the type of crustacean.

TYPES OF CRUSTACEANS

Crabs

Most restaurants in the United States use blue crabs, which are native to the East Coast. There are other crabs used in the same way, but blue crabs are cheap, no doubt in part because they are so hard to shell. Extracting the meat requires expert technique and patience. Those on the West Coast of the United States eat Dungeness crab. However, even there it isn't cheap, and its hard shell makes it of little use in sauce making. Although there are few sauce recipes designed specifically for crabs, blue crabs are useful for making crustacean sauces because they are easy to clean and are usually inexpensive. To clean them, make an incision directly behind the eyes with a sharp knife or ice pick. Turn the crab over and unfold the apron—the small flap clinging to the underside of the body—and make another incision into the body of the crab; this cuts the major ventral nerves and kills them instantly. Twist off the apron while pulling. The crab's intestine should come with it. Grip the crab firmly and pull off the top shell. This will expose the gills clinging to the bottom section and allow the remainder of the inedible intestine to fall out. Pull the gills off with your fingers. After cleaning, the crab can be used in the same way as other crustaceans.

Crayfish

Crayfish live in fresh water and vaguely resemble miniature lobsters. Their flavor, however, is distinctly different. They have long been popular in France and Italy, where they have been almost completely fished out. Nowadays European crayfish comes mostly from Eastern Europe. The United States still has an abundance of crayfish in its streams and lakes, probably because Americans have ignored them for so long. (Louisianans, who call them "crawfish," are an exception.) They are becoming increasingly popular as interest in European and regional American cuisine increases. Although some suppliers market crayfish tails, these are useless for sauce preparation.

Because removing the meat from crayfish is labor intensive, many restaurant chefs buy a quantity of live crayfish with which to prepare sauce along with some prepared tails for use in the final dish. When buying whole crayfish, make sure they are alive. Many cookbook authors insist that a gritty vein—actually the intestine—running through the tail be removed from the live crayfish before it is used in sauce making. Not only is this inhumane, it is unnecessary, as the intestine is easily removed after cooking.

Langoustines

Also known as Dublin prawns, Norway lobsters, or *scampi* (singular, *scampo*), langoustines are similar in appearance to crayfish except that they swim in saltwater. Although langoustines can be found all over the world, only three American species are large enough to be marketable, and even these are hard to find. Most of the langoustines found in American markets have been flown in from Europe, where they are more widely available, though never inexpensive. The tails can be used in the same way as shrimp or crayfish tails. The shells are pale and so contribute little color to a crustacean sauce.

Lobsters

There are two primary species of lobster, *Homarus americanus*, which is found in American waters, and *Homarus gammarus*, found in European waters. These two types are similar and can be cleaned and cooked in the same way. Many recipes call for cooking lobster in a pot of boiling water for 10 to 15 minutes, depending on its size. Although the result may be suitable, the lobster's juices are lost in the pot, the coral is cooked to a red, hard, practically tasteless mass, and none of the flavor is extracted from the shell. The recipes in this chapter are designed so that the flavors from the lobster can be converted into sauces. To accomplish this, the lobster is usually cut apart while alive (not as brutal as it sounds—the lobster is killed instantly).

Practically all of the lobster can be used. Only the small stomach sac in the middle of the head (more accurately called the "carapace") should be discarded (see Classic Sauce Américaine, page 335).

Selecting lobsters depends on eventual use. It is not necessary to buy perfect 2-pound (1 kilogram) lobsters to use in lobster salad. For salads, sauces, and lobster ragoûts, it is a good idea to buy culls—lobsters that are missing a claw or have one claw that has atrophied. They are considerably less expensive and, provided they are still alive, work just as well as larger, more expensive lobsters for making sauces.

Female lobsters, because they provide coral, are essential for making certain lobster sauces. To tell the difference between a male and female lobster, turn the lobster over and examine the small legs lining each side of the bottom of the tail. The pair of legs closest to the head (where the tail and head join) are hard and firm on the male and soft and flexible on the female. European recipes sometimes call for lobsters that are spawning. The underside of a spawning lobster's shell is thickly encrusted with eggs. Marketing of spawning lobsters is, however, illegal in the United States. When buying lobster, don't insist on more females than you need. Half the number is usually enough to supply plenty of coral for the whole recipe.

Coral, the the lobster eggs, is very dark green, almost black, when raw; it turns bright orange when cooked, making for beautifully colored sauces. Tomalley, an internal organ, is pale green. While delicious, it does not change color when heated, a factor to consider when using it in sauces.

Rock Lobsters

Also known as spiny lobsters, rock lobsters are similar to regular lobsters but have no claws. They are available fresh in Europe and on the Pacific coast of the United States. Frozen rock lobster tails from South America, South Africa, and New Zealand are often served in the United States, but they have little value in sauce making.

Shrimps

Unfortunately, shrimps are usually marketed with their heads removed, which leaves little that can be used for sauce making. It is possible to buy frozen shrimp heads to use for soups and sauces, but these are taken from farmed shrimp and have a monotonous sameness about them that wild shrimp do not. Finding wild shrimp—which have a delightfully crunchy texture and a distinct nutty flavor—with the heads can be difficult. The best shrimp are sent to Italy. In a pinch, however, a suitable stock can be made with the shells, providing the shrimps are impeccably fresh.

CRUSTACEAN BUTTER

Crustacean butter is used for finishing and adding complexity not only to crustacean sauces but to fish and certain meat sauces as well. It is also useful for last-minute sauces, to which the flavor of crustaceans can be added without starting an américaine-style sauce from scratch.

Crustacean butter is prepared from cooked crustacean shells. Shells with a bright orange color, such as lobster and crayfish, are best. Because crustacean butter takes considerable time to prepare, it is best to save the shells when preparing lobster for salads and other dishes in which the shells are removed and freeze them until needed. However, avoid hard claw shells, which can damage your mixer.

Crustacean butter is valuable in sauce making not only for its flavor, but also for its bright color. By cooking crustacean shells with butter, flavor and color are extracted that would be left behind if the shells were cooked only in stock or other water-based liquids.

Because crustacean butter is intensely flavored, a little goes a long way. It can be prepared in batches and refrigerated or frozen until needed. It keeps in the refrigerator for up to a month and can be frozen almost indefinitely.

YIELD: 1 POUND (450 GRAMS)

cold butter	1½ pounds	675 grams
cooked crustacean shells, preferably lobster or crayfish	3 pounds	1.3 kilograms
hot water	2 quarts	2 liters

1. Cut the butter into large chunks and add it to the lobster or crayfish shells in the bowl of a stand mixer. **(A, page 332)** The shells should not come more than two-thirds up the sides of the bowl or they might fly out while the mixture is being worked. If your mixer is small, you may need to work in batches.

2. Attach the paddle blade to the mixer and start on slow speed. Work the shells with the butter until the mixture starts to hold together in a single mass, usually after about 5 minutes. **(B, page 332)**

3. Turn the mixer speed up slightly and work the shells with the butter for 20 to 30 minutes. The butter should take on a salmon color. **(C, page 332)**

4. Transfer the mixture to a heavy-bottomed pot. Place the pot on the stove and gently heat it **(D, page 332)** until the butter has melted. Cook the butter for about 30 minutes. If there is any sign of boiling or if the butter starts to brown around the edges, immediately turn down the heat.

(continued)

5. Add enough hot water to cover the shells by about 2 inches (5 cm). (E)

6. Chill the pot with the butter in the refrigerator or in a bowl of ice until the butter floating on the surface congeals into a hard, solid mass. (F)

7. Carefully remove the butter (which should be bright orange) from the surface of the water in the same way as removing fat from a chilled stock. (G) Discard the crustacean shells and the liquid.

8. Put the congealed butter into a small saucepan and gently bring it to a simmer. Be careful not to overheat it or it may brown and lose its flavor and color. On the other hand, be sure that you boil off any water in the butter or it can cause the butter to turn rancid. The butter is ready when it stops sputtering. The very moment this becomes perceptible, plunge the bottom of the saucepan in a bowl of cold water to stop the cooking.

9. Strain the butter through a fine-mesh strainer or fine chinois to remove fragments of shell and other particles. (H)

10. The crustacean butter is best stored in small, tightly sealed mason jars kept in a cool place or in the refrigerator. When you first open the butter, give it a sniff to see if it's rancid. When well sealed, crustacean butter keeps for up to a year. If more has been prepared than will be needed over a year, the excess can be frozen. (I)

CRUSTACEAN OIL

Crustacean butter cannot be used in cold sauces such as mayonnaise and vinaigrette because it congeals. For these sauces it is better to prepare a crustacean oil. Crustacean oil is prepared by replacing the butter in the crustacean butter recipe with the same amount (3 cups/750 milliliters) of inert-tasting oil. When preparing crustacean oil, break up the shells by wrapping them in a kitchen towel and beating them with a rolling pin before combining them in the mixer with the oil. It can be helpful to freeze the mixing bowl beforehand so the oil congeals and holds onto the shells. Otherwise the shells can just slide around in the mixer and fail to release their pigment and flavor.

BUTTERS WITH WHOLE CRUSTACEANS

Occasionally a classic recipe will call for a compound butter made with the flesh of cooked crustaceans. To prepare these butters, purée equal parts butter and shelled, cooked crustacean meat (by volume; it's okay to eye it) in a food processor. Work the butter through a drum sieve with a plastic pastry scraper.

Sauce Américaine

Although there are many variations of this classic sauce, the recipe that follows demonstrates many of the techniques used for preparing crustacean sauces. This recipe uses lobster, which is the traditional crustacean used for Sauce Américaine. Other crustaceans such as crabs, shrimps (if they have their heads), and crayfish can be substituted.

Sauce Américaine can be thickened and flavored in many ways (although some will argue it is then no longer Sauce Américaine). Many recipes include either veal or fish stock. Older recipes usually call for thickening the sauce with beurre manié or roux, while some newer versions are thickened with starches such as arrowroot. Some contemporary chefs use hydrocolloids. This recipe uses none of those options but relies on reduction to concentrate the sauce's flavors, and on whole butter and crustacean butter to give a smooth texture and a final thickening. Cream is added to the lobster coral (more traditional recipes combine it with butter) to prevent it from curdling on contact with the hot sauce. Although classic recipes for Sauce Américaine do not usually use crustacean butter, the butter adds an extra note of complexity and contributes to the color.

Recipes for Sauce Américaine always call for Cognac, which has an amazing affinity for crustaceans. Other sauces use other flavorful liquids (Madeira is common), but again, if the Cognac is replaced, the sauce should be given another name. Tarragon and fennel, which have similar anise-like notes, go extremely well with crustaceans. Herbs such as chervil and parsley, whose flavor is fleeting, should be worked with butter first. Other more intensely flavored herbs, such as marjoram, oregano, or wild thyme, should be added earlier; they can be bundled into a bouquet garni.

Although traditional Sauce Américaine is normally quite thick so that it can coat pieces of lobster, modern chefs and their clientele are often pleased to have lobster in a sauce with a more broth-like consistency. If a lighter sauce is wanted, reduction of the lobster cooking liquid should stop earlier.

Traditionally, lobster à l'américaine is served in the shell, but this is a messy process. A better approach is to cook the lobster pieces lightly—enough to get the meat out of the shells—then return the shells to the pan for making the sauce. This also helps prevent overcooking the lobster.

CLASSIC SAUCE AMÉRICAINE

YIELD: 3 CUPS (750 MILLILITERS) SAUCE; ABOUT 8 SERVINGS

wine vinegar	1 teaspoon	5 milliliters
cognac	9 tablespoons	140 milliliters
lobsters, 2 female and 2 male	6 pounds	2.5 kilograms
olive or vegetable oil	¼ cup	60 milliliters
shallots, finely chopped	5	5
garlic cloves, crushed	2	2
white wine	1 cup	250 milliliters
large bouquet garni (page 52)	1	1
tomato purée	1 cup	250 milliliters
chicken or good-quality fish stock (optional)	up to ½ cup	up to 125 milliliters
heavy cream	½ cup	125 milliliters
lobster or other crustacean butter (page 331)	1 ounce	30 grams
parsley butter	1 ounce	30 grams
tarragon butter	1 tablespoon	15 grams
chervil butter	1 ounce	30 grams

1. Put the vinegar and 1 teaspoon (5 ml) Cognac into the bottom of a bowl that will be used to catch the lobster juices and place a strainer over the bowl. Kill the lobsters and extract the coral and tomalley as described on page 338. Press the coral and tomalley from all the lobsters through

(*continued*)

the strainer, working it through using a small ladle or, better yet, your fingers. **(A)**

2. When all the tomalley and coral have been strained, put the bowl immediately over ice. Do not try to keep them for more than a few hours. (The mixture will probably have an ugly blue-green color, but it will turn bright orange once heated.)

3. Cut the lobster tails into sections about 1 inch (2.5 cm) long. **(B)** Cut the heads in half lengthwise and remove the stomach sacs. **(C)** Crack the claws with a chef's knife.

4. Heat the olive oil in a flat sauté pan that will hold all the pieces of lobster in one layer. Sauté the lobster sections, including the cracked claws, the pieces of tail, and the halved heads, until the shells turn red (usually about 5 minutes). **(D)**

5. Take the meat out of the lobster pieces and reserve. Return the shells to the pan. Break them up with a rolling pin (the European kind without

handles) or the handle of a cleaver held up on end. **(E)** Sprinkle the shells with the shallots and the garlic and stir over the heat for 2 to 3 minutes.

6. Place the remaining Cognac in a small saucepan and bring it to a simmer. Tilt the pan slightly over the flame to ignite it. (Cognac should always be flamed before adding it; if flamed with the shells, it can cause the tiny hairs on the lobster shells to burn and give a bitter taste to the sauce. It can also flare up dangerously.) **(F)**

7. Add the flamed Cognac, white wine, bouquet garni, and tomato purée to the lobster shells. **(G)** Cover the pan and cook gently for 20 minutes. **(H)**

8. Strain the liquid through a coarse chinois, pushing down on the solids with a rolling pin, **(I)** and then through a fine chinois into a small saucepan; there should be about 2 cups (500 milliliters) liquid. If there is less, add stock. Reduce the sauce by half, until 1 cup (250 milliliters) remains. Sample it to see whether further reduction is necessary; the sauce should be full flavored and have a silky consistency. (It is better to overreduce the sauce slightly at this point rather than to underreduce it, because once the butters and lobster coral are added, further reduction will be impossible.)

9. Whisk in the cream and reduce slightly. **(J)**

10. Whisk in the crustacean butter and the herb butters. **(K)**

(continued)

11. Carefully ladle the hot sauce into the strained coral (off the ice) while whisking. Notice that the blue-green purée will first discolor the sauce, but once the purée is heated by the hot sauce, the sauce will turn orange. If this color change does not occur, it means that there was not enough coral, as only the coral—not the tomalley—changes color. Although the color of the sauce will be a pale green instead of orange, its flavor will still be excellent. It is unlikely that the sauce will require the addition of salt.

12. Serve the sauce with the barely warmed lobster in hot soup plates.

Sauce Cardinal and Sauce Nantua

Sauce Cardinal and Sauce Nantua are crustacean-flavored white sauces. They are similar in that they are both based on Sauce Béchamel, but finished with lobster or crayfish butter for Cardinal and Nantua, respectively. Sauce Cardinal also contains fish stock and truffle essence, whereas Sauce Nantua contains a large proportion of heavy cream. Nouvelle cuisine versions never contain flour but are usually based on reduced cream flavored with reduced court-bouillon, reduced fish stock, or the cooking liquid from steamed or stewed crustaceans. Modernist chefs are likely to leave out much of the cream and achieve some of the thickening with hydrocolloids such as xanthan gum or lambda carrageenan.

PREPARING LIVE LOBSTERS

While most home cooks boil their lobsters in a large pot, more sophisticated recipes, especially those that derive their flavor from the lobster juices and coral, require breaking up the live creature. This isn't as gory as it sounds since the lobster is killed humanely before anything else is done to it.

Rinse the lobsters under cold running water. (Lobsters are often kept in tanks for long periods and should be thoroughly rinsed.) To prevent the lobster juices from clotting, put 1 teaspoon (5 milliliters) wine vinegar and 1 teaspoon (5 milliliters) of Cognac into the bottom of a bowl that will be used to catch the juices. Place a strainer over the bowl. Use a chef's knife to cut through the bottom of the lobster's "head," the carapace. Hold the lobster firmly by the back of the head with one hand and the back of the tail with the other. Twist quickly while holding both the tail and the head over the strainer. Squeeze the head firmly so that any juices run into the strainer. (If the lobster is cut with a knife on a cutting board, some of the juices run out and are lost.) Reach into both the head and the tail of the lobster with a forefinger, pull out the coral and tomalley, and place them in the strainer. Use a small ladle to work the contents of the strainer into the bowl. You now have a broken-up lobster, which can be cooked as desired, and the juices, which can be used to finish a sauce.

CLASSIC SAUCE CARDINAL

YIELD: 2 CUPS (500 MILLILITERS)

sauce béchamel (page 133)	1½ cups	375 milliliters
fish stock	¼ cup	60 milliliters
truffle juice or cooking liquid (see page 58)	¼ cup	60 milliliters
heavy cream	6 tablespoons	90 milliliters
lobster butter (see page 331)	1½ ounces	45 grams
salt and white pepper	to taste	to taste

Combine the béchamel, fish stock, truffle juice or cooking liquid, and cream in a 2-quart (2 liter) saucepan. Reduce the sauce to bring it to the desired consistency. Whisk in the lobster butter and season with salt and pepper.

CLASSIC SAUCE NANTUA

YIELD: 2 CUPS (500 MILLILITERS)

heavy cream	1 cup	250 milliliters
sauce béchamel (classic or otherwise; page 133)	2 cups	500 milliliters
crayfish butter (see page 331)	2 ounces	60 grams
salt and white pepper	to taste	to taste

Combine half the cream with the béchamel in a 2-quart (2 liter) saucepan and reduce the mixture until 2 cups (500 milliliters) remain. Thin the sauce with the remaining cream and whisk in the crayfish butter. Season with salt and pepper and strain through a fine-mesh strainer.

Note: To be honest, there is little difference between crayfish butter and lobster butter; both have a generic crustacean flavor. One can be easily substituted for the other.

NOUVELLE CUISINE SAUCE CARDINAL OR SAUCE NANTUA

This recipe is based on the classic sauces but is made with heavy cream and finished with chopped fines herbes. It is presented as a model and can be varied following the needs and whims of the cook.

YIELD: 1 CUP (250 MILLILITERS)

full-flavored court-bouillon (page 366), full-flavored fish stock (page 93), or appropriate crustacean cooking liquid	1 cup	250 milliliters
heavy cream	1 cup	250 milliliters
appropriate crustacean butter (page 331)	2 ounces	60 grams
parsley	½ bunch	½ bunch
tarragon sprig, leaves only	1	1
chervil	½ bunch	½ bunch
whole butter	2 tablespoons	30 grams
salt and pepper	to taste	to taste

Combine the flavor base liquid with the cream in a 2-quart (2 liter) saucepan. Reduce the mixture until it takes on a sauce-like consistency. Whisk in the crustacean butter and strain the sauce through a fine chinois. Chop the parsley, tarragon, and chervil with the whole butter (this seals in their flavor and keeps them from turning black) and whisk the resulting herb butter into the sauce. Season with salt and pepper.

Note: Contemporary cooks are less likely to serve this style of sauce, but are probably going to thicken the court-bouillon or cream (less of it) with a hydrocolloid such as lambda carrageenan.

NOUVELLE CUISINE CRAYFISH SAUCE

Although crayfish are prepared much like lobsters and other crustaceans, certain techniques differ. Because crayfish are available whole, the tails can be lightly cooked, and the remaining parts of the crayfish—the head and claws—can be used to create a crayfish sauce base. The basic technique resembles the method used for the preparation of Sauce Américaine (page 335). In this recipe the crayfish heads and claws are puréed after cooking and used to prepare a rich, full-flavored crayfish sauce.

If the tails contain an unsightly intestine, it can be easily removed after they are cooked by pinching the tip of the tail and pulling it out.

YIELD: 1 QUART (1 LITER); SERVES 20

live crayfish	3 pounds	1.4 kilograms
olive or vegetable oil	¼ cup	60 milliliters
shallots, finely chopped	2	2
carrot, finely chopped, 1 small	3 ounces	75 grams
celery, finely chopped	2 ounces	60 grams
garlic cloves, crushed	2	2
large bouquet garni (page 52)	1	1
cognac	½ cup	125 milliliters
white wine	1½ cups	375 milliliters
tomato purée	1 cup	250 milliliters
heavy cream	2 cups	500 milliliters
parsley	½ bunch	½ bunch
tarragon sprig, leaves only	1	1
chervil	¼ bunch	¼ bunch
whole butter	2 ounces	60 grams
crayfish or other crustacean butter (page 331)	2 ounces	60 grams

1. Eliminate any dead crayfish. To do this, spill them out on a large table and quickly sort through them. Throw out any that are limp or obviously dead. Rinse the live crayfish in a colander under cold running water.

2. Heat the oil in a 5-quart (5 liter) pot and sweat the shallots, carrot, celery, and garlic. When the vegetables begin to soften, add the bouquet garni and continue sweating the mixture for 5 minutes more.

3. Place the Cognac in a small saucepan and flame off the alcohol.

4. When the vegetables have softened but not browned, add the white wine and flamed Cognac and bring the mixture to a rapid boil.

5. Add the crayfish to the pot, cover the pot firmly, and steam the crayfish. While the crayfish are steaming, toss them several times, holding the lid tightly in place, so they are redistributed and cook evenly. Check the crayfish after 5 minutes. When they have all turned red, remove the pot from the heat.

6. Place a large colander over a bowl and drain the crayfish, reserving the cooking liquid in the bowl and the crayfish, vegetables, and bouquet garni in the colander.

7. Let the crayfish cool for several minutes, then twist off their tails. Remove the meat from the tails by gently squeezing them to crack the shells and pulling the shells away from the meat. Remove the intestine at this point by tugging gently on the rear-most tail flap. (The intestine should just pull out.) Separately reserve the meat and the shells.

(*continued*)

8. Traditionally, crayfish heads and claws are crushed with a heavy pestle in a mortar, but today a food processor is often used. (If using a food processor, however, be sure to remove the claws from the crayfish—they are extremely hard and can damage the blade.) Put the crayfish heads and tail shells in a food processor and purée them to a coarse paste. Crack open the claws with a heavy pestle or by wrapping them in a kitchen towel and hitting them with the side of a cleaver.

9. Combine the paste and cracked claws with the cooking liquid, the vegetables and bouquet garni left from cooking the crayfish, and the tomato purée. Bring the mixture to a slow simmer and simmer for 15 minutes.

10. While the puréed crayfish mixture is simmering, reduce the cream in a saucepan on the stove. Stir it every minute or so to keep it from breaking.

Reduce it by one-third to one-half, depending on the desired consistency of the final sauce.

11. Strain the crayfish shell mixture through a coarse chinois and then a fine chinois. Finally, strain the liquid through a carefully rinsed wet cloth napkin. (The best way to do this is to line a chinois with the napkin, add the liquid, and then carefully twist the napkin at the top. Continue twisting to squeeze out the liquid.) There should be about 2 cups (500 milliliters) of strained liquid.

12. Add the reduced cream to the strained crayfish liquid. Reduce the sauce more if necessary.

13. Chop the parsley, tarragon, and chervil with the whole butter.

14. Swirl in the herb butter and crustacean butter.

Crayfish Sauce, a Modernist Approach

It's easy to adapt the above recipe to a modernist approach. If you execute the recipe through step 11, you'll end up with 2 cups (500 milliliters) of flavorful liquid. Instead of reducing the cooking liquid and finishing it with cream, you would thicken this liquid, at least partially, with a hydrocolloid, such as 0.1% xanthan gum or 0.15% lambda carrageenan. Smaller amounts of cream and/or butter could then be used to give the sauce its characteristic richness without being overbearing. The balance between the two—the amount of cream versus the percentages of hydrocolloids—is for the saucier to determine.

LEEKS WITH LOBSTER CORAL SAUCE

One of the great things about crustaceans is their ability to perfume other foods in a way that extends the flavor of the crustaceans without additional expense. A good example of this is the Chicken with Crayfish on page 349. This is an even simpler dish, in which the flavors of the lobster are extended in its sauce. The sauce perfumes the leeks as much as the lobster itself.

YIELD: 4 SERVINGS

342

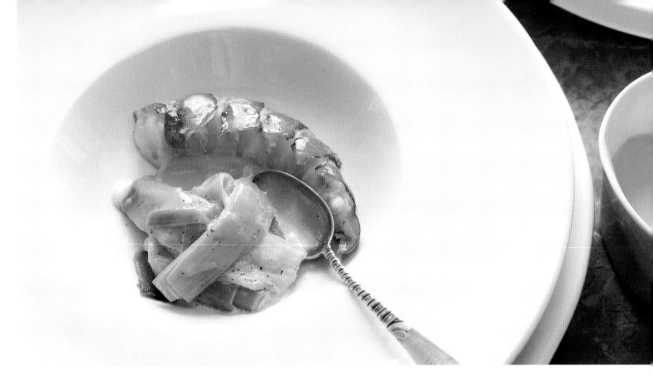

leeks	2	2
chicken stock, fish stock, or court-bouillon	2 cups	500 milliliters
cognac	1 teaspoon	5 milliliters
white wine vinegar	1 teaspoon	5 milliliters
beurre blanc, reduced cream, or modern or traditional béchamel	½ cup	125 milliliters
lobsters, both female or one of each sex	2	2

1. Preheat the oven to 325°F (160°C). Cut the greens off the leeks and cut the white sections in half lengthwise. Rinse out any sand or grit contained in the leeks. Arrange the leeks in a baking dish, pour over 1 cup (250 milliliters) of chicken stock or other liquid, and cover loosely with foil. Bake for 30 to 40 minutes, until the leeks are soft. If they start to brown, add a little water. Remove from the oven and keep warm. Reduce the oven temperature to 200°F (95°C).

2. Add the Cognac and vinegar to a bowl that will catch the lobster juices, and set a strainer over the bowl. Kill the lobsters, discard the grain sac (see photo page 336), and extract the coral and tomalley as described on page 338. Work the coral and tomalley through the strainer.

3. Put the lobster parts in a straight-sided sauté pan with the remaining 1 cup (250 milliliters) of chicken stock or other liquid. Cover the pan and simmer over medium heat until the lobster turns red, about 5 minutes. Let cool slightly. Strain and reduce any leftover liquid to about 2 tablespoons (30 milliliters). Stir into the beurre blanc.

4. Whisk the hot beurre blanc into the coral and transfer the mixture to a saucepan with sloping sides. Whisk over low heat until the sauce turns bright orange. Don't let it boil.

5. Gently warm the lobster tails, and claws if desired, covered with foil, in the oven. When warm, arrange the tails (split in half lengthwise), leeks, and lobster sauce in heated soup plates.

Classic Crustacean Sauce Variations

Sauce Américaine, Sauce Nantua, and Sauce Cardinal are the classic crustacean mother sauces from which other sauces are derived. Other variations are based on classic fish sauces, such as Sauce Normande, which can be finished with crustacean butter and truffles to produce Sauce Diplomate and Sauce Joinville.

SAUCE HOMARD (LOBSTER SAUCE)

Lobster sauce (Sauce Homard) differs from a classic Sauce Cardinal in that the béchamel base is replaced with a fish velouté. If the Sauce Cardinal is based on reduced cream, as in the nouvelle cuisine version of the recipe, a small spoonful of lobster butter is added to give the sauce the character of a classic lobster sauce. To reduce the amount of cream or velouté, hydrocolloid thickeners can be used to thicken the sauce base.

SAUCE NEWBURG

The technique for preparing a Sauce Newburg is essentially the same as that for a Sauce Américaine except that the tomatoes are replaced with Madeira and heavy cream. The sauce is then finished with lobster coral and tomalley in the same way as the Américaine.

SAUCE ORIENTALE

A Sauce Orientale is a Sauce Américaine to which a small amount of curry powder, first heated in butter, is added at the end.

SAUCE BAVARIAN

A Sauce Bavarian is based on an infusion of horseradish, thyme, bay leaf, and parsley in wine vinegar. The mixture is then beaten with egg yolks into a sabayon and finished with Crustacean Butter (page 331).

TIPS FOR THE RESTAURANT CHEF

Crustacean sauces can be expensive to prepare. Much of the cost can be defrayed by using the crustacean meat for other dishes, especially cold dishes such as salads that will not require reheating. Crustacean shells can also be saved and converted into crustacean butter. If lobster is being presented in lobster stews or in other dishes for which it is cut into pieces, buying lobster culls instead of perfectly intact whole lobsters is far more economical.

If you are using lobster for sauce making but saving the meat for another dish or to use as a garniture, a helpful cooking method is to leave the lobster tails whole and slide a wooden skewer into each tail, between the inner-side membrane and the flesh (see photo). This prevents them from curling in the pot and makes it easier to slice presentable medallions.

Depending on the style of restaurant service, a crustacean sauce can be finished to order. It is very difficult to keep coral-thickened sauces warm during a restaurant service. Even when they can be kept from curdling (with very careful attention to temperature), they lose a great deal of finesse. To prevent these problems, the liquid used to braise or steam the crustacean is thickened with some whole butter and crustacean butter, plus a hydrocolloid if desired, kept warm, and only combined with a small amount of the coral purée after an order is placed. Remember, the coral purée should be kept on ice at all times. Alternatively, the sauce base can be held in a whipping siphon in a sous vide immersion bath at no more than 133°F (56°C), and piped out into a bowl containing a measured amount of coral.

Sauce Cardinal and Sauce Nantua, although lacking the complexity of Sauce Américaine and Crayfish Sauce, are convenient to prepare and keep well during a restaurant service. They also lend themselves well to last-minute variations for special crustacean and fish dishes. Provided a reserve of crustacean butter is on hand, Sauce Cardinal variations can be made in only a few minutes.

Some crustacean sauces, if left over after a restaurant service, can be used the next day. Sauce Cardinal and Sauce Nantua can be reheated and brightened with a few freshly chopped herbs and a few drops of lemon juice. Américaine-style sauces, especially when they contain lobster coral, cannot be reused as is, but can be saved and added to the moistening liquids in the next batch of Sauce Américaine.

Sous vide cookery has revolutionized many modern kitchens. Lobster tails and other cooked crustaceans can be reheated in a sous vide immersion bath to a specific temperature to prevent overcooking. Keep in mind, however, that the flesh from raw lobster is almost impossible to get out of the shell. Crustaceans need to be at least partially cooked before they can be heated sous vide.

TIPS ON COOKING LOBSTERS

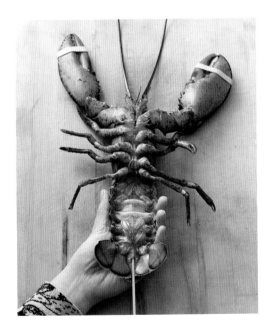

Novice cooks usually cook lobsters by throwing them into a pot of boiling water—usually for longer than necessary—and then serve them with melted butter. This method is straightforward and gives satisfactory results, but unfortunately many of the lobsters' flavorful juices are released in the boiling water during cooking and never recovered. Melted butter contributes flavor and richness but does little to underline or accent the natural flavors of the lobster. If you want to boil the lobsters—which is, after all, the simplest method—boil only for 4 minutes, following the directions on page 347.

An equally efficient but more versatile method is to steam lobster in a small amount of white wine, court-bouillon, stock, or even water. The briny lobster juices are released into the steaming liquid during cooking. Because relatively little liquid remains in the pot after the lobster has been steamed, it can quickly and easily be converted into a sauce. Once a natural cooking liquid is available as a base for a sauce, a wide variety of sauce-making techniques can be used to vary the sauce's consistency and shape its final flavor. In the recipe that follows, the steaming liquid is lightly reduced and finished with heavy cream and freshly chopped parsley.

STEAMED LOBSTER WITH PARSLEY SAUCE

YIELD: 4 MAIN-COURSE OR 8 FIRST-COURSE SERVINGS

live lobsters, 2 female and 2 male	4	4
white wine	1 cup	250 milliliters
shallots, finely chopped	3	3
heavy cream	½ cup	125 milliliters
parsley, finely chopped	1 bunch	1 bunch
white pepper	to taste	to taste

1. Lobsters require little preparation before steaming, but they should be rinsed in cold running water and then quickly and painlessly killed by inserting a sharp knife in the underside where the tail and head join. Do not kill the lobsters until the last minute; otherwise they will lose juices and flavor while waiting to go into the pot.

2. Put the wine and shallots in a pot with a tight-fitting lid that holds the lobsters without too much leftover space. Cover with the lid and simmer for 2 to 3 minutes, to infuse the shallot flavor into the wine.

3. If you want the lobster tails to remain straight, insert skewers along the underside of the tails, between the membrane and the flesh (see photo, page 345). Add the lobsters to the simmering wine, turn the heat to high, and replace the lid. (Even though the lobsters have been killed, they may still kick around a bit, so be careful to secure the lid. It might even be necessary to hold it down during the first few minutes of cooking.)

4. After 5 minutes of steaming, remove the lid and rotate the lobsters so that the ones on the bottom are shifted to the top of the pot (those directly in the steaming liquid cook faster). Cover again and steam for 5 minutes more. At this point, the lobsters should all be bright red. Do not remove the lid any more often than necessary or too much steam will be released and the cooking will be slowed.

5. Remove the lid and wait 30 seconds or so for the steam to dissipate (steam can burn you very quickly). Wrap a kitchen towel around your hand and remove the lobsters from the pot. Cover the lobsters with a towel to keep them warm and prevent them from drying out while you finish the sauce.

6. Add the cream to the cooking liquid from the lobster. Bring to a simmer.

7. Strain the liquid mixture through a fine-mesh strainer into a 2-quart (2 liter) saucepan. Taste the sauce to see if it needs reduction. (It is usually quite salty, so reduction should be avoided.) Add the chopped parsley, simmer the sauce for about 1 minute to infuse the parsley flavor, and season with white pepper.

8. Cut the lobsters lengthwise down the middle. Remove the stomach sac from each side of the head. If desired, remove the lobster from the shell.

9. Because the parsley sauce is very thin, it is best to serve the lobster in large, flat soup bowls with the sauce either underneath it in the bowl or passed at the table in a sauceboat.

Other possibilities for converting the strained lobster steaming liquid into a sauce include:

• Beating it with egg yolks to convert it into a sabayon, which can be left as is or finished with yogurt, herb butter, whole butter, clarified butter, or crustacean butter (for these last two, an emulsion must be in place before they are added).

• Finishing the steaming liquid with less cream and using butter to produce a sauce with more luster and a richer consistency.

• Thickening the sauce with hydrocolloids such as xanthan gum and lambda carrageenan and then finishing it with a small amount of butter, crustacean butter, or cream.

• Adding a generous helping of chopped fresh herbs at the end. Herbs shape the flavor of a finished sauce in sometimes dramatic and sometimes subtle ways. Fines herbes (chervil, chives, tarragon, parsley) give the sauce delicacy, finesse, and freshness, while Provençal herbs (savory, marjoram, oregano, thyme, hyssop, rosemary, and lavender) may be used in combination or alone to add their dramatic southern French associations.

• Finishing the steaming liquid with flavored mayonnaise. The mayonnaise can be stabilized as described on page 417. Lobster oil can be worked in at the end.

FOUR-MINUTE LOBSTER WITH A SAUCE MADE FROM ITS CORAL

While the French and other cultures have devised elaborate and delicious methods for cooking lobsters, one of the simplest remains the best: boiling. While boiling often results in dry, cottony flesh, this is usually due to overcooking. Most books recommend about 20 minutes, but here a 2-pound lobster is cooked for 4 minutes, just long enough to cook the flesh and leave it moist and delicate. There is, however, one result of this process that some consider a curse and others a blessing: the coral inside female lobsters remains raw and dark green—almost black—from the relatively low internal temperature. While some cooks might be tempted to discard the coral, keep in mind that it's the tastiest part of the lobster. It also lends itself to making an impeccable lobster sauce. You're also likely to encounter tomalley inside the lobsters—pale, green, amorphous—which is delicious and can also be used in the sauce, although it can dampen the color somewhat. If color is of extreme importance, leave the tomalley out.

Beurre blanc and hollandaise work especially well as a base sauce for incorporating the coral, but the coral can also be worked into any number of seafood-based sauces such as veloutés, and even hot mayonnaise emulsions.

YIELD: 4 SERVINGS

(continued)

TIPS ON COOKING LOBSTERS

347

live lobsters, 2 pounds (1 kilogram) each, at least 2 female	4	4
cognac or wine vinegar	4 drops	4 drops
beurre blanc (page 434), hollandaise (page 398), or other base sauce	1½ cups	375 milliliters
salt and pepper	to taste	to taste

1. Bring a large pot of water (enough to submerge all the lobsters) to a hard boil. Submerge the lobsters and boil for 4 minutes. (Count from the moment you add the lobsters to the hot water.) Drain in a colander. **(A)** Cover the lobsters loosely with a dry towel and let them rest for 5 to 10 minutes.

2. Add the Cognac or wine vinegar to a bowl and set a strainer over the bowl. Twist open the female lobsters **(B)** and gently tug on the coral hanging out of the tail and from the opening in the head where the tail joins. **(C)** (Whether to leave the tomalley in the lobster or to use it in the sauce is up to you. It will add flavor to the sauce but may discolor it.) Work the coral through the strainer into the bowl. If you're serving the lobster later (cold or reheated sous vide), keep the coral, covered with plastic wrap, on a bowl of ice. The coral is extremely perishable and shouldn't be held for more than 6 hours.

3. Warm the base sauce gently. Slowly whisk about half the base sauce into the coral **(D)**, then return the mixture to the remaining base sauce, off the heat. Whisk the sauce until it turns

from a rather sullen green to bright orange. **(E)**
If it doesn't turn orange, heat the sauce gently
(remember that coral consists of eggs, which
will curdle as the sauce approaches a boil), while
whisking, until the color changes. The coral will
also thicken the sauce (in the manner of egg
yolks), so it may need to be thinned with more
base sauce, cream, stock, or water. Season with
salt and pepper and serve the sauce with the
lobsters, either on the plate or on the side.

USING CRUSTACEAN FLAVORS WITH MEAT AND FISH

In traditional classic and regional French cooking, the flavorful liquid extracted from lobster, crayfish, or other crustaceans is usually converted into an integral sauce, such as Sauce Américaine (page 335), served with the crustaceans themselves. Crustacean Butter (page 331), on the other hand, is used as a staple ingredient in professional kitchens as a last-minute flavoring for classic sauces and contemporary or improvised variations.

In certain older or regional recipes, crustacean cooking liquid is also used to moisten fish and poultry. This excellent technique will give a finished dish a deeper, more complex flavor than simply swirling in crustacean butter at the end.

CHICKEN WITH CRAYFISH

This classic Lyonnais dish has been made popular by a number of chefs, including Paul Bocuse. The flavors of crayfish and chicken can be combined by lightly searing, without browning, the pieces of chicken in crayfish butter and moistening the chicken pieces with crayfish cooking liquid in the manner of a fricassée. This dish can also be approached as a sauté by cooking the pieces of chicken completely in crayfish butter and making the sauce in the pan with crayfish cooking liquid. The chicken can also be roasted in the oven and basted with crayfish butter. The drippings are caramelized at the end of cooking, the roasting pan deglazed with crayfish cooking liquid, and cream whisked in along with more crayfish butter. Crayfish tails are the obvious garniture for either version. The following version is a fricassée.

YIELD: 8 SERVINGS

(*continued*)

chickens, 3½ pounds (1.75 kilograms) each	2	2
crustacean butter (page 331)	6 tablespoons	90 grams
steaming liquid from crayfish or other crustacean, or fish stock	2 cups	500 milliliters
whole butter	4 tablespoons	60 grams
finely chopped fines herbes	2 tablespoons	30 milliliters
salt and pepper	to taste	to taste
crayfish tails, cooked	40	40

1. Quarter the chickens and lightly sear the pieces on both sides in 4 tablespoons (60 grams) of the crustacean butter in a straight-sided sauté pan.

2. Add the crayfish steaming liquid or other liquid to the pan, cover, and gently simmer the chicken for 15 to 20 minutes, until firm to the touch. Transfer the chicken to a platter and cover it with aluminum foil to keep it warm.

3. Reduce the cooking liquid until 1 cup (250 milliliters) remains. Carefully skim off any fat or froth that floats to the surface. If you would like more body in the finished sauce, continue to reduce the liquid as desired before adding the butter.

4. Whisk the whole butter into the sauce until completely emulsified, then whisk in the remaining 2 tablespoons (30 grams) of crustacean butter.

5. Strain the sauce through a fine chinois into a 1-quart (1 liter) saucepan. Whisk in the fines herbes. Season with salt and pepper.

6. Heat the crayfish tails in the sauce. Serve over or around the chicken.

VARIATIONS

Other herbs can be used instead. The sauce for the crayfish can remain somewhat soup-like (these kinds of sauces are often referred to as "long"). Or the cooking liquid can be reduced so that the sauce comes out relatively thick ("short"). Cream can be added to the base and be more or less reduced. Other thickeners, such as hydrocolloids, can be added to the sauce base to minimize the need for rich (and expensive) ingredients such as cream and butter. You can also make a more exciting crayfish base: Steam the crayfish, twist off the tails and claws, and simmer the crushed heads (carapaces) in liquid (cream works amazingly well because its fat extracts color and flavor from the shells). Use this liquid as the base for simmering the chicken.

JAPANESE-STYLE CRAB SAUCE

This very fluid sauce is best served around and under seafood rather than on top.

YIELD: 6 SERVINGS

dashi (page 576)	2 cups	500 milliliters
mirin	1 tablespoon	15 milliliters

soy sauce	1 tablespoon	15 milliliters
potato starch	2 tablespoons	30 milliliters
water	2 tablespoons	30 milliliters
shredded crabmeat, preferably snow or king crab	1 cup	250 grams

1. Bring the dashi to a simmer and add the mirin and soy sauce. Work the starch to a smooth paste with the water and whisk the mixture into the barely simmering dashi; simmer for just a second or two more.

2. Whisk in the crabmeat and serve immediately over fish or shellfish such as scallops.

IMPROVISING CRUSTACEAN SAUCES

After analyzing and preparing the classic crustacean sauces—Cardinal, Américaine, and Nantua—the basic techniques used for crustacean sauces should be familiar. Once these techniques have been mastered, it is relatively simple to change one or more of the ingredients to give a sauce a new twist or a personal touch.

Moistening Liquids

One of the components most frequently replaced when preparing an américaine- or nantua-style sauce is the preliminary moistening liquid. In a Sauce Américaine, tomato pulp, flamed Cognac, and white wine are used. It is possible to replace these moistening liquids with various table wines (Sauternes adds a subtle sweetness and complexity to the sauce), fortified wines such as Madeira or sherry, or hard cider. The flamed Cognac can be replaced with other liquors, such as whiskey or Armagnac. Remember, however, that complex, expensive liquors and wines should not be added during the early stages of preparing a sauce, because their nuances will be wasted.

Recipes for crayfish sauce and sauce américaine usually call for stock such as fish or chicken stock. Be especially careful when using fish stock: It must be made from only the

JAPANESE-STYLE CRUSTACEAN SAUCES FOR SEAFOOD

Japanese cooks flavor dashi with mirin and soy sauce and thicken it with a small amount of potato starch to come up with a sauce base that is then varied by adding shredded crustacean, often crab. These sauces are light and elegant alternatives to French-style butter sauces.

freshest fish or bones. Because the sauce will undergo reduction, if only fish stock is used, the resulting sauce may have a strong fishy taste that will overwhelm the more subtle flavors of the crustaceans. If you are uncertain about the quality of available fish stock, it is better to use a more subtle stock, such as veal or chicken, or court-bouillon. Some chefs like to use some mussel cooking liquid in crustacean sauces. Mussel liquor gives a lively, sea-like flavor to a sauce, but be careful, especially if the sauce is going to be reduced at a later stage—mussel-cooking liquid is very salty.

Aromatics

When preparing Sauce Américaine and Crayfish Sauce, shallots and garlic are used for the Américaine and a mirepoix—in this case, a mixture of chopped carrots, shallots, garlic, and celery—is used for the Crayfish Sauce. These elements provide complexity and help round out the flavors of the sauces. It is possible to add other flavorings to these initial ingredients, such as extra garlic, chopped fennel (which beautifully accents the flavors of crustaceans), and a variety of herbs. Once these ingredients are moistened, a classic bouquet garni of parsley, fresh thyme, and bay leaf is added during the cooking. This bouquet garni can be altered to give the sauce a different character. Sprigs of fresh marjoram, wild thyme, or oregano can be used to give it an Italian or southern French accent. Fennel greens or tarragon can also be used to liven up the sauce. Remember, again, when flavoring a sauce at this early stage, only the more aggressively flavored herbs (see "Herbs," page 51) will contribute flavor that will last through all the stages of making the sauce. When using delicate herbs such as chervil and chives, or herbs whose flavor is extremely volatile, such as basil, add them near the end of the sauce's preparation. It also helps to incorporate these herbs into compound butters, chopping the herbs and butter together so that the herbs have little contact with air. The butter prevents the herbs from darkening and seals in their flavor until the last minute when the butter is whisked into the sauce.

Liaisons and Thickeners

Once the crustaceans have been cooked in a moistening liquid, the chef must decide on the consistency he or she wants for the final sauce. If the final dish is to be presented in the style of a soup, light stew, or pot au feu, then obviously little liaison is necessary—a few tablespoons of cream or a swirl of butter will be sufficient to smooth out the sauce's texture and give it an appealing sheen. If, however, it is important that the sauce coat the final preparation, then a greater amount of liaison or a more powerful one must be used. Beurre manié provides a quick, inexpensive liaison without making the sauce overly rich. Be sure to reduce the sauce to concentrate its flavors before adding the beurre manié, since beurre manié should not be cooked more than a second or it will taste starchy. Roux can also be used. Newer modernist thickeners such as xanthan gum and lambda carrageenan will give the sauce the desired consistency without a starch muting or interfering with its flavor.

When beurre manié or roux is used to thicken a crustacean sauce, the resulting sauce often has a slightly matte appearance. In some cases, where a certain rusticity is wanted—in regional French, Italian, or Spanish cooking—this effect is desirable. If, however, you want a sauce with more sheen without resorting to butter, another starch such as cornstarch or arrowroot, or hydrocolloid thickeners such as Ultra-Sperse 3, can be used. Be sparing in the use of each of these, as too much will give the sauce a slippery texture and an artificial appearance. Remember, when using starch, to bring the sauce to a full boil. Hydrocolloids should be well blended into the liquid using an immersion blender or rotor stator homogenizer (see page 35).

Crustacean sauces can also be thickened with cream, butter, or both. Remember the techniques for using butter: It should be added only after the sauce has been reduced. If you add the butter and then discover that the sauce is too thin or its flavor is not concentrated enough, you will not be able to reduce it further to thicken it. If cream is used, it is advisable to reduce it separately before adding it to the crustacean sauce reduction—long reduction with the sauce can cause the cream to turn granular or break. And remember, never cover a sauce containing cream while it is cooking.

Classic sauces are often thickened with egg yolks. Although the classic method (beating the egg yolks with a small amount of the sauce liquid and returning the mixture to the hot sauce) works for crustacean sauces, the resulting sauce is often undesirably rich. Alternative methods using egg yolks can also be used to thicken crustacean sauces (see "Contemporary Variations," page 401). The reduced crustacean cooking liquid can be beaten with egg yolks to form a sabayon—an extremely light, almost dietetic sauce. This sabayon can also be finished with butter, crustacean butter, and herb butters to produce a crustacean-flavored hollandaise-type sauce.

A modernist approach to egg yolk–thickened sauces may include hydrocolloids and/or emulsifiers to stabilize the yolks and prevent them from curdling. This involves using one emulsifier for the fat (the egg yolks are stabilized with liquid lecithin) and another type of emulsifier (propylene glycol alginate) for the liquids that are going to be combined with the yolks. Work 1% to 2% liquid lecithin into the butter or egg yolks (whatever fat is being used to finish the sauce) and 0.5% propylene glycol alginate into the liquid base. Whisk the yolks and base together into a sabayon and whisk in melted or clarified butter (or crustacean butter) in a steady stream.

Another method for binding a crustacean sauce with egg yolks is to finish the sauce with a mayonnaise (see "Mayonnaise-Based Seafood Sauces," page 425). This method will not only lightly bind the sauce but can be used to incorporate final flavorings and nuances into the finished sauce. A saffron-flavored mayonnaise works particularly well.

Finishes and Final Flavors

Once the liaison has been added to the sauce (or the decision has been made to dispense with it), it is time for the final shaping of the sauce's flavor. In some cases, the liaison and final flavoring of the sauce will occur simultaneously, such as when herb butter, crustacean butter, or a flavored mayonnaise is being used. The final flavorings of a crustacean sauce should never mask the intrinsic crustacean flavors that the chef has worked so hard to extract, but should bring them into focus. Fines herbes are especially useful for this. Fines herbes without tarragon can always be used to finish a crustacean sauce, regardless of the ingredients used to flavor the sauce. Their flavor is so delicate that they add subtlety, freshness, and complexity to the sauce while never taking over. If tarragon is used, more thought should be given to whether it complements the other flavor components—usually it does; tarragon and crustaceans work extremely well together. If you want a more assertive, direct sauce, other herbs and herb butters can be used to contribute a final accent. Chopped fresh marjoram or oregano (used sparingly) gives the sauce a distinct, unmistakable character.

One of the classic flavorings used for crustaceans is Cognac. It is a magic marriage, as the flavors merge in amazing, subtle ways. However, if Cognac is used in the preliminary moistening of the crustaceans, many of its nuances will have been lost by the time the sauce is ready for final flavoring. Toward the end of cooking, depending on the budget, a finer Cognac can be used. In any case, avoid using an extremely old Cognac. It is preferable to use a young, full-bodied Cognac with considerable fruit.

The classic Cognac used in flavoring crustacean sauces can be replaced with other liquors, such as Armagnac, whiskey, Calvados, aquavit, or Pernod, to give the sauce individuality. Remember, when choosing these flavorings, to use good judgment—do not use whiskey to finish a sauce moistened with cider, use Calvados. Do not use Calvados to finish a sauce that has been moistened largely with tomato pulp. Be careful when using Pernod or other anise flavors: Unlike with Cognac or whiskey, if you add too much, their flavor is difficult to cook off.

Regardless of what other flavors are used to finish a sauce, lobster coral should be added at the very end, because it is so sensitive to heat.

GARNITURES FOR CRUSTACEANS

Many chefs and home cooks like to vary the classic crustacean preparations by adding vegetables or even fruits and presenting these with the finished crustaceans. When preparing dishes such as these, you should decide whether to incorporate the flavor of these components into the crustacean sauce or simply serve them as garnitures on the side. If, for example, you want to serve a lobster with fresh morels or other wild mushrooms, there are two routes to follow: The mushrooms can be sautéed in an appropriate oil or fat, sprinkled with herbs, and simply presented on the side of the plate along with the lobster. This is a perfectly acceptable method. On the other hand, morels have a delicate complexity that works well in sauces. If you want to exploit that flavor, the morels should be cooked so that their flavor can be incorporated into the sauce. To do this, take a few tablespoons of the crustacean cooking liquid (or other liquid such as cream, fish stock, or court-bouillon if another base is being used), and cook the morels in a covered saucepan with the liquid. When they are finished cooking, this liquid should be returned to the crustacean sauce base.

It has become common to see crustaceans served with fruits—mango is especially popular and surprisingly good. When using fruit, the cooking liquid from the fruit can be returned to the sauce to give it a subtle, underlying sweetness. A fruit-based eau-de-vie can also be used to finish the sauce when the flavor is appropriate; for example, do not finish your crayfish with pineapple with Poire William.

Stew-like preparations that contain two or more types of crustaceans have become extremely popular in French restaurants, because the customer can taste a variety of different crustaceans on the same plate. When well prepared, they are extremely labor intensive, both in preparation and when the order is placed.

ADDITIONAL SAUCES FOR CRUSTACEANS

The sauces described previously are based on flavors extracted from crustaceans such as lobster, crayfish, crab, and shrimp. They follow the French tradition of using a sauce to accentuate, nuance, and extend the flavors of the basic ingredients. Because these sauces are time-consuming and expensive to prepare, the home cook or restaurant chef may want to resort to a simple sauce that can be prepared at the last minute and served with the crustacean as an alternative to the ubiquitous drawn butter. Some ideas follow; other chapters in this book describe the methods for making these sauces.

EMULSIFIED SAUCES

HOLLANDAISE. Plain; sabayon made with crustacean liquid; flavored with garlic; finished with crustacean butter; finished with tomato purée; flavored with curry or saffron

BÉARNAISE-STYLE. Practically any of the classic versions

MODERN. Emulsified or stabilized with agar, lambda carrageenan, gelatin, xanthan gum, guar gum, locust bean gum, mono- and diglycerides (Glice), Polysorbate 80, propylene glycol alginate, lecithin, or gum arabic; puréed with stabilized egg yolks (cooked sous vide at 140°F (60°C)

BEURRE BLANC AND DERIVATIVES

Finished with crustacean butter, Pernod, Cognac, or tomato coulis; flavored with garlic or Provençal herbs

MAYONNAISE-FINISHED SAUCES

HOT FISH OR CHICKEN STOCK. Finished with appropriately flavored mayonnaise; saffron- and herb-flavored mayonnaises work especially well

VINAIGRETTE-FINISHED SAUCES

Vinaigrettes are particularly versatile when served with cold crustaceans. The vinegar can be cooked lightly with strained lobster coral to create a colorful orange base for the vinaigrette. The oil can be lobster oil (see page 334), nut oils, or olive oil. The oil should be whisked or blended into the vinegar, a small amount at a time.

REDUCED-CREAM SAUCES

Infused with herbs, black or green peppercorns, white wine and shallot reductions

BROWN SAUCES

Containing wild mushrooms, truffles, or herbs and lightly finished with crustacean butter

COMBINING CRUSTACEANS WITH OTHER SHELLFISH

All the techniques used for extracting the flavor from crustaceans can be used to create braising liquids that in turn are used to cook other shellfish. The complexity of flavor, when combining shellfish in this way, is overwhelming and well worth the (considerable) effort.

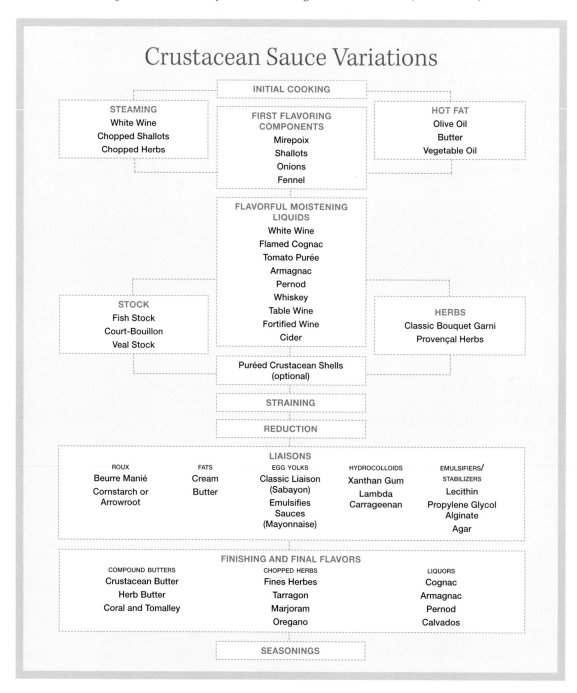

Crustacean Sauce Variations

INITIAL COOKING

STEAMING
White Wine
Chopped Shallots
Chopped Herbs

FIRST FLAVORING COMPONENTS
Mirepoix
Shallots
Onions
Fennel

HOT FAT
Olive Oil
Butter
Vegetable Oil

FLAVORFUL MOISTENING LIQUIDS
White Wine
Flamed Cognac
Tomato Purée
Armagnac
Pernod
Whiskey
Table Wine
Fortified Wine
Cider

STOCK
Fish Stock
Court-Bouillon
Veal Stock

HERBS
Classic Bouquet Garni
Provençal Herbs

Puréed Crustacean Shells
(optional)

STRAINING

REDUCTION

LIAISONS

ROUX	FATS	EGG YOLKS	HYDROCOLLOIDS	EMULSIFIERS/ STABILIZERS
Beurre Manié	Cream	Classic Liaison (Sabayon)	Xanthan Gum	Lecithin
Cornstarch or Arrowroot	Butter	Emulsifies Sauces (Mayonnaise)	Lambda Carrageenan	Propylene Glycol Alginate
				Agar

FINISHING AND FINAL FLAVORS

COMPOUND BUTTERS	CHOPPED HERBS	LIQUORS
Crustacean Butter	Fines Herbes	Cognac
Herb Butter	Tarragon	Armagnac
Coral and Tomalley	Marjoram	Pernod
	Oregano	Calvados

SEASONINGS

MIXED SHELLFISH FRICASSÉE

T his dish is called a fricassée because it sounds prettier than "stew," not because it follows the stricter definition given on page 275. The idea is to cook each shellfish in a way that suits it best and then combine the liquids released by all the shellfish to form the sauce. A piece of each crustacean is served on the same plate. Remember when cooking mollusks, such as clams, cockles, and mussels, that they must be scrubbed and thoroughly rinsed. Sort through them to make sure there are no bad ones.

YIELD: 4 SERVINGS

cockles, rinsed	1 pound	450 grams
or	or	or
littleneck clams, scrubbed	12	12
mussels, preferably green-lipped new zealand, rinsed	4 large	4 large
white wine	½ cup	125 milliliters
water	1 cup	250 milliliters
lobster, 1	1½ pounds	675 grams
cognac or white wine vinegar	a few drops	a few drops
tomatoes, peeled, seeded, chopped	2 large	2 large
heavy cream	½ cup	125 milliliters
sea scallops, shucked	4 large	4 large
shrimp, peeled and deveined	4 jumbo	4 jumbo

1. Steam open the cockles or clams and the mussels in the white wine and water. Remove the bivalves and set aside. Reserve the steaming liquid. If it has sand or grit, decant it into a clean container, rinse out the pot, and put it back in.

2. Put the lobster in the pot with the steaming liquid. Cover and steam it over medium heat until it turns bright red, about 5 minutes. Remove, cover with a towel, and let rest for 5 minutes.

3. Put the Cognac or vinegar in a bowl and place a strainer over the bowl. Take the lobster meat out of the shell, working over the strainer to capture any coral. Reach your fingers into the base of the head (carapace) and tail and pull out any coral and/or tomalley. Work the coral and/or tomalley through the strainer.

4. Combine the tomatoes with the steaming liquid and simmer gently for 10 minutes. Work through a strainer into a saucepan and add the cream. Simmer slightly to concentrate the flavor but not so much as to thicken it or make it too salty. Poach the scallops and shrimp in the sauce for about 2 minutes. Remove the scallops and shrimp.

5. Thoroughly whisk half the sauce base into the bowl containing the strained coral/tomalley. Transfer this mixture to a saucepan, ideally one with sloping sides. Whisk the sauce over medium heat. Don't let the sauce get too hot; cook it only until it turns from pink to orange.

6. Arrange the shellfish in heated soup plates and pour the sauce over and around them.

GELÉES AND CHAUDS-FROIDS

Natural meat and fish gelées (sometimes called aspics) are among the most subtle and delicious of foods, and can be the most beautiful: A breast of chicken or fillet of fish surrounded by a golden herb-specked gelée is a delightful sight. Because aspics lend themselves to manipulation—their intrinsic quality compromised by the addition of excess gelatin—they are thought of more as building materials for the far-flung fantasies of late-nineteenth-century French cooking than as delicate accompaniments to cold meats or fish. An authentic gelée is the natural cooking liquid from meat or fish that sets when cold. In France, the term *aspic* usually refers to a meat or fish preparation that has been molded and held together with the appropriate gelée. In the United States, where the word *jelly* brings to mind fruit preserves, *aspic* is most often used to refer to any dish that includes meat or fish gelée.

The most common way to prepare a meat or fish gelée is to take clear stock and add enough gelatin to set it. The resulting gelée may look passable but will have less flavor than the stock would if served hot. If the stock is weakly flavored initially, the peculiar flavor of commercial gelatin will come through, and the too-stiff texture given the gelée by the gelatin creates a nauseating glue-like mass.

Unfortunately, the dining public has grown to dislike gelées because few people have ever tasted an authentic meat or fish gelée. A properly prepared gelée should be deeply flavored and only slightly gelatinous; it should barely hold together when served.

With the advent of modernist cuisine in recent years, other compounds than gelatin are being used to set gelées. These gelling agents—sodium alginate and agar, to name a couple—can be used to make both cold and hot gelées, and to create foams that can be used to coat foods in the same way as gelées, effects that were unthinkable not so many years ago. They are remarkably powerful and can be used in minute amounts.

Like gelatin, these new—or, rather, recently discovered—compounds need to be worked in solution. This process happens in several stages. First there is dispersion, which is the simple combining of the compound with liquid so that it's broken apart and no lumps remain. The second stage is hydration, when liquid penetrates the particles. Last, there is gelatinization, which occurs as the minute particles of compound swell and become at least partially soluble. This is usually the result of heating the solution, but it can also occur in a cold medium. Once the gelling agent has dissolved and gelatinized, the liquid is allowed to set. Each of these stages has optimum temperatures that differ among gelling agents. For example, some compounds require gentle constant heat in sous vide bags in order to dissolve, while others, like xanthan gum, can be added at virtually any temperature and without much ado. Gelatin sets in the refrigerator, but some other gelling materials, such as agar, set at relatively high temperatures and can be left out of the refrigerator without melting.

Once the gel has set, it can be used a small amount at a time to add body to sauces. Some gels also act as emulsifiers, making it possible to whip them together with fats to obtain various butters and creams.

Some gelling agents work better in combination—for example, a mixture of kappa and iota carrageenans, of low- and high-acyl gellans, of locust bean gum with agar and xanthan gum, or of locust bean gum with kappa carrageenan. It's worthwhile to experiment with various gelling ingredients both alone and in combination.

Some gelées can be served hot. This is particularly attractive when you want to create the impression that the food was prepared en gelée or, when opaque, as chaud-froid. Hot gelées are typically prepared using combinations of agar, sorbitol, and xanthan gum. Low- and high-acyl gellans are also used.

NATURAL MEAT GELÉES

In most professional settings, meat and fish gelées are prepared—or at least begun—independently of what they will accompany, in the same way that stocks are prepared in advance and eventually used in stock-based (nonintegral) sauces or in integral sauces. Several methods can also be used to make meat or fish gelée.

The best gelées are "natural gelées" derived from the poaching or braising liquids from meat or fish. These gelées have a deep, complex flavor. However, keep in mind that stocks are essentially poaching liquids. If they are well made, from something other than just bones, they will replicate the effect of an integral sauce. In any case, start with a deeply colored and flavored liquid. To take things to an extreme, prepare a basic meat or fish broth and use it as the moistening liquid for more meat or fish. The process is repeated until the liquid contains the right amount of natural gelatin. The flavor is superlative.

Gelées can also be prepared by reducing stocks or braising liquids to concentrate both the flavor and the natural gelatin, but this method cooks out much of the aromatic flavor of the stock and gives it a flat taste.

The gelée stock also can be prepared with meat for flavor (veal or beef shanks, pork shoulder, turkey wings, or duck thighs, for example) and pork rinds or a split veal foot for texture and consistency. These additions provide natural gelatin and give a somewhat more fragile texture to the stock than commercial gelatin, but do little to enhance its flavor.

In a restaurant setting, if cold meats are poached for other dishes, the jelled poaching liquid can be used when it contains enough natural gelatin. This method not only provides the best gelée but costs nothing more to prepare. It can be used only in settings where the poached meats and poultry are served without gelée or an integral sauce of their own (such as cold beef, chicken for chicken salad, turkey breast, or veal shank with tomato sauce).

Begin by preparing a full-bodied white or brown stock using meat and appropriate trimmings. The meat and trimmings can be browned or not, along with aromatic vegetables, depending on the use and style of the gelée (see Chapter 4, "Stocks, Glazes, and Essences," page 81). Remember to moisten the stock with cold water, and prevent it from boiling at any point. If the stock is kept at a slow simmer and not allowed to boil during its initial preparation or the subsequent poaching of the meats, and if it is carefully skimmed, it will not require clarification.

Use the stock over the course of several days for poaching meats. To keep it clear, it is best to start poaching the meats in cold or lukewarm stock; if the stock is already simmering when the meat is added, it may cloud. Again, be careful not to let the stock boil while poaching the meat. When the stock has been used several times for poaching, it should be tested to determine whether it is ready to be used as a gelée. Taste it to see if it is full flavored. It may be necessary to revitalize it from time to time by adding additional aromatic vegetables or a bouquet garni.

The consistency of the gelée also needs to be checked at each stage by placing a few tablespoons of the liquid in a small bowl and putting it in the refrigerator or over a bowl of ice. When the gelée has set, remove it from the refrigerator or ice for about 5 minutes and check the consistency. It should be as delicate as possible without being liquid. If the gelée is too thick (this is unlikely if it has not been reduced), it can be lightened with some clear stock. If it is too thin, continue to poach more meat in it, or gently reduce it until it has the necessary consistency when set.

When the gelée has the correct consistency, salt and other flavorings can be added. Remember that salt is much less assertive in cold preparations than hot, so be certain to adjust the salt after the gelée has cooled but not set.

When looking for inspiration when making gelées, keep in mind that most of the brown sauces in Chapter 7 can be served as gelées. Simply leave out any fats, coat the bottom of soup plates with the fatless sauce, and let set. Arrange the cold food and garniture on top.

CLASSIC MEAT GELÉE

Classic recipes for meat gelées are almost identical to basic brown and white stocks except that a gelatinous element is added. It is then clarified with additional meat and egg whites, although properly made stock—carefully skimmed and never allowed to boil—should not require the addition of egg whites.

The following recipe calls for moistening 3 pounds (1.5 kilograms) of meat, such as veal or beef shanks, stewing hens, or chicken carcasses, with water or stock. If water is used, extra gelatin is provided by combining a split and blanched veal foot with the meat. One veal foot, split into halves and cooked for 6 hours, will set 4 quarts (4 liters) liquid, so it is necessary to gauge the amount of gelatin that will be in the finished gelée; if gelatinous cuts of meat are used or an already gelatinous stock is used to moisten the meat, then adding a veal foot will make the finished gelée too gelatinous.

As the gelée stock cooks, it loses a certain natural vitality that is best restored by adding a small amount of chopped mirepoix or coarsely chopped fines herbes.

YIELD: 2 QUARTS (2 LITERS)

veal foot, split in half lengthwise (for water-based gelée only)	1	1
meat	3 pounds	1.5 kilograms
onion, halved	1 medium	1 medium
clove	1	1
carrot, 1 medium, coarsely chopped	4 ounces	125 grams
clear veal, beef, or chicken stock, or water, cold	4 quarts	4 liters
large bouquet garni (page 52)	1	1

1. If using water to moisten the meat, blanch the veal foot, starting it in cold water.

2. Preheat the oven to 400°F (200°C). Place the meat, onion halves (one studded with the clove) and carrot in a roasting pan, and lightly brown them in the oven.

3. Transfer the meat and vegetables, and blanched veal foot, if using, to a 15-quart (14 liter) stockpot and add the cold stock. Slowly bring the mixture to a simmer. This should take at least 20 minutes; it should *never* boil. Skim off any scum or fat that floats to the surface.

4. Add the bouquet garni and continue simmering the stock for 5 hours. Skim every 15 minutes or so. Add water or stock as needed to keep the ingredients covered.

5. If the gelée stock is perfectly clear, carefully ladle it through a coarse chinois, then a fine chinois, and finally a fine chinois lined with cheesecloth. If for some reason the stock is cloudy, it will need to be clarified (see "Clarifying Gelées," opposite).

Finishing the Gelée

Once the gelée stock has been strained, chill some of it in the refrigerator or over a bowl of ice so that it sets and its consistency can be checked. If a fairly gelatinous stock was used to moisten the meats or a veal foot was used, the gelée will probably set firmly and in fact may need to be lightened. If water alone was used, however, the gelée may not be stiff enough, in which case adjust its consistency by:

1. Putting it back on the stove, reducing it by one-fourth, and rechecking its consistency, repeating the process again if necessary.

2. Using the gelée stock to moisten additional meat or lean meat trimmings and cooking it again for 2 to 4 hours (preparing a double or triple stock).

3. Adding powdered or sheet gelatin (soaked first in cold water and drained) to the still-hot gelée stock. Use the gelatin sparingly, adding only a small amount at a time. Remember that even if the gelée stock does not set, it still contains natural gelatin of its own.

Clarifying Gelées

When gelées are prepared using carefully defatted meat, clarification takes place naturally: The proteins contained in the meat combine with any loose fat in the surrounding stock and float to the surface, to be skimmed off. When gelées are prepared with carcasses or with stock whose clarity has been compromised by inadequate skimming or by boiling, the final gelée must be clarified.

Often a stock that is only slightly cloudy can be clarified by straining through a chinois lined with a cloth napkin, a sheet of muslin, or a triple layer of cheesecloth. When using any of these, be sure to rinse the cloth thoroughly to eliminate any traces of soap or bleach. After several minutes of straining, the cloth will become clogged with minute particles. When this happens, gently pull on one side of the cloth so the liquid moves to a clean section. It may be necessary to do this several times during the straining.

The traditional method for clarifying stocks (also used for consommé) is to combine the lukewarm gelée stock with perfectly lean chopped meat and egg whites. The meat and egg whites are whisked with the stock while it is being gently heated, and the whole mixture is cooked long enough to coagulate any soluble protein. The finished gelée stock is then strained through cheesecloth.

Many authors suggest combining the chopped meat with mirepoix and fresh herbs to compensate for the flavor lost during long cooking and clarification, but these ingredients should be added judiciously, taking into consideration the flavor of the stock and its eventual use.

CLARIFICATION FOR MEAT GELÉE

YIELD: TO CLARIFY 5 QUARTS (5 LITERS) STOCK

lean beef (such as rump)	1 pound	500 grams
egg whites	3	3
fresh tarragon (optional)	3 sprigs	3 sprigs
onion, finely chopped (optional)	1 small	1 small
celery, finely chopped (optional)	½ stalk	½ stalk
carrot, finely chopped (optional)	½	½
gelée stock, warm	5 quarts	5 liters

1. Carefully remove any fat from the beef, and chop the meat finely. (A meat grinder or food processor can be used to chop it.)

2. Stir together the meat, egg whites, and the tarragon, onion, celery, and carrot, if using.

3. Place the clarification in the bottom of a 10-quart (10 liter) stockpot and add the stock to be clarified. Whisk the clarification into the stock to ensure that the egg white is evenly distributed throughout.

4. Bring the mixture slowly to a simmer, and let it simmer slowly for 20 minutes, without disturbing it.

5. Cut a hole in the crust (known as a "raft") that will have formed on the surface of the gelée stock to see whether the mixture is clear. Once the stock is perfectly clear (don't worry about larger particles floating around in it), use a skimmer to gently remove clumps of the congealed raft. Strain the gelée through a coarse chinois lined with three layers of well-rinsed cheesecloth.

FISH GELÉES

Fish gelées are prepared with essentially the same methods used for meat gelées, except that veal feet are never cooked with the fish bones. (Fish bones cook in 30 minutes and veal feet take 6 hours.) Because the gelatin contained in fish bones rapidly dissolves into the surrounding liquid, it is rarely necessary to add extra gelatin.

Fish gelée has traditionally been prepared by making a double fish stock (moistening inexpensive fresh fish with a previously made stock) and then clarifying that stock with puréed whiting flesh (Escoffier called for fresh caviar!) and egg whites in the same way as for meat stock. Excellent fish gelée can still be prepared using this method, but the danger lies in the unavailability of fresh ingredients. Because the fish flavors will be intensified by three moistenings, it is essential that the fish be impeccably fresh—caught the same morning—or the resulting gelée will have a strong fishy taste. Avoid, also, cooking the fish bones too long—no more than 20 minutes—or the gelée will taste too fishy.

Because fish stock contains finely divided particles of protein that are hard to strain out, it is usually clarified with lean chopped fish flesh and egg whites. If the fish stock is carefully prepared, clarification can be dispensed with, as the gelée stock is simply strained through cheesecloth or a napkin. If only a small amount of fish gelée is needed, a double fish stock can be allowed to settle and the clear liquid on the top carefully drawn off with a ladle.

Some chefs use dashi (Japanese seaweed and bonito stock) instead of fish stock to make gelées. Dashi is especially dramatic when combined with lime juice and clarified. Since dashi contains no natural gelatin, gelatin must be added. These dashi combinations can also be combined with cream and used for chaud-froid or for cold or hot soups.

CLASSIC FISH GELÉE

YIELD: 4 QUARTS (4 LITERS)

very fresh lean fish or fish trimmings (no skin)	3 pounds	1.5 kilograms
onion, 1 medium, chopped	8 ounces	250 grams
fresh fish stock (page 93), cold	5 quarts	5 liters
medium bouquet garni (page 52)	1	1
lean white fish, finely chopped (optional)	8 ounces	250 grams
egg whites (optional)	2	2

1. Make sure the gills, skin, and all traces of blood have been removed from the fish. Combine the fish with the onion in a 10-quart (10 liter) stockpot. Cover with the cold fish stock. Add the bouquet garni.

2. Slowly bring the mixture to a very slow simmer. Skim off any froth that floats to the surface.

3. Simmer gently for 30 minutes. Strain the stock through a fine chinois.

4. The stock can now either be strained through a napkin or cheesecloth, allowed to settle, and the top half carefully drawn off with a ladle, or it can be clarified with the fish and egg whites.

5. To clarify the stock, allow the strained stock to cool slightly; it can be tepid but should not be boiling hot.

6. Combine the chopped fish and egg whites in an 8- to 10-quart (8 to 10 liter) stockpot, and cover with the strained fish stock. Bring the mixture slowly to a simmer. When it has reached a simmer, gently scrape against the bottom of the pot with a long spoon to make sure the fish–egg white mixture has not formed a clump and stuck to the bottom, where it might burn. Allow the mixture to simmer for 30 minutes.

7. When the stock is clear, carefully ladle it through a strainer lined with cheesecloth. (Be sure to rinse the cheesecloth in cold water first to eliminate any chemical taste.)

Alternatives to Traditional Fish Gelée

Because fresh fish for fish gelée is difficult to obtain, many chefs have worked out alternative gelées to accompany cold fish dishes in the same way as traditional fish gelée. One excellent method is to prepare a light gelée stock by simply cooking a veal foot in water and using the resulting stock to moisten an abundance of herbs and vegetables combined with a small amount of egg white and acidulated with lime juice, lemon juice, or verjuice.

This gelée can also be prepared by adding commercial gelatin to court-bouillon, but a certain suaveness of texture and flavor is lost.

COURT-BOUILLON GELÉE

YIELD: 3 QUARTS (3 LITERS)

veal foot, split in half lengthwise, blanched, and drained	1	1
water	4 quarts	4 liters
onion, 1 large, chopped	8 ounces	225 grams
leeks, including several inches of green, chopped	2	2
carrots, 2 medium, chopped	8 ounces	250 grams
garlic cloves, chopped	2	2
fennel bulb, chopped	1 small	1 small
fresh tarragon, chopped	3 sprigs	3 sprigs
fresh parsley, chopped	½ bunch	½ bunch
fresh thyme, chopped	2 sprigs	2 sprigs
egg whites	4	4
juice of 2 to 3 limes or lemons, or verjuice	to taste	to taste
salt and pepper	to taste	to taste

1. Combine the blanched veal foot with the water and simmer it for 6 hours. Skim carefully, adding cold water from time to time to compensate for evaporation.

2. Combine the onion, leeks, carrots, garlic, fennel, tarragon, parsley, and thyme. Add the egg whites and lime juice. Thoroughly work in the egg whites with a wooden spoon or clean hands. Place in a 6- to 8-quart (6 to 8 liter) stockpot.

3. If the gelée stock was chilled, heat it just enough to melt it and facilitate pouring. Stir the lukewarm veal gelée stock into the clarification.

4. Slowly bring the mixture to a low simmer. Allow it to simmer for 20 minutes.

5. Cut into the raft of coagulated egg white that forms on the surface with a spoon to make sure the liquid beneath is clear.

6. Gently pull out the bulk of the coagulated egg white with a skimmer and discard. Strain the stock through a coarse strainer and again through a wet napkin or a cheesecloth-lined chinois.

7. Chill some of the gelée stock to verify its consistency. If it is too stiff, thin with court-bouillon. If the gelée is too light, add additional reduced and especially gelatinous veal gelée or commercial gelatin. (The mixture can also be reduced, but much of its vitality will be lost.)

8. Season with salt and pepper, and adjust the acidity of the gelée stock if necessary.

FLAVORING GELÉES

Because they are served cold, gelées can be flavored using a wide variety of techniques and ingredients, including some that would be destroyed in a sauce served hot. Many ingredients, such as wines, herbs, truffles, and wild mushrooms can be added to the gelées either near the end of cooking or when the gelée has completely cooled.

The same principles apply to determining a gelée's final flavor as to preparing hot sauces. In most cases, the gelée should enhance and extend the flavor of the food it accompanies. For example, a gelée made to accompany a dish of cold rabbit should capture the flavor of the rabbit and not be dominated by wine, herbs, or other ingredients. In some cases, however, the gelée's flavor can be manipulated to contrast with the flavor of the central ingredient rather than extend it, such as an acidic gelée based on court-bouillon and verjuice served with a cold fish fillet.

Wines

When wine is used to prepare gelées, it is often added at the end so that volatile compounds such as alcohol and certain flavor components remain in the gelée; these would be lost if the wine were added to a hot sauce. For this reason, gelées are an exception to the informal rule that expensive, rare, and old wines have no place in cooking.

Choose a wine with little or no tannin. Be careful also with very acidic white wines, which will sometimes cloud the gelée; the acidity denatures the soluble proteins contained in the gelée. If this happens, bring the gelée to a simmer and reduce it slightly while skimming; if it still remains cloudy, strain it through a napkin. As a general rule, the ratio of wine to gelée should be one part wine to nine parts gelée stock, but the real criterion is taste. Avoid adding so much wine that the flavor of alcohol remains in the gelée.

Because the flavor of the wine used for making gelées is well diluted, it is best to use wine with an assertive character. Fortified wines such as port, sherry, and Madeira work especially well. Wines with a distinct varietal character, such as Gewürztraminer, late-harvest Riesling, and Sauternes, can also be used.

Red wine–flavored gelées are somewhat more complicated. Gelées are best flavored with a mature red wine whose tannin has almost completely disappeared. Avoid red wines that contain a high percentage of alcohol. Big-bodied California wines or Rhône wines that work beautifully in red wine sauces because their alcohol is cooked off are often too alcoholic for gelées. To obtain a deeply colored gelée, a full-bodied, deeply colored red wine should be used, but such a wine will usually be too tannic to be added to a gelée stock at the end. It should first be simmered with meat trimmings or stock. The cooked wine, which will give body and color to the gelée, can be used in conjunction with raw wine that will contribute individuality and finesse.

After adding wine, check the consistency of the gelée. The gelatinous components will be diluted, and the alcohol may also interfere slightly with setting. If the gelée refuses to set, use a small amount of commercial gelatin, or remove one-fourth of the gelée stock, reduce it by half, and return it to the original batch.

RED WINE MEAT GELÉE

The best red wine meat gelée is a natural by-product of braising a large quantity of beef in red wine (as in Boeuf Mode, page 379), but this method is expensive and not often practical. A simpler version can be made with red wine and gelée stock. When red wine is combined with meat gelée stock, the resulting mixture often tastes acrid and acidic. The best way to deal with this problem is to combine the red wine with a light gelée stock (the stock should not contain too much gelatin, or it will end up being overreduced) and reduce the two together. As the acid contained in the red wine combines with the stock, soluble proteins will coagulate and make the stock cloudy, so the gelée stock will have to be strained through cloth. If the wine is very alcoholic—it burns in the mouth or going down—you can reduce the alcohol content by boiling it off in a vacuum for 20 minutes (see page 36). Alternatively, the wine can be simmered to eliminate the alcohol, but much of its finesse and complexity will be lost.

YIELD: 2 CUPS (500 MILLILITERS)

deep-colored, full-bodied red wine	2 cups	500 milliliters
medium bouquet garni (page 52; optional)	1	1
onion, chopped (optional)	1 small	1 small
carrot, chopped (optional)	1 small	1 small
garlic clove, crushed (optional)	1	1
light-bodied clear gelée stock	1 quart	1 liter

1. In a 4-quart (4 liter) saucepan, combine the red wine with the bouquet garni, onion, carrot, and garlic, if using.

2. Reduce the wine by half.

3. Add 2 cups (500 milliliters) of the gelée stock to the wine and reduce the mixture for about 20 minutes, until only 1 cup (250 milliliters) remains.

4. Add the remaining stock to the reduction and reduce again for 20 minutes, until 2 cups (500 milliliters) remain.

5. Strain the gelée stock through a wet napkin or a triple layer of cheesecloth. Set a small amount in the refrigerator and check its consistency.

Note: If desired, additional raw wine can be added to the strained gelée stock to give the final gelée complexity and finesse. When using raw wine, which is often unpredictable, work with a small amount of the gelée stock at first, adding wine and tasting as you go, before flavoring the whole batch. Don't bother with this method if you're using nondescript wine; because the wine is not cooked, this is one of the rare exceptions to the rule that alcohol should always be cooked off when making sauces.

PORT AND CRACKED PEPPER GELÉE FOR FOIE GRAS

Some recipes for preparing fresh foie gras suggest wrapping it tightly in a clean towel and poaching it (foie gras en torchon). If you use this method, be sure to poach the foie gras in the natural gelée stock, to enhance the gelée's flavor. If the foie gras is baked in a terrine, add the natural gelée that floats to the top of the terrine to the gelée stock in this recipe. I recommend exposing the port to vacuum for 20 minutes in order to make it less alcoholic, but this isn't essential if you don't have the requisite equipment.

YIELD: 2 CUPS (500 MILLILITERS), ENOUGH TO ACCOMPANY 6 SLICES FOIE GRAS

natural veal, chicken, or game gelée stock	2 cups	500 milliliters
cracked black pepper	1 teaspoon	5 milliliters
tawny port (or to taste)	½ cup	125 milliliters
salt and pepper	to taste	to taste

1. Bring the gelée stock to a simmer. Add the cracked pepper and turn off the heat. Cover the pot with a lid so that the stock cools slowly, giving the pepper time to infuse.

2. When the gelée stock has cooled to room temperature, add the port to taste. The exact amount will depend on the flavor and style of the port.

3. Strain the gelée stock. Test a small amount in the refrigerator to judge the consistency. Season with salt and pepper as the stock cools. Serve the chopped gelée on the plate next to slices of the foie gras.

LOBSTER WITH SAUTERNES GELÉE

YIELD: 2 CUPS (500 MILLILITERS), ENOUGH TO ACCOMPANY 4 LOBSTERS

live lobsters	4	4
natural veal or chicken gelée stock	enough to cover	enough to cover
finely chopped parsley (optional)	2 tablespoons	30 milliliters
sauternes (or to taste; see note)	½ cup	125 milliliters
salt and pepper	to taste	to taste

1. Kill the lobster by inserting a knife under the bottom of the carapace and rapidly pulling it forward. Separate the heads, tails, and claws of the lobsters. Remove the stomach sacs and save any juices that run out, but leave the tomalley and coral in the lobster.

2. Tie the lobster tails together with string in sets of two or slide skewers along the inside of the tails, between the flesh and the membrane along the base of the tail. (See photo on page 345; this keeps them straight while they are cooking, making it easier to slice even medallions.)

3. Combine the lobster sections, lobster juices, and the gelée stock in a large saucepan; the parts should be completely covered with the gelée stock. Bring the stock to a slow simmer and poach the lobster parts until they turn red, about 4 minutes after they reach a simmer.

4. Turn off the heat, remove the lobster parts, and let them cool slightly. Remove the meat from the claws and tails, reserving it to serve with the gelée. Coarsely chop the lobster shells with the end of a European rolling pin or a cleaver, and return them to the hot gelée stock.

5. Gently cook the shells for 20 minutes. (The chopped shells should flavor and clarify the stock.)

6. Strain the gelée stock through cheesecloth, stir in the parsley, if using, and let it cool to room temperature.

7. Add Sauternes to taste; the exact amount will depend on the particular Sauternes being used.

8. Check the gelée's flavor and consistency. Season with salt and pepper. Chill the gelée. If the gelée is too thin or refuses to set, add some reduced gelée or commercial gelatin.

9. Slice the reserved lobster meat into medallions and chill. Spoon over enough of the barely set gelée to coat the medallions. Slide the medallions into the fridge or freezer for 5 minutes to allow time for the gelée to set up. Repeat the process, coating the lobster with more gelée, until all the gelée is used up.

Note: Other sweet wines, such as a beerenauslese, late-harvest California Riesling, or Muscat de Beaumes de Venise, may be used instead of Sauternes, with the recipe title changed accordingly.

SHERRY-DUCK GELÉE

This full-flavored, golden gelée, although never inexpensive to prepare, is an excellent way for a restaurant to use extra duck thighs. Use a good-quality dry sherry—a fino, Manzanilla, or amontillado would work well. If desired, expose the sherry to vacuum for 20 minutes (see page 36) to eliminate some of the alcohol.

YIELD: 2 CUPS (500 MILLILITERS)

whole duck legs	6	6
dry sherry (if using pekin duck legs)	2 cups	500 milliliters
or	or	or
dry sherry (if using moulard duck legs)	1 quart	1 liter
brown chicken, beef, or veal gelée stock	2 cups	500 milliliters
salt and pepper	to taste	to taste

1. Trim all the skin and fat off the duck legs, and separate the drumsticks from the thighs.

2. Place the thighs and drumsticks snugly in a 2-quart (2 liter) pot with a tight-fitting lid and no long handle. Add the sherry, making sure it completely covers the duck, and put on the lid. If there isn't enough sherry to cover, supplement it with a little stock or water.

3. Place the pot in a larger pot. Pour enough water into the larger pot to reach halfway up the sides of the small pot.

4. Place the lid on the large pot and bring the water to a simmer. Simmer in this way for 5 hours, replacing the water in the outer pot as needed. Do not open the inner pot.

5. While the duck is cooking, place the gelée stock in a 1-quart (1 liter) saucepan and carefully reduce it by three-quarters, until almost a glaze. Strain through a chinois if necessary.

6. Remove the inner pot and cool, covered, in the refrigerator or in an ice bath.

7. When the contents of the inner pot have cooled, carefully separate the liquid and solid ingredients. The duck meat can be saved for another use. The liquid should be either completely liquid or barely set.

8. Melt the reduced brown gelée and stir it into the cold sherry-duck liquid. Strain through a chinois lined with a wet napkin or a triple layer of cheesecloth. Season with salt and pepper if necessary. Chill the gelée to adjust its consistency.

Herbs

Herbs can be used in gelées in much the same way as when preparing hot sauces. Some such as thyme and savory, should be included in the bouquet garni while the gelée stock is cooking so they can meld into the flavor structure. Fines herbes, whose volatile flavors dissipate quickly when exposed to heat, are best added as the gelée is cooling to freshen and enliven it. If they are added when the gelée is cool, however, their flavor will not infuse in the gelée. Others, such as marjoram, become an assertive accent when a generous amount is infused in the gelée stock near the end, then strained out.

FINES HERBES GELÉE

To capture the flavor of delicate herbs, many chefs like to infuse the hot gelée stock with the herbs in tightly sealed containers, as this recipe demonstrates. When an herb gelée will be strained, as is this one, include the stems as well as the leaves.

YIELD: 1 QUART (1 LITER)

gelée stock	1 quart	1 liter
fresh chervil	1 bunch	1 bunch
flat parsley	1 bunch	1 bunch
fresh chives	1 bunch	1 bunch

1. Bring the gelée stock to a slow simmer in a 2-quart (2 liter) saucepan.

2. While the stock is heating, finely chop the herbs. (This must be done at the last minute.)

3. Put the chopped herbs in a large (2-quart/2 liter) mason jar and pour the simmering stock over them. Seal the lid.

4. Let the gelée stock cool at room temperature in the jar. Gently turn the jar over from time to time during cooling to redistribute the herbs.

5. When the gelée is completely cool but not set, strain out the herbs through a chinois. If you decide to retain the herbs, continue to turn the jar while the gelée is setting so they are distributed evenly throughout.

Spirits

Many of the nuances of old or delicate spirits that would be lost if used to finish a hot sauce can be better appreciated in a gelée. When preparing gelées, spirits are used at two stages. Full-bodied spirits, such as young Cognac or whiskey, can be added near the beginning so that they blend into the background; more delicate spirits, such as older Cognacs, Calvados, and marc or grappa (especially good with game), can be added almost near the end so their nuances are not lost from prolonged exposure to heat. When using spirits, experiment with a small amount of the gelée before adding spirits to the whole batch. Choose the most flavorful spirits available so that you do not have to add too much; otherwise, the gelée will have an unpleasant taste of alcohol.

Other Flavorings for Gelées

Because of their delicacy, gelées can be flavored with almost any ingredient that will not cause them to cloud or otherwise interfere with their appearance. Cracked pepper is popular with chefs. If you are tempted to substitute green peppercorns, make sure they are well rinsed, and do not crush them or they will cloud the gelée.

Wild mushrooms—and even cultivated mushrooms—lend depth and complexity when added near the end of cooking. Dried morels are particularly excellent, but dried cèpes (porcini) also work well. The stems from cultivated mushrooms can be used, but be sure they are fresh or they will color the gelée an unpleasant gray.

Gelées used for fish can be enhanced by adding saffron (preferably in threads) while the gelée stock is still warm. When used by itself in gelées or cold sauces, saffron has an aggressive quality that is not as apparent when used in hot sauces. It is therefore best used in conjunction with typically Provençal flavors, such as basil, tomatoes, fennel, and marjoram.

MOREL GELÉE

YIELD: 2 CUPS (500 MILLILITERS)

fresh morels	8 ounces	225 grams
or	or	or
dried morels, 20 medium	½ ounce	14 grams
port or madeira (optional; for dried morels)	as needed	as needed
brown meat gelée stock, hot	2 cups	500 milliliters

1. If fresh morels are being used, inspect them for sand and dirt. Check the insides for bugs. If they need to be cleaned, put them in a colander and quickly rinse them with cold running water. If dried morels are being used, rinse them quickly in cold running water and place them in a bowl. Sprinkle them with the port and let them soften for 20 minutes. When they are soft, gently squeeze them to eliminate grit.

2. Infuse the morels into the almost-simmering gelée stock (the stock has to be hot to cook the alcohol out of the morels) in a covered 1-quart (1 liter) saucepan for 10 minutes. Strain the gelée stock through a fine chinois. Chop the morels, not too fine, and stir into the finished gelée as it sets in the refrigerator.

SAFFRON AND TOMATO FISH GELÉE

This gelée is analogous to a Mediterranean fish soup and is excellent when served with an assortment of cold poached fish. Although the recipe calls for concentrated fish stock (which should be made from very fresh fish), the gelée is even better if the poaching liquid from several batches of fish is used as a base. This gelée can also be used in the layers of a cold terrine or hure (see page 381).

YIELD: 2 CUPS (500 MILLILITERS)

concentrated fish stock, warm	2 cups	500 milliliters
or	*or*	*or*
fish poaching liquid, warm	2 cups	500 milliliters
finely chopped fresh marjoram leaves	1 tablespoon	15 milliliters
saffron threads	1 pinch	1 pinch
tomatoes, peeled, seeded, and diced	½ cup	125 milliliters
salt and pepper	to taste	to taste

1. Let the fish stock settle in a glass jar. It will clarify itself by leaving sediment near the bottom and clear liquid at the top. Carefully ladle off the top, clear portion and strain it first through a fine chinois, then through a chinois lined with a wet napkin or a triple layer of cheesecloth.

2. Tie the marjoram leaves in a small square of cheesecloth.

3. Heat the stock in a 1-quart (1 liter) saucepan and stir in the saffron, tomatoes, and the sachet of marjoram leaves. Remove the pan from the heat and cover it with a lid. Let the flavors infuse for 10 minutes. Gently strain the stock through a fine chinois. Don't press down in the strainer or you will cloud the gelée.

4. When the gelée stock has cooled, remove the marjoram and check the gelée's consistency. Season with salt and pepper.

WORKING WITH GELÉES

Meat and fish gelées can be used to accompany cold foods in several ways. The simplest method is to serve the chopped gelée next to the food being served, such as a terrine or slice of foie gras. When chopping gelée, some chefs like to sprinkle a few drops of Cognac over it before chopping to help prevent the little chunks of gelée from melting back together. Chopped gelée will also contribute suavity when tossed with cold cooked vegetables to form a kind of salad.

When chopped gelée is served with vegetables, the distinction between gelée-accompanied vegetables and cold consommé is simply a matter of proportion. A cold consommé consists traditionally of mostly consommé with an almost insignificant amount of garniture incorporated at the last minute. When gelées are used in vegetable, meat, or fish salads, the solid elements are in the forefront and the gelée in the background.

When a gelée is made with certain modernist ingredients that set at a high temperature, ingredients such as seafood or chicken that have been coated with gelée can be cooked sous vide to an exact temperature without melting the gelée.

SALADE GRECQUE IN COURT-BOUILLON GELÉE

Because court-bouillon contains no gelatin of its own, it must be combined with commercial gelatin or gelée stock made with veal feet (see page 362). A delicate court-bouillon gelée, lightly acidulated with lime juice or verjuice, not only makes an excellent accompaniment to cold raw or poached fish (it can even be served atop raw oysters), but it can be a semiliquid medium for a salade grecque. A traditional salade grecque is prepared by braising vegetables with herbs, white wine, olive oil, and coriander. In this version, a court-bouillon gelée stock is used to moisten the vegetables and the salad is served in its own glistening gelée.

YIELD: 8 SERVINGS

fennel bulb	1	1
juice of 1 lemon		
artichokes	2 large	2 large
pearl onions	24	24
zucchini	2 medium	2 medium
carrots	2 medium	2 medium
coriander seeds	1 tablespoon	15 milliliters
court-bouillon gelée (page 366)	3 cups	750 milliliters
cayenne pepper	to taste	to taste
flat parsley leaves	2 tablespoons	30 milliliters
chervil leaves	2 tablespoons	30 milliliters

1. Preheat the oven to 300°F (150°C). Cut the fennel bulb into 8 wedges. Make sure to leave some of the central core attached to each wedge to hold it together. Put the wedges in a 4-quart (4 liter) bowl; sprinkle and toss them with a few drops of lemon juice.

(continued)

2. Turn the artichokes and rub them with lemon juice. Add them to the bowl with the fennel.

3. Peel the pearl onions.

4. Cut each zucchini lengthwise into 4 sections. Bevel the edges for a decorative effect.

5. Peel and slice the carrots.

6. Spread the vegetables in a single layer over the bottom of a 6-quart (6 liter) rondeau or straight-sided sauté pan. Add the coriander seeds, court-bouillon gelée, and cayenne. Cover with a sheet of parchment paper cut into a round, and put the lid on the pan.

7. Bring the vegetables to a slow simmer. As soon as they simmer, place them in the oven.

Braise in the oven for about 20 minutes. Check the vegetables after 20 minutes; be careful not to cook out all of their texture.

8. When the vegetables are still slightly crunchy, take the pot out of the oven and remove the artichokes with a slotted spoon; reserve them.

9. While the mixture is cooling at room temperature, add the parsley and chervil.

10. Remove the choke from each artichoke bottom with a spoon. Cut each bottom into 4 or 8 wedges and return them to the other vegetables.

11. When the vegetables have cooled, transfer them with the braising liquid to a mixing bowl or a decorative terrine, and let set in a cool place or in the refrigerator.

Coating Foods with Gelées

In more formal French cooking, gelées have long been used to coat fish and meats such as trout, chicken breasts, and game. The piece of meat is first chilled and then placed on a rack over a sheet pan. The cold but still-liquid gelée is spooned over and allowed to set; the process is repeated until the meat or fish is coated with a smooth layer. Most diners today are more excited by a piece of meat or fish embedded in its own natural gelée, taken from a terrine or gratin dish, than by the presentations of the past, but a slice of cold meat coated with a sparkling herb gelée is still a striking sight.

Gelées that are used to coat chilled meats, fish, or vegetables, chopped and presented as an accompaniment to pâtés and terrines, or integrated into salads can often be enhanced with the addition of chopped or cubed ingredients such as truffles, carrots, mushrooms (diced or left whole if small), grilled peppers of various colors, tomatoes (peeled, seeded, chopped, and salted to remove excess water; see page 506), chopped herbs, prosciutto, or cubes of foie gras. Some of these garnitures (peppers, tomatoes, foie gras) are best stirred into the gelée just before it sets, while others, such as morels, truffles, or prosciutto, should be stirred into the gelée stock while it is still hot, so their flavors can infuse into the gelée. These garnished gelées can then be used in the same ways as plain gelées.

Gelées are also used to coat the insides of molds that are then filled with mousses, vegetables such as artichokes or mushrooms, pieces of lobster, crayfish tails, and the like. The molds should first be chilled, and the cold-but-not-set gelée spooned over the insides of the molds in several stages.

FOIE GRAS EN GELÉE

The ideal gelée for foie gras would be derived from the poaching liquid for the foie gras itself (see page 117), but since this is rarely practical, here we use a classic brown meat gelée. If you like, add chopped morels or truffles to the gelée.

YIELD: 4 FIRST-COURSE SERVINGS

terrine of foie gras, 3-ounce (100 gram) slices	4	4
brown meat gelée, melted	1 cup	250 milliliters

1. Assemble four ramekins just large enough to hold the slices of foie gras. If the slices won't fit, cut the foie gras into large cubes. Pour about a third of the gelée into the ramekins and let it set in the refrigerator.

2. When the gelée is well set, arrange the foie gras on top in the ramekins and pour over the rest of the gelée stock. Allow to set in the refrigerator.

3. Unmold the foie gras en gelée onto cold plates and serve immediately.

PARSLEYED HAM TERRINE (JAMBON PERSILLÉ)

Jambon persillé is a terrine of ham, chopped parsley, and gelée. The ham is cut into strips and placed in alternating layers with the meat gelée and a large amount of chopped parsley. In the traditional version from Burgundy, the terrine is sliced, necessitating a rather stiff gelée to hold it together. Although the traditional version is wonderful, the version that follows is prepared with prosciutto instead of cooked ham and is served in individual portions, so the gelée can be kept fragile and trembling.

YIELD: 10 SERVINGS

raw cured ham, such as prosciutto di parma	8 ounces	250 grams
brown meat gelée	3 cups	750 milliliters
large artichoke hearts, cooked and diced	2	2
reconstituted dried mushrooms, such as morels or porcini (cèpes)	1 ounce (dry weight)	30 grams
flat parsley, finely chopped	1 large bunch	1 large bunch

1. Cut the ham slices into strips about ¼ inch (5 mm) wide.

2. If the ham is salty, soak the strips in cold water for 10 minutes to eliminate the salt; pat them dry with paper towels.

(continued)

FLAVORING GELÉES

3. Melt the gelée in a 2-quart (2 liter) saucepan, holding it at a temperature that keeps it on the verge of setting.

4. Chill 10 dariole molds and line them with gelée. Coat them as often as necessary to produce a ⅛-inch-thick (3 mm) layer of gelée. **(A, B)**

5. Fill the gelée-lined dariole molds with alternating layers of ham strips, diced artichoke hearts, mushrooms, and parsley (about 1 tablespoon/15 milliliters of parsley per mold). Fill them with the chilled-but-not-set gelée. **(C)** Tap the molds firmly against a table to eliminate air pockets.

6. Refrigerate the molds for 2 to 3 hours to set. **(D)**

7. Unmold the jambon persillé onto cold plates and serve.

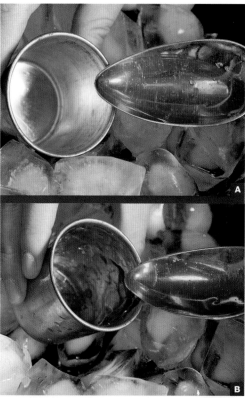

Integral Gelées

A gelée that is the natural outcome of a preparation that has been allowed to set is an excellent method of presentation. Cold leftover stews can be spooned out as they are, provided all fat is taken off the top. A slightly more sophisticated method is to melt the natural gelée surrounding the meat and add decorative garnitures, such as freshly chopped herbs, freshly cooked baby carrots (stewed in some of the melted gelée), turnips, fennel, or julienned vegetables. The whole thing can then be reconstructed in an attractive dish (a copper braisière, perhaps) and presented at the table. The boeuf mode en gelée that follows exemplifies this method.

COLD BRAISED BEEF (BOEUF MODE)

This home-style French dish is a model of simple, natural cooking, in which the braising liquid is served along with the cold beef. The dish can also be prepared in the same way using white wine instead of red; it is then called boeuf à la bourgeoise.

In rustic preparations of this dish, the carrots and onions used in the braising are returned to the gelée and constitute part of the garniture for the finished dish. In a restaurant, a new set of carrots and sometimes onions (pearl onions are most attractive) are simmered in the degreased braising liquid and used as the garniture.

YIELD: 8 SERVINGS

fatback	7 ounces	200 grams
cognac	¼ cup	60 milliliters
parsley, chopped	1 small bunch	1 small bunch
garlic cloves, chopped	3	3
red wine	7 fluid ounces	200 milliliters
onions, chopped coarsely	6 ounces	175 grams
carrots, 2 medium, chopped coarsely	8 ounces	250 grams
large bouquet garni (page 52)	1	1
boneless rump roast	4 pounds	1.8 kilograms
veal foot, split and halved crosswise (4 pieces)	1	1
vegetable oil	3 tablespoons	45 milliliters
brown stock	1 quart	1 liter
salt and pepper	to taste	to taste
carrots, sliced crosswise	4 medium	4 medium

(continued)

1. Cut the fatback into strips for larding. Combine the Cognac, parsley, and garlic, and marinate the fatback overnight in the mixture.

2. (This marinating step is optional.) Combine the red wine, onions, chopped carrots, and the bouquet garni, and marinate the roast in the mixture for 6 hours. Drain the roast and pat it dry, reserving the marinade.

3. Lard the roast in the direction of the grain with the strips of fatback.

4. Blanch the veal foot pieces and rinse them in cold water. Preheat the oven to 275°F (135°C).

5. In a 4-quart (4 liter) heavy-bottomed pot, brown the roast in the oil. Discard the oil and add the red wine, onions, chopped carrots, and bouquet garni (or the marinade), the veal foot, and the stock. The liquid should reach just to the top of the meat.

6. Bring the liquid to a slow simmer, skimming any froth that floats to the surface. Cover the pot with a sheet of aluminum foil and then with a lid. Transfer to the oven and continue cooking for 4 hours or until the roast is easily penetrated with a skewer. Remove the lid and foil every 15 minutes and check to make sure the liquid is not boiling. If it starts to simmer, turn down the oven.

7. Remove the roast from the pot and cover it with plastic wrap to prevent it from drying out.

8. Strain the cooking liquid and carefully skim any grease from it. (The easiest way to do this is to let it set in the refrigerator overnight, removing the solidified grease when it is cold.) Reserve the veal foot pieces.

9. If the gelée is too light or does not jell when it is cool, reduce it by one-fourth to one-third to concentrate its natural gelatin. When it sets to the correct consistency, season with salt and pepper.

10. Strain the gelée through a fine chinois lined with a wet cloth napkin or a triple layer of cheesecloth.

11. Simmer the sliced carrot rounds in the gelée until they are soft.

12. Bone the cooked veal foot. Cut the gelatinous flesh into strips or cubes and stir into the gelée.

13. When the braised beef has cooled, slice and layer it in a terrine with the carrots and barely melted gelée, chill to set, and slice or spoon out to serve (like an hure; see page 381). Alternatively, mold the sliced beef and carrots in individual oval gratin dishes.

VARIATIONS

A larded and braised piece of beef assembled in a terrine with its natural gelée and aromatic garniture can be used as a model for an almost infinite variety of cold meat terrines and hures. The gelée can be flavored with wine, which can be added at the beginning of the braising or at the very end during the final flavoring of the gelée.

In a traditional boeuf mode, carrots and onions constitute the principal garnitures, but obviously these can be modified according to season, location, and occasion. A southern French or California version might be garnished with tomatoes (peeled, seeded, and salted to remove excess moisture), fennel (cut into wedges and precooked in braising liquid or stock), garlic cloves (peeled and poached), or wild mushrooms, for example.

The gelée almost always benefits from a generous quantity of freshly chopped herbs added while it is cooling. Parsley works beautifully, but chervil, tarragon, or a combination of classic fines herbes also works well.

Hures (*Terrines in Gelée*)

Meat, vegetable, and fish terrines held together with gelée (in French, *hures*) have become increasingly popular. They are beautiful, require no cream or butter, and can be adapted to a wide range of ingredients. Their one drawback is that to produce firm, even slices, the gelée must be stiff enough to bind the various components. If a gelée is too stiff, its cool, melting suavity is lost, and it instead feels rubbery in the mouth.

An alternative to gelée-based terrines is to make individual portions in small ramekins or molds. They can then be unmolded at the last minute. Because no slicing is involved, the gelée can be left fragile and shimmering.

SALMON AND TRUFFLE HURE

This hure is made by layering very thin, lightly cooked slices of salmon with sliced truffles and truffle-flavored meat gelée. The hure is then allowed to set in a truffle-lined bowl so that once unmolded, it is completely black and shining with gelée.

YIELD: 4 FIRST-COURSE SERVINGS

skinless salmon fillet	8 ounces	250 grams
extra-virgin olive oil	2 tablespoons	30 milliliters
salt and pepper	to taste	to taste
fresh black truffle	1 large	1 large
brown veal or beef gelée	1 cup	250 milliliters

1. Preheat the oven to 300°F (150°C). Slice the salmon into squares about 5 inches (12.5 cm) on each side and ⅛ inch (3 mm) thick. Place each slice on a small individual sheet of aluminum foil that has been very lightly brushed with olive oil.

2. Sprinkle the salmon with salt and pepper. Place the sheets of aluminum foil with the salmon slices on a sheet pan and place in the oven for approximately 20 seconds, until the surface of the salmon has begun to cook slightly. Do not cook the slices all the way through. Remove from the oven and let cool.

3. Slice the truffle—there's no need for peeling—with a Japanese mandoline. (A large truffle should yield approximately 60 paper-thin slices.)

4. Cover each of the salmon slices with the sliced truffles, reserving 20 to 30 truffle slices to line the mold. Gently stack the truffle-covered slices of salmon, leaving them on the bottom piece of foil. Place the stack on a plate and cover with plastic wrap. Refrigerate for 2 to 3 hours, so the truffles permeate the salmon with their perfume.

5. Bring the gelée to a simmer in a 1-quart (1 liter) saucepan. Remove it from the heat and add the reserved truffle slices. Cover the saucepan and let it cool.

6. Strain the infused gelée into a mixing bowl, reserving the truffle slices. Place the bowl with the gelée over a bowl of ice. Stir the gelée until it is just on the verge of setting.

(continued)

7. Place a 2-cup (500 milliliter) round-bottomed bowl in another bowl of ice. Line the inside of the bowl with a piece of plastic wrap and then line with the gelée. Coat the bowl as often as necessary to produce a ¼-inch-thick (5 mm) layer of gelée.

8. Line the bowl with the reserved truffle slices until none of the interior of the bowl is visible.

9. Layer the inside of the bowl with the truffled salmon slices and the almost-set gelée. Take one slice at a time, leaving the truffles clinging to the salmon, and arrange the slices in the bowl so that you end up with a stack with gelée and truffles between the layers. Continue until the bowl is full and all the ingredients have been used.

10. Cover the bowl with plastic wrap and refrigerate for 2 hours to set.

11. When ready to serve, place the bowl in another bowl of hot water for 10 to 15 seconds. Turn the salmon hure onto a round silver tray and remove the plastic wrap. (Silver contrasts well with the black truffles.) Serve the hure at the table with a spoon.

Note: This salmon and truffle hure can also be made in ramekins and served in individual portions.

Smoked Gelées

A natural gelée flavored with the smokiness of grilled foods is analogous to the smoke-scented broth that accompanies grilled game birds (see page 289). To prepare a smoke-flavored gelée, a natural gelée is prepared in advance; smoked or grilled meats or fish are then gently stewed in the melted gelée until they impart the flavor of the smoker or grill. The gelée can be used to coat or accompany the grilled or smoked meats or fish or as an accent to other cold foods.

CHICKEN BREASTS WITH SMOKED GELÉE

In this recipe, chicken wings and backs are grilled and used to prepare a smoke-flavored gelée. The gelée can then be used to coat the poached chicken breasts. The breasts can also be grilled, but the smoke-flavored gelée will provide a less striking contrast. As in many gelée and stock recipes, use a pot that closely fits the size of the ingredients. Pack the ingredients in so as little liquid as possible is needed to cover. This renders a more concentrated stock or gelée.

YIELD: 8 SERVINGS

split boned breasts, wings, and backs	4 chickens	4 chickens
clear brown chicken stock (see note)	6 cups	1.5 liters
salt and pepper	to taste	to taste

1. Poach the chicken breasts for about 8 minutes in 2 cups (500 milliliters) of the stock. They are done when they bounce back to the touch. Remove them from the stock and chill on a plate in the refrigerator.

2. Grill the chicken wings and backs over wood coals (aromatic woods—fruitwoods, hickory, vine cuttings, and mesquite—are best).

3. Place the grilled chicken in a close-fitting pot (a 2-quart [2 liter] saucepan is usually about right) and cover them with the remaining clear stock. (Do not use the poaching stock for the gelée, as it will be cloudy.) Bring the stock to a slow simmer for 15 minutes. Skim off any fat or froth that floats to the surface.

4. Strain the stock first through a fine chinois and then through a chinois lined with a wet napkin or a triple layer of cheesecloth. Chill the stock in a bowl over ice or in the refrigerator until it barely starts to set. It will set on the sides of the bowl first.

5. Place the cold chicken breasts on a cake rack placed on a sheet pan. Spoon a layer of gelée over the breasts and return them to the refrigerator for 10 minutes to give the gelée time to set. Repeat this process until there is a ¼-inch-thick (5 mm) layer of gelée on the top of each breast.

It may be necessary to melt the gelée gently in the bowl from time to time by placing it over the stove or a bowl of hot water. Do not let it get too hot or it will melt the gelée already on the breasts and you will have to start over. Turn the remaining melted gelée out into a pan or plate just large enough to hold the gelée in a ¼-inch-thick (5 mm) layer.

6. Serve the gelée-coated breasts on chilled plates. Cut the remaining gelée into ¼-inch (5 mm) cubes or just chop it randomly, like parsley, but not too fine. Use it to surround each of the breasts.

Note: The chicken stock should be gelatinous enough to set firmly in the refrigerator; if it is not, reduce it.

VARIATION

Smoked gelée can be used to coat the chilled chicken breasts, served chopped on the side, or used to construct an hure. Garniture such as diced grilled peppers, ham, tomatoes, mushrooms, or even fruits such as peaches can be incorporated into the gelée or served on the side. Avoid using tropical fruits, however, because the protease they contain will break down the natural gelatin contained in the gelée, causing it to melt.

IMPROVISING GELÉES

Because of their subtlety, natural gelées can be used as a medium for virtually any flavor. As with hot sauces, the aesthetic spectrum for making gelées runs between two poles. At one end of the spectrum are gelées prepared so that they are actually or seemingly derived from the meats or fish they accompany. Remember that a gelée was originally created directly from the cooking process—stews left to set in their own juices or chicken sautés allowed to congeal and then spooned out the next day.

On the opposite end of the spectrum are gelées designed to contrast with the foods they accompany. Popular in eighteenth-century France, dishes with contrasting gelées, such as pigeon with crayfish gelée, are still occasionally served in contemporary French restaurants. Between these two poles are gelées whose flavor is gently shaped so that the flavor of the ingredient they accompany is accented while remaining intact, such as the braising liquid from a rabbit accented with a grassy-flavored Sauvignon Blanc or Sancerre.

It is always valuable for the chef to keep in mind a historical, regional, or well-known dish as a reference point during improvisation. As an example, imagine preparing a dish of cold chicken to be accompanied by a gelée. It may be useful to think first of hot chicken dishes appropriate to the setting or style of the restaurant. A chicken sautéed with mushrooms and tarragon (chasseur) could be reinterpreted as a cold dish by deglazing the pan with a natural gelée stock and infusing the mushrooms and tarragon. In the hot version, the sauce would often be finished by swirling in a chunk of butter; for the cold version, the surrounding gelée would simply set. The traditional mushrooms could be set in the gelée as components in an hure or cut into cubes as garniture.

CHAUDS-FROIDS

The fundamental difference between gelées and chauds-froids is that chauds-froids are opaque, usually because they contain cream, although some older versions contain egg yolks or even mayonnaise. Originally, chauds-froids were leftover cream-finished stews such as chicken fricassée, served cold, surrounded by their natural (and delicious) congealed cooking liquid. During the nineteenth century and up to the end of the twentieth century, overly gelatinous and inedible chaud-froids were used at food shows to demonstrate elaborate décor and complication, replacing the spontaneous and eminently satisfying cold chicken with its congealed sauce. It is little wonder that chaud-froid is rarely served in restaurants when its origin as a natural cold sauce has been forgotten. Like gelées, if it is prepared at all, it is too often done with characterless stock and too much gelatin. An authentic natural chaud-froid is one of the finest things of the kitchen.

In classic French cooking, chauds-froids are divided into white and brown. White chauds-froids are analogous to white sauces and are prepared with white stock, without browning any of the components. Brown chauds-froids have been almost entirely abandoned because they form a less impressive backdrop for decoration than the white versions; their flavor, however, is usually better, more assertive as it is.

In the same way as natural gelées, authentic chaud-froid may function as a medium for finely chopped herbs, cubes of mushrooms, grilled peppers, truffles, and other ingredients. These are not only delicious, but they provide contrasting texture. They can also contribute dramatic colors.

Preparing Chauds-Froids

Chaud-froid is made by adding heavy cream to either white or brown meat or fish gelée stock. (A) Usually one-tenth to one-eighth cream by volume is the appropriate amount. Because cream softens the flavors of the gelée, be sure to adjust the seasonings and flavorings after the cream is added. Also, both the seasonings and flavorings are more subtle when the chauds-froids and gelées have set, so chauds-froids should be slightly overseasoned. In some ways, chauds-froids are easier to prepare than aspics because the gelée used as the base need not be perfectly clear. Use the chaud-froid in the same way as a gelée, either as a base or to coat meat or other foods. (B)

Adding Purées to Chauds-Froids

The color and flavor of chauds-froids can be enhanced by stirring in a full-flavored vegetable purée just before adding the cream. Tomato purée gives the chaud-froid a lovely pink color and a touch of sweetness and acidity that goes well with chicken and fish. A chaud-froid to which a quantity of puréed grilled red or yellow peppers has been added is an excellent accent to strongly flavored meats or grilled foods; using a smoke-flavored gelée (page 382) as the base would make a worthwhile experiment.

Puréed black truffles infused in a small amount of still-hot gelée before the cream is added provides a sublime coating for game.

SORREL CHAUD-FROID

Sorrel purée gives this chaud-froid an irresistible acidity that offsets its richness; the color is somewhat drab, but the flavor compensates for it. It is an excellent coating for cold barbecued chicken or fish.

YIELD: 2 CUPS (500 MILLILITERS)

heavy cream	½ cup	125 milliliters
sorrel leaves, 2 large handfuls	3 ounces	75 grams
full-flavored gelée	1½ cups	375 milliliters
salt and pepper	to taste	to taste

1. Combine the cream and sorrel leaves in a 2-quart (2 liter) saucepan.

2. Bring the mixture to a simmer for 5 minutes.

3. If you have access to a rotor stator homogenizer (see page 35), shear the hot mixture to completely integrate the sorrel. If you don't have a rotor stator homogenizer, purée for 30 seconds in a blender or with an immersion blender. Do not try to blend the mixture when it is cold or the cream may curdle.

4. Stir in the gelée and bring the mixture to a simmer. Reduce as needed to thicken, or thin with water or more cream if too thick.

5. Strain through a fine chinois and season well with salt and pepper.

Hot Gelées and Chauds-Froids

Hot gelées are one of the latest contributions of modernist chefs. This is because certain modernist ingredients such as agar, sorbitol, xanthan gum, and low- and high-acyl gellans can set gelées at higher temperatures and subsequently be served warm. These hot gelées can be served much like their cold counterparts, for example, cut into decorative cubes for garniture. However, unlike cold gelées, hot gelées tend to slip off the top of food in one solid sheet—an unpleasant effect. A safer approach is to place the gelée under the food, much like the fluid bouillon-like sauces used as modern brown sauces. A second sauce, one that coats the food from the top, can also be applied; it should contrast in flavor and texture with the gelée. One approach, in fact, is to take one of the components out of the coating sauce, such as domestic or wild mushrooms, truffles, or saffron or other spice, and work it into the gelée so that the experience of the dish is complete only after biting into the gelée.

A hot gelée can also be served in a soup bowl under the soup itself. In this way, the diner can probe the bottom of the dish and release a whole new set of flavors and texture.

In the same way as cold gelées, a hot gelée should be clear. If the basic liquid comprising the gelée is cloudy, then it makes sense to turn it into a chaud-froid with heavy cream or an opaque hydrocolloid.

Just as with cold gelées, the consistency of a hot gelée is important—there's nothing worse than biting down on a hot and rubbery (and possibly slimy) gel. This is accomplished by choosing the right gelling agent for the task and getting the proportions right.

All gelling agents have their pros and cons. According to The Cooking Lab, in their magnificent five-volume set, *Modernist Cuisine*, various combinations of xanthan gum and low- and high-acyl gellans create different textures and different effects. When an aspic-like texture is wanted, xanthan gum is combined with low-acyl gellan, but when the emphasis is on mouthfeel, low- and high-acyl gellan are both used along with xanthan gum. Keep in mind that because high-acyl gellan is opaque, it can't be used in clear gelées. When a firmer gelée is appropriate, a little locust bean gum will improve the efficacy of xanthan gum.

Last, a cellulose compound such as methylcellulose will gel at a high temperature but turn liquid as it cools. In this way it's possible to serve a gelée that starts out firm and ends up liquid as it cools in the plate.

HOT EMULSIFIED SAUCES

ost of us associate hot emulsified sauces with such delights as hollandaise sauce and béarnaise sauce. All of the great hot emulsion sauces are based on eggs, usually chicken eggs, and just the yolks, but emulsions can also be made with duck eggs, lobster coral, or sea urchin roe.

A hot emulsified sauce without eggs can be based on certain vegetable purées such as roasted garlic, cooked-down onions (soubise), reduced tomato concassée, and potato purée (see Chapter 18, "Purées and Purée-Thickened Sauces") or on hydrocolloids, a broad family of polysaccharides that includes agar and xanthan gum.

There are two types of emulsifiers: emulsion stabilizers and true emulsifiers (sometimes called surfactant emulsifiers). An emulsion stabilizer works by thickening the sauce (that is, increasing its viscosity) so that lighter compounds, like oil, will take longer to separate out and float to the top. In essence, the mixture becomes so stiff that the two mutually insoluble components are trapped and cannot coalesce. Examples of this are starches and hydrocolloids, which hold mixtures in an emulsified state. A true emulsifier, called a surfactant, on the other hand, works because half its molecules are soluble in (or attracted to) oil and half are soluble in water. The molecules, each half embedded in either oil or water, prevent the minute globules from touching each other and coalescing. Egg yolks are an example of true emulsifiers.

In addition to the classic emulsifiers, modernist cuisine chefs are now working with a large collection of new emulsifiers and stabilizers. Devices such as the rotor stator homogenizer (see page 35), once found only in the laboratory, are so powerful that they create emulsions with no emulsifier or stabilizer at all. Many fluid gels, made from hydrocolloids, make excellent stabilizers but aren't in fact emulsifiers in the true sense of the word. They do, however, work beautifully with emulsifiers such as propylene glycol alginate, lecithin, Polysorbate 80, and sucrose esters.

Modernist Emulsions

Modernist cooks use a number of emulsifiers, some of them hydrocolloids, some of them true emulsifiers, usually proteins. Some of these, such as agar, are first dissolved with liquid such as water or stock, allowed to gel, and the gel then pureed to make what's called a fluid gel. Agar can also be dissolved in warm fat. This fat can then be emulsified with other ingredients. When reheated, this agar mixture functions as a powerful emulsifier. Xanthan gum is one of the easiest hydrocolloids to incorporate (it can be hydrated in either cold or hot water) and is highly effective even at low concentrations. Mono- and diglycerides (Glice), which are not hydrocolloids, are often incorporated into recipes for butter-like spreads and to stabilize custards or ice cream. Polysorbates such as Polysorbate 80 make excellent emulsifiers for mayonnaise, vinaigrettes, and shortenings made from novel ingredients such as nut oils. Propylene glycol alginate stabilizes melted butter and prevents it from breaking. Lecithin is also useful in butter or egg yolk sauces in which instability is a liability.

When deciding on which hydrocolloid to use and in what concentration, keep in mind the desired viscosity of the final sauce and adjust the recipe to include just enough of the appropriate thickener. For example, when thickening relatively thin sauces such as beurre blanc or other sauces that have been purposely left thin so they can be served in wide soup bowls, it may be appropriate to use about 0.5% agar and convert the mixture to a fluid gel along with an emulsifier such as propylene glycol alginate. The chart on page 637 shows the relative thickening power of various hydrocolloids, starches, and fatty emulsifiers such as butter.

HOT EMULSIFIED EGG-BASED SAUCES

Traditional hot emulsified egg sauces are made by quickly beating egg yolks and liquid over heat to form an airy foamy emulsion called a sabayon (see photos, opposite). Fat, usually melted or clarified butter, is then slowly whisked in. The sauce can then be flavored with a wide range of ingredients and preparations. Hot emulsified egg yolk sauces are among the richest and most luxurious sauces—but they can be the most difficult to make well. The technique of emulsifying fats and liquids with egg yolks can also be adapted and used for contemporary sauce innovations. Sauce béarnaise and sauce hollandaise are the best known of the hot emulsified egg sauces, but there are many classic and contemporary variations. The technique of combining flavor components into a hot emulsion of egg yolks, liquid, fat, and air remains the same regardless of the particular sauce being prepared.

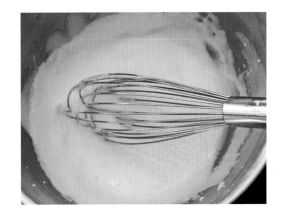

In addition, new techniques, such as cooking the yolks sous vide and adding stabilizers, can make these sauces more reliable and less intimidating. Effective stabilizers, which thicken the basic liquid (such as water or broth) from which the sauce is made, include agar, carrageenans, gelatin, gellan, guar gum, sodium alginate, and xanthan gum. Perhaps the easiest approach for stabilizing egg yolk–thickened sauces is to stir a small amount of liquid lecithin (about 1% the amount of butter) into the melted butter before whisking it into the sabayon.

Precautions for Making Hot Emulsified Egg Yolk Sauces such as Béarnaise and Hollandaise

1. Make sure that the sabayon is completely cooked. If it is not cooked enough, it will separate, and the sauce will be too thin or will break completely.

2. Remember that one egg yolk can absorb about ½ cup (125 milliliters) clarified butter (the equivalent of 5 ounces/150 grams whole butter). If too much butter is added, the sauce is likely to break.

3. Egg yolks curdle above 185°F (85°C), so make sure the butter is not too hot before stirring it into the sabayon.

4. Do not add the butter to the sabayon all at once, or the sauce will break. Conversely, it should not be added too slowly, or the sauce will be heavy.

5. Keep the sauce at the correct temperature, about 145°F (63°C), during restaurant service. If it gets too hot, it will break. The best way to keep it at the correct temperature is to place it in a pan of water on a low flame or somewhere near the back of the stove. Check it from time to time to make sure that it is not too hot.

6. Keep emulsified sauces covered while they are being held for use. Otherwise, a skin may form on the surface. Stir them gently before serving.

7. Hot emulsified sauces tend to cook and thicken while being held warm before service. They should be thinned about every hour with a little water or heavy cream. If allowed to sit for too long without being thinned, they will break.

8. Even well-made sabayon sauces will not remain frothy during a long dinner service. For this reason, keep them in a whipping siphon (hold in a bain-marie kept below 140°F/60°C) and pipe out to order.

Repairing Broken Sauces

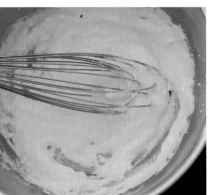

If an emulsified egg yolk sauce is prepared incorrectly—for example, if the clarified butter is too hot or too much is added at once—the tenuous emulsion will destabilize and the sauce will "break." A broken sauce is easy to recognize because it suddenly thins and takes on a grainy appearance. When confronted with a broken emulsified sauce, it is important to diagnose the problem first. Check the temperature of the sauce by feeling the outside of the saucepan. If it seems too hot, let the sauce cool before trying to repair it.

Provided the sauce didn't get too hot (if it has curdled, it is irreparable), a broken emulsified sauce can usually be repaired by beating the warm sauce into an egg yolk that has first been beaten with a little cold water or 1 tablespoon (15 milliliters) heavy cream. The resulting sauce will not be as light as a sauce made correctly initially, but it will be acceptable for most uses. Stirring a few drops of liquid lecithin into the broken sauce will help stabilize the emulsion as you add the butter.

If the problem seems to be that the butter was added too quickly, gradually beat the broken sauce into 1 tablespoon (15 milliliters) heavy cream (a few drops of liquid lecithin dissolved in the cream would also help), adding the sauce a bit at a time. Once the mixture starts to thicken, the broken sauce can be added more quickly. Provided that the broken sauce contains a minimum amount of egg yolk (1 yolk per ½ cup/125 milliliters clarified butter), any amount of sauce can be repaired starting with 1 tablespoon (15 milliliters) heavy cream. If you are doubtful whether the broken sauce contains enough egg yolk, work the broken sauce into an egg yolk instead of the heavy cream.

If a sauce seems to be only on the verge of breaking, it can often be brought back together by slowly whisking in 1 tablespoon (15 milliliters) cold water or heavy cream. A tiny bit of xanthan gum (about 1.5 grams per liter/¼ teaspoon per quart) will help pull the sauce together, but will make it thicker. If it becomes too thick, just add a little liquid.

Storage

When preparing hot emulsified egg yolk sauces, make as much as is needed. Although these sauces can be stored overnight in the refrigerator and melted and beaten into a fresh egg yolk the next day, the longer a sauce is kept, the greater the danger of bacterial contamination. Because these sauces are kept warm rather than hot while being held before service, they are a perfect medium for bacteria. If sauce has been kept warm for more than two or three hours, it is best to discard any that is left over. If only a small amount of sauce was prepared and it was not held for more than two hours, it can be stored overnight and reconstituted the next day. Remember, when storing emulsified egg yolk sauces overnight, to date the container with the date the sauce was first made. An emulsified egg yolk sauce should never be reconstituted more than once.

To reconstitute a hot emulsified egg yolk sauce, gently heat it in a pan set over another pan containing warm water. While the sauce is melting, put 1 egg yolk in a sloping-sided saucepan. Beat in 1 tablespoon (15 milliliters) cold water and, optionally, 0.15 gram liquid lecithin to help stabilize the emulsion. Put the saucepan over high heat. Continue whisking until the yolk begins to stiffen. When the sauce has melted—it will be severely broken with bits of egg yolk floating around in the melted butter—whisk it gradually into the beaten egg yolk. A reconstituted sauce will never be as light as the original sauce, but piping with a whipping siphon will restore much of its airiness. Keep in mind that if the sauce has turned to scrambled eggs, there is no recourse—your sauce is doomed.

Serving

Hot emulsified egg yolk sauces are traditionally served with grilled meats, poached or grilled fish, and hot vegetables. Tangier sauces, such as béarnaise and choron, go well with meats, while more delicate variations accompany vegetables or fish. Sauce Maltaise (page 399) is almost always served with hot asparagus.

In traditional restaurant service, foods should never be served already coated with a hot emulsified egg yolk sauce. These sauces should be either served in a sauceboat or to the side of the meat or fish on the plate. In this way the diner can regulate the amount of sauce he or she wants to eat.

CLASSIC HOT EMULSIFIED EGG YOLK SAUCES

Sauce Béarnaise

Sauce béarnaise is made by preparing an intensely flavored infusion of tarragon, chopped shallots, white wine, wine vinegar, and cracked pepper. These ingredients are simmered and slowly reduced to extract the flavor from the herbs and shallots and to concentrate the acidity of the vinegar and white wine. While traditionally performed on the stove, the herbs and shallots can also be infused with into the vinegar by cooking sous vide at 140°F (60°C) for about an hour before incorporating into the sauce.

Many chefs and cooks know how to prepare an acceptable béarnaise or hollandaise but rarely understand what is required to prepare a perfect airy sauce. Many recipes for hot emulsified sauces simply say to beat melted butter into gently warmed egg yolks. Sauces prepared in this way contain no air and thus tend to be heavy and thick. To prepare a light, delicate, emulsified sauce, it is essential to first prepare a frothy emulsion of egg yolks, liquid, and air. This emulsion is called a sabayon. Once the sabayon is correctly prepared, the addition of flavorings and fat is a straightforward process.

Chefs sometimes differ as to whether to use clarified butter, melted butter, or cold butter. There are advantages and disadvantages to each. Clarified butter gives the smoothest-textured sauce, but many flavor components and nutrients that are contained in the milk solids are lost. Clarified butter is almost always used if a sabayon, which contains water or another liquid, is being used as the sauce base. Whole butter, whether cold or melted, contains only 75 percent pure fat; the remaining 25 percent is mostly water, which results in a thinner sauce. So if a thick sauce is required, clarified butter is traditional. Melted butter will give a more delicate-tasting sauce, but its extra water content can often make the sauce runny. (Nowadays the sauce can be quickly thickened with a little xanthan gum.) Emulsified sauces made with cold butter will often have the best flavor, but much of the airiness of the sauce will be lost because the butter will require more whisking as it is added to the sabayon. Again, holding the sauce in a bain-marie in a whipping siphon takes care of the lightness problem.

When using clarified butter for hot emulsified egg yolk sauces, allow approximately ½ cup (125 milliliters) clarified butter per egg yolk. To stabilize the sauce, add 1% to 2% liquid lecithin to the melted butter. When using whole or melted butter, use 6 egg yolks for approximately 1 pound (500 grams) butter. For either method, use 1 to 1½ tablespoons (15 to 25 milliliters) liquid (usually water) per egg yolk when preparing the sabayon. If clarified butter is used, the sauce will be extremely thick—the consistency of a traditional mayonnaise—but since the base is usually thinned by adding other liquids to flavor it, it is better to start out with a thick mixture than one that is too thin. It is also possible to add less than the full amount of butter, which will result in a lighter, airier sauce. One tablespoon (15 milliliters) liquid added to ½ cup (125 milliliters) of an emulsified sauce base made with clarified butter will result in a perfect texture for most dishes.

Either of two methods can be used to flavor emulsified egg yolk sauces. Some recipes suggest whisking the basic flavors, such as a lemon juice, tarragon, and vinegar infusion or orange zests, with the egg yolks when preparing the sabayon, and then straining the sauce after adding the butter. The disadvantage to this method is that the sauce loses

STABILIZING EGG YOLKS BY COOKING SOUS VIDE

Usually the trickiest part of making an emulsified egg yolk sauce is preparing the sabayon. If it overcooks for just a second, it turns into scrambled eggs.

When making large amounts of emulsified egg sauces, it often makes sense to cook the yolks (or whole eggs) sous vide so that you can be assured that they will be heated to the exact temperature needed to make the emulsion. Then, once you have the cooked yolks on hand, it's simply a matter of whisking butter or oil into the yolks. Ten egg

yolks are enough for 1 quart (1 liter) hollandaise or related sauce.

Whisk together the yolks until smooth and put them in a 1-quart (1 liter) heavy plastic bag. Force as much air out of the bag as possible when sealing it, or use a vacuum sealer (see page 35). Submerge the bag in a sous vide tank set to 140°F (60°C) for 30 minutes.

Use as needed for emulsified sauces. Simply whisk in butter or other fat as though making a traditional sauce.

some airiness when it is strained. In the recipes that follow—the béarnaise recipe is a model for the others—a sauce base is prepared with clarified butter and the flavoring is added at the end. This eliminates the need for straining the sauce and also makes it possible to prepare a quantity of flavoring to be added to the sauces as they are prepared over the course of several days.

Some recipes suggest combining the reduction with the egg yolks before cooking them into a sabayon. Because the reduction is extremely acidic, it tends to "cook" the yolks prematurely, so the resulting sabayon contains less air and is heavier. Some other recipes suggest combining the unstrained reduction with the sauce and then straining the entire sauce, but this method has the disadvantage of forcing air out of the sauce.

SAUCE BÉARNAISE

The emulsified sauce base that is prepared here is used for all of the sauces that follow; the flavor reduction of herbs, vinegar, white wine, and shallots makes this sauce specifically a sauce béarnaise. Traditional recipes for sauce béarnaise call for chervil in the flavor reduction, but in this recipe it is optional. The flavor of tarragon is so much more assertive that the flavor of the chervil is usually overpowered and lost. While the traditional approach is to prepare the reduction on top of the stove, this causes many aromatic compounds to volatilize and be lost. Consider cooking the infusion, sous vide, for about an hour at 140°F (60°C).

YIELD: 1 QUART (1 LITER)

whole butter	21 ounces	600 grams
or	or	or
clarified butter	2 cups	500 milliliters
liquid lecithin (optional)		6 grams
shallots	3 medium	3 medium
fresh tarragon	1 bunch	1 bunch
fresh chervil (optional)	½ bunch	½ bunch
whole black peppercorns	1 teaspoon	5 milliliters
white wine	¾ cup	185 milliliters
tarragon vinegar or white wine vinegar	¾ cup	185 milliliters
egg yolks	6	6
cold water	6 tablespoons	90 milliliters
salt and white pepper	to taste	to taste

(continued)

1. (This step is optional if you already have clarified butter on hand.) To clarify the butter, melt it in a straight-sided saucepan over medium heat. Check it from time to time to make sure that it does not become too hot and burn. Remove it from the heat and skim off any froth that has floated to the top with a ladle; then carefully remove the clarified butter (the water contained in the butter will be on the bottom) with a ladle. There should be about 2 cups (500 milliliters).

2. Stir the lecithin, if using, into the butter. Keep the clarified butter warm until needed.

3. To prepare the flavor reduction, peel and chop the shallots. This should be done as close to the last minute as possible. If the shallots are chopped more than a few hours in advance, they should be kept in a plastic or stainless-steel container and covered with wine vinegar to help keep their flavor intact.

4. Remove the leaves from the tarragon and the chervil, if using, and reserve. (They will later be chopped and added to the sauce at the end.) Reserve the stems.

5. Crush the peppercorns by placing them on a cutting board and crushing them with the bottom of a small pot or saucepan.

6. Combine the white wine, vinegar, herb stems, shallots, and peppercorns in a stainless-steel or stainless steel-lined copper 1-quart (1 liter) straight-sided saucepan. (Avoid aluminum, which turns the yolks gray.) Heat the mixture over a medium flame until it comes to a simmer. Continue simmering the mixture for 15 to 20 minutes, until it is reduced by about two-thirds so that about 3 fluid ounces (90 milliliters) remain. Be careful to prevent the flame from wrapping around the outside of the saucepan, which can cause any of the mixture that has stuck to the sides of the saucepan to brown, giving an off flavor and color to the finished sauce.

7. Strain the reduction through a fine chinois and reserve until needed. (A)

8. Combine the egg yolks with the cold water in a 2-quart (2 liter) saucepan with sloping sides. Whisk the mixture until it becomes light and frothy. This usually takes about 30 seconds.

9. Heat over a medium to high flame, whisking rapidly (see Notes). The mixture will triple in volume. As the sabayon approaches the correct temperature, it will suddenly thicken; you will start to see the bottom of the saucepan while whisking. When the sabayon starts to stiffen, continue whisking as rapidly as possible over the heat for about 5 seconds, to ensure it is completely cooked. (If the sabayon is undercooked, the process tends to reverse itself and the sauce will be runny and may even break.)

10. Remove the sabayon from the heat and whisk for about 20 seconds to cool it. (Otherwise it may curdle, being overcooked by the residual heat in the saucepan.)

11. Ladle the clarified butter into the sabayon while gently stirring with the whisk. (B) It is not necessary to work the butter into the sabayon drop by drop, because the sabayon is already an emulsion that will readily combine with fat. In fact, the butter should be added fairly rapidly to avoid overworking the sauce, which would force out air.

12. When all the butter has been added, the sauce will have a very stiff texture. Add the tarragon-vinegar reduction until the sauce has the right flavor and desired consistency. (C) If it is too stiff, it can be thinned with water or with the liquid that settles to the bottom of a new batch of clarified butter. Do not thin the sauce until the flavor has been adjusted.

13. Chop the reserved tarragon leaves and the chervil leaves, if using, and add them to the sauce. (D)

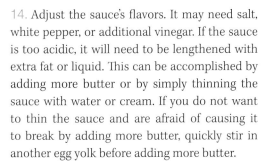

14. Adjust the sauce's flavors. It may need salt, white pepper, or additional vinegar. If the sauce is too acidic, it will need to be lengthened with extra fat or liquid. This can be accomplished by adding more butter or by simply thinning the sauce with water or cream. If you do not want to thin the sauce and are afraid of causing it to break by adding more butter, quickly stir in another egg yolk before adding more butter.

Notes: Some restaurants prepare enough flavor reduction (steps 3 through 7) to last several weeks (it keeps well) instead of preparing a batch for each sauce.

Many recipes suggest cooking the egg yolks over low heat or even over a pan of simmering water. This is a nuisance in a professional kitchen, where these sauces often must be prepared at the last minute. Slow heating of the sabayon is also detrimental to the sauce. A sabayon should be completely cooked in about 2 minutes. If whisked and cooked any longer, the egg yolks lose their ability to emulsify with air, and the resulting sauce is heavy. If you are not confident working with high heat, practice making sabayons with 2 or 3 egg yolks at a time.

Sauce Hollandaise

This sauce is one of the simplest and most delicious of the emulsified sauces. Because the flavor of hollandaise is subtle—only a bit of lemon juice is used—it is especially important to use the best butter available. It is best to use clarified butter; melted whole butter will produce a sauce that is too thin once the lemon juice has been added.

Prepare a sabayon using only egg yolks and water, as in steps 8 through 10 for Sauce Béarnaise (page 395). (Older recipes use a vinegar reduction, but most modern chefs dispense with it.) Stir in clarified butter to prepare a sauce base, as in step 11 for Sauce Béarnaise. Finish the sauce with approximately 2 tablespoons (30 milliliters) lemon juice per 2 cups (500 milliliters) sauce; if making the quantity in the Sauce Béarnaise recipe, add ¼ cup (60 milliliters) lemon juice to the sauce. Taste the sauce while adding the lemon juice, so as not to add too much; if the sauce is too lemony, much of the subtlety and buttery nuances will be lost. Adjust the seasoning with salt and freshly ground white pepper. Yield: 1 quart (1 liter)

MODERNIST STABLE HOLLANDAISE

There are several tricks and ingredients that will stabilize an emulsion. One is to cook the egg yolks sous vide at a temperature of 140°F (60°C) as described on page 394. When it's time to add the butter, use a rotor stator homogenizer (see page 35) or immersion blender with the flat blade and slowly add the butter to the yolks. This recipe uses propylene glycol alginate as a stabilizer, but you can also experiment with adding various emulsifiers such as Glice, lecithin, Polysorbate 80, or gum arabic. Some can be stirred directly into the egg yolks, while others need to be dissolved in a small amount of water before they are stirred into the yolks. This technique can be used for hollandaise, all of its derivatives, and, for that matter, virtually any emulsified sauce.

YIELD: 1 QUART (1 LITER)

egg yolks, lightly beaten	6	6
lemon juice	1 tablespoon	15 milliliters
propylene glycol alginate		5 grams
clarified butter	3 cups	750 milliliters
salt and pepper	to taste	to taste

1. Blend together the egg yolks, 1 teaspoon (5 milliliters) of the lemon juice, and the propylene glycol alginate until the propylene glycol alginate dissolves. Seal the mixture in a heavy plastic bag and place in a sous vide bath set to 140°F (60°C) or a bain-marie and cook for 30 minutes.

2. Transfer the egg yolk mixture to a bowl and beat in the butter in a slow, steady stream using a rotor stator homogenizer or an immersion blender with the flat blade. Add more lemon juice, if needed, to taste. Season with salt and pepper.

VARIATION

Make the hollandaise frothy and foamy by piping it with a whipping siphon.

Derivatives of Béarnaise and Hollandaise

Most classic emulsified egg yolk sauces are prepared in the same way as béarnaise or hollandaise—only the flavoring is different. Unless otherwise noted, each of the following classic recipes makes approximately 2 cups (500 milliliters) sauce.

SAUCE CHORON (SAUCE BÉARNAISE WITH TOMATO)

The natural sweetness of ripe tomatoes goes well with the vinegar and tarragon flavor of sauce béarnaise. Prepare a tomato purée by slicing the tomatoes in half crosswise and squeezing out the seeds. (It is not necessary to peel the tomatoes, because the purée will be strained.) Coarsely chop the seeded tomatoes and gently stew them in a small amount of olive oil. They will first release water. Continue cooking until the water has evaporated and the purée begins to thicken. Strain the

purée and stir it into the sauce béarnaise. Use approximately one part strained tomato purée to three parts Sauce Béarnaise: For 2 cups (500 milliliters) Sauce Choron, use 1½ cups (375 milliliters) Sauce Béarnaise and ½ cup (125 milliliters) tomato purée (2 medium tomatoes will produce this much purée). Taste while adding the purée, because the amount of purée needed will depend on the ripeness and flavor of the tomatoes and on personal taste.

SAUCE MALTAISE (ORANGE-FLAVORED SAUCE HOLLANDAISE)

Sauce Maltaise is prepared in the same way as hollandaise except that orange juice cooked with orange zest is added to the sauce instead of lemon juice. Traditionally blood oranges, which give this sauce a distinctive reddish tint, are used, but if they are unavailable, a delicious sauce can still be made with regular oranges. In classic French cooking, this sauce is served with asparagus.

Prepare an infusion from the juice of 2 large oranges (about 5 fluid ounces/150 milliliters) and the julienned zest from half of 1 orange. Gently reduce this infusion until ¼ cup (60 milliliters) remain. Stir this reduction into 2 cups (500 milliliters) unflavored sauce base. Yield: 2¼ cups (560 milliliters)

SAUCE MOUSSELINE (HOLLANDAISE WITH WHIPPED CREAM)

Sauce hollandaise can be lightened with whipped cream just before serving. To lighten 2 cups (500 milliliters) hollandaise, whip approximately ½ cup (125 milliliters) heavy cream. The whipped cream should be folded into the hollandaise just before serving. (If added earlier, it will release water into the sauce and the air contained in the whipped cream will be lost.) Be sure to adjust the seasoning after adding the whipped cream. This sauce is traditionally served with hot vegetables, but it also makes an excellent accompaniment for fish. Yield: about 3 cups (750 milliliters)

SAUCE NOISETTE (BEURRE NOISETTE SAUCE)

Although this sauce is traditionally based on hollandaise, any hot emulsified egg sauce can be given added complexity by finishing it with a small amount of beurre noisette. Reserve one-fourth of the whole butter being used to prepare the clarified butter for the base, and cook it gently to the noisette stage. (For a description of how to prepare Beurre Noisette, see page 438.) Do not add lemon, which, if the butter is still very hot, will cause it immediately to burn. Strain the beurre noisette through a fine chinois and use it to finish the sauce. To prepare 2 cups (500 milliliters) sauce, use 2 egg yolks, 2 tablespoons (30 milliliters) water, ¾ cup (185 milliliters) clarified butter, 2 ounces (60 grams) butter cooked to the noisette stage, and salt and pepper to taste.

Because beurre noisette gives sauces an intensely buttery flavor, it can be used to flavor emulsified sauces that have less than the full amount of butter. These sauces, although they will taste very buttery, will actually be lighter.

BEURRE NOISETTE EMULSION

This foam is almost identical to a classic emulsified egg yolk sauce except that the yolks are precooked sous vide, and once thus stabilized are combined with the beurre noisette. Use it as a model for making just about any stabilized egg yolk foam. Other fats can include foie gras fat, goose fat, olive oil, or cocoa butter.

Whisk together 3 egg yolks and seal them in a heavy plastic bag, forcing as much air out of the bag as you can (or use a vacuum sealer, page 35). Submerge the bag in a sous vide tank and cook for about 30 minutes at 140°F (60°C). Warm the butter to the temperature of a hot bath. Transfer the egg yolks to a mixing bowl and whisk in the butter. Transfer to a whipping siphon and heat the siphon to 138°F (59°C) in a water bath or sous vide tank. Pipe out as needed to order.

SAUCE FOYOT OR VALOIS (SAUCE BÉARNAISE WITH MEAT GLAZE)

Sauce béarnaise can be given a fuller, meaty flavor by adding meat glaze (glace de viande). The amount to add depends on the consistency and flavor of the glaze, but 3 tablespoons (45 milliliters) added to 2 cups (500 milliliters) Sauce Béarnaise is usually correct. This sauce is excellent with grilled or sautéed meats.

SAUCE TYROLIENNE (OIL-BASED SAUCE BÉARNAISE)

Although this sauce is technically a mayonnaise (because oil is used instead of butter), it is included here because it is served hot and because it is traditionally classified in the béarnaise family. Prepare the reduction and sabayon used for Sauce Béarnaise (steps 3 through 10), but instead of finishing the sabayon with butter (step 11), use the same amount of oil. Flavor the sauce with 3 tablespoons (45 milliliters) reduced tomato purée for every 2 cups (500 milliliters) sauce base. A pinch of cayenne pepper added at the end helps enliven the sauce and bring out the flavor of the other ingredients. Traditionally, this sauce is used for grilled fish and meats. The sauce is very thick and may be thinned with stock, cooking liquids, or other liquids.

SAUCE RUBENS (ANCHOVY AND CRUSTACEAN SAUCE FOR FISH)

This unusual sauce is an excellent accompaniment to fish. It is based on an infusion of chopped onions, carrots, and celery (a mirepoix) and white wine, which is then combined with egg yolks and finished with crustacean butter and (optionally) anchovy paste.

Gently stew ½ cup (125 milliliters) mirepoix in ½ ounce (15 grams) butter. Do not let the mirepoix brown. When the mirepoix is cooked, after about 10 minutes, add 1 cup (250 milliliters) white wine and 1 cup (250 milliliters) fresh fish stock. Gently reduce this mixture until only 3 tablespoons (45 milliliters) syrupy glaze remain in the saucepan. Add 1 tablespoon (15 milliliters) Madeira and cook for 1 minute more to remove the alcohol from the Madeira. Strain this mixture through a fine-mesh strainer, let it cool, and combine it with 2 egg yolks. Whip this mixture into a sabayon and finish it with ½ cup (125 milliliters) clarified butter and 1 ounce (30 grams) Crustacean Butter (page 331). Traditionally, 1 teaspoon (5 milliliters) anchovy paste is called for, but for some, it detracts from the sauce. Yield: 2½ cups (360 milliliters)

CONTEMPORARY VARIATIONS

The techniques used to prepare classic hot egg yolk sauces can be modified to make lighter contemporary variations. There are no rules about serving contemporary hot emulsified egg yolk sauces, but often they are served on the plate rather than on the side, because they are lighter than their classic cousins. The first step in preparing a classic emulsified sauce is the preparation of the sabayon. In classic recipes, the egg yolks are combined with a small amount of cold water and the mixture is beaten over heat to form a preliminary, extremely airy emulsion, the sabayon. Water works well because it contains no acid, which tends to stiffen the yolks prematurely, or gelatin, which can make the sabayon too heavy. It is possible, however, to prepare a sabayon with a more flavorful liquid. If the sauce is to be served with poached fish, it makes good culinary sense to use some of the poaching liquid instead of water to give the sauce more character. If the sauce is to be used for meat, then a small amount of appropriate stock or the liquid from a deglazed roasting or sauté pan can be used to give the sauce extra flavor and complexity.

Fats

Classic emulsified sauces call for a large amount of fat, usually butter, added to a given number of egg yolks. In the nineteenth century, when these sauces were standardized, people were less concerned with eating fat and in fact associated rich sauces with luxury and wealth. One of the most obvious modifications of classic egg yolk sauces is simply to add less fat. The result is a sauce that contains a higher proportion of air and hence fewer calories.

Because much of the flavor of these sauces depends on the type and quality of the fat used, serious thought should be given to which type of fat to use, even if the proportion of fat is less than in a traditional sauce. When using butter, use the best quality available. Never use salted butter in sauce making; the salt interferes with the seasoning of the sauce, and salted butter has a less delicate flavor and is often less fresh than sweet butter.

It is also possible to replace butter with oils or other fats to lighten the sauce and give it a different flavor. A delicious emulsified egg yolk sauce can be made with olive oil instead of butter. The resulting sauce is identical to a mayonnaise except that it is served hot. Olive oil has a full, distinctive flavor, however, so it should replace butter only when its flavor is appropriate. In Gascony, a region in southwestern France, the butter for these sauces is sometimes replaced with a small amount of goose fat. A small amount of the fat that is rendered when preparing terrines of foie gras will give a wonderful flavor to a sauce. Because the flavor of foie gras is extremely full and intense, very little is needed to make a deeply flavored sauce. A small amount of Beurre Noisette (page 438) also can be whisked into butter sauces to give them a full, buttery taste, without using too much butter.

The idea of reducing the amount of fat added to the initial sabayon can be taken to its logical extreme. It is possible to make a sabayon and add no fat at all. Such a sauce will be extremely light and airy, containing only a small amount of fat from the egg yolks.

This technique can be used to thicken cooking liquids. A classic preparation, sole bonne femme, can be used to exemplify the technique. To prepare sole bonne femme, either a whole sole (with the dark skin removed) or sole fillets are quickly baked with some chopped shallots, sliced mushrooms, chopped parsley, white wine, and fish stock. As soon as the sole is done, it is transferred to a plate or platter and the cooking liquid is quickly reduced on top of the stove. Heavy cream is then added, the sauce is again reduced until it thickens, and butter is swirled in to finish the sauce. The sole is then coated with the sauce and quickly glazed under the broiler before serving (see page 305 for a recipe). To lighten this recipe, the cooking liquid needs to be reduced only slightly, allowed to cool, and then combined with an egg yolk and beaten into a sabayon. Butter can then be added to the sabayon before glazing, but this is optional. The recipe for Braised Fillets of Sea Bass with Sabayon Sauce (page 404) also exemplifies this technique.

Alternative Flavors

Many chefs have neglected the wide range of flavoring possibilities that can be used for hot emulsified sauces. These sauces can be strongly flavored (such as a sauce choron) or very delicately flavored (sauce mousseline). One flavor that has become justifiably popular with contemporary chefs is saffron. Curry also works extremely well, as do truffles.

Adding Vegetable Purées

Much of the butter or oil used to prepare these sauces can be replaced with various purées, which contribute flavor without making the sauce excessively rich. Mushroom purée, carrot purée, onion purée (soubise), garlic purée, freshly prepared parsley purée, asparagus purée, artichoke purée, watercress purée, puréed tomatoes, puréed tomatillos, and truffle purée can all be used to finish emulsified sauces (see Chapter 18, "Purées and Purée-Thickened Sauces").

Adding Whipped Cream, Sour Cream, Yogurt, or Fresh Cheese

For a lighter effect, hot emulsified egg yolk sauces can be finished with sour cream, yogurt, or fresh cheese in the same way that a classic sauce mousseline is finished with whipped cream. Use these ingredients sparingly, however. Yogurt and sour cream will give an unpleasant acidity to the sauce if too much is used. Fresh cheese will give delicacy and lightness to a sauce, but again, be careful not to use too much, or the sauce will have a fine graininess or a chalky texture. Keep in mind also that any of these ingredients may separate in the sauce. To prevent this, blend 1% lambda carrageenan into the cheese, yogurt, or sour cream before whisking them into the sauce.

Combining Emulsified Sauce with Stock or Other Sauces

One of the most fundamental changes in the aesthetics of sauce making has been an acceptance of thinner sauces. Not too many years ago, it would have been unacceptable to serve a sauce that would not cling to the surface of whatever food was being served. Nowadays, it is acceptable for a sauce to be served under or around a piece of meat, fish, or vegetable. Modern sauces often resemble intensely flavored broths that capture or accent the flavor of the dish being served without masking either its appearance or flavor.

Hot emulsified sauces can be readily combined with other liquids—other sauces, broths, and stocks. These thinned sauces will be lighter textured but have the intensity of flavor of the original thicker versions. It is often convenient, especially in a restaurant setting, to prepare a standard sauce and whisk it with another liquid to order. Emulsified sauces, hot sauces, and mayonnaise have a tendency to break if too thin; the emulsion can exist only in a particular range of densities. For this reason, thinner emulsified sauces should be prepared to order.

Emulsified sauces can be combined with other sauces, providing an excellent method of making use of broken butter sauces, which would be difficult to reconstitute. Leftover beurre blanc can be melted and used instead of melted butter to finish a hot emulsified egg yolk sauce.

Special Flavors and Finishes for Fish Sauces

Hot emulsified sauces work well with fish and shellfish. Fish sauces are traditionally based on fish stock (usually reduced or thickened with roux) or the natural cooking liquid derived from cooking the fish itself (integral sauces). Fish stock, because it is usually made with fish bones, often has a fishy taste instead of the delicate sea-like flavor that gives fish sauces their finesse and vitality.

To impart a natural sea-like flavor to a hot emulsified sauce, several ingredients and techniques can be used. One technique, discussed below, is to prepare a sabayon with the cooking liquid from the fish. The sauce is then seasoned and served as a light, almost fat-free sabayon, or butter is added in the style of a more traditional sauce. Such a sauce is a sauce vin blanc (see page 221).

If it is impractical to prepare an integral hot emulsified sauce with the cooking liquid from the fish, the cooking liquid from clams, mussels, or oysters works extremely well—far better than ordinary fish stock does. If full-flavored, briny oysters are available (Belons from Maine are excellent), shuck one directly into the saucepan of the finished sauce. The oyster will give the sauce the delicate flavor of the sea. A small quantity of sea urchin roe (1 tablespoon/15 milliliters per 1 cup/250 milliliters sauce), first passed through a fine-mesh strainer, can be used to finish hot emulsified sauces for fish. Sea urchin roe must be impeccably fresh and should have a delicate, slightly sweet taste, vaguely reminiscent of milk chocolate. Always taste it before using it in a sauce. If scallops with roe are available, the roe can be puréed, passed through a fine-mesh strainer, and used to finish the sauce.

Hot emulsified sauces can also be finished with Crustacean Butter, page 331 (about 1 ounce/30 grams per cup/250 milliliters sauce), or with lobster coral and tomalley that have first been passed through a fine-mesh strainer.

SABAYON SAUCES

When a cooking liquid is allowed to cool, it can be combined with egg yolks and quickly whisked over heat to form a sabayon. In classic sauce making, the sauce would then be completed by adding fat, usually clarified butter. It is possible to eliminate most or all of the fat. The resulting sauce is extremely light and airy. Although egg yolks are extremely rich, two or three egg yolks form enough sabayon sauce to serve six to eight diners.

BRAISED FILLETS OF SEA BASS WITH SABAYON SAUCE

YIELD: 4 SERVINGS

shallot, chopped	1	1
sea bass fillets, 6 to 8 ounces (150 to 225 grams) each	4	4

fish stock or court-bouillon	½ cup	125 milliliters
white wine	¼ cup	60 milliliters
egg yolks	2	2
whole butter (optional)	1 ounce	30 grams
or	or	or
extra-virgin olive oil (optional)	2 tablespoons	30 milliliters
or	or	or
crème fraîche (optional)	1 tablespoon	15 milliliters
salt and pepper	to taste	to taste

1. Preheat the oven to 500°F (260°C). Place the shallots in the bottom of a straight-sided sauté pan or flameproof oval baking dish. (Use a container that fits the dimensions of the fish fillets as closely as possible or too much liquid will be needed to moisten the fish. The natural flavors of the fish will then be lost, and an inordinate amount of time will be needed to reduce the cooking liquid before it is combined with the egg yolks.) Place the fillets atop the shallots.

2. Add fish stock and wine until the liquid comes halfway up the sides of the fish fillets. (If you do not use all the liquids called for here, do not worry. It is best to use as little liquid as possible, to concentrate the flavors of the fish and the resulting sauce.)

3. Heat the fish on top of the stove until the liquid comes to a slow simmer. Cover the pan loosely with aluminum foil and place it in the oven.

4. While the fillets are still slightly underdone, after about 8 minutes of cooking per inch (2.5 cm) of thickness, remove them from the oven and transfer them to a plate. Cover them with aluminum foil to keep warm while preparing the sauce. (They will continue cooking while the sauce is being prepared.)

5. Strain the fish cooking liquid into a measuring cup. If more than ½ cup (125 milliliters) remains, reduce it on top of the stove to concentrate its flavors.

6. Transfer the fish cooking liquid to a mixing bowl to cool it more rapidly. (If a large number of these sabayon sauces are being prepared during a restaurant service, it might even be convenient to keep a bowl of ice handy to speed up the cooling.) When the liquid is cool, combine it with the egg yolks in a sloping-sided saucepan.

7. Heat the mixture over high heat while quickly beating with a sauce whisk.

8. When the sabayon begins to stiffen and the bottom of the saucepan starts to be visible while whisking, remove the pan from the heat. Continue whisking for about 20 seconds more, to cool the sabayon slightly.

9. The sabayon can be served as is, or it can be finished with the butter, olive oil, or crème fraîche. Season with salt and pepper.

Note: Sabayon sauces contain such a high proportion of air that they do not pour easily—they are too light. It is often best to serve them on the plate with the fillets rather than at the table, as is traditional with classic emulsified sauces. One method that works well is to coat the tops of the fish fillets with the sabayon and then quickly slide the fillets under the broiler to brown them lightly.

SEA SCALLOPS WITH SEA URCHIN EMULSION

Until recently, sea urchin sauce relied on the sea urchin roe itself to form and stabilize the emulsion. At the height of nouvelle cuisine, this natural sea urchin roe emulsion would have been reinforced with reduced cream, butter, or both. Nowadays, propylene glycol alginate, in combination with the roe, can be used to emulsify the sauce. The roe should be treated with the same care as egg yolks, that is, no overheating.

The base for this sauce is a court-bouillon, but there's no need to adhere to a prescribed recipe. Roasted in-season vegetables, simmered for a few minutes in water, will also do the trick. Fennel stalks (save the bulbs for salads, braising, or roasting) add a note of anise that works well with the marine notes from the sea urchin roe. Roast garlic purée can augment the liaison provided by the propylene glycol alginate, but don't overdo it. If you're braising seafood, use the braising liquid here instead of the court-bouillon.

Depending on how the sauce is to be used, many chefs like to serve sea urchin–derived sauces in the scooped out sea urchin shells.

YIELD: 6 MAIN-COURSE SERVINGS

cold court-bouillon (page 366)	2 cups	500 milliliters
propylene glycol alginate		2.5 grams
cold butter	2 tablespoons	30 grams
golden roe from 6 sea urchins, worked through a fine-mesh strainer or drum sieve		
sea scallops or other shellfish (steamed, sautéed, braised, etc.)	6 servings	6 servings

1. Whisk together the court-bouillon and propylene glycol alginate. Bring to a simmer while blending with an immersion blender until the powdered alginate is completely mixed in with no specks. If you see specks, strain the mixture through a chinois.

2. Whisk in the butter. Slowly pour the court-bouillon mixture into the sea urchin roe while blending with the immersion blender.

3. Serve immediately with the prepared scallops or other shellfish.

ROAST CHICKEN WITH GARLIC AND SAFFRON NAGE

Garlic and saffron work well together in virtually any situation, including in sauces for chicken or seafood. Here, garlic is roasted in the skin and the pulp, once squeezed out, is used to emulsify the sauce. A small amount of lecithin and Ultra-Sperse 3, worked into the garlic purée, facilitate and stabilize the emulsion with chicken stock and chicken juices from the deglazed roasting pan.

Normally the saffron might be added directly to the emulsified sauce, but here, the elements are deconstructed and the saffron is instead enclosed in tiny spheres. In this way, as the diner sips the thickened broth, the saffron aroma and flavor are released only after the spheres are gently crushed against the roof of the mouth.

YIELD: 4 MAIN-COURSE SERVINGS

roasting chicken (4 pounds/2 kilograms), trussed	1	1
garlic head, broken into cloves, unpeeled	1	1
chicken stock or jus	1½ cups	375 milliliters
powdered lecithin		4 grams
Ultra-Sperse 3		2 to 4 grams
saffron threads, soaked for an hour in 1 teaspoon (5 milliliters) water	1 pinch	0.2 gram
salt and pepper	to taste	to taste
calcium gluconate		8 grams
sodium alginate		3 grams
cold distilled water	2 cups	500 milliliters

1. Surround the chicken with the garlic cloves in a roasting pan just large enough to hold the chicken and garlic in a single layer. Roast in a hot oven. If at any point the garlic threatens to burn, add about a cup (250 milliliters) water to the roasting pan. Keep a close eye.

2. Scoop the garlic cloves out into a strainer. Degrease the juices in the pan and deglaze the roasting pan with 1 cup (250 milliliters) of the chicken stock. Strain and reserve the deglazing liquid.

3. Use a small ladle to work the garlic pulp through the strainer into a small mixing bowl to get rid of the peels. Blend in the lecithin and the Ultra-Sperse 3 until smooth. If necessary, work the purée with an immersion blender to dissolve the lecithin and Ultra-Sperse 3. If the purée is too stiff to work, add a little of the reserved deglazing liquid.

4. Whisk the reserved deglazing liquid into the garlic purée a bit at a time until the mixture is smooth.

(*continued*)

5. Combine the saffron and its soaking liquid with the remaining ½ cup (125 milliliters) chicken stock. Season the mixture with salt and pepper. Blend in the calcium gluconate until completely dissolved.

6. In a 1-quart (1 liter) bowl or beaker, dissolve the sodium alginate in the distilled water. Set up two additional bowls filled with cold tap water with which to rinse the spheres once they come out of the setting solution.

7. Use a Finnpipette to sprinkle drops of the saffron solution into the sodium alginate solution (see page 32). Give the globules about 90 seconds to set, then scoop them out with a skimmer (with a screen) or small strainer and transfer them to the first bowl of cold water. Gently stir the water to dissolve any remaining sodium alginate. Transfer to the second bowl of cold water to reserve.

8. When ready to serve, arrange a piece of chicken in each of four wide soup bowls. Heat the reserved garlic-deglazing liquid mixture while stirring. Do not let it come to a boil or you may denature the lecithin. The sauce should have a frothy, creamy consistency. Spoon the saffron spheres into the sauce, season with salt and pepper, and ladle over the chicken.

IMPROVISING HOT EMULSIFIED SAUCES

Improvisation requires an ability to imagine gustatory rather than visual images—a kind of thinking with the mouth and stomach. The technique of recalling tastes, textures, and colors takes practice, but once mastered it allows the chef to review mentally a variety of flavor combinations, checking and discarding until some exciting juxtaposition begins to form. Because the art of cookery relies on an aesthetic invariably linked with appetite, this technique works best on an empty stomach. The stomach and salivary glands are quick to respond to mental taste images and, when it comes to cooking, are far more reliable than the intellect.

The modern chef is often overwhelmed by the variety of available ingredients and finds it difficult to cook in a cohesive way with a kind of natural culinary logic underlying his or her cuisine. Many a chef has made the mistake of inventing for invention's sake in this era when something seemingly new and outlandish is revered more than a well-prepared classic. The best way to keep this wayward tendency in check is to work within limits. Traditional regional cooks have always had the natural advantage of working with a limited variety of ingredients, restricted by what nature provides.

One useful method for improvising a sauce is to consider whether the ingredients grow (or could grow) in the same region. Nature usually shows good taste, so ingredients that grow in the same region are likely to work well together in the kitchen.

An example of this method of checking the regionality of a dish can be used when devising modifications to a classic sauce béarnaise. Perhaps the béarnaise is to be served with a grilled steak, and the more assertive fresh marjoram is used to replace the tarragon. Marjoram is a Mediterranean herb. In traditional Mediterranean cooking, butter is rarely used; rather, extra-virgin olive oil is the cooking fat most often used. So perhaps the butter in the "béarnaise" can be replaced with olive oil. Technically it would no longer be sauce béarnaise but rather a hot mayonnaise or a kind of sauce tyrolienne, but in the realm of improvisation, these designations become cloudy.

An improvised sauce may often start as a modification of a classic or traditional recipe. Sometimes the improvisation stems from a happy accident—a missing ingredient, an apprentice using the wrong herb, or just the sudden whim of adding something because it seems good.

A classic sauce can be personalized by changing one or more of the ingredients. For example, try replacing the tomato purée in a sauce choron with a purée of tomatillos.

When altering a classic sauce, be sure that the newly improvised sauce is an appropriate accompaniment. Do not try to make a sauce delicate and subtle if it is going to be served with a full-flavored piece of meat. On the other hand, a piece of poached fish should not be served with a sauce that has been too strongly flavored with herbs.

If a sauce is being invented from scratch, the chef should consider several key points.

WITH WHAT IS THE SAUCE TO BE SERVED? A sauce intended to accompany a leg of lamb grilled over vine cuttings and fresh herbs should obviously be more assertive than a sauce served with spears of freshly picked wild asparagus. Here is where the chef needs to envision the flavors of the sauce, trying to determine whether they work with the food being served.

WHAT IS THE SETTING? Taste and flavor are not independent of other experiences. Certain sauces are better served in a formal restaurant setting, where foods are carefully presented to the diners, than at outdoor barbecues. A delicate and subtle sabayon may be wasted on a socializing barbecue crowd, whose food needs to be more assertive for its flavor to be noticed. Conversely, a full-flavored, straightforward sauce may seem ordinary in a fancy restaurant, where diners may be looking to be surprised.

WHO ARE THE DINERS? Some people are so intimidated by fats that a classic béarnaise will frighten them off. If this is so, a lightened version of an emulsified sauce may be appropriate.

MAYONNAISE-BASED SAUCES

Mayonnaise is an emulsion of oil and a water-based liquid. Because liquids such as lemon juice, vinegar, and wine do not mix readily with oil, a third component, an emulsifier (traditionally egg yolks), is required to bind the two. The egg yolks are first seasoned with salt and pepper, and a small amount of lemon juice or vinegar is added. Oil is then slowly stirred or beaten into the yolks until the mixture starts to thicken. At this point, the emulsion is established and the oil can be added more quickly.

Many home cooks and beginning chefs associate mayonnaise with the commercial bottled variety. Bottled mayonnaise is made with whole eggs and a high proportion of oil, giving it little of the flavor of authentic, freshly made mayonnaise. Fresh mayonnaise made with egg yolks and good-quality oil is often a revelation.

Mayonnaise is a versatile sauce. Its flavor, texture, and color can all be adjusted according to traditional recipes—of which there are many—or the whim of the chef. Traditionally, mayonnaise is used to accompany cold meats, fish, and vegetables and to bind composed salads.

When preparing mayonnaise, make sure the egg yolks are fresh. Always use a good-quality oil. Many commercially available vegetable oils have an unnatural taste or may even taste rancid (see "Oils," page 45). Safflower, canola, or avocado oil is recommended in the recipes that follow. Carefully taste and smell any oil before using it in the mayonnaise.

Making a stabilized mayonnaise is useful for large amounts or for when the mayonnaise will be in and out of the refrigerator—shifting from cold to warm can cause a traditional mayonnaise to break. For a stabilized mayonnaise, egg yolks are precooked sous vide at 140°F (60°C) for 30 minutes. This makes emulsifying easier and makes the sauce less likely to break. For additional stability, you can also work 1% to 2% liquid lecithin into the egg yolks.

Precautions for Preparing Traditional Mayonnaise

1. All the ingredients for making mayonnaise should be at room temperature.

2. Never use aluminum bowls or saucepans to prepare mayonnaise, as they will turn it gray.

3. Add the oil very slowly, especially at the beginning.

4. In general, 1 quart (1 liter) of oil should be emulsified with at least 4 egg yolks. However, if you want a mayonnaise with fewer yolks, keep in mind that a single yolk will set at least 10 liters of oil.

5. As you add the oil, the mayonnaise will become thicker. If it becomes too thick, the minute globules of oil will coalesce and the sauce will break. If the mayonnaise starts to get as thick as bottled mayonnaise, stir in a tablespoon or so (the amount will depend on how much mayonnaise you're making) water, lemon juice, or other flavorful liquid.

Repairing Broken Mayonnaise

If mayonnaise breaks at any point, it can be brought back together by beating the broken mixture bit by bit into a fresh egg yolk or a small amount of other emulsified liquid such as heavy cream. As soon as this new mixture begins to thicken, the broken mayonnaise can be added more quickly. Mayonnaise, especially traditional mayonnaise made without hydrocolloid thickeners and emulsifiers, frequently breaks when stored overnight in the refrigerator and should be reconstituted before being used.

Storing Mayonnaise

Many cases of food poisoning have resulted from improperly handled and stored mayonnaise. When correctly stored, mayonnaise is less perishable than people usually assume. It most often becomes contaminated when used in salads or other prepared dishes that are left for long periods at room temperature. Contaminated mayonnaise may smell and taste perfectly normal, adding to the danger. To keep mayonnaise fresh and safe, keep it cool and well covered in a plastic container with a tight-fitting lid. Never use aluminum containers to store mayonnaise—they will turn it gray. Mayonnaise should be stored for no more than three days in the refrigerator and never for more than 4 hours at room temperature. Make small batches so there is no temptation to store it for too long a period.

TRADITIONAL MAYONNAISE

YIELD: 1½ CUPS (375 MILLILITERS)

egg yolks	4	4
mustard (optional)	2 tablespoons	30 milliliters
fine salt (or to taste)	1 to 2 teaspoons	5 to 10 milliliters
finely ground white pepper	1 pinch	1 pinch
wine vinegar or lemon juice	2 tablespoons	30 milliliters
safflower or other inert-tasting oil	1½ cups	375 milliliters
flavorful liquid for thinning (optional)		

1. Combine the egg yolks, mustard, if using, salt, pepper, and 1 tablespoon (15 milliliters) of the wine vinegar. (A, B, page 414) Blend with a whisk or immersion blender until the mixture is smooth. (If using an immersion blender, put the mayonnaise in a narrow container to make

(*continued*)

it easier for the blender to reach down into the mixture.) If using an electric mixer, use the whisk attachment on medium speed.

2. If needed, transfer the egg yolk mixture to a larger bowl. Slowly beat the oil into the egg yolk mixture. Add about a tablespoon (15 milliliters) of oil at a time while beating, and wait for the oil to combine with the yolks before adding more. If preparing the mayonnaise by hand, it is best to pour several tablespoons of oil down one side of the bowl and whisk the yolks in such a way as to avoid mixing more than a tablespoon of oil into the mixture at once.

3. When the mixture begins to thicken, the emulsion has been established, meaning it is

now relatively stable. The oil can now be added in a thin but steady stream.

4. As more oil is added, the mayonnaise may become so thick that it will be difficult to work. Unless the mayonnaise is already too acidic, add the remaining wine vinegar. If the mayonnaise is still too thick or it is already acidic enough, you can add other liquid, such as water, infused flavorful mixtures, or vegetable purées. Continue beating and adding oil until all the oil has been incorporated. Adjust the seasoning.

Note: Mayonnaise can also be made using a mortar and pestle.

LIGHTENING MAYONNAISE

Making mayonnaise with a sabayon results in a lighter, airier sauce. A sabayon is made by whisking egg yolks with a small amount of liquid (about 1 tablespoon/15 milliliters per yolk) over a carefully controlled heat source. The technique is the same as that used for preparing hot emulsified sauces such as béarnaise and hollandaise. This method causes the egg yolks, water, and air to emulsify; the resulting mayonnaise is then technically a foam, since the emulsion contains air. Conveniently, heating the egg yolks also kills any salmonella bacteria.

A sabayon-based mayonnaise should contain far less oil than traditional mayonnaise, about ¼ cup (60 milliliters) per yolk. If too much oil is added, the sauce will be

heavy and the air that has been beaten into the sabayon will be lost. Although a sabayon-based mayonnaise is usually prepared by first combining water with the egg yolks, it is also possible to use other flavorful liquids appropriate to the sauce's final flavor. Cooking liquids from fish or meat or various stocks can all be used. Unlike a traditional mayonnaise, in which acidic ingredients, such as vinegar or lemon juice, are added at the beginning, in a sabayon they should not be added until near the end; otherwise they will cause the egg yolks to thicken prematurely and result in a heavier sauce. Once the sabayon-based mayonnaise is prepared, it can be flavored in the same way as a traditional mayonnaise. (Recipes and techniques for hot sabayon sauces are given in Chapter 13, "Sabayon Sauces.")

Because sabayon-based mayonnaise is relatively unstable, it should not be kept for more than a few hours or it will lose its airiness and light texture. Consequently, it is best to prepare only a small amount at a time.

If mayonnaise is being served on the side as an accompaniment to cold meats, fish, or vegetables, it can be lightened by folding it with beaten egg whites. Beating the egg whites and the final folding with the mayonnaise should be done as near to the last minute as possible. One egg white will lighten approximately ½ cup (125 milliliters) mayonnaise. When it's time to serve the sauce, gently fold in the beaten egg whites with a rubber spatula. The resulting sauce is extremely light and works well with delicate flavorings. One excellent flavoring is ½ teaspoon (3 milliliters) grated orange zest and 1 tablespoon (15 milliliters) orange juice per cup (250 milliliters) lightened mayonnaise. The lightened orange-flavored mayonnaise is excellent with cold asparagus. Mayonnaise that has been lightened with beaten egg whites should not be used to prepare hot mayonnaise-finished sauces, though, because the egg whites will coagulate when they come in contact with hot liquid.

The fat content and richness of mayonnaise can be reduced by combining it with one or more vegetable purées (see Chapter 18, "Purées and Purée-Thickened Sauces"). The ratio of purée to mayonnaise depends on the purée, the final use of the sauce, and the desired consistency, but using equal parts of each is a good place to start. Make sure that the purée is perfectly smooth and not too liquid. It is better to produce a sauce that is too thick than one that is too thin, as a thick sauce can easily be thinned. If using a green vegetable purée, do not add vinegar to the sauce until the last minute or the sauce will turn gray.

One of the oldest combinations of mayonnaise and a vegetable purée is aïoli made with a cooked potato (see page 417), a method popular in Provence.

Fresh cheese or yogurt can be added to mayonnaise to give it a lighter texture and make it less caloric. The ratio of cheese or yogurt to mayonnaise should be adjusted according to taste, but one part yogurt to four parts mayonnaise is usually about right. Yogurt gives the mayonnaise a pleasant tang, which makes it an excellent medium for spicy flavorings and curries. Plain regular yogurt, without stabilizers, or Greek or Middle Eastern leben yogurt can be used. If using regular yogurt, make sure it doesn't contain stabilizers. Drain it in a coffee filter for an hour before you use it.

416

EMERGENCY "HOMEMADE" MAYONNAISE

If guests make a sudden appearance or you've run out of aïoli for your platter of cooked vegetables, you can fake it by stirring a little extra-virgin olive oil and a little chopped garlic into bottled mayonnaise. Bottled mayonnaise is made with such a stabile emulsion that it's unlikely to break. You may find, however, that it becomes too thick. Simply dilute it with a teaspoon or two (5 to 10 milliliters) water, lemon juice, vinegar, heavy cream, or a combination.

Lightening Mayonnaise with Potato Purée

Potato purée is often used in Provence to lighten strong mayonnaises such as aïoli so they can be dolloped more generously on the hot vegetables, fish, and eggs served at a traditional aïoli dinner. The method can also be used to make other full-flavored mayonnaises less rich.

To lighten a Sauce Aïoli (page 418), combine two parts of the sauce with one part potato purée (page 517). If the mayonnaise becomes too stiff, thin it with an appropriate liquid, such as fish broth, stock, potato cooking liquid, heavy cream, or lemon juice. Peeled and still-warm cooked red potatoes can also be added directly along with the oil when preparing aïoli with a mortar and pestle.

STABILIZED MAYONNAISE

Many stabilizers and emulsifiers are available for keeping a mayonnaise from breaking, but one of the best emulsifiers is egg yolk. Unfortunately, egg yolks can be persnickety and refuse to emulsify (this seems to be especially true when the cook is in a hurry). To stabilize them, cook them, sous vide, for 30 minutes at a temperature of 140°F (60°C).

CLASSIC MAYONNAISE-BASED SAUCES

Basic unflavored mayonnaise is useful because of its versatility, but other ingredients are usually added to flavor it and make it more appropriate for a particular preparation. Many different flavorings can be incorporated into the mayonnaise base as need and inspiration suggest. Some flavored mayonnaises, however, have become standards, and their recipes follow. Most have French names, but they may also be named for the principal flavoring.

Sauce Verte (*Green Mayonnaise*)

This mayonnaise tastes the same as basic unflavored mayonnaise—only the color is different. Stir 2 teaspoons (10 milliliters) chlorophyll (page 445) into 1 cup (250 milliliters) mayonnaise. It may be necessary to add more chlorophyll, but it is best to start with a small amount; surprisingly little is needed. Don't add the chlorophyll until you're almost ready to serve the mayonnaise or the acidity may cause it to turn gray. Yield: 1 cup (250 milliliters)

Sauce Aïoli (*Garlic Mayonnaise*)

This mayonnaise is a specialty of Provence, where it accompanies platters of hot vegetables and poached salt cod, and octopus daube. To prepare 1 cup (250 milliliters) aïoli, peel 3 medium garlic cloves and work them into a smooth paste with a pinch of coarse salt with a mortar and pestle. If a mortar and pestle are not available, finely chop the garlic, then crush it on a cutting board with the side of a chef's knife. Combine the garlic paste with 2 egg yolks and gradually work 1 cup (250 milliliters) extra-virgin olive oil into the mixture. If using a mortar and pestle, do this directly in the mortar. Add 1 tablespoon (15 milliliters) or more lemon juice or water to the mayonnaise after adding half the oil, to prevent the mayonnaise from becoming too thick.

Although garlic mayonnaise is traditionally prepared directly in a mortar while the oil is gently worked in with the pestle, modern recipes frequently suggest using a blender, electric mixer, or hand whisk. Olive oil is a surprisingly fragile substance and will often turn bitter if beaten or overworked. When using extra-virgin olive oil, work it into the yolks with a wooden spoon if a mortar and pestle are not available. You may also want to start the mayonnaise with an inert-tasting oil in a blender and finish the sauce by working in olive oil by hand. Yield: 1 cup (250 milliliters)

If you don't want to start aïoli from scratch, simply stir garlic purée into an already prepared mayonnaise. For extra subtlety and nuance, you may want to add cooked garlic purée (page 515) squeezed out of roasted garlic cloves to replace some or all of the raw garlic called for in the classic recipe.

SAFFRON-FLAVORED AÏOLI

Aïoli can be flavored with saffron by adding a pinch of saffron threads or powder to the garlic–egg yolk mixture before adding the oil. When using saffron threads, soak them for 30 minutes in 1 tablespoon (15 milliliters) warm water **(see photo)** and add both water and threads to the egg yolks. Do not add the saffron to the mayonnaise after the oil has been added, as it will take too long for the color and flavor of the saffron to dissolve into the mayonnaise. Yield: 1 cup (250 milliliters)

Sauce Andalouse (*Tomato and Sweet Red Pepper Mayonnaise*)

This lively flavored mayonnaise is prepared by adding reduced tomato purée and peeled and diced sweet red peppers to basic mayonnaise. It is, of course, possible to prepare the sauce with canned pimentos and tomato paste, but much of the spirit and vitality of the sauce is then lost. Use 1½ sweet red peppers (4 ounces/125 grams, peeled and diced), ¼ cup (60 milliliters) tomato purée (see photos, page 507), and 1 cup (250 milliliters) mayonnaise base. This sauce also benefits from the addition of an extra tablespoon or two (15 to 30 milliliters) good wine vinegar and a good pinch of cayenne pepper or dash of hot pepper sauce. Yield: 1¾ cups (450 milliliters)

Sauce Chantilly (*Mayonnaise with Whipped Cream*)

Mayonnaise can be lightened by folding in whipped cream at the last minute. Although traditional recipes suggest folding the mayonnaise with only one-fourth its volume of whipped cream, it is possible to use more—up to one part cream (before whipping) to two parts mayonnaise. Mayonnaise lightened with whipped cream has a delicate, melting texture, making it an excellent accompaniment to cold or warm vegetables and fish. When folding mayonnaise with whipped cream, it is best to lighten the mayonnaise by thoroughly stirring a third of the whipped cream into the mayonnaise before folding it with the last two-thirds. The whipped cream, medium stiff, should be seasoned with salt and white pepper before being combined with the mayonnaise.

Whipped cream should never be combined with mayonnaise until the last minute, as it tends to break down and lose its airiness.

Mustard-Flavored Mayonnaise

Mustard is an excellent and surprisingly subtle flavoring for mayonnaise. When used in small amounts, it brightens the flavor of the mayonnaise while remaining in the background. Any variety of mustard can be used. Maille brand Dijon mustard, homemade mustard, and whole-grain Meaux-style mustard all provide different nuances. Green mustard, sold by Maille, is colored with chlorophyll and can also be used for color and flavor. Flavored mustards can be used in mayonnaise, but a better flavor is often obtained by adding the fresh flavor component directly to the mayonnaise instead of relying on the mustard to provide it. For example, tarragon-flavored mustard will not provide as clear and bright a flavor as mayonnaise flavored with plain mustard and fresh tarragon. The total amount of mustard to use—including any that was added when preparing the mayonnaise base—depends on the strength of the mustard and the whim of the chef, but 4 teaspoons (20 milliliters) per cup (250 milliliters) mayonnaise is a good place to start.

Sauce Rémoulade (*Caper and Herb Mayonnaise*)

This sauce can accompany cold meats, fish, and vegetables. Although a traditional celeriac rémoulade is prepared with mayonnaise well flavored with mustard (Sauce Dijonaise), combining the celeriac with Sauce Rémoulade can be more exciting. Flavor 1 cup (250 milliliters) basic mayonnaise with 2 tablespoons (30 milliliters) mustard and ¼ cup (60 milliliters) chopped capers. Add 1 teaspoon (5 milliliters) anchovy paste and 2 tablespoons (30 milliliters) mixed finely chopped parsley, chervil, and tarragon. If fresh chervil and tarragon are not available, it is better to leave them out rather than use dried. Tarragon preserved in vinegar, however, makes an acceptable substitute for fresh. Yield: about 1½ cups (375 milliliters)

Sauce Suédoise (*Apple-Horseradish Mayonnaise*)

Although it may sound like a bizarre juxtaposition, the combination of apple purée and mayonnaise makes an excellent sauce for cold meats, especially pork and game. It is best to use sour baking apples (Reinettes de Canada are among the best), but if they cannot be found, Granny Smiths will produce a very satisfactory sauce. Prepare the apple purée by first peeling, coring, and slicing the apples. Coat the sliced apples with a few drops of lemon juice to prevent them from turning brown, as well as to add a note of acidity to the finished sauce. (Never soak sliced apples in water, or their natural sugars and flavor will leach out.) Cook the apples gently in a covered saucepan with 1 tablespoon (15 milliliters) white wine. (Use this amount of wine regardless of how many apples you use.) This may seem like a small amount of liquid, but remember that the apples themselves will release liquid as soon as they are heated by the steaming wine. As soon as the apples are soft, usually after about 10 minutes, purée them in a food processor or food mill, or through a drum sieve. Return the purée to the saucepan and reduce it until it is stiff and no liquid remains. Be careful to stir the mixture constantly with a wooden spoon and not allow it to burn. Allow to cool before incorporating into the mayonnaise.

The proportion of apple purée to mayonnaise will vary depending on the apples' flavor; anywhere from one part apple purée and three parts basic mayonnaise to equal parts of each will work. One pound (450 grams)—about 2 large apples—provides approximately 1 cup (250 milliliters) purée. Flavor the apple mayonnaise with grated horseradish, about 1 tablespoon (15 milliliters) per cup (250 milliliters).

Mayonnaise Made with Hard-Boiled Egg Yolks

Some traditional mayonnaises are made with hard-boiled yolks. Creating an emulsion with cooked yolks is difficult and unreliable; it is better to cheat a little and begin with a combination of raw and cooked yolks—or for that matter, with raw egg yolks alone. Sauces prepared using all raw egg yolks will differ only slightly from the hard cooked-yolk variety. In any case, hard-boiled yolks will absorb not even half as much oil as raw yolks, so adjust proportions accordingly. Be sure to sieve the cooked egg yolks to eliminate lumps.

SAUCE GRIBICHE

While capable of forming emulsions, cooked egg yolks are far less efficient emulsifiers than raw. To circumvent this problem, include a raw egg yolk to make the sauce easier to emulsify. Although this sauce is traditionally served with cold fish, its tangy acidity works well with deep-fried foods (even french fries). Both the whites and yolks of hard-boiled eggs are used. Prepare a mayonnaise base with 3 sieved hard-boiled egg yolks, 1 raw egg yolk, 1 tablespoon (15 milliliters) mustard, 1 tablespoon (15 milliliters) wine vinegar, 1 teaspoon (5 milliliters) fine salt, pepper to taste, and 1 cup (250 milliliters) safflower oil. Make sure the mixture is worked to a smooth paste before adding the oil. Add 2 tablespoons (30 milliliters) chopped capers, 2 tablespoons (30 milliliters) chopped sour gherkins (cornichons), and 2 tablespoons (30 milliliters) mixed chopped fresh parsley, chervil, and tarragon. (If all three are not available fresh, do not substitute dried herbs; just add a little more of the other two.) Finish the sauce with a julienne of the 3 cooked egg whites. Yield: 1¾ cups (450 milliliters)

SAUCE TARTARE (TARTAR SAUCE)

Traditional recipes for sauce tartare vary: Some call for a mayonnaise made with hard-boiled egg yolks, whereas others use all raw yolks. Flavorings for tartar sauce also differ: Older recipes call for puréed scallions or chives (a food processor cannot be used for this purée—you need a mortar and pestle), whereas others prepare tartar sauce with the same additions as Sauce Rémoulade, but replace the anchovy paste with a teaspoon or two (5 to 10 milliliters) mustard. Although not classic, probably the easiest and most satisfying method is to flavor 1 cup (250 milliliters) mayonnaise base with 2 finely chopped shallots and finish the sauce with a heaping tablespoon (20 milliliters) finely chopped chives and 2 teaspoons (10 milliliters) mustard. Yield: 1¼ cups (300 milliliters)

MAYONNAISE VARIATIONS

Using Various Oils

Basic mayonnaise can be prepared or flavored with a wide variety of oils, including extra-virgin olive oil, nut oils such as toasted walnut or hazelnut, toasted sesame oil, and relatively inert-tasting oils such as grapeseed or avocado oil, as well as certain brands of vegetable oil and peanut oil. Because nut oils and sesame oil are strongly flavored and expensive, it is usually best to prepare a base mayonnaise with three parts inert-tasting oil and then finish the mayonnaise with one part of the more strongly flavored oil. Sesame oil is very strong and should be added a drop at a time, to taste.

A NOTE ON USING EXTRA-VIRGIN OLIVE OIL

Extra-virgin olive oil imparts an unmistakable full flavor to mayonnaise. Some chefs find the flavor overbearing and prefer to use half olive oil and half safflower oil. Mayonnaise containing extra-virgin olive oil should be gently worked by hand, using a wooden spoon or a mortar and pestle. When olive oil is beaten with a whisk or in a machine, it loses its fruitiness and turns bitter. To avoid this, make a mayonnaise with an inert-tasting oil using a blender or other device and add the extra-virgin olive oil by hand.

HAZELNUT MAYONNAISE

This sauce works well brushed on grilled or broiled fish (full-flavored fish, such as salmon, are the best). Prepare a mayonnaise using three parts inert-tasting oil and one part hazelnut oil. Stir mustard into the sauce (Dijon or Meaux-style work equally well)—about 2 tablespoons (30 milliliters) per cup (250 milliliters) mayonnaise. Thin the sauce with a little fish stock or court-bouillon, or other appropriately flavored liquid, and a good-quality wine vinegar; the sauce should be quite acidic, to give it lightness and bring out the flavor of the fish. Season well with salt and white pepper. This sauce can be colored green by adding chlorophyll or by using a commercially available green mustard (the Maille brand of fines herbes also works well).

Alternative Flavors

Because the flavor and consistency of mayonnaise are so malleable, mayonnaise makes the perfect medium for a variety of both subtle and assertive flavorings and garnitures.

CILANTRO AND HOT PEPPER MAYONNAISE

This mayonnaise is excellent with grilled or deep-fried fish or vegetables. Combine 1 cup (250 milliliters) mayonnaise with 1 bunch cilantro, finely chopped (optional), ¼ cup (60 milliliters) cooked tomato coulis (page 508), 1 crushed garlic clove, and 2 seeded and finely chopped jalapeños. Finish with 1 to 2 tablespoons (15 to 30 milliliters) wine vinegar, to taste. Season with salt. Yield: 1½ cups (375 milliliters)

For variations, use different chiles. To use dried chiles, seed them, chop them fine, and infuse them into a small amount of hot cream. The mixture can be puréed with a blender or immersion blender. Strain the chile cream and add it to the mayonnaise.

MOREL MAYONNAISE

This works better with dried morels (which have an intense smoky flavor) than with fresh. It is excellent with grilled vegetables and fish. Rinse ½ ounce (15 grams) dried morels under cold running water and soak them in a bowl with ½ cup (125 milliliters) Madeira. When the morels are soft, put them in a saucepan with the Madeira (be careful to leave any grit in the bottom of the bowl), partially cover, and cook them for 5 minutes. Remove the morels and cook down the Madeira until only 1 tablespoon (15 milliliters) remains. Chop the cooked morels and add them and the reduced Madeira to 1 cup (250 milliliters) mayonnaise. Add 1 to 2 tablespoons (15 to 30 milliliters) wine vinegar, to taste. Season with salt and pepper. Yield: 1¼ cups (300 milliliters)

GREEN SAUCE

Combine ¼ cup (60 milliliters) mayonnaise (homemade or bottled) with 3 tablespoons (45 grams) each minced chives, drained and chopped capers, chopped parsley, and chopped sorrel (optional); 2 tablespoons (30 grams) each chopped tarragon and chopped chervil (optional); 1 tablespoon (15 milliliters) prepared mustard; and 1 tablespoon (15 milliliters) wine vinegar, or more as desired. Gently whisk in 1 cup (250 milliliters) extra-virgin olive oil in a steady stream. Season with salt and pepper. For a greener, more subtly flavored sauce, purée the sauce with an immersion blender. Yield: 1½ cups (375 milliliters)

CURRY YOGURT MAYONNAISE

Gently cook 2 tablespoons (30 milliliters) good-quality curry powder with 2 tablespoons (30 milliliters) safflower oil for 30 seconds to 1 minute. Combine the curry mixture with 1 cup (250 milliliters) mayonnaise. Stir in ¼ cup (60 milliliters) yogurt. Yield: 1¼ cups (300 milliliters)

Thinning Mayonnaise with Liquids

The thick consistency of traditional mayonnaise limits its use as a sauce, and in some contexts can be unappealing. Fortunately, traditional mayonnaise can be thinned to virtually any consistency. Thinning mayonnaise with either hot or cold liquids is a useful sauce-making technique. When mayonnaise is thinned and correctly flavored, it becomes a light, digestible sauce that can be varied almost endlessly. Highly flavored oils such as olive oil or nut oils can also be worked in, in small amounts, to a hot sauce. The sauce should never be allowed to boil or the egg yolks will curdle.

HOT LIQUIDS

An example of combining hot liquids with mayonnaise is using mayonnaise-based sauces for fish. Cooking liquids from fish soups and stews can be lightly thickened with mayonnaise and the remaining mayonnaise passed at the table. When serving poached or braised fish, place ½ cup (125 milliliters) mayonnaise (flavored to your liking) in the bottom of a saucepan or a stainless-steel mixing bowl. Slowly pour 1 cup (250 milliliters) of the hot poaching or braising liquid over the mayonnaise, whisking rapidly. **(see photo)** Whisk the mixture continuously while pouring in the hot liquid; otherwise, the mayonnaise may break. (Consider using the stabilized mayonnaise on page 417, which will not break so easily.) When all the hot liquid has been added, place the bowl or saucepan over low heat or a bain-marie and continue whisking until the mixture begins to thicken. Do not overheat the mixture; by no means should it boil. The sauce, which has the consistency of heavy cream, can then be served over or under the fish. This technique works especially well with full-flavored mayonnaises such as saffron, garlic (aïoli), or curry; see also Bourride, page 427.

The ratio of mayonnaise to cooking liquid can, of course, be varied, depending on the desired final consistency of the sauce. The foregoing method uses mayonnaise to lightly thicken the cooking liquid from fish. It is also possible to prepare a light-style mayonnaise by whisking up a sabayon (see page 404) and replacing the water with a flavorful liquid, such as the cooking liquid from fish, crustaceans, or meat. You can also thicken the liquid with a small amount (0.15% or more as needed) of xanthan gum and 1% lambda carrageenan before adding it to the mayonnaise. In this way, less mayonnaise will be required to create a creamy consistency.

An often-encountered difficulty when making this sauce in advance is keeping it warm without it breaking. An effective way of doing this is to put the sauce into a whipping siphon (charged or not with nitrous oxide) and keep it warm (no more than 137°F/57°C) in a bain-marie. If you charge the siphon, the sauce will come out foamy when served.

COLD LIQUIDS

Mayonnaise can be thinned with a wide variety of flavorful cold liquids, such as mushroom cooking liquid (see page 100), cold stocks, court-bouillon, truffle juice, and vinegar (sherry and balsamic are especially good). Wine can be used to thin and flavor mayonnaise, provided the alcohol is cooked off first; fortified wines, such as Madeira and sherry, work the best. Cognac and anise-flavored spirits such as Pernod or Ricard can provide flavor, but they should be used sparingly—add them a drop at a time.

MAYONNAISE-BASED SEAFOOD SAUCES

Mayonnaise, long used as an accompaniment to shellfish and other seafood, can be enhanced with braising liquids, stocks, tomalley, and coral. Cooking liquids from shellfish can be used to flavor mayonnaise using one of two methods: The first is simply to whisk the cooking liquid into a mayonnaise made in advance. The second is to make a sabayon (see page 404) by whisking shellfish cooking liquid (about a tablespoon/15 milliliters per yolk) into the egg yolks over medium heat to form a foamy emulsion before the oil is added.

The cooking liquid that results from steaming mussels or clams in a small amount of wine or other liquid, or from poaching or steaming scallops, can be reduced and used to flavor mayonnaise. When using the cooking liquid from mussels or clams, let the liquid settle a minute before carefully decanting it into a clean container, leaving any grit behind. Also, remember that the cooking liquid from clams and mussels is extremely salty, so do not add salt to the mayonnaise at the beginning. Keep tasting while adding the cooking liquid to regulate the saltiness. Mussel, clam, or scallop cooking liquid can be also be used to braise fish. The braising liquid is then whisked into the mayonnaise.

Mayonnaise made with seafood cooking liquid can be served either hot or cold. This seafood sauce can be used as a base for light fish and shellfish stews or simply as sauce for fish. Various mayonnaises have long been used in elaborately presented cold lobster dishes. Unfortunately, the mayonnaise used is often thick and carelessly flavored, so it does little more than mask both the appearance and taste of the lobster and add unwanted richness and calories.

It is possible to prepare a delicately textured, full-flavored mayonnaise from crustaceans. One method of making these sauces is to whisk the egg yolks with the cooking liquid from the crustaceans. This sauce can be further flavored with herbs, Cognac, Pernod, crustacean oil, and/or sea urchin roe.

Crustacean-flavored mayonnaise can be finished with Crustacean Oil (page 334), which is prepared in the same way as Crustacean Butter (page 331), with olive oil replacing the butter.

Sea urchin roe that has first been forced through a fine-mesh strainer gives a delicate, sea-like sweetness to seafood mayonnaise. Be sure that the sea urchins are impeccably fresh. Some sea urchin roe has an aggressive taste of iodine, so be sure to taste it before adding it to a sauce.

SABAYON-BASED LOBSTER MAYONNAISE

YIELD: 2 CUPS (500 MILLILITERS)

lobster cooking liquid (see page 334)	1 cup	250 milliliters
egg yolks	6	6
safflower or other inert-tasting oil	½ cup	125 milliliters
extra-virgin olive oil	6 tablespoons	90 milliliters
cooked tomato coulis (page 508)	½ cup	125 milliliters
crustacean oil (page 334; optional)	2 tablespoons	30 milliliters
wine vinegar	to taste	to taste
salt and pepper	to taste	to taste

1. Reduce the lobster cooking liquid to ½ cup (125 milliliters). Let it cool.

2. Combine the reduced cooking liquid with the egg yolks in a 2-quart (2 liter) saucepan with sloping sides. Whisk off the heat until frothy.

3. Beat the mixture over medium heat until it froths and stiffens slightly. Immediately remove from the heat and continue whisking for about 20 seconds, to cool it slightly.

4. Whisk in the safflower oil, then stir in the olive oil with a wooden spoon. Stir in the tomato coulis and the crustacean oil, if using.

5. Add vinegar to taste. Season with salt and pepper.

Note: A sabayon can be tricky because it can turn into scrambled eggs in seconds. Do not use too heavy a pan, because it will retain heat and continue cooking the egg yolks, causing them to curdle. While it may sound contradictory, a sabayon is best made in a relatively light stainless-steel bowl. In this way, the bowl (hold it with a towel) can be moved quickly on and off the heat source to closely control the cooking of the yolks.

BOURRIDE SÈTOIS
NAGE BOUND WITH MAYONNAISE

This bourride comes from Sète, in the south of France along the western end of the Mediterranean coast. It is prepared by poaching fish in a nage made with aromatic vegetables and herbs. Once the fish is cooked, the poaching liquid is then strained and whisked into an aïoli, which lightly binds it and contributes to its flavor. This is a model for finishing fish poaching liquid with mayonnaise. Any of the classic mayonnaises in this chapter can be used, as well as improvised mayonnaises using different oils and flavorings for new variations.

Bourride sétoise, often made with monkfish (*baudroie*), may also include the puréed monkfish liver, a delicacy somewhat like foie gras from the sea. If you're using the liver, purée it with about the same volume of the nage and work the mixture through a drum sieve or large strainer. You can stabilize the mixture with 0.5% propylene glycol alginate in the court-bouillon (nage) and/or 2% liquid lecithin to the mayonnaise.

Fennel adds an ineffable freshness to stocks. Because the fennel isn't eaten in the finished dish, you can use the branches and fronds and save the bulbs for something else. (Whenever you use fennel bulbs in other recipes, it's worth saving the branches in the freezer for stocks.)

YIELD: 6 SERVINGS

whole monkfish tails, 1 or 2	6 pounds	3 kilograms
onion, coarsely chopped	1 medium	1 medium
fennel branches, 12 inches (30 centimeters) each, chopped	2 or 3	2 or 3
large bouquet garni (page 52), with a strip of dried orange rind	1	1
water	3 cups	750 milliliters
monkfish liver, 1 (optional)	5 ounces	150 grams
liquid lecithin (if using the liver)		1.5 grams
propylene glycol alginate (if using the liver)		1.5 grams
saffron-flavored aïoli (page 419; see step 4)	1 cup	250 milliliters
egg yolks (optional)	3	3
french bread (large round or fat loaf)	6 slices	6 slices
salt and pepper	to taste	to taste

(continued)

1. Cut the skin off the monkfish tails and slide a knife along each side of the central vertebral column, detaching the meaty fillets as you go.

2. Combine the onion, fennel, bouquet garni, and water in a small pot and simmer, covered, for 25 minutes. Strain through a fine chinois.

3. If you're using the liver, purée it in a food processor with an equal amount (by volume) of nage. Purée in the liquid lecithin and work the mixture through a fine strainer or a drum sieve. Use an immersion blender to blend the propylene glycol alginate into the hot nage for about 5 minutes.

4. Prepare the aïoli. To prepare a thicker, more stew-like sauce, whisk the extra egg yolks into the aïoli. If you're using the liver, work it into the aïoli.

5. Toast the slices of bread.

6. When it is time to present the bourride, put the nage into a straight-sided sauté pan and bring it to a simmer on top of the stove. Place a slice of toasted bread in the bottom of each heated soup plate. Poach the monkfish fillets in the stock, then slice them into ½-inch-thick medallions. Place the pieces of monkfish on the bread in the serving plates.

7. Whisk a cup (250 milliliters) of the fish poaching liquid into the saffron aioli in a saucepan with sloping sides. Gently heat the sauce while whisking; by no means let the sauce boil. Season with salt and pepper to taste. When the sauce is hot enough to serve, ladle it over the monkfish in the soup plates.

VARIATIONS

The seafood used in a bourride is not limited to the traditional monkfish. Virtually any flavorful fish or other seafood can be used. If using fish that provide bones (monkfish only has the central vertebrae), it's possible to make a fish broth rather than a nage using the same ingredients as above but also adding the fish bones.

It is especially exciting to use seafood, such as scallops, with coral or roe that can be used in the sauce. If you encounter coral while shucking fresh scallops, integrate it into the mayonnaise (work it through a drum sieve first) as you would the monkfish liver above. Poach the scallops in the nage and transfer them to hot soup plates. Spoon over the sauce.

Lobster Coral Mayonnaise

A sublimely flavored mayonnaise can be prepared by simply whisking strained raw lobster coral and tomalley into raw egg yolks, as when making a traditional mayonnaise, or into a sabayon (see page 404), before adding the oil.

The color will be a somewhat odd gray green, but the sauce will be complex, with an intense lobster taste. Keep in mind, however, that a mayonnaise made with raw coral is extremely perishable and shouldn't be kept (even cold) for more than a few hours. The coral can also be whisked with twice its volume of heavy cream over low heat until it turns orange, then cooled and folded into the mayonnaise base.

MAYONNAISE-BASED MEAT SAUCES

Highly flavored mayonnaise is wonderful with grilled and sautéed meats. An assortment of flavored mayonnaises can even be served in lieu of the more typical American condiments, mustard and ketchup. Making an assortment of mayonnaises is simpler than it sounds because one mayonnaise base can be made for all the varieties and then each flavored sauce derived from it.

IMPROVISING MAYONNAISE-BASED SAUCES

A walk-in refrigerator containing fruits and vegetables, leftover sauces, varieties of fish and shellfish, and perhaps an array of well-made stocks can be a powerful inspiration to a chef looking to devise a new and interesting mayonnaise-based sauce. Often a particular ingredient will stand out and suggest itself as the focal point of the sauce. Perhaps there are some wild mushrooms, some smoked fish, or too many sweet peppers—any of which can be used to make an original sauce. Once the central flavor of the sauce has been decided, peripheral ingredients and components can be added to the sauce to shape its final flavor, texture, and color.

Traditional recipes are also a valuable source of ideas. One method for inventing sauces is to imagine a traditional dish—even one you don't like—and deconstruct it in your mind while imagining what can be done to improve it. For example, the diced apples, celery, and walnuts in a Waldorf salad are traditionally bound together with mayonnaise, but many people find the mayonnaise to be a needless addition of fat and calories, as well as heavy in texture. The mayonnaise contributes little to the final flavor of the dish and in fact does more to obscure the clean flavor and crisp texture of the salad's components than to lend them finesse or excitement. However, small modifications to a mayonnaise may improve the overall dish. The added richness and calories of mayonnaise are justified if the mayonnaise contributes more flavor—for example, if it is flavored with herbs, curry, truffles, or wild mushrooms. Perhaps the mayonnaise can be flavored with walnut or hazelnut oil to accentuate the walnuts, or maybe a teaspoon (5 milliliters) of Calvados or reduced cider can be added to underline the character of the apples. Another possibility is to convert the Waldorf salad into a sauce by chopping the nuts, apples, and celery very finely and combining them with a mayonnaise that has been thinned with a little cider or cream or lightened with yogurt. This sauce can then be used for cold fish or meats.

Once the basic flavor of a sauce has been determined, the chef should decide its use and final texture and color. Are lightness and delicacy important? Will the diners be calorie conscious, or are they more interested in robust, traditional fare? In some cases a traditional mayonnaise with classic flavoring may be more appropriate than a modern improvised version, no matter how delicious. The type of oil must be determined before either of the bases can be prepared. If the flavor of the oil is not needed to contribute to the final flavor of the mayonnaise, an inert-tasting oil such as safflower oil, French peanut oil (*huile d'arachide*), avocado oil, or grapeseed oil should be used for the base. If the oil will give character to the sauce, then the chef must determine how assertive the final flavor should be and what proportion of flavorful oil to use.

Once the base mayonnaise has been prepared, the chef must decide whether the sauce should be lightened, perhaps with vegetable purée, whipped cream, beaten egg whites, fresh cheese, or yogurt. Should the finished sauce be light and frothy? Thin, with a soup-like consistency? Stiff, in the traditional style? And a colored mayonnaise is often more appealing than the pale yellow of traditional plain mayonnaise. Chlorophyll, green mustard, chopped tomatoes, reduced tomato purée, tomato paste, saffron, curry, and finely chopped truffles can all be used to provide color (so long as the flavor is appropriate, of course). Avoid preparing sauces with too deep or intense a color, as they may look artificial and unappetizing.

When all the major components have been integrated into the sauce, its flavor and texture should be fine-tuned. It may need only something obvious, such as salt or pepper (always use freshly ground white pepper). If you are uncertain about adding a particular ingredient, work with only a small amount of the mayonnaise until you have a sense of how the ingredient will behave and work in the finished sauce. Good-quality vinegar and mustard will almost invariably enliven the flavor of mayonnaise. If the mayonnaise tastes flat, try adding these ingredients first. They will often bring out the flavor of other ingredients in the sauce. Finely chopped fresh herbs add subtlety and an ineffable complexity to a finished sauce. They will often make the difference between a very good sauce and a great one. Mushroom cooking liquid, truffle essence, or good-quality truffle juice will usually give a seemingly complete sauce a whole new dimension. As extravagant as it may sound, good truffle juice will go a long way in sauce making, especially in cold sauces, where none of the flavor is lost in cooking.

While the final flavor of the sauce is taking shape, pay close attention to its color and texture. Do not become so carried away by adding liquid flavorings that you find the sauce has suddenly become too thin—this can be a difficult problem to fix. If adding stock or mushroom cooking liquid, keep an eye on the sauce's color. As delicious as mushroom cooking liquid is, it can give an unsightly gray cast to the finished sauce.

If you have decided to lighten the sauce, remember that some lightening agents, such as beaten egg whites or whipped cream, should be added to the sauce only just before serving. When using lighteners, their airiness can be exploited by piping the sauce out of a whipping siphon.

TIPS FOR THE RESTAURANT CHEF

Because mayonnaise is a cold sauce, it is easy to work with in a restaurant setting. It need not be kept on the stove or in a steam table during a restaurant service, and it can usually be prepared well in advance. It will sometimes break when held overnight in the refrigerator, but it can be easily reconstructed by gently working it into an egg yolk or a tablespoon or two (15 to 30 milliliters) heavy cream. However, rather than reconstructing the mayonnaise (and this shouldn't be done more than once or twice, or bacteria will accumulate) each day it is used, it is better to start out with the stabilized mayonnaise on page 417.

In restaurants where a large number of mayonnaise-based sauces are being prepared, it is often convenient to prepare a relatively large quantity of mayonnaise base and then flavor it as needed to construct derivative sauces.

Because mayonnaise can be reconstituted almost indefinitely, kitchen personnel are often tempted to keep it on hand for too long. Mayonnaise, especially when left unrefrigerated, can become contaminated with staphylococci and other bacteria—particularly treacherous because they do not produce an off-odor or taste in the mayonnaise. Mayonnaise should be stored in the refrigerator and never be kept on hand for more than four days.

BUTTER SAUCES

Butter sauces can be classified into four categories. In *beurre blanc–type sauces*, cold butter is whisked into a flavorful liquid base; *broken butter sauces* are made by cooking whole butter in a sauté pan so that the butter breaks—these sauces are then usually finished with lemon juice or wine vinegar; *compound butters* are prepared by working cold whole butter with flavorful ingredients such as herbs or reduced vegetable purées; *whipped butters* are prepared in almost the same way as compound butters, except that a hot flavorful liquid is also incorporated into the butter.

BEURRE BLANC SAUCES

Until the late 1960s, beurre blanc (also called *beurre nantais*) was little known outside Brittany, the Loire Valley, and a few specialized Parisian restaurants. Because it contains no emulsifier other than butter itself, it was considered extremely difficult to make. In fact, there was a certain amount of mystique surrounding its preparation, usually concerning magic wrists or the need for a half-century's experience. Gradually, a few of the more adventurous Parisian chefs discovered that the sauce was not so difficult to make after all, and beurre blanc, along with an array of obvious derivatives, took Paris by storm. Whether this sudden mass discovery of beurre blanc started flour's banishment from the kitchens of Michelin-starred restaurants or simply coincided with it is hard to say, but once beurre blanc emerged from obscurity, it played a leading role in French kitchens in much the same way as béchamel and velouté did years before.

As beurre blanc became firmly established in contemporary kitchens, chefs realized that the technique used to whip the sauce into an emulsion (*monter au beurre*; see page 114) was applicable to an almost infinite variety of sauce bases, including traditional and newly innovated brown and white sauces.

TRADITIONAL BEURRE BLANC
BEURRE NANTAIS

The original version, from Brittany, is almost always prepared with Muscadet wine, which is made from grapes grown in the area surrounding the city of Nantes on France's Atlantic coast. Muscadet has the crisp, clean flavor and the acidic edge essential to a successful beurre blanc. If Muscadet is unavailable or too expensive, other wines can be used, but if only wines containing relatively little acidity are available, it may be necessary to add a few additional drops of vinegar to wake up the sauce at the end.

The recipe that follows contains a small amount of heavy cream, which, although not essential, will help start the emulsion. A great deal of myth still surrounds the addition of the butter to the flavor base. Many authors insist that the butter be added in tiny increments, often as little as a tablespoon (15 milliliters) at a time, over low heat, and imply that the sauce will break if the butter is added any faster. In fact, the butter can be cut into relatively large cubes (about 1 inch/2.5 cm on each side) and added all at once over high heat. The keys are to not stop whisking and not let the sauce boil. Seasonings can be added at the end. Traditionally, 1 teaspoon (5 milliliters) fine salt is added per 2 cups (500 milliliters) sauce, but diners today often find this to be slightly too much.

YIELD: 2 CUPS (500 MILLILITERS)

shallot, finely chopped	3 ounces	75 grams
white wine	½ cup	125 milliliters
white wine vinegar	½ cup	125 milliliters
heavy cream or other liquid	¼ cup	60 milliliters
butter, cut into 1-inch (2.5 cm) cubes	1 pound	500 grams
salt and pepper	to taste	to taste

1. Combine the shallots with the wine and vinegar in a heavy-bottomed saucepan. Gently simmer the mixture until practically all the liquid has evaporated (reduce by about 90 percent). (A)

2. Add the cream. If cream is not being used, the same amount of another liquid, such as water, must be added, or the sauce will be too thick. (B)

3. Check the inside of the saucepan to make sure it has not browned, which would discolor the sauce. Wipe off any browning with a wet towel.

4. Add the butter to the shallot infusion. Quickly whisk the sauce over high heat until all the butter has been incorporated. (C, D)

5. Season with salt and pepper. If the sauce seems flat, add more vinegar, a few drops at a time. If the sauce tastes harsh or overly acidic, whisk in more butter.

6. Most chefs prefer to strain the beurre blanc, but for some dishes the minced shallots provide an appealing contrast to the pale sauce.

Holding and Saving Beurre Blanc

If held properly, beurre blanc prepared just before a restaurant service or lengthy meal will stay intact for several hours. Leave it in the saucepan, covered, in a warm area such as a warm oven, plate warmer, or on the back of the stove. If necessary, the saucepan can be placed in a pan of hot water.

When beurre blanc is held for any length of time, it will begin to thicken and must be thinned periodically with heavy cream, water, court-bouillon, or another appropriate liquid, either cold or hot. If it is not thinned and stirred approximately every 30 minutes, it is likely to break. Broken beurre blanc can be repaired by whisking it into several tablespoons of reduced heavy cream, but this can be done only once.

Leftover beurre blanc, with the shallots strained out, can be used in hollandaise- or béarnaise-type sauces. It can also be cooked on the stove until it breaks completely and separates; it can then be used for clarified butter, although it will taste like shallots.

Stabilizing Beurre Blanc

To stabilize a beurre blanc—a good idea when anticipating a busy service or when you won't have time to give the sauce the necessary occasional stirring—work 2% liquid lecithin into the butter before using it to mount the sauce. This not only stabilizes the sauce, but also allows you to construct the sauce over a base of flavorful broth, as in the recipe that follows, instead of just the limited amount of shallot reduction. Blend 0.5% propylene glycol alginate into the vinegar-shallot reduction before whisking in the butter.

STABILIZED COURT-BOUILLON BEURRE BLANC

There are two great things about this sauce. It won't break unless wildly abused, and it allows you to incorporate flavorful liquids that, at least when used in any quantity, would otherwise cause the sauce to break. Here the sauce is combined with court-bouillon, but virtually any flavorful liquid will work. Consider using poaching liquids, braising liquids, or jus.

YIELD: 4 CUPS (1 LITER)

shallot, minced	1 large	1 large
white wine vinegar	¼ cup	60 milliliters
dry, acidic white wine	6 tablespoons	90 milliliters
liquid lecithin		6 grams
cold butter	6½ ounces	200 grams
propylene glycol alginate		2 grams
flavorful court-bouillon (page 366), hot (at least 140°F/60°C)	¾ cup	185 milliliters

Combine the shallot, vinegar, and wine in a small saucepan. Simmer the mixture down to about one-quarter its original volume. Work the lecithin into the butter. Use an immersion blender to blend the propylene glycol alginate into the court-bouillon until no specks of propylene glycol alginate remain in the liquid. Add this to the shallot infusion. Blend in the butter all at once.

Beurre Blanc Variations

Beurre Blanc lends itself to several obvious variations, such as Beurre Rouge (red wine replaces the white), Beurre Citron (lemon juice replaces wine and vinegar), and Beurre à l'Ail (garlic replaces the shallots). Any of the flavor bases for emulsified egg sauces can be used as the base for beurre blanc–style sauces.

BEURRE ROUGE (RED WINE–BUTTER SAUCE)

The most obvious variation of Beurre Blanc involves replacing the white wine with red wine and the white wine vinegar with red wine vinegar. The resulting sauce, however, has a pale purple cast that reminds some people of Pepto-Bismol. To deepen the color of the sauce, reduce a bottle of full-bodied red wine with no tannin and low acidity to ½ cup (125 milliliters). Replace the vinegar called for in a classic beurre blanc with red wine vinegar. Combine the vinegar, red wine reduction, and shallots in a saucepan. Reduce as needed and whisk in the butter.

Unfortunately, Beurre Rouge often has a one-dimensional flavor and may even have an unpleasant metallic taste, because the wine is reduced without any protein that would remove the astringent tannins and deepen the flavor. A better approach is to make a red wine brown sauce containing reduced stock or demi-glace.

BEURRE CITRON (LEMON BEURRE BLANC)

This sauce is prepared in the same way as Beurre Blanc except that the white wine and vinegar are replaced with lemon juice. Use the juice of 1 lemon for 1 pound (500 grams) butter. Many beginning chefs incorrectly assume that lemon juice will impart a distinct lemon flavor to the sauce. In fact, lemon juice contributes only acidity—a more direct, less subtle acidity than that provided by vinegar. For lemon flavor, grated or blanched julienned lemon zest can be infused in the lemon juice before whisking in the butter.

BEURRE FONDU (EMULSIFIED BUTTER)

In many sauce-making settings, it is convenient to have on hand already emulsified butter, which does not necessarily have the distinct character of a classic beurre blanc. Butter can be emulsified by whisking it into almost any liquid, such as court-bouillon, various stocks or cooking liquids, and of course, lemon juice, vinegar, or water. Whatever liquid base is used, some acidity derived from wine, vinegar, verjuice, or citrus juice will help stabilize the emulsion. The butter can also be stabilized with 2% liquid lecithin and the liquid phase with 0.5% to 1% propylene glycol alginate. Emulsified butter is handy for finishing last-minute sauces or cooking liquids, rather than enriching with cold butter each time.

CLARIFIED BUTTER

Butter is said to be "clarified" once the milk solids, which are proteins, and the water contained in the butter are removed. Clarified butter can be used for sautéing because it burns at a very high temperature—much higher than whole butter, which, because it contains milk solids, burns at a lower temperature. It can also be added to emulsified egg yolk sauces, to which it adds body and its beautiful buttery flavor without thinning the sauce (whole butter, which contains water, will thin an emulsified egg yolk sauce).

One of the easiest methods of preparing clarified butter, and one that is particularly convenient for the home cook, is simply to prepare beurre noisette.

In situations where a relatively large amount of clarified butter—5 pounds or more—is being clarified, the simplest approach is simply to melt the butter. Once melted, most of the milk solids will float to the top where they're easily skimmed off. Once skimmed, the clarified butter (the pure butterfat) is easily ladled out. A layer of water and milk solids will remain at the bottom. Most of the time this is discarded, although some cooks use the milk solids for bread making.

BROKEN BUTTER SAUCES

These sauces are prepared by cooking butter until it breaks, then flavoring it with an acidic ingredient such as lemon juice or wine vinegar. Broken butter sauces are less popular than they used to be, yet there are preparations for which no other kind of sauce will do: sole (or other fish) meunière, sauce grenobloise (with broken butter, capers, and lemon), and skate with brown butter (the butter is cooked slightly beyond the noisette stage) are a few examples.

Beurre Noisette

The French name for this butter sauce translates literally as "hazelnut butter," not because it contains nuts but because of the characteristic nutty smell—like butterscotch—of the butter when it is cooked to just the right stage. Do not confuse Beurre Noisette with *beurre de noisette*, which is actually made with puréed hazelnuts. Usually Beurre Noisette is prepared directly in the pan used for cooking fish or white meats à la meunière (as in the recipe that follows), but it can also be prepared separately, especially for banquets or when a large number of guests is being served at one time. Beurre noisette is also used for innumerable Indian preparations, and in Indian cuisine is known as *ghee*.

To prepare Beurre Noisette separately, on the stove, slowly melt whole butter in a heavy-bottomed saucepan. (A) Continue cooking the butter over medium heat until the water has boiled off (usually 15 to 18 percent of whole butter is water) and the butter froths up. (B, C) When the water has evaporated and the milk solids have begun to coagulate into small white specks, turn down the flame. (D) Watch the specks carefully while the butter is cooking. (E) When the specks turn a medium brown and cling to the sides and bottom of the pan, remove the saucepan from the heat. (F) Plunge the bottom of the saucepan into a bowl of cold water to stop the cooking. (G) Strain the butter through a fine-mesh strainer into a clean container. (H)

439

FILLETS OF DOVER SOLE À LA MEUNIÈRE

While beurre noisette can be made on its own, it is sometimes the result of a cooking process. Sole meunière is a dish in which beurre noisette is prepared to order in the pan used to sauté the sole filets.

Beurre noisette is sometimes finished with elements that counteract its richness. The best-known variations on the meunière theme are à la *grenobloise*, which is beurre noisette to which capers, miniature croutons, and lemon cubes have been added; *amandine*, made with slivered almonds that have been cooked in the hot beurre noisette; and à *la polonaise*, finished with breadcrumbs.

This dish calls for Dover sole, which is the only authentic sole sold commercially (unlike American "sole," which is really flounder).

YIELD: 2 SERVINGS

fillets of sole, 3 to 4 ounces (100 to 125 grams) each	4	4
salt and pepper	to taste	to taste
flour (for dredging)	as needed	as needed
clarified butter	¼ cup	60 milliliters
whole butter	2½ ounces	75 grams
juice of ½ lemon		
chopped parsley	1 tablespoon	15 milliliters

1. Season the fillets with salt and pepper and dredge them in flour. Pat them to remove excess.

2. Sauté the fillets in the clarified butter (oval sauté pans are best for this), and transfer them to serving plates or a platter. Discard the cooked butter and wipe out any particles of burned flour with a paper towel.

3. Let the sauté pan cool slightly, then add the whole butter. Cook the whole butter until it froths and the froth begins to subside. While the butter is cooking, sprinkle the cooked fillets with lemon juice (see Note) and the parsley.

4. Pour the hot beurre noisette over the fillets.

Note: The lemon juice can also be added directly to the butter in the sauté pan, but be sure to let the cooked butter cool 30 seconds or so before adding the lemon juice, which can cause the butter to burn if the butter is too hot.

Beurre Noir

Many chefs confuse Beurre Noir, which literally means "black butter," with burned butter. Correctly prepared Beurre Noir is made in the same way as Beurre Noisette except that when it is served, the lemon juice is replaced with vinegar. Full-flavored vinegars, such as sherry and balsamic vinegars, work especially well. In classic French cooking, Beurre Noir is most often served with fish (especially skate), and as a sauce for poached brains.

Alternative Flavorings

Beurre Noisette and Beurre Noir can be garnished with herbs other than the traditional chopped parsley. Tarragon, chervil, marjoram, and oregano all provide different nuances. Other components, such as chopped garlic, diced gherkins (cornichons), diced mushrooms (wild or otherwise), diced truffles, and chopped shallots can be added to the butter while it is being heated. Acidic liquids such as verjuice or reduced red or white wine can replace the traditional lemon juice and vinegar.

COMPOUND BUTTERS

Compound butters are prepared by working whole butter with flavorful ingredients such as herbs, vegetable purées, reduced wines or stocks, anchovies, spices, or coral. Depending on the desired consistency of the butter or the finesse of the dish, compound butters may be worked through a drum sieve so that they end up perfectly smooth. They can be used by themselves as "sauces" for grilled meats, fish, and vegetables, or swirled in at the end to complete more complex sauces.

It is often convenient to add compound butters, rather than flavoring ingredients alone, to sauces. This is especially true for herbs such as basil or tarragon, which turn black if chopped in advance. If the herbs are chopped into butter, they are protected from the air and their color and flavor stay intact. **(A)** It is also useful to prepare a compound butter when using fragile ingredients that may coagulate in contact with a hot liquid. Sea urchin roe, sea scallop coral, and foie gras should be combined with at least one-half their weight in butter before being whisked into a sauce.

Compound butters served over grilled or sautéed meats or fish can be presented in one of two ways. The first is to roll the softened compound butter in a sheet of plastic wrap, parchment paper, or aluminum foil to form a compact cylinder. **(B)** Chill the cylinder and slice it into miniature disks. Place the disks over hot meat or fish just before serving. The second method is to warm the butter slightly and then whip it with a whisk. Avoid overworking the butter, or it will develop an unpleasant clinging feel in the mouth. The flavor of the butter itself will also lose some of its finesse. Worked or whipped compound butters are traditionally served on the side in a sauce boat, but today's chefs will often put them directly on the meat or fish.

Compound butters are also useful as a decorative and flavorful finish for hot soups.

The flavor base for compound butters was traditionally prepared with a mortar and pestle and then usually strained through a fine-mesh drum sieve after being combined with the butter. Today a food processor is usually used instead of the mortar and pestle, but to obtain a perfectly smooth texture, a fine-mesh drum sieve is still necessary for straining the butter at the end.

Compound butters are almost always seasoned with salt and pepper. Recipes vary and suggest anywhere from ½ teaspoon to 1 tablespoon (3 to 15 milliliters) fine salt to 1 pound (500 grams) butter. If a whole tablespoon is used, the butter will be extremely salty; this is appropriate only if the butter is being used as the only seasoning on grilled or deep-fried foods. Cayenne pepper, wine vinegar, and lemon juice will often wake up the flavor of a compound butter.

Compound butters by nature are susceptible to breaking. One look at a steak topped with maître d' butter (parsley butter) will show the butter turning to oil and froth with the parsley throughout. While many of us appreciate this—it's part of the effect—compound butters can be stabilized so they remain intact and don't break. Working 2% liquid lecithin into the cold butter will usually do the trick.

Crustacean butters, which are similar to compound butters, are found on pages 331 and 447.

Classic French Compound Butters

The classic French repertoire contains approximately forty compound butters. Some of these, such as maître d' butter (*beurre maître d'hôtel*) and Montpellier Butter, continue to be widely used, whereas others, though more obscure, provide inspiration by reminding us of sometimes exotic combinations that can be expressed in today's style.

ALMOND BUTTER

Finely grind 5 ounces (150 grams) peeled and toasted almonds in a food processor for 5 minutes (this sounds like a long time but is necessary to achieve the right texture). Scrape the walls of the food processor from time to time and grind until a smooth paste is obtained. Add 8 ounces (250 grams) cold butter, cut into cubes, to the almond paste, and process the mixture until it is perfectly homogeneous. Season with salt. The butter can be used as is or made perfectly smooth by working it through a fine-mesh drum sieve with a plastic pastry scraper or rubber spatula. This butter is excellent on grilled fish and vegetables. Yield: 13 ounces (400 grams)

ANCHOVY BUTTER

Select the best anchovies available (see page 70). Soak 24 anchovy fillets (2½ ounces/60 grams) in cold water for 5 minutes to eliminate excess salt and oil. Dry the anchovies on paper towels and purée them in a food processor with 8 ounces (250 grams) butter. Work the butter through a fine-mesh drum sieve with a plastic pastry scraper or rubber spatula. When used sparingly, anchovy butter is excellent for finishing fish sauces. Yield: 11 ounces (310 grams)

BERCY BUTTER

Reduce 1 cup (250 milliliters) white wine with 2 finely chopped shallots until only 2 tablespoons (30 milliliters) liquid remain. Let the reduction cool (do not strain it), then work it into 7 ounces (200 grams) creamed butter. Add 1 tablespoon (15 milliliters) chopped parsley and 2 teaspoons (10 milliliters) lemon juice. Season with salt and pepper. Older recipes incorporate diced and poached marrow into the butter along with the other ingredients. The only difference between a Bercy Butter without marrow and a shallot butter is that the Bercy Butter is flavored with reduced white wine. Season with ½ teaspoon (2 milliliters) salt. Yield: 9 ounces (255 grams)

CHIVRY BUTTER

This butter is also sometimes called Ravigote Butter. Mince 1 shallot and blanch for 1 minute. Blanch 1 heaping tablespoon (20 milliliters) each of fresh tarragon, chervil, parsley, chives, and salad burnet in boiling salted water for 15 seconds. Quickly refresh the herbs and minced shallot in a strainer with cold running water and dry them on towels. The herbs and shallot are best ground with a mortar and pestle before being worked with 4 ounces (125 grams) butter, but if a mortar and pestle are unavailable, the herbs and shallot can be puréed along with the butter in a food processor. After the herbs and shallot have been puréed with the butter, force the butter through a fine-mesh drum sieve. Yield: 5 ounces (145 grams)

CHLOROPHYLL BUTTER

This butter is good to have on hand for coloring hot sauces green. (Plain chlorophyll can be used for cold sauces.) Work chlorophyll into butter until you get the color you're looking for. Typically, a tablespoon of chlorophyll colors 4 ounces (120 grams) butter, although you may want to adjust the amounts according to the exact shade you're looking for. Yield: 4 ounces (120 grams)

COLBERT BUTTER

Work 2 tablespoons (30 milliliters) melted glace de viande (page 97) and 1 tablespoon (15 milliliters) chopped blanched tarragon leaves into 8 ounces (250 grams) Maître d' Butter (page 444). Yield: 11 ounces (300 grams)

GARLIC BUTTER

Traditional recipes call for blanching peeled garlic cloves and combining them with an almost equal weight of butter (7 ounces/200 grams garlic to 8 ounces/250 grams butter) before straining the butter through a drum sieve. For some applications, such as snail butter or for garlic bread, garlic butter can be prepared by grinding and working unblanched cloves with butter, 2 cloves per 4 ounces (125 grams) butter. Yield: 16 ounces (450 grams)

HAZELNUT BUTTER (BEURRE DE NOISETTE)

Don't confuse *beurre de noisette*, which is made with hazelnuts, with *beurre noisette*. Beurre noisette is butter cooked until it takes on a nutty, butterscotch-like flavor (see page 438); it contains no other ingredients than butter.

Beurre de noisette is made with hazelnuts, usually about 1 part nuts to 3 parts butter. The hazelnuts should first be toasted in the oven to bring out their flavor. Remove as much of the dark skins as possible by rubbing the hot nuts against each other in a kitchen towel. Grind the nuts with the butter in a food processor for about 5 minutes, stopping when needed to keep the butter from melting. Alternatively, since a food processor can't produce a perfectly smooth paste, you can substitute unsweetened praline paste for the hazelnuts.

MAÎTRE D' BUTTER (BEURRE MAÎTRE D'HÔTEL)

This is probably the best known of the compound butters, as it is the usual accompaniment to *steak frites* (grilled steak with french fries). Work 8 ounces (250 grams) butter with ¼ cup (60 milliliters) finely chopped parsley and 1 teaspoon (5 milliliters) lemon juice. Season with salt and pepper. Some recipes suggest adding mustard to the butter. Yield: 11 ounces (300 grams)

MARCHAND DE VIN BUTTER

This butter is excellent served on top of grilled steaks. Reduce 1 cup (250 milliliters) full-bodied red wine with 1 minced large shallot and 5 cracked peppercorns. When the wine is three-quarters reduced, add 1 tablespoon (15 milliliters) glace de viande (page 97) and a good pinch of salt. Continue reducing until a few tablespoons of syrupy mixture remain. Let cool. Work the mixture with 5 ounces (150 grams) butter, 2 teaspoons (10 milliliters) lemon juice, and 1 tablespoon (15 milliliters) finely chopped parsley. Yield: 6 ounces (180 grams)

MONTPELLIER BUTTER

This, the most elaborate of the classic compound butters, is well worth the effort. It is excellent served on hot or cold fish and meats. It has a softer texture than most compound butters because of the olive oil it contains.

Crush 1 small peeled garlic clove in a mortar and work to a paste. Add 4 anchovy fillets, 1 chopped chornichon (sour gherkin), and 1 tablespoon (15 milliliters) capers and work again to a paste. Blanch the leaves from ½ small bunch each parsley, watercress, chervil, chives (chopped before blanching); 1 sprig tarragon; 1 small handful spinach leaves; and 2 chopped shallots in boiling salted water for 30 seconds. Drain, rinse with cold water, and wring dry in a kitchen towel. Combine with the garlic mixture and grind to a paste in the mortar or in a food processor. Add 1 raw egg yolk and 2 cooked egg yolks and work again until smooth. Add 6 tablespoons (90 grams) butter and work through a drum sieve. Gently work ¼ cup (65 milliliters) extra-virgin olive oil into the butter with a wooden spoon (remember, whisking turns olive oil bitter). Season with salt, pepper, cayenne, and a little lemon juice or good wine vinegar. Yield: 9 ounces (275 grams)

MUSTARD BUTTER

This simple butter is excellent served atop grilled foods for which straight mustard would be too strong. Mustard butter can be prepared with smooth Dijon mustard or whole-grain Meaux-style mustard. Traditional recipes call for 2 to 3 tablespoons (30 to 45 milliliters) mustard per 8 ounces (250 grams) butter, but more can be added according to taste. Yield: 10 ounces (300 grams)

PAPRIKA BUTTER

Most commercially available paprikas have so little flavor that the spice is used in the kitchen primarily for its color. Spanish pimentón, however, is smoked paprika and has a distinct smoky flavor that's delicious in sauces. Some chefs prepare paprika butter, using 1 teaspoon (5 milliliters) paprika to 8 ounces (250 grams) butter, for coloring sauces at the last minute or for decorating soups. Yield: 9 ounces (250 grams)

PREPARING CHLOROPHYLL

Purée 1 pound (500 grams) raw spinach leaves with 1 quart (1 liter) water in a blender or food processor. Strain the liquid through a clean kitchen towel and twist the towel to extract green liquid from the spinach. Gently heat the green liquid in a saucepan until it coagulates. **(A)** Strain the liquid through a strainer lined with a wet towel or coffee filter. **(B)** Gently scrape the chlorophyll off the inside of the towel with a spoon. Chlorophyll can be stored in the refrigerator, covered with a thin coating of oil, for a week or so. **(C)** Yield: 1 to 2 ounces (30 to 60 grams)

SMOKED SALMON BUTTER

This butter can be used to add an extra dimension to fish sauces or can be served as is atop grilled or sautéed fish. Purée 4 ounces (125 grams) smoked salmon in a food processor. Work the paste with 8 ounces (250 grams) butter and strain the mixture through a drum sieve. Yield: 13 ounces (375 grams)

SNAIL BUTTER

Combine 2 finely chopped shallots, 1 garlic clove worked to a paste (in a mortar or crushed with the side of a knife on a cutting board), and 2 tablespoons (30 milliliters) finely chopped parsley with 12 ounces (350 grams) butter. Season with salt and pepper. Yield: 14 ounces (400 grams)

SWEET RED PEPPER BUTTER

This butter is excellent on grilled fish and vegetables or for finishing more complex fish sauces. Combine 4 ounces (125 grams) grilled and peeled sweet red peppers with 8 ounces (250 grams) butter. Force the butter through a drum sieve. Yield: 13 ounces (375 grams)

TARRAGON BUTTER

This is, justifiably, one of the most popular of the herb butters. Blanch 2 ounces (50 grams) fresh tarragon leaves for 1 minute in boiling salted water. Refresh the leaves and dry them on a towel. Grind the blanched leaves with a mortar and pestle or in a food processor. Combine the tarragon paste with 8 ounces (250 grams) butter. Yield: 11 ounces (300 grams)

TOMATO BUTTER

Combine ¼ cup (60 milliliters) thick tomato coulis (page 507) with 8 ounces (250 grams) butter. This butter is excellent on all grilled foods and as a decorative finish for hot soups. Adding 1 teaspoon (5 milliliters) good wine vinegar will enhance its flavor. Yield: 10 ounces (300 grams)

TRUFFLE BUTTER

Traditional recipes combine 4 ounces (125 grams) fresh black truffles with 8 ounces (250 grams) butter strained through a drum sieve. This is an extravagance that few restaurants (even those that serve truffles) can afford. A more economical method, which is exciting in its subtlety, is to unwrap butter and store it overnight in a tightly sealed jar with fresh truffles. The next day the butter will reek of the truffles and can be used on top of grilled or sautéed foods, or to give an ineffable, fleeting complexity to other sauces. Yield: 8 ounces (225 grams)

Coral Butters

Coral butters can be approached in several ways, depending on how they will be used. When destined to finish a sauce, the raw coral is typically worked with an equal amount of butter (by volume—it's okay to eye it) and forced through a fine-mesh drum sieve.

When coral butters are served as an accompaniment to foods such as grilled fish, some chefs prefer to cook the coral for a minute or two before working it with the butter. Raw coral will, however, always have more subtlety and a brighter flavor than cooked. When using raw coral to prepare compound butters, it must be impeccably fresh. Raw coral, especially lobster coral, is extremely perishable and should be used within hours of killing the lobsters.

Lobster coral that has been forced through a sieve along with the tomalley, however, will be too liquid to be added in any quantity to butter. This mixture is best combined with a small amount of cream rather than butter for use in sauce making.

When a hot sauce is finished with coral butter, do not allow the sauce to come to a boil or the coral will curdle and break. (For more about working with lobster coral, see page 330 in "Crustacean Sauces.")

SEA SCALLOP CORAL BUTTER

In the United States, sea scallops are usually sold already shucked without their bright orange coral. Not only is the coral wasted, but the scallops are never fresh, because they are extremely perishable, and once removed from the shell, they die.

When fresh scallops are available in the shell, they can be served with their coral, or the coral can be converted into a compound butter and used to finish a sauce or the scallops' poaching liquid. Purée equal parts by volume (exactness isn't important) of scallop coral and butter. Cream the two together and force the butter through a fine-mesh drum sieve. Don't use coral that's gray or unsightly.

SEA URCHIN ROE BUTTER

Sea urchin roe has a delicate, almost sweet sea-like flavor, making it perfect for fish sauces. If incorporated directly into a hot sauce, it will curdle, so it should first be strained through a drum sieve with approximately an equal amount of butter by volume **(see photo)**. Taste the sea urchin roe before using it in a sauce. If it has a strong, iodine flavor, it should not be used.

CAVIAR BUTTER

To make an authentic caviar butter with sturgeon caviar is an extravagance whose sum is worth less than its parts. The delicacy and complex flavor of sturgeon caviar is lost when it is heated, and its texture is completely eradicated when preparing the butter. Some chefs have prepared "caviar" butters with lumpfish roe, trout roe, salmon roe, and others, but the resulting butters can be only as good (and are rarely as good) as the raw ingredients.

Spice Butters

Practically any spice can be ground and creamed with butter so that it can be easily incorporated into a sauce at the last minute without the risk of forming lumps. Spices can be freshly ground in a small home coffee grinder. Some spices, such as those contained in curry—cardamom, fenugreek, coriander, cumin, turmeric, nutmeg—should be cooked for about a minute in a small amount of butter on the stove before being incorporated into the rest of the butter. This wakes up their flavor, especially if they are a bit stale.

Herb Butters

Almost any herb can be chopped and worked with butter to form a compound butter. The method works especially well with such herbs as basil, thyme, and tarragon, which quickly turn black once chopped. Certain classic green butters, such as Chivry Butter and Montpellier Butter (pages 443 and 444), make use of several herbs that are first blanched in boiling salted water before being chopped or crushed in a mortar and worked with the butter. Traditionally, herb butters were prepared by first crushing the herbs with a mortar and pestle before combining them with the butter and straining through a drum sieve. Nowadays most chefs chop the herbs, combine them with the butter in a food processor, and omit the last step of straining. Whichever method is used, it is best to let herb butters sit for an hour or two before they are used to allow the herb flavors to permeate the butter.

Liver Butters

Many sauces, especially deeply flavored sauces for game, benefit by being finished with a compound butter prepared with the animal's liver. Sometimes the heart and gizzard can also be used, as well as a small amount of ground juniper berries, which help reinforce the sauce's gamy flavor. Sauces finished with liver butter have an opaque, almost muddy appearance that is sometimes startling to people used to translucent brown sauces finished with butter.

PIGEON SAUCE

The most obvious method for cooking a tender young pigeon is to roast it and prepare a jus. The jus can then be finished with a compound butter prepared with approximately equal parts of butter and the pigeon's liver, heart, gizzard, and lungs. In a restaurant setting, it is often more practical to remove the pigeon suprêmes and to prepare the giblet-juniper butter and a jus with the pigeon carcass in advance. The suprêmes are then sautéed to order, the pan deglazed with the jus, and the sauce finished with the giblet-juniper butter. (See Sautéed Pigeon Breasts with Giblet Sauce, page 116.)

FOIE GRAS BUTTER

Foie gras is excellent for finishing sauces. Because of its high fat content, it will thicken a sauce and remain smooth provided it is not allowed to boil. When using partially cooked foie gras (*mi-cuit*) or terrine of American foie gras, mash together about equal parts foie gras and butter, then force the mixture through a fine-mesh drum sieve. Avoid using raw foie gras, which contains too much water.

Because foie gras butter is inherently unstable, it is a sound idea to add 2% liquid lecithin to the foie gras–butter mixture. Propylene glycol alginate (0.5%) can also be blended into a sauce's hot liquid base for further stability.

WHIPPED BUTTERS

These butters are essentially compound butters that have been lightened and flavored with a relatively large amount of flavorful liquid, and to which whipped cream is added. They are usually served in a sauceboat, so diners can serve themselves, but they can be made especially dramatic and frothy by piping with a whipping siphon. Whipped butters offer a greater range of possibilities than the better-known compound butters because of the flavorful liquids they contain.

WHIPPED BUTTER FOR GRILLED OR SAUTÉED FISH

YIELD: 8 TO 10 SERVINGS

butter	8 ounces	250 grams
warm (not hot) flavorful liquid (see note)	½ cup	125 milliliters
good-quality wine vinegar (or to taste)	3 tablespoons	45 milliliters
salt and pepper	to taste	to taste
heavy cream	½ cup	125 milliliters

1. Soften the butter in a stand mixer equipped with a paddle blade.

2. When the butter is soft, put the whisk attachment on the mixer and whip the butter while slowly adding the flavoring liquid. Slowly add vinegar to taste. Whip the butter until it is light and airy, usually for about 8 minutes. Season with salt and pepper.

3. Season the cream with salt and pepper. Whip the cream and fold it with the butter.

Note: Any appropriate flavorful liquid, such as mussel or clam cooking liquid, reduced court-bouillon, good fish stock, or fish cooking liquid, can be used.

Whipped Butter Variations

Whipped butters can be based on stocks, cooking liquids, vegetable purées, or infusions whipped into appropriate compound butters. A whipped butter for grilled chicken might consist of brown chicken stock reduced with shallots or garlic and finished with tarragon, tomato, sweet red pepper, or mustard butter. Whipped butters for fish can be based on court-bouillon, fish stock, or the fresh cooking liquid from the poached or braised fish. Red wine whipped butter for fish can be prepared using red wine fish sauce (see page 224) as a base and finished with herb butters, crustacean butters, or coral butters.

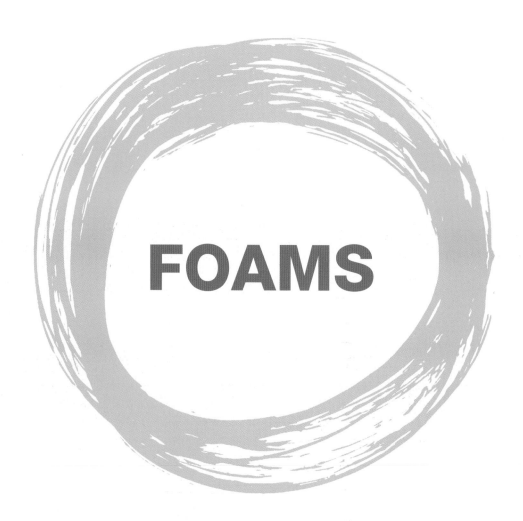

FOAMS

A foam or froth (a froth is simply a foam with larger bubbles) is like an emulsion, except that it includes a gas, usually air, carbon dioxide, or nitrous oxide. Whether fluid or stiff, foams may function as sauces because they provide flavor and textural contrast. To stabilize the foam and prevent the bubbles from coalescing and collapsing, hydrocolloids are often added. Ideally, they should be surfactants that coat the gas bubbles and keep them from deflating.

While many of us associate culinary foams with the delicate and rarefied versions served as a part of modernist cuisine, foams have long been used in traditional cooking. Culinary uses of foams include cakes, breads, marshmallows, soufflés, and mousses.

Modernist foams differ from traditional foams because they contain any number of novel compounds unheard of in the classic kitchen. While traditional foams are based on beaten egg whites (soufflés, mousses) or whipped cream (mousses, frozen soufflés), modernist foams use a number of foaming agents (methylcellulose, xanthan gum, alginates, albumin, lecithin, and carrageenans, to name a few) and stabilizers. The kind of stabilizer used for a foam depends on the nature of the foam—what's holding it together.

Modernist culinary foams include fat-based foams (cream, cocoa butter, coconut cream, foie gras fat, butter), starch-based foams (potato starch, gelatinized starch such as Wondra), egg foams (egg yolks, egg whites), and foams made from methylcellulose. Each of these foams reacts differently to stabilizers. For example, a stabilizer used for a fat-based foam may have an entirely negative reaction with a protein-based foam such as an egg foam.

In addition to these odd-sounding compounds, modernist foams also use some different devices than traditional foams such as that for a soufflé. When choosing what instrument to use to make a foam, consider how it will incorporate air or the appropriate gas. Traditional implements such as whisks and immersion blenders can sometimes be used to make modernist foams, but in many cases, there are more efficient implements. The classic whipping siphon used in restaurants for whipped cream may very well be the most useful foam-making instrument in the modernist kitchen. It forces pressurized nitrous oxide into whatever liquid is placed in the container. When the liquid is ejected into the atmosphere, the nitrous oxide expands and turns the liquid into a foam.

At times, foams are made in a vacuum chamber. When a liquid is placed in a sealed container that is connected to a vacuum pump, it will expand into a foam. The problem is getting the foam to set so it keeps its shape and consistency when the vacuum is removed. The usual solutions, depending on the nature of the foam, are to either heat or chill the foam, so that it sets, before releasing the vacuum.

When making a foam, remember that you must incorporate gas. While highly useful for making emulsions, devices such as blenders and rotor stator homogenizers (see page 35) are useless for making foams because they don't beat in enough air. You can prepare a foam with an immersion blender as long as you use the flat blade, which incorporates more air, and hold it near the surface of the liquid so that air is introduced into the liquid.

Foams are divided into several categories. Fat-based foams include cream or cocoa butter or foie gras fat. When a foaming agent and stabilizer are added to the fat base, novel effects, such as hot whipped cream, can be achieved. Egg foams are familiar—egg yolks make sabayon, egg whites make meringue, and whole separated eggs make soufflés—but piping with a siphon allows almost any liquid that contains fat to expand into a foam once released from the siphon. Most sauces can be held in a whipping siphon and the siphon held sous vide to an exact temperature without the risk of the sauce breaking.

Some foams can be served hot or cold, while others are limited to a more narrow range of temperatures. A fat-based foam, for example, mustn't get too hot or the sauce will break and the fat separate. Gelatin foams must be kept cold or the gelatin will melt and the foam fall apart.

Most foams benefit from some kind of stabilizer. Carrageenan and locust bean gum stabilize hot dairy foams. Alginates stabilize hollandaise, whipped cream, and beer foam.

One of the most difficult problems when making foams is a lack or lightness of flavor. This is because most of a foam's volume is flavorless gas. Relatively little liquid remains (liquid is the main carrier of flavor) and the foam may have too little taste. Foams reinforced with sugar, such as meringue, often circumvent this problem because they can be made with strongly flavored ingredients such as chocolate or coffee. But savory foams, in addition to being less stable, carry flavor less efficiently than liquid. Hence, foams are often flavored with essential oils, which can be extremely strong. Foams also work well with roasted nut oils (Leblanc brand are the best) and flavorful ingredients such as garlic, truffles, reduced mushroom cooking liquid, reduced seafood braising liquids, grated orange zest (or orange essential oil), and chiles.

When buying essential oils, make sure they are food safe. Some natural and anodyne-sounding extracts can actually be toxic. When working with a natural oil or absolute (see page 72), dilute it with ethanol (not denatured) or 100-proof vodka to 20%. To flavor your foam, add the alcohol dilution a drop at a time until the foam has the right flavor intensity.

TRUFFLE BUTTER FOAM

One of the great things about this foam is that you don't need to cut into your truffle to get at its flavor. The aroma of a nice stinky truffle is infused directly into butter by storing it overnight with the truffle, sealed in an airtight jar. This recipe is also a template for converting any full-flavored liquid, such as juices, infusions, and full-flavored stock (or, better, consommé), into a foam. It can also be flavored rather strongly with ingredients like herbs, spices, or mushrooms. Stabilizers thicken the full-flavored liquid and make it receptive to emulsification with butter.

YIELD: ABOUT 2¼ CUPS (560 MILLILITERS) LIQUID; TWICE AS MUCH WHEN CONVERTED INTO A FOAM

smelly truffle	1	1
unsalted butter	8 ounces	250 grams
versawhip (modified soy protein)		1.75 grams
locust bean gum		0.7 gram
water	¼ cup	60 milliliters
hot flavorful liquid, such as stock infused with full-flavored herbs or spices or truffle juice	1 cup	250 milliliters
salt	to taste	to taste

1. Store the truffle with the butter overnight in a tightly sealed jar.

2. Combine the Versawhip, locust bean gum, and water to make a slurry. Incorporate the slurry into the hot flavorful liquid and heat gently until the mixture thickens.

3. Remove the truffle from the butter and melt the butter. In a blender, blend the thickened liquid into the melted butter. Season with salt.

4. Put in a siphon and let cool for 30 minutes before piping out.

COLD NEROLI FOAM

Unlike *petitgrain*, a relatively inexpensive orange essential oil distilled from orange leaves and twigs, neroli is an essential oil made from the flowers. It is not cheap, but it has an exquisite aroma and is so potent that just a drop of 20% solution (as described on page 452) will perfume a lot of foam. You could also add a drop or two of tuberose essential oil, although it is intensely floral and not to everyone's taste. Add it to the base a drop at a time and evaluate the intensity of the aroma before adding more. Don't expect to get a lot of flavor out of this foam, but the aroma, wafting up as the foam is served, perhaps with a delicate dessert, is irresistible.

YIELD: ABOUT 1¼ CUPS (300 MILLILITERS) LIQUID; TWICE AS MUCH WHEN CONVERTED INTO FOAM

water	¾ cup	200 milliliters
versawhip		4 grams
xanthan gum		0.4 gram
20% neroli essential oil	6 drops (or to taste)	6 drops (or to taste)
sugar	½ cup	100 grams
citric acid		1 gram

Combine the water, Versawhip, and xanthan gum in a stand mixer and beat until fluffy. The foam should have the consistency of beaten egg whites. Add the essential oil, sugar, and citric acid. Beat until the sugar and citric acid are dissolved. (Some people like the crunch of undissolved sugar and citric acid, while others prefer them totally integrated.) Use immediately. Pipe with a pastry bag or siphon.

WHITE WINE FOAM

Most wine used in the kitchen ends up being exposed to heat, which destroys its identity and character. Wines used in cold dishes, however, do not require heat, and so their individuality is retained.

Wine alone in a cold dish usually tastes sour, which may be fine if you're serving the foam with shellfish or delicate seafood. Sugar attenuates this acidity and brings out the flavor of the wine. The sugar in this foam may need to be adjusted. This foam also contains xanthan gum to help stabilize it. When this foam is released from a whipping siphon, it has the consistency of shaving cream.

YIELD: 1¾ CUPS (400 MILLILITERS) LIQUID; TWICE AS MUCH WHEN CONVERTED INTO FOAM

sugar	½ cup	125 milliliters (or as needed)
hot, but not boiling, water	½ cup	115 milliliters
gelatin, preferably sheet		6 grams
xanthan gum		0.4 gram
white wine (see note)	1¼ cups	300 milliliters

1. Stir the sugar into the hot water until it dissolves; if it has trouble dissolving, heat the mixture as needed. Set aside until barely warm.

2. Soften the gelatin in a bowl of cold water for about 5 minutes, then wring out excess water. (If you're using powdered gelatin, combine it with 2 tablespoons [30 milliliters] cold water and let it "bloom" for 10 minutes.)

3. Blend the xanthan gum into the sugar-water mixture until dissolved. Add the wine and gelatin. If necessary, warm the mixture, while stirring, just enough to dissolve the gelatin. Don't let it get too hot or you'll compromise the foam's flavor; the wine should never get much hotter than body temperature. If the liquid is still warm, let it cool to room temperature.

4. Transfer to a siphon; charge with 1 to 2 cylinders for a pint (500 milliliter) siphon. Chill overnight for best results before piping to serve.

Note: Wines such as Riesling (Alsatian or German), Chablis, Gewürztraminer, white Burgundy (if feeling extravagant) such as Meursault or Puligny-Montrachet, Sauternes, and Coteaux Champenois (still Champagne) all work well.

COLD FRUIT JUICE FOAM

Fruit juice foams are easy to make because they only involve combining the juice with gelatin. Some juices, such as passion fruit, are very intense and very sour and will require sugar, best dissolved into a thick syrup, before it is added. Other juices, such as orange or grapefruit juice, may not seem flavorful enough and can be reduced, ideally in a vacuum (see page 36). Citrus juices also benefit from the flavor of blanched zest, infused in a small amount of water and strained into the juice.

YIELD: ABOUT 3 CUPS (700 MILLILITERS) LIQUID; TWICE AS MUCH WHEN CONVERTED INTO FOAM

powdered gelatin or leaf gelatin	¼ ounce	8 grams
cold water for blooming powdered gelatin	6 tablespoons	90 milliliters
fruit juice	2½ cups	625 milliliters
concentrated sugar solution	as needed	as needed

1. Bloom the powdered gelatin in the cold water or soak leaf gelatin in a bowl of cold water for about 5 minutes.

2. Barely warm the juice to body temperature. (Heating the juice unnecessarily destroys much of its fresh flavor.)

3. Remove the juice from the heat and stir in the gelatin until dissolved(if using leaf gelatin, wring out excess water first). Sweeten with sugar solution as desired. Put the mixture into a siphon and chill the siphon so the mixture sets, for about an hour or, better, overnight, before piping to serve.

TOMATO (OR OTHER JUICE) FOAM

This recipe illustrates the efficacy and versatility of powdered lecithin to create foams from a variety of juices.

YIELD: 1 QUART (1 LITER) LIQUID; TWICE AS MUCH WHEN CONVERTED INTO FOAM

tomato juice, or other juice	1 quart	1 liter
powdered lecithin		5 grams
sugar	to taste	to taste

Combine all the ingredients in a mixing bowl. Blend the mixture with an immersion blender until well combined. Transfer to a stand mixer and beat until a foam forms on top, where it can be skimmed off. Let rest for 1 minute before serving.

COLD LEMON PASTIS FOAM

At Chez Panisse, chef Jeremiah Tower served a plate of raw oysters, each one anointed with one drop of pastis, the inspiration for this foam. This foam is very delicate, and great on seafood such as oysters or cold lobster. Pastis is the generic name for anise-flavored aperitifs such as Ricard and Pernod; any of these will do the trick.

The foam given here is emulsified with lecithin. This is a very light foam, but it can be made more or less substantial by increasing or decreasing the amount of lecithin. This foam also contains a small amount of xanthan gum to stabilize it, but it can be left out if you're looking for a very delicate froth.

The base liquid can be virtually anything, provided it contains no fat, which would interfere with the lecithin. For seafood, mussel cooking liquid is particularly good, but court-bouillon (ideally concentrated by reduction under vacuum; see page 36) works well, as do fish stock (which must be impeccably fresh) and the liquor released by oysters when they're shucked. Reduced mushroom cooking liquid can also be used (alone or in combination with other flavorful liquids), but it lends a rather sad, muted color to the whole thing.

YIELD: 1 CUP (250 MILLILITERS) LIQUID; TWICE AS MUCH WHEN CONVERTED INTO FOAM

xanthan gum		0.6 gram
lemon juice	3 tablespoons	45 milliliters
pastis, such as ricard or pernod	8 to 12 drops (to taste; must be subtle)	
sugar	2 teaspoons (or more to taste)	10 grams (or more to taste)
powdered lecithin		2.5 grams
flavorful liquid (see note)	¾ cup	200 milliliters

1. Blend the xanthan gum, lemon juice, pastis, sugar, and lecithin into the base liquid until all the ingredients dissolve. The pastis should be barely perceptible. If you can't taste the pastis at all, add more, one drop at a time, until you just reach the taste threshold and you can barely taste it.

2. Beat with a stand mixer, electric whisk, or balloon whisk until you see copious foam. Once the amount of foam you're producing no longer seems to increase, stop beating. Wait a couple of minutes for the foam to settle. (Liquid will be released underneath the foam.) Serve immediately.

Note: Choose an appropriately flavored liquid such as raw oyster liquor, mussel cooking liquid, reduced mushroom cooking liquid, court-bouillon (ideally, reduced), fish or chicken stock or broth (carefully skimmed of fat), fennel braising liquid, or seafood braising liquid.

HOT CURRY AND COCONUT FOAM

Cooking curry powder in a little butter before adding it to a mix of coconut milk and coconut cream brings out the curry's flavor and creates a fat-based foam. This foam makes a delicate topping for seafood and chicken.

YIELD: 1¼ CUPS (300 MILLILITERS) LIQUID; TWICE AS MUCH WHEN CONVERTED INTO FOAM

curry powder	1 heaping teaspoon	5 grams
butter	1 tablespoon	15 grams
coconut cream	3 fluid ounces	100 milliliters
coconut milk	3 fluid ounces	100 milliliters
powdered lecithin		3 grams
iota carrageenan		0.75 gram
cold water	¼ cup	60 milliliters

1. Heat the curry powder in the butter in a small saucepan until the curry aroma wafts from the pan. Immediately cool by plunging the bottom of the pan in a bowl of cold water (don't bother with ice) and leaving it there for a few seconds.

2. Blend together the coconut cream and coconut milk and whisk in the curry mixture until evenly distributed. Blend in the powdered lecithin.

3. In a separate saucepan, blend together the iota carrageenan and the water. Heat the mixture to 176°F (80°C) and blend the dissolved carrageenan into the coconut mixture. Immediately (the iota carrageenan must be hot and sets very quickly) transfer to a siphon and charge with 2 cylinders for a 1-pint (500 milliliter) siphon or 4 cylinders for a 1-quart (1 liter) siphon. Hold the siphon in a bain-marie or sous vide immersion bath at 158°F (70°C) for 2 hours before piping.

SABAYON FOR FOAMS AND EMULSIFIED SAUCES

For many of us, the notion of preparing a sabayon—in which a degree or two shift in temperature may cause it to fail—is intimidating, to say the least. Take this to a grand scale—you have to make a sabayon with, say, a hundred egg yolks—and you've a recipe for terror, not sabayon.

To alleviate this worry, you're best off cooking the egg yolks sous vide. In this way you can be sure to hit the temperature right on. There's no chance of curdling or undercooking because the temperature of the surrounding water bath is set to the exact needed temperature.

In classic French cooking, savory sabayons are mainly used as precursors to emulsified egg yolk sauces such as hollandaise. But in today's more foam-centric kitchens, a sabayon is often served, seasoned and flavored, with no additional fat at all.

In modernist cooking, a sabayon is often made by combining barely cooked yolks with flavorful liquids. The mixture, instead of being beaten directly into a foam, is combined with small amounts of flavorful liquids and piped out at the last minute from a siphon. This last-minute use of the siphon is what gives the foam its final airiness, meaning once cooked to the appropriate temperature, virtually any flavorful liquid can be integrated into the sabayon. Instead of being beaten over heat on the stove, frothing occurs by nitrous oxide expanding as the sabayon is ejected from the nozzle. Sabayons made in this way are much more stable than those made by hand. They are also more convenient during a busy service than whisking up individual sabayons by hand.

HOT SAVORY SABAYON AS A SAUCE BASE OR SIMPLE FOAM

Use flavorful liquid such as broth, infusions of herbs and teas, vinegar (diluted with water), fortified wines (especially fino sherry—which is dry—or Madeira) with the alcohol burned off, fruit or vegetable juices (reduced or not, with heat or vacuum or shellfish cooking liquid. In a pinch, use water.

YIELD: 1¾ CUPS (450 MILLILITERS) LIQUID; TWICE AS MUCH WHEN CONVERTED INTO FOAM

egg yolks	20	20
water or flavorful liquid	1¼ cups	300 milliliters
salt and pepper	to taste	to taste

1. Whisk the egg yolks until smooth and seal in a heavy plastic bag. Cook sous vide for 30 minutes at 140°F (60°C).

2. Warm the liquid to the same temperature (or a little lower) than the sous vide water (just put your hand in the water and do it by feel; err on the side of being too cool). If the liquid is too hot, it may curdle the yoks.

3. Whisk together the yolks and liquid in a mixing bowl until the yolks are evenly dispersed. Season with salt and pepper. Transfer to a whipping siphon and hold in a bain-marie or sous vide immersion bath at 140°F (60°C). Use as needed.

VARIATION

This sauce is similar to Sauce Vin Blanc (page 221), in which white wine is whisked up into a sabayon and butter added in the manner of a hollandaise. Sauce Marguery (page 304) is similar except that it is based on a white wine braising liquid from sole. Virtually any proportion of butter can be added to the recipe above, as a little as a teaspoon per serving to eight times as much; a sabayon is able to absorb a large amount of butter.

HOT FOIE GRAS FOAM

You don't need to use beautiful whole slices of foie gras to make this foam; just the fat will do. Foie gras fat—the fat that is rendered when foie gras is cooked in a terrine or *en torchon*—is a delicious alternative to butter, duck fat, or goose fat. While normally insoluble in liquid, here Glice (mono- and diglycerides) helps the fat to emulsify.

YIELD: ABOUT ½ CUP (100 MILLILITERS) LIQUID; TWICE AS MUCH WHEN CONVERTED INTO FOAM

foie gras fat	3½ ounces	100 grams
liquid lecithin		2 grams
mono- and diglycerides (glice)		1.7 gram

Heat the foie gras fat to 140°F (60°C) and stir in the lecithin and Glice until they dissolve. Transfer to a siphon and hold in a sous-vide bath at 140°F (60°C) for at least 20 minutes. Pipe as needed.

WARM CARAMELIZED BUTTER (GHEE) FOAM

Ghee, or caramelized butter (sometimes called beurre noisette) in which the milk solids have been allowed to brown, lends a nutty, buttery flavor to all manner of sauces and foams. Normally, ghee doesn't dissolve in water or other liquid. However, in the presence of the right compounds (such as egg yolks or certain hydrocolloids such as the sucrose esters used here) it can be used to create an emulsion.

YIELD: 1¼ CUPS (280 MILLILITERS) LIQUID; TWICE AS MUCH WHEN CONVERTED INTO FOAM

heavy cream	¼ cup	60 milliliters
skim milk	¼ cup	60 milliliters
sucrose esters		0.7 gram
ghee (page 438), warm but not hot	¾ cup	175 milliliters

Combine the cream and skim milk and warm over medium heat; do not boil. Off the heat, blend in the sucrose esters. Once the sucrose esters have been incorporated, blend in the ghee in a steady stream. Chill overnight in a whipping siphon. The next morning, warm in a sous vide immersion bath at 95°F (35°C) for about an hour before piping to serve.

RIESLING SPOOM

Most of the time the particular character of a wine is lost in cooking: The basic structure and body may remain, but any finesse and identity are lost. Strangely, however, when fine wines are sweetened with sugar syrup, the character of the wine emerges in such a way that it's easy to identify the varietal and even the region. Alsatian Riesling is a good choice for this foam because of its strong varietal character and its high acidity; the high acidity allows the addition of more sugar, which stabilizes the spoom.

This recipe uses a vacuum method in which the spoom expands considerably. Unlike the usual method of applying vacuum to a liquid in an Erlenmeyer flask, a spoom or other foam requires a vessel you can ultimately reach into with a spoon to serve. You'll need a large jar or beaker (at least 1½ quarts/1.5 liters), with a tight-fitting stopper; the stopper should have a hole in the middle with a tight-fitting 6-inch (9 centimeter) piece of glass tubing to connect with the vacuum pump, usually via rubber tubing. This may require an adapter. If you don't have a setup for vacuum, prepare the spoom in the same way and just leave out the vacuum step and freeze the mixture in a bowl. The spoom won't be as impressively foamy, but it will be as delicious.

YIELD: 5 CUPS (1.25 LITERS), 10 SERVINGS

sugar	1¾ cups	340 grams
water	¾ cup	180 milliliters
alsatian riesling or other wine with strong varietal identity, 1 bottle	3 cups	750 milliliters
albumin powder		2 grams

1. Combine the sugar and water and bring to a simmer. Stir until the sugar dissolves. Remove from the heat and let cool.

2. Combine the sugar syrup with the Riesling and taste the mixture to make sure it has the right balance of acidity and sweetness. Add more sugar (dissolve it first in water) if need be.

3. Stir in the albumin and beat the mixture in a stand mixer for 4 minutes on high speed, until fluffy.

4. Transfer to a vacuum chamber—be sure to leave room for the mixture to expand by as much as 100%—and apply a vacuum. (See page 36 for instructions.)

5. Once the mixture has expanded, seal off the rubber tubing leading to the vacuum pump so the vacuum doesn't come undone, and detach the tubing from the pump. Put the mixture in the freezer for about 4 hours to firm up.

6. Take off the lid and serve as you would if serving sorbet.

461

SALAD SAUCES, VINAIGRETTES, SALSAS, AND RELISHES

These sauces are also called simple or independent sauces because they are prepared independently of the foods they accompany. They are the opposite of integral sauces, because they derive none of their character from the preparation itself. They do not require stock, because they are designed to contrast and complement rather than underline and reinforce a food's basic flavors. (Other sauces, such as mayonnaise, béchamel, and hollandaise, also function in this way.) Independent sauces can be simple or complex. Sometimes the simplest natural products make the best sauces. Cold-pressed extra-virgin olive oil dribbled over a piece of grilled fish can be more appropriate and satisfying than a complicated, artfully prepared lobster sauce.

Independent sauces can be prepared from an infinite variety of flavorful ingredients that are usually infused in an appropriate medium such as cream, vinegar, oil, or vegetable purée. They can also be simple mixtures of finely chopped fruits and vegetables (as in salsas), combinations of pickled ingredients (relishes), or more elaborate sweet-and-sour concoctions (chutneys).

Hydrocolloids such as Ultra-Sperse 3 (a tapioca derivative) and xanthan gum can be added to these sauces to prevent syneresis (the tendency of purée-based sauces to separate) and, when appropriate, to function as thickeners.

CREAM-BASED COLD SAUCES

Cream is an excellent medium for cold sauces because it both emulsifies and carries flavor. Because of its delicate, almost neutral taste, it is a useful backdrop for flavorful ingredients that would be too aggressive if used alone.

American heavy cream is usually too thin to be used directly for a cold sauce base. Several methods can be used to thicken it to the desired consistency. One of the simplest is to combine it with a small amount of acidic liquid such as lemon juice, lime juice, verjuice, or vinegar. Cream thickened in this way can then be used as a medium for a wide variety of flavorful ingredients and can then be served with cold meats, fish, and vegetables and as a salad dressing. Heavy cream can also be thickened in the same way as crème fraîche, by inoculating it with an active culture found in buttermilk, sour cream, or yogurt. The bacteria secrete lactic acid that causes the cream to thicken. To achieve these results instantaneously, simply add lactic acid to the cream and it will thicken. The quickest method for thickening cream without adding any other ingredients is, of course, to whip it lightly. When whipping cream, make sure that the cream, the bowl, and the whisk have been well chilled. In hot weather, it is a good idea to whisk the cream over ice. You can also use a whipping siphon (see page 32).

HERB-SCENTED THICKENED CREAM FOR SALADS

Several kinds of herbs can be infused and used to flavor heavy cream or crème fraîche. The herbs are first crushed with a mortar and pestle or finely chopped with lemon juice, lime juice, or vinegar. The cream is then whisked into the infusion. If regular heavy cream is used, it will thicken after a few minutes.

Herb-scented cream can be lightly spooned over cold fish and meats, but it is most often used as a sauce for salads. When flavored with mint or dill, it can be served with sliced cucumbers that have been seeded, salted, and drained to remove excess water. When flavored with freshly chopped cilantro and Tabasco, it makes an excellent dressing for a salad of tomatoes, cucumbers, grilled peppers, onions, garlic, and fennel. Or it can be used as a dressing for a simple green salad.

YIELD: 1 CUP (250 MILLILITERS)

fresh herb leaves (see note)	1 to 2 tablespoons	15 to 30 milliliters
coarse salt	½ to 1 teaspoon	3 to 5 milliliters
lemon or lime juice, wine vinegar, or verjuice	2 tablespoons	30 milliliters
heavy cream	1 cup	250 milliliters

1. Combine the herb leaves and coarse salt in a mortar or wooden bowl. Grind the herbs with the salt (the salt helps work the mixture into a purée) using a pestle or the back of a wooden spoon.

2. Stir in the lemon juice. Continue stirring until the salt dissolves. Stir in the cream.

3. Let the mixture rest for 5 to 10 minutes in the refrigerator, until the cream thickens.

Note: Marjoram, oregano, mint, thyme, and dill are some of the possibilities. The amount to use depends on the strength of the herb's flavor; for example, marjoram is stronger than mint, so a smaller amount of marjoram would be used. A tiny pinch of sugar will sometimes pick up and amplify an herb's flavor; this works especially well with mint.

CULTURED CREAM

When Americans see crème fraîche, the French equivalent of American heavy cream, they usually assume that because it is thick, it is richer and more flavorful than its American counterpart. The thick texture results not from richness but from the bacterial culture it contains, which contributes acidity. The acidity in turn causes the cream to thicken and gives it a delicate tang.

Although the flavor of authentic crème fraîche cannot be duplicated with American ingredients, heavy cream can be cultured so that it thickens. Combine 2 tablespoons (30 milliliters) buttermilk or sour cream with 2 cups (500 milliliters) heavy cream, and gently heat the mixture to body temperature in a saucepan. Transfer the cream to a stainless-steel, glass, or porcelain container. Keep it covered in a warm place until it thickens, usually about 24 hours. As soon as the cream thickens, refrigerate it. It will keep for at least a week, usually longer. Yield: 2 cups (500 milliliters)

If you're in a mad rush and need crème fraîche right away, consider working in a small amount of lactic acid (which you can buy in powdered form online). Lactic acid is the same compound produced by bacteria during fermentation, so the effect is almost identical.

YOGURT-BASED COLD SAUCES

In addition to its usefulness as a thickener for hot sauces, yogurt is an excellent medium for cold sauces and can be used in much the same way as thickened cream. It is less rich than cream and has a refreshing tang that is especially pleasant in the summer. It is often used in Indian and Middle Eastern cooking.

There are several types of yogurt available, ranging from very light yogurt made from skimmed milk to thick Middle Eastern–style leben yogurt that almost has the consistency of fresh cheese. When using yogurt in salads, a thicker yogurt works best because the vegetables in the salad will continue to release liquid into the sauce, thinning it and diluting its flavor.

One of the simplest yogurt sauces is for the Indian raita, a cucumber salad flavored with mint or cilantro and sometimes minced garlic and hot peppers. The Greeks have another version, a sort of light-style skorthaliá that contains garlic, almonds, and parsley, which they serve over cold vegetables. Yogurt can also be flavored with herbs, with colorful purées made from sweet peppers or tomatoes, with onions, or with shallots, to create a variety of light spreads for cold or grilled foods. These simple sauce variations can also be used to finish hot sauces for fish and vegetables (see "Finishing Sauces with Yogurt," page 125).

Because yogurt contains a relatively high amount of protein compared to heavy cream, it tends to separate when heated. To prevent this, add a small amount of lambda carrageenan (about 2%) to the yogurt to stabilize it.

MINT AND CILANTRO YOGURT SAUCE

This bright green sauce is excellent served with barbecued foods such as chicken or full-flavored fish. If desired, you can include lambda carrageenan to stabilize the sauce.

YIELD: 1½ CUPS (375 MILLILITERS)

plain yogurt	10 tablespoons	150 milliliters
lambda carrageenan (optional)		3 grams
water (optional)	2 teaspoons	10 milliliters
onion, finely chopped	2 tablespoons	30 milliliters
fresh ginger, finely chopped	¼ teaspoon	2 milliliters
jalapeños, finely chopped	2	2
fresh mint, leaves only	1 bunch	1 bunch
fresh cilantro, leaves only	1 bunch	1 bunch
salt and pepper	to taste	to taste

Drain the yogurt in a coffee filter for an hour or so to eliminate excess water. If using the carrageenan, soak it in the water until smooth and hydrated. Combine the drained yogurt, onion, ginger, jalapeños, mint, cilantro, and the carrageenan and its soaking liquid, if using, in a food processor. Process for 15 to 30 seconds, until the ingredients are finely chopped and the mixture is smooth. Season with salt and pepper.

OILS, VINEGARS, AND VINAIGRETTES

Oil and vinegar have long been used as condiments for grilled foods and salads. First-pressed extra-virgin olive oil has a finesse and depth of flavor that surpass those of many a more complicated sauce. Because it is a completely natural product subject to variations in climate and soil, its flavor, like that of wine, is never completely predictable. Perhaps it is these subtle variations in flavor that make it possible to use olive oil throughout the year in all sorts of preparations without the flavor ever becoming monotonous.

Other flavorful oils, such as nut oils, can of course be used alone as condiments or combined with vinegar in vinaigrettes. Inert-tasting oils, such as grapeseed or safflower oil, are sometimes used to attenuate their more assertive cousins.

If you're using extra-virgin olive oil, avoid using a blender or rotor stator homogenizer (see page 35). When beaten, extra-virgin olive oil turns bitter. (Not everyone perceives this, but for those who do, it ruins the oil.) To avoid this, make a vinaigrette base using an inert-tasting oil such as safflower oil; avocado oil is the best of all because it's tasteless (it is, however, expensive). Then work the olive oil into it with a wooden spoon.

Flavored Oils

For centuries, Mediterranean cooks have been putting sprigs of herbs in jars of olive oil and using the infused oils for salads, to baste roasting meats, and as condiments for grilled fish. Recently chefs have taken a more aggressive approach to infused oils and have been experimenting with blanching and puréeing a wide variety of herbs and vegetables to create full-flavored and brightly colored oils that can be emulsified with other ingredients or served on their own. Flavored oils can also be prepared from a variety of spices and from concentrated vegetable juices. Although no less rich than butter, these oils contain no cholesterol and have a brightness of color and flavor that is a welcome relief to the butter-weary diner.

Several approaches can be used when preparing flavored oils. The first and more traditional method is a simple infusion: Flavorful ingredients are left to steep in the oil for up to several weeks. Similarly but less traditionally, they may be cooked together sous vide for several hours. The oil is then strained or poured off as it is needed. Another method involves combining a purée with the oil (for example, basil, truffle, stewed red peppers). The purée is then either strained out or left dispersed in the oil, resulting in a full-flavored and often brightly colored oil that can be used alone or in combination with other ingredients as a decorative sauce. Spice-scented oils can also be prepared by first moistening a ground spice with part of the oil, then combining it with the remainder and allowing it to infuse for several days. Crustacean-flavored oils can be prepared in the same way as crustacean butter, by simply replacing the butter with an inert-tasting oil or a good olive oil. Some infused oils are best if the oil is kept cool while it is infusing—the delicacy of herbs such as basil or chervil is damaged by heat—but other ingredients require that the oil be warm so that it extracts the flavor of the ingredient more efficiently.

OILS FOR INFUSING

Select an oil whose flavor goes well with the ingredient being infused. Extra-virgin olive oil makes sense when the infusion is made with full-flavored herbs such as marjoram, thyme, lavender, rosemary, sage, basil, and oregano—typically Mediterranean flavors—but might take over the flavor of more delicate herbs such as chervil or parsley. For these, a less flavorful pure olive oil, perhaps with a small amount of extra-virgin olive oil added, allows the flavors of the herbs to come through more clearly. For other ingredients, such as spices, it makes more sense to use a completely inert-tasting oil such as canola, safflower, or grapeseed oil. For Asian ingredients such as ginger, Sichuan peppercorns, lemongrass, or star anise, an inert-tasting oil or peanut oil, perhaps with some dark sesame oil added for flavor, is far better than olive oil.

COLD-INFUSED METHOD

This is the most straightforward method for making infused oils and usually consists of simply shoving sprigs of herbs or coarsely chopped ingredients (such as orange rinds) through the neck of a bottle of oil. Some cold-infused oils (for example, basil oil) take only a day to make because the ingredients release their aroma and flavor very quickly into the surrounding oil. Other ingredients may require a week or two of infusion to reach optimum flavor. If the herbs are finely chopped or the leaves are detached from the branches, the oil will need to be strained through a fine-mesh strainer before it is used. Never use ground dried herbs. Because herb oils, especially cold-infused versions, may strengthen or weaken over time, it is best to taste them each time before they are used. Using a sous vide tank will shorten the infusion time from days to hours.

COLD-INFUSED HERB OIL

This oil is one of the simplest to make. Simply slide sprigs of full-flavored herbs through the neck of the bottle into the oil.

YIELD: 1 QUART (1 LITER)

fresh or dried marjoram, thyme, sage, lavender, rosemary, or oregano (enough so that the herbs loosely fill the bottle)	4 bunches	4 bunches
or	or	or
loose dried herbs	¼ cup	60 milliliters
extra-virgin olive oil	1 quart	1 liter

1. Wash the herbs under cold running water (use a strainer if the herbs are off the stem). Dry them thoroughly on a towel.

2. Combine the herbs with the olive oil (simply slide sprigs of herbs through the neck of the bottle).

3. Cork the bottle and store in a cool place, but not in the refrigerator, for at least a week or two and up to several months. Alternatively, cook the herb-oil mixture sous vide at 140°F (60°C) for 24 hours.

BASIL OR CHERVIL OIL

Basil and chervil have delicate flavors that infuse quickly into the surrounding oil. The herbs can be chopped in a blender or food processor, but they should not be processed for too long or the moisture contained in the herbs will emulsify with the oil and the finished oil will be cloudy.

YIELD: 1 QUART (1 LITER)

fresh basil leaves (6 large bunches)	6 tightly packed cups	1.4 liters
or	or	or
fresh chervil (15 large bunches)	6 tightly packed cups	1.4 liters
extra-virgin olive oil	4½ cups	1.1 liters

1. Wash and dry the herbs.

2. Sprinkle the herbs with 1 tablespoon (15 milliliters) of the olive oil to prevent them from turning dark, and chop them finely by hand or chop them not too finely in a blender or food processor. If using a blender or food processor, add enough of the olive oil to help the herbs to circulate, but don't use more oil than necessary.

3. Combine the chopped herbs with the rest of the olive oil and allow to sit at room temperature for 24 hours. Alternatively, cook the herb-oil mixture sous vide at 140°(60°C) for 3 hours.

4. Strain through a fine chinois, or a strainer lined with a triple layer of cheesecloth. Don't push on the herbs in the strainer because too much moisture will be extracted. Instead, let the oil drain through naturally, for about an hour. This oil keeps for up to 2 weeks in a cool place.

HOT-INFUSED METHOD

Some ingredients release their flavor into the surrounding oil so slowly that it's impractical to use them to make infused oils using the cold method. For these ingredients, the oil is gently heated—but not so much that the delicacy of the oil or ingredients is lost—and the ingredients are allowed to lightly sizzle for 10 seconds (for finely chopped herbs and ground spices) up to 1 hour (for vegetables such as tomatoes).

For more precise control when infusing ingredients in hot oil, cook the mixture sous vide at 140°F (60°C) for about 3 hours. (The exact cooking time depends on the herb and its freshness.) This will allow for a consistent temperature and provide the opportunity to find the exact best times and temperatures.

CHILE AND SWEET PEPPER OILS

Because chiles come fresh, dried, and smoked in so many varieties and colors, they can be used to make an array of subtly flavored oils that in turn can be used as seasonings in vinaigrettes, as additions to purée sauces (such as tomato sauce) or emulsified sauces (such as hollandaise-based sauces, reduced-cream sauces, or beurre blanc and its derivatives), as components in pasta sauces, or in Chinese cooking.

Chinese chile oils generally contain additional ingredients such as ginger, and usually include dark sesame oil. Sweet red peppers can be infused in olive oil for a sweet and delicate oil that makes a perfect component in vinaigrettes, or that can simply be sprinkled on sliced tomatoes or fresh Italian-style cheeses such as mozzarella. Dried and smoked chiles are used to make hot and spicy yet subtly flavored oils that can be used as sauces for grilled meats and seafood.

Fresh pepper oil keeps for 2 weeks in a cool place and dried pepper oils for several months.

ANCHO CHILE OIL

Because ancho chiles (dried ripe poblano chiles) are easy to find and flavorful, and give a deep ruby glow to infused oils, they make a perfect starting point for experimentation. But almost any dried or fresh chile can be used to make a distinctive oil. Chipotle chiles or pasillas de Oaxaca (both of which are smoked) make especially delicious hot and smoky oils. Adjust the chile amounts depending on the size of the chiles. Dried pasillas, for example, are at least twice the size of dried chipotles. Adjust the proportions of pure olive oil and extra-virgin olive oil to taste.

YIELD: 1 QUART (1 LITER)

dried chiles such as ancho, guajillo, mulato, pasilla, chipotle, or pasillas de oaxaca	20 to 40	20 to 40
pure olive oil	3 cups	750 milliliters
extra-virgin olive oil	1 cup	250 milliliters

1. Rinse and dry the chiles or wipe them with a moist towel. Cut off the stems.

2. Chop the chiles for about 30 seconds in a food processor, until they flake but aren't powdered, or chop them finely by hand. There should be 1½ cups (375 milliliters) flakes, so if necessary, grind or chop a few more.

3. Combine the chile flakes with the pure olive oil in a saucepan and place over medium heat. When the chiles are sizzling and begin to float, turn the heat down very low and let the chiles sizzle gently for 3 to 10 minutes. Keep sniffing the oil and as soon as the chiles begin to smell

toasty, take the pan off the heat. Let cool for 30 minutes. Alternatively, cook the chiles and pure olive oil sous vide at 140°F (60°C) for 3 hours.

4. Stir the extra-virgin olive oil into the chile mixture. Strain through a fine chinois or a strainer lined with a triple layer of cheesecloth. If there are still specks floating in the oil, strain the oil again through a strainer lined with a cloth napkin.

CHINESE-STYLE CHILE OIL

Because most commercial Chinese chile oil is harsh (and often rancid), conscientious Chinese cooks make their own. Recipes for the oil range from simple (hot chiles heated in peanut oil) to relatively complex (garlic, ginger, sesame oil, and black beans added to the mix). This recipe falls between the two extremes.

The chiles suggested below can be combined for different flavor nuances and degrees of heat. Chipotles and pasillas de Oaxaca will lend a characteristic smoky note to the oil. If using all small or relatively mild chiles, add a few extra.

YIELD: 1 QUART (1 LITER)

dried chiles such as ancho, guajillo, mulato, pasilla, chipotle, or pasillas de oaxaca	20 to 40	20 to 40
fresh ginger, coarsely chopped	3 tablespoons	45 milliliters
garlic cloves, peeled	5	5
peanut oil	1 quart	1 liter
dark Asian sesame oil	½ cup	125 milliliters

1. Rinse and dry the chiles or wipe them with a moist towel. Cut off the stems.

2. Chop the chiles, ginger, and garlic for about 30 seconds in a food processor or chop everything finely by hand. If there is less than 1¾ cups (450 milliliters) of the mixture, add more chiles.

3. Combine the chile-garlic-ginger mixture with the peanut oil in a saucepan. Place the pan over medium heat. When the solids are sizzling and beginning to float, turn the heat down to low and allow the ingredients to sizzle gently for about 5 minutes, until they smell toasty. Take the pan off the heat and let cool for 30 minutes. Alternatively, to avoid overcooking the chiles, cook the mixture sous vide at 140°F (60°C) for 12 hours.

4. Strain the infused oil through a fine-mesh strainer or a strainer lined with a triple layer of cheesecloth. Combine with the sesame oil.

SWEET RED PEPPER OIL

This brightly colored oil captures the flavor of sweet red peppers. Unlike chile oil, which is hot and spicy, red pepper oil is mild and sweet. It is best when served with grilled fish or used as the oil in preparing a vinaigrette.

YIELD: 2 CUPS (500 MILLILITERS)

sweet red peppers	1 pound	500 grams
olive oil	2 cups	500 milliliters

1. Halve the peppers, remove the stems and seeds, and chop coarsely.

2. Combine the chopped peppers with the olive oil in a 2-quart (2 liter) saucepan. Cook the peppers over a low flame for about 1 hour, until they are soft. Alternatively, cook the peppers and oil sous vide at 140°F (60°C) for 12 hours.

3. Let the peppers and oil cool. Pour into a blender and blend for 30 seconds.

4. Return the mixture to the saucepan and cook gently for 15 to 20 minutes, until the particles of pepper separate from the oil. Do not overcook the oil or its flavor will be compromised.

5. Strain the oil through a fine chinois. The oil will keep for months in the refrigerator.

VEGETABLE-INFUSED OILS

Aromatic vegetables, especially garlic, tomatoes, and mushrooms, make marvelous oils that in turn can be used in vinaigrettes, as flavorings in vegetable purées, or as simple sauces for vegetables, seafood, or even meats.

TOMATO OIL

Tomato oil makes a lovely accent in vinaigrettes that in turn can be used as sauces for grilled seafood, chicken, or vegetables. Tomato oil can also be used alone.

YIELD: 2 CUPS (500 MILLILITERS)

ripe red tomatoes	7 pounds	3 kilograms
extra-virgin olive oil	2 cups	500 milliliters

1. Preheat the oven to 400°F (200°C). Wash the tomatoes, cut them in half crosswise, and squeeze out the seeds. Oil a heavy-bottomed roasting pan with 1 tablespoon (15 milliliters) of the olive oil and spread over the tomato halves, cut side down, in a single layer.

2. Bake the tomatoes for 1½ to 2 hours, until the juices released by the tomatoes have evaporated into a small amount of syrupy liquid. Do not allow the liquid on the bottom of the pan to brown.

3. Scrape the tomatoes into a heavy-bottomed saucepan and add the remaining olive oil. Cook over low heat (the tomatoes should slowly release small bubbles) for 1 to 1½ hours, until the bubbles dissipate and the tomatoes begin to darken very slightly. Be careful at this point not to burn the tomatoes or oil. Alternatively, to avoid overcooking, cook the roasted tomatoes and oil sous vide at 140°F (60°C) for 12 hours.

4. Gently pour the ingredients in the pan into a fine-mesh strainer set over a bowl and let drain, without pushing on the tomatoes, for about 1 hour. (The drained tomatoes can be worked through a food mill or strainer to eliminate peels; they make a delicious sauce.)

5. Reserve the oil in a cool place for up to 2 weeks. If liquid settles to the bottom of the bottle, carefully transfer the oil to another bottle, leaving the liquid behind.

MOREL OR PORCINI OIL

Most dried mushrooms infuse oil with a surprisingly full-flavored yet delicate aroma, but dried morels and porcini (cèpes) work the best. Dried mushroom oil can be used in salad dressings, pasta sauces, or in emulsified egg, butter, or cream sauces. Mushroom oils can be kept in a cool place for up to 2 weeks.

YIELD: 1 QUART (1 LITER)

dried morels or porcini (cèpes), rinsed, patted dry	3 to 6 ounces	90 to 175 grams
pure olive oil	1½ cups	375 milliliters
extra-virgin olive oil	3½ cups	875 milliliters

1. Combine the mushrooms with the pure olive oil in a blender and purée to a coarse paste, about 1 minute.

2. Transfer the mushroom-oil paste to a 2-quart (2 liter) saucepan and place over low heat while stirring gently. One minute after the paste starts bubbling, take the pan off the heat and let cool. Alternatively, cook the mushroom-oil paste sous vide at 140°F (60°C) for 12 hours.

3. Stir the extra-virgin olive oil into the mushroom paste. Strain the mixture through a fine chinois, then again through a strainer lined with a triple layer of cheesecloth or a carefully washed and rinsed kitchen towel.

SPICE-INFUSED OILS

Pungent and finely ground spices can be quickly infused in oil by heating the spices in the oil until the spices sizzle; the mixture is then strained. Any of the spices used in Indian curry mixtures (pages 607 to 615), or the mixtures themselves, can be infused into an inert-tasting oil such as French *huile d'arachide*, grapeseed oil, or good-quality safflower oil. If experimenting with an unknown spice or spice mixture, heat the spices in a small amount of oil so that if you accidentally overheat the spices you won't waste a large amount of oil.

YIELD: 1 QUART (1 LITER)

ground spices such as cardamom, cumin, star anise, cinnamon, cloves, or spice mixtures such as garam masala (page 607)	1 cup	250 milliliters
inert-tasting oil such as grapeseed, safflower, or canola	4½ cups	1.1 liters

1. Combine the spices with 2 cups (500 milliliters) of the oil in a small, heavy-bottomed saucepan. Heat, while stirring, over medium heat until the spices begin to sizzle. Continue cooking for about 2 minutes, until the spices smell aromatic. Remove from the heat and let cool. Alternatively, to avoid overcooking, cook the spices and oil sous vide at 140°F (60°C) for 6 hours.

2. Taste the oil to make sure it hasn't burned (in which case it has to be thrown out) and that it tastes strongly of the spices. If it isn't very spicy, repeat the heating and cooling until the oil is intensely flavored. (Remember, this oil-spice mixture will be diluted with the rest of the oil.)

3. Combine with the remaining oil and strain first through a fine chinois, then again through a strainer lined with a triple layer of cheesecloth or a carefully washed and rinsed kitchen towel.

Infused Vinegars

Like cold-pressed natural oils, vinegar can be used as a condiment in itself. It can be especially lovely when sprinkled over grilled or sautéed fish instead of the ubiquitous squeeze of lemon. Many people like to sprinkle both vinegar and olive oil over grilled foods. Depending on the setting, the effect can be far more satisfying than that of a premade vinaigrette.

Vinegars infused with herbs, garlic, and flowers have long been kitchen staples. Fruit vinegars, popular in the seventeenth and eighteenth centuries, have reentered the culinary mainstream, with sometimes dubious results. Whether the flavor of a particular herb or ingredient is best introduced into a sauce by first infusing it in vinegar or by using the herb directly depends on the herb or ingredient. Infused vinegars may have first been used as a method of preserving seasonal herbs, rather than ends in themselves. Tarragon and Provençal herbs such as thyme, rosemary, oregano, marjoram, savory, and lavender seem to take best to preservation in vinegar. The flavor of certain other herbs, such as basil, is distorted by vinegar and would be more likely to stay intact if the herb were puréed and held in oil.

The vinegars given here are made by infusing the ingredients for at least a week. However, you can achieve the same effect more quickly by cooking the vinegar mixture sous vide at 140°F (60°C) for 12 hours.

PROVENÇAL HERB VINEGAR

Vinegars can be made from a single herb or from a combination, as in this recipe. This method is also excellent for preserving herbs.

YIELD: 1 QUART (1 LITER)

fresh thyme	1 bunch	1 bunch
fresh savory	1 bunch	1 bunch
fresh marjoram	1 bunch	1 bunch
bay leaf	1	1
garlic clove, peeled	1	1
shallot, peeled and halved	1	1
good-quality wine vinegar	1 quart	1 liter

1. Force the thyme, savory, marjoram, bay leaf (all of which should be left on the stems), garlic, and shallot through the mouth of a magnum wine bottle or other bottle of suitable size.

2. Fill the bottle with the vinegar and cork it. Let the vinegar steep for at least 1 week before use.

ORANGE VINEGAR

Vinegar can be flavored with orange or other citrus fruits by allowing strips of zest to infuse the vinegar for several days. Citrus vinegars are especially lovely used on endive.

YIELD: 1 QUART (1 LITER)

oranges	4	4
good-quality wine vinegar	1 quart	1 liter

1. Peel the zests from the oranges with a sharp paring knife or vegetable peeler.

2. Push the zests through the mouth of a vinegar or wine bottle. Pour over the vinegar, and cork the bottle. Let the zests infuse the vinegar for 1 week before use.

RASPBERRY VINEGAR

Practically any fruit, chopped or left whole, can be infused into a bottle of vinegar. Commercially available raspberry vinegar is often made with raspberries that have been cooked to concentrate their sweetness and flavor. Unfortunately, the result is often too sweet and strongly flavored. A more subtle version can be made by simply steeping fresh raspberries in good-quality wine vinegar. The vinegar should have a good concentration of acetic acid (7%), because the water contained in the raspberries tends to dilute it.

YIELD: 1 QUART (1 LITER)

fresh raspberries	1 cup	250 milliliters
white wine vinegar	3 cups	750 milliliters

1. Crush the raspberries in a stainless-steel bowl with the back of a wooden spoon.

2. Add the vinegar, stir the mixture, and pour it through a funnel into a 1-quart (1 liter) bottle. Cork the bottle.

3. Let the raspberries steep in the vinegar for a week. Strain the vinegar through a fine chinois or, if it needs to be perfectly clear, through a triple layer of cheesecloth.

Vinaigrettes

Strictly speaking, vinaigrettes are emulsions of vinegar and oil, but in contemporary kitchens the definition is often stretched to include an emulsion of an acid, such as lemon juice or verjuice, containing not only oil but sometimes cream. Long relegated for use as dressings for green salads and cold foods, vinaigrettes have come into their own as both hot and cold sauces that can be served with meats, fish, and vegetables. Vinaigrettes are relatively unstable emulsions that break if left to sit. The most common emulsifier is mustard, but many contemporary vinaigrettes are constructed around vegetable purées, such as tomato, sweet pepper, or garlic. Modernist vinaigrettes may contain lecithin, xanthan gum, propylene glycol alginate, or other stabilizing ingredients. When using these ingredients, water-soluble thickeners (propylene glycol alginate, sucrose esters, and xanthan gum) should be added to the aqueous phase (the vinegar or other liquid), and oil-soluble ingredients (such as liquid lecithin and mono- and diglycerides [Glice]) to the oil. So-called vinaigrettes that have been stabilized with egg yolks are, strictly speaking, light-style mayonnaises.

In addition to using vegetable purées as starting points for contemporary vinaigrettes, chefs often use vinaigrettes in conjunction with other sauces, such as beurre blanc and its derivatives. Because vinaigrettes are unstable, especially when served hot, combining them with an emulsified butter sauce helps stabilize the emulsion.

Integral sauces made from roasting juices and cooking liquids can also be quickly finished as vinaigrettes by combining the cooking liquid in a blender with cooked vegetables or herbs, which act as emulsifiers, then slowly adding vinegar and oil.

VINAIGRETTES FOR GREEN SALADS

Beginning cooks often prepare vinaigrette by nervously whisking oil into a mixture of vinegar and mustard, ever fearful that the tenuous emulsion will break. It often does. Since the components in a vinaigrette will be evenly spread over the surface of a salad anyway, it is not necessary to work them into an emulsion. In fact, extra-virgin olive oil loses much of its delicacy and may even turn bitter if overbeaten. The easiest and most obvious sauce for a tossed green salad is to dribble over a few tablespoons of good extra-virgin olive oil, sprinkle over about one-third as much good wine vinegar (infused herb vinegar is great), sprinkle on some salt and freshly ground pepper, and toss. However, thanks to the availability of modern stabilizing ingredients such as lecithin, xanthan gum, propylene glycol alginate, and mono- and diglycerides (Glice), vinaigrettes can easily be made more stable. It is also possible to make a vinaigrette with no emulsifier at all by puréeing with a rotor stator homogenizer (see page 35).

The most important flavors of a vinaigrette are usually those provided by the vinegar and oil. The best-quality extra-virgin olive oil and good aged vinegar are the most natural sauces, although some chefs find extra-virgin olive oil has too much character (or is too expensive) and insist that it be used exclusively for Provençal cooking. Nut oils can also be used but can become monotonous if used regularly. They are best served with distinctly bitter or particularly aggressive greens. Some people think that a vinaigrette should be almost tasteless and insist on using inert-tasting, chemically extracted vegetable oils, either alone or in conjunction with natural full-flavored oils.

To vary the flavor of a salad vinaigrette beyond the natural characteristics of the oils and vinegars, flavored vinegars and oils can be used, or additional ingredients can be infused into the vinegar before the salad is tossed. Two of the most common ingredients are mustard and garlic. Garlic should be worked to a paste or finely chopped before it is combined with the vinegar. It is then strained out before the vinegar is added to the salad. Herbs should be finely chopped and allowed to infuse the vinegar for varying lengths of time: Provençal herbs, such as marjoram, thyme, and savory, for several hours; fines herbes (tarragon, chives, parsley, and chervil), for 5 to 10 minutes. It is best to avoid using mustard in delicately flavored vinaigrettes containing extra-virgin olive oil, as the delicacy of the oil will be lost.

BASIC VINAIGRETTE FOR GREEN SALADS

Plain vinaigrettes can be varied by balancing the flavors of various vinegars and oils. Some chefs use only extra-virgin olive oil for their salads, while others like to attenuate the full flavor of olive oil with relatively inert-tasting oils such as safflower, avocado (the best choice), or French *huile d'arachide*. Some chefs are fond of nut oils, such as walnut or hazelnut.

Most people use mustard when making a vinaigrette (not only for flavor but because it acts as an emulsifier), but mustard can obscure the flavor of good-quality oils and is best left out when using the sauce for green salads. When preparing vinaigrette to be served with cold meats, mustard is a welcome addition. Either finely ground Dijon or whole-grain Meaux-style mustard can be used.

Depending on taste and the strength of the vinegar, most vinaigrettes contain one part vinegar to three or four parts oil.

YIELD: 1 TO 1¼ CUPS (250 TO 325 MILLILITERS)

vinegar	¼ cup	65 milliliters
mustard (optional)	1 to 2 teaspoons	15 to 30 milliliters
salt and pepper	to taste	to taste
oil	¾ to 1 cup	190 to 250 milliliters

Combine the vinegar, mustard, if using, and salt and pepper in a bowl. **(A)** Slowly stir in the oil with a whisk. **(B, C)** Do not beat. When most, but not all, of the oil has been added, start tasting the vinaigrette. It may not be necessary to add all the oil. Do not worry if the vinaigrette separates. When it is tossed with the salad greens, all of its components will coat the greens even if the vinaigrette has not been thoroughly emulsified.

Note: Vinaigrette that's stored in the refrigerator almost inevitably breaks. To avoid this, follow the stable vinaigrette recipe on page 479.

STABLE VINAIGRETTE

When making a vinaigrette without mustard there is no emulsifier. To make a stable vinaigrette, blend the vinegar first with an emulsifier such as propylene glycol alginate (0.5% of the vinegar). Heat the oil to 140°F (60°C) and stir in lecithin (2% of the oil) and Glice (2% of the oil). Blend the oil into the vinegar using a rotor stator homogenizer (see page 35) or immersion blender. Once inert-tasting oil has been added, other delicate oils such as extra-virgin olive oil can be stirred in with a wooden spoon.

Low-fat versions of vinaigrettes can be prepared by substituting a thickened flavorful liquid (use about 2 grams xanthan gum per quart/liter) for some of the oil.

1 CUP (250 MILLILITERS)

xanthan gum		0.5 gram
flavorful vinegar	6 tablespoons	90 milliliters
safflower, canola, or avocado oil	8 tablespoons	100 milliliters
liquid lecithin		2 grams
mono- and diglycerides (glice)		2 grams
salt and pepper	to taste	to taste
extra-virgin olive oil	¼ cup	60 milliliters

1. Use an immersion blender to work the xanthan gum into the vinegar. Warm the safflower oil to approximately 140°F (60°C) and add the lecithin and Glice. Stir until they are completely dissolved. Blend the safflower oil, in a steady stream, into the vinegar mixture. A rotor stator homogenizer (page 35) is ideal for this, but an immersion blender will also work.

2. Once the vinaigrette comes together, it will look somewhat like mayonnaise but can be diluted and seasoned with salt and pepper. Gently work in the olive oil, a bit at a time, with a wooden spoon.

CREAMY VINAIGRETTE FOR SALADS

Heavy cream, alone or in conjunction with oil, can be added to vinegar and mustard, producing a vinaigrette that is excellent with delicately flavored salads. Because of its subtlety, creamy vinaigrette can be flavored easily with herbs such as mint, chives, or chervil. It is also excellent for showcasing a special vinegar.

YIELD: 1½ CUPS (375 MILLILITERS)

mustard	2 teaspoons	10 milliliters
salt and pepper	to taste	to taste
vinegar	¼ cup	60 milliliters
heavy cream	1 cup	250 milliliters
extra-virgin olive oil	¼ cup	60 milliliters
chervil or other delicate herb, chopped	2 tablespoons	30 milliliters

Combine the mustard, salt and pepper, and vinegar. Whisk in the cream. Gently stir in the olive oil. Stir in the chervil. Unlike standard vinaigrette, creamy vinaigrette is relatively stable and will keep in the refrigerator for up to 5 days or so.

HONEY-MUSTARD VINAIGRETTE

This savory vinaigrette is delicious in salads and when tossed with cold cooked vegetables. If you make your own infused vinegar, which I highly recommend, don't hesitate to use it here.

YIELD: ¾ CUP (185 MILLILITERS)

garlic clove, minced	1	1
fresh ginger, minced	½ teaspoon	2 milliliters
balsamic, homemade, or banyuls vinegar	3 tablespoons	45 milliliters
honey	1 tablespoon	15 milliliters
dijon or whole-grain meaux-style mustard	1 tablespoon	15 milliliters
soy sauce	2 tablespoons	30 milliliters
dark asian sesame oil	1 tablespoon	15 milliliters
extra-virgin olive oil	¼ cup	60 milliliters
bonito flakes (optional)	½ cup	125 milliliters

Whisk together the garlic, ginger, vinegar, honey, mustard, soy sauce, and sesame oil, Stir in the olive oil. Use as is. Or stir in the bonito flakes, let the mixture sit for an hour or overnight at room temperature or in the refrigerator, then strain them out.

VARIATION

For a more stable version, heat the olive oil to about 140°F (60°C) and stir in 0.6 gram Glice and 0.6 gram liquid lecithin until dissolved. Let cool before adding the olive oil to the vinaigrette.

MORE ELABORATE VINAIGRETTES

Vinaigrettes often provide the necessary accent for leftovers and have long been popular with cold foods such as brains, leftover poached meats, and cold roast chicken. Because no cooking is involved, the preparation of an impromptu sauce based on oil and vinegar lends itself to improvisation. Vinaigrettes for cold meats and fish are usually best when more aggressively flavored than a vinaigrette for a green salad. Mustard is one of the best and most obvious flavorings, but other briny ingredients, such as cornichons (sour gherkins), capers, anchovies, and grilled peppers, are excellent when finely chopped and incorporated into the sauce. Herbs, finely chopped or crushed at the last minute into a paste with a mortar and pestle, provide exciting flavor and color.

Cold vinaigrettes can also be constructed around vegetable purées (which act as emulsifiers), bits of leftover roasting juices or braising liquids, reduced court-bouillon, or leftover cream sauces.

WILD MUSHROOM AND WALNUT OIL SALAD

Be sure to use walnut oil made from roasted nuts (see "Nut Oils," page 46) when flavoring this salad. The greater your collection of wild mushrooms, the tastier the salad. The confit is optional.

YIELD: 4 FIRST-COURSE SERVINGS

wild mushrooms	1½ pounds	675 grams
duck fat, olive oil, or bacon fat	3 tablespoons	45 milliliters
red wine vinegar or sherry vinegar	¼ cup	60 milliliters
roasted walnut oil, preferably from leblanc	3 tablespoons	45 milliliters
extra-virgin olive oil	3 tablespoons	45 milliliters
confit duck legs, meat shredded (optional)	2	2
salt and pepper	to taste	to taste
salad greens	as needed	as needed

(continued)

1. Clean the mushrooms and cut them into thick slices; if they are small, leave them whole. When cutting them in pieces, follow the contours of the mushroom to respect its shape.

2. Heat the duck fat in a large sauté pan until it ripples and toss in the mushrooms. Sauté over high heat until browned and fragrant, about 10 minutes.

3. Pour the vinegar and walnut and olive oils into the pan, add the duck meat, if using, and season with salt and pepper. Heat until the vinegar comes to a boil, then dump over the salad greens and toss gently.

NEROLI, PETITGRAIN, AND ORANGE BLOSSOM VINAIGRETTE

Any number of approaches can be used for making an orange vinaigrette. Orange zests can be infused into the oil, reduced orange juice (by vacuum if you have the equipment; see page 36) can be added to or used to replace the vinegar, and citric acid (sour salt) can be added to add an extra tart citrus dimension.

Perhaps most exciting, essential oils and absolutes can be whisked into the vinaigrette to give it depth and dimension that would be next to impossible otherwise. This recipe features three derivatives of the orange. Petitgrain is made by distilling the twigs and leaves of the tree. It has a clean, vibrant aroma, orange-like but with other aspects. Neroli is expensive because it is distilled from the orange flowers, not the branches. Most expensive of all is orange blossom absolute; it offers an entirely different aroma than neroli even though its source is the same.

YIELD: 1 CUP (250 MILLILITERS)

orange juice	½ cup	125 milliliters
lemon juice	¼ cup	60 milliliters
xanthan gum		0.1 gram
liquid lecithin	2 drops (about 0.1 gram)	
inert-tasting oil such as avocado	1 cup	125 milliliters
diluted petitgrain solution (or more as needed)	1 drop	1 drop
20% neroli solution (or more as needed)	1 drop	1 drop
20% orange blossom absolute solution (or more as needed)	1 drop	1 drop
salt and pepper	to taste	to taste

FLAVORING STABILIZED VINAIGRETTES WITH ESSENTIAL OILS

If you're making a vinaigrette with stabilizers such as xanthan gum and lecithin, you will end up with a very stable emulsion, which makes it easy to work in any number of ingredients without the risk of breaking the sauce. Among these, are essential oils (see page 72), an excellent source of flavorings for vinaigrettes and other emulsified sauces.

Keep in mind that most essential oil and absolutes are very powerful, so much so that you're unlikely to need more than a drop to flavor a cup (250 milliliters) or more of vinaigrette, mayonnaise, or other sauce. In fact, it is best to start out with a diluted solution of 20% essential oil in high-proof drinking alcohol such as Everclear. Don't use isopropyl alcohol or denatured alcohol and certainly don't use methyl alcohol (which can cause blindness).

1. Combine the orange and lemon juices and reduce down to 1 tablespoon (15 milliliters), under vacuum if you have one (see page 36). Stir the xanthan gum into the reduction.

2. Stir the lecithin into the oil, then blend the oil into the juice reduction. If you're whisking or using an immersion blender, add the oil slowly as though making mayonnaise. If you're using a rotor stator homogenizer (see page 35), just mix everything together and blend until the vinaigrette is white and thick.

3. Whisk in the essential oil solutions to taste and season with salt and pepper.

GREEN SAUCES

Some of the oldest European sauces are vinaigrettes containing finely chopped herbs; older recipes also used verjuice. These were usually called green sauces. Any of the many herb-anchovy-caper-cornichon–hard-boiled egg combinations found as the basis for mayonnaises and compound butters such as Montpellier Butter (page 444) can be used for vinaigrettes.

SALSA VERDE

Recipes for this Italian green sauce vary widely, depending on the source, but the sauce is basically a vinaigrette that is well flavored with herbs and pickled vegetables such as capers and cornichons (sour gherkins). It often contains mustard and anchovies, but these are not essential. Breadcrumbs are sometimes worked into the sauce to give it a thicker texture so that it can be dolloped onto foods at the table. It is excellent with cold boiled meats and grilled foods, especially full-flavored fish such as tuna and mackerel.

YIELD: 3 CUPS (750 MILLILITERS)

garlic cloves, peeled	2	2
fresh flat parsley leaves	3½ ounces	100 grams
fresh basil leaves	3½ ounces	100 grams
extra-virgin olive oil	9 fluid ounces	280 milliliters
capers, drained	3 tablespoons	45 milliliters
cornichons	2 ounces	50 grams
mustard	1 tablespoon	15 milliliters
wine vinegar	½ cup	125 milliliters
salt and pepper	to taste	to taste
breadcrumbs (optional)	¼ to ½ cup	60 to 120 milliliters

1. Chop the garlic and crush it into a paste in a mortar or on a cutting board with the side of a knife.

2. Wash and dry the parsley and basil. Sprinkle the leaves with 2 tablespoons (30 milliliters) of the olive oil (to prevent the basil from turning black during chopping). Chop the herbs, capers, and cornichons together until they are the size of large grains of sand.

3. Put the mixture into the mortar with the garlic (or into a bowl, along with the garlic, if you used a knife to crush the garlic) and stir in the mustard and vinegar.

4. Gently stir in the remaining cup (250 milliliters) olive oil while working gently with a pestle or wooden spoon. Season with salt and pepper. If a thicker vinaigrette is desired, work in breadcrumbs until the appropriate consistency is achieved.

VARIATION

A small amount of xanthan gum (about 1.5 grams) and Ultra-Sperse 3 (about 3.5 grams) can be blended into the sauce to prevent syneresis. You may also want to use a rotor stator homogenizer (see page 35) to create a smoother and better emulsified sauce.

SAUCE RAVIGOTE

There are two classic versions of sauce ravigote, one a velouté flavored with herbs and served hot (page 153) and this probably earlier version, which is a type of vinaigrette, served cold. This French version of green sauce is similar to the Italian salsa verde, except that it contains onions and is never bound with breadcrumbs.

YIELD: 2 CUPS (500 MILLILITERS)

wine vinegar	½ cup	125 milliliters
capers, drained and chopped	2 heaping tablespoons	40 milliliters
fresh flat parsley	1 bunch	1 bunch
fresh chervil, chopped	2 heaping tablespoons	40 milliliters
fresh chives, chopped	2 heaping tablespoons	40 milliliters
onion, finely chopped	1 medium	1 medium
extra-virgin olive oil	1 cup	250 milliliters
salt and pepper	to taste	to taste

Stir together the vinegar, capers, parsley, chervil, chives, and onion. Gently stir in the olive oil. Season with salt and pepper.

VARIATION

For a more stable version, heat the olive oil to 140°F (60°C) and stir in 2.5 grams mono- and diglycerides (Glice) and 2.5 grams liquid lecithin. Let cool before stirring, a little at a time, into the vinaigrette.

MINT SAUCE FOR LAMB

Older recipes for English green sauce vaguely recommend finely chopping or grinding together herbs, vinegar or verjuice, and usually a bit of sugar or sometimes orange juice. Sorrel was most frequently called for, but parsley, spinach, and sometimes mint were also used. Green sauces were usually served with veal or roast lamb. The mint in this green sauce can be replaced with dill, sorrel, parsley, or spinach.

YIELD: ½ CUP (125 MILLILITERS)

fresh mint	1 large bunch	1 large bunch
coarse salt	½ teaspoon	2 milliliters
sugar	1 teaspoon	5 milliliters
vinegar, lemon juice, or verjuice	¼ cup	60 milliliters

1. Remove the leaves from the mint. Wash them if necessary, and make sure they are perfectly dry.

2. Grind the mint leaves with the salt and sugar with a mortar and pestle.

3. When the mint has been ground to a fine paste, mix in the vinegar or juice. If the sauce seems too acidic, dilute it with water.

HOT VINAIGRETTES

Because vinaigrettes are relatively unstable emulsions, they have been little used as hot sauces for fear they will separate on a hot plate—even though vinegar and oil have long appeared separately as condiments on Mediterranean tables. For vinegar and oil to remain combined, it is necessary to have an ingredient that will stabilize an emulsion of the two. Mustard is the emulsifier most often used, but it is too aggressive to use with delicate sauces and oils. Vegetable purées and herbs, combined using a blender or with a rotor stator homogenizer (see page 35) just before serving, can also emulsify vinaigrettes, but most of these are imperfect emulsifiers and are better when augmented with compounds such as propylene glycol alginate, xanthan gum, and lecithin. Because the flavor of extra-virgin olive oil is distorted when the oil is worked in a blender or rotor stator homogenizer, it is often necessary to use another type of oil for the first stage of the blending and then to stir in extra-virgin olive oil by hand.

Several factors in the changing aesthetic of how a sauce should look and taste have contributed to the acceptance of hot vinaigrettes in contemporary kitchens. At one time, a trace of fat on the surface of a sauce meant that the sauce had broken, because it had been carelessly prepared. Nowadays, certain foods are sometimes presented surrounded with a small amount of fat. This is especially true for naturally fatty foods such as foie gras or vegetables cooked à la grecque with olive oil. Hence it is acceptable to serve the components of a vinaigrette—oil and vinegar—so that they appear separate on the plate. Moreover, diners no longer expect food to be served swimming in sauce or napped with a sauce that covers it. A small amount of sharply flavored, tangy sauce on the bottom of the plate has become acceptable. Finally, chefs have taken to combining vinaigrettes with other sauces to stabilize them. For example, the hot tomato vinaigrette recipe that follows is stabilized with hot emulsified butter.

HOT TOMATO VINAIGRETTE

This vinaigrette uses hot tomato coulis as the emulsifier and is given extra flavor and complexity with reduced court-bouillon. The vinaigrette is then combined with emulsified butter (beurre fondu; see page 437), and the flavor is adjusted with seasonings or by adding more of certain ingredients. This vinaigrette is best brushed on hot fish fillets or shellfish.

YIELD: 2 CUPS (500 MILLILITERS)

court-bouillon (page 366)	2 cups	500 milliliters
shallot, minced	1 medium	1 medium
garlic clove, crushed, peeled	1	1
extra-virgin olive oil	5 tablespoons	75 milliliters
ripe tomatoes	4	4
fresh thyme	1 sprig	1 sprig
lemon juice	2 tablespoons	30 milliliters
water	1 tablespoon	15 milliliters
butter	2 ounces	60 grams
sherry vinegar or balsamic vinegar	2 tablespoons	30 milliliters
salt and pepper	to taste	to taste

1. Reduce the court-bouillon to ½ cup (125 milliliters) in a 2-quart (2 liter) saucepan.

2. Sweat the shallot and garlic in 1 tablespoon (15 milliliters) of the olive oil in another 2-quart (2 liter) saucepan.

3. Cut the tomatoes in half crosswise and squeeze out the seeds. Chop the tomatoes coarsely and add them to the shallots and garlic. Add the thyme.

4. Cook the tomatoes until any excess liquid evaporates. Strain the mixture through a fine chinois, drum sieve, or food mill into the reduced court-bouillon.

5. While the tomatoes are cooking down, prepare the emulsified butter by heating the lemon juice and water over medium heat and whisking in the butter.

(continued)

6. Add the emulsified butter to the tomato–court-bouillon mixture. **(A)** Whisk in the vinegar and then the remaining ¼ cup (60 milliliters) olive oil. **(B, C)**

7. Adjust the sauce's flavors by adding additional vinegar, olive oil, or whole butter. Season with salt and pepper.

VARIATION

For a more stable version, work 0.6 gram liquid lecithin into the butter before preparing the beurre fondu. Heat ¼ cup (60 milliliters) of the oil to 140°F (60°C) and mix in 0.75 gram mono- and diglycerides (Glice). In step 6, whisk in the emulsified butter and then the oil-Glice mixture.

WARM SWEET RED PEPPER AND GARLIC VINAIGRETTE

This sauce illustrates the use of infused oils and garlic purée in a hot vinaigrette. The vinaigrette can be served hot on grilled foods, or it can be used as a thickener for roasting juices or for poaching liquids for fish.

YIELD: 1 CUP (250 MILLILITERS)

garlic cloves, peeled	10	10
champagne vinegar	3 tablespoons	45 milliliters
fresh marjoram, finely chopped	1 tablespoon	15 milliliters
sweet red pepper oil (page 472)	10 tablespoons	150 milliliters
roasting juices (optional)	to taste	to taste
salt and pepper	to taste	to taste

1. Simmer the garlic cloves in enough water to cover by 2 inches (5 cm) for about 20 minutes, until they are soft. Drain the garlic and force it through a drum sieve with a plastic pastry scraper into a stainless-steel bowl.

2. Combine the garlic pulp with the vinegar and marjoram.

3. Whisk in the oil and the roasting juices, if using. Season with salt and pepper.

VARIATION

To stabilize the vinaigrette, heat the oil to 140°F (60°C) and stir in 1.5 grams mono- and diglycerides (Glice) and 1.5 grams liquid lecithin. Let cool before proceeding as directed.

FINISHING INTEGRAL SAUCES AS VINAIGRETTES

The cooking liquids from braised fish, vegetables, and meats and the roasting juices from meats can be converted into savory vinaigrettes by last-minute puréeing in a blender with vinegars, oils, cooked vegetables (such as the mirepoix vegetables used in cooking the meat or fish), and herbs. These delicate yet full-flavored sauces are excellent alternatives to flour-thickened gravies or butter-enriched roasting juices.

BASIL VINAIGRETTE FOR ROAST LAMB

In this recipe a jus prepared from a roast leg, rack, saddle, or shoulder of lamb is finished as a basil-flavored vinaigrette. The resulting sauce may be served hot or cold. The recipe can be adapted by using roasting juices from other meats, different herbs, and various oils.

Because the only emulsifier is basil, a blender is used to quickly homogenize the mixture. Because the flavor of extra-virgin olive oil is compromised by the action of the blender, pure olive oil (which is virtually flavorless) is puréed in a blender first and then extra-virgin olive oil is whisked in by hand. It is also possible to omit the oils completely. For a more stable version, see the variation that follows, which features xanthan gum and Ultra-Sperse 3 to prevent syneresis.

YIELD: ¾ CUP (165 MILLILITERS)

full-flavored lamb roasting juices, hot	¼ cup	60 milliliters
wine vinegar	3 tablespoons	45 milliliters
salt and pepper	to taste	to taste
leaves from 1 small bunch basil or parsley	1	1
pure olive oil	2 tablespoons	30 milliliters
extra-virgin olive oil	2 tablespoons	30 milliliters

(continued)

1. Combine the roasting juices, vinegar, salt and pepper, and basil leaves and blend with an immersion blender or rotor stator homogenizer (see page 35) for 15 to 20 seconds, until the basil is finely chopped and a creamy emulsion is formed.

2. Pour the pure olive oil into the mixture in a steady stream while blending.

3. Transfer the sauce to a mixing bowl and use a wooden spoon to stir in the extra-virgin olive oil by hand.

4. Taste the sauce to see whether it needs additional vinegar or oil. Adjust the seasonings.

VARIATION

To make a stabilized version, add 0.8 gram xanthan gum and 2 grams Ultra-Sperse 3 to the hot roasting juices and vinegar along with the salt, pepper, and basil, and blend as directed.

HOT HAZELNUT AND PARSLEY VINAIGRETTE

This is an excellent method for finishing the cooking liquids from roast meats or braised fish and fish fillets cooked *en sauce* (see "Braising," page 301). The sauce, which is bound and flavored with parsley, can be flavored with different oils, vinegars, lemon or lime juice, verjuice, or herbs. Because the sauce is unstable and its flavor fragile, serve it immediately after blending. Fish and meats can be lightly brushed with this sauce, or they can be surrounded with a thin layer of sauce spread on the plate.

YIELD: ¾ CUP (185 MILLILITERS)

flat parsley, leaves only	1 bunch	1 bunch
meat roasting juices or fish braising liquid, hot	¼ cup	60 milliliters
vinegar	2 tablespoons	30 milliliters
hazelnut oil	¼ cup	60 milliliters
salt and pepper	to taste	to taste

1. Combine the parsley leaves with the hot meat juices in a blender. Add the vinegar and blend on high speed for 15 to 20 seconds.

2. Pour the hazelnut oil into the liquid through the top of the blender, while blending. Strain the sauce through a regular mesh strainer to eliminate any large pieces of parsley or through a fine chinois to eliminate the parsley completely.

3. Taste the sauce and season with the salt and pepper. More oil or vinegar can be added if necessary.

VARIATION

For additional stability, blend 0.5 gram xanthan gum into the hot meat juices along with the parsley and vinegar. Heat the hazelnut oil to 140°F (60°C) and stir in 1.2 grams liquid lecithin and 1.8 grams mono- and diglycerides (Glice). Blend the oil into the vinegar mixture, a bit at a time, with an immersion blender or rotor stator homogenizer (see page 35). Strain and season as directed.

SALSAS

Mexican salsas are combinations of more or less finely chopped vegetables and sometimes fruits. They are seasoned and flavored in many different ways, but usually contain hot peppers, cilantro, lime juice, and tomatoes. The ingredients, instead of being puréed or infused into a liquid, are allowed to retain their texture and individuality within the salsa. Salsas are usually brightly colored and have a direct and refreshing flavor. Because of this, the more traditional salsas are excellent with grilled and highly flavored foods.

MEXICAN SALSA

There are many recipes and variations for Mexican salsa, some cooked, some raw. The following recipe is a mixture of raw ingredients that are allowed to macerate.

YIELD: 1 QUART (1 LITER)

tomatoes, peeled, seeded, and coarsely chopped	6 large	6 large
garlic clove, crushed to a paste	1	1
sweet red pepper, seeded and finely chopped	1	1
jalapeño, seeded and finely chopped	1	1
cuban long pepper, seeded and finely chopped	1	1
red onion, chopped	1 medium	1 medium
avocado, pitted, peeled, and chopped	1	1
fresh cilantro, chopped	1 small bunch	1 small bunch
juice of 2 limes		
extra-virgin olive oil	3 tablespoons	45 milliliters
salt	to taste	to taste

Combine all the ingredients and let the mixture steep for an hour or two before serving. This salsa is best served right away so the avocado doesn't turn black. It can be stored for a night or two in the refrigerator; cover with plastic wrap pressed directly on the surface.

VARIATIONS
There are many possible variations of Mexican salsa. One of the best is to replace the tomatoes in the recipe with small tomatillos, cooked, which give the salsa a delightful sour taste and characteristic green color. Yellow tomatoes and different-colored chiles and peppers can be used for exciting color combinations. Cilantro is the most commonly used Mexican flavoring for salsa. Other herbs, such as parsley, chopped fresh thyme, or oregano, can be substituted, giving the salsa a Mediterranean rather than a Mexican character.

Improvising Salsas

The concept of chopping ingredients and then serving the mixture as a sauce opens up a whole range of possibilities for sauce making. The ingredients retain their color, texture, and individual flavor but are cut small enough for the mixture to take on an identity of its own. It can then be spread over foods and eaten like a sauce.

Almost any vegetable or fruit can be chopped and served in the juices it releases during maceration; vegetables and fruits such as cucumbers, tomatoes, papayas, and mangoes release liquid when tossed with salt. Vegetables and fruits can also be lightly bound with another sauce. Although no one would ever call it a salsa, a mushroom duxelles lightly bound with cream could be thought of as an extension of this concept.

When improvising salsas, the difference between soup, salad, and salsa becomes hazy. Gazpacho, a spicy Spanish soup of raw chopped garlic, onions, cucumbers, and tomatoes, can be served as a summer sauce for grilled foods. Fruit salads can be converted to sauces by chopping or cutting the fruits into smaller pieces and seasoning them with herbs. The ingredients in guacamole, instead of being mashed, can be coarsely chopped so they retain their color and texture. The mixture can then be served as a sauce for other foods instead of always being relegated to before-dinner chips-and-dip.

Chefs in France sometimes use a mixture of vegetables cut into brunoise (cubes measuring $\frac{1}{16}$ to $\frac{1}{8}$ inch/about 2 millimeters on each side) as a light and decorative treatment for grilled or sautéed meats and fish. Likely vegetables for this treatment are tomatoes, sweet peppers, cucumbers, mushrooms, truffles, and cornichons (sour gherkins). Capers are also sometimes added to these mixtures for their direct flavor and contrasting shape. These mixtures of vegetable brunoise are usually scented with a variety of herbs and moistened with an acidic ingredient such as lemon or lime juice, various vinegars, or, most recently, verjuice. Olive oil and nut oils as well as stocks and roasting juices are also used.

TRUFFLE SALSA

When truffles are chopped and used to finish a classic brown sauce, the sauce is called *Périgueux* (page 200); the same sauce, finished with sliced truffles, becomes a Périgourdine. When the truffles are puréed with a natural jus, contemporary (and seventeenth-century) chefs call it a truffle coulis. To call the following recipe a truffle salsa may be carrying poetic license too far, but the term is used here to imply that the truffles are cut into tiny cubes. The salsa may be served hot or cold, spread over hot or cold meats or fish.

YIELD: 1 CUP (250 MILLILITERS)

fresh or preserved black truffles	7 ounces	200 grams
full-flavored stock	2 tablespoons	30 milliliters
heavy cream	2 tablespoons	30 milliliters
extra-virgin olive oil	1 tablespoon	15 milliliters
excellent vinegar (sherry or authentic balsamic)	a few drops	a few drops
salt and pepper	to taste	to taste

1. Peel the truffles and slice them into ⅟₃₂-inch (1 mm) slices with a Japanese mandoline. Julienne the slices and then cut them into tiny dice. Chop the peels very fine.

2. Combine the stock and cream and bring the mixture to a simmer. Add the diced truffles and chopped peelings and stir the mixture over low heat for 1 minute.

3. Cover the saucepan and remove the salsa from the heat. Let it sit for 15 minutes.

4. Stir in the olive oil and the vinegar with a wooden spoon. Add salt and pepper.

TROPICAL FRUIT SALSA

The idea for making salsas with fruit stemmed from a delicious summer salad of tropical fruit highly seasoned with grilled peppers and cilantro and tossed with lime juice and olive oil. Barbecued chicken or shrimp is tossed into the salad just before serving.

To convert a salad into a salsa, simply cut the pieces of fruit or vegetable small enough so that the mixture, although comprising small pieces of solid food, gives the impression of being semiliquid, so it can be poured or spooned over foods.

If preparing the salsa in advance, it is best to keep the fruits separate. The cilantro should be chopped just before serving, and the fruits seasoned only at the end. In this recipe the fruit is cut into ¼-inch (5 mm) cubes—the French call this size cube *macédoine*—but for less formal presentations, the ingredients can simply be chopped until the salsa has the right consistency.

This tropical fruit salsa comprises several different fruits. The fruits can also be kept separate, each seasoned differently, for a variety of fruit salsas to serve with grilled meats or fish. In restaurant settings or in situations where this is impractical, the individual fruit salsas flavored with different herbs or tossed with different-colored peppers and tomatoes can be arranged directly on the plate.

This recipe is only a model; almost any type of fruit can be used.

YIELD: 1 QUART (1 LITER)

(continued)

fresh pineapple, peeled and cored	¼ small	¼ small
hawaiian papaya, peeled and pitted	1	1
kiwis, peeled	2	2
mango, peeled and pitted	1	1
sweet red pepper, grilled, peeled, and seeded	1	1
fresh hot chiles, seeded	2 or 3 small	2 or 3 small
fresh cilantro	1 small bunch	1 small bunch
red onion	1 medium	1 medium
juice of 2 limes		
salt	to taste	to taste

1. Cut the fruits into small cubes or chop until they come together to produce a semiliquid consistency.

2. Chop or cube the red pepper and the chiles. Chop the cilantro. Finely chop the onion.

3. Combine all the ingredients.

CHUTNEYS AND RELISHES

The distinction among chutneys, relishes, salsas, pestos, and purées is often hard to establish because the terms are all used somewhat interchangeably.

Although in some languages the term *salsa* describes any sauce, it is used here to refer to a Mexican-style sauce of chopped herbs, vegetables, and sometimes fruits. Mexican salsas are usually served raw or only lightly cooked. Salsas can be made exclusively with Mexican-style ingredients, or the concept and style can be stretched and used with other ingredients for a distinctly non-Mexican result, such as Truffle Salsa (page 492).

A relish is similar to a salsa except that some of the ingredients have usually been pickled in brine or vinegar—pickles (often French cornichons), capers, pickled onions, peppers, and pickled beets are likely candidates.

Chutneys are usually divided into three types. The most familiar kind—of which Major Grey's is the best-known—is sweet and sour and usually contains fruit cooked with a sweetener such as sugar or molasses, spices, and an acidic ingredient such as vinegar. A second variety, made by tossing vegetables such as onions with herbs (usually mint or cilantro), spices, chiles, and acidic ingredients such as lemon juice, vinegar, or tamarind, is more akin to a relish or simple salad designed to accompany richer foods. A third kind consists mostly of finely chopped herbs (again, usually cilantro or mint) simply tossed with lemon juice or given body with coconut or mango.

Pesto is the Italian word for "pestle," which makes the term applicable to sauces other than the familiar Genoese version made of basil, cheese, and pine nuts; any mixture that has been ground to a paste with a mortar and pestle or food processor can be called a pesto (see "Pestos," page 535).

Sweet-and-Sour Chutneys

Almost any fruit or vegetable can be cooked and seasoned with sugar, vinegar, and spices to provide an acceptable chutney. Sweet-and-sour chutneys make a perfect vehicle for underripe fruits, including pears, peaches, or mangoes. Because of the sugar and vinegar they contain, sweet-and-sour chutneys will keep for several months, tightly covered, in the refrigerator.

SWEET-AND-SOUR FRUIT CHUTNEY

Although many Indian classics have been carefully standardized, it's possible to improvise a sweet-and-sour chutney by adjusting some of the standard ingredients to taste and by using virtually any underripe fruit.

YIELD: ABOUT 2 CUPS (500 MILLILITERS)

sugar	2 tablespoons	30 milliliters
good-quality white wine vinegar, cider vinegar, or sherry vinegar	½ cup	125 milliliters
underripe fruit, cut into ¼ × ½-inch (5 mm × 1 cm) cubes (see note)	2 cups	500 milliliters
serrano chile, stemmed, seeded, finely chopped *or* thai chiles, stemmed, seeded, finely chopped	1 *or* 2	1 *or* 2
fresh ginger, grated	2 teaspoons	10 milliliters
garam masala (page 607) or basic curry powder (page 614)	1 tablespoon	15 milliliters
white or dark raisins (optional)	½ cup	100 grams

1. Combine the sugar and vinegar in a stainless-steel saucepan large enough to hold the fruit and simmer gently to dissolve the sugar.

2. Stir the fruit into the sugar-vinegar mixture and simmer gently until the cubes soften but retain some texture, 5 to 15 minutes. Drain the fruit in a strainer set over another saucepan. Combine the chiles, ginger, and spice mixture with the liquid released by the fruit and, if necessary, reduce the liquid by two-thirds to three-quarters, until it is syrupy.

3. Stir the raisins, if using, into the hot reduced liquid and let the mixture cool. Stir the fruit into the cooled mixture.

Note: For the fruit, use 2 pears (8 ounces/225 grams) each; 2 mangoes (14 ounces/400 grams) each; or 3 peaches (6 ounces/175 grams) each. Peel and core or pit the fruit as necessary before dicing.

GREEN TOMATO CHUTNEY

This chutney, using underripe tomatoes (not tomatillos), is flavored with garam masala (pages 607 and 608) or mild curry powder, but other spices and flavors can be used. It is served cold with meats and curries.

YIELD: 3 CUPS (750 MILLILITERS)

onion, finely chopped	1 large	1 large
olive oil	¼ cup	60 milliliters
green (underripe) tomatoes	2 pounds	1 kilogram
garam masala or good-quality mild curry powder	1 tablespoon	10 grams
sugar	6 tablespoons	90 milliliters
vinegar	¼ cup	60 milliliters
salt and pepper	to taste	to taste

1. Gently sweat the onion in the olive oil for 20 minutes. Do not allow it to brown.

2. Peel the tomatoes by plunging them into boiling water, then into cold water, and sliding off the skins. Cut them in half crosswise and squeeze out the seeds. Chop them coarsely.

3. Add the garam masala to the onions and cook for 1 minute.

4. Add the chopped tomatoes, sugar, and vinegar to the onion mixture, and cook for about 30 minutes, until the chutney thickens.

5. Season with salt and pepper, and adjust the the sugar and the vinegar. Allow to cool. Store for up to 2 nights in the refrigerator.

KUMQUAT RELISH

Kumquats are not to everyone's taste, but their tartness coupled with a subtle bitterness makes them perfect for relishes that can be served with grilled foods or leftover roast meats. This relish is a little like a marmalade but not as sweet and with more texture.

YIELD: 2 CUPS (500 MILLILITERS)

kumquats	1 pound	450 grams
sugar	⅓ cup	80 milliliters
star anise pods, crushed and tied in cheesecloth (optional)	3	3
orange juice	3 cups	750 milliliters

1. Rinse the kumquats and slice them the thickness of a quarter (about ¹⁄₁₂ inch/2 millimeters).

2. Combine the kumquats with the sugar, star anise sachet, if using, and orange juice and bring to a gentle simmer. Skim off any froth that floats to the surface.

3. When the kumquats soften, after about 15 minutes, drain them in a colander set over a clean saucepan. Boil down the liquid until it's thick and syrupy, to about ½ cup (125 milliliters), and combine it with the kumquats. Serve cold. This sauce can be stored for at least several weeks, refrigerated in a tightly covered jar.

MOSTARDA DI CREMONA

This ancient fruit sauce is the classic accompaniment to bollito misto. It is sold by online gourmet stores, but you can also make it yourself if it's summer and you have access to the fruit. If you can't find all the fruit, just substitute more of the others.

YIELD: 6 CUPS (1.5 LITERS)

underripe pears, peeled, cored, cut into wedges	2	2
quince or large apple, peeled, cored, cut into wedges	1	1
sugar	3 cups	600 grams
white wine vinegar or sherry vinegar	2 cups	500 milliliters
fresh cherries, pitted	1 cup	140 grams
fresh apricots, halved and pitted	8 ounces	225 grams
fresh peach, pitted and cut into wedges	1 large	1 large
fresh figs, halved	5 large	5 large

Simmer the pears and quince with the sugar and vinegar until soft. Add the remaining fruit and simmer gently for 10 minutes. Gently remove the fruit with a skimmer or spider and reserve in a bowl while you boil down the poaching liquid until it is syrupy. Put the fruit back in the syrup and simmer for 5 minutes. Put the fruit in sterile jars, pour over the syrup, and seal. The mostarda should keep in the refrigerator for weeks.

Vegetable Chutneys

Some chutneys function as relishes or even salads and provide a bright, refreshing flavor and a crunchy texture that contrasts with the main course. Although many chutneys are traditional and don't allow for much variation, the concept of thinly slicing, cubing, or grating raw vegetables such as cucumbers, tomatoes, onions, and carrots and flavoring them with spices lends itself to improvisation. In addition to spices, most Indian vegetable chutneys contain chiles to provide heat, and an acidic ingredient such as lemon juice or vinegar.

CAPER AND CORNICHON RELISH

YIELD: 2 CUPS (500 MILLILITERS)

red onion	1	1
capers, drained	8 tablespoons	125 grams
cornichons (sour gherkins)	8 tablespoons	125 grams
vinegar	¼ cup	60 milliliters
extra-virgin olive oil	¼ cup	60 milliliters
fresh dill, chopped	2 tablespoons	30 milliliters

Finely chop the onion, capers, and cornichons. Combine them with the vinegar, olive oil, and dill. Cover and let macerate overnight in the refrigerator.

TOMATO AND ONION CHUTNEY

The combination of onions and tomatoes is an Indian favorite. Each region—and even each cook—stamps a unique identity on the mixture by using different spices, and sometimes yogurt, grated coconut, or nuts. This version is one of the simplest and most popular.

YIELD: ABOUT 1 QUART (1 LITER), ENOUGH FOR 6 TO 8 SIDE-DISH SERVINGS

red onions, thinly sliced	2 medium	2 medium
tomatoes, peeled, seeded, chopped	4 medium	4 medium
fresh cilantro leaves, coarsely chopped	¼ cup	60 milliliters
lemon juice	1 tablespoon	15 milliliters

serrano chiles, stemmed, seeded, very finely chopped	2	2
or	or	or
thai chiles, stemmed, seeded, very finely chopped	4	4
or	or	or
jalapeños, stemmed, seeded, very finely chopped	4	4
fine salt	1 teaspoon	5 milliliters

1. Soak the onion slices for 1 hour in ice water to give them crunch and attenuate their flavor.

2. Heat the tomatoes in a small heavy-bottomed saucepan over medium heat, and stir until they thicken into a sauce. Remove from the heat and stir in the cilantro, lemon juice, chiles, and salt.

3. Within an hour of serving, drain the onions, spin them dry in a lettuce spinner (or pat them with towels), and stir them into the cooled tomato sauce. This sauce will keep, refrigerated, for 2 to 3 days.

Herb Chutneys

Anyone who's eaten in an Indian restaurant has encountered the runny and flavorful green sauces served as relishes at the beginning of the meal. Mint and cilantro are the herbs most often used in these sauces, but the idea of puréeing fresh green herbs, sweetening them slightly, and thinning the mixture with water, yogurt, or coconut milk can be used to improvise very light sauces with other herbs.

CILANTRO OR MINT CHUTNEY

YIELD: 1 CUP (250 MILLILITERS), ENOUGH FOR 4 TO 6 SERVINGS

fresh cilantro or mint leaves, tightly packed	1 cup	250 milliliters
sugar (optional)	1 teaspoon	5 milliliters
cold water, plain yogurt, or coconut milk	¾ cup	185 milliliters
onion, peeled, finely chopped	1 small	1 small
serrano chile, stemmed, seeded, finely chopped	1	1
or	or	or
thai chiles, stemmed, seeded, finely chopped	2	2
or	or	or
jalapeños, stemmed, seeded, finely chopped	2	2
lemon juice	2 tablespoons	30 milliliters

Within an hour of serving the sauce, purée the herbs in a blender with the sugar, if using, and water for 1 minute on high speed. Stir in the onion, chiles, and lemon juice.

FRUIT SAUCES

Savory fruit sauces have long been popular in England and the United States as accompaniments to roasts and pâtés. Everyone is familiar with mint jelly served with roast lamb, and cranberry sauce served with roast turkey. The more elaborate Cumberland sauce, although less well known, has long been served with pâtés and cold roast meats.

Most cold fruit sauces contain pectin, a naturally occurring sugar-like substance that causes acidic fruit mixtures to jell. Because most fruits contain insufficient pectin, most fruit sauces contain jelly to help them set.

CUMBERLAND SAUCE

Centuries ago, fruit sauces were common in French cooking, and they are still popular today in England. Fruit sauces are particularly tasty with game, especially venison. This sauce is best served cold with cold meats.

YIELD: 1 CUP (250 MILLILITERS)

shallot, minced	1	1
zest of 1 orange, finely julienned		
zest of 1 lemon, finely julienned		
red currant jelly	¼ cup	60 milliliters
port	6 tablespoons	90 milliliters
juice of 1 orange		
wine vinegar	2 tablespoons	30 milliliters
dijon mustard	1 teaspoon	5 milliliters
ground ginger	1 pinch	1 pinch

Blanch the shallots and the orange and lemon zests for 2 minutes in boiling water. Drain in a strainer. Combine with the jelly, port, orange juice, vinegar, mustard, and ginger in a small saucepan. Bring the sauce to a slow simmer and simmer long enough to cook the alcohol off the port and to dissolve the jelly. Serve cold.

CRANBERRY SAUCE

This straightforward sauce is the one served in England and the United States with roast turkey. It should not be confused with more elaborate French cranberry sauces, which are actually brown sauces garnished with whole cranberries.

YIELD: 1 QUART (1 LITER)

cranberries	1 pound	500 grams
sugar	1 cup	200 grams
water	as needed	as needed

1. In a heavy-bottomed saucepan, combine the cranberries, sugar, and enough water to cover the mixture by 1 inch (2.5 cm).

2. Bring the mixture to a slow simmer and cook for about 20 minutes. Stir every couple of minutes to keep the sauce from sticking.

3. Taste the sauce and add more sugar if needed. Cook until the sugar dissolves.

4. Allow to cool. The sauce can be served as is, or for a smooth sauce, pass through a food mill or drum sieve. Serve cold.

TAMARIND SAUCE

YIELD: 1 CUP (250 MILLILITERS)

tamarind pulp	2 walnut-size pieces	
water	1 cup	250 milliliters
garlic clove, minced	1	1
sugar	3 tablespoons	45 milliliters
fish sauce	3 tablespoons	45 milliliters
thai chiles, stemmed, seeded, minced	3	3
fresh ginger, grated	3 tablespoons	45 milliliters

1. Combine the tamarind pulp and water in a small saucepan and bring to a simmer. Poke at the pulp with a wooden spoon to get it to dissolve. Strain into a clean saucepan.

2. Add the garlic, sugar, fish sauce, chiles, and ginger and bring to a simmer. Simmer gently for 3 minutes, then let cool. Serve at room temperature.

FRUIT SAUCES

501

PURÉES AND PURÉE-THICKENED SAUCES

P urées of vegetables, nuts, legumes, and sometimes fruits are used either as sauces in themselves or to thicken and flavor more complex sauces or cooking liquids. Tomato and sorrel sauces are examples of purées that provide the base and essential character of the sauce; the purée functions as both a thickener and the primary flavor. Purées can also be used to finish sauces, or to lightly thicken braising liquids or roasting juices without distracting from the cooking liquid's intrinsic flavor. Because most purées, depending on the amount and type of starch they contain, are less efficient emulsifiers than hydrocolloids or purified starches such as flour, cornstarch, or arrowroot, they give body to a sauce by dispersing large amounts of insoluble components—often proteins or cellulose-related compounds—into the liquid medium. For this reason sauces based on or thickened with vegetable purées usually have a matte appearance rather than the smooth, transparent look associated with starch-, hydrocolloid-, and butter-thickened sauces.

The advantage of using vegetable purées rather than starch or hydrocolloids as thickeners is that they provide flavor of their own and a natural, wholesome texture to the sauce. Diners have become wary of artificially thickened sauces that have the texture of a carefully reduced jus, stock, or cooking liquid but that, when tasted, show themselves for what they are—thin, carelessly prepared stocks thickened at the last minute. A purée-thickened sauce will have a more rustic appearance but a more natural flavor than a starch- or hydrocolloid-thickened one. Purées are also almost completely free of fat; a purée-thickened sauce will be much less rich than one thickened with butter or cream. Purées can be used in conjunction with starches or cream and butter; the finished sauce will not be as rich as one thickened with cream and butter alone nor as completely lean as a sauce thickened with purée alone.

One of the simplest and most obvious ways to use a purée to give body to a sauce is to purée the aromatic vegetables used in a stew or the mirepoix cooked along with a roast to enhance the flavor of the finished jus. The purée is then stirred, bit by bit, into the roasting juices or braising liquid to achieve the desired thickness. As a result, the aromatic vegetables are not wasted and the sauce is lightly thickened without resorting to starches or other flavorless ingredients. The one drawback to this method, however, is that the aromatic vegetables used in roasting or braising often contain fat released by the meat during cooking. They should therefore be heated with the jus or braising liquid and the fat carefully skimmed off before the vegetables are puréed.

In large restaurants and catering operations, last-minute thickening of roasting and braising juices is rarely practical. Consequently, purées are often prepared in advance and used to thicken sauces or cooking liquids as they are needed.

Some sauces derive not only their texture but also their flavor and color from a purée. The best-known examples of this are tomato sauces, but almost any vegetable, legume, nut, or fruit can be cooked, puréed, and converted into a sauce. Some purée-based sauces combine the purée with other thickeners, such as reduced cream, Sauce Béchamel, hydrocolloids, emulsifiers, emulsion stabilizers, or Sauce Velouté. The best-known example of this is Sauce Soubise, which is Sauce Béchamel combined with onion purée.

Because vegetable and fruit purées often lack the necessary compounds to create emulsions, it often helps to include hydrocolloids—such as xanthan gum or Ultra-Sperse 3—in the purée to ensure that they emulsify the sauce at hand. In addition to acting as emulsifiers, these ingredients help prevent syneresis (the separation of the pulp from the liquid). Hydrocolloids, emulsifiers, and emulsion stabilizers can also be added to a purée to provide the necessary consistency. Sucrose esters and propylene glycol alginate are efficient additions to the aqueous phase of the emulsion while Glice (mono- and diglycerides) and liquid lecithin are added to the oil phase. (When it comes to vegetable and fruit purées, the aqueous phase refers to the moisture contained in the purée itself, plus any additional liquids—for example, stock added to thin the purée. The oil phase refers to any fats, such as butter, oils, coconut oil, or heavy cream, that may be added to the purée.)

Most purées, unless they are starchy enough to act as emulsifiers on their own, require an additional agent to help them absorb fats into an emulsion. These emulsifiers include cream, butter emulsified into a sauce (such as a beurre blanc or beurre fondu), hydrocolloids, or a starch such as flour.

Much of the time, a single emulsifier added to the aqueous phase of the purée is sufficient to create an emulsion. It is also possible to add an emulsifier to any fat being worked into the purée. Lecithin and egg yolks are examples of fat-based emulsifiers. In most situations, a single stabilizer does the trick, but when stability over an extended period of, say, several hours is essential, it may be necessary to add emulsifiers to both phases.

EQUIPMENT FOR PREPARING PURÉES

A mortar and pestle can always be relied on for grinding nuts, puréeing vegetables, and converting various ingredients into pastes and purées. They are a most reliable tool because they allow easy control of the consistency of ingredients and avoid the sometimes brutal action of machines, which can damage the flavor of certain ingredients such as extra-virgin olive oil and basil. Their main disadvantage is that using them can be time-consuming when preparing large quantities; moreover, a large, good-quality mortar and pestle can be hard to find.

Blenders or immersion blenders work extremely well for moist purées, when there is no danger of making the purée too thin or smooth. If too dry or stiff, some mixtures are difficult to work in a blender or with an immersion blender. When making a thin purée (such as watercress sauce), put the solid ingredients in first, turn on the blender or immersion blender, and slowly add the liquid (through the top if you're using a blender). If too much liquid is added at the beginning, the solid ingredients may churn around and escape the blades. When adding cream to a purée, remember to make sure it is hot; otherwise it will turn into butter. Do not use a blender for potatoes or other starchy vegetables, because it tends to overwork the mixture and make it gluey. Do not make sauces containing extra-virgin olive oil in a blender.

While it is more convenient to use an immersion blender—there are fewer dishes to wash—some powerful stand mixers are more efficient. A stand blender also has its dangers—hot liquid can shoot out the top as the rapid blending causes it to combine with air and expand. Ideally, let the mixture cool before blending, but if this isn't practical, wrap a kitchen towel tightly around the lid and start the blender on its slowest speed.

Food processors often are the most efficient tools for chopping and puréeing. When using a food processor, it is very easy to overwork some mixtures and eliminate texture completely. When preparing coarse purées (such as tomato), use the pulse mechanism on the food processor and continually scrape the sides with a rubber spatula so that none of the ingredients escape the blade. As with blenders, do not use a food processor for starchy vegetables or mixtures containing extra-virgin olive oil.

Food mills, a hand-driven precursor to the food processor, are excellent for puréeing and simultaneously straining a variety of mixtures. Their action is more delicate than that of a blender or food processor, making them useful for starchy purées, tomato sauces, sorrel mixtures, and other purées in which the ingredients are already soft and do not require much force to crush them into a paste.

Drum sieves provide the only reliable means of obtaining perfectly smooth thick purées. They are also excellent for making perfect mashed potatoes: The vertical pressure used to force the potatoes through the sieve does not cause the purée to become sticky and elastic, as does a food processor. More-liquid mixtures can be worked through a fine chinois; however, beware that this may strain out too much of the purée itself.

TOMATOES

There are many types of basic tomato sauces. Some are uncooked, lumpy mixtures of raw tomatoes, while others are delicate, smooth purées or long-cooked versions flavored with meats, aromatic vegetables, and herbs. The best way to approach a tomato sauce depends on the time of year and the type and quality of tomatoes that are available. One axiom of cooking might be: The better the ingredients, the less treatment they require. This is especially true when preparing tomato sauce.

The best tomatoes for sauces are usually the small, pear-shaped plum tomatoes, but more important than the type are ripeness and gardening methods. Most tomatoes on the market are picked—and used—before they are ripe. Tomatoes are best used when they are so ripe that they seem ready to burst out of their skin and so soft that they must be handled very carefully (a condition that is not optimum for mass shipping to the nation's supermarkets). Most tomatoes are also overwatered before they are picked. The water dilutes their flavor and must be eliminated later.

Most tomato sauces are spoiled by overcooking and by including too many ingredients, so that the natural delicacy of the tomato is lost—although admittedly a tomato sauce made with canned tomatoes or pale winter fresh tomatoes will need some reinforcement.

Raw Tomato Concassée

The simplest tomato sauce is a raw or barely cooked concassée. *Concasser* means "to crush, break, or grind" and, when applied to cooking, implies that the original texture of the food is still somewhat intact.

When ripe end-of-summer tomatoes are in season, the best way to prepare them and keep all their bright, natural flavor intact is to prepare a raw concassée. Raw tomato concassée can be served as a cold sauce for meats and fish or gently warmed and served with hot foods. Because raw tomato concassée is not strained, the tomatoes must be peeled and seeded before they are chopped. The best way to peel tomatoes is to plunge them in boiling water for 10 or 15 seconds (the exact amount of time depends on how ripe they are; the riper they are, the shorter the time) or, if only one or two tomatoes are involved, rotate them over a gas flame with a fork. Plunge the tomatoes immediately into cold water to prevent the pulp from cooking, and then pull off the peel with your fingers.

To seed tomatoes, cut them in half crosswise and squeeze the seeds from each half. Chop the tomatoes coarsely with a chef's knife. When raw tomato concassée is made with ripe summer tomatoes, any additional flavoring other than salt and pepper may seem superfluous, but a sprinkling of freshly chopped parsley or basil and a dribble of extra-virgin olive oil will not do any harm.

When preparing tomato concassée with less-than-perfect tomatoes, several methods can be used to reduce the water content and concentrate the tomatoes' flavor. Coarse salt can be used to eliminate excess liquid. After peeling the tomatoes, cut them into wedges as for a salad. Pull the seeds from each of the wedges with the tip of a finger. Toss the wedges with salt and place them in a colander set over a bowl to catch any liquid they release. Let the tomatoes sit for 30 minutes, tossing them every 10 minutes. After they have drained, chop them to the desired texture.

Cooked Tomato Concassée

There are two approaches. Shown here, the chopped tomatoes are simply cooked down to a paste. (A, B, C) Alternatively, when you want to preserve the freshness of the tomatoes, cook the concassée for 2 minutes over high heat, just long enough for the tomatoes to release their liquid. Strain, reserving the liquid, then boil the liquid until it is reduced to a syrup. Combine it with the strained tomatoes.

Tomato Coulis

The word *coulis* describes any sort of smooth purée that has been strained to eliminate seeds and bits of peel. A tomato coulis is perfectly smooth and can be used alone either hot or cold, or to flavor other sauces, such as aurore and choron, mayonnaises, and beurre blanc. Depending on the quality of the tomatoes, tomato coulis can be raw or cooked. When preparing tomato coulis, you need only seed the tomatoes to eliminate excess liquid; peeling is not necessary because the skins will be strained out anyway. Tomato coulis can be used as the starting point and emulsifier for a hot or cold vinaigrette or stirred into whipped cream or crème fraîche and served as a cold sauce; mustard whisked in at the end lends a discreet tang.

RAW METHODS. To prepare raw tomato coulis, cut the tomatoes in half crosswise, squeeze out the seeds, and chop the halves with a chef's knife. It is best to chop the tomatoes by hand; if dealing with a large quantity, a food processor can be used, but work the mixture as little as possible or the blade will break up any remaining seeds, making the mixture bitter. Strain the mixture through a fine strainer or a food mill with the finest plate.

Raw tomato coulis contains a large proportion of water, which will tend to separate out as the coulis sits in storage or, worse, while the coulis sits on the plate. Excess water can be eliminated in several ways.

- Coarsely chop and salt the tomatoes, as for tomato concassée, and allow them to drain before straining them.

- Place the tomato coulis in a chinois suspended over a pot or bowl for 2 to 3 hours. Gently stir the mixture inside the chinois every 20 minutes or so.

- Transfer the coulis to a tall container and ladle off the water as it gradually floats to the top.

- Blend 0.5% xanthan gum and 1% Ultra-Sperse 3 into the coulis.

Even when excess water has been eliminated from a raw tomato coulis, the microscopic particles of pigment tend to separate from the surrounding liquid, a phenomenon called syneresis. In some situations this will probably not even be noticed, but in more formal settings, in which a coulis is spread over the bottom of a large plate, it can be unsightly. For this reason some chefs combine raw tomato coulis with an emulsifier such as reduced heavy cream, a very small amount of egg yolk, or an appropriate hydrocolloid thickener or emulsifier.

COOKED METHOD. Rinse the tomatoes, cut them in half crosswise, and squeeze out the seeds. Chop them coarsely, skins and all, and stew them with olive oil or another fat until they are completely soft and release all their liquid. Strain the mixture and reduce the liquid that runs through the strainer until it is syrupy. Purée the solids by working them through a food mill or a drum sieve. Combine the purée with the reduced liquid.

Traditional Tomato Sauces

Most of the better-known Italian sauces, such as *sugo finto*, *salsa di pomodoro*, and *ragù*, are constructed around a flavor base of one or more mirepoix vegetables (celery, carrots, onions), in some cases pork or veal, sometimes garlic, various herbs, and a bouquet garni.

In French cooking, tomatoes are more often used as a flavoring or secondary component added to a more complex sauce, rather than as a sauce base. Despite this seemingly secondary role, tomatoes enter into a classic Sauce Espagnole and hence into practically every classic French brown sauce. Tomato concassée and coulis are also used to moisten meat and chicken stews, such as marengo and chasseur, but in each of these examples the sauce is balanced with other ingredients and flavors. Mexican and Spanish tomato sauces, such as salsa (see page 491), are often raw concassées seasoned with appropriate herbs and spices.

Tomato concassée or coulis is sometimes, in both sauces and soups, emulsified with cream. It is usually best to add the tomatoes to reduced cream to maintain an emulsion and to create a delicious sauce. **(A)** Adjust the consistency of the sauce by reducing it to thicken it **(B)** or by thinning with liquid such as more (unreduced) cream.

Improving the Flavor of Tomato Sauces

Regardless of the type of tomato sauce being prepared, its flavor can usually be improved in several ways.

1. Use the best, ripest fresh tomatoes. When this is not possible, canned tomatoes can be used. There is much argument as to the best brands of canned tomato or tomato purée, but Redpack, Hunt's, Pomi, and Delverde are well rated and seem like good ones to start using and comparing. Fresh tomato coulis or concassée can also be prepared in the summer and frozen for winter use if there is enough freezer space available for this to be practical.

2. Avoid overcooking the tomatoes. Most recipes suggest preparing some kind of flavor base, adding the tomatoes, and cooking the mixture down until it thickens. It is best to precook and strain the liquid released by the tomatoes (as described for Cooked Tomato Concassée, page 507) and cook the liquid down with the flavor base before adding the tomato pulp.

3. The better the tomatoes, the less they benefit from additional flavoring and manipulation. But less-than-excellent tomatoes can still be used in an almost endless variety of ways. They can be cooked with meats and vegetables (either as a flavor base or in a stew); different herbs can enter into the bouquet garni (sage, oregano, marjoram, hyssop, basil) or be chopped and added to the sauce near the end (tarragon, chives, parsley, chervil); the sauce can be finished with cream, butter (plain or compound), hydrocolloids, or olive oil (flavored or not, or emulsified into a mayonnaise such as Aïoli, page 418, or Rouille, page 127). The sauce can be lent body and suavity by adding reduced stock or by combining it with stock and carefully reducing the two together (as in a classic espagnole). White or red wine can be added at the beginning and simmered with the flavor base.

4. Some tomato sauces, especially pasta sauces, are made by slowly roasting tomatoes in the oven, where they release a surprising amount of liquid. This liquid is ladled off, simmered down to a syrup on top of the stove, and combined with the chopped roasted tomatoes. This slow cooking lightly caramelizes the tomatoes and magnifies their flavor in a way that simple stove-top stewing will not.

Caramelization also enhances the flavor of sauces made with tomato paste (whole tomatoes contain so much water that they can be caramelized only by very long cooking). An excellent method for starting a traditional French or Italian tomato sauce is to sweat onions, carrots, celery, and garlic in olive oil until lightly caramelized, stir in tomato paste, and continue cooking until the tomato paste browns and smells toasty. A small amount of wine can be stirred in and quickly reduced to dryness before relatively neutral liquids such as stock or water are added and the sauce simmered just long enough to extract the flavor of the caramelized ingredients.

5. The flavor of a tomato sauce can usually be improved by increasing both its sweetness and acidity and making sure the two are in balance. Chefs and home cooks have long added sugar to tomato sauces, especially when the tomatoes are underripe. What is less obvious is that even the flavor of acidic tomatoes is improved by adding a small amount of wine vinegar. Start by adding sugar, a small amount at a time, while tasting. As soon as you can taste the sugar, add vinegar a bit at a time, until you can taste it. Then balance the taste of the vinegar with an additional small amount of sugar. By increasing both the acidity and sweetness of the sauce, the flavor of the tomatoes will come into focus.

EMULSIFIED TOMATO PURÉE

This purée is based on a tomato coulis that has been reduced down to the consistency of ketchup. It is designed to be whisked into sauces (such as the Tomato-Thickened Almond Sauce that follows) as an emulsifier and/or thickener. Xanthan gum, Ultra-Sperse 3, and lecithin are added as stabilizers.

YIELD: ABOUT ¾ CUP (200 MILLILITERS)

tomatoes, peeled, seeded and chopped, 4 large	2 pounds	1 kilogram
ultra-sperse 3		0.5 gram
xanthan gum		0.2 gram
vegetable oil	3 fluid ounces	100 milliliters
liquid lecithin		1 gram
wine vinegar (or to taste)	2½ teaspoons	12 milliliters

1. Spread the tomatoes in a wide sauté pan and reduce until no more liquid is released and the mixture appears dry. Work the tomatoes through a food mill to obtain a thick coulis. Put the coulis in a beaker or other container with the Ultra-Sperse 3 and the xanthan gum and purée with an immersion blender until smooth.

2. Combine the vegetable oil with the lecithin and stir until the lecithin is dissolved, then purée the oil into the tomato mixture with an immersion blender (see photo). Add the vinegar to taste.

TOMATO-THICKENED ALMOND SAUCE

YIELD: ⅓ CUP (150 MILLILITERS)

almond milk	3 fluid ounces	100 milliliters
emulsified tomato purée (page 510)	1½ fluid ounces	50 milliliters
wine vinegar (or more to taste)	1 teaspoon	5 milliliters

Heat the almond milk in a small saucepan without letting it boil. Whisk in the tomato purée.

Add vinegar to taste. If the sauce isn't thick enough, reduce it.

TOMATILLOS

Tomatillos are more closely related to gooseberries than to regular tomatoes. They are not underripe tomatoes, but a separate fruit entirely. They have long been popular in Mexican cooking, where they are usually lightly stewed and flavored with various combinations of garlic, peppers, onions, and cilantro.

Tomatillos can be prepared in much the same way as tomatoes, except that their paper-like sheath should be removed and they should be lightly cooked, as they are usually too tough to eat raw. They can be gently stewed and puréed into a colorful tangy sauce that can be flavored with traditional Mexican flavors or adapted in other ways.

TOMATILLO SAUCE

YIELD: 2 CUPS (500 MILLILITERS)

fresh or canned tomatillos	1 pound	500 grams
onion, chopped	1 small	1 small
garlic cloves, chopped	2	2
fresh chiles, seeded and chopped	2 small	2 small
olive oil	3 tablespoons	45 milliliters
cilantro, finely chopped (optional)	¼ cup	60 grams
heavy cream (optional)	½ cup	125 milliliters

1. If using fresh tomatillos, remove the papery sheath from the outside. If using canned, drain them. Chop the tomatillos coarsely.

2. Sweat the onion, garlic, and chiles in the olive oil in a wide heavy-bottomed sauté pan for 10 minutes.

(continued)

3. Add the tomatillos and stew over medium heat until the mixture is completely soft. Continue to stir over the heat until the mixture becomes stiff. Add the cilantro, if using, and cook for about 10 minutes. (If you like to see the cilantro in the finished purée, add it at the end as described in the next step.) Work the tomatillo mixture through a drum sieve or coarse strainer to get rid of the seeds and peels.

4. Finish the purée with the cream, if using. If you prefer a richer puree, add more cream and simmer until the purée has the consistency you like. If you want the cilantro to be visible in the finished purée, add it here.

SORREL

Sorrel is undeservedly ignored by American cooks, who in all fairness have little access to it, even in summer when it is in season and easy to grow. It has a sharp, tangy flavor that makes it an excellent accompaniment to fish and white meats. It softens as soon as it comes in contact with heat, so it is easy to purée and use as both a flavoring and a thickener.

Sorrel is used in sauce making in two ways. In one method, the raw leaves are rolled and cut into thin strips (chiffonade) and added to white sauces at the end; in the other method, the sorrel is stewed by itself or with a touch of cream or butter, finely chopped or puréed with a food processor, and, for a more refined texture, forced through a drum sieve or coarse strainer.

Buy sorrel in large quantities from a greenmarket around May, when it should be cheap (it grows like a weed), stew it for 10 minutes in its own juices, and freeze it in tightly sealed plastic bags or clamp jars.

SORREL PURÉE

This is a simple purée used for finishing sauces. It must be thinned and enriched with butter or cream, and/or thickened with a hydrocolloid, if it is to be used alone to accompany meats or fish.

YIELD: 2 CUPS (500 MILLILITERS)

fresh sorrel leaves	1 pound	500 grams
butter	1 ounce	30 grams
liquid lecithin (optional)		0.6 gram

1. Wash the sorrel leaves and drain them thoroughly.

2. Melt the butter in a straight-sided sauté pan, stir in the lecithin if using, and add the sorrel leaves. If they do not all fit, add some, wait a minute until the first batch starts to wilt, and add the rest in batches.

3. When all the sorrel leaves have softened and turned a dull green-gray, take them out of the pan with a slotted spoon, pressing them against

the side of the pan to extract any liquid. Put the leaves in a bowl.

4. Reduce the liquid remaining in the sauté pan until it becomes syrupy, and add it to the sorrel leaves.

5. The leaves can be puréed in a food processor or blender, with an immersion blender, or chopped by hand. Force the mixture through a fine-mesh drum sieve.

Note: If the purée is to be used within a day or two, keep a sheet of plastic wrap directly on its surface; otherwise a black crust will form. To store the purée longer, keep it in a jar, refrigerated, covered with a thin film of oil, or freeze it in resealable plastic freezer bags.

Sorrel Sauces

Sorrel purée is used in sauce making as both a flavoring and thickener. Depending on the style of a restaurant, sorrel purée can be kept on hand and stirred into last-minute reductions or used to thicken and flavor sauces made in advance. It is almost always used in conjunction with butter or cream and is often thickened with a hydrocolloid.

The amount of sorrel purée to use will vary, depending on the desired thickness of the finished sauce. For a thick purée that should be served on the side, add 1 cup (250 milliliters) liquid to 2 cups (500 milliliters) purée. For a thin, almost broth-like consistency, 1 cup (250 milliliters) purée can be used to thicken 3 cups (750 milliliters) liquid.

SORREL SAUCE FOR FISH

YIELD: 2 CUPS (500 MILLILITERS)

flavorful liquid (see notes)	1 cup	250 milliliters
sorrel purée	¾ cup	185 milliliters
heavy cream	¼ cup	60 milliliters
liquid lecithin (optional)		0.6 gram
butter	1 ounce	30 grams
juice of 1 lemon (see notes)		
salt and pepper	to taste	to taste

1. Heat the flavorful liquid base.

2. Whisk in the sorrel purée until it is evenly distributed.

3. Heat the cream until hot but not boiling. If using the lecithin, stir it into the cream. Add the cream to the sauce base and check the consistency. If the sauce is too thin, add more purée. If it is too thick, thin it with more of the liquid base or cream.

4. Whisk in the butter. Whisk in the lemon juice and season with salt and pepper.

(continued)

Notes: The liquid base can be any appropriate flavorful liquid, such as fish stock, shellfish cooking liquid, court-bouillon, or mushroom cooking liquid, alone or in combination.

Lemon juice may seem redundant in an already acidic sauce, but it sharpens and brings into focus the flavor of the sorrel without making it aggressively acidic.

STABILIZED SORREL SAUCE FOR FISH

There are times, especially during a long dinner service, when the sauce may sit in a steam table for hours and separate. To avoid this, and to assist the purée in functioning as a thickener and emulsifier, hydrocolloids—here xanthan gum, Ultra-Sperse 3, and liquid lecithin—can be added to the purée before it is used.

YIELD: 2 CUPS (450 MILLILITERS)

court-bouillon or fresh fish stock (page 366 or 93)	1 cup	250 milliliters
sorrel purée (page 512)	¾ cup	185 grams
xanthan gum		0.9 gram
ultra-sperse 3		0.4 gram
heavy cream	¼ cup	60 milliliters
liquid lecithin		1 gram
lemon juice	1 tablespoon	15 milliliters
butter	1 ounce	30 grams
salt and pepper	to taste	to taste

1. Heat the court-bouillon and whisk in enough sorrel purée to give it the consistency you're looking for. Use an immersion blender to blend in the xanthan gum and Ultra-Sperse 3.

2. Heat the cream in a small saucepan until it comes to a simmer, then stir in the lecithin. Blend the cream into the purée. Add the lemon juice and swirl in the butter. Season with salt and pepper.

GARLIC

When raw garlic cloves are crushed or chopped, a series of chemical reactions produces their familiar assertive aroma and flavor. By cooking garlic cloves whole, either peeled or unpeeled, these reactions are bypassed, and the resulting flavor is surprisingly mild.

The easiest and most flavorful method for preparing cooked garlic purée is to wrap four or five heads together in aluminum foil and roast them for about 1 hour, until they are soft. The pulp is then extracted with a food mill or drum sieve. If a paler purée is needed for finishing cream sauces, unpeeled garlic cloves can be cooked in simmering water until they are soft. Some recipes suggest peeling the cloves and simmering them in several changes of water to attenuate their flavor. This usually is not necessary because whole cooked cloves are quite mild.

Buy garlic with large cloves surrounded with white skin and preferably a little violet near the base. The best garlic is the freshly harvested spring garlic, which has large, fresh-smelling cloves, and is sticky to the touch. Do not confuse this with elephant garlic, which also has large cloves but a peculiar taste; it should be avoided.

Garlic purée is delicious when served alone as a condiment to smear on grilled foods or on croutons. It should be well seasoned and is best when finished with extra-virgin olive oil or a little heavy cream. It also goes well with Provençal herbs such as thyme, marjoram, or oregano.

Garlic purée can also be used to finish soups and sauces or to thicken roasting juices or braising liquids. It works especially well with full-flavored fish and chicken dishes. One very direct method of using garlic purée for thickening roasting juices is to surround the uncooked roast with unpeeled garlic cloves and strain the roasted cloves along with the roasting juices through a sieve or food mill.

When garlic is puréed raw, it is so strong that it is used primarily as a flavoring for mayonnaise (Aïoli, page 418) or in conjunction with milder purées such as potatoes. Raw garlic can also be worked to a paste with a mortar and pestle or with the side of a knife and combined with finely chopped herbs to sprinkle over sautéed vegetables. A persillade is a classic mixture of raw garlic purée, chopped parsley, and sometimes breadcrumbs, but this mixture can be made with almost any full-flavored herb, such as thyme, marjoram, oregano, or lavender.

BAKED GARLIC PURÉE

YIELD: 1 CUP (250 MILLILITERS)

garlic heads	15	15
olive oil	1 tablespoon	15 milliliters

1. Preheat the oven to 325°F (160°C). Peel the outside papery skin off the garlic heads. Create 3 packets of garlic by wrapping 5 heads together in aluminum foil.

2. Bake the garlic until the cloves are soft, usually about 1 hour.

3. Extract the purée from the cloves with a food mill, or by pushing the garlic flesh through a drum sieve with a plastic pastry scraper or a strainer with the back of a ladle.

4. To store the purée in the refrigerator, place in mason jars or narrow containers, smooth the top with the back of a spoon, and dribble over the olive oil. Seal the jars or cover with plastic wrap. The purée darkens when exposed to air.

SWEET PEPPERS

In recent years, many different-colored sweet bell peppers have become available in American markets. Chefs have taken to them not only for their flavor but for the sunny, summery look they give to a finished plate. Sweet pepper purée can be used to finish cooking liquids, giving them color, flavor, and texture. It works especially well in sauces for grilled or sautéed foods. It can be incorporated into an already prepared sauce, such as a mayonnaise, or used as a sauce base in itself, with ingredients added to it (as for vinaigrette). The simplest way to use sweet pepper purée is to whisk it into a flavor base such as a stock, wine used to deglaze a sauté pan, or a little heavy cream. Exciting presentations can be made using different-colored sweet pepper purées together on the plate.

Thick sweet pepper purée can be chilled and stirred into whipped cream to form a delicate cold sauce for meats or fish. Sweet pepper purée can also be served alone as a condiment for barbecued or other full-flavored foods.

SWEET PEPPER PURÉE

When served alone, this sauce can be made hotter and more exciting by including some chiles, fresh Provençal herbs (fresh thyme, marjoram, or oregano), chopped garlic, onions, or hot pepper sauce such as Tabasco. Roasted and peeled peppers have a more intense and complex flavor, but if speed is an issue, make the purée with unpeeled raw peppers and then strain out the peels (through a drum sieve is best) after cooking.

YIELD: 3 CUPS (750 MILLILITERS)

sweet peppers of a single color	6 to 8	6 to 8
extra-virgin olive oil	¼ cup	60 milliliters

1. Grill the peppers or roast them on a gas stove (see page 420) until the skin is burnt and black all over. Scrape away the peel and rinse under cold water. Cut around and remove the stems from the peppers. Cut the peppers in half lengthwise and pull out the seeds and pulp.

2. Purée the peppers in a food processor or work them through a food mill or drum sieve. If an extremely stiff purée is needed, cook the purée while stirring constantly to reduce it. Just before serving or using, slowly stir in the oil.

POTATOES

Potato purée is used as a thickener for sauces and cooking liquids. It is also used as the base for thick strongly flavored sauces, especially those containing garlic, such as Skorthaliá (page 517). In hot sauces, it is often used in conjunction with cream and butter, but it can also be used alone. Sauces thickened with potato purée lack the perfectly smooth texture of starch-thickened sauces or of sauces thickened with cream and butter. Potato purée does, however, give a sauce a satisfying subtlety and depth of flavor without being too rich. Sauces that have been lightly thickened with potato purée can also be strained through a chinois to eliminate some of its mealy texture. The best potatoes for making purées for sauces are Yukon Golds or Yellow Finns.

POTATO PURÉE

YIELD: 2 CUPS (500 MILLILITERS)

potatoes	1 pound	500 grams
salt and pepper	to taste	to taste

1. Peel the potatoes. Keep them in a bowl of cold water until needed. If they are large, cut them into quarters.

2. Put the potatoes in a pot, and add just enough cold water to cover. Cook the potatoes at a slow simmer for 30 to 40 minutes, until they are easily penetrated with a knife.

3. Drain the potatoes, being sure to save the cooking liquid. (If a thinner purée is desired, the cooking liquid can be used instead of cream or butter to thin the finished purée.)

4. Purée the cooked potatoes by forcing them through a drum sieve or ricer. Using a drum sieve produces the finest texture and is also the least likely to break cell walls and release starch and thus give the purée a gluey consistency. A ricer prepares a lovely purée (it doesn't turn the purée gluey), but the purée will still have small lumps that are inappropriate for a sauce. If the purée is being beaten into a sauce to act as a thickener, the sauce should be strained through a chinois to eliminate the lumps. Never use a blender, food mill, or food processor, as these overwork the purée. Season the purée with salt and pepper.

SKORTHALIÁ
POTATO-GARLIC PURÉE

Stiff purées redolent of raw garlic can be found all along the Mediterranean, where they accompany grilled and sautéed vegetables such as eggplant and zucchini, cold vegetables such as beets and artichokes, meat, and fish, especially poached salt cod. A variety of ingredients are used to give the sauces body. An aïoli may contain only egg yolks and oil as thickeners, whereas the Greek version, skorthaliá, may contain ground almonds. This recipe uses potatoes for body.

The consistency of skorthaliá can be adjusted by adding stock or cooking liquid. The flavor and color can be enhanced by adding Sweet Pepper Purée (page 516), made with red peppers, to taste. Basil Oil (page 468) can also be added for flavor and color.

YIELD: 1 QUART (1 LITER)

(continued)

517

small firm-fleshed unpeeled potatoes	2 pounds	1 kilogram
garlic cloves, peeled	8	8
fine salt	1 tablespoon	15 milliliters
extra-virgin olive oil	1 cup	250 milliliters
wine vinegar or lemon juice	½ cup	125 milliliters
white pepper	to taste	to taste

1. Cover the potatoes with cold water and bring to a simmer. Cook for 20 to 30 minutes, until easily penetrated with a knife but before the skins begin to split.

2. Work the garlic to a paste with a mortar and pestle or by crushing the cloves with the side of a knife on a cutting board.

3. When the potatoes are done, peel them while they are still warm and add them a few at a time to the garlic paste in the mortar or in a bowl. Crush them with the pestle or the back of a wooden spoon, adding the salt while crushing them.

4. When the potato-garlic mixture is smooth, gradually work in the olive oil and vinegar. Season with pepper.

POACHED CHICKEN WITH TARRAGON

YIELD: 4 SERVINGS

whole chicken, 1	4 pounds	2 kilograms
tarragon	1 bunch	1 bunch
white chicken stock (page 88), warm	1 quart	1 liter
heavy cream	¼ cup	60 milliliters
potato purée (page 517)	½ cup	125 milliliters

1. Separate the chicken skin from the meat of the chicken with a forefinger. Do not try to pull the skin away from the breast bone or from the back, as it may tear.

2. Remove the tarragon leaves from the stems and place them between the skin and meat of the chicken.

3. Truss the chicken and place it in a tight-fitting, tall but narrow pot. Pour over just enough of the chicken stock to cover the chicken.

4. Slowly bring the stock to a simmer, skimming off any froth that floats to the surface. Poach the chicken for approximately 40 minutes. Transfer it to a plate and cover it lightly with foil to keep warm.

5. Reduce the poaching liquid while skimming carefully, until 1½ cups (375 milliliters) remain.

6. Add the cream to the reduced poaching liquid and whisk in the potato purée a bit at a time, until the sauce has the desired consistency. The sauce can be left very light—almost the consistency of a soup—or made thick enough to coat the pieces of chicken. For a very thin, light-textured sauce, strain through a chinois.

7. Remove and discard the skin from the chicken, carve the meat, and serve it with the sauce in hot bowls or wide deep plates.

POTATO-THICKENED SAUCE FOR PORK

Potato purée can be used as a light thickener for pork sauces, added to the cooking juices from a roast loin of pork, or used to thicken pan-deglazed sauces.

YIELD: 2 TO 4 SERVINGS

pork chops	4	4
clarified butter or oil	2 tablespoons	30 milliliters
full-bodied brown pork or chicken stock	¾ cup	185 milliliters
heavy cream	¼ cup	60 milliliters
potato purée (page 517)	3 tablespoons	45 milliliters
salt and pepper	to taste	to taste

1. Sauté the pork chops in the butter or oil. Transfer them to a plate and keep them warm while preparing the sauce.

2. Discard the fat in the sauté pan. Deglaze the pan with the stock and reduce by about one-third.

3. Whisk in the cream and potato purée. Reduce the sauce if it is too thin, or add more stock if it is too thick. Season with salt and pepper, and serve the sauce over the pork chops.

ONIONS

Onions that have been gently stewed develop a delicate sweetness and depth of flavor that make them a perfect foil for roast meats. The best-known onion sauce is Sauce Soubise I (page 139), which is made especially delicate and discreet by preliminary sweating of the onions (browning is avoided at all costs), which are then combined and puréed with Sauce Béchamel. A more rustic and assertive sauce can be prepared by simply stewing onion slices in butter until they are soft, cooking them for a few minutes longer with some heavy cream, and puréeing the mixture in a food processor. Both Sauce Soubise and a simple stewed onion purée can be flavored with roasting juices or stock and enriched with varying amounts of cream and butter. Onion purée served with grilled foods can be made more assertive by adding tomato purée, wine vinegar, or Provençal herbs.

Variations of sauce soubise and onion purée can be prepared with leeks, shallots, rocambole, and other similarly flavored vegetables.

Stewed Onion Purée

Traditional sauce soubise is quite thick by today's standards because it was often used to coat roasts (such as veal Orloff) or chops. A more contemporary version can be made by puréeing stewed onions with heavy cream and omitting the béchamel. This sauce can then be served as is or reduced to the desired consistency.

Peel and slice 5 pounds (2.25 kilograms) onions, and sweat them in 4 ounces (125 grams) butter. Be sure to use a heavy-bottomed pot and stir the onions almost constantly to prevent them from browning. The onion slices will shrink to about one-sixth of their original volume. When the onions are completely soft and there is no liquid left on the bottom of the pot, add ½ cup (125 milliliters) heavy cream. The sauce can be seasoned and served as is, or puréed in a blender or food processor or with an immersion blender, and strained. Be sure to purée it while it is still hot, or the cream will turn to butter. For a tangy sauce that is more appropriate for grilled foods, wine vinegar, red pepper purée, or tomato purée can be added to the onion sauce. The sauce can also be made more complex by adding reduced stock or roasting juices. Yield: 1 quart (1 liter)

SAUCE SOUBISE III

This modernist Sauce Soubise (see Chapter 6, "White Sauces," for the other two versions) is based on a fluid gel made from "milk" extracted from onions. Agar is the emulsifier. This recipe is adapted from one invented by Heston Blumenthal.

YIELD: 1 CUP (250 MILLILITERS)

white onion(s), peeled, sliced	1 pound	500 grams
butter	2 ounces	60 grams
milk	2 cups	500 milliliters
powdered agar		1.75 grams
salt	to taste	to taste

1. In a wide, heavy, straight-sided sauté pan, sweat the onions in the butter until the onions are completely soft but not at all browned. Pour over the milk and maintain at a very low simmer for 20 minutes or until the milk has reduced by about half.

2. Strain the onions through a chinois, pressing down on them, and measure out 1 cup (250 milliliters) of the liquid. Transfer to a small saucepan and let cool.

3. Use an immersion blender to blend the agar into the milk. Bring to a simmer and boil for about 3 minutes while blending with the immersion blender. Season with salt to taste. Pour the mixture into a baking dish to set, about 20 minutes.

4. Purée the gel in a blender until smooth and use it, cold or warm, as a sauce.

PARSLEY

Parsley that is puréed in a blender or with an immersion blender just before serving is an excellent flavoring for fish sauces or delicate meat sauces, especially for sweetbreads. Its flavor is robust yet subtle and complex. Once puréed, parsley quickly loses its pungent aroma and flavor and so should be used immediately. Parsley purée can be presented in two ways: as a stiff purée to be served alongside fish and meats, or as a thickener, blended directly into a sauce at the last minute.

STIFF PARSLEY PURÉE

This purée can be dolloped directly on the plate alongside hot foods, passed at the table in a sauceboat, or used as a thickener for thinner sauces and cooking liquids.

YIELD: 2 CUPS (500 MILLILITERS)

flat parsley	2 large bunches	2 large bunches
heavy cream	½ cup	125 milliliters
lambda carrageenan (optional)		2.5 grams
stiff potato purée (page 517)	1 cup	250 milliliters
salt and pepper	to taste	to taste

1. Pick the parsley leaves and discard the stems (or save for stock). Wash and dry the leaves thoroughly.

2. Bring the cream to a simmer with the lambda carrageenan, if using.

3. Put the parsley leaves in a blender. Turn the blender to slow speed and slowly pour in the hot cream through the hole in the center of the lid.

4. When all the cream has been added, turn the blender to high speed and purée for 1 minute.

(continued)

Alternatively, you can purée the parsley-cream mixture using an immersion blender.

5. Strain the purée through a fine chinois.

6. Transfer the parsley purée to a saucepan and whisk in the potato purée until the mixture has the desired consistency. Season with salt and pepper.

Finishing Sauces and Cooking Liquids with Parsley Purée

Parsley purée can be used as a thickener and flavoring for light-textured sauces using one of two methods. The first consists of blanching and puréeing parsley, then working it through a fine-mesh drum sieve. The purée is then whisked into made-to-order sauces as needed. Although convenient to use at the last minute, working the purée through the sieve is laborious and time-consuming.

The second method involves pouring hot cooking liquids, stocks, or court-bouillon over raw parsley leaves in a blender and puréeing at high speed for 2 minutes; an immersion blender can also be used. The hot sauce is then quickly strained through a strainer or chinois. This method sidesteps the drum sieve and captures the flavor of the parsley at its freshest, but it has the disadvantage of requiring considerable last-minute manipulation.

PLAIN PARSLEY PURÉE FOR FINISHING SAUCES
METHOD 1: USING A DRUM SIEVE

YIELD: 2 CUPS (500 MILLILITERS)

flat parsley	1 large bunch	1 large bunch
court-bouillon (page 366) or stock	¼ cup	60 milliliters
flavorful liquid sauce base	1½ cups	375 milliliters

1. Pick the parsley leaves and discard the stems (or save for stock). Blanch the leaves for 1 minute in boiling salted water. Drain the parsley in a colander and rinse with cold running water. Gently squeeze dry.

2. Put the blanched parsley in the blender with the court-bouillon and blend at high speed, stopping every 10 to 15 seconds to scrape the inside of the blender. Blend until the liquid is green and contains only tiny specks of parsley; this usually takes about 2 minutes.

3. Work the purée through a fine-mesh drum sieve with a plastic pastry scraper.

4. Heat the flavorful base in a saucepan and, just before serving, whisk in purée to taste.

METHOD 2: USING A BLENDER ALONE

YIELD: 1 CUP (250 MILLILITERS)

flat parsley	1 large bunch	1 large bunch
flavorful liquid sauce base	¾ cup	185 milliliters
sucrose esters (optional)		0.5 gram

1. Wash the parsley and pick the leaves, discarding the stems (or save for stock). Dry the leaves in a towel.

2. Bring the flavorful base and the sucrose esters, if using, to a simmer in a saucepan. Add the leaves and bring the liquid back to a simmer.

3. Strain out the leaves from the liquid, immediately rinse them with cold water, and return the liquid to the saucepan on the stove.

4. Put the leaves in a blender. Turn the blender on high and slowly pour in the simmering liquid through the small hole on top. Blend for 15 to 30 seconds. Strain through a medium-mesh strainer. Serve immediately.

Note: Because parsley contains no starch and contributes little bulk, liquids finished with parsley purée tend to be quite thin. If a thicker sauce is needed, thicken the sauce, using one of many methods, and add the parsley puree only a few seconds before serving. The perfume of parsley purée is lost after about 5 minutes, so if another liaison is being used, work quickly and do not overcook the purée. In a restaurant, these purées must be made to order or at regular intervals.

WATERCRESS

Like parsley, watercress can be puréed, thickened with potatoes, and served as an accompaniment, or it can be used directly to finish cooking liquids and sauces.

Sauces finished with watercress purée have become popular because of their bright color and delicate flavor. Like parsley, watercress purée used to finish sauces can be prepared in two ways: The first and easiest is to add the hot sauce base to blanched watercress in a blender (see method 2 for Parsley Purée, page 523). The second is to prepare a separate watercress purée and whisk it into the sauce base at the last minute. Watercress sauces and purées should not be kept hot for more than 1 hour or they lose their vibrant color and flavor.

Watercress Purée

When watercress purée is served on the side, as an accompaniment to meat or fish, its texture is reinforced by combining it with a starchy purée (usually potato), like the Stiff Parsley Purée (page 521). If the purée is being used to finish a sauce, it can be used alone. Usually, however, watercress sauces contain cream, butter, hydrocolloids such as xanthan gum, or other purées that attenuate watercress's sometimes bitter flavor.

Watercress purée is prepared in the same way as parsley purée: Simply blanch the watercress leaves (the stems tend to be bitter) for 2 minutes in boiling salted water, drain, and refresh them in cold running water. Purée them in a blender or with an immersion blender with a small amount of court-bouillon or stock, and force the mixture through a drum sieve. This purée will keep for several days in the refrigerator and can be used for finishing sauces (such as mayonnaise, hot emulsified egg sauces, beurre blanc–type sauces) or cooking liquids from fish, chicken, and delicately flavored meats. Keep the purée well covered until it is needed.

MUSHROOMS

While coarsely chopped mushrooms are often used in cooking (they're called "duxelles"), a finer purée is used to finish sauces. Fresh or dried mushrooms can be puréed and used as flavorful thickeners for a variety of sauces and cooking liquids. The mushrooms can first be cooked in a small amount of stock or water and drained; the cooking liquid is then reduced and puréed with the mushrooms in a blender or food processor or with an immersion blender. Or the mushrooms can be puréed raw and cooked in butter with lemon juice over high heat to eliminate their moisture.

For a fine-textured purée, purée cooked mushrooms in a food processor and then work them through a drum sieve. Almost any type of mushroom can be used to make purée, but always try to use them when they are fresh, especially when using the ordinary cultivated kind, which give an off-gray cast to the purée if they are old. Cooking mushrooms with lemon juice helps prevent them from turning dark, but too much juice may affect the final flavor. Dried wild mushrooms should be well rinsed and soaked; they can then be used in the same way as fresh.

Purées made from more assertive mushrooms such as morels, cèpes (porcini), and chanterelles make an excellent flavoring and thickener for brown sauces, red wine sauces, meat stews, or even as a finish for roasting juices. Cultivated mushrooms and delicately flavored wild varieties are excellent for finishing fish sauces.

Although many chefs often use vegetable purées as a way to avoid adding too many rich ingredients to their sauces, mushroom purées are best used in conjunction with a small amount of cream or butter, or xanthan gum.

MUSHROOM PURÉE

YIELD: 2 CUPS (500 MILLILITERS)

mushrooms	20 ounces	550 grams
stock or water or madeira (for wild mushrooms)	½ cup or ½ cup	125 milliliters or 125 milliliters
juice of 1 lemon		
xanthan gum (optional)		0.6 gram
butter (method 2 only)	1 ounce	30 grams

METHOD 1: USING COOKED MUSHROOMS

1. Thoroughly rinse the mushrooms. If they are large, halve or quarter them.

2. Put the mushrooms in a saucepan with the stock or Madeira and the lemon juice. Cover the saucepan and simmer for 10 minutes.

3. Drain the mushrooms and reduce the cooking liquid to about 2 tablespoons (30 milliliters).

4. Purée the mushrooms, the xanthan gum, if using, and the cooking liquid in a food processor for about 3 minutes. Scrape the sides of the food processor every 15 seconds. Force the purée through a drum sieve with a plastic pastry scraper. Keep the purée well covered with plastic wrap until needed.

METHOD 2: USING RAW MUSHROOMS

1. Rinse the mushrooms and cut them into quarters.

2. Purée the mushrooms with the stock or Madeira in a blender or in a tall, narrow container with an immersion blender.

3. Combine the puréed mushrooms, lemon juice, xanthan gum, if using, and butter in a straight-sided sauté pan. Cook the purée until all the moisture evaporates.

4. Use the purée as is, or work it through a drum sieve if a very fine purée is needed.

Red Wine–Mushroom Sauces

Deeply flavored brown sauces and red wine sauces take especially well to thickening with mushroom purée. The braising liquid from a red wine stew or the concentrated red wine base for Sauce Bordelaise or Meurette Sauce (pages 186 and 189) can be thickened using this method.

Use approximately one part mushroom purée to thicken three parts braising liquid or sauce base. Heat the liquid or sauce base to a simmer and whisk in the mushroom purée until the sauce has the desired consistency.

CAULIFLOWER

Cooked cauliflower can be puréed with a blender or immersion blender and then strained to give body and a subtle flavor to sauces. In the sauce below, it is combined with coconut milk and flavored with galangal.

CAULIFLOWER AND GALANGAL SAUCE

This exotic sauce captures the flavor of galangal, a rhizome that looks a lot like ginger but has a different flavor (see page 42). The cauliflower and coconut milk give consistency to this broth-like sauce, which is best on seafood.

YIELD: 2 CUPS (500 MILLILITERS)

cauliflower, ½ small	about 10 ounces	about 280 grams
white onion, chopped	1 small	1 small
chicken stock (page 88)	1 cup	250 milliliters
coconut milk	1 cup	250 milliliters
liquid lecithin (optional)		3.75 grams
1 piece fresh or frozen galangal	2 ounces	50 grams

1. Cut the small cauliflower florets away from the large stem at their base. Blanch the florets in boiling water for 1 minute. Drain.

2. Combine the cauliflower, onion, and stock in a small pot and simmer until the cauliflower softens, about 15 minutes.

3. Gently heat the coconut milk until hot to the touch, but not boiling, and whisk in the lecithin, if using.

4. Peel the galangal and slice into rounds the size of quarters. Add to the cauliflower, stir in the coconut milk, and simmer for 5 minutes more. Purée with an immersion blender and strain.

ROOT VEGETABLES

Flavorful root vegetables such as turnips, celeriac, and carrots can be puréed either alone or in combination and used to thicken sauces. One of the most useful techniques for thickening a braising or stewing liquid is to purée the aromatic vegetables included in the mirepoix and use these as the thickener. In this way the vegetables are not wasted; they will always provide more flavor than a thickener based on starch.

Root vegetables can also be glazed with stock and a small amount of butter before being puréed and used to finish sauces for roasted meats.

PURÉES AND PURÉE-THICKENED SAUCES

Thickening Meat Stews

Most meat stews contain aromatic vegetables—usually carrots, onions, and garlic—which are used to flavor the marinade and are eventually cooked along with the meat. In homemade versions, the aromatic vegetables are left in the stew when it is served. In more formal settings, the stewed meat, poultry, or fish is sorted out, and the aromatic vegetables are discarded and replaced with more "presentable" vegetables that have often been turned and cooked separately. The braising liquid is then usually reduced and thickened with beurre manié or cream and egg yolks (for a blanquette).

To thicken the stew with its own vegetable purée, sort the cooked meat from the vegetables. Put the vegetables in a pot with the braising liquid. Bring the liquid to a slow simmer and skim off the fat over a period of about 20 minutes. This step is designed to eliminate most of the fat contained in the vegetables. Strain out the vegetables and continue reducing the braising liquid (unless too little is left or it is already thick enough). Purée the vegetables in a blender or food processor, or with an immersion blender, or by forcing them through a drum sieve. When the braising liquid has been reduced enough and has a full flavor, whisk in the vegetable purée bit by bit, until the sauce has the desired consistency. To obtain a perfectly smooth texture, the sauce can be strained through a chinois. Because straining will make the sauce much thinner, it may be necessary to add more purée and strain it again until the consistency is right.

If the vegetables fail to emulsify the braising liquid, you can blend a small amount (0.5%) of xanthan gum into the warm sauce.

NUTS AND SEEDS

Nuts have been used in sauce making since Roman times and are still used in rough-textured purées—the best known is pesto—and to thicken Indian curries. In medieval European cooking, they were often used in conjunction with bread and sometimes cooked egg yolks to thicken sauces and cooking liquids. In seventeenth-century recipes for roux, almond flour was often included along with wheat flour. Gradually, classical French cooking abandoned nuts as thickeners in favor of starches and eventually cream, butter, and now hydrocolloids, but the use of nuts in sauce making is still common in European regional cooking and in Indian cooking. Sauces made with almonds, sesame seeds, pine nuts, pistachios, chestnuts, cashews, hazelnuts, and walnuts are the most common. In rough-hewn sauces, such as pestos, the nuts are ground or pounded with the other ingredients.

Buy shelled nuts in cans or tightly sealed bags. Taste them as soon as possible—a surprisingly large percentage of commercially available nuts are rancid. Nuts should be stored in a cool place.

Some nuts, such as hazelnuts, almonds, and walnuts, are covered with a thin skin that should be removed. To peel almonds, plunge them into boiling water for 1 minute, drain, and rub them in a wet towel. Hazelnuts are best toasted for 5 minutes and then rubbed together in a towel while still hot. Walnuts require longer blanching and meticulous scraping—most cooks do not bother peeling them. The flavor of nuts is often improved by lightly toasting them in a 350°F (175°C) oven for 5 to 10 minutes.

Nut Butters

When nuts are used as a thickener, they are often puréed into nut butters. To prepare a nut butter, purée peeled and lightly toasted nuts in a food processor for 3 to 5 minutes, stopping every 30 seconds to scrape the sides with a rubber spatula. To produce 1 cup (250 milliliters) of nut butter, use 8 ounces (250 grams) of nuts. Nut butters can be used to give a velvety texture to sauces that might otherwise be thickened with cream, butter, or starch. The subtle flavor of nuts goes especially well with spices and curries.

CARDAMOM–NUT BUTTER SAUCE

YIELD: 1 CUP (250 MILLILITERS)

full-flavored stock or cooking liquid	1 cup	250 milliliters
husked cardamom seeds	1 teaspoon	3 grams
almond, hazelnut, or cashew butter	1 tablespoon	15 milliliters
heavy cream (optional)	2 tablespoons	30 milliliters

1. Heat the stock in a 1-quart (1 liter) saucepan and add the cardamom seeds. Gently simmer the stock with the seeds for 15 minutes to infuse their flavor.

2. Whisk in the nut butter and cream, if using. Thin the sauce as needed with additional stock, or thicken it with slightly more nut butter.

3. Strain through a fine chinois.

NUT CURRY SAUCE

YIELD: 1 CUP (250 MILLILITERS)

onion, chopped	1 small	1 small
butter (if using glice) *or* butter (if not using glice)	4 tablespoons *or* 1 tablespoon	60 grams *or* 15 grams
curry powder	2 teaspoons	10 milliliters
freshly grated coconut	¼ cup	60 milliliters
stock or cooking liquid	1½ cups	375 milliliters
mono- and diglycerides (glice) (optional)		0.6 gram
nut butter	1 to 2 tablespoons	15 to 30 milliliters
salt and pepper	to taste	to taste

1. Sweat the onion in 1 tablespoon (15 grams) of the butter until translucent. Do not allow the onion to brown.

2. Add the curry powder and cook for 3 minutes more.

3. Add the coconut and stock and cook at a slow simmer for 15 minutes to infuse the flavor of the grated coconut.

4. If you're using Glice, heat the remaining butter in a very small pan to about 140°F (60°C).

Work the Glice into the butter and stir until it dissolves.

5. Whisk the nut butter into the coconut-stock mixture, then whisk in the Glice-butter mixture. Stir the sauce until it has the desired consistency. Reduce to thicken if needed or thin with additional stock, water, or coconut milk.

6. Season with salt and pepper and strain through a coarse strainer. If you want a very smooth purée, work the mixture through a chinois or, if it's stiff enough, a drum sieve with a fine mesh screen.

CASHEW SAUCE

I n southern India, cashews are ground to a paste and used to thicken sauces. Here is a typical Keralan sauce used for chicken.

YIELD: ENOUGH SAUCE FOR 4 SERVINGS (1 CUP/250 MILLILITERS)

cardamom pods, crushed, seeds reserved	6	6
minced fresh ginger	1 teaspoon	5 milliliters
minced garlic	1 teaspoon	5 milliliters
ground cumin	1 teaspoon	5 milliliters
minced onion	3 tablespoons	45 milliliters
clarified butter	3 tablespoons	45 milliliters
salt and pepper	to taste	to taste
sugar	¼ teaspoon	2 milliliters
dried fenugreek leaves (optional)	1 big pinch	1 big pinch
milk	½ cup	125 milliliters
cashew paste (recipe follows)	2 tablespoons	30 milliliters

1. Gently sauté the cardamom seeds, ginger, garlic, cumin, and onion in the butter for about 5 minutes.

2. Season with salt and pepper, sugar, and fenugreek leaves, if using, and stir in the milk and cashew paste. Whisk until smooth.

(continued)

Purée 1 cup (250 milliliters) roasted cashews with ½ cup (125 milliliters) water in a food processor for about 2 minutes, until smooth. Store in a jar in the refrigerator. Expect the mixture to separate somewhat over time. Stir the paste until smooth before using. Yield: 1 cup (250 milliliters)

Almonds

Almonds have long played a role in European, Middle Eastern, and Indian cookery. In European cooking, before the development of roux, ground almonds, along with egg yolks and breadcrumbs, were used to give body to sauces.

A large number of sauces containing almonds can be found in Europe's regional cuisines. Spanish romesco is a well-seasoned purée of almonds, hazelnuts, peppers, garlic, and breadcrumbs, often flavored with tomatoes. It is usually served with grilled or poached fish and shellfish. Picada (page 530) is a similar mixture, used to thicken soups and stews.

Bitter almonds are unavailable in the United States because of their high cyanide content, so here only sweet almonds are used. For a more pungent almond flavor, a drop or two of almond extract can be added, but be careful or it may mask the flavor even of garlic.

Almonds are excellent in curry sauces, where they soften the flavor of the spices and add an ineffable subtlety to the sauce. They are surprisingly efficient as thickeners, so they can be used to thicken without making the sauce too rich.

PICADA
GARLIC-ALMOND PURÉE

This mixture is used as a thickener. All of the ingredients except the olive oil can be puréed in a food processor until smooth. The olive oil is stirred in by hand at the end.

Picada can be used as a thickener for meat and fish stews and soups in much the same way as an aïoli is used to thicken bourride. To thicken fish soups and stews, it is best to whisk the hot cooking liquid into the picada in a bowl. To thicken meat stews, be sure to strain and thoroughly degrease the liquid before combining it with the picada. Again, the liquid should be whisked into the picada, not the other way around. For a perfectly smooth sauce, strain through a fine chinois. One to 2 tablespoons (15 to 30 milliliters) of picada can be used to thicken ½ cup (125 milliliters) broth or cooking liquid.

YIELD: 2 CUPS (500 MILLILITERS)

garlic cloves, peeled	4	4
peeled and toasted almonds	4 ounces	125 grams
parsley, leaves from	1 bunch	1 bunch
white bread, lightly toasted, crusts removed	3 slices	3 slices
water	½ cup	125 milliliters
extra-virgin olive oil	½ cup	125 milliliters

1. Put the garlic, almonds, parsley, and bread into a food processor. Purée for 4 to 5 minutes, until smooth.

2. Add the water 2 tablespoons (30 milliliters) at a time, and continue puréeing until the picada is stiff but no longer oily. Scrape down the sides of the food processor from time to time for an evenly textured mixture. Transfer the picada to a mixing bowl and slowly stir in the olive oil with a wooden spoon.

3. Keep the picada covered until needed. It is best used the same day.

Chestnuts

Chestnut purée has long been the traditional accompaniment to roast game. It usually has the texture of mashed potatoes and is eaten along with the meat as a vegetable. The chestnuts are often glazed with a flavorful stock and sometimes port wine to underline their natural sweetness before they are puréed. Bacon or smoked ham is sometimes cooked along with the chestnuts to accent the purée with an agreeable smoky flavor.

Chestnut purée is commercially available—do not confuse it with the sweetened version, *crème de marrons*—or can be prepared from scratch. Because of the effort required to make purée starting with whole chestnuts, it is usually worthwhile to buy them already shelled with the inner "nut" peeled.

To pull away the outer peel, make a slit with a sharp paring knife on the rounded outer side (be sure to add the slit or the chestnuts are likely to explode in the oven) and roast the chestnuts for about 10 minutes in a 400°F (200°C) oven in a roasting pan. It is easiest to shell and peel the chestnuts while they are still hot, so work quickly or take only a few out of the oven at a time. Use a kitchen towel to hold each chestnut while pulling apart each side of the slit so the chestnut core pops out. Do your best (it isn't always easy) to remove the inner membrane by rubbing the hot chestnuts together in a towel. If the inner skin sticks, plunge the shelled chestnuts into boiling water for 1 or 2 minutes, or simply leave it.

CHESTNUT PURÉE

YIELD: 2 CUPS (500 MILLILITERS)

shelled and peeled chestnuts	1 pound	500 grams
celery, 1 stalk, thinly sliced	3 ounces	100 grams
full-flavored brown stock	2 cups	500 milliliters
port	½ cup	125 milliliters
butter	2 ounces	60 grams

1. Combine all the ingredients in a straight-sided sauté pan and bring to a simmer. Cover the chestnuts with a round of parchment paper or half-cover the pan with a lid. Simmer until the chestnuts are soft and easily crushed with a fork and the liquids have reduced and formed a syrupy glaze on the bottom of the pan.

2. Purée the chestnut mixture in a food processor until smooth, about 3 minutes. (The resulting purée is very fine, so it is not necessary to force it through a drum sieve.) When storing chestnut purée, be sure to cover it with a sheet of plastic wrap directly on its surface, to prevent a skin from forming.

Coconut

Coconut water taken from the inside of the coconut and coconut milk extracted from grated coconut pulp have long been used as a moistening liquid and flavoring for curry sauce (page 151). The coconut pulp, finely puréed in a food processor and forced through a drum sieve, can also be used as a thickener. The shrimp sauce that follows is a variation of the traditional Brazilian fish stew *vatapá*.

SHRIMP WITH COCONUT AND PEANUT SAUCE

YIELD: 8 FIRST-COURSE SERVINGS

shrimp, preferably with heads	32	32
onion, chopped	1 small	1 small
garlic cloves, crushed, peeled	2	2
fresh ginger slice	¼ inch	5 millimeters
peanut oil	2 tablespoons	30 milliliters
fish stock, chicken stock, or court-bouillon (page 93, 88, or 366)	1 cup	250 milliliters
sucrose esters (optional)		1.25 grams
tomatoes, peeled, seeded, coarsely chopped	3 medium	3 medium
jalapeños, seeded, finely chopped	1 or 2	1 or 2
peanuts	4 ounces	125 grams
puréed pulp from 1 coconut or one 10-ounce (280-gram) bag dried grated coconut		
cilantro, finely chopped	1 small bunch	1 small bunch
salt and pepper	to taste	to taste

1. Peel and devein the shrimp, saving the shells and heads (if available). Refrigerate the shrimp.

2. Gently sweat the shrimp shells and heads with the onion, garlic, and ginger in the peanut oil for 15 minutes.

3. Moisten the mixture with the stock and simmer for 15 minutes. Strain through a chinois into a second saucepan. Discard the solids. Use an immersion blender to blend in the sucrose esters, if using. Continue blending while bringing the liquid to a simmer, about 2 minutes.

4. Add the tomatoes and jalapeños to the sauce base. Simmer for 15 minutes.

5. Purée the peanuts and coconut in a food processor for 3 minutes. Force the coconut-peanut purée through a drum sieve with a plastic pastry scraper.

6. Put the shrimp in a straight-sided sauté pan and cover with the hot sauce base. Poach for 1 to 2 minutes. Transfer the shrimp to hot soup plates.

7. Whisk the coconut-peanut purée and cilantro into the hot poaching liquid. Season with salt and pepper. Ladle over the shrimp in the soup plates.

Pine Nuts

Pine nuts, sometimes called *pignolia* or *pignoli*, are actually the seeds of pine trees. They are used in Mediterranean sauces, for which they are crushed with a mortar and pestle with a variety of herbs and sometimes olives. They are best known as one of the ingredients in Genoese pesto sauce (page 535). Pine nuts, except for inferior Chinese examples (the best pine nuts come from Italy), are expensive. In many recipes, walnuts can be substituted.

Pistachios

Pistachios are sometimes used in the same way as almonds or walnuts, as the basis for pestos. Like pine nuts and almonds, they were often called for in medieval cooking. Even though they were more expensive than almonds, they were appreciated for their distinctive green color. (Pistachios turn green only after they are cooked.) They should be blanched and peeled in the same way as almonds. Beautiful roasted green pistachio oil is available from Leblanc.

Walnuts

Like pine nuts and pistachios, walnuts are excellent when coarsely pounded or chopped, contributing both texture and flavor to a finished sauce. They are often used in Italian cooking, in sauces for pasta.

WALNUT AND PARMESAN CHEESE SAUCE FOR PASTA

A dry, well-aged goat or sheep's milk cheese may be substituted for the Parmesan cheese in this sauce. Don't worry if this sauce separates; that's part of its rustic charm.

YIELD: 2 CUPS (500 MILLILITERS)

shelled walnuts	8 ounces	250 grams
extra-virgin olive oil	½ cup	125 milliliters
heavy cream	¼ cup	60 milliliters
freshly grated parmigiano-reggiano	2 ounces	50 grams
finely chopped parsley leaves	3 tablespoons	45 milliliters
salt and pepper	to taste	to taste

1. Chop the walnuts in a food processor; use the pulse mechanism to avoid turning the walnuts into a purée. The pieces should be about the size of peppercorns.

2. Gently heat the chopped walnuts in the olive oil and cream. Do not let the sauce boil.

3. Stir in the grated cheese and the parsley. Simmer for 1 minute. Season with salt and pepper.

PESTOS

Although most people associate pesto with the traditional Genoese version of crushed pine nuts, garlic, basil, cheese, and olive oil, *pesto* simply means "pestle." The term's meaning is, in fact, applied to a whole family of sauces made of solid ingredients crushed to a paste in a mortar or food processor. Perhaps it is the rough-and-tumble last-minute character of these sauces or the brightly flavored ingredients they contain that make them among the most satisfying of foods.

Pistou is the southern French version of pesto and differs from Genoese pesto only in that it sometimes contains tomatoes but never pine nuts. It is used almost exclusively to finish the French version of minestrone, called *soupe au pistou*.

Although tapenades and anchoïades are usually not referred to as pestos, the principles and techniques used to prepare them are the same: A variety of solid ingredients are worked to a paste with a mortar and pestle. A food processor should be used cautiously so as not to risk chopping the ingredients too fine such that the sauce ends up looking like a purée. This is particularly important when chopping olives, since overworking olives can cause bitterness.

GENOESE PESTO

Genoese pesto is not only wonderful over pasta but makes an excellent sauce for grilled meats, fish, and vegetables. It can also be stirred into soups at the last minute.

YIELD: 1 QUART (1 LITER)

basil leaves	1 pound	500 grams
garlic cloves, peeled	5	5
toasted pine nuts	3 tablespoons	45 milliliters
coarse salt	1 teaspoon	5 milliliters
freshly grated parmigiano-reggiano	8 ounces	250 grams
extra-virgin olive oil	1 cup	250 milliliters

(continued)

1. Wash the basil leaves and make sure they are well dried. (If they are wet, some of their pungent flavor will be lost.)

2. Put all the ingredients except the olive oil in a mortar or food processor. If not all the basil fits, it may be necessary to start grinding and add it a bit at a time. Work or pulse the mixture to a coarse paste. If using a food processor, scrape the paste into a mixing bowl.

3. Gently work in the olive oil with a pestle or wooden spoon.

Pistou/Pesto Variations

Thick, intensely flavored pastes can be made with other ingredients using pesto and pistou as models. In French cooking, many of these mixtures have an *-ade* ending and are used in various ways, sometimes for finishing more complex sauces and sometimes served atop strongly flavored grilled or sautéed foods.

INDIAN MINT PESTO

YIELD: 1 CUP (250 MILLILITERS)

mint leaves, tightly packed	1 cup	250 milliliters
finely chopped jalapeños	2 tablespoons	30 milliliters
finely chopped onion	2 tablespoons	30 milliliters
finely chopped fresh ginger	½ teaspoon	3 milliliters
lemon juice	4 teaspoons	20 milliliters
almond butter (page 442)	3 tablespoons	45 milliliters
salt	to taste	to taste

Combine all the ingredients in a food processor. If you prefer a coarse paste, pulse the food processor until you get the consistency you like; if you prefer a fine paste, just purée until smooth, about 20 seconds.

ANCHOÏADE

An anchoïade is prepared by chopping or crushing salt-cured or oil-packed anchovies into a paste with garlic, and sometimes other ingredients such as herbs and olives. Olive oil is then stirred into the mixture. The finished anchoïade is served with grilled vegetables or on croutons. Salted or canned anchovies should be soaked in cold water and then drained on towels to eliminate the salt or oil before using.

TAPENADE

This mixture of finely chopped olives makes a marvelous spread for toasted croutons, hot pasta, and grilled vegetables, fish, and meats. This recipe uses a mortar and pestle, but a food processor can be used, although the texture will be more homogeneous and much of the rustic, rough-hewn quality of the sauce will be lost. Tapenade recipes always contain capers—*tapéno* means "caper" in the Provençal dialect—but the dried currants, which add a note of sweetness that relieves the saltiness of the mixture, are not traditional.

YIELD: 1 QUART (1 LITER)

dried currants	6 ounces	175 grams
oil-cured Moroccan olives	2 pounds	1 kilogram
salt-cured or oil-packed anchovy fillets	4 ounces	125 grams
garlic cloves, peeled	2	2
capers, drained	3 ounces	75 grams
extra-virgin olive oil	½ cup	125 milliliters
salt and pepper	to taste	to taste

1. Soak the currants in just enough warm water to cover for 1 hour, to plump and soften them.

2. Pit the olives by tapping them with a mallet or a heavy pan to push the pits through the flesh.

3. Soak the anchovies in cold water to eliminate salt and oil (see Note).

4. Work the garlic and anchovies to a paste with a mortar and pestle.

5. Drain the currants and add them, the pitted olives, and the capers to the anchovy-garlic paste. Work the mixture to the desired consistency with the pestle; the sauce is always better when left coarse, containing irregular bits and pieces of olive.

6. Work in the olive oil and season with salt and pepper.

Note: Salted anchovies should be soaked for 30 minutes, oil-packed anchovies for 10 minutes.

GREEN OLIVE AND CAPER TAPENADE

The green olives in this recipe are unusual, as is the hard-boiled egg, which softens the flavor and helps bind the mixture. Green olive and caper tapenade can be used on grilled foods and as a quick finish for full-flavored fish broths and poaching liquids.

YIELD: 2 CUPS (500 MILLILITERS)

green olives (see note)	1 pound	500 grams
capers, drained	4 ounces	125 grams
garlic clove, peeled	½	½
parsley, chopped	1 small bunch	1 small bunch
hard-boiled eggs	3	3
whole-grain mustard	2 tablespoons	30 milliliters
extra-virgin olive oil	¼ cup	60 milliliters
salt and pepper	to taste	to taste

1. Pit the olives by first hitting them with a mallet or heavy pan, then cutting around the pits with a paring knife if necessary.

2. Put the olives, capers, garlic, parsley, eggs, and mustard in a mortar or food processor. Work the mixture to a stiff paste, making sure that little pieces of each component are left intact; the mixture should not be a purée.

3. Stir in the olive oil by hand and add salt and pepper as needed.

Note: Use Picholine or other natural olives; do not use canned California varieties of green olives.

BEANS AND OTHER LEGUMES

Almost any variety of bean or legume can be cooked, puréed, and whisked into a sauce to give it body, flavor, and/or color. In most areas of the United States, dried beans are the most commonly available, but fresh lima beans, cranberry beans, and fava beans often appear in spring and summer in local greenmarkets. Fresh and frozen peas can also be used as sauce thickeners.

Dried beans must be soaked for 2 to 3 hours in warm water to soften them before cooking. They have soaked long enough when the skins start to wrinkle. Longer soaking can cause the beans to start germinating, so it is best not to soak beans overnight. Lentils do not require softening.

Dried beans will not soften if cooked with acidic ingredients, so do not add wine or tomato purée until the beans have already completely softened. Some chefs add a pinch of baking soda to the water, which makes it alkaline and helps soften the beans.

Dried beans usually require about three times their weight of water for cooking: For example, 1 pound (500 grams) beans should be cooked in 6 cups (1.5 liters) water. Always start dried beans in cold water and bring the water to a simmer over a 45-minute period. Do not rush the cooking or the beans will harden. Depending on how the bean purée is to be used, other ingredients such as onions, celery, carrots, garlic, and fennel can be added. A bouquet garni is almost always a welcome addition. Many recipes for bean purées suggest adding smoked meats, such as ham, ham hocks, or bacon, but these are inappropriate if the purée will be used to finish a delicate sauce.

Bean purées should be kept covered with plastic wrap pressed down against the surface to prevent a skin from forming.

Fava Beans

Fava (broad) beans are one of the few varieties of bean that are not native to the Americas; they have been used in European cooking for centuries. They are often available fresh, in spring and summer, in local greenmarkets. When properly prepared, they have a bright green color and a subtle, complex flavor. Their main disadvantage is that they must be peeled twice, so preparing a substantial amount of purée can be time-consuming. Much of the weight of the unshelled bean will also be lost: 2 pounds (1 kilogram) unshelled beans yields 1 pound (500 grams) shelled beans, which in turn yields 20 percent less (13 ounces/400 grams) when the inner skin is removed. Unlike dried beans, which are slowly simmered, fresh fava beans should be cooked for 1 minute, like most green vegetables, uncovered in a large pot of boiling salted water (a sprig of fresh winter savory in the water will add an interesting note). Rinse the beans immediately with cold water so they don't lose their color or overcook and become aggressive. The recipe that follows can be used for thickening sauces; if the purée is to be served alone as an accompaniment, it should be enriched with butter or cream.

FAVA BEAN PURÉE

This recipe can also be used to prepare a purée of fresh or frozen peas. If using frozen peas—which can be excellent—skip the preliminary blanching and simply purée the thawed peas.

YIELD: 1 CUP (250 MILLILITERS)

fresh fava beans in the pod	1 pound	500 grams
appropriate liquid (see step 4)	½ cup	125 milliliters

1. Remove the beans from the pods.

2. Remove the skin from each of the beans. This is best done with a small paring knife or a thumbnail.

3. Cook the beans for about a minute in a pot of rapidly boiling salted water. Drain the beans in a colander and rinse them with cold running water to cool them.

4. Purée the beans in a food processor. Thin the purée with liquid if desired; cream, butter, stock, roasting juices, or braising liquids are some of the possible options.

5. If you want the puree to be perfectly smooth, force it thorough a drum sieve. Keep it in a bowl, covered with plastic wrap, until needed.

Lentils

Lentils are easy to cook—they require no presoaking—and come in several colorful varieties. The type most familiar to Americans is the common brown lentil, but the French have a tiny green variety called Le Puy that is particularly tasty. In India, a striking orange variety is sometimes used. Lentils cook faster than most types of dried beans, usually within 1 hour.

Lentil purée can be served as an accompaniment to red meats (it is best with game) or used to finish sauces. When served as a purée, it should be well enriched with butter or cream and preferably some roasting or braising juices. It can also be improved by gently sweating mirepoix with ham or bacon before adding the lentils. A note of sweetness from Madeira, port, or sugar will often enhance the flavor of the purée.

LENTIL PURÉE

YIELD: 2 CUPS (500 MILLILITERS)

lentils	1 cup	250 milliliters
carrot (optional)	½	½
onion (optional)	1 medium	1 medium
medium bouquet garni (page 52)	1	1
butter	2 ounces	60 grams
water	3 cups	750 milliliters

1. Rinse the lentils and peel and coarsely chop the carrot and onion, if using.

2. Combine all the ingredients in a heavy-bottomed saucepan. Bring to a slow simmer and cook until the lentils crush easily between thumb and forefinger.

3. Remove the bouquet garni and purée the mixture in a food processor or food mill.

4. Force the purée through a drum sieve. Keep it well covered with plastic wrap until needed.

RED WINE SAUCE FINISHED WITH LENTIL PURÉE

The earthy flavor of lentils makes them an excellent liaison for full-bodied brown and red wine sauces. Thicken 1 cup (250 milliliters) of either Sauce Bordelaise (page 186) or Meurette Sauce base (page 189) with ½ cup (125 milliliters) lentil purée. Strain the finished sauce through a chinois.

White Beans and Flageolet Beans

After soaking for 2 hours, white beans and flageolet beans can be softened and made easier to digest by precooking them for 15 minutes with a pinch of baking soda, draining them, and then moistening them again with fresh boiling water. If the purée is being used to finish other sauces, no other ingredients need be added, but if the purée is being served on its own, it is best combined with mirepoix vegetables (sectioned and simmered with the beans), cubes of ham (preferably smoked), bacon lardons, and/or herbs before puréeing. The purée can also be enriched with cream, butter, roasting juices, reduced stock, or other flavorful liquids if it is to be served as an accompaniment.

WHITE OR FLAGEOLET BEAN PURÉE

YIELD: 2 CUPS (500 MILLILITERS)

white or flageolet beans	1 cup	200 grams
baking soda	1 teaspoon	5 milliliters
onion, chopped (optional)	1 small	1 small
carrot, chopped (optional)	1 small	1 small
celery, chopped (optional)	½ stalk	½ stalk
ham, chopped (optional)	2 ounces	60 grams
bacon, diced (optional)	2 ounces	60 grams
butter	1 ounce	30 grams
large bouquet garni (page 52; optional)	1	1
cold water	3 cups	750 milliliters
assorted chopped herbs (optional)	to taste	to taste
salt and pepper (optional)	to taste	to taste

1. Soak the beans for 2 hours in lukewarm water.

2. Drain the beans and put them in a pot with the baking soda and enough water to cover. Bring the water to a simmer, cook the beans for 15 minutes, and drain.

3. If using any of the optional ingredients—the onion, carrot, celery, ham, or bacon—sweat them in the butter until the vegetables have softened and/or the bacon has rendered.

4. Add the beans, and any additional ingredients you've decided to include, and the bouquet garni.

5. Cover with the water. Cook the beans, partially covered to prevent the mixture from frothing up and overflowing, at a slow simmer for an hour or until they are easily crushed between thumb and forefinger. If at any point they threaten to run dry, add more water.

6. Drain the beans, remove the bouquet garni, and add the chopped herbs, if using. Purée the beans and any added ingredients in a food processor. If you want the purée to be perfectly smooth, force it though a drum sieve. Season with salt and pepper.

7. Put the purée in a bowl and cover it with plastic wrap until needed.

USING PURÉES WITH OTHER METHODS

Most purées have a distinct character of their own that can sometimes interfere with the flavor of a delicate sauce. For this reason chefs often combine different purées or use them with different types of liaisons. They are excellent when used in conjunction with butter, cream, hydrocolloids, or egg yolks because they lend support to the final texture of the sauce, so less of the rich ingredients needs to be used to achieve the same effect.

WATERCRESS AND MUSHROOM SAUCE FOR FISH

This sauce can be treated as a stock-based sauce, or the same method can be used to finish the cooking liquid for integral fish sauces. Lambda carrageenan keeps this relatively unstable sauce from separating.

YIELD: 1¼ CUPS (285 MILLILITERS)

fish cooking liquid, court-bouillon (page 366), or fish stock (page 93)	¾ cup	185 milliliters
leben yogurt	4 teaspoons	20 milliliters
mushroom purée (page 525)	¼ cup	60 milliliters
lambda carrageenan (optional)		0.4 gram
watercress purée (page 523)	4 teaspoons	20 milliliters
salt and pepper	to taste	to taste

Heat the cooking liquid in a 1-quart (1 liter) sloping-sided saucepan. Whisk in the yogurt, mushroom purée, and lambda carrageenan, if using. Simmer the mixture until it has the consistency you like. If it remains too thin, or threatens to separate, whisk in another 0.2 gram of lambda carrageenan and bring back to a simmer. Add the watercress purée just before serving to prevent the purée from turning gray. Season with salt and pepper.

PARSLEY EMULSION

Few of us recognize the complex and beguiling aroma and flavor of fresh parsley. In restaurants, it is usually chopped in advance so that it loses its delicacy and takes on the smell of lawnmower clippings. Because of this, chopped parsley, parsley purées, and this emulsion must be prepared within 15 minutes of serving. Because parsley contains no starch or natural emulsifiers, any sauce based on it must use another thickener that will hold the puréed parsley in suspension—here, xanthan gum and Ultra-Sperse 3.

This sauce can be used for either fish or white meat such as veal or chicken. It goes especially well with sweetbreads. Unless gelatinous stock is used (which would remain gelled when cool), this emulsion can be served hot or cold.

YIELD: 1 CUP (250 MILLILITERS)

xanthan gum		0.5 gram
ultra-sperse 3		1.25 grams
stock or court-bouillon, hot	1 cup	250 milliliters
parsley, leaves from	1 bunch	1 bunch
salt and pepper	to taste	to taste

1. Use an immersion blender to blend the xanthan gum and Ultra-Sperse 3 into the hot liquid. Return the mixture to a simmer in a 2-quart (2 liter) sloping-sided saucepan, whisking all the while. Take off the heat and let cool.

2. If you're serving the sauce hot, bring the liquid to a simmer; if serving cold, start with cold liquid. Immediately before serving, add the parsley leaves and purée with an immersion blender. Strain through a chinois, season with salt and pepper, and serve.

PASTA SAUCES

Every region of Italy has its traditional pasta favorites. Although pasta sauces are easy to invent and improvise, it is helpful to keep in mind certain principles and time-proven traditions. All pasta dishes contain a liquid component that functions as a carrier for flavor and prevents the pasta from sticking to itself. Cooked and drained pasta tossed only with solid ingredients will soon become a gummy mess. In Italy, a popular method of serving pasta, especially stuffed pasta, is in a *minestra*. A minestra is simply a broth to which a simple garniture such as vegetable cubes, a spoonful of Parmesan cheese, or several pieces of stuffed pasta is added. For stuffed pasta, the broth and a little grated Parmesan cheese are the only "sauce."

We Americans, however, are more familiar with pasta served with a limited amount of a savory sauce or sauce-like liquid. The most familiar sauces are based on tomatoes or olive oil, but other ingredients such as cream, butter, the cooking liquid from shellfish, meat juices, and rendered fats (especially pancetta and prosciutto fats) are all used to create a flavorful medium for a pasta sauce. Once the basic liquid medium is established, the sauce can be augmented with herbs, vegetables, shellfish, salty condiments such as capers or olives, and chopped meats.

PASTA STYLES

Although cooks in America tend to combine sauces with any variety of pasta that comes to mind, most Italians associate particular kinds of pasta with a region's own specialties and sauces. In northern Italy, fresh pasta made with eggs is more popular than the dried pasta, often made only with water, usually served in the south. To delineate which sauces are traditionally served with what pasta would be the subject of an entire book, but there are a few principles and traditions that help make a judicious pairing of pasta and sauce.

Fresh pasta is usually cut in strands and served with the richer sauces—often containing cream, butter, and meats—associated with northern Italian cooking, whereas dried pasta, which comes in a myriad of shapes (often contorted) and sizes, is usually associated with the tomato-based and vegetable sauces of the south. One reliable approach when deciding what pasta to use is to consider how much of the sauce will cling to the pasta and how rich the sauce is. A pasta with a lot of nooks and crannies such as *radiatore* ("little radiators") will hold onto too much of a very rich sauce based on butter or cream. A light tomato sauce, on the other hand, will slide off a smooth, slippery fettuccine or spaghetti. If pasta with a meat sauce is being served as a first course, a smooth-strand pasta and relatively little sauce will be appropriate, while the same dish served as a main course might be better with an irregularly shaped pasta and relatively more sauce.

A NOTE ABOUT SERVING SIZES

In Italy, pasta is always served in relatively modest amounts before the main course—never with the main course or as the main course itself, as it is sometimes served in the United States. The amount of pasta served in Italy as a first course (or second course if it follows antipasti) is about two-thirds the amount served in the United States as a main course. One pound (450 grams) of dried pasta or 1½ pounds (675 grams) of fresh is usually about right for four main-course or six pasta-course servings.

OLIVE OIL AND BUTTER: THE BASE FOR THE SIMPLEST SAUCES

One of the simplest and most satisfying ways to eat pasta is to toss it with the best extra-virgin olive oil or sweet butter and sprinkle it with freshly grated Parmesan cheese. Butter is the basis for the famous (or nowadays perhaps infamous) fettuccine Alfredo, which is simply cooked fettuccine tossed with triple the amount of butter normally served with buttered pasta, plus reduced heavy cream, cheese, and other seasonings.

PASTA SHAPES

ACINI DI PEPE	peppercorns	ORZO	barley
ANELLI	little rings	PAPPARDELLE	wide strips
BUCATINI	little hollows	PENNE	quill pens
CANNELLONI	large reeds	PERCIATELLI	small pierced
CAPELLINI	fine hairs	RADIATORE	radiators
CONCHIGLIE	shells	RIGATONI	large grooves
DITALI	thimbles	ROTELLE	spiral shapes
DITALINI	little thimbles	ROTINI	little spiral shapes
ELBOW MACARONI	dumplings	RUOTE	wagon wheels
FARFALLE	butterflies or bowties	SPAGHETTI	length of rope
FETTUCCINE	small ribbons	STELLINE	little stars
FUSILLI	twisted spaghetti	TAGLIATELLE	cut noodles
GEMELLI	twins	TRIPOLINI	little bows
LINGUINE	small tongues	TUBETTI	little tubes
MAFALDA	flat, ripple-edged	TUBETTINI	very little tubes
MANICOTTI	small muffs	VERMICELLI	little worms
MOSTACCIOLI	small mustaches	ZITI	bridegrooms
ORECCHIETTE	little ears		

PASTA WITH BUTTER OR OLIVE OIL

YIELD: 6 PASTA-COURSE OR 4 MAIN-COURSE SERVINGS

fresh pasta	1½ pounds	675 grams
or	or	or
dried pasta	1 pound	450 grams
sweet butter, cut into small chunks (or to taste)	6 ounces	180 grams
or	or	or
extra-virgin olive oil (or to taste)	¾ cup	185 milliliters
salt and pepper	to taste	to taste
freshly grated parmigiano-reggiano		

Boil the pasta in salted water until al dente, drain, and toss with the butter or oil and salt and pepper. Pass the Parmesan cheese at the table.

Simple Additions to Pasta with Butter or Olive Oil

Many of the best pasta sauces are made by adding one or more simple ingredients to cooked pasta that has simply been tossed with butter or olive oil. Much of the time, these ingredients can be tossed raw with the cooked pasta. Other ingredients, such as garlic or sage, may also be gently cooked first in the butter or olive oil before being tossed with the pasta. Remember, however, that extra-virgin olive oil should be cooked very gently so that its perfume isn't destroyed by the heat. The creamy texture of sweet butter is also lost when the butter is overheated rather than simply allowed to melt on the pasta. However, butter can be cooked to the noisette stage (until lightly browned) before being tossed with the pasta (see Pasta with Butter and Sage, page 551).

ANCHOVIES. Italians, especially those from the south, are fans of both fresh and salted anchovies. In the United States, fresh anchovies are almost impossible to find, so we must rely on anchovies packed in oil or preserved in salt. Anchovies packed whole in salt have a deeper, more complex flavor than anchovies packed in oil (see page 70).

SWEET PEPPERS. Grilled and peeled sweet red peppers—in Italian, called *peperoni*—are cut into strips or cubes, quickly simmered with tomatoes and garlic, and used as a pasta sauce.

CAPERS. These miniature salted or brine- or vinegar-soaked berries give a savory accent to pasta sauces based on simple combinations of fresh tomatoes, herbs, olives, and anchovies. Italian cooks prefer the small nonpareil capers, which in Italy are available packed in salt, but in the United States are usually found packed in brine and vinegar in jars.

GARLIC. So often used in Italian cooking that it's almost universal, finely chopped or sliced garlic gently cooked in olive oil or butter makes a simple and satisfying sauce. Italian cooks often cut the garlic into paper-thin slices and cook them very slowly until they turn pale brown and develop a nutty flavor.

HERBS. The simplest way to give distinction to simple butter- or olive oil–coated pasta is to add fresh herbs. Basil is the best known—just add a small handful of whole leaves to the basic pasta tossed with olive oil—but finely chopped marjoram (especially with garlic) works magic with pasta tossed with butter or olive oil. Throughout Italy, sage and butter are cooked together in one of the best and simplest of pasta sauces. Mint and oregano are also popular herbs for flavoring pasta.

OLIVES. A variety of green and black olives are found throughout Italy, and each variety can be used to give its own particular nuance to a pasta sauce. The olives are pitted—easy to accomplish by just squeezing the pointier ends together between thumb and forefinger—and left otherwise whole, coarsely chopped, or on occasion ground to a paste. Olives give a salty and bitter note to pasta sauces, which makes them excellent in combination with basil, tomatoes, garlic, and anchovies.

PEPERONCINI. These little dried red peppers, found in any Italian grocery, are a favorite condiment for simple Italian pasta sauces. The peppers are coarsely chopped and need very little if any cooking before being tossed with the pasta. Red pepper flakes make a good substitute.

PINE NUTS. In addition to their use in pesto sauce, pine nuts are a popular ingredient in pasta sauces (especially those made with vegetables and garlic) to provide texture. The flavor of pine nuts is enhanced when they are lightly toasted in a dry sauté pan or in the oven.

TOMATOES. In many Italian sauces, chopped tomatoes are gently stewed with aromatic vegetables, often combined with meats and wine, into deep-flavored and complex sauces such as ragù or Bolognese sauce. But for simpler sauces, tomatoes can peeled and seeded, cut into cubes, and tossed with pasta—often in conjunction with other condiments such as olives and anchovies—producing pasta sauces that are fresh and light.

TRUFFLES. The most famous truffles used in pasta dishes are the pungent white truffles from the Piedmont region of northern Italy. Umbria, in central Italy, is also renowned for its winter black truffles, the same species (*Tuber melanosporum*) as French truffles from the Perigord and other regions. Tuscany is also gifted with summer truffles (*Tuber aestivum*), which, although less aromatic than white truffles or winter black truffles, are much less expensive. White truffles are shaved raw over simple dishes of fresh pasta tossed with butter or olive oil, whereas black truffles are more likely to be cooked in preparations such as Spaghetti alla Norcina (page 553).

PASTA WITH BUTTER AND SAGE
FETTUCCINE CON BURRO E SALVIA

This simple but delicious pasta sauce shows off the combination of sage and garlic. The secret to success is that both the butter and garlic should be lightly browned before they're tossed with the pasta.

YIELD: 6 PASTA-COURSE OR 4 MAIN-COURSE SERVINGS

unsalted butter	6 ounces	175 grams
fresh sage leaves	12	12
garlic cloves, very thinly sliced	4	4
fresh pasta *or* dried pasta	1½ pounds *or* 1 pound	675 grams *or* 450 grams
salt and pepper	to taste	to taste
freshly grated parmigiano-reggiano		

(continued)

551

1. Bring a large pot of salted water to a rapid boil for cooking the pasta.

2. Heat the butter with the sage leaves in a small saucepan or sauté pan over medium heat. When the butter starts to froth, stir in the garlic.

3. Cook the pasta in the boiling water while the butter is cooking. Drain when al dente.

4. When the butter stops frothing, the garlic is pale brown, and light brown specks of coagulated milk solids appear along the bottom and sides of the pan, toss the butter, garlic, and sage with the pasta. Season with salt and pepper. Pass the Parmesan cheese at the table.

SPAGHETTI WITH STREETWALKER'S SAUCE
SPAGHETTI ALLA PUTTANESCA

This sauce, said to be from the island of Ischia (off the coast of Naples), has become popular not only in Naples but in all of Italy and even abroad. The name *puttanesca*, usually translated somewhat less delicately than "streetwalker," comes from the fact that the ladies of the night, after whom this sauce is named, had little time to shop and had to rely on ingredients such as olives and anchovies that would keep without spoiling. Or so the story goes.

YIELD: 6 PASTA-COURSE OR 4 MAIN-COURSE SERVINGS

extra-virgin olive oil	¼ cup	60 milliliters
garlic cloves, crushed to a paste	2	2
dried peperoncini, chopped or red pepper flakes	2 teaspoons or 2 teaspoons	10 milliliters or 10 milliliters
anchovy fillets, drained, patted dry, coarsely chopped	24	24
plum tomatoes, peeled, seeded, coarsely chopped	1½ pounds	675 grams
brine-cured (not oil-cured) black olives such as gaeta, pitted, coarsely chopped, about 60	6 ounces	175 grams
capers, drained	¼ cup	60 milliliters
dried spaghetti or other strand pasta or fresh strand pasta such as fettuccine or linguine	1 pound or 1½ pounds	450 grams or 675 grams
salt	to taste	to taste

1. Bring a large pot of salted water to a rapid boil for cooking the pasta.

2. Heat the oil over medium heat in a sauté pan large enough to hold the cooked pasta, and stir in the garlic, peperoncini, and anchovies. Let the garlic sizzle for about 1 minute, then stir in the tomatoes, olives, and capers.

3. Cook the spaghetti in the boiling water while continuing to stir the sauce over medium heat. Season the sauce with salt—it may not need any because of the olives and anchovies. Drain the spaghetti when al dente and toss with the sauce.

SPAGHETTI WITH BLACK TRUFFLES, GARLIC, AND ANCHOVIES
SPAGHETTI ALLA NORCINA

This dish is named after Norcia, a town in Umbria famous not only for its black truffles but for its excellent pork and pork products. The slightly dissonant flavor of the anchovies is lovely with the truffles and garlic.

YIELD: 6 PASTA-COURSE OR 4 MAIN-COURSE SERVINGS

black truffle	1	1
extra-virgin olive oil	1 cup	250 milliliters
garlic cloves, crushed to a paste	2	2
anchovy fillets (optionally soaked for 5 minutes in cold water), patted dry, finely chopped	12	12
dried spaghetti or fresh strand pasta such as fettuccine or linguine	1 pound or 1½ pounds	450 grams or 675 grams
salt and pepper	to taste	to taste

1. Bring a large pot of salted water to a rapid boil for cooking the pasta.

2. If the truffle has dirt in its crevices, scrub it with a small brush, quickly rinse it, and pat it dry. Grate it with the small teeth of a hand grater.

3. Gently heat ¼ cup (60 milliliters) of the olive oil over low heat in a pan large enough to hold the cooked pasta and stir in the garlic and anchovies. Stir the sauce for about 4 minutes, until the garlic sizzles and releases its aroma. Stir in the grated truffle for 1 minute, then pour in the rest of the olive oil.

4. Cook and drain the spaghetti. Toss it with the sauce in the pan. Season, while tossing, with salt and pepper.

CREAM-BASED PASTA SAUCES

Heavy cream, because it is so receptive and forms so perfect a medium for other flavors, is often simmered with one or more aromatic ingredients to make a rich and flavorful pasta sauce. Unlike butter, which turns oily if overheated, cream thickens just enough so that it coats the pasta with a suave and velvety sauce. Pasta cream sauces require little effort—ingredients are simply infused in the simmering cream until the sauce thickens slightly. Almost any flavorful ingredient can be infused in cream, but here are a few suggestions. The following ingredients can be used alone or in combination.

DRIED MUSHROOMS. Dried mushrooms, especially porcini (cèpes), rinsed and soaked in barely enough water to cover, make a full-flavored pasta sauce that is especially delicious when the chopped mushrooms and their soaking liquid are simmered in heavy cream. Dried mushrooms can also be tossed in butter- or olive oil–based sauces.

PROSCIUTTO. Tiny slivers or cubes of prosciutto, simmered in cream, give pasta sauces an inimitable depth of flavor.

WALNUTS. Ground walnuts are used in Genoa and the surrounding region of Liguria to make pasta sauces. Traditionally, raw walnuts are ground to a paste, but it's also possible to leave them slightly chunky so the sauce has some texture. The walnuts can also be roasted to bring out their flavor.

PAPPARDELLE WITH DRIED PORCINI MUSHROOMS
PAPPARDELLE AI PORCINI SECCHI

Pappardelle are flat long noodles, originally from Tuscany, measuring about ¾ inch (2 cm) wide. Any flat strand pasta, such as linguine or tagliatelle, can be substituted. Dried porcini mushroom sauces often contain tomatoes, but the simplest and perhaps most delicious versions are made with only cream and seasonings.

YIELD: 6 PASTA-COURSE OR 4 MAIN-COURSE SERVINGS

dried porcini mushrooms (about 1½ ounces/ 45 grams)	1 cup	250 milliliters
water, warm	¼ cup	60 milliliters
heavy cream	2 cups	500 milliliters
salt and pepper	to taste	to taste
fresh pappardelle or strand pasta such as fettuccine or linguine *or* dried pappardelle or strand pasta	1½ pounds *or* 1 pound	675 grams *or* 450 grams
freshly grated parmigiano-reggiano		

1. Rinse the mushrooms under cold running water and place them in a small bowl with the warm water. Turn the mushrooms around in the water every 5 minutes and soak for a total of 20 minutes, until soft and pliable.

2. Bring a large pot of salted water to a rapid boil for cooking the pasta.

3. Heat the cream over medium heat in a pot large enough to hold the drained pasta.

4. Squeeze the soaking liquid out of the mushrooms and reserve both mushrooms and liquid.

5. Coarsely chop the mushrooms. Pour the liquid slowly into the cream, leaving any grit or sand behind. Add the chopped mushrooms to the cream and simmer until the cream thickens slightly, about 5 minutes. Season with salt and pepper.

6. Cook and drain the pasta, toss with the sauce, and serve. Pass the Parmesan cheese at the table.

TORTELLINI OR TAGLIATELLE WITH WALNUT SAUCE
TORTELLINI O TAGLIATELLE CON SALSA DI NOCI

Traditional with tortellini, ravioli, or tagliatelle, walnut sauce is delicious on any flat strand, preferably fresh, pasta. The consistency of the chopped walnuts is largely a matter of taste; some Italian recipes recommend puréeing them to a paste, whereas some chefs leave them in lentil- to pea-size crunchy pieces.

YIELD: 6 PASTA-COURSE OR 4 MAIN-COURSE SERVINGS

shelled walnuts	1⅔ cups	200 grams
heavy cream	2 cups	500 milliliters
garlic cloves, finely chopped	2	2
finely chopped fresh marjoram or sage (optional)	2 teaspoons	10 milliliters
salt and pepper	to taste	to taste
small to medium tortellini *or* fresh fettuccine *or* dried fettuccine	48 *or* 1½ pounds *or* 1 pound	48 *or* 675 grams *or* 450 grams
butter (optional)	as needed	as needed
freshly grated parmigiano-reggiano		

(continued)

1. Preheat the oven to 350°F (175°C). Spread the walnuts on a sheet pan and bake for 15 minutes, until they smell fragrant and darken very slightly. Chop the walnuts by hand or in a food processor to about the size of peas, and reserve.

2. Bring a large pot of salted water to a rapid boil for cooking the pasta.

3. Heat the cream over medium heat in a pot large enough to toss the drained pasta. Stir in the garlic, marjoram, if using, and the walnuts. Simmer until the cream thickens slightly, about 5 minutes, and season with salt and pepper.

4. Cook and drain the pasta and toss with the sauce. Ravioli can be tossed with a little butter and the sauce spooned over on the plates. Pass the Parmesan cheese at the table.

SAUCES BASED ON PRESERVED PORK PRODUCTS

Although the best-known pasta sauces are based on olive oil, butter, cream, or tomatoes, Italy has delicious ham (prosciutto, both raw cured—*crudo*—and cooked—*cotto*), savory unsmoked bacon (pancetta), and a version of lard (*strutto*) far superior to the soapy-tasting American version. Good-quality American bacon can be used in pasta sauces, but unless first blanched, it will give the sauce a pronounced smoky flavor that, although not authentic, is quite tasty.

Pork products such as pancetta or prosciutto are gently cooked so they render their delicious fat, which is then incorporated into the sauce. Pancetta is quite fatty and can be cut into cubes or strips and rendered in the same way as bacon. Prosciutto, on the other hand, is very lean, except for a layer of fat surrounding the meat just under the rind. This fat can be finely chopped or puréed to a paste in a food processor and then gently rendered and used as a cooking fat for sauces. It's important that the fat from pancetta or prosciutto be exposed to only very gentle heat—as with extra-virgin olive oil—or it will lose flavor and finesse.

SPAGHETTI WITH PANCETTA, EGGS, AND PARMESAN CHEESE
SPAGHETTI ALLA CARBONARA

This famous Roman dish is traditionally made with guanciale, a kind of unsmoked bacon made from pork cheeks. Guanciale is obtainable at some local specialty butchers and online, but if you cannot get it, pancetta or prosciutto makes a more than adequate substitute.

YIELD: 4 PASTA-COURSE OR 2 MAIN-COURSE SERVINGS

guanciale, pancetta, or prosciutto (such as prosciutto di parma with fat attached), cut into ⅛-inch-thick (3 mm) slices	⅓ pound	150 grams
garlic clove, finely chopped	1 small	1 small
large eggs, beaten	3	3
salt and pepper	to taste	to taste
freshly grated parmigiano-reggiano	¾ cup	185 milliliters
dried spaghetti *or* fresh strand pasta such as fettuccine or linguine	8 ounces *or* 1 pound	225 grams *or* 450 grams

(continued)

SAUCES BASED ON PRESERVED PORK PRODUCTS

557

1. Cut the guanciale or pancetta into 1-inch-wide (2.5 cm) strips. If using prosciutto, cut off and discard the rind (or save it for braises), remove and finely chop the fat, and cut the meat into 1-inch (2.5 cm) strips. Bring a large pot of salted water to a rapid boil for cooking the pasta.

2. Render the guanciale, pancetta, or prosciutto fat in a heavy-bottomed pan large enough to hold the cooked pasta over low to medium heat, until the fat becomes slightly crispy, 10 to 15 minutes. Remove the meat from the pan. If using a very fatty guanciale or pancetta, drain off all but ⅓ cup (80 milliliters) of the fat. Stir the garlic into the remaining fat and cook for 1 minute.

3. Season the eggs with salt and pepper and stir in half of the grated Parmesan cheese. Cook and drain the pasta, and quickly toss with the rendered fat and garlic. Add the beaten eggs; guanciale, pancetta, or prosciutto; and the remaining cheese and toss again. Season with salt and pepper and serve on hot plates.

SEAFOOD SAUCES

Fresh shellfish sauces and, to a lesser extent, sauces made from fresh fish—especially fresh anchovies and sardines—are popular in regions of Italy that border the sea. Preserved seafood, especially salted anchovies and tuna preserved in oil or brine, are more typical in those inland areas with limited access to fresh seafood.

Fresh shellfish sauces are approached in several ways. One typical method, usually used for clams and mussels, consists of steaming open the shellfish with a little water or white wine, combining the cooking liquid with olive oil, butter, or occasionally cream, and tossing the cooked pasta with the liquid (sometimes reduced but often not). Crustacean sauces are often nothing more than the whole crustacean—shrimp, scampi (langoustines), or mantis shrimp (Mediterranean shrimp-like crustaceans)—sautéed in olive oil and sprinkled with chopped herbs, and perhaps some chunks of tomato. The whole combination is then tossed with the pasta. Occasionally, crustacean shells are infused into cream or used to make a crustacean butter, either of which is then used in the sauce (see Fettuccine and Shrimp with Crustacean Cream Sauce, page 561).

Italians are fond of tentacled creatures. Squid and octopus are familiar to Americans, but cuttlefish, which looks like squid but is fatter and more squat, isn't found in American waters and must be imported; it's hard to find in the United States except in East Coast ethnic markets. Cuttlefish ink is much darker, thicker, and more abundant than squid ink, so it works better in black Italian sauces and as a coloring for fresh pasta. Squid and baby octopus are usually lightly sautéed with olive oil, herbs, and white wine—they can also be grilled—and simply tossed with the cooked pasta. Cuttlefish, which is meatier and tougher, is braised in stews with tomatoes and occasionally red wine, and finished with its ink in a method analogous to making a civet. Squid can also be trimmed, the hoods cut into rings, the cluster of tentacles sectioned (if large), and braised in red wine, with the sauce reduced and tossed with pasta. Large octopus, a favorite Italian antipasto and salad ingredient, is also best when braised—much like a red wine beef stew—and the full-flavored and gelatinous braising liquid reduced and used as a sauce. The braised octopus sections can also be quickly grilled and combined with their reduced braising liquid just before tossing with the pasta.

SPAGHETTI WITH CLAMS OR MUSSELS
SPAGHETTI ALLE VONGOLE O COZZE

Americans are probably most familiar with the classic linguini with clam sauce, but in Rome and Naples, clams and mussels are usually served with spaghetti. Virtually any cooked strand pasta can be tossed with steamed mussels or clams and their delicious briny liquid. This version is based on olive oil, but it is also possible to combine the cooking liquid with butter or heavy cream (reduced until slightly thickened), flavor it with chopped herbs—especially parsley—and toss with the pasta.

YIELD: 6 PASTA-COURSE OR 4 MAIN-COURSE SERVINGS

garlic cloves, finely chopped	2	2
water	⅓ cup	80 milliliters
small clams or mussels, scrubbed and sorted	4 pounds	1.8 kilograms
tomatoes, peeled, seeded, coarsely chopped	2 medium	2 medium
extra-virgin olive oil or heavy cream	⅔ cup	165 milliliters
finely chopped parsley or basil (chopped at the last minute)	2 tablespoons	30 milliliters
salt and pepper	to taste	to taste
dried spaghetti or other strand pasta *or* fresh strand pasta such as fettuccine or linguine	1 pound *or* 1½ pounds	450 grams *or* 675 grams
butter *or* olive oil	½ ounce *or* 1 tablespoon	15 grams *or* 15 milliliters

1. Bring a large pot of salted water to a rapid boil for cooking the pasta.

2. Combine the garlic with the water in a pot large enough so that the shellfish come only halfway up its sides (to leave room for them to open). Add the shellfish, cover the pot, and cook over medium to high heat until all the shellfish have opened, about 10 minutes for clams or 6 minutes for mussels.

3. Remove the shellfish from the pot with a big spoon or skimmer, put them in a bowl or pot, cover, and keep them warm. (You can take the cooked clams or mussels out of the shells—or just remove the top shell—but the dish looks more festive when they're left in their shells.) Slowly pour the shellfish cooking liquid into a small saucepan, leaving the garlic and any grit behind in the pot (if the liquid is very gritty, strain it).

4. Combine the tomatoes, extra-virgin olive oil, and parsley with the cooking liquid and bring to a simmer. Season with salt and pepper (salt may not be necessary).

5. Cook and drain the pasta, toss with the butter or olive oil, and distribute in hot bowls. Ladle the sauce over the pasta and arrange the shellfish over and around.

SPAGHETTI WITH SQUID OR BABY OCTOPUS
SPAGHETTI AL RAGÙ DI TOTANO

This dish, from the southern Italian region of Calabria, can be made with squid (called *totani* in the regional dialect), baby octopus, or cuttlefish. Unlike many Italian pasta dishes that use quickly sautéed squid, this version calls for gently braising it in tomato sauce. One difference between this dish and classic French stews is that French stew recipes call for cooking the ingredients in a minimum of fat and skimming off the fat during or after cooking so that little if any ends up in the final sauce. In this stew, a large amount of olive oil is used and the stew is gently cooked, uncovered, until the olive oil separates out. This separated mixture—heresy to a French cook—becomes the sauce.

YIELD: 6 PASTA-COURSE OR 4 MAIN-COURSE SERVINGS

squid or baby octopus	2 pounds	900 grams
onion, finely chopped	1 medium	1 medium
garlic cloves, finely chopped	2	2
extra-virgin olive oil	½ cup	125 milliliters
tomatoes, peeled, seeded, chopped *or* drained and chopped canned tomatoes	4 medium *or* 2 cups	4 medium *or* 500 milliliters
dried spaghetti or other strand pasta	1 pound	450 grams
chopped basil leaves (chopped at the last minute)	3 tablespoons	45 milliliters
salt and pepper	to taste	to taste

1. Clean the squid by pulling out the innards and cutting off the tentacles just above where they join into a cluster. The purple skin may be scraped off the hoods, but this is only for appearance—some cooks insist that the flavor is improved by leaving this skin attached. Cut the hoods into ¼-inch-wide (5 mm) rings. Clean baby octopus in the same way as squid but leave the hoods and tentacle clusters whole.

2. Heat the onion and garlic over medium heat in 2 tablespoons (30 milliliters) of the olive oil in a heavy-bottomed pot large enough to hold the drained pasta until translucent, about 10 minutes. Stir in the tomatoes and the rest of the oil and bring to a gentle simmer. Stir in the squid or octopus, partially cover the pan, and simmer very gently, stirring every few minutes, until the oil and tomatoes separate and the seafood is tender, about 45 minutes. (If the seafood is cooked before the sauce separates, continue cooking uncovered; if the sauce runs out, add a tablespoon or two of water.)

3. While the seafood is cooking, bring a large pot of salted water to a rapid boil for cooking the pasta. Cook and drain the pasta.

4. Stir the basil into the sauce, season with salt and pepper, add the pasta, and toss.

FETTUCCINE AND SHRIMP WITH CRUSTACEAN CREAM SAUCE
FETTUCCINE ALLA CREMA DI SCAMPI

Scampi are crayfish-like saltwater crustaceans, not the shrimp that are usually served as a substitute in the United States. The correct English name for *scampi* is "lobsterettes," but most of the time the French name, langoustines, is used instead. Although some langoustines are imported into the United States (mostly from New Zealand), they are difficult to find. Shrimp, crayfish, and lobster can all be substituted. This sauce is made with crustacean butter made from shells (page 331); the shells needn't be from the same crustacean.

YIELD: 6 PASTA-COURSE OR 4 MAIN-COURSE SERVINGS

shelled raw shrimp, cooked crayfish tails, or cooked lobster meat	1½ pounds	675 grams
heavy cream	1½ cups	375 milliliters
ripe tomatoes, seeded, finely chopped *or* drained and chopped canned tomatoes	2 medium *or* 1 cup	2 medium *or* 250 milliliters
chopped fresh thyme *or* chopped fresh marjoram	½ teaspoon *or* 1 teaspoon	3 milliliters *or* 5 milliliters
crustacean butter (page 331)	4 ounces	125 grams
salt and pepper	to taste	to taste
fresh fettuccine (tagliatelle) or linguine *or* dried fettuccine or linguine	1½ pounds *or* 1 pound	675 grams *or* 450 grams

1. Bring a large pot of salted water to a rapid boil for cooking the pasta. If the shrimp are very large, cut them into ½-inch (1 cm) sections. If using crayfish tails, leave them whole. Slice lobster tails into ¼-inch-thick (5 mm) medallions. Leave lobster claws whole.

2. Combine the cream, tomatoes, and thyme or marjoram in a medium saucepan over medium heat and cook until the mixture thickens to a sauce-like consistency, about 10 minutes. Whisk in the crustacean butter and strain the sauce through a fine-mesh strainer. Season with salt and pepper and reserve.

3. Just before serving, boil and drain the pasta. Very gently heat the shellfish in the sauce, never letting it boil for even a second—which would cause the shellfish to curl up, harden, and dry out. Toss the pasta with the sauce and shellfish and serve.

SPAGHETTI WITH TUNA
SPAGHETTI COL TONNO

This Roman dish is traditionally made with tuna packed in oil, but nowadays in the United States fresh tuna is so widely available that it's worth making this dish with fresh tuna or, for that matter, any full-flavored, firm-fleshed fresh fish. Avoid overcooking fresh tuna or it will turn very dry.

YIELD: 6 PASTA-COURSE OR 4 MAIN-COURSE SERVINGS

garlic cloves, finely chopped	2	2
extra-virgin olive oil	½ cup	125 milliliters
tomatoes, peeled, seeded, coarsely chopped or drained, seeded, and chopped canned tomatoes	3 medium or 1½ cups	3 medium or 375 milliliters
dried spaghetti or other strand pasta or fresh spaghetti or other strand pasta	1 pound or 1½ pounds	450 grams or 675 grams
fresh tuna, cut into ½-inch (1 cm) cubes	1 pound	450 grams
finely chopped parsley (chopped at the last minute)	1 tablespoon	15 milliliters
finely chopped fresh basil (chopped at the last minute)	2 tablespoons	30 milliliters
salt and pepper	to taste	to taste

1. Bring a large pot of salted water to a rapid boil for cooking the pasta.

2. Sweat the garlic in 2 tablespoons (30 milliliters) of the olive oil over medium heat in a heavy-bottomed pot large enough to hold the drained pasta. When the garlic turns translucent and smells aromatic (don't let it brown), after about 5 minutes, add the tomatoes and the rest of the olive oil. Stew over medium heat, uncovered, until the tomatoes and oil separate, about 15 minutes.

3. Cook and drain the pasta. Immediately before draining the pasta, add the tuna and herbs to the sauce and stir over medium heat for 30 seconds. Season with salt and pepper, add the pasta, and toss.

VEGETABLE SAUCES

Many of the best pasta sauces are simple vegetable dishes made by chopping the vegetables somewhat more finely than if they were being served as a side dish, then tossing the vegetables with cooked pasta. Tomatoes, chopped and gently stewed into a sauce, are the best-known example, but greens such as spinach, chard, broccoli raab, kale, artichokes, asparagus, peas, green beans, and fennel can all be cooked and used alone or in combination as simple sauces. Mushrooms and truffles are also used to make simple but extraordinarily delicious sauces.

Most vegetable sauces are made by gently stewing the vegetable in olive oil, butter, or sometimes cream. Sometimes chopped garlic or other condiments such as anchovies, pine nuts, or raisins are added, and sometimes herbs such as sage or marjoram. The sauce is then tossed with the cooked pasta.

SPAGHETTI WITH ARTICHOKES, GARLIC, AND PARSLEY
SPAGHETTI E CARCIOFI

The suave delicacy of artichokes makes a luxurious pasta sauce that can be served with spaghetti—the pasta used for this dish in the far southern region of Calabria, where it is popular—but the sauce's richness makes it even better served with fresh flat strand pasta such as fettuccine. In typical southern Italian style, this sauce is based on olive oil—pancetta is optional—but the cubes of cooked artichokes can also be simmered in cream to make a delicate cream-based pasta sauce.

YIELD: 6 PASTA-COURSE OR 4 MAIN-COURSE SERVINGS

artichoke bottoms (leaves trimmed off the sides, top two-thirds of the artichoke cut off)	4 large	4 large
juice of 1 lemon		
olive oil (for cooking the artichokes)	2 tablespoons	30 milliliters
extra-virgin olive oil or heavy cream	⅔ cup or 1 cup	165 milliliters or 250 milliliters
garlic clove, finely chopped	1	1
dried spaghetti or other strand pasta or fresh fettuccine or other strand pasta	1 pound or 1½ pounds	450 grams or 675 grams
finely chopped parsley (chopped at the last minute)	2 tablespoons	30 milliliters
salt and pepper	to taste	to taste
freshly grated parmigiano-reggiano		

1. Toss the artichoke bottoms with lemon juice immediately and put the artichoke bottoms, lemon juice, 1 tablespoon (15 milliliters) of the olive oil, and enough cold water to cover the artichokes by several inches in a large nonaluminum pot. Put a plate directly over the artichokes to keep them submerged. Simmer the artichokes for about 20 minutes from the time the water comes to a boil, until they can be easily penetrated on the bottom with a sharp knife. Drain and let cool.

(*continued*)

563

2. While the artichokes are cooling, bring a large pot of salted water to a rapid boil for cooking the pasta.

3. Scoop the chokes out of the artichoke bottoms with a spoon and cut the bottoms into ⅓-inch (1 cm) dice. Toss with the remaining 1 tablespoon (15 milliliters) olive oil and reserve.

4. Heat the extra-virgin olive oil or cream over medium heat in a pot large enough to hold the drained pasta. Add the garlic and cook until it smells aromatic, or until the cream thickens to a sauce-like consistency, about 5 minutes. Meanwhile, cook and drain the pasta.

5. Stir the parsley and artichoke cubes into the sauce and bring it back to a simmer. Season with salt and pepper, add the pasta, and toss. Pass the Parmesan cheese at the table.

ORECCHIETTE WITH COOKED GREEN LEAFY VEGETABLES
ORECCHIETTE CON CIME DI RAPA

Orecchiette (the word means "little ears") are popular in Puglia, the region of Italy that Greece-bound travelers vaguely remember passing through on their way to the ferry in Bari. Many of Puglia's pasta dishes are based on vegetables and olive oil; Puglia is famous for both. Although the Pugliese have their favorite greens—broccoli raab among them—this simple method of combining greens and pasta can be used for chard, arugula, kale, turnip or beet greens, or even spinach.

YIELD: 6 PASTA-COURSE OR 4 MAIN-COURSE SERVINGS

greens such as chard, kale, turnip or beet greens, or spinach	2 pounds	900 grams
or	*or*	*or*
arugula	4 bunches	4 bunches
or	*or*	*or*
broccoli raab	2 pounds	900 grams
garlic cloves, very thinly sliced	4	4
peperoncini, stemmed and chopped	2	2
or	*or*	*or*
red pepper flakes	2 teaspoons	10 milliliters
extra-virgin olive oil	½ cup	125 milliliters
dried orecchiette or short tubular pasta such as macaroni, ziti, or penne	1 pound	450 grams
salt and pepper	to taste	to taste
freshly grated parmigiano-reggiano		

1. Bring a large pot of salted water to a rapid boil for cooking the pasta. Remove the heavy stems from the greens, arugula, or broccoli raab, wash and drain, and chop the leaves and/or flowers coarsely.

2. Heat the garlic and peperoncini over medium heat in 2 tablespoons (30 milliliters) of the olive oil in a heavy-bottomed pot large enough to hold the drained pasta. When the garlic smells aromatic and begins to turn very slightly brown, about 3 minutes, stir in the chopped vegetables. Continue stirring over medium heat until the vegetables release their moisture and become tender, about 5 minutes.

3. Cook and drain the pasta. Season the vegetables with salt and pepper and stir in the remaining olive oil. Add the pasta and toss. Pass the Parmesan cheese at the table.

FETTUCCINE WITH PEAS
FETTUCCINE CON PISELLI

This simple dish, best known in the Veneto (the region surrounding Venice), is based on a mixture of pancetta and butter, but lightly reduced cream can replace the butter and even the pancetta. This approach need not be limited to peas; other delicately flavored green vegetables such as asparagus tips, baby string beans, or baby green onions or leeks can be quickly blanched or boiled and tossed with the pasta. Parsley is called for in the traditional recipe, but other herbs such as chervil or chives can be used to give this dish a vaguely French touch.

YIELD: 6 PASTA-COURSE OR 4 MAIN-COURSE SERVINGS

pancetta, 1 slice, finely chopped	2 ounces	60 grams
onion, finely chopped	1 small	1 small
fresh peas, 2 to 3 pounds (1 to 1.5 kilograms), shelled or frozen baby peas, thawed	2 to 3 cups or about 1¼ pounds (two 10-ounce packages)	500 to 750 milliliters or 525 grams
chicken stock (page 88)	½ cup	125 milliliters
fresh fettuccine, linguine, pappardelle, or other strand pasta	1½ pounds	575 grams
unsalted butter	1 ounce	30 grams
finely chopped parsley (chopped at the last minute)	1 tablespoon	15 milliliters
salt and pepper	to taste	to taste
freshly grated parmigiano-reggiano		

(continued)

1. Bring a large pot of salted water to a rapid boil for cooking the pasta. If using fresh peas, bring another large pot of salted water to a boil.

2. Cook the pancetta over medium heat for about 5 minutes in a heavy-bottomed pot. Stir in the onion and continue cooking, stirring occasionally, until the onion turns translucent, about 7 minutes.

3. Blanch the fresh peas for 1 to 2 minutes, then drain.

4. Add the stock and the peas to the onion mixture, turn the heat to high, and cook for 3 to 5 minutes, gently folding the peas over so they cook evenly.

5. Cook and drain the pasta. Toss the pasta with the butter and arrange in wide soup bowls (they must have rims because the sauce is very liquidy).

6. Stir the parsley into the peas and season with salt and pepper. Ladle the peas and their cooking liquid over the pasta. Pass the Parmesan cheese at the table.

MEAT SAUCES

Italian meat sauces, ragù, are usually made by gently cooking chopped meat with aromatic vegetables (the Italian equivalent of a mirepoix is a *soffritto*) and adding liquids such as red or white wine and chopped tomatoes. What distinguishes ragù from French sauces is that the meat is left in the sauce, whereas French brown sauces are based on the extract—the braising or poaching liquid (stock)—that has been separated from the cooking meats. This Italian method of including the meat right in the sauce makes ragù a substantial sauce, perfect for pasta. (A French brown sauce wouldn't cling to pasta and would lack substance.) Italian cooks do sometimes, however, serve pasta in the broth from gently simmered meats (such combinations of pasta in broth are called *minestre*) and then serve the meat after the pasta with condiment-like sauces such as the Salsa Verde on page 484.

It's useful to think of a ragù as analogous to a ragoût (a stew), in which the meat is cut up so finely that it becomes an integral part of the sauce. In fact, many ragù recipes are far better if the meat is cut into small cubes by hand, rather than being chopped. Better yet—and taking the ragù/ragoût analogy a step further—large pieces of meat or meat cubes can be braised and then chopped and combined with the reduced braising liquid after cooking. Using this system, any French stew or braise can be converted into a delicious pasta sauce. Italian meat sauces are based not only on the familiar beef or veal (Bolognese sauce) or pork (popular in Naples) but also on rabbit, duck, hare, and variety meats such as sweetbreads, brains, kidneys, and chicken and duck livers.

RAGÙ

Although recipes for this famous Bolognese sauce vary, they all begin with the preparation of a flavor base with ground beef (or sometimes leftover cubes of cooked beef) and mirepoix vegetables. This recipe is slightly different from the classic one in that the flavor base is first cooked with the liquid released by the tomatoes; the pulp is added later. This recipe calls for ground beef, but the sauce will have more texture and an appealing hand-hewn quality if the meat is cut by hand into ¼-inch (5 mm) cubes.

YIELD: 1 QUART (1 LITER)

(*continued*)

onion, finely chopped	1 medium	1 medium
carrot, chopped	1 small	1 small
prosciutto, chopped	2 ounces	50 grams
extra-virgin olive oil	3 tablespoons	45 milliliters
lean chopped or ground beef	12 ounces	350 grams
large bouquet garni (page 52), with a few sprigs marjoram	1	1
raw tomato concassée (page 506), liquid drained and reserved	3 cups	750 milliliters
heavy cream	¼ cup	60 milliliters
salt and pepper	to taste	to taste

1. Gently sweat the onion, carrot, and prosciutto in the olive oil until the vegetables soften. Add the beef and stir the mixture until the juices released by the meat evaporate and only fat is left. Do not cook beyond this stage.

2. Add the bouquet garni and the liquid from the tomato concassée and simmer the mixture for about 30 minutes, until the liquid evaporates and again only fat is visible.

3. Add the tomato pulp and continue simmering the sauce until it has the right thickness. This should not take longer than 15 minutes.

4. Add the cream and cook for 2 minutes more.

5. Season with salt and pepper. If the sauce seems to lack flavor, follow the recommendations for using sugar and vinegar (see "Improving the Flavor of Tomato Sauces," page 509).

PAPPARDELLE WITH TUSCAN DUCK SAUCE
PAPPARDELLE ARETINE

Duck is cooked into pasta sauces in many regions of Italy. Each region has its preferred pasta shape and its own style of cooking and serving the duck. In some regions, the duck is left in large chunks—even on the bone—whereas in other places the duck flesh is finely chopped. This recipe falls somewhere in between.

Most Italian recipes call for removing the duck skin and cooking the whole duck, but this sauce is especially good when made with leftover duck thighs, which can be saved in the freezer if the breasts are being used for other dishes. In general, duck thighs are better for braising because they tend to stay more moist, although if the duck meat is being finely chopped, any dryness will be imperceptible. Making a stock from the duck carcass, reducing it, and adding it to the sauce is an ultimate, but not essential, refinement.

YIELD: 1 QUART (1 LITER) SAUCE, ENOUGH FOR 6 PASTA-COURSE OR 4 MAIN-COURSE SERVINGS

whole Pekin duck	5 pounds	2.3 kilograms
or	*or*	*or*
thighs and drumsticks from 2 ducks	5 pounds	2.3 kilograms
olive oil	2 tablespoons	30 milliliters
onion, finely chopped	1 medium	1 medium
carrot, finely chopped	1 small	1 small
celery, finely chopped	½ stalk	½ stalk
garlic cloves, finely chopped	3	3
prosciutto, 1 slice (⅛ inch/3 mm thick), finely chopped (optional)	2 ounces	50 grams
ripe tomatoes, peeled, seeded, chopped	3 pounds	1.35 kilograms
or	*or*	*or*
drained and seeded canned tomatoes, chopped	2 (28-ounce) cans	1 liter
red wine	1 cup	250 milliliters
sage leaves	3	3
fresh pappardelle, fettuccine (tagliatelle), or linguine	1½ pounds	675 grams
or	*or*	*or*
dried tubular pasta such as penne or rigatoni	1 pound	450 grams
salt and pepper	to taste	to taste
freshly grated parmigiano-reggiano		

1. If using a whole duck, remove the breasts, thighs, and the first (thicker) wing joints. Reserve the giblets. The carcass can be used for making stock or discarded.

2. Brown the giblets, if using, and the duck pieces, skin side down, in the olive oil in a heavy-bottomed pot. Remove and reserve the giblets as soon as they are browned. Brown the duck pieces as long as possible without letting the skin burn, about 20 minutes. Keep the breasts skin side down over moderate heat so they render the maximum of fat. Turn the pieces over and brown them for 5 minutes more on the meat side. Take the duck pieces out of the pan and reserve. Pour off all but 2 tablespoons (30 milliliters) of the fat and add the onion, carrot, celery, garlic, and prosciutto. Sweat over medium heat until the onion turns translucent, about 10 minutes.

3. Put the browned duck pieces and giblets, except for the liver, back into the pot with the vegetables. Add the tomatoes, wine, and sage. Cover the pot and simmer very gently for 2 hours. Be sure regularly to skim off fat. Don't let the broth boil.

4. Remove the duck pieces. Reduce the sauce gently, skimming every 15 minutes, until only 1 quart (1 liter) of sauce remains.

5. While the braising liquid is reducing, bring a large pot of salted water to a rapid boil for cooking the pasta. Pull off and discard any fat and skin clinging to the duck pieces, take the meat off the bones, and chop the duck meat, giblets, and liver into roughly ¼-inch (5 mm) pieces.

6. Cook and drain the pasta.

(continued)

7. Stir the chopped duck into the sauce. Just before serving, season with salt and pepper. Add the pasta, toss, and serve immediately. Pass the Parmesan cheese at the table. The giblets can be either incorporated into the sauce or sprinkled over the finished plates.

TOMATO SAUCES

Italian cooks use tomatoes in several ways: as a moistening liquid in braises, stews, and meat (ragù) and seafood sauces; raw, coarsely chopped and simply tossed with pasta, usually olive oil, and often with herbs or other ingredients such as olives, anchovies, or capers; added to a soffritto and gently simmered until thick; and baked or dried, then more or less finely chopped to a sauce-like consistency (see also "Tomatoes," page 506).

MACARONI WITH BAKED TOMATO SAUCE
MACCHERONI CON POMIDORI AL FORNO

Tomatoes become intensely sweet and savory when gently baked—the oven baking seems to concentrate their flavor more than simply stewing or simmering them on the stove, as in most tomato sauces. This dish comes from Puglia.

YIELD: 6 PASTA-COURSE OR 4 MAIN-COURSE SERVINGS

ripe tomatoes, peeled	4 pounds	1.8 kilograms
extra-virgin olive oil	¼ cup	60 milliliters
dried macaroni or short tubular pasta, such as ziti, rigatoni, or penne *or* fresh macaroni or pasta	1 pound *or* 1½ pounds	450 grams *or* 675 grams
garlic cloves, finely chopped	3	3
finely chopped parsley (see note)	2 tablespoons	30 milliliters
freshly grated parmigiano-reggiano		

1. Preheat the oven to 400°F (200°C). Cut the tomatoes in half crosswise, squeeze out and discard the seeds, and chop the tomatoes coarsely into chunks.

2. Brush a baking dish or roasting pan just large enough to hold the tomatoes in a single layer with 1 tablespoon (15 milliliters) of the olive oil.

3. Bake the tomatoes for 1½ to 2 hours, until the liquid released by the tomatoes has almost completely evaporated and only a couple tablespoons of syrupy liquid remain.

4. Bring a large pot of salted water to a rapid boil. Cook and drain the pasta.

5. Heat the remaining olive oil in a wide skillet large enough to hold the drained pasta and stir in the garlic. Stir the garlic for about 2 minutes, until it releases its aroma. Stir in the parsley and tomatoes.

6. Stir the tomatoes with a wooden spoon—this will cause them to break down into a sauce. Add the pasta and toss. Pass the Parmesan cheese at the table.

Note: Most of us relegate parsley to a secondary role and rarely give it the attention it deserves. Ideally, parsley should be chopped just before it is used, as it quickly loses its fresh aroma and ends up smelling like lawnmower clippings. However, in a fast-paced kitchen, it isn't practical to stop and chop parsley for 10 minutes. One trick: Chop the parsley a little coarsely ahead of time, then at the last minute, chop it for 30 seconds so it again releases its aroma.

ASIAN
SAUCES

Many classically trained cooks are perplexed when confronted with an Asian sauce recipe. Not only are the ingredients sometimes completely unrecognizable, but the approach and logic are profoundly different from those used in making Western sauces. Unlike European sauces, especially French classic sauces, which are designed to concentrate the flavors of the main ingredients (in integral sauces) or at least emulate the flavors of the main ingredients through the preparation and careful reduction of stocks (in nonintegral sauces), Asian sauces are designed to accent or contrast with the main ingredient. Japanese cooks use dashi, a smoky fish broth, for both meats and fish; Southeast Asian cooks flavor most of their curries, soups, and stews with fish sauce; Indian cooks use elaborate combinations of spices; and Chinese cooks are likely to use an array of bottled sauces, often in subtle and delicious combinations, but again as an accent to, rather than intensification of, the main ingredient's inherent flavor. With this in mind, it's essential for the cook who sets out to make an Asian sauce to avoid masking the flavors of the main ingredient with too many strong or disparate flavors. Although Asian sauces don't emphasize the careful sculpting of the main ingredient's inherent flavors in the way of classic French sauces, the best Asian sauces use their own palette of ingredients with great subtlety and finesse to accent the main ingredient without masking its flavor or appearance.

Although many of the ingredients used are radically different, Western and Asian sauces share many of the same techniques. Asian sauces are often begun by "sweating" mixtures of aromatic ingredients in a small amount of fat before liquids are added—in much the same way as when making the sauce base for any number of classic European sauces. Whereas in France this basic mixture will likely contain onions, carrots, and celery (a classic mirepoix) or in Italy, a fair amount of garlic (a *soffritto*), Asian base mixtures may contain an array of ingredients including shrimp paste, galangal, ginger, chiles, and curry leaves. Asian cooks sometimes add liquids directly to stir-fried meats, vegetables, and seafood in the same way a French chef adds broth and other liquids to a fricassée. In other instances, the stir-fried foods are completely removed from the wok (or sauté pan) before liquids are added, in the manner of a sauté. Thickeners are also used, but instead of flour, butter, or cream, Asian sauces may be thickened with coconut milk, cooked lentils, kuzu root (a starch much like arrowroot), or nut butters.

Fortunately, a trained cook who sets out to make an Asian sauce for the first time won't have to master an array of new techniques, but will need only familiarize himself or herself with a new palette of ingredients. Other than painstakingly following basic recipes, it is useful for beginning cooks to travel, so that in addition to tasting foods in situ, they can experience the context of how the food is served—to see and taste those foods that precede, accompany, or follow a particular dish—and to experience how people eat and what foods give them pleasure. Short of traveling thousands of miles, eating in Asian restaurants in the United States will also introduce the beginning cook to the flavors and rituals of a particular cuisine. Once a palette of flavors and ingredients becomes familiar, the cook can work within it, improvising here and there, to come up with authentic dishes stamped with his or her own particular style.

Many cooks, having newly discovered an Asian ingredient previously unknown to them, set out to integrate it into the tried-and-true sauces of their own repertory with results that are bizarre at best. These attempts often fail because the context of the sauce is from one place and the flavors from another. But although this skewing of flavors and context has led to many of the most ill-conceived mishmashes of "fusion" cooking, it is possible to cautiously add an Asian ingredient to a Western sauce to provide a note of unfamiliar intrigue. (A few bonito flakes infused in a fish sauce do wonders.) The influence of Japanese cooking on French classic cuisine, one of the most successful interactions of two seemingly disparate approaches to food, led to the light touch and elegant simplicity of the most successful plates of nouvelle cuisine. This Japanese influence, more an aesthetic seen in the almost stark simplification of presentations, has irreversibly influenced the refined cooking found in classic French restaurants. For those attempting the "fusion" of disparate cuisines, it's essential to keep the context of one cuisine intact. If the context becomes clouded so that no one particular cooking tradition predominates, the diner may be left weary and confused. A fine meal should follow a single tradition and aesthetic, and evoke a history, a place, and a people, not serve as an experimental testing ground for bizarre juxtapositions of flavors and styles.

JAPANESE SAUCES

Whereas most Western sauces are made by thickening a liquid, such as stock or milk, and infusing the mixture with flavorful ingredients, Japanese sauces are often served as light broths (Japanese foods are often served in small bowls) with little or no thickener. When Japanese sauces are thickened or reduced, they are used as savory glazes, brushed on foods while they cook, rather than as liquid sauces. Teriyaki sauce is the most familiar of these glazes. Japanese sauces are also often served as dipping sauces or as salad dressings containing no oil. And while European sauces are constructed using an almost infinite variety of ingredients, most Japanese sauces are made using relatively few.

Dashi

Traditional European sauces rely on broths, either made in advance as stocks or the result of the cooking process, but Japanese cooks rely almost exclusively on a universal broth called *dashi*. Dashi is the most fundamental component in Japanese sauce making and, in fact, in most Japanese cooking. Although dashi's universality may surprise Western-trained cooks, who take great care and time to distill the flavor of a particular food into a broth or jus, most recipes for dashi take only about 15 minutes to make and lend themselves to great subtlety.

In the most classic dashi recipe, only two ingredients are needed: dried bonito (a fish closely related to tuna) and *konbu*, a variety of kelp sold dried in long strips. Bonito destined for making dashi is slowly and carefully dried and smoked until it shrinks and hardens into something looking vaguely like an overripe banana but with the texture of wood. In the most traditional kitchens, the hardened chunk of bonito, *katsuo-bushi*, is shaved as it is needed on a plane-like gadget with a drawer attached to its base. But nowadays, even serious Japanese cooks who insist that the flavor of hand-shaved bonito flakes is better often rely on preshaved flakes. Bonito flakes, *hana-katsuo* or *kezuri-katsuo*, are sold in cellophane bags and look like pink wood shavings. Large pink flakes are usually more subtle and inviting, whereas brownish or very small flakes sometimes have a fishy smell and flavor. Instant dashi (*dashi-no-moto*) is sold in little bags, and although it has none of the inviting subtlety of dashi made from bonito flakes, it's a usable substitute and infinitely better than its Western equivalent, the bouillon cube.

The second dashi ingredient, konbu, is a kind of dried kelp sold in dark brown, almost black, strips a couple of inches (5 cm) wide and about 18 inches (45 cm) long. The best strips come from Hokkaido, Japan's northernmost island, and are lightly coated with a thin white mineral layer that should be left on. These strips are gently wiped with a moist towel—never rinsed—before they are cooked.

Classic dashi is prepared in two stages. In the first stage, konbu is steeped in hot water for about 15 minutes as though making tea. This first infusion, konbu dashi, is sometimes used alone (it's a favorite of vegetarians), but bonito flakes are generally added to the hot mixture, steeped for about 1 minute, and strained out. The result is primary dashi. Secondary dashi, made by using the bonito flakes and kelp a second time, is sometimes used in long-simmering soups and stews, where the subtlety of primary dashi would be lost. Dashi will keep in the refrigerator for two weeks, or it can be frozen indefinitely.

PRIMARY DASHI

konbu (kelp), 1 strip	18 inches	45 centimeters
cold water	5 cups	1.2 liters
bonito flakes (about 4 loosely packed cups/1 liter)	1 ounce	25 grams

1. Wipe the konbu with a barely moistened towel. Fold the konbu in half, place it in a 2-quart (2 liter) saucepan, and pour over the water. **(A)** Place the pan over low to medium heat (or higher heat if you're scaling up the recipe) so that the water comes to a slow simmer after 15 minutes.

2. As soon as the water reaches a simmer, take out the konbu (reserve it for secondary dashi, or discard) and take the pan off the heat. Stir in the bonito flakes **(B)** and let them infuse for 1 minute. Strain. **(C)** The bonito flakes can be discarded or saved for secondary dashi.

Note: If desired, you can prepare a preliminary infusion by first adding anchovies or other small anchovy-like fish, and simmering for 20 minutes before adding the konbu.

Constructing a Japanese Sauce

Once the basic dashi is on hand, most Japanese sauces are easily constructed by adding two or three additional ingredients. Only rarely is additional cooking required, and never the long cooking needed to make Western stocks and reductions.

The four most popular additions to dashi are sake (rice wine), soy sauce, miso, and mirin. Sake is used in much the same way as wine is used in Western cooking. It's simmered long enough for the alcohol to cook off and, like grape wine, is appreciated for its ability to give a bright freshness to sauces and broths, especially those containing fish—no rarity in Japan.

Soy sauce is used in Japan much as salt is used in the West. It gives an intriguing savor to sauces and broths. Dark soy sauce can also be used to deepen the color of a sauce. (Japanese soy sauce comes both light and dark.)

Miso is made by fermenting soy beans with grains and then grinding the mixture to a peanut butter–like paste. It comes in a variety of colors, each with a different salt content and depth of flavor. Lighter misos, called "white" or "yellow" miso, are less salty than darker varieties and are often used for cold dressings; darker miso has a deeper flavor and is used for more strongly flavored, usually cold-weather, dishes. Japanese chefs usually combine more than one miso (as Western cooks might carefully balance mixtures of herbs) to come up with their own nuances of flavor. Because miso is salty and full flavored, it is used sparingly, with rarely more than a couple of tablespoons (30 grams) added to 1 cup (250 milliliters) liquid.

Mirin, an extremely sweet type of sake, is sold in Japanese grocery stores (and often in American groceries as well) as a cooking wine. Used in small amounts to give sweetness to Japanese sauces, it is a perfect counterpoint to the saltiness of ever-present soy sauce and dashi. Sugar can be used instead of, or in addition to, mirin (see Chapter 3, "Ingredients," for more about soy sauce, miso, and mirin).

Presenting and Serving Japanese Broth-Like Sauces

Much of the appeal of Japanese seafood and meat dishes is the lightness of an accompanying broth-like sauce that surrounds the food rather than covering it. It may be for this reason that so many Japanese dishes are served in small and elegant—often handmade—pottery or lacquer bowls.

Because broth-like sauces are served in a small bowl with hot foods, there is always the risk of the sauce causing the food (especially delicate seafood) to overcook while it makes its way from kitchen to dining room, and even while it sits in front of the diner. To avoid this, foods are often placed on mounds of cooked vegetables (such as julienned carrots or daikon, or greens such as spinach or watercress) or atop Japanese noodles so the meat or seafood is held elevated above the hot broth.

BASIC JAPANESE BROTH-LIKE SAUCE WITH MIRIN, SOY SAUCE, AND SAKE

This sauce, actually a cross between sauce and soup, is fundamental to Japanese cooking. It can be subtly varied to taste or to go with particular ingredients by adding more or less of the three primary ingredients: soy sauce, mirin, and sake. In addition to these ingredients, the sauce is infused with extra bonito flakes to give it a more pronounced smokiness. Finely chopped scallions are added at the end for color and additional flavor.

YIELD: 2 CUPS (500 MILLILITERS), ENOUGH FOR 8 FIRST-COURSE SERVINGS OR 4 MAIN-COURSE

dashi (page 576)	1¼ cups	300 milliliters
mirin	¼ cup	60 milliliters
sake	¼ cup	60 milliliters
dark japanese soy sauce	¼ cup	60 milliliters
dried bonito flakes	¾ cup	185 milliliters
scallions, including green parts, finely sliced	2	2

Combine the dashi with the mirin, sake, and soy sauce in a small saucepan and bring to a simmer. Remove from the heat, stir in the bonito flakes, and let sit for 1 minute. Strain. Stir in the scallions and use immediately.

SALMON WITH BASIC JAPANESE BROTH-LIKE SAUCE

This dish is inspired by a classic recipe in Shizuo Tsuji's excellent book, *Japanese Cooking: A Simple Art.* Mr. Tsuji uses steamed sea bream, but any firm-fleshed fish works well. Scallops are also excellent. Alternative cooking methods can also be employed—the seafood can be sautéed (the crispy skin provides textural contrast), poached, baked, or even grilled. Soba (buckwheat) noodles prop up the fish and provide starch; julienned vegetables or cooked leafy greens can also be used. Double the amounts to produce main-course servings.

YIELD: 8 FIRST-COURSE SERVINGS

squares of salmon fillet with skin (scaled), or other firm-fleshed fish, all the same thickness, 3 ounces (75 grams) each	8	8
dried soba noodles	8 ounces	225 grams
japanese broth-like sauce (page 578)	2 cups	500 milliliters

1. Steam, sauté, poach, bake, or grill the fish. If you sauté the fillets, pat off any excess oil with paper towels. (The fish can also be teriyaki glazed, as on page 580.)

2. Cook the noodles as you would pasta, and drain. Arrange the noodles in mounds in small hot bowls.

3. Place a piece of salmon, skin side up, on each mound and ladle the sauce around. Serve immediately.

GRILLED SWORDFISH WITH CLAMS AND BROTH-LIKE MISO SAUCE

Miso provides a simple and savory addition to the cooking liquid from fish and shellfish. Keep in mind, however, that miso is very salty, so it must be used sparingly, especially with the salty cooking liquid from clams or mussels. This technique—surrounding grilled seafood with miso- and shellfish-scented broth—can be used with any firm-fleshed fish. Shiso or kinome leaves are typical Japanese garnitures, but tiny watercress or mint sprigs will also work. The swordfish steaks may also be glazed with Teriyaki Sauce (page 580). If the ingredient amounts in this recipe are halved (cut the clams down to 12 and use smaller swordfish steaks), the dish works well as a first course.

YIELD: 4 MAIN-COURSE SERVINGS

littleneck clams, scrubbed	20	20
basic dashi (page 576)	3 cups	750 milliliters
swordfish steaks, 6 to 8 ounces (175 to 250 grams) each	4	4
peanut oil or vegetable oil	2 teaspoons	10 milliliters
sansho powder or black pepper	1 teaspoon	5 milliliters
red miso	2 tablespoons	30 grams
kinome leaves, shiso leaves, or watercress sprigs	4	4

1. Simmer the clams in a covered pot with the dashi for about 12 minutes. When the clams have all opened, remove the top shell from each clam and reserve the clams, nestled in their bottom shells. Slowly pour the cooking liquid into a small saucepan, leaving any grit or sand behind.

2. Brush the swordfish steaks with the oil and sprinkle with the sansho powder or pepper. Grill or sauté the swordfish.

(continued)

3. While the swordfish steaks are grilling, work 2 tablespoons (30 milliliters) of the clam cooking liquid into the miso and return this mixture to the rest of the cooking liquid. Gently reheat the clams in the miso broth.

4. Place the swordfish steaks in wide soup plates and ladle the miso broth around them. Place 5 clams around each serving. Garnish with the kinome leaves.

Using Japanese Sauces as Glazes

Because of the sugar or mirin they contain, Japanese sauces are easily cooked down into thick and syrupy, sweet and savory glazes.

TERIYAKI SAUCE

Teriyaki sauce, a mixture of mirin, sake, soy sauce, and sometimes sugar, may be brushed on meats, fish, or vegetables while they are grilling so that it concentrates on their surface into a thick, syrupy glaze. It can also be prepared in the still-hot pan used for sautéing—in the same way a French sauce is made by deglazing—but instead of the sauce being then poured over the meat or fish, the meat or fish is put back in the pan and the sauce reduced to a glaze. The meat or fish comes out of the pan coated with a shiny sweet-and-savory glaze. This glazing method is especially effective on the crisp skin of chicken or salmon.

YIELD: ½ CUP (125 MILLILITERS)

sake	3 tablespoons	45 milliliters
mirin	3 tablespoons	45 milliliters
dark japanese soy sauce	3 tablespoons	45 milliliters

Combine all the ingredients and refrigerate until needed (the sauce will keep indefinitely). Or use the mixture of ingredients to deglaze the hot sauté pan, as in the following recipe.

TERIYAKI-GLAZED FISH, STEAK, OR CHICKEN

Teriyaki glazing works best for relatively thick cuts of fish, steak, or chicken. It's easy to overcook thinner cuts because they must be sautéed in two stages—first in hot oil, second with the teriyaki ingredients.

YIELD: 4 SERVINGS

thick fish or meat steaks	4	4
or	*or*	*or*
chicken, quartered	1	1
vegetable oil	2 tablespoons	30 milliliters
ingredients for teriyaki sauce (mirin, soy sauce, sake), either combined or separate		

1. Sauté the fish, meat, or chicken in the oil in a large heavy-bottomed sauté pan over medium to high heat so the pieces are well browned on both sides. Leave underdone by about 3 minutes. Remove from the pan.

2. Pour out the cooked oil and pour the teriyaki sauce or ingredients (there's no need to combine them) into the still-hot pan. Put the fish, meat, or chicken back in the pan and boil the teriyaki mixture over high heat for about 1½ minutes, until it looks thick and syrupy.

3. Turn over the fish, meat, or chicken and boil for another 1½ minutes, until there's practically no sauce left in the pan. Be careful at this point (keep sniffing) to permit the glaze to caramelize only slightly, not to burn.

YAKITORI SAUCE

Yakitori are small skewers of meat, usually chicken but sometimes beef—or even horse—or vegetables, quickly grilled and glazed with a sweet and savory sauce. Yakitori sauce contains ingredients common to many Japanese sauces: sake, soy sauce, mirin, and sugar, but it is thicker than most Japanese sauces.

The skewers of yakitori are brushed with or dipped into the yakitori sauce at least twice during grilling: once when the food is three-quarters done and once again 1 minute before serving. If using wooden skewers, be sure to push the pieces of meat or vegetables right next to one another so the wood between the pieces doesn't burn. The ends of wooden skewers should also be wrapped in aluminum foil so they don't burn.

YIELD: 1 CUP (250 MILLILITERS)

sake	½ cup	125 milliliters
dark japanese soy sauce	1 cup	250 milliliters
mirin	¼ cup	60 milliliters
sugar	3 tablespoons	45 milliliters

Combine all the ingredients in a small saucepan and simmer for about 10 minutes, until reduced by half. Let cool. Yakitori sauce keeps indefinitely in the refrigerator.

CHICKEN, MEAT, OR VEGETABLE YAKITORI

Yakitori make savory predinner hors d'oeuvre and can be made with small cubes of meat or chicken, or pieces of vegetables such as peppers, onions, or mushrooms.

YIELD: 8 SERVINGS

boneless chicken breast, cubed	12 ounces	350 grams
or	or	or
beef steak such as sirloin, cut into ¾-inch (2 cm) cubes	12 ounces	350 grams
or	or	or
vegetables, cut into cubes or strips	12 ounces	350 grams
yakitori sauce (page 581)	1 cup	250 milliliters

1. Marinate the cubes of meat, chicken, or vegetables in the yakitori sauce for 30 minutes.

2. Thread the cubes on 8 presoaked wooden or metal skewers. If you're using wooden skewers, be sure the pieces of meat are right up against each other so the wood doesn't burn. Grill over high heat until lightly browned but not cooked through, about 3 minutes, turning after 1½ minutes.

3. Brush the skewers with the yakitori sauce or roll the skewers in the sauce on a plate. Grill until almost done, about 2 minutes more, and again coat with sauce. Grill for at least 30 seconds more over high heat and serve.

Japanese Dipping Sauces

Although many of the best Japanese sauces are broth-like affairs, served hot and surrounding the food in small bowls, the Japanese also use an array of dipping sauces for raw fish and simmered meats and seafood. Some of these sauces are as simple as a tiny mound of wasabi combined with soy sauce by the diner at a sushi bar; others are more complex and thicker, containing miso, ground sesame seeds or peanuts, egg yolks (these sauces are thickened much like a crème anglaise), and kuzu starch (a root-derived starch that behaves much like arrowroot).

Many of the dipping sauces traditionally served with sashimi (raw fish) are also served with cold or hot grilled or fried seafood and meats or with cold vegetables—even as salad dressings. Tosa sauce is a smoke-flavored sauce made by infusing dark soy sauce with sake, mirin, konbu, and bonito flakes. The basic ingredients are almost the same as those used for making dashi, but instead of the bonito and konbu being simmered, they are left to infuse in the cold soy sauce for anywhere from a day to a year. Tosa sauce is more deeply flavored and complex than the simple soy sauce and wasabi usually served as an accompaniment to raw fish.

TOSA SAUCE

Tosa sauce is best after it has aged for 6 months, but it can be used right away or for up to 1 year. It is used as a dipping sauce for raw fish or hot or cold seafood, meats, or vegetables.

YIELD: 1¼ CUPS (300 MILLILITERS), 8 SERVINGS

konbu (kelp), 1 strip	3 inches	8 centimeters
mirin	¼ cup	60 milliliters
sake	¼ cup	60 milliliters
dark japanese soy sauce	1 cup	250 milliliters
bonito flakes (about 1 loosely packed cup/ 250 milliliters)	¼ ounce	7 grams

1. Wipe the konbu with a barely moist towel and snap it into several pieces.

2. Combine all the ingredients in a stainless-steel mixing bowl, cover with plastic wrap, and let sit for 24 hours at room temperature.

3. Strain through a fine-mesh strainer or cheesecloth. Refrigerate in a bottle with a tight-fitting cap.

PONZU SAUCE

In addition to many of the basic dipping sauce ingredients—soy sauce, mirin, bonito flakes, and konbu—Ponzu Sauce contains a large amount of lemon juice. In Japan, yuzu, a very sour lemon, is used, so recipes adapted for American readers usually call for a combination of lemon and lime juice.

In Japan, Ponzu Sauce is served as a dipping sauce for raw, very firm–fleshed fish that are sliced very thinly and traditionally served in a rosette pattern. (Fugu, the blowfish known to be fatal if improperly cleaned, is the most notorious and expensive example.) Very thinly sliced fish has too delicate a flavor to match the combination of soy sauce and wasabi or Tosa Sauce (page 583) served with the more familiar, thicker-sliced raw fish such as tuna. Ponzu Sauce also lends a bright yet subtle complexity when dribbled over hot grilled or sautéed seafood in the same way as lemon juice in the West. A drop or two also makes a delicious accent to a raw oyster.

Like Tosa Sauce, Ponzu Sauce is best when allowed to mature for several months, but it can be used right away or as long as 1 year after it is made.

YIELD: 2 CUPS (500 MILLILITERS), ENOUGH FOR ABOUT 10 SERVINGS

(continued)

lime juice	½ cup	125 milliliters
lemon juice	½ cup	125 milliliters
rice vinegar or sherry vinegar	2 tablespoons	30 milliliters
dark japanese soy sauce	½ cup	125 milliliters
mirin	½ cup	60 milliliters
bonito flakes (about 1 loosely packed cup/ 250 milliliters)	¼ ounce	7 grams

1. Combine all the ingredients in a stainless-steel mixing bowl, cover with plastic wrap, and let sit at room temperature for 24 hours.

2. Strain through a fine-mesh strainer and store in the refrigerator in a bottle with a tight-fitting cap.

MISO SAUCE

Miso (fermented soy bean sauce) is often used in both cold and hot Japanese sauces. Miso is often combined with mirin or sugar to provide a sweet relief to miso's strong saltiness. Sweetened miso combined with toasted and ground sesame seeds is a popular sauce for cold vegetables such as asparagus, string beans, or okra. Miso sauce can also be used as a dipping sauce for hot steamed or boiled vegetables. Don't use salt anywhere else in a dish served with miso—miso sauce is very salty.

YIELD: ⅔ CUP (165 MILLILITERS), 4 SERVINGS

white sesame seeds	6 tablespoons	90 milliliters
red miso, or a mixture of brown and white miso	2 tablespoons	30 grams
mirin	¼ cup	60 milliliters
water (optional)	1 to 2 tablespoons	15 to 30 milliliters

1. Toss the sesame seeds in a dry sauté pan over high heat until they smell toasty and turn pale brown, about 5 minutes. Grind them to a paste in a coffee grinder or in a traditional *suribachi* (Japanese mortar and pestle; see page 32).

2. Stir the sesame paste with the miso and the mirin until smooth. Add water, if necessary, to thin to desired consistency.

Japanese Salad Dressings

Japanese salad dressings are acidic in the same way as Western dressings, but unlike vinaigrette and its variations, Japanese salad sauces rarely contain oil. In addition to the familiar Japanese standbys—soy sauce, dashi, and mirin—Japanese salad dressings almost always contain rice vinegar or lemon or lime juice to provide the necessary acidity. And although the most basic dressings contain no thickeners, more elaborate versions are thickened or given body with egg yolks, starch (kuzu starch or cornstarch), ground sesame seeds, puréed tofu, mustard (for the closest equivalent to vinaigrette), and wasabi.

BASIC JAPANESE SALAD DRESSING

In the same way that a Western vinaigrette might be balanced, the amounts of each of the ingredients in a Japanese salad dressing can be varied to taste; more soy sauce can be added for a pronounced saltiness, more dashi to soften the effect of the vinegar and to lend a subtle smokiness, and more vinegar if the dressing needs an emphasized acidic zing. Rice vinegar is traditionally used, but sherry vinegar makes a delicious accent to the smokiness of the dashi.

Unlike Western vinaigrettes that take on a stale quality when stored overnight, Japanese salad dressings keep in the refrigerator almost indefinitely, unless they contain egg yolks.

YIELD: 1 CUP (250 MILLILITERS)

rice vinegar or sherry vinegar	6 tablespoons	90 milliliters
japanese soy sauce	1 tablespoon plus 1 teaspoon	20 milliliters
japanese broth-like sauce (page 578), cold	½ cup	125 milliliters

Combine all the ingredients.

VARIATIONS

Some salads or vegetables benefit from extra sweetness in the dressing (cold beets and cucumbers come to mind). Varying amounts of mirin, or smaller amounts of sugar, dissolved into the basic salad dressing will contribute a contrasting sweetness. The delightful smokiness of most Japanese salad dressings can be increased by infusing a handful of dried bonito flakes in the hot dressing and straining after 1 minute. (If infusing in a cold sauce, strain after 24 hours.) This is an alternative to adding dashi, which would dilute the sauce's acidity.

Japanese salad dressings can also be thickened and used to coat cooked vegetables or as dipping sauces. To thicken the basic dressing, bring it to a simmer, beat 3 egg yolks until pale, and whisk them into the sauce off the heat. Return the mixture to the heat and stir gently with a wooden spoon (as though making crème anglaise) until the sauce thickens. Let cool.

A basic Japanese salad dressing can also be thickened and flavored with sesame paste, a popular ingredient in Japanese sauces. To make a sesame-flavored and thickened salad dressing, toast two-thirds the amount of white *(continued)* sesame seeds as there are liquid ingredients (for example, ⅔ cup/165 milliliters seeds to 1 cup/250 milliliters liquid ingredients) by tossing the seeds in a hot skillet until lightly browned and fragrant, about 5 minutes. Grind the seeds to a flaky paste in a coffee grinder (or blender for larger amounts) or in a traditional Japanese suribachi (see page 32). (Peanut butter can be substituted for the sesame paste with delicious, if not strictly authentic, results.)

Miso is also used as a thickener and flavoring for Japanese salad dressings. To make a miso-flavored dressing, work 2 tablespoons (30 milliliters) of the basic dressing into ¼ cup (60 milliliters) of brown, red, or white miso and stir this mixture into 1 cup (250 milliliters) of the basic dressing. (This dressing tends to be quite salty.)

KOREAN SAUCES

Korean cooking is more appreciated for its variety of side dishes, pickles, and condiments than for an elaborate system of sauce making. Most Korean sauces are simple dipping sauces, salad dressings (very similar to their Japanese equivalents), or seasoning mixtures for pickles, especially *kimchi*.

In many ways, Korean cooking is similar to that of Japan, but there are two important and particularly Korean ingredients that give many Korean dishes a character that sets them apart. Red chile paste known as *kochujang* (see page 41), an everyday condiment in Korea, is used to flavor soups, one-pot dishes, and as a dipping sauce. Soy bean paste, or *twoenjang* (see page 42), is the Korean equivalent of Japanese miso, but Korean paste is stronger and more distinctive—no dish made with twoenjang would be mistaken for a Japanese relative made with miso.

KOREAN VINEGAR DIPPING SAUCE

Korean dipping sauces are similar to many Japanese dipping sauces in that they share the common ingredients of soy sauce, rice vinegar, sugar, ginger, and sesame (either sesame oil or ground sesame seeds). One difference, however, is that Korean sauces often contain hot chiles that are finely chopped, powdered, or in kochujang paste form. Another difference is that neither dashi nor bonito flakes ever appear in Korean sauces, while they are staple ingredients in Japanese sauces.

Recipes for Korean dipping sauces vary from household to household, and any of the ingredients in the following recipe can acceptably be adjusted to taste. This sauce is used for dipping grilled or fried meats, fish, or vegetables. It also makes a delicious condiment for cold leftover grilled or roasted meats or fish. It will keep for at least a week in the refrigerator.

YIELD: ⅔ CUP (165 MILLILITERS)

sesame seeds	1 tablespoon plus 1 teaspoon	20 milliliters
japanese dark soy sauce	6 tablespoons	90 milliliters
rice vinegar	¼ cup	60 milliliters
sugar	2 teaspoons	10 milliliters
grated fresh ginger *or* grated garlic	2 teaspoons *or* 2 teaspoons	10 milliliters *or* 10 milliliters
toasted sesame oil, preferably japanese brand	2 teaspoons	10 milliliters
serrano chile, finely chopped *or* thai chiles, finely chopped *or* kochujang (or to taste)	1 or 2 *or* 2 to 4 *or* 1 teaspoon to 2 tablespoons	1 or 2 *or* 2 to 4 *or* 5 to 30 milliliters
chopped cilantro (optional) *or* scallions, chopped (optional)	2 tablespoons *or* 2	30 milliliters *or* 2

1. Toast the sesame seeds by tossing them in a dry skillet over high heat for about 5 minutes, until they turn pale brown and smell toasty.

2. Combine the sesame seeds, soy sauce, vinegar, sugar, ginger or garlic, sesame oil, chiles or kochujang, and cilantro or scallions and let sit for at least 30 minutes before serving.

THAI AND VIETNAMESE SAUCES

To group these countries together is somewhat like trying to characterize in a few short pages the cooking of all of Europe. But there are certain ingredients and techniques that, if not identical, are similar enough to give these cuisines characteristics in common.

The ingredient most central to Thai and Vietnamese sauces is fish sauce, known respectively as *nampla* or *nuoc mam*, which is made from the liquid released by fermenting fish (see page 40 for buying tips). When combined with other ingredients, fish sauce settles into the background in much the same way that salted anchovies lend a subtle note to Mediterranean sauces with garlic and perhaps tomatoes. But fish sauce has such a full flavor and is so much the heart and soul of Southeast Asian cooking that it allows for the creation of sauces and soups completely without broth or stock, never mind the long-simmered reductions of Western sauce making.

Other ingredients used in Southeast Asian sauces, such as garlic and shallots, are familiar Western staples, but Southeast Asian cooks also rely on a variety of flavorings that until recently were never seen in the United States. Two aromatic ingredients— lemongrass and makrut lime leaves—are used throughout Southeast Asia to give sauces a delicate citrus flavor. A stalk of lemongrass looks like an elongated, very immature ear of corn. Usually only the tender section (which is several inches long, near the base) is thinly sliced and simmered in liquids or ground into a curry paste to lend a subtle lemony flavor and aroma. Makrut lime leaves look like bay leaves but have a distinct lime aroma. They can be simmered whole in soups or sauces, they can be thinly sliced, or they can be ground up with other ingredients in curry pastes. Like Chinese cooks, Southeast Asian cooks use fresh ginger, but they are also fond of galangal (sometimes spelled "galanga"). This rhizome looks very much like ginger but has a subtle and distinctive pine-resin flavor.

Whereas European cooks use heavy cream to give body, richness, and unctuosity to their sauces, Southeast Asian cooks use coconut milk. Coconut milk has a gentle sweetness and richness that softens the often incendiary heat of spicy sauces and soups. Shrimp paste is also popular in Southeast Asian cooking, although in many restaurants in America it seems to be left out or is used only in very small amounts. Made from fermented shrimp, shrimp paste gives a distinctive aroma to Southeast Asian foods, but most Westerners find the aroma too strong (the kitchen will smell like something went terribly wrong). Southeast Asian cooks also like to finish their sauces with herbs. Cilantro is probably the most popular—the leaves are typically added at the end—but the roots and stems are also used, ground into curry pastes. Mint and two Asian varieties of basil are also well liked (see Chapter 3, "Ingredients," for more about each of these ingredients).

Southeast Asian Dipping Sauces

Many of the most popular Southeast Asian sauces are simple dipping sauces, based on fish sauce of course, and made as everyday accompaniments to a bowl of rice, which is the main staple. In the West, these sauces are more likely to be served with richer fare such as fried or grilled fish, shellfish, or chicken.

Every Southeast Asian country has its own classic dipping sauces, but the most often used dipping sauces in each country do have certain characteristics and ingredients in common. Most dipping sauces are simple mixtures of chopped herbs (cilantro is a favorite, but mint and basil are also popular), aromatic vegetables such as shallots and garlic (at times in prodigious amounts), and ginger. Burmese and Vietnamese sauces sometimes reveal their country's proximity to China by including soy sauce or even hoisin sauce.

Almost all Southeast Asian dipping sauces include an acidic ingredient, which makes them lovely accents to seafood. Vinegar (namely harsh distilled white vinegar) is often used and is the one ingredient that might be better replaced with good cider vinegar or white wine vinegar. Lime juice is popular (in Southeast Asia the small makrut lime is sometimes used, but the juice of Western limes is milder and, to some cooks, preferable. The most distinctive acidic ingredient is tamarind. Tamarind pods look vaguely like wizened fava beans, the beans surrounded in the husk with a brown sticky paste. It's the paste rather than the bean that is used as a souring agent, and since fresh tamarind is sometimes difficult to find outside of ethnic markets, it is fortunate that the paste itself is sold inexpensively in small packages. The packaged paste, which is sometimes sold with chunks of seeds and fibers, must be soaked in boiling water and strained before it can be used.

Chiles are also an almost universal ingredient in Southeast Asian dipping sauces. The most popular chiles—small bird chiles, sometimes called Thai chiles—make up in heat for what they lack in size. Larger serrano chiles are also used in Southeast Asian cooking and are easier to find than the Thai variety in some parts of the United States. Peanuts—either coarsely chopped and chunky, or roasted and ground into peanut butter—are also added to dipping sauces in small amounts to give the sauces a bit of texture and sweetness. Sugar is another popular ingredient used in Southeast Asian dipping sauces, often serving to strike the perfect balance between sour ingredients (vinegar, lime, or tamarind), savory ingredients (primarily fish sauce), hot ingredients (chiles), and aromatic ingredients (herbs, garlic, and ginger).

VIETNAMESE SPICY FISH SAUCE
NUOC CHAM

This basic sauce has the same essential flavors that are included in most Southeast Asian dipping sauces. Americans who are unfamiliar with Vietnamese food may prefer a sauce with less fish sauce, or a sauce made with Thai fish sauce, which is milder. In fact this sauce is very similar to one of the most popular Thai dipping sauces, *nam prik*. In Vietnam, nuoc cham might be served with a bowl of rice to constitute a simple meal, but it is also an almost universal sauce for salads—it's perfect with cucumbers—and grilled and fried seafood or meats. It will keep for up to 2 weeks, well covered, in the refrigerator.

YIELD: ¾ CUP (185 MILLILITERS)

garlic cloves, crushed to a paste	2	2
fresh red or green thai chiles, finely chopped *or* serrano chiles, finely chopped	4 *or* 2	4 *or* 2
sugar	3 tablespoons	45 milliliters
lime juice	6 tablespoons	90 milliliters
vietnamese or thai fish sauce	¼ cup	60 milliliters

Combine all the ingredients in a small bowl. Stir until the sugar is dissolved.

Note: To prepare ½ cup (125 milliliters) tamarind extract, pour ½ cup (125 milliliters) boiling water over 2 tablespoons (30 milliliters) tamarind paste in a small mixing bowl. Let sit for 15 minutes, stir thoroughly, and strain.

VARIATIONS
The amounts of each of the ingredients can be increased or decreased to produce spicier, hotter, more sour, or sweeter versions. The lime juice can be replaced with vinegar (distilled white vinegar is typically used, but white wine vinegar or cider vinegar will give the sauce more finesse), or with tamarind extract (see Note). Water can also be added to the sauce for a lighter version, and chopped cilantro will give the sauce a refreshing bite. A finely chopped 1-inch (2.5 cm) slice of peeled fresh ginger can be stirred into the sauce to make the classic Vietnamese *nuoc mam gung*—a sauce sometimes served with plain rice and also with seafood.

589

Thai Curry Pastes

Unlike Indian curries, which are almost always made from a combination of dried and powdered spices, Thai curries are pastes with a consistency much like stiff peanut butter. Instead of relying entirely on dried spices, Thai cooks also include fresh ingredients such as chiles, garlic, and shallots in their pastes. Thai curry pastes are usually freshly made using a traditional mortar and pestle, so their pungent aroma and flavor stay intact.

Curry pastes are very strong and are never served alone. Rather, they are combined at the last minute with liquids such as water, seafood or meat stock, fish sauce, lime juice, and coconut milk. Although the ingredients that go into a Thai curry paste can be used separately as flavorings, a premade paste makes the complicated assortment of flavorings easier to use. And because the pastes have a relatively smooth consistency achieved from long pounding and grinding, they can be incorporated into sauces without interfering with the consistency.

Red curry paste—red because it contains a large number of red chiles—is the best-known and most popular Thai curry paste. It is traditionally made by slow grinding with a mortar and pestle, but in modern kitchens the grinding is sometimes started in a food processor. Don't try to use the food processor for the whole process, because it won't grind the ingredients to a smooth enough consistency. Other curry pastes, made using the same techniques, contain additional ingredients and different proportions of many of the same ingredients found in red curry paste. Green curry paste contains green chiles (often serranos) instead of red chiles, and it is even hotter than red curry paste. Yellow curry contains many of the same ingredients contained in green and red curry pastes, but also includes an array of Indian curry spices.

THAI RED CURRY PASTE

Red curry paste (as all curry paste) is somewhat labor intensive because there is no adequate substitute for slow grinding with a mortar and pestle. Curry pastes do freeze well, however, so the slow grinding process isn't necessary every time a dish calls for one. It's worth making a large batch, freezing it in smaller quantities, and using it as needed.

Dried guajillo chiles are suggested here, but it's worthwhile experimenting with different dried red chiles to come up with varying nuances and heat.

Shrimp paste, listed here as optional, is traditionally cooked in a skillet before it is combined with the other ingredients. To avoid an aroma that many Western cooks find unpleasant, do this in a well-ventilated kitchen, or simply add the shrimp paste to the curry without cooking it. (Some cooks wrap the shrimp paste in aluminum foil and toast it in a skillet so the aroma doesn't escape.)

YIELD: 1 CUP (250 MILLILITERS)

guajillo or ancho chiles, about 10	2½ ounces	70 grams
coriander seeds	1 tablespoon	15 milliliters
lemongrass	2 stalks	2 stalks
thai chiles, stemmed and seeded *or* serrano chiles, stemmed and seeded	6 *or* 3	6 *or* 3
peeled galangal, sliced ¼-inch (5 mm) thick	8 slices	8 slices
shallots, peeled	4	4
garlic cloves, peeled	4	4
cilantro roots *or* cilantro stems, coarsely chopped	2 *or* about 2 heaping tablespoons	2 *or* 40 milliliters
zest of 1 lime, cut in strips *or* makrut lime leaf	*or* 1	*or* 1
shrimp paste (optional)	1 tablespoon	15 milliliters

1. Wipe the guajillo chiles with a dry towel. Cut off the stems and slice the chiles in half lengthwise. Shake out the seeds.

2. Put the guajillo chiles and coriander seeds in a food processor and grind to a powder, about 3 minutes.

3. Peel the outermost sheath off the lemongrass stalks and discard. Cut off 5 inches (12.5 cm) of the tender end and thinly slice. Discard the rest of the stalks or dry them and reserve them to add them to broths for other Southeast Asian dishes. Add the slices to the chile mixture.

4. Add the rest of the ingredients to the chile-lemongrass mixture and purée for about 10 minutes, scraping the inside of the food processor bowl with a rubber spatula every minute.

5. Transfer one-third of the paste to a mortar and grind with a pestle to a smooth paste, about 10 minutes. Repeat with the remaining two-thirds, a third at a time. (If a very large mortar is available, grind the paste all at once.)

THAI GREEN CURRY PASTE

Green curry paste is made in the same way as red curry paste—preliminary grinding in a food processor, final grinding with a mortar and pestle—but some of the ingredients and their proportions are different. Most important, green curry is made with fresh green chiles (usually serranos) rather than dried red ones. The proportion of chiles is also higher, so green curry is even hotter than red.

YIELD: 1 CUP (250 MILLILITERS)

coriander seeds	1 tablespoon	15 milliliters
white peppercorns	1 teaspoon	5 milliliters
lemongrass, outer sheath removed and discarded	3 stalks	3 stalks
green serrano chiles, seeded, coarsely chopped	12	12
zest of 1 lime, coarsely chopped *or* makrut lime leaf, coarsely chopped	*or* 1	*or* 1
shallots, coarsely chopped	6 medium	6 medium
garlic cloves, coarsely chopped	6	6
cilantro roots *or* cilantro stems, coarsely chopped	5 *or* about 2 heaping tablespoons	5 *or* 40 milliliters
peeled galangal, sliced ¼-inch (5 mm) thick	4 slices	4 slices
gently packed cilantro leaves	1 cup	250 milliliters
shrimp paste (optional)	1 tablespoon	15 milliliters

1. Put the coriander seeds and peppercorns in a food processor and grind to a powder, about 1 minute.

2. Thinly slice 3 inches (8 cm) of the tender ends of the lemongrass and add to the processor bowl. Discard the rest of the lemongrass stalks.

3. Put the remaining ingredients in the food processor and purée for about 10 minutes, scraping the inside of the bowl with a rubber spatula every minute.

4. Transfer the paste to a mortar—don't fill it more than one-third full; work in batches if necessary—and grind to a smooth paste; this will take about 20 minutes (see note).

Note: Because grinding some aromatic ingredients such as makrut lime leaves, tamarind, and lemongrass stalks requires hard hand work, it is helpful to have good tools. Buy the largest mortar and pestle you can find. Make sure that the inside of the mortar isn't glazed.

The best "gadget" of all, often used in India, is a coarse-grained flat rock that looks a bit like a tombstone. With it is used a stone cylinder that looks much like a European-style rolling pin without handles. The herbs and aromatic ingredients are placed on the stone and the cylinder is pushed and pulled (not rolled) back and forth. These are available from Indian supply stores.

Using Curry Pastes: Thai Meat and Seafood Sauces and Stews

Once Thai curry pastes are on hand, a Thai-style sauce can be assembled in minutes. Most Thai sauces are used as part of stew-like "curries" rather than sauces prepared separately for ladling, Western style, over cooked meats and seafood. Thai sauces are only lightly thickened with either curry paste or coconut milk, having the consistency of creamy soup. This characteristic makes Thai curries perfect for serving with rice.

There are numerous traditional and standard recipes for Thai curries, but these curries can be improvised once the function of the basic ingredients is grasped. Other than the curry paste itself, Thai curries almost always contain fish sauce and an acidic ingredient such as tamarind, vinegar, or lime juice. They also usually contain coconut milk (which gives them a delicate sweet richness), a little sugar, additional makrut lime leaves (which add flavor and look pretty), chopped or whole basil, mint, and/or cilantro leaves, and perhaps most important, a vegetable or nut garniture to provide contrasting flavor and texture. Garnitures for Southeast Asian stews function in the same way as they do for European stews but instead of carrots, pearl onions, or mushrooms, a Southeast Asian stew might contain cashews, bamboo shoots, miniature eggplants, pineapple, long beans, or cucumbers.

THAI CURRY MODEL

This basic model can be used for seafood, poultry, red meat, or vegetables. Meats, poultry, and seafood can be browned first or simply simmered directly with the stew's liquid ingredients. Poultry, seafood, and tender cuts of meat can be quickly stir-fried or sautéed before they are simmered in the curry, but tough cuts of meat should be gently braised in stock or water in the same way as for a European-style stew. The stewing liquid is then used as the liquid component in the curry.

YIELD: 6 SERVINGS

MAIN INGREDIENT
to be used alone or in combination

2¼ pounds/1 kilogram (6 ounces/175 grams per serving) of one of the following, cut into 2 × ½-inch (5 × 1 cm) strips:

boneless chicken breasts		
firm-fleshed fish such as swordfish or shark		
tender cut of beef such as sirloin, flank, or sirloin strip *or* shellfish such as scallops, left whole or cut into disks		
squid, cut into rings		
shrimp (left whole)		
peanut or vegetable oil (if meat or seafood is being browned first)	2 tablespoons	30 milliliters

COOKING OIL, BASIC FLAVORING, AND COOKING LIQUID

peanut or vegetable oil	1 tablespoon	15 milliliters
red or green thai curry paste	¼ to ½ cup	60 to 125 milliliters
appropriate liquid or water	1 cup	250 milliliters
fish sauce	2 to 6 tablespoons	30 to 90 milliliters

ENRICHER AND THICKENER

coconut milk *or* fresh coconut milk (see page 43)	1 (14-ounce) can *or* 2 cups	425 milliliters *or* 500 milliliters

SWEET-AND-SOUR INGREDIENTS

juice of 2 limes *or* tamarind extract (see note, page 589) *or* wine vinegar or cider vinegar	*or* ½ cup *or* 2 tablespoons	*or* 125 milliliters *or* 30 milliliters
sugar (optional)	1 to 2 tablespoons	15 to 30 milliliters

SLOW-COOKING AROMATIC INGREDIENTS
optional

makrut lime leaves	6	6
peeled galangal, sliced ¼-inch (5 mm) thick	3 slices	3 slices

GARNITURES
to be used alone or in combination

bamboo shoots

sweet bell peppers

broccoli, cut into florets

cashews

eggplant, peeled, cut into 1-inch (2.5 cm) cubes

long beans or string beans

mushrooms

pineapple, cut into wedges or cubes

spinach

tofu, cut into 1-inch (2.5 cm) cubes

FAST-COOKING AROMATIC INGREDIENTS
optional

cilantro or thai basil leaves, whole or coarsely chopped, or mint leaves, torn into pieces	3 tablespoons	45 milliliters

1. If desired, brown the main ingredient in oil in a skillet or wok. Set it aside on a plate. Pour off the used oil.

2. Heat the cooking oil (in the same skillet used for browning the main ingredient) and stir the curry paste over medium heat for about 4 minutes, until it smells fragrant. Stir in the liquid and fish sauce and bring to a gentle simmer.

3. Stir in the coconut milk, the sweet-and-sour ingredients, and the slow-cooking aromatic ingredients, if using, and bring back to a simmer.

4. Add one or more of the garnitures and simmer until almost done.

5. Add back the main ingredient and simmer until done or heated through.

6. Stir in the herb, if using. Simmer for 30 seconds. Serve immediately.

IMPROVISING THAI CURRIES WITHOUT CURRY PASTES

Curry pastes offer an easy method for quickly incorporating a complex mixture of ingredients into stew-like curries. But these same ingredients can be finely chopped or even left whole and then be simmered directly in broth or even water to make a sauce.

Here is a broth-like sauce that's quick to make and can be served around pieces of cooked meat and fish. Adjust, add, or omit ingredients to taste.

YIELD: 3 TO 4 CUPS (750 MILLILITERS TO 1 LITER); 1 QUART (1 LITER)
IF THE TOMATOES ARE USED; ENOUGH FOR 6 TO 8 SERVINGS

chicken, fish, or meat broth, cooking liquid from meat stew, or water	1 cup	250 milliliters
coconut milk	1 (14-ounce) can	425 milliliters
tomatoes, peeled, seeded, chopped (optional)	1 cup	250 milliliters
garlic cloves, crushed to a paste	4	4
shallots, finely chopped	2	2
thai chiles, seeded, finely chopped *or* serrano chiles, seeded, finely chopped	2 to 8 *or* 1 to 4	2 to 8 *or* 1 to 4
lemongrass, outer sheath removed and discarded, 3 inches (8 cm) of root end thinly sliced	2 stalks	2 stalks
makrut lime leaves	6	6
sliced peeled galangal (¼-inch/5 mm thick)	6	6
lime juice or tamarind extract (see note, page 589)	2 to 4 tablespoons	30 to 60 milliliters
thai fish sauce	2 to 4 tablespoons	30 to 60 milliliters
sugar	½ to 2 tablespoons	7.5 to 30 milliliters
cilantro, mint, or thai basil leaves	3 tablespoons	45 milliliters

1. Bring the broth, coconut milk, and tomatoes, if using, to a slow simmer in a medium pot.

2. Stir in the garlic, shallots, chiles, lemongrass, lime leaves, and galangal, the minimum amounts of lime juice, fish sauce, and sugar. Adjust the acidity with lime juice or tamarind, the saltiness with fish sauce, and the sweetness with sugar.

3. Stir in the cilantro, mint, or basil, simmer for 30 seconds, and serve.

INDONESIAN SAUCES

Any cook familiar with Thai curry pastes and sauces will find the ingredients and techniques for making Indonesian sauces very similar to those used in Thailand. Indonesian cooks are forever grinding aromatic ingredients with a mortar and pestle to create an Indonesian spice paste (generically called *bumbu*), then heating the mixture in oil before adding liquid, usually coconut milk. But while Thai curries are somewhat standardized, Indonesians make a different spice mixture for every dish.

There are, however, several ingredients that give Indonesian dishes their own identity and make Indonesian cuisine distinct from other Southeast Asian cuisines. Bottled fish sauce, an indispensable flavoring in Thai and Vietnamese cooking, is rarely used in Indonesia. Indonesian cooks rely instead on shrimp paste, called *terasi*, to give dishes much of their depth of flavor. While it's possible to get by without shrimp paste in Thai and Vietnamese cooking (fish sauce fills the gap somewhat), it's an essential ingredient in Indonesian cooking. Traditional Indonesian recipes often include shrimp paste in the bumbu, which is fried before liquids are added. The aroma released by the shrimp paste is so pungent and unfamiliar to Western noses that a safer approach is to wrap the shrimp paste tightly in a square of aluminum foil, heat it in a dry sauté pan, and unwrap it and combine it with the other ingredients when it has cooled and the liquids have been added. Another trick—frowned upon by purists—is to simply stir the uncooked shrimp paste into the simmering sauce.

Kemiri nuts, sometimes called candlenuts, are another particularly Indonesian ingredient. These waxy nuts have very hard shells, but fortunately they're always sold out of the shell. They are ground to a paste using a mortar and pestle (although nowadays the grinding is sometimes initiated in a food processor) and used to thicken sauces. Macadamia nuts can be used as a substitute, but they don't thicken as well and won't impart the particular authentic flavor of kemiri nuts. Kemiri nuts are mildly toxic when raw and should always be cooked.

Salam leaves contain a subtly flavored oil that imparts a distinct character to Indonesian stews and sauces. They are used in the same way as bay leaves in Western cooking and curry leaves in Indian cooking. Imported bay leaves can be used as a substitute.

Like the Chinese, Indonesians are also fond of soy sauce and have two versions of their own: *kecap asin*, relatively light and salty, and a heavier, sweeter version, *kecap manis*. Both versions are used in marinades and in sauces. *Kecap*, pronounced "ketchup," is the origin of the Western word *ketchup*, but Indonesian soy sauces are very different from tomato ketchup.

Indonesian cooks share the Thai passion for galangal, but they are more likely to buy it in powdered form (called *laos*) than they are in fresh or frozen chunks.

The satay (or *saté*) is the Indonesian preparation best known in the West. A satay is made by marinating cubes of meat or seafood with spices, kecap, and aromatic vegetables, and then skewering the cubes and grilling them. The distinct flavor of the marinade contributes to the satay's character, but much of its special character comes from the sauce. Most satay sauces are based on ground peanuts flavored with spices, made hot with chiles, and sweetened with sugar.

Indonesians also have their own set of relishes, most of them hot and spicy, called *sambals*. Most sambals are used as condiments for other foods.

CHINESE SAUCES

It's obviously difficult to describe even the most basic sauces of a country as huge and diverse as China in a few short pages. It can be helpful, however, to see how profoundly the Chinese approach to sauce making differs from the traditions of Europe. Whereas many of the best European sauces are made by careful and systematic concentration of a product's natural flavors, many Chinese sauces are designed to accent and provide contrast to the ingredients rather than to distill their essence. And although few condiments are used in classic French cooking (mustard is the only one used with any regularity), Chinese kitchen cabinets are filled with bottled seasonings, sauces, oils, and relishes. Some are homemade, but others, having been made commercially for centuries, are trusted standby condiments much as mustard and ketchup are in the West.

Another well-known factor that has influenced the evolution of Chinese cooking is the scarcity of cooking fuel. Many Chinese sauces are the result of a quick stir-fry and a few simple seasonings or condiments sprinkled toward the end of cooking.

Making Sauces for Stir-Fries

Even though Chinese cooks rely on a variety of techniques, stir-frying is probably the one most associated with Chinese cooking. It's essential to understand stir-frying to get a sense of how Chinese sauces are made.

Stir-frying is almost identical to sautéing—sautéing in the most literal sense, wherein the foods are tossed in the hot pan over high heat—except that a wok is used instead of a frying pan and the foods are stirred (often with chopsticks) instead of being tossed. (A, B) Chinese cooks introduce flavor into stir-fries by lightly frying finely minced aromatic ingredients (especially ginger and garlic) in the oil before the main ingredients are added. This technique is essentially what an Italian cook does when gently sautéing sliced garlic in olive oil before stirring in vegetables. These aromatic ingredients can also be stir-fried along with the rest of the ingredients. To make a sauce for a stir-fry, the cooking oil is drained out and liquids are added—essentially the same method used in Western fricassée.

Liquids, which almost always include soy sauce, are then quickly stirred with the food, and the dish is served immediately. The liquids added to a stir-fry are sometimes left

unbound—they remain completely liquid and surround the foods on the serving dish—but often a thickener (usually cornstarch) is used to get them to cling around the foods. Cornstarch can be added to a stir-fry in two ways. It can be dissolved in a small amount of liquid (typically 1 tablespoon/15 milliliters cornstarch is dissolved in 2 tablespoons/30 milliliters liquid) and stirred into the stir-fry a minute before the cooking is completed. (C) Alternatively, it can be incorporated into a marinade. In addition to cornstarch, marinades for stir-fries typically contain soy sauce.

BASIC STIR-FRY SAUCE VARIATIONS AND FLAVORINGS

The Basic Stir-Fry recipe (page 600) is to Chinese cooking what a simple sauté recipe is to French cooking—a base upon which unlimited variations can be built. Here are some of the more common ingredients added to stir-fries (see Chapter 3, "Ingredients," for more information, including best brands).

CHILES, CHILE PASTES, AND CHILE OIL. Many stir-fries are enhanced by a little spicy heat. Depending on the regional cooking style, Chinese cooks may use black pepper (for example, in hot-and-sour soup), Sichuan peppercorns, fresh or dried chiles, or chile oil. Chiles are most popular in the regions of Sichuan and Hunan. Chinese cooks also use bottled chile pastes. Chiles and chile-based condiments are added to stir-fries at different stages. Chile oil can replace the vegetable oil used for stir-frying, or whole dried or chopped fresh chiles can be added at the same time as the garlic and ginger. Chile pastes can be stirred into the stir-fry, to taste, a minute or two before serving.

FERMENTED BLACK BEANS. Rinsed and lightly chopped, fermented black beans are best when soaked in a little sherry before they are added to stir-fries near the end of cooking. Because fermented black beans are very salty, the soy sauce called for in the basic stir-fry recipe should be left out initially, then added to taste at the end of cooking. Two tablespoons (30 milliliters) rinsed and crushed or lightly chopped black beans, soaked in the same amount of sherry, is usually just about the right quantity for the Basic Stir-Fry (page 600). The black beans should be added at the same time as the meat. Their soaking liquid, which will be very salty, can be added near the end, to taste.

HAM. Slivers of salty ham can make the perfect accent to stir-fried foods, especially vegetables. China has an array of excellent hams, but none of them is as yet imported into the United States, so Smithfield ham is the best available substitute. Black Forest ham runs a close second. These hams should be thinly sliced, cut into slivers, and added to stir-fries a minute or two before the end of cooking.

HOISIN SAUCE. Like so many Chinese sauces, this sweet anise-scented sauce is made with soy beans. A tablespoon or two (15 to 30 milliliters) of hoisin sauce added to a stir-fry during the last minute of cooking will give the sauce a subtle sweetness. Hoisin sauce is best used in conjunction with a small amount of dark sesame oil.

ORANGE PEEL. Dried orange and tangerine peels are sold at Asian groceries as a seasoning for stir-fries. Slivers of dried orange peel (or, in a pinch, slivered fresh zests) are especially good in stir-fries containing chiles (or chile paste) and sesame oil. Orange zests can be cut off in strips with a paring knife or vegetable peeler and allowed to dry for 2 to 3 days on a rack. Tightly sealed, they can then be stored for several months.

OYSTER SAUCE. One to 2 tablespoons (15 to 30 milliliters) of oyster sauce added to a stir-fry during the last minute of cooking will give the sauce a

MODEL FOR A BASIC STIR-FRY

There are dozens of variations on this basic theme, and a couple of different approaches for incorporating the cornerstone ingredients of ginger, garlic, and cornstarch. Both the ginger and garlic can be left in thick slices, gently fried for a minute or two in hot oil, and fished out before other ingredients are added, or they can be peeled, finely chopped, and added to the stir-fry with the other ingredients. The cornstarch is combined with soy sauce (or another cool liquid) and used as a marinade, or the mixture may simply be added to the stir-fry near the end so the cornstarch thickens the sauce. Stir-fries require very high heat so that the ingredients will brown quickly without overcooking.

YIELD: 4 SERVINGS

MAIN INGREDIENTS		
boneless chicken breasts, beef (a medium-tender cut such as flank steak or sirloin steak), boneless and skinless duck breast, shrimp, or scallops	1½ pounds	675 grams
green vegetables such as bok choy, broccoli (domestic or chinese), watercress, chard (weight after trimming)	1 pound	500 grams
MARINADE		
dark soy sauce	2 tablespoons	30 milliliters
cornstarch	2 teaspoons	10 milliliters
dry sherry or chinese rice wine	2 tablespoons	30 milliliters
INGREDIENTS FOR STIR-FRYING		
peanut or vegetable oil	2 tablespoons	30 milliliters

distinctive seafood character. Oyster sauce is especially good when used in conjunction with dark sesame oil.

PEANUTS AND OTHER NUTS. Sichuan cooks are fond of peanuts and like to combine them with garlic, sesame oil (or paste), and chile paste in fiery sauces for cold meats or noodles. Peanuts and other nuts are also added to stir-fries for their flavor and to provide a contrasting texture. Peanuts (start out with raw peanuts) are most easily incorporated into a stir-fry by frying them, with their papery red skins left on, in a few tablespoons of hot oil. Drain off the oil and add the peanuts to the rest of the stir-fry near the end. Or, to simplify things, add roasted peanuts to the stir-fry just before serving. (They will lose their crunch if added sooner.)

SESAME OIL. Dark Asian sesame oil has an intense flavor that gives stir-fries a savory accent and a characteristic northern Chinese character. Sesame oil is

finely chopped fresh ginger	1 teaspoon	5 milliliters
finely chopped garlic	2 teaspoons	10 milliliters
chicken stock, seafood or fish stock, or water	¼ cup	60 milliliters
soy sauce (optional)	to taste	to taste

1. Cut the poultry or meat into strips about 2 × ⅜ inches (5 cm × 5 mm). Shellfish such as shrimp or scallops may be left whole or, if very large, cut into 1-inch (2.5 cm) sections or ½-inch-thick (1 cm) disks. Cut the vegetables into manageable pieces, but not so small that they lose their identity.

2. Work the marinade ingredients together into a smooth paste and work the mixture into the meat or seafood. Marinate for 10 to 30 minutes.

3. Heat the oil in a large wok or skillet over very high heat. When the oil begins to ripple, stir in the protein, leaving any excess marinade behind in the bowl—don't throw it out. When the protein begins to brown, add the ginger, garlic, and vegetables.

4. Quickly stir the protein with the vegetables until both are done, 3 to 6 minutes. Chicken strips should lose their flexibility and become stiff to the touch; duck and beef should remain rare or medium rare; shrimp should turn orange. If there is oil left in the bottom of the wok or skillet after stir-frying, spoon it out and discard it.

5. Stir in the stock and simmer for 30 seconds more. If the stir-fry needs salt, add a teaspoon (5 milliliters) or more soy sauce. If the sauce is too runny, stir in a teaspoon or two (5 to 10 milliliters) of the marinade left in the bottom of the bowl. Stir while cooking for another 30 seconds, and serve.

very powerful—½ to 2 teaspoons (3 to 10 milliliters) added to a stir-fry during the last few seconds of cooking is usually sufficient.

SUGAR AND HONEY. Sauces for stir-fried meats or vegetables are often enhanced with a little sugar or honey. Start out adding ½ teaspoon (3 milliliters) of either to a stir-fry a minute before the cooking is completed.

VINEGARS. Chinese cooks use a variety of vinegars and often combine them with sugar to come up with sweet-and-sour sauces. Rice vinegar, Chinese black vinegar, and balsamic vinegar can all be used to season stir-fries.

Chinese Cold Sauces

Whereas Western cooks (especially French) have for centuries emphasized the importance of warm and hot sauces and have come up with elaborate systems and hierarchies for their use, Chinese cooks have put much of their energy into developing cold sauces. The Chinese also lack the aversion to bottled sauces that Western chefs feel, and will often combine these bottled sauces and condiments to make variations. Many of these cold sauces can be tossed with cold meats, poultry, or noodles, and others can be used as simple dipping sauces for items such as wontons or deep-fried dishes, or as salad dressings (see also "Flavored Oils," page 467).

CHINESE GINGER- AND GARLIC-FLAVORED "VINAIGRETTE"

One of the easiest and most versatile dipping sauces is a simple mixture of soy sauce, vinegar, and fresh ginger. This sauce is excellent with Chinese black vinegar (see page 48), but balsamic vinegar makes an acceptable substitute.

YIELD: 1 CUP (250 MILLILITERS)

japanese dark soy sauce (see note)	⅔ cup	165 milliliters
chinese black vinegar or balsamic vinegar	⅓ cup	80 milliliters
grated fresh ginger	2 teaspoons	10 milliliters
finely chopped garlic	2 teaspoons	10 milliliters
sesame oil (see page 47)	1 teaspoon	5 milliliters

Combine all the ingredients. Let sit for an hour, then serve. This sauce will keep for at least a week in the refrigerator.

Note: Japanese soy sauce is popular even in Chinese sauces because it is less salty than Chinese. When substituting Chinese soy sauce (see page 41), use half as much as called for, then add more to taste, if desired.

SWEET AND SPICY SESAME SAUCE

Inspired by a recipe in Barbara Tropp's excellent *The Modern Art of Chinese Cooking*, this sauce has a complex sweetness but enough heat to prevent the sweetness from being cloying. This sauce can be tossed with or brushed on cold chicken, or used as a dipping sauce for grilled foods or as a salad dressing.

YIELD: ¾ CUP (185 MILLILITERS)

sesame seeds	2 tablespoons	30 milliliters
or	*or*	*or*
asian sesame paste (see page 41)	¼ cup	60 milliliters
sugar	1 tablespoon	15 milliliters
water, hot	2 tablespoons	30 milliliters
dark sesame oil	2 tablespoons	30 milliliters
hoisin sauce	1 tablespoon	15 milliliters
japanese dark soy sauce	¼ cup	60 milliliters
chile oil	1 tablespoon	15 milliliters
or	*or*	*or*
thai chiles, very finely chopped	2 to 4	2 to 4
or	*or*	*or*
serrano chiles, very finely chopped	1 or 2	1 or 2

1. If using whole sesame seeds, toss them in a dry skillet over high heat until they are lightly brown and smell fragrant, about 5 minutes. Cool, then grind them to a paste in a coffee grinder.

2. Dissolve the sugar in the water. Whisk all the ingredients into a smooth paste or purée in a food processor, scraping down the sides with a rubber spatula a few times during the processing. Keep the sauce in the refrigerator until needed. It typically will last several weeks.

CHINESE MUSTARD SAUCE

Most Chinese mustard sauces are made with dry mustard and flavored with sesame oil and chile oil. Barbara Tropp (*The Modern Art of Chinese Cooking*) recommended replacing the dry mustard with Dijon (specifically Maille brand) for a truer mustard flavor. Ms. Tropp used a sauce similar to this one for a number of cold salads (some with chicken, others with duck) and as a dipping sauce for fried pork balls. Dipping sauce keeps indefinitely in the refrigerator, but it is better if the fresh cilantro is added shortly before serving. For homemade Chinese-Style Chile Oil, see page 471.

YIELD: 1 CUP (250 MILLILITERS)

(continued)

603

dijon mustard	¾ cup	185 milliliters
chile oil	3 tablespoons	45 milliliters
chinese black vinegar or balsamic vinegar	1 tablespoon	15 milliliters
finely chopped cilantro	3 tablespoons	45 milliliters

Combine the mustard, chile oil, and vinegar 1 or 2 hours before serving. Just before serving, stir in the cilantro.

INDIAN SAUCES

Because India is a huge and diverse country with well over a dozen languages and several major religions (each with its own culinary taboos and traditions), it would seem impossible to make generalizations about Indian cooking as a whole. And although any serious discussion of Indian cooking requires a close look at the cooking of individual regions, many of the same techniques and ingredients are used throughout the country, making it possible to take a broad overview and at least get a sense of how an Indian sauce is put together.

Curries

The most famous Indian sauces are the natural products of making curries. In essence, curries are stews made by simmering meat, seafood, or vegetables (or a combination) in flavorful liquid in much the same way as a French cook might simmer meat or seafood in wine and then add a variety of garnitures for flavor, contrasting texture, and color. But while much of the subtlety and variety of the best French cooking lies in the careful combination of herbs, the genius of Indian cooking is based on the subtle use of spices, many of which are rarely if ever used in European cooking.

A European or American cook's experience with Indian cooking is likely to be throwing a dash of curry powder into an essentially Western dish (curry powder is in fact marvelous in cream and butter sauces; see Curry Sauce, page 151), but in India, bottled curry powder—essentially an Anglo-Saxon adaptation—is never used. Instead, each region (and even each cook) relies upon a unique combination of spices, which gives Indian sauces distinct regional character.

Except for the use of spices, an Indian curry is made in much the same way as any stew. While European cooks start most stews by gently sweating aromatic vegetables such as onions, carrots, celery, and garlic as a gently flavored mirepoix or soffritto, most Indian cooks rely most heavily on onions. And instead of the gentle sweating that prevents the onions from turning brown, Indian cooks use higher heat so the onions do brown. A French or Italian cook would probably sweat the vegetables in butter or olive oil, but an Indian cook might use ghee (beurre noisette), mustard oil, coconut oil, or sesame oil, depending on the region where he or she lives. Nowadays, inert-tasting vegetable oils are replacing many of these regional preferences.

While a Western cook might add a little fresh or dried thyme or marjoram to an aromatic vegetable base, an Indian cook will most likely add chopped chiles, garlic, and ginger to the browning onions. At this point, the Indian cook may begin to add spices. Spices are typically added at different stages of cooking. Again, the incorporation of spices into an Indian curry is analogous to the use of herbs in European cooking. Herbs or spices that release their flavor slowly (thyme in France, cinnamon in India) are added first so they can meld with the flavors of other ingredients. Those spices whose flavor the cook wishes to magnify are stirred in the hot fat to accentuate their flavor. Other spices whose flavor the cook wishes to mollify may be worked to a paste with water and stirred into the stew later during cooking. Other spices may be worked to a paste with water or cooked in ghee and stirred in at the very end so their delicacy or forthrightness isn't lost.

Meat, seafood, or vegetables are usually added to the curry after cooking the vegetables, aromatics (such as ginger, garlic, chiles) and, usually, the first round of spices. The meat or seafood may be lightly browned in the oily spice mixture, but much of the time this preliminary browning is minimal (like a fricassée) or it is skipped entirely (like a blanquette). At this point, a European cook is likely to add stock, wine, or water, or perhaps a mixture of wine and herbs that had been used for marinating the meat, but the Indian cook may use one or more of an array of liquids. Tomatoes are well liked in India and often constitute the only liquid. In Southern India, coconut milk is often used, either in purely liquid form or as a pasty purée of whole coconut pulp (see "Coconut Milk," page 43). In Northern India, yogurt and dairy products, including whole milk and cream, are also popular.

Once the meat, seafood, or vegetables are simmering in spice-flavored liquid, the Indian cook may add one or more ingredients to thicken the curry. A traditional European cook would have likely floured the meat before browning it, or might whisk the finished braising liquid into a roux, as when making a blanquette. Indian cooks have a far more imaginative array of thickeners and techniques, many of which are only recently being incorporated into Western cooking. In some Indian curries, the cooked onions are puréed into a thickening paste before being combined with the simmering meat. Nuts, especially cashews, peanuts, and almonds, and seeds, such as sesame, poppy, mustard, or fenugreek, are ground into pastes and used as thickeners. Lentils, especially pink or yellow Indian lentils, are simmered, puréed, and added to curries. Coconut milk and coconut paste are often used as thickeners in Southern Indian cooking. Dairy products such as cream, milk, or yogurt, especially when drained in cheesecloth, are also effective thickeners.

It's appropriate to mention at this point that the criteria for an Indian curry differ somewhat from those for a Western stew. The fat contained in Western stews—for example, those containing cream—must never separate, but in Indian cooking the oil or fat used for the initial cooking of aromatic vegetables and the principal ingredient(s) may very likely separate out, especially during long cooking. When yogurt or other dairy products are used, this leaves a stew with the coagulated milk solids clinging to the solid ingredients (such as meat or seafood) and a rather oily sauce. This effect is often unappealing to Westerners, but quite acceptable in India. (In Western cooking, this could be remedied by spooning out and discarding the separated fat and adding liquid and an emulsifier such as heavy cream to at least partially re-emulsify the coagulated milk solids.)

As with a discerning European cook who understands how to wake up the flavor of a stew or brown sauce with a splash of good wine vinegar, or a white sauce with a squeeze of lemon, the use of acidic ingredients has long been recognized as an important element in Indian cooking. Some of the acidic ingredients used in Western cooking are also used in India. Underripe tomatoes, vinegar, lime or lemon juice, and yogurt (used also as a moistening liquid and thickener) often provide curries with the essential acidic bite. Other ingredients, unfamiliar to Western cooks, are also used in India. Tamarind pulp, sold as a paste (see page 44), is especially popular in Southern India and also used throughout Southeast Asia. In some regions of India, the pulp is combined with spices. The pulp from fresh mangoes is sometimes simmered in curries for its freshness and tang. Dried mango and dried mango powders are also used.

Indian cooks are keenly aware of color, and because many of the ingredients used in Indian curries sometimes give the stew an unpleasant off-gray or brown hue, some ingredients are used primarily for the bright colors they impart. Powdered turmeric, often included in commercial curry powders, will give a drab-looking curry an appealing yellow brightness; saffron is not only delicious but creates an exotic orange-colored sauce, even when used in very small quantities; a wide assortment of fresh herbs may be puréed with liquid ingredients, or just very finely chopped to add a green hue or green specks (cilantro is the most popular); and tomatoes contribute an appealing pink.

Finely chopped herbs are the most popular last-minute finishes for Western stews and sauces, but Indian cooks are more likely to use spices. The spices can be worked with water into pastes and added in the same way that spices are added earlier during the cooking, or they can be cooked into a flavorful *tadka* (also spelled *tarka*). A tadka is made by heating ghee in a skillet and stirring in spices—especially cumin seeds, mustard seeds, cloves, and asafetida—and aromatic vegetables such as chiles, garlic, and onions, and then quickly blending this mixture into vegetarian stews and lentil dishes.

Spice Mixtures

The subtlety and variety of Indian food reveals itself only when spices are carefully balanced to achieve a particular effect or to enhance a particular flavor. Spice mixtures, if used to the exclusion of other spices, or if used for every dish (the ubiquitous bottle of curry powder is the best example), will leave Indian dishes with a tiring sameness. On the other hand, it can be tedious to combine an array of spices for every dish. What is typical in India is to use a spice mixture—the particular blend will depend largely on the traditions of the cook's region—and then add one or more other spices or aromatic ingredients to give the dish distinction.

Indian cooks are fond of roasting spices. This is easy to do by stirring the raw whole spices in a dry hot skillet until they brown ever so slightly and smell fragrant, but it is also possible to cook the ground spices or finished spice mixtures, Western style, in a little butter or oil until they release their flavor. One disadvantage to this quick-and-easy method, however, is that some spices release their aroma and flavor more quickly than others. So-called sweet spices such as cinnamon and cloves release their aroma quickly and need no roasting, whereas "spicier" spices such as cumin or coriander are greatly enhanced by roasting. Consequently, sweeter and delicate spices can be left raw and spicier spices can be roasted and combined in the same spice mixture.

Although purists insist on roasting and combining their spices every day, roasted and ground spices and the derivative spice mixtures will keep with very little alteration in their flavor for several months, tightly wrapped, in the freezer.

TRADITIONAL GARAM MASALA
MOGHUL GARAM MASALA

G *aram masala* means "hot spice mixture," a somewhat misleading Western translation because Indian cooks talk about spices that either heat or cool the body—distinctions that have little to do with how hot they are in the mouth. Garam masala is the spice mixture most often used in Northern Indian cooking. None of the spices for the following garam masala need be roasted, because they are all intensely aromatic.

YIELD: ⅓ CUP (80 MILLILITERS)

cinnamon sticks, 2 inches (5 cm) long, coarsely chopped	4	4
black peppercorns	1 rounded tablespoon	20 milliliters
whole cloves	1 tablespoon	15 milliliters
black cardamom pods, husks removed	3	3
fennel seeds (optional)	1 rounded tablespoon	20 milliliters

Blend the spices in a blender at high speed for about 3 minutes. Work the mixture through a fine-mesh strainer. Zap what doesn't go through the strainer a second time in the blender and work it through the strainer. Reserve the garam masala, tightly sealed, in the freezer.

MODERN GARAM MASALA
PUNJABI GARAM MASALA

I n addition to the "sweet" and aromatic spices combined to make traditional garam masala, many contemporary versions of garam masala contain green cardamom instead of the traditional black cardamom, and also contain a large proportion of cumin and coriander—spices that give traditional garam masala a sharper and more "curry-like" flavor and aroma. It's possible to get by without roasting the spices (especially if the spice mixture is being cooked in fat before being combined with moist ingredients), but Punjabi garam masala will have more distinction if the coriander and cumin seeds are stirred in a hot skillet for a few minutes first, until they release their aroma.

YIELD: ¼ CUP (60 MILLILITERS)

(continued)

607

black or white cumin seeds	2 tablespoons	30 milliliters
coriander seeds	2 tablespoons	30 milliliters
cinnamon sticks, 2 inches (5 cm) long, coarsely chopped	4	4
black peppercorns	1 tablespoon	15 milliliters
whole cloves	1 tablespoon	15 milliliters
green cardamom pods, husks removed	1 tablespoon	15 milliliters

Stir the cumin seeds in a hot dry skillet until they smell aromatic and brown very slightly. Transfer the cumin seeds to a bowl and repeat with the coriander seeds. Let cool. Grind all the spices together in a coffee grinder or blender on high speed for about 3 minutes. Strain through a fine-mesh strainer, grind again, and strain out what doesn't go through. Punjabi garam masala may be frozen, tightly sealed, for several months.

BENGALI FIVE-SPICE MIXTURE
PANCH PHORAN

YIELD: ½ CUP (120 MILLILITERS)

fennel seeds	2 tablespoons	30 milliliters
brown mustard seeds	2 tablespoons	30 milliliters
fenugreek seeds	2 tablespoons	30 milliliters
cumin seeds	2 tablespoons	30 milliliters
nigella (black cumin) seeds	2 tablespoons	30 milliliters

Stir together all the ingredients and store in a tightly sealed container. Shake before using. Just before using, toast the spice mix in a dry sauté pan while continuously stirring until it smells fragrant. If appropriate for the recipe at hand, the mixture can also be heated in a small amount of oil in the same way as curry powder.

SAMBAAR POWDER

This is a spicy mixture based largely on the flavor of certain dried peas. Sambaar powder is especially popular in Southern India, where it is used to flavor an array of vegetarian dishes. It is often used in conjunction with cooked hulled mung beans (*moong dal*) and lentils, which are then puréed and used to thicken vegetarian stews. Three tablespoons (45 milliliters) of sambaar powder is usually enough to flavor about 1 quart (1 liter) liquid.

YIELD: ½ CUP (125 MILLILITERS)

coriander seeds	¼ cup	60 milliliters
brown mustard seeds	1 teaspoon	5 milliliters
moong dal (split and hulled yellow variety)	1 teaspoon	5 milliliters
channa dal (yellow split peas)	1 teaspoon	5 milliliters
urad dal (split and skinned gram beans)	1 teaspoon	5 milliliters
fenugreek seeds	1 teaspoon	5 milliliters
cumin seeds	2 teaspoons	10 milliliters
powdered asafetida	¼ teaspoon	1 milliliter
curry leaves	20	20
dried guajillo chiles, stems and seeds removed	6	6
black peppercorns	1 teaspoon	5 milliliters

1. Stir the coriander, mustard seeds, moong dal, channa dal, urad dal, fenugreek, and cumin in a hot dry skillet for about 3 minutes, until the spices smell aromatic. Stir in the asafetida, curry leaves, and chiles and stir for another 2 minutes.

2. Remove from the heat, let cool, and combine with the peppercorns. Grind in a coffee grinder or blender at high speed for about 3 minutes and work through a fine-mesh strainer. Store, tightly sealed, in the freezer.

CURRY MODEL

Although it's impossible in a short space to include a collection of authentic Indian dishes and to explain the traditions that give each one its character and dictate the spices, spice mixtures, and other ingredients that go into their preparation, it is possible to outline a basic system that is common to most Indian curries. The resulting dish may not be identical to any particular authentic and regional Indian dish, but the ingredients and techniques will be authentically Indian, and the cook who experiments with the basic ingredients will develop a sensitivity to the balance of spices in the same way a European-trained cook will have developed an almost instinctual sensitivity to herbs. The amounts of each of the following ingredients will vary enormously depending on which of the other ingredients are being included. Cooking times will also vary. Shellfish such as shrimp or scallops may only need a minute or two, strips of tender meats about 5 minutes, a quartered chicken about 40 minutes, and stewing meats about 2 hours. Slow-cooking meats should be gently stewed in stock or water following the techniques for any stew (that is, careful degreasing, and never allowing it to boil; see "Methods and Ingredients for Braises and Stews," page 259) and the braising liquid then converted into a curry.

YIELD: 6 TO 8 SERVINGS

MAIN INGREDIENT

2¼ to 4 pounds/1 to 2 kilograms (6 to 8 ounces/175 to 225 grams per serving) of one of the following:

chicken, quartered or sectioned into small pieces

lamb cubes or strips from the leg or shoulder

stewing beef (chuck, shank, or other stewing cut), cut into cubes or thick strips

tender beef (sirloin, strip, rib), cut into cubes or strips

shrimp and other shellfish (left whole)

firm-fleshed fish fillets, cut into cubes or strips

vegetables, cut into chunks, florets, or strips

COOKING FAT

About 2 tablespoons/30 milliliters:

ghee

mustard oil

sesame oil

coconut oil

vegetable oil

FRESH AROMATIC INGREDIENTS

onions, thinly sliced, chopped, or puréed	2 large	2 large
finely chopped garlic	1 teaspoon to 3 tablespoons	5 to 45 milliliters
finely chopped fresh green chiles such as serrano	1 teaspoon to 3 tablespoons	5 to 45 milliliters
grated peeled fresh ginger	1 teaspoon to 1 tablespoon	5 to 15 milliliters

SPICE MIXTURE

1 teaspoon to 2 tablespoons/5 to 30 milliliters or more to taste:

traditional garam masala (page 607)

modern garam masala (page 607)

bengali five-spice mixture (page 608)

sambaar powder (page 609)

basic curry powder (page 614)

INDIVIDUAL SPICES AND HERBS

any of the spices contained in spice mixtures above	¼ teaspoon to 2 tablespoons	2 to 30 milliliters
curry leaves	10 to 30	10 to 30
fresh or dried fenugreek leaves, soaked in water with a pinch of salt for 30 minutes to remove the slightly bitter taste	½ cup	125 milliliters
saffron	1 pinch	1 pinch
ground turmeric (for color)	1 teaspoon to 1 tablespoon	5 to 15 milliliters
cinnamon leaves, gently fried for 10 minutes	1 or 2	1 or 2
bay leaf	1 or 2	1 or 2
ground mace	⅛ to ½ teaspoon	1 to 3 milliliters
grated nutmeg	⅛ to ½ teaspoon	1 to 3 milliliters
star anise pods, crushed	1 or 2	1 or 2

(continued)

LIQUIDS AND MOIST INGREDIENTS
1 to 3 cups/250 to 750 milliliters:

stock

tomatoes, peeled, seeded, and chopped

coconut milk

yogurt

milk

NUTS
optional

slivered almonds

cashews

pistachios

THICKENER
1 to 3 tablespoons/15 to 45 milliliters:

nut butter (peanut, almond, cashew)

ground seed paste such as sesame, poppy, mustard, or fenugreek

cooked and puréed onions

dried legumes, cooked separately and puréed, especially pink or
yellow indian lentils, hulled mung beans (moong dal), yellow split peas
(channa dal), or split gram beans (urad dal)

coconut paste (ground coconut pulp)

ACIDIC INGREDIENT
2 teaspoons to 2 tablespoons/10 to 30 milliliters:

vinegar

lime juice

underripe tomatoes

tamarind extract (see note, page 589)

green mangoes (fresh, dried, or powdered)

AROMATIC FINISHES (TADKA)
optional

cumin seeds	1 to 2 teaspoons	5 to 10 milliliters
brown mustard seeds	½ to 2 teaspoons	3 to 10 milliliters
cloves	¼ to ½ teaspoon	2 to 3 milliliters
asafetida	⅛ to ¼ teaspoon	1 to 2 milliliters

aromatic vegetables such as chiles, garlic, and onions

FINAL HERBS
optional

1 to 3 tablespoons/15 to 45 milliliters whole or chopped leaves:
cilantro, mint, basil

FINAL ADDITION OF SPICES

salt

any of the foregoing spices or spice mixtures worked to a smooth paste with water
(if the spices in the mixtures have not been roasted, the spice mixtures should be
gently cooked in oil or butter until they release their perfume)

1. (Optional) Brown the meat or seafood in one of the cooking fats and reserve.

2. Cook one or more of the fresh aromatic ingredients in fresh cooking oil or in the fat left in the pan. The ingredients can be gently sweated or quickly sautéed.

3. Stir the spice mixture and the additional spices and herbs into the hot vegetables and cook gently until the spices release their aroma. If the base is being used for a long-cooking stew, the spices are better added at the end.

4. Return the meat to the pan (seafood should be added later because it cooks so quickly) and add one or more of the liquids. Simmer gently until the meat has finished cooking. (Thickeners can be added at the same time as the meat or added when the meat is done.)

5. Add nuts, if using, one of the thickeners, and an acidic ingredient.

6. (Optional) Cook one or more of the tadka ingredients in hot ghee until they release their aroma. Stir the hot tadka into the finished curry.

7. (Optional) Add chopped herb or whole leaves.

8. Season to taste with salt and, if necessary, final additional spices.

BASIC CURRY POWDER

This homemade curry powder is far better than any commercial bottled version. Because the spices are roasted, this curry powder can be stirred into liquids to taste without first being cooked. Two teaspoons to 1 tablespoon (10 to 15 milliliters) is usually appropriate for 1 cup (250 milliliters) liquid.

YIELD: ⅓ CUP (80 MILLILITERS)

coriander seeds	¼ cup	60 milliliters
cumin seeds	2 teaspoons	10 milliliters
brown mustard seeds	2 teaspoons	10 milliliters
fenugreek seeds	2 teaspoons	10 milliliters
green cardamom pods (husks removed)	10	10
cloves	12	12
cinnamon sticks, 2 inches (5 cm) long, coarsely chopped	2	2
black peppercorns	2 teaspoons	10 milliliters
ground turmeric	1 tablespoon	15 milliliters

Stir the coriander, cumin, mustard seeds, fenugreek, and cardamom in a hot dry skillet until the spices smell aromatic, about 5 minutes. Let cool. Combine with the cloves, cinnamon, peppercorns, and turmeric in a coffee grinder or blender and blend at high speed for about 3 minutes. Strain through a fine-mesh strainer. Blend again and strain what doesn't go through the strainer the first time. Store, tightly sealed, in the freezer.

LAMB CURRY WITH GARAM MASALA AND MIXED VEGETABLES

This stew is an example of one of the many possibilities that can be derived from the foregoing curry model. One of the advantages to this dish is that it's self-contained, so there's no need to prepare an accompanying starch (potatoes are simmered in the curry) or green vegetables, which are also cooked directly in the curry. The effect of including vegetables right in the curry is also an impressive sight.

YIELD: 6 SERVINGS

lamb shoulder, boneless (from 3 pounds/ 1½ kilograms thick bone-in shoulder chops)	2 pounds	1 kilogram
salt	to taste	to taste
ghee or vegetable oil	2 tablespoons	30 milliliters
onion, thinly sliced	1 medium	1 medium
garlic cloves, chopped	2	2
serrano chiles, stemmed, seeded, finely chopped or jalapeños, stemmed, seeded, finely chopped	1 to 3 or 2 to 6	1 to 3 or 2 to 6
finely chopped fresh ginger	1 tablespoon	15 milliliters
water	1 cup	250 milliliters
fingerling potatoes, about 1 ounce/ 25 grams each	1 pound	450 grams
coconut milk or fresh coconut milk (see page 43)	1 (14-ounce) can or 2 cups	425 milliliters or 500 milliliters
cremini or domestic mushrooms, quartered	½ pound	225 grams
garam masala (page 607)	1½ tablespoons	25 milliliters
cashew or other nut butter	3 tablespoons	45 milliliters
snap peas or snow peas, ends broken off	½ pound	225 grams
spinach leaves, blanched, drained, refreshed	1 bunch	1 bunch
coarsely chopped cilantro leaves	3 tablespoons	45 milliliters

1. Cut the lamb into 1-inch (2.5 cm) cubes. Sprinkle with salt and brown in the ghee on all sides in a heavy-bottomed sauté pan, uncovered and over high heat. Remove the meat from the pan and reserve.

2. Pour all but 2 tablespoons (30 milliliters) of the fat out of the pan and stir in the onion, garlic, chiles, and ginger. Cook over medium heat, stirring, for about 15 minutes, until the onions lightly caramelize.

3. Add the water and potatoes to the onion mixture. Cover the pan and simmer gently over low to medium heat until the potatoes are barely done, about 20 minutes. Add the coconut milk and mushrooms and simmer for 5 minutes more.

4. Work together the garam masala, cashew butter, and 3 tablespoons (45 milliliters) of the liquid from the pan into a smooth paste in a small bowl. Whisk this mixture into the rest of the liquid in the pan.

5. Stir in the snap peas and the reserved lamb and simmer for 2 minutes. Stir in the spinach and cilantro and simmer for 1 minute more. Season with salt.

DESSERT SAUCES

Many desserts can be enhanced with an appropriate sauce, to provide contrast, extra sweetness or acidity, moistness, and extra color. Fruit tarts, especially if they do not contain too much sugar, are best served with a sweet sauce such as a crème anglaise or a sabayon that will round out the acidic flavor of the fruit. Very sweet desserts, such as cakes or pastries containing chocolate or elaborate creams, are best served with a relatively acidic sauce, such as an unsweetened fruit coulis. Dessert sauces can be served at the table in a sauceboat or directly on the plate.

CRÈME ANGLAISE

Crème anglaise is one of the most delicious and versatile of the dessert sauces. Although traditionally flavored with vanilla, it is adaptable for a variety of flavor combinations. It is excellent when served with fruit tarts and pastries that are not too sweet. It is also the base for French-style ice cream.

Traditional crème anglaise is made with a vanilla bean, sugar, milk, and egg yolks. The amounts of each can be changed to taste. The recipe that follows contains less sugar and more vanilla than older recipes, which tend to be sweeter and less extravagant with the vanilla. Acceptable crème anglaise can be made with vanilla extract, but it will never have the depth of flavor that the cream has when infused with vanilla beans. The recipe that follows uses 12 egg yolks per quart (liter) of milk, which produces a fairly rich cream. Acceptable crème anglaise can be made with as few as 8 yolks per quart (liter). Richer versions also exist, using as many as 16 yolks per quart (liter) and replacing half of the milk with heavy cream.

CRÈME ANGLAISE

YIELD: 6 CUPS (1.5 LITERS)

vanilla beans	2	2
milk	1 quart	1 liter
sugar	¾ cup plus 2 tablespoons	175 grams
egg yolks	12	12

1. Cut the vanilla beans in half lengthwise and add them to the milk in a 2-quart (2 liter) saucepan. Bring the milk to a simmer.

2. While the milk is heating, whisk together the sugar and egg yolks in a heatproof bowl until the sugar dissolves and the yolks are pale yellow.

3. As the milk approaches a simmer, remove the vanilla beans and scrape the inside of each half with a paring knife to release the tiny seeds. Return the seeds to the milk.

4. When the milk simmers, pour half of it over the egg yolk–sugar mixture, gently whisking.

5. Add the egg yolk–sugar-milk mixture to the saucepan and stir it over medium heat with a wooden spatula or spoon. Stir constantly, being careful to reach around and into the corners, where the cream is most liable to coagulate and separate into coarse aggregates.

6. *Do not let the cream boil.* Check the consistency of the cream by holding up the spatula sideways and making a streak along the back with your finger. When the streak remains without the cream running down and obscuring it, the cream is ready.

7. Immediately remove the cream from the heat. Continue stirring for 1 to 2 minutes, so the heat retained in the bottom of the saucepan won't cause the crème anglaise to curdle.

8. Strain the cream through a strainer. Do not use a chinois or the specks of vanilla will be strained out.

9. Set the cream over a bowl of ice to cool it quickly, stirring to prevent a skin from forming.

VARIATION

This is the classic and traditional way of making a crème anglaise. Another method is to cook it sous vide, which allows you to poach the milk-yolk-sugar-vanilla mixture in a well-sealed plastic bag at a precise temperature. One advantage to this technique is that you can then keep the sauce in the immersion bath until needed.

Whisk together the yolks, milk, split vanilla bean, and sugar and vacuum-seal in a heavy plastic bag. Cook the mixture sous vide at a temperature of 156°F (70°C) for 40 minutes. At this point, you can use the crème anglaise right away, you can keep it in the sous vide tank for up to a couple of hours until you need it, or you can transfer it to a bain-marie (water bath) to keep it warm. If you're serving it cold, or not using it right away, transfer the crème anglaise to a mixing bowl and let cool, stirring every minute or two to keep a skin from forming on the surface.

Coconut Crème Anglaise

Crème anglaise made with coconut milk is said to be healthier than the milk version. When using coconut milk to replace all or part of the milk, it is usually stabilized with hydrocolloids such as 2% liquid lecithin (worked into the egg yolks) and 0.5% propylene glycol alginate (blended into the coconut milk). Or blend in equal parts sucrose esters (1%) into both the egg yolks and the coconut milk. Proceed as though using milk.

EGGLESS CRÈME ANGLAISE

Some less-scrupulous chefs used to add cornstarch to their crème anglaise to give it extra body without having to use more egg yolks. The cornstarch stabilized the crème anglaise but also sometimes imparted a starchy taste or off mouthfeel.

By using xanthan gum instead, it's possible to make a crème anglaise with all the creaminess of the original without either egg yolks or cornstarch.

YIELD: 1 QUART (1 LITER)

milk	1 quart	1 liter
sugar	7 ounces	200 grams
xanthan gum		2 grams
vanilla beans	2	2

(continued)

Use an immersion blender to blend together the milk, sugar, and xanthan gum. Split the vanilla beans in half lengthwise and add them to the milk mixture. Bring to a simmer to infuse the beans for about 5 minutes. Whisk continuously until the mixture thickens, as soon as it approaches a simmer. Strain through a chinois. Stir while cooling (if you are cooling) to prevent a skin forming on the surface.

Crème Anglaise Variations

Crème anglaise is the most versatile of all the dessert sauces because it is a perfect medium for other flavors. Traditionally thickened with only egg yolks, crème anglaise lends itself to modernist thickeners as well. Flavors should be added to taste, but a few parameters are listed below. The vanilla contained in the crème anglaise will usually enhance whatever additional flavor is used, but if pure flavor is wanted, the vanilla can be omitted.

SPIRITS

Make sure the crème anglaise is cool before adding spirits; otherwise their flavor, most of which is volatile, will evaporate.

- Whiskeys (such as bourbon or Irish whiskey; Scotch isn't recommended because of its smoky flavor): Add ½ cup (125 milliliters) per quart (liter) of crème anglaise or to taste.

- Grape brandies (such as Cognac or Armagnac): Add ½ cup (125 milliliters) per quart (liter) of crème anglaise.

- Fruit brandies (such as framboise, mirabelle, Kirsch, Poire William, or Calvados, not fruit-flavored brandies): Add 6 tablespoons (90 milliliters) per quart (liter) of crème anglaise.

- Liqueurs (such as Cointreau, Grand Marnier, Chartreuse, amaretto, or anisette): Add ½ cup (125 milliliters) per quart (liter) of crème anglaise; decrease the sugar contained in the crème anglaise basic recipe by ⅓ cup (60 grams).

- Rum (white or dark pot-distilled rums; Martinique rum is the best): Add ½ cup (125 milliliters) per quart (liter) of crème anglaise.

FRUITS

Crème anglaise can be flavored with fruit in several ways. The first and most obvious is to add fruit purée, but good-quality fruit brandy can also be used (see preceding list). The flavor of citrus fruits is best imparted by replacing the vanilla bean with the grated zest of the appropriate fruit.

- Berries (such as raspberries, strawberries, or blueberries): Add ¾ cup (185 milliliters) strained purée (coulis) per quart (liter) of crème anglaise.

- Citrus fruits (such as oranges, tangerines, lemons, or limes): Replace the vanilla beans in the basic recipe with the grated zests of 2 oranges, 3 tangerines, or 4 lemons or limes. Strain the cream through a chinois.

CHOCOLATE

Chocolate can be added to a crème anglaise in two ways. The first is to stir cocoa powder into the egg yolks along with the sugar. The second is to add chunks of chocolate to the finished cream while it is still hot and stir the mixture until they melt. Remember to use the best-quality chocolate (see page 71).

- Using cocoa powder: Combine ½ cup (125 milliliters) of the milk called for in the recipe with the egg yolks and sugar. Add ½ cup (125 grams) cocoa powder to the mixture and stir with a whisk until smooth. Continue as for a regular crème anglaise.

- Using bar chocolate: Break up 8 ounces (250 grams) bittersweet chocolate into small chunks. Add these to the crème anglaise as soon as it thickens. Stir off the heat with a whisk until the chocolate is completely and evenly dissolved in the cream. Strain through a chinois. If bittersweet chocolate is not available, sweet or baking chocolate can be used, but remember to adjust the amount of sugar contained in the crème anglaise accordingly.

COFFEE

Crème anglaise can be flavored with coffee in several ways: Strong espresso can be added to the crème anglaise at the end; ground coffee beans can be infused in the milk along with or instead of the vanilla (this method provides the best flavor); or coffee extract or dissolved instant coffee can be added to the cream at the end.

- Using brewed espresso: Add ½ cup (125 milliliters) strong espresso per quart (liter) of crème anglaise.

- Using coffee beans: Finely grind 3 ounces (75 grams) dark-roasted coffee beans. Stir the ground coffee into the cold milk before heating. Once the crème anglaise has thickened, strain out the coffee through a chinois.

- Using coffee extract or instant espresso coffee: Dissolve 2 heaping tablespoons (40 milliliters) instant espresso granules in 3 tablespoons (45 milliliters) water. Stir slowly into the finished crème anglaise, to taste.

HERBS

Herb-flavored crème anglaise is wonderful served with fruits and delicately flavored pastries. Mint, spearmint, lavender, verbena, thyme, and lemon thyme can all be used to replace the vanilla in a traditional crème anglaise. Simply tie up the herbs like a bouquet garni, or in cheesecloth if they are loose, and simmer with the milk.

CARAMEL

Crème anglaise can be prepared with caramel syrup instead of sugar. Prepare a caramel, using 25 percent more sugar than called for in the crème anglaise (see "Caramel Sauces," page 626). Prepare a caramel syrup by dissolving the still-hot caramel in a small amount of water and then combining the resulting syrup with the hot milk for the crème anglaise.

NUTS

The two most common nut flavorings for crème anglaise are hazelnut and almond. Bitter almonds are unavailable in the United States because of the cyanide they contain. For this reason, most chefs use almond extract, almond paste, marzipan, or praline to impart the full flavor of almonds. If you're using almond paste or marzipan, cut the sugar used in the crème anglaise by half the amount of almond paste or marzipan that you are using.

The flavor of hazelnuts is best imparted using hazelnut praline, which is available from suppliers of imported foods. If imported hazelnut praline is unavailable, it can be prepared by cooking coarsely chopped hazelnuts in plain caramel for a minute or two, pouring the hot mixture onto an oiled marble, letting it cool and solidify, and pounding it with a rolling pin to prepare nougatine. The nougatine is then coarsely chopped with a knife and ground to a powder in a food processor. The result is never as smooth and unctuous as commercially available praline, but it will impart flavor. When used in a sauce, it should be strained out after it has infused its flavor into the liquid.

SPICES

Cinnamon and cloves are often found in sweet desserts, but it is surprising how rarely other spices are used. Ginger is magnificent (infuse fresh ginger in hot milk; combine powdered ginger with the egg yolks), as is a mixture of saffron and cardamom, a flavor combination used in India for ice cream. The best way to experiment with flavoring with spices is to make small amounts of individual infusions, using ½ cup (125 milliliters) milk and 1 teaspoon (5 milliliters) ground spice for each and then combining the infusions to devise interesting flavor combinations.

TRUFFLES

The flavor of black truffles has an amazing affinity for sweet, creamy desserts, including crème anglaise. Infuse ¾ ounce (20 grams) grated or finely julienned fresh truffles (first sliced on a Japanese-style mandoline, then julienned with a knife) in a hot mixture of 1 cup (250 milliliters) milk and 1 cup (250 milliliters) heavy cream. Convert the infusion into a crème anglaise by cooking with 6 egg yolks in the usual way. Do not strain. Serve with poached or caramelized fruits. This crème anglaise can also be turned into ice cream. When making ice cream, replace the cream called for in the recipe with milk or the ice cream may end up with small particles of congealed fat.

ALTERNATIVE SWEETENERS

Crème anglaise can be made with honey or maple syrup (great when flavored with bourbon) instead of sugar. When substituting either of these, use 1¼ cups (300 milliliters) to replace 1 cup (200 grams) granulated sugar.

SABAYONS

Sabayons are among the few sauces in which the character of the wine used in preparation is not lost. They are delicious even when prepared with ordinary white wine, but when distinctively flavored wines are used, they are magnificent. Because of the acidity contained in wine (even sweet wines), a well-made sabayon will always have a nervous, vinous edge that makes it the perfect accompaniment to fruits and fruit pastries. If not made too sweet, it is also a good foil for a glass of dessert wine.

Even though the recipe that follows contains less sugar than classic versions, the amount of sugar should be decreased even more when sweet wines are used in its preparation. When Marsala is used, the sabayon becomes a traditional Italian zabaglione. Although traditional sabayons are prepared with wine as the only flavoring, some chefs like to flavor the sabayon with fruit brandies or liqueurs after it has cooled. Although the techniques are the same, sabayons—which always contain sugar—should not be confused with savory sabayons or the preliminary stage in the preparation of emulsified egg sauces.

SABAYON

YIELD: 6 CUPS (1.5 LITERS)

egg yolks	12	12
sugar	1½ cups	300 grams
white wine	2½ cups	625 milliliters

1. Whisk together the egg yolks and sugar in a saucepan with sloping sides or a stainless-steel bowl.

2. Pour in the wine and whisk the mixture continuously over medium heat. The sabayon will expand and become fluffy. As soon as it begins to lose volume, or if the bottom of the pan becomes visible while whisking, remove it from the heat. Whisk for 15 seconds more to prevent it from curdling. At this point, the sabayon can be used as is—served hot or cold—or you can flavor it with other ingredients as described below. If you're serving it cold, keep it covered with plastic wrap touching its surface to prevent a skin from forming.

VARIATIONS

Although almost any wine can be used to make a suitable sabayon; white wines with good acidity and a distinctive character will give subtlety and nuance to the sauce. Many recipes suggest making sabayon sauce with Champagne, which is delicious. It is best to use a mature (even slightly madeirized) French Champagne, but since this is rarely practical, a good-quality Coteaux Champenois (see page 68) will produce excellent results. Do not substitute a sparkling wine other than Champagne. If Champagne is unavailable or too expensive, it is better to substitute a good-quality still wine.

Chablis, Vouvray (demi-sec), Riesling (German or Alsatian), Gewürztraminer, and Muscadet will all make interesting sabayon sauces. Sweet wines can also be used: Sauternes, late-harvest Rieslings (including German Beerenauslese and Trockenbeerenauslese), Muscat de Beaumes de Venise, and madeirized wines (Madeira, Marsala, and sherry) will all impart their own character and distinction to the sauce. If you use sweet wine, cut the sugar by about half the weight of the wine.

Sabayon can also be flavored with fruit brandies, such as Calvados, Poire William, or Kirsch, after it has cooled; fruit purées and coulis (equal parts coulis and sabayon); and spices, first infused in a small amount of water or cream and strained into the sabayon. It can also be lightened by folding it with an equal volume of whipped cream.

CHOCOLATE SAUCES

Most chocolate sauces are made by combining melted chocolate with varying proportions of heavy cream, butter, egg yolks, or other liquids. The amount of each of these ingredients depends on the desired consistency of the sauce and whether the sauce is being served hot or cold.

Bittersweet (sometimes called semisweet) chocolate is the type of chocolate most often called for in chocolate sauce recipes, but other chocolates can be substituted and the recipe modified if bittersweet is unavailable. Always use the best-quality chocolate.

When melting chocolate, make sure that all the utensils are perfectly dry. Even a drop or two of liquid will cause chocolate to pull together into a lumpy mass. Once this occurs, extra liquid has to be added to the chocolate (at least 1 tablespoon/15 milliliters liquid per ounce/30 grams chocolate) to thin it out. In most sauce recipes this is not a problem because sufficient liquid is usually added anyway. Chocolate is also sensitive to heat and will scald at relatively low temperatures. For this reason, it is best to heat chocolate in a double boiler when it is being melted alone. Chocolate can also be easily melted in a microwave oven. Place the chocolate in a microwave-safe dish and heat on the high setting. Allow 1 minute for the first ounce (30 grams) of chocolate, an additional 10 seconds for each additional ounce (30 grams). Heat until almost melted, stirring once, and then stir until smooth.

In addition to the following recipes, chocolate-flavored Crème Anglaise (page 621) can also be used as a chocolate sauce, especially when a less rich sauce is needed for fruits or fruit pastries, or if the sauce is to be served cold.

GANACHE

This is the simplest and one of the best chocolate sauces. It can be made with different proportions of chocolate and liquid; equal parts heavy cream and bittersweet chocolate are most common for frosting cakes or for a chocolate filling for candies, for which the ganache needs to be stiff. For chocolate sauce, a higher proportion of cream can be used.

YIELD: 1 QUART (1 LITER)

bittersweet chocolate (see notes)	1 pound	450 grams
heavy cream or crème fraîche	2 cups	500 milliliters

1. Chop the chocolate into medium-size chunks.

2. Bring the cream to a simmer in a 2-quart (2 liter) saucepan.

3. As soon as the cream comes to a simmer, remove from the heat and add the chocolate.

4. Let the chocolate sit in the liquid for 5 minutes, then stir the mixture with a rubber spatula or wooden spoon until it is perfectly smooth.

5. Serve or use immediately. Ganache tends to break when chilled and reheated.

Notes: When using bitter (unsweetened) chocolate, substitute 10 ounces (300 grams) bitter chocolate and ¾ cup plus 2 tablespoons (200 grams) sugar for the bittersweet chocolate. Dissolve the sugar in the cream while it is heating. Make sure the sugar is completely dissolved before adding the chocolate.

Flavoring Ganache

Ganache can be flavored at the end with liquid such as spirits or extracts, added to taste. Ganache can also be flavored by infusing flavorings such as vanilla beans, orange zests, mint leaves, or ground coffee into the cream-milk mixture, then straining them out before the chocolate is added.

CHOCOLATE BUTTER SAUCE
HOT FUDGE SAUCE

Chocolate Butter Sauce has a richer texture and more luxurious sheen than ganache. The liquid in this recipe can be anything with which the sauce might be flavored, such as strong coffee, brandy, whiskey, or liqueur; water can also be used for a plain chocolate flavor. Chocolate butter sauce, when cold, is stiffer than regular ganache, hence its appeal to those who like ice cream with hot fudge sauce.

YIELD: 1 QUART (1 LITER)

bittersweet chocolate (see note)	1 pound	500 grams
heavy cream	1½ cups	375 milliliters
butter	12 tablespoons	175 grams

1. Chop the chocolate into chunks with a large heavy knife. Bring the cream to a simmer, remove from the heat, and add the chocolate. Let sit for 5 to 10 minutes, until the chocolate has melted, then stir the mixture with a rubber spatula or wooden spoon until it is perfectly smooth.

2. When the mixture is perfectly smooth, use a small whisk to stir in the butter, one-fourth at a time. While the sauce can be kept warm for an hour or so, it is best served right away.

Note: If using bitter (unsweetened) chocolate, use 10 ounces (300 grams) chocolate and dissolve ¾ cup plus 2 tablespoons (200 grams) granulated sugar in the cream.

White Chocolate

White chocolate can be substituted in either of the preceding recipes. It is even more sensitive to heat than dark chocolate because of the milk solids it contains. White chocolate that has been overheated will coagulate irreversibly. When preparing ganache with white chocolate, grate the white chocolate or chop it very finely. Let the cream cool to 120°F (50°C) before stirring in the chocolate.

If preparing white chocolate butter sauce, carefully monitor the temperature of the liquids and melting chocolate. Do not let the temperature exceed 120°F (50°C).

White chocolate is extremely sweet, lacking the bitter flavors that balance the sweetness of dark chocolates. White chocolate sauces are best flavored with fruit brandies (eaux-de-vie) such as Kirsch, framboise, or mirabelle. Only add spirits after the sauce has chilled.

CARAMEL SAUCES

The easiest way to prepare caramel is to simply stir granulated sugar in a heavy-bottomed saucepan over medium heat. When the sugar melts and turns deep brown, add water, cream, or fruit juice to dissolve the caramel into a sauce.

Many recipes for caramel suggest that the sugar first be dissolved in water and that any crystals that form on the inside of the saucepan be continuously brushed off with a pastry brush to prevent the sugar from recrystallizing. Both of these steps can be eliminated by simply melting the sugar without liquid. The most important precautions to follow when preparing caramel in this way are to stir the mixture continuously, and not use too high a heat; otherwise the sugar will burn rather than caramelize evenly.

Because liquid caramel is burning hot (320°F/160°C), it must be combined with other liquids when it is used to flavor a sauce. Some recipes add heavy cream to the hot caramel, which dissolves the caramel and simultaneously reduces the cream. Other recipes add water, fruit juice, or fruit purée to the caramel to dissolve it and serve it as is, or then finish it with cream, butter, or both. Caramel sauces are often flavored with vanilla, but bourbon or malt whiskey can be used with excellent results.

CARAMEL CREAM SAUCE

YIELD: 2 CUPS (500 MILLILITERS)

granulated sugar	1 pound	500 grams
heavy cream	2 cups	500 milliliters
vanilla extract or other flavoring (optional)	2 teaspoons	10 milliliters

1. Melt the sugar in a 4-quart (4 liter) heavy-bottomed saucepan or copper poêlon. (A large saucepan or poêlon is necessary because the cream boils up when added to the caramel.) **(A)** Stir the sugar constantly over medium heat with a wooden spoon until any lumps have melted. **(B)** Continue stirring until the caramel is a deep reddish brown. **(C)**

2. Standing back from the saucepan, add half the cream. The cream will boil vigorously and dissolve the hot caramel. When the boiling slows down, add the rest of the cream. **(D)**

3. Whisk the sauce until the caramel is thoroughly dissolved in the cream. Check the consistency of the sauce and reduce it slightly if necessary. Add the vanilla extract or other flavoring if desired. Let the sauce cool. It can be stored for weeks in the refrigerator.

Caramel Butter Sauce

Caramel butter sauce is prepared in the same way as caramel cream sauce except that the heavy cream is replaced with 2 cups (500 milliliters) water, fruit juice, coffee, or other flavored liquid, and the mixture is reduced to a syrup. It is then finished with 4 ounces (125 grams) butter plus the vanilla extract. Interesting flavor combinations can be invented by infusing the water with spices such as cloves and star anise. The butter can also be omitted and the sauce served simply as a caramel syrup.

BUTTERSCOTCH SAUCE

Butterscotch is similar to caramel sauce except that butter is cooked along with the sugar, so that the milk solids caramelize and impart the characteristic flavor of noisette butter (see "Beurre Noisette," page 438) to the sauce. Some recipes use brown sugar to give the sauce a deeper color and flavor, but brown sugar tends to obscure the flavor of the butter, which is what makes butterscotch sauce so delicious.

This recipe uses a caramel base that is cooked a second time with butter. Cream is added near the end to emulsify the butter.

YIELD: 1 QUART (1 LITER)

granulated sugar	1 pound	450 grams
water	2 cups	500 milliliters
butter	8 tablespoons	125 grams
heavy cream	2 cups	500 milliliters
vanilla extract	2 teaspoons	10 milliliters

1. Prepare a caramel by melting the sugar in a 4-quart (4 liter) heavy-bottomed saucepan (large enough to prevent boiling over). Stir constantly as the sugar melts so that the caramel cooks evenly and doesn't burn. When the caramel is a deep reddish brown, stand back and pour in half the water.

2. When the water has stopped boiling, add the rest of the water and the butter. Cook the mixture to the soft-ball stage (234° to 240°F/112° to 116°C; see Note). If at any point it smells like the butter may be burning, remove from the heat.

3. Add the cream and vanilla. Continue to simmer the sauce until it attains the desired thickness. Let cool; the sauce can be stored in the refrigerator for several weeks.

Note: To judge when sugar syrup has reached the soft-ball stage without using a thermometer, dip the back of a spoon into the syrup and then quickly into a glass of cold (but not iced) water. Pinch the end of the spoon between two fingers. The syrup should form a gum-like mass on the end of the spoon.

PEAR-BUTTERSCOTCH SAUCE

This sauce is the natural outcome of caramelizing pears with sugar and butter. Pear-Butterscotch Sauce could be described as an integral dessert sauce. Pears prepared in this way are much more exciting than poached pears.

YIELD: 12 SERVINGS

pears	6	6
lemon	½	½
granulated sugar	1 cup plus 2 tablespoons	225 grams
butter, cut into large chunks	5 ounces	150 grams
heavy cream	1 cup	250 milliliters
poire william (optional)	to taste (about 3 tablespoons)	to taste (about 50 milliliters)
raspberry coulis (page 631; optional)	as needed	as needed
whipped cream (optional)	as needed	as needed

1. Preheat the oven to 375°F (190°C). Peel the pears, cut them in half lengthwise, and remove the cores with a paring knife. Rub them with the lemon.

2. Spread the pear halves, round side down, in a single layer in a heavy-bottomed pot. Do not leave any section of the pot bottom uncovered, or the sauce will burn.

3. Sprinkle the pears with the sugar and butter.

4. Bake the pears until they soften and begin to brown slightly. This can take anywhere from 15 minutes to 1 hour, depending on the ripeness of the pears. Remove them from the pot with a slotted spoon.

5. When the pears are cooked, the butter should be clear and the sugar should be lightly caramelized on the bottom of the pot. If not, cook the mixture on top of the stove until the liquids on the bottom are well browned.

6. Pour in the cream while the pot is still hot. Whisk the mixture while scraping the bottom of the pot to dissolve the caramelized sugar.

7. Strain the sauce and let it cool slightly. Flavor it with Poire William, if desired.

8. Serve the sauce over the hot pears. Raspberry coulis and whipped cream may be served alongside if desired.

629

FRUIT COULIS AND SAUCES

Fruits can be used to prepare the simplest and most satisfying of dessert sauces. Although they can be sweetened to taste, their natural acidity makes them an excellent accompaniment to sweet desserts. The most straightforward fruit sauces are simple fruit purées. For a slightly more sophisticated version called a *coulis*, the purée is strained to eliminate seeds or fragments of peel.

Purées and coulis are prepared in different ways, depending on the type of fruit. Some fruits, such as raspberries or strawberries, can be simply forced through a strainer with a ladle or wooden spoon. Other fruits, such as ripe pears and melons, will be easier to strain if they are first puréed in a food processor or blender. Some firm fruits, such as underripe pears or apples, must be stewed cooked before they are puréed or strained.

Depending on their consistency and hardness, fruit purées and coulis can be strained in various ways. If the mixture is stiff and difficult to work, use a drum sieve. If, on the other hand, the mixture remains liquid but still contains plenty of softened solids, use a food mill. If the mixture is thin and easy to work, work it directly through a chinois. All fruit mixtures must be strained through a chinois as the final step. The other methods pre-strain the coulis and make it less likely to damage the chinois.

The flavor of fruit purées and coulis can be adjusted depending on the foods they are accompanying. When served with sweet desserts such as ice creams, an unsweetened fruit purée provides a welcome contrast. For less sweet desserts, such as brioche or certain fruit tarts, a sweetened fruit coulis may provide the appropriate sauce. Some chefs may decide to go even further and finish a fruit coulis with cream or butter, to produce a richer and fuller-textured sauce. When making sweet coulis, sugar not only adds the requisite sweetness, but also pulls out the perfume in the fruit, making it more aromatic. You'll get an even more dramatic result if you use fructose instead of sucrose, because fructose is sweeter than sucrose. When sweetening fruit coulis and purées, always prepare a sugar syrup with granulated sugar rather than adding the sugar directly to the purée, where it will take longer to dissolve. The sugar syrup should be added to the coulis to taste; the amount will vary depending on the ripeness and natural acidity of the fruit. Most fruit coulis are improved by adding a small amount of lemon juice (oddly, this is true even for coulis that are initially acidic).

When good-quality ripe fruit is used to prepare purées and coulis, little needs to be done to improve their flavor. On the other hand, a purée or coulis made from underripe or out-of-season fruit can sometimes be improved by adding a small amount of appropriate flavored fruit brandy, such as Kirsch, framboise, or mirabelle. These flavorings should be added only once the fruit purées and coulis are cool, because heat quickly causes the volatile fruit flavors of these brandies to evaporate.

At times you may want to concentrate your fruit coulis or purée to bring out its natural sweetness, flavor, and delicacy. The obvious way to do this would be to reduce the mixture by boiling, in the same way you would for stock to make glace de viande. The problem is that this requires heat, and heat denatures the flavor of fruit and gives it a distinct cooked and "jammy" flavor. One solution, used in modernist cuisine, is to apply vacuum so you can reduce at a much lower temperature than would otherwise be possible (see page 36).

You may also want to serve your fruit coulis as a gel, spread out on a cold plate, with a cold dessert on top. If the gel is well executed and melts as soon as it hits the tongue, the effect can be dramatic. (See "Dessert Gelées," page 634.)

When fresh berries are out of season, coulis and purées can be prepared with frozen berries. There are also some excellent commercially available frozen purées, which are especially practical for out-of-season or tropical fruits. Quality varies; some of these purées have been cooked (which destroys much of their finesse) or contain too much sugar, so a bit of comparative testing is advisable before settling on a particular brand.

Raspberry Coulis

Force 2 cups (500 milliliters) raspberries through a strainer with a ladle or large wooden spoon. When using frozen raspberries, make sure they are completely thawed before straining. To eliminate the tiny seeds, strain the coulis a second time through a chinois. Do not try to strain the raspberries through a chinois initially, as too much force may damage the fragile mesh screen. Adjust the flavor and consistency of the coulis with sugar syrup or plain water (when it needs to be thinned without being made any sweeter) and lemon juice. This technique can be used for strawberries, blueberries, black currants, and other soft berries. If any of the berries are hard or underripe, they can be puréed first in a food processor.

Cranberry Coulis

The preparation of cranberry coulis is similar to that for other berries, except that the cranberries must be cooked to soften them before they are strained. Put the cranberries in a heavy-bottomed saucepan with enough water or sugar syrup to come halfway up the sides. Cover the pan and simmer them for 20 to 30 minutes, until they are soft. Keep an eye on the berries so they don't scald. If the liquid runs dry and they start to stick to the pan, add 3 tablespoons water. Strain the cooked cranberries through a chinois (or, if the mixture is too firm to work through a chinois, force it through a regular strainer first and then through the chinois) and adjust the flavor with sugar syrup or water. Cranberry coulis made with water alone is extremely acidic and almost always needs to be sweetened. When left on the sour side, it is excellent served with hot sweet desserts such as vanilla soufflé or bread pudding. This same technique can be used with fruits that need to be softened before they can be strained, such as underripe apricots and red currants.

Pear Coulis

Peel and core pears and rub the cut sides with half a lemon. Poach them in a sugar syrup (equal parts sugar and water by weight) until they are soft. Purée them in a food processor and strain. Sweeten the purée with the syrup used for poaching.

Strawberry Coulis

Work the strawberries—frozen are fine if thawed completely—through a strainer or fine-mesh drum sieve. **(A, B)** Adjust the flavor and consistency of the coulis with sugar syrup or water and lemon juice. To further clarify the coulis, if desired, use a Büchner funnel to suck the remaining coulis through the filter (see page 30). Store overnight in the refrigerator.

Kiwi Coulis

Kiwis should not be puréed in a food processor or blender before being strained; these cause the small black seeds to break open, giving the purée a peculiar bitter flavor. Crush peeled kiwis in a bowl with a large wooden spoon, then force them through a strainer. To eliminate the seeds (although they can be attractive), strain the mixture a second time through a chinois.

BLOOD ORANGE CONCENTRATE

Blood oranges not only have their own distinct flavor, but they often taste more concentrated than the more familiar orange orange juice. This concentration method takes that aspect and exaggerates it still further. Use this method to concentrate juices to various degrees, depending on your needs.

YIELD: ½ CUP (125 MILLILITERS)

blood orange juice, strained through a chinois	2 cups	500 milliliters

1. Put the juice in a 2-quart (2-liter) Erlenmeyer flask (the flask is intentionally large to increase the surface area of the juice and speed its evaporation) with a sidearm.

(continued)

CONCENTRATING COULIS AND FRUIT JUICES IN A VACUUM

To concentrate the flavor of a fresh fruit coulis, avoid the obvious reflex to boil it down to concentrate it. This will only result in a cooked, jam-like flavor and aroma. Likewise, reducing fruit juices in the kitchen takes away from their natural flavor and makes them taste cooked. Think of the difference between fresh juice and the same juice out of a bottle. A better approach is to evaporate the coulis or juice with a vacuum pump. Aqueous liquids (those containing water) boil at different temperatures depending on the surrounding air pressure. At lower pressure, such as one created with a vacuum pump, such liquids boil at room temperature. Keep in mind that this is a somewhat time-consuming process—it may take 20 minutes to evaporate a cup of liquid—but if you're using fruit juices in small amounts to make fruit juice "consommé," the technique is well worth the effort. This method is also excellent for reducing the alcohol content of certain wines, making them more adaptable for use in gelées.

When evaporating under vacuum, use an Erlenmeyer flask with a sidearm (see page 28) and make sure the flask is larger than you need so the coulis or juice only comes about an inch up the sides. This increases the surface area and makes evaporation go more quickly. You should also use a trap, another container to which you attach the hose coming from the flask and another hose that leads to the pump. The trap keeps liquid from being accidently sucked into the pump.

Transfer 2 cups (500 milliliters) fresh fruit coulis to a 2-quart (2 liter) Erlenmeyer flask. Insert a tight-fitting cork in the top of the flask. Hook one end of a piece of rubber tubing to the sidearm and the other end to the trap, a flask with a two-holed stopper in the top with glass tubing coming through each hole, as shown in the photograph. Attach the other end of the tubing to one of the glass tubes coming out of the cork of the second flask. Attach another length of rubber tubing to the other glass tube sticking out of the two-holed stopper. Place the trap—the flask with the two tubes sticking out the top—in a bowl of ice water.

Run the vacuum pump. You should immediately see the coulis or juice come to a boil. As it continues to boil, it will become colder and the boiling will stop. Apply a small amount of heat under the Erlenmeyer flask, just enough to get the coulis to boil again, and continue until the coulis is reduced by half. Use low heat, at least from time to time, to compensate for the cooling caused by evaporation under vacuum. If at any point the liquid stops boiling, heat it ever so slightly. In any case, adjust the temperature so the liquid maintains a boil.

Note: Erlenmeyer flasks have the disadvantage of being difficult to clean because it's hard to get a brush up against the inside wall. This may be a particular difficulty if the flask was used to concentrate citrus juices, which, as the pulp boils up, stick to the inside of the flask and oxidize. Citrus juices should be strained through a chinois to eliminate pulp before boiling in an Erlenmeyer flask.

2. Place a cork in the top of the flask and, using rubber tubing, hook a vacuum pump to the side-arm (see page 36). Turn on the vacuum. You'll need to place the flask over low heat because the vacuum and the concurrent evaporation cool the liquid. Simmer the liquid to the consistency and strength you need.

DESSERT GELÉES

It makes sense that any coulis can be converted to a gelée by having a little gelatin worked in. These gelées can be served on their own, or used to coat the bottom of a chilled plate upon which other desserts are served. Some tropical fruits, such as pineapple, papaya, or mango, contain protease enzymes that break down the amino acid structure of the gelatin. These coulis must be brought to a boil before they are used so that the enzyme is denatured and can no longer affect the gelatin.

Berry Gelée

Depending on the berries' texture, work them through a food mill with the finest insert or purée them in a food processor, and then work them through a chinois to obtain a coulis. Start with 2½ teaspoons (7 grams) powdered gelatin or 2 sheets gelatin, and 1 cup (250 milliliters) coulis. Bloom the gelatin (see Note below). To preserve the bright flavor of uncooked fruit, heat only a small amount of the coulis (about four times the volume of the bloomed gelatin). Add the gelatin and let it dissolve. Stir the gelatin mixture into the rest of the cold coulis and stir thoroughly so the gelatin doesn't clump up. Chill in the refrigerator for 30 minutes or more to set.

Note: To bloom gelatin, combine powdered gelatin with about three times its volume cold water in a small bowl, or combine sheet gelatin with water to cover. Soak for about 5 minutes. Add the powdered gelatin mixture to the coulis, or wring out the soaked sheet gelatin and then incorporate it into the coulis.

Wine Gels

Because the wine is not cooked when making a gelée, wine gels provide one of the few contexts in which the character of the wine is kept intact. One difficulty when making these gels is getting the amount of gelatin just right. If the gelée ends up too stiff or rubbery, it should be melted and more wine added. If it is too liquid, it should be melted and more gelatin added. This recipe may require some tweaking since the alcohol content of the wine is liable to change from year to year, throwing off the calculations. The most practical approach is to keep notes so that you can make future adjustments to the recipe. To serve, let set on chilled plates and then serve a chilled dessert, such as panna cotta, on top. The gelée can also be chopped or cut into cubes and used to garnish plates of other desserts.

SAUTERNES GELÉE

Sauternes is a magnificent sweet wine from the area around Bordeaux. Use the best you can afford or substitute something less expensive such as Montbazillac, Muscat de Baumes de Venise, or fine fino sherry. You can also use a dry wine and add sugar to it to taste.

The alcohol in wine gelées can cause a burning sensation on the tongue and in the nose. This effect is disagreeable when drinking the wine and even more so when the wine is used in a gelée. You can bring the wine to a simmer for a couple of minutes to cook off some of the alcohol (you want to leave some), but this can also affect the delicacy of the wine. A better method is to use vacuum to evaporate off some of the alcohol. The alcohol will boil off before the rest of the flavor components.

YIELD: 2½ CUPS (550 MILLILITERS)

sauternes, ½ bottle	1½ cups	375 ml
powdered gelatin or sheet gelatin	2 teaspoons or 2 leaves	10 grams or 10 grams
cold water if blooming powdered gelatin or bowl of cold water if blooming sheet gelatin	3 tablespoons or to cover	45 milliliters or to cover
warm water	½ cup	125 milliliters

1. If desired, put the Sauternes in a sidearm flask over the lowest possible heat and use a vacuum pump to evaporate most of the alcohol (see page 36). This should take about 20 minutes.

2. Bloom the gelatin in the cold water for about 5 minutes (see Note, page 634). If you're using powdered gelatin, add it, along with the water used for blooming, to the warm water and stir until dissolved. If using sheet gelatin, drain and wring out the sheets, then add them to the warm water. Stir the warm water–gelatin mixture into the room-temperature Sauternes until it dissolves. Transfer to the vessel of your choice, depending on how you plan to serve the gelée, such as molds, chilled plates, or other dishes, and allow to set in the refrigerator.

THE RELATIVE THICKENING POWER OF LIAISONS

HOW TO READ THE LIAISONS CHART

The thickening power of liaisons is determined with a viscometer (see page 36), which measures the resistance of a mixture to a rotating flat probe. The series of numbers running horizontally along the top of the following chart represents the viscosity—thickness—of various liquids, usually water or stock, thickened with starches, hydrocolloids, nuts, fats, or emulsifiers.

Zero represents no viscosity at all (apparently liquid helium gets close), while the number one represents the viscosity of water. The numbers increase exponentially and thus grow large very quickly. The chart is meant as a relative guide because it is best to get a sense of thickness based on those mixtures you already know—such as béchamel, hollandaise, mayonnaise, etc. For example, if you want to use sodium alginate as a thickener and for its emulsifying properties, the chart indicates that you will get the consistency of beurre blanc by using 1 percent (10 grams/liter) sodium alginate to water, broth, or other sauce.

The viscosity of emulsifiers is sometimes hard to measure. This is because emulsions are frequently non-Newtonian. Non-Newtonian liquids behave in myriad complex ways and may change viscosity based on agitation or other factors. Ketchup, which must be shaken to get it out of the bottle, is an example of a non-Newtonian liquid because it behaves in an unanticipated way. It is stiff when still and begins to flow when shaken. The chart does its best to give at least a general sense of the viscosity of emulsions such as mayonnaise.

The chart gives the relative viscosity of compounds, mixtures, and sauces, simplifying the task of which liaisons to choose and in what quantities. The thicknesses have been measured at 68° F (20°C) unless otherwise noted. Temperatures are given in Celsius. Because the viscosity of certain substances is a function of temperature, their viscosity readings may need to be reevaluated if they are heated or chilled. Many mixtures fail when the temperature is too low, or become thinner as they are heated.

A couple of entries require additional explanation. Heavy cream, for example, is given as a percent of reduction. If the chart says 0.66, it means that the cream has been reduced to 66 percent (two-thirds) its original volume. Butter may also present some confusion. The amounts are given as percentages in relation to water or other liquid. As an example, when a mixture is 70 percent butter and 30 percent liquid, as when a sauce is montée au beurre, it has a thickness similar to hot heavy cream. As the percentage of butter increases, the sauce thickens more. For example, a sauce montée au beurre with 80 percent butter is going to have a thickness around that of a beurre blanc.

Relative Viscosity

0–1	1–2	2–4	4–8	8–16	16–32	32–64	64–128	128–256
	1 = water			**8** = heavy cream	**18** = 0.25% konjac gum (at 90°C)	**40** = cream reduced to 88% (at 90°C)	**70** = brown stock reduced × 30 (at 80°C)	**140** = cream reduced to 66% (at 90°C)
						60 = 2% kappa carrageenan (at 90°C)	**75** = 0.25% lambda carrageenan	**150** = 0.5% locust bean gum (at 80°C)
						78 = 3% tapioca flour		**150** = 2% propylene glycol alginate (at 60°C)
						80 = cream reduced to 75% (at 90°C)		**160** = 3% Ultra Tex 3
						100 = 2% agar (at 40°C)		**185** = 5% N-Zorbit in oil (at 35°C)
						110 = vegetable oil		**190** = 1% carrageenan
						110 = brown stock reduced × 30 (at 60°C)		**200** = 0.25% konjac gum
						125 = 2% kappa carrageenan (at 40°C)		**220** = 0.5% lambda carrageenan
								240 = 1% sodium alginate
								250 = heavy cream (at 10°C)
								250 = 2.5% Ultra Sperse 3
								250 = 1% locust bean gum (at 90°C)

(continued)

Relative Viscosity (*continued*)

256–512	512–1024	1024–2048	2048–4096	4096–8192	8192–16384	16384–32768	32768–65532	65532–131640
270 = beurre blanc	**550** = 1% guar gum (at 60°C)	**1200** = 0.75% xanthan gum (at 90°C)	**2125** = 1% guar gum (at 40°C)	**4100** = 5% cornstarch	**16000** = 20% roux	**22000** = light mayonnaise		**92000** = 1.5% konjac gum
300 = 0.5% locust bean gum (at 35°C)	**625** = Tomato-Thickened Almond Sauce (page 511)	**1500** = cream reduced to 36% (at 90°C)	**2500** = 2% carrageenan	**5400** = 1% xanthan gum (at 60°C)				
340 = cream sauce–like	**625** = 0.5% xanthan gum (at 90°C)	**1575** = 1% guar gum (at 50°C)	**3000** = crème anglaise (18 yolks/liter)	**6400** = 1.5% xanthan gum				
340 = 5% roux	**750** = cream reduced to 50%		**4000** = 5% Ultra Sperse 3	**6600** = 5% cornstarch				
350 = 0.5% guar gum	**750** = 3% Ultra Tex 3			**7500** = 0.5% low-acyl gellan (at 10°C)				
350 = 1% xanthan gum								
350 = 2% propylene glycol alginate (at 50°C)								
370 = 2% propylene glycol alginate (at 40°C)								
425 = 8% N-Zorbit in oil (at 30°C)								
400 = 1% guar gum (at 90°C)								
500 = almond milk								
500 = 1% locust bean gum (at 55°C)								

GLOSSARY

ASPIC (GELÉE) In America, aspic is the chilled coating applied to various cold meats and fish. For example, one might say that a food is "coated with aspic." In France, an "aspic" refers to the whole dish. For example, one would consider a "fish aspic" an entire course at a dinner. While aspic's original purpose was to reinforce and provide delicate nuances to cold dishes, this vision was largely lost and aspics became merely decorative. A classic aspic is clarified gelatinous bouillon, chilled and allowed to set.

BARD To wrap foods, usually meat roasts or birds, with a thin sheet of fatback. This prevents the surface of the food from drying out, protects from direct heat, and bastes the food as the fat renders. Traditionally, a bard is used to cover the breasts on a roast chicken to slow down their cooking so it matches that of the thighs.

BARDING FAT A thin sheet of fatback used to wrap meats to be roasted or braised.

BEURRE MANIÉ A paste made of equal parts butter and flour, used to thicken sauces and braising liquids. It is not cooked, but is whisked into a sauce or braising at the very last minute.

BLANCH Briefly cooking in boiling water. Can be done for several purposes: to cook completely, to partially precook, or, when cooking vegetables, to preserve their color. Green vegetables should be tossed into boiling water; root vegetables must be started in cold water and then the heat gradually increased.

BLANQUETTE Traditionally, a French veal stew made by poaching veal in stock or water, binding the poaching liquid with roux, and finishing it with a liaison of egg yolks and cream. A classic of French country cooking. The term sometimes appears on contemporary menus to mean any stew of meat, fish, or vegetables that is presented in a white sauce containing cream.

BOUQUET GARNI A bundle of herbs, tied up with string, used for flavoring stocks and other liquids. A classic bouquet garni contains varying amounts of fresh parsley, thyme, and bay leaf. Some recipes include a stalk of celery or leek greens, but these are usually superfluous, especially if the liquid has been flavored with mirepoix. The contents of a bouquet garni can also be changed to give ethnic or regional nuances to a cooking liquid.

BRAISE Unlike poaching, which is to cook submerged in a large amount of liquid, braising is cooking in a small amount of liquid so the braising liquid is easily concentrated before serving. The adjectives *white* or *brown* describe whether the meat has been browned; *short* or *long* braises refer to the length of the cooking time. The finished braising liquid is often enhanced with herbs, butter, or cream. *See also* Casserole Braising; Cuillère, à la; Étuver; Poêler; Pot Roasting.

BRAISIÈRE A vessel for braising meats.

BROTH A flavorful liquid made by simmering meat or seafood in water. Broths and stocks are virtually the same thing. The word *stock* simply implies that it is being saved (stocked) for another preparation, such as a sauce or soup. *See also* Stock.

BROWN STOCK A stock made by first browning the ingredients (usually meat, meat bones, or poultry) on the stove or in the oven, before moistening them with water, more stock, or, on occasion, wine.

CASSEROLE BRAISING A method for cooking poultry and meats in a covered, close-fitting casserole; also known as *en cocotte*. Casserole-braising can be carried out with butter alone (poêlage) or with a small amount of liquid (étuver).

CHAUD-FROID Gelée (aspic) that is made opaque by adding ingredients such as cream, egg yolks, or béchamel. There are both brown and white chauds-froids.

CHIFFONADE A style of cutting leafy greens into fine shreds, a chiffonade is made by rolling up a leaf and slicing it crosswise.

CIVET A stew, usually containing red wine, that is finished and thickened at the end with blood. The best-known is civet de lapin (rabbit civet).

COLLOID A mixture in which fine particles of fats or insoluble solids are dispersed in liquid and remain suspended indefinitely or for at least a long time. There are two types: In one, fat particles are dispersed in liquid (such as a sauce finished with a little butter); in the other, water particles are dispersed in fat (hollandaise). Particles in liquids may also be gasses such as air, carbon dioxide, or nitrous oxide; these colloids are usually called

639

foams. Don't confuse colloids with solutions, which are stable and never separate. Milk is a colloid, Coca-Cola is a solution. *See also* Hydrocolloids.

COULIS In pre-classic French cooking, a coulis was a concentrated stock made by repeatedly moistening meats with stock and double stock. When well made, it has a natural demi-glace consistency and intense flavor. It was the predecessor of classic demi-glace, which contains roux. More recently, a coulis is a purée or stewed mixture, usually of tomatoes, other fruit, or vegetables that has been strained to eliminate seeds, peels, and other solids. *See also* Demi-Glace.

CUILLÈRE, À LA Meats braised for so long they can be served with a spoon are said to be cooked à la cuillère.

DASHI A broth used in classic Japanese cooking, made from a combination of seaweed, dried bonito, and at times other ingredients such as dried anchovies. *See* page 575.

DECONSTRUCTION The process of separating elements in a recipe so that each retains its own identity yet contributes to the whole, deconstruction provides an avenue for rethinking many dishes. Spherification (see page 182) is one exciting technique for deconstruction because it allows one element (such as truffles or saffron) to be held apart in the spheres until the moment the diner bites down on one.

DEGLAZE To add liquid to a sauté or roasting pan to dissolve the flavorful coagulated juices, which the French call *sucs*; an important stage in making jus, integral sauces, and stews.

DEGREASE To remove fat from a simmering stock by skimming, or to eliminate rendered fats from roasting or saute pans before deglazing.

DEMI-GLACE Reduced stock having the consistency of a light syrup, demi-glace today is simply a reduction of a brown stock by about fifteen times. In classic French cooking (circa 1900), demi-glace was prepared by reducing espagnole (see page 163), a full-bodied stock thickened with flour. Because the liquid was already partially thickened, less reduction was required and money was saved. The result, however, wasn't as tasty as well-made modern versions. Demi-glace can also be prepared by repeated moistenings of more meat or fish rather than reduction.

DENATURE When exposed to heat or aggressive ingredients (think how lemon clouds a broth), proteins denature by spooling apart and clumping or coagulating. Once denatured, proteins lose their structure and their effectiveness. Broken crème anglaise is an example.

DISPERSE The act of breaking apart in a liquid. Any number of implements such as a whisk, electric whisk, blender, or rotor stator homogenizer (see page 35) may be used for this depending on the ingredient's solubility.

EMULSION A stable mixture of two mutually insoluble liquids, such as oil and water, emulsions are stabilized by certain ingredients such as egg yolks, mustard, or any of a number of hydrocolloids or modernist emulsifiers. Beurre blanc, sauces montée au beurre, hollandaise, mayonnaise, and vinaigrette are a few examples.

EN COCOTTE *See* Casserole-Braising.

EN SAUCE Braising fish fillets and then converting the braising liquid into a sauce.

ESPAGNOLE Highly concentrated meat stock lightly bound with roux, espagnole was, until the mid-twentieth century, the cornerstone of French sauce making. Recipes vary over the centuries, but the use of roux, originally introduced as an alternative to the extravagant braises and sauces of pre-classic French cooking, is common to all of them. Escoffier's espagnole contains tomatoes (a later addition) and an enormous quantity of meat. Over time, espagnole has been so bastardized and cheapened that contemporary chefs rarely use it.

ESSENCE A concentrated stock or extract of a flavorful ingredient such as mushrooms, truffles, celery, or leeks; in nineteenth-century French cooking, essences were used as flavorings for classic sauces. Today they are sometimes used as light sauces in themselves, perhaps lightly bound by whisking in a small cube of butter before serving or emulsified with other ingredients for contemporary vinaigrettes.

ESTOUFFADE A stew in which the pieces of meat are first browned in fat before being cooked in liquid, usually red or white wine. Also, a concentrated brown stock made with both beef and veal. The term is rarely used in this sense in modern kitchens.

ÉTUVER In the strictest and simplest sense, to étuver is to cook in a covered container. More often, however, it means that a small amount of liquid has also been included. Sometimes spelled *étouffer*, "to smother," the word functions as both verb (*étuver* or *étouffer*) and noun (*étuvé* or *étouffée*). Étouffées are not to be confused with estouffade, a type of stew.

FLUID GEL A gel made with agar that has set and then been puréed until fluid, so that it behaves both like a liquid and a pliable solid. A fluid gel has a mouthfeel all its own and should liquefy as soon as it hits the mouth. Usually the mixture is quite viscous and is used much like a thick sauce. It is often applied in small smears designed to accompany various dishes.

FOAM/FROTH Foams and froths (a froth is an especially airy foam with big bubbles; think cappuccino) are like emulsions except that one of the components is a gas such as air, carbon dioxide, or nitrous oxide. Foams are made using any number of devices, including an immersion blender (for a rather coarse froth-like foam), a whipping siphon, or a rotor stator homogenizer (for a very fine foam; see page 452).

FRICASSÉE Traditionally, a fricassee is a specific dish, made with chicken or veal. The meat or poultry is first cut into pieces and gently sweated in butter without coloring, then gently simmered in a mixture of flour, butter, and stock. The cooking liquid is finished with a cream and egg yolk liaison, and the finished dish garnished with pearl onions and mushrooms. The term is used in this book in a wider, more generic sense, to distinguish a fricassee from a sauté.

FUMET Today, the word simply describes a fish stock, but in nineteenth-century cooking, the term referred to small amounts of concentrated stock made from game or poultry and used to finish mother sauces, such as espagnole or velouté.

GARNITURE In English, a decoration, such as a sprig of parsley, usually superfluous, placed on the side of a plate or platter. In French, the entire accompaniment to a preparation of meat or fish. Much of the vocabulary of classic French cuisine exists only to describe variations in garniture, the basic cooking method remaining the same.

GASTRIQUE A mix of sugar and vinegar used as a base for sweet-and-sour sauces or fruit sauces for duck and other meats. Most recipes suggest cooking sugar with vinegar until the sugar caramelizes. However, this drives off the flavor and the volatile acidity of the vinegar. A sounder approach is to cook the sugar until it caramelizes and then deglaze the pan with vinegar.

GEL A solution that has been set into a solid with a gelling agent. The gelling agent typically has long molecules that align or tangle with each other to cause the liquid to set. Some gelling agents are proteins (gelatin, egg whites,

egg yolks, agar), while others are starches (corn starch, flour, tapioca starch) with long polysaccharide chains that help the liquid to set, while still others are enzymes (rennet).

GELATINIZATION Once a gelling agent such as a hydocolloid has been hydrated, it must be gelatinized. This usually requires heating the gel so that any particles swell and completely disperse in the liquid, causing the gel to set.

GLAZE (GLACE DE VIANDE, GLACE DE POISSON) Stock or poaching liquid that has been reduced to the consistency of a syrup when hot and the texture of hard rubber when cold; an intensely flavored glaze used to reinforce the flavor and consistency of sauces, usually brown sauces. Especially useful for sauces made "à minute," because they are already reduced and will pull a sauce together in seconds.

GRAVY A jus that has been thickened with flour, by either adding flour to the roasting pan before deglazing (usually making a roux with the flour and the fat in the pan) or by making a roux in a saucepan and whisking in the jus.

HURE Meat, fish, or vegetables incased in gelée. A typical hure is served in slices. For a lighter effect, an hure can also be prepared in individual molds, which makes it possible to use a more fragile and hence more appealing gelée. Most cooks have never heard of an hure and would call one presented in individual molds an aspic.

HYDRATION The initial moistening of such ingredients as hydrocolloids and gelatin. Many thickeners and emulsifiers, especially hydrocolloids, need to be hydrated before they can be used, or they will remain undissolved. Some ingredients must be hydrated in hot or boiling liquid, or at a specific temperature (in which it can be useful to hydrate sous vide); others can be hydrated in liquid at any temperature.

HYDROCOLLOID An ingredient used to thicken, emulsify, or stabilize sauces and other liquids. Hydrocolloids, of which starches are a type, are a large category that includes alginates, gums, resin (gum arabic), and methylcellulose. *Hydrocolloid* also refers to the mixture itself, a colloid (see page 73) in which the particles are distributed in water.

INFUSE To soak or steep an ingredient in a liquid, to flavor a sauce or cooking liquid; tea is a common infusion.

INTEGRAL SAUCES Sauces derived directly from the juices released during the cooking of the main ingredients. The liquid from stews and braises, the jus or gravy from a roast, the reduced or bound poaching liquid for seafood or meat are all integral sauces or bases for integral sauces. *See also* Nonintegral Sauces and Simple Sauce.

IONS When an acid reacts with an alkali, it creates a salt. When a salt is dissolved in water, it splits into two ions. Table salt, sodium chloride, for example, separates into sodium ions (Na+) and chlorine ions (Cl-). Once free from the tight crystalline structure of solid salt, these electrically charged ions are able to enter into chemical reactions.

JUS The natural juices released by meat during roasting. In some instances, a jus remains in the bottom of the roasting or dripping pan and is simply degreased and served. In others, the juices are caramelized, the fat poured off, and the pan deglazed.

LARD To insert strips of fat into meats to keep them moist. The French recognize two methods: larding proper (*larder*), which consists of inserting a large larding needle (*lardoire*) into the interior of meats such as pot roasts and quickly removing it, leaving the fat embedded in the meat; and interlarding (*piquer aux lardons*), which consists of sewing tiny strips of fatback into the surface of meats with a second type of larding needle (*aiguille à piquer*). While some chefs and butchers consider larding archaic, there is no other way to make braised meat more moist.

LARDONS Strips of bacon, usually about an inch (2.5 centimeters) long and ¼ inch (0.6 centimeters) wide, that are gently sweated until barely crispy and used as a garniture for stews, braises, and sautés. If you want to avoid a strong smoky taste, blanch the lardons for 10 minutes in boiling water.

MAILLARD REACTION When cooking liquids are exposed to oxygen, they form complex compounds derived from peptides (shortened, broken-up protein strands), sugars, amino acids, and air. These compounds are formed when meats or fish are roasted, sautéed, or grilled.

MARINATE To surround meats and fish with aromatic liquids (marinades).

MATIGNON An old term used to designate a coarsely chopped mirepoix containing ham. This mixture is still useful for making flavor bases for sauces and braised dishes.

MINESTRA In Italian cooking, this is simply a broth, lightly garnished with vegetables or pasta. Serving stuffed pasta in broth is a light and elegant alternative to tossing the pasta with a thicker sauce. Pasta served in broth is called *en brodo*.

MIREPOIX A mixture of chopped onions, carrots, and celery, used as a flavor base for sauces, braises, and roasts. Mirepoix is chopped into various sizes. For a small batch of sauce, the vegetables should be cut quite fine—about ¼ inch (0.5 centimeter)—while mirepoix for a big pot of stock can be introduced with hardly any chopping at all. Older recipes include cubes of lean salt pork or ham.

MODERNIST CUISINE Sometimes called "molecular cuisine," modernist cuisine is characterized by the use of heretofore exotic ingredients such as gelling agents, stabilizers, and thickeners. Many modernist kitchens contain ingredients and equipment (often very expensive) that have allowed for the innovation of new processes such as spherification.

MODIFIED STARCH Many of the hydrocolloid thickeners in use in today's modernist kitchens are pre-treated starches (such as tapioca), which dissolve more readily than the original starch. Wondra brand is an example of flour that has been pre-hydrated, gelatinized, and toasted. Once made into a smooth slurry with water, its rather large particles are stirred directly into a sauce, gravy, or jus without lumping. This is a boon to those who don't want to bother using a roux or beurre manié. Modified starches are useful because they can be used without pre-gelatinization or hydration.

MONTER AU BEURRE To swirl butter into a sauce. This thickens the sauce slightly, unites disparate flavors, and adds an ineffable finesse. It also functions as a final liaison.

NAGE, À LA Method of poaching and presenting food, usually fish and seafood, in a court-bouillon surrounded by the aromatic vegetables used in the court-bouillon's preparation. It is popular in contemporary kitchens because it is attractive on the plate and contains no fat.

NAP (NAPPER) To coat. When a sauce coats a food, it is said to *napper*. The correct consistency can be verified by dipping a spoon in the sauce and gauging how long and how thickly the sauce clings to the spoon. Until forty years ago, all sauces were required to nap. The use of sauce spoons now allows the saucier to make thinner and lighter sauces. In modern kitchens, dishes that were originally served on plates with a sauce stiff enough to nap the food are now sometimes served in soup plates, allowing for a light, almost broth-like sauce.

NONINTEGRAL SAUCES Sauces that are not derived directly from the cooking juices of the main ingredient. Such sauces are based on stock or its derivatives such as demi-glace or meat glaze (stock-based sauces are designed to emulate integral sauces), or on completely unrelated ingredients, as in salsa, called simple sauces. *See also* Integral Sauces and Simple Sauce.

PEPTIDES Fragments of protein as small as two amino acid molecules attached to one another. Peptides, in combination with oxygen and natural sugars, are responsible for the Maillard reaction (see page 642).

PINCER When meats are browned in the oven as the first stage of a braise, they release a considerable amount of liquid. This liquid has little flavor unless it is boiled down until it caramelizes. This preliminary caramelization enhances the flavor of braised meats and certain stews but must be carried out carefully to avoid burning the juices. Nowadays, ingredients for stocks and braised dishes are usually browned separately or in stages, so there is less risk of over- or undercooking.

POACH To cook foods gently, completely covered in barely simmering liquid. Poaching differs from braising only in the amount of liquid used.

POÊLER The closest English translation of this very specific French culinary term is "pot roasting." In classic French recipes, it includes a large amount of butter. In modern culinary usage, *poêler* means simply to cook in a frying pan.

POT AU FEU A French country dish of poached beef. Traditionally, it is served in two courses: the first, a bowl of broth; the second, a plate of the poached meat. In recent years, chefs and menu writers have used the term more liberally to mean an assortment of meat or fish served surrounded by an unbound broth or poaching liquid.

POT ROASTING This confusing term is used to describe a range of often conflicting techniques. In some cases it describes poêlage, an old-fashioned method by which meats are braised with a large amount of butter. Nowadays, however, the term is used to describe braising a relatively large piece of meat in a covered pot.

PURÉE Solid ingredients that have been worked with a blender, food processor, or mortar and pestle and strained with a drum sieve (when stiff) or a chinois (when liquid). Strained purées, especially of fruits or tomatoes, are sometimes called coulis.

REDUCE To simmer a stock or braising liquid in order to evaporate water and concentrate the liquid's flavor.

ROUX Equal parts flour and butter cooked to varying degrees; the most traditional liaison for sauces.

SABAYON A dessert sauce made by whisking egg yolks, dry white wine, and sugar over heat until the mixture becomes a foam. Sabayon is the French equivalent of Italian zabaglione. Also, the preliminary emulsion used as a base for hot emulsified egg yolk sauces, such as hollandaise, in which egg yolks are combined with a small amount of cold water and beaten over medium heat until the mixture becomes an airy foam.

SALMIS Usually applied to game and poultry, a salmis combines two cooking methods, roasting and braising. The bird is partially roasted, the meat is removed and a sauce made from the carcass, sometimes by compressing it in a duck press. Just before serving, the meat is quickly reheated in the sauce.

SAUTÉ To cook in a pan over high heat so the food's surface lightly browns and caramelizes. Sometimes the foods, especially vegetables, are tossed or quickly stirred during cooking (*sauter* in French means "to jump"). Much of the time, however, sautéing is a bit more systematic and may involve careful turning of meats and poultry and close regulation of temperature, such as when sautéing a steak or pieces of chicken. A small amount of oil or other fat is usually used to lubricate the pan and prevent sticking.

A sauté is also a kind of dish, of poultry, veal, or rabbit, in which the cut-up pieces are cooked in butter or another fat, uncovered, on top of the stove. Once cooked through, the meat is removed and kept warm, the fat discarded, and the pan deglazed for the sauce. *See also* Fricassée and Stir-Fry.

SEQUESTRANT A substance added to a hydrocolloid emulsifier or thickener to aid in hydration. While many emulsifiers and thickeners require calcium ions in order to work, if these ions are present (either in the hydrocolloid or the liquid) before hydration, the hydrocolloid may be more difficult to dissolve, requiring very hot liquid or a long time to do so. To modify this effect, a sequestrant—usually sodium citrate or sodium hex-ametaphosphate—is added to "tie up" the stray calcium ions and allow the compound to hydrate more easily. Once the compound is hydrated, if it needs calcium to act, the calcium can be added.

SIMMER To bring a liquid to a temperature just below a boil. The surface of a simmering liquid should just shake a little or, as the French say, "smile." Most recipes referring to boiled foods really mean simmered foods. Foods, except green vegetables, are rarely boiled.

SIMPLE SAUCE A sauce made of ingredients that are derived neither from stock nor from the food with which it is being served is called a "simple" sauce. Salsa, chutney, and pesto are examples of simple sauces.

SINGER To sprinkle browning meats or poultry parts with flour as they cook in fat, the idea being to thicken an eventual braising liquid as for a stew or pot roast. Sometimes, the flour is added to the fat left in the pan to make a roux before liquids such as stock are added. This remains a viable technique provided that just enough fat is left in the pan for cooking the flour.

SOFFRITO The Italian version of mirepoix, soffrito may also contain garlic, pancetta, and herbs such as parsley, sage, or rosemary. *See also* Mirepoix.

SOUS VIDE Literally "under vacuum," sous vide is a technique in which foods are placed in tightly sealed bags and cooked in a circulating water bath at a specific, relatively low temperature. Because the temperature of the water bath can be adjusted to match the eventual internal temperature of meats or fish, they will not overcook even after several hours. Sous vide cookery is also excellent for infusing ingredients in vinegars and oils and for stabilizing egg yolks to make sabayons and hollandaise.

SPHERIFICATION A method by which a small amount of liquid is encapsulated in a sphere (see page 182). Spherification is often used to "deconstruct" dishes into their individual elements.

STABILIZER An ingredient added to an emulsion to help the emulsion stay in place without breaking. While most true emulsifiers are surfactants, in which one half of the molecule is soluble in water and the other half in oil, a stabilizer works by thickening the emulsion in such

a way that lighter components cannot float to the top, which would break the sauce. As an example, the egg yolk in mayonnaise is a true emulsifier, but a mayonnaise may still break; xanthan gum can be used as a stabilizer to hold the emulsion in place.

STEW Meat, fish, or vegetables cut into pieces and cooked in a small amount of liquid. *See also* Braise.

STIR-FRY Virtually the same as sautéing, except that the ingredients are stirred instead of tossed. Many cooks assume that stir-frying must be done in a wok, but an iron skillet works just as well. *See also* Sauté.

STOCK A more or less gelatinous and aromatic liquid, prepared by poaching meat, poultry, fish, or bones in water or additional stock. Virtually the same as a broth or bouillon, except those terms imply that the liquid will be served as is. "Stock" implies eventual use in another preparation. *See also* Broth, Brown Stock, White Stock.

SWEAT To cook slowly in fat, often covered, without browning, so that ingredients such as mirepoix release their juices. Ideally, the liquids released by the food should lightly caramelize on the bottom of the pan.

SYNERESIS The gradual leaking of liquid out of a gel, foam, purée, or sauce. This causes an unsightly rim of transparent liquid (mostly water) to encircle the sauce once on the plate. This effect is especially pronounced when a sauce gets its body from a large number of minute particles. Vegetable purée sauces and any sauce thickened with a purée are susceptible to syneresis. Many hydrocolloids and other thickeners and emulsifiers inhibit syneresis, allowing the particles in particle-thickened sauces to stay evenly distributed.

VACUUM The absence of air or other gas creates a vacuum. Vacuum pumps are useful in modernist cooking to create vacuums in which alcohol is boiled off from wine, or certain sauce bases or coulis are reduced without needing to be raised to too high a temperature. *See also* Sous Vide.

WHITE STOCK A stock made by moistening meat, seafood, or vegetables with water or additional stock without first browning the ingredients. Bones used for white stock must be blanched or the stock will come out gray and inedible. White stocks are used when a clear, very pale liquid is required. *See also* Brown Stock.

BIBLIOGRAPHY

Adrià, Ferran, and Juli Soler and Albert Adrià. *El Bulli 2003*. elBulli books, 2003

Adrià, Ferran, and Juli Soler and Albert Adrià. *El Bulli 2004*. elBulli books, 2004

Aduriz, Andoni Luis. *Mugaritz*. Phaidon, 2012

Ali-Bab. *Gastronomie Pratique*. Flammarion, 1928

Anderson, Burton. *The Wine Atlas of Italy*. Simon and Schuster, 1990

Andoh, Elizabeth. *An American Taste of Japan*. William Morrow, 1983

Andrews, Colman. *Catalan Cuisine*. Atheneum, 1988

Apicius. *L'Art Culinaire*. Translated by Jacques André. Société dEdition "Les Belles Lettres," 1987

Aron, Jean-Paul. *Le Mangeur du XIXe Siècle*. Robert Laffont, 1973

Artusi, Pellegrino. *The Art of Eating Well*. Translated by Kyle Phillips III. Random House, 1996

Asher, Gerald. *On Wine*. Random House, 1982

——. *Vineyard Tales*. Chronicle Books, 1996

Bayless, Rick. *Authentic Mexican*. William Morrow, 1987

——. *Mexican Kitchen*. Scribner, 1996

Beauvilliers, A. *L'Art du Cuisinier*: 2 volumes. Paris, 1814

Beef and Veal. Time-Life Books, 1979

Beeston, Fiona. *Mes Hommes du Vin*. Plon, 1989

Bertolli, Paul, with Alice Waters. *Chez Panisse Cooking*. Random House, 1988

Bhumichitr, Vetcharin. *The Taste of Thailand*. Pavillion Books Ltd., 1988

Bisson, Marie-Claude. *La Bonne Cuisine Française*. Solar, 1988

Blanc, George. *Ma Cuisine des Saisons*. Robert Laffont, 1984

Blumenthal, Heston. *The Fat Duck Cookbook*. Bloomsbury, 2007

Bocuse, Paul. *La Cuisine du Marché*. Flammarion, 1976

Boni, Ada. *Italian Regional Cooking*. Dutton, 1969

Bonnefons, Nicholas de. *Les Delices de la Campagne*. Paris, 1679

Bourin, Jeanne. *Les Recettes de Mathilde Brunel*. Flammarion, 1983

Boussel, Patrice. *Les Restaurants dans la Comédie Humaine*. Editions de la Tournelle, 1950

Bremzen, Anya Von, and John Welchman. *Terrific Pacific Cookbook*. Workman, 1995

Brennan, Jennifer. *The Original Thai Cookbook*. Putnam, 1981

——. *The Cuisines of Asia*. St. Martin's Press, 1984

——. *One-Dish Meals of Asia*. Times Books, 1985

Brillat-Savarin, Jean Anthèlme. *Physiologie du Goût*. Julliard, 1965

——. *The Philosopher in the Kitchen*. Translated by Anne Drayton. Penguin, 1970

Brown, James. *Fictional Meals and Their Function in the French Novel*. University of Toronto Press, 1984

Bugialli, Giuliano. *Classic Techniques of Italian Cooking*. Simon and Schuster, 1982

——. *Foods of Italy*. Stewart, Tabori and Chang, 1984

Carême, Antonin. *L'Art de La Cuisine Française au XIXe Siècle*. 5 volumes. Paris, 1843-1847

Casas, Penelope. *The Foods and Wines of Spain*. Knopf, 1988

Chang, Wonona W., Helen W. Irving, and Austin Kutscher. *An Encyclopedia of Chinese Food and Cooking*. Crown, 1970

Chiarello, Michael. *Flavored Oils*. Chronicle Books, 1995

Claiborne, Craig, and Virginia Lee. *The Chinese Cookbook*. Lippincott, 1972

——. and Pierre Franey. *Classic French Cooking*. Time-Life International, 1978

The Cooking of Provincial France. Time-Life Books, 1968

Cost, Bruce. *Bruce Cost's Asian Ingredients*. William Morrow, 1988

Courtine, Robert. *Balzac à Table*. Robert Laffont, 1976

——. *Feasts of a Militant Gastronome*. William Morrow, 1974

——. *Zola à Table*. Robert Laffont, 1978

——. *Mon Bouquet de Recettes*. Marabout, 1977

——. *The Hundred Glories of French Cooking*. Translated by Derek Coltman. Farrar, Straus and Giroux, 1973

——. and Céline Vence. Translated and adapted by Philip Hyman and Mary Hyman. *The Grand Masters of French Cuisine: Five Centuries of Great Cooking*. G.P. Putnam's Sons, 1978

La Cuisinier Gascon. Amsterdam, 1740

David, Elizabeth. *French Provincial Cooking*. Penguin, 1968

——. *An Omelette and a Glass of Wine*. Viking, 1985

——. *Italian Food*. Harper and Row, 1954

Davidson, Alan. *Fish and Fish Dishes of Laos*. Tuttle, 1975

De Croze, Austin. *Les Plats Régionaux de France*. Paris. Reprint, Daniel Morcrette, n.d.

De Groot, Roy Andries. *Revolutionizing French Cooking.* McGraw Hill, 1975

De la Reynière, Grimod. *L'Almanach des Gourmands 1803.* Paris, 1803

Del Conte, Anna. *Gastronomy of Italy.* Prentice Hall, 1987

Delfs, Robert A. *The Good Food of Szechwan.* Kodansha International, 1974

De Rabaudy, Nicolas. *Léonel, Cuisinier des Grands.* Presses de la Renaissance, 1978

Diat, Louis. *Sauces French and Famous.* Dover, 1951

Dictionnaire de Vins. Larousse, 1969

Le Dictionnaire portratif de cuisine. . . . Paris, 1767

Dion, Roger. *Histoire de la Vigne et du Vin en France.* Flammarion, 1977

Dried Beans and Grains. Time-Life Books, 1982

Dubois, Urbain. *Cuisine Artistique.* 2 volumes. Paris, 1988

Dumas, Alexandre. *Grand dictionnaire de cuisine.* Paris, 1873

Duong, Binh, and Marcia Kiesel. *Simple Art of Vietnamese Cooking.* Prentice Hall, 1991

Fisher, Mary Frances Kennedy. *The Art of Eating.* World Publishing, 1954

Foo, Susanna. *Chinese Cuisine.* Chapters Publishing Ltd. 1995

The Food of China. Periplus Editions, 1995

Franklin, Alfred. *La Vie Privée d'Autrefois: Modes, Moeurs, Usages des Parisiens.* Plon, 1889

Freson, Robert. *The Taste of France.* Stewart, Tabori and Chang, 1983

Gilbert, Philéas. *L'Alimentation et la Technique Culinaire à Travers les Siècles.* Société des Cuisiniers de Paris, 1928

Gouffé, Jules. *Le Livre des Soupes et des Potages.* Hachette, 1875

Gringoire, Th., and L. Saulnier. *Le Répertoire de la Cuisine.* Dupont et Malgat, 1914

Guérard, Michel. *Cuisine Minceur.* Translated by Narcisse Chamberlain. William Morrow, 1976

——. *La Cuisine Gourmande.* Robert Laffont, 1978

Guillot, André. *La Grande Cuisine Bourgeoise.* Flammarion, 1976

——. *La Vrai Cuisine Légère.* Flammarion, 1981

Guy, Christian. *Almanach Historique de la Gastronomie Française.* Hachette, 1981

Haeberlin, Paul et Jean-Pierre. *Les Recettes de L'Auberge de L'Ill.* Flammarion, 1981

Hahn, Emily. *The Cooking of China.* Time-Life International, 1969

Hanson, Anthony. *Burgundy.* Faber and Faber, 1982

Hazan, Marcella. *The Classic Italian Cookbook.* Random House, 1973

——. *More Classic Italian Cooking.* Random House, 1984

Humm, Daniel, and Will Guidara. *Eleven Madison Park.* Little, Brown and Company, 2011

Hyman, Philip, and Mary Hyman. "La Chapelle and Massialot: An 18th Century Feud." *Petits Propos Culinaires 2,* 1979

——. "Long Pepper: A Short History." *Petits Propos Culinaires 6,* 1980

——. "Vincent La Chapelle." *Petits Propos Culinaires 8,* 1981

I Secondi con il Pesce. Editoriale Del Drago, 1993

Jaffrey, Madhur. *Flavors of India.* Crown, 1961

——. *A Taste of India.* Athaneum, 1988

Jeffs, Julian. *Sherry.* Faber and Faber, 1961

Kasper, Lynne Rosetto. *The Splendid Table.* William Morrow, 1992

Kennedy, Diana. *The Cuisines of Mexico.* Harper and Row, 1972

——. *The Art of Mexican Cooking.* Bantam, 1989

King, Shirley. *Dining with Marcel Proust.* Thames and Hudson, 1979

La Chapelle, Vincent. *Le Cuisinier modern. . . .* The Hague, 1742

Lamb. Time-Life Books, 1981

La Varenne, François Pierre de. *Le Cuisinier francois. . . .* Paris, 1651

——. *Le Parfaict confiturier. . . .* Paris, 1667

Le Divellec, Jacques, and Celine Vence. *La Cuisine de la Mer.* Robert Laffont, 1982

Le Manuel des officier de bouche. . . . Paris, 1759

Le Ricette Regionali Italiane. Solares, 1967

Lichine, Alexis. *New Encyclopedia of Wines and Spirits.* Knopf, 1974

Livingstone, John, and Melvin Master. *The Wines of the Rhône.* Faber and Faber, 1978

L.S.R. *L'Art de bien traiter. . . .* Paris, 1674

Lune, Pierre de. *Le Cuisinier ou il est tratté de la veritable méthode de apprester toutes sortes de viands, gibbier, volatiles poisons tant de mer que d'eau douce. . . .* Paris, 1656

Maffioli, Giuseppe. *La Cucinia Veneziana.* Franco Muzzio, 1982

Manjon, Maite. *The Gastronomy of Spain and Portugal.* Prentice Hall, 1990

Marin, François. *Les Dons de Comus ou les dés de la table.* Paris, 1739

Marks, Copeland, and Aung Thein. *The Burmese Kitchen.* M. Evans and Company, 1987

——. *The Exotic Kitchens of Indonesia*. M. Evans and Company, 1989

Massialot, François. *Le Cuisinier roïal et bourgeois. . . .* Paris, 1691

May, Tony. *Italian Cuisine*. Italian Wine and Food Institute, 1990

Menon. *La Cuisinière bourgeoise*. Paris, 1756

——. *La Science du Maître d'Hôtel, Confiseur*. Paris, 1739

——. *La Science du Maître d'Hôtel, Confiseur*. Paris, 1749

——. *Les Soupers de la Cour. . . .* Paris, 1755

Miller, Gloria Bley. *The Thousand Recipe Chinese Cookbook*. Simon and Schuster, 1966

Millon, Marc and Kim. *Flavours of Korea*. André Deutsch, 1991

Minchelli, Jean and Paul. *Le Duc: Toute la Cuisine de la Mer*. Olivier Orban, 1986

Montagné, Prosper, and Alfred Gottschalk, eds. *Larousse Gastronomique*. Paris: Larousse, 1938

——. *Larousse Gastronomique*. Translated by Nina Froud, Patience Gray, Maud Mordoch, and Barbara Macrae Taylor. Crown, 1961

Myhrvold, Nathan and The Cooking Lab. *Modernist Cuisine*. 5 volumes. The Cooking Lab, 2011

Nignon, Eduard. *Eloges de la Cuisine Française*. Piazza, 1933

Nostradamus, Michel de. *Excellent et moult utile opuscule à touts necessaire. . . .* Lyons, 1555

Oliver, Raymond. *Gastronomy of France*. Translated by Claude Durrell. World Publishing, 1967

Olney, Richard. *The French Menu Cookbook*. William Collins Sons, 1975

——. *Simple French Food*. Atheneum, 1974

——. *Yquem*. Flammarion, 1985

——. *Ten Vineyard Lunches*. Interlink Books, 1988

——. *Romanée-Conti*. Flammarion, 1991

——. *Lulu's Provençal Table*. HarperCollins, 1994

Owen, Sri. *Indonesian Food and Cookery*. Prospect Books, 1976

Panjabi, Camellia. *The Great Curries of India*. Simon and Schuster, 1995

Parienté, Henriette, and Geneviève De Ternant. *La Fabuleuse Histoire de La Cuisine Française*. O.D.I.L., 1981

Le Pâtissier François. Lyons, 1695

Pennin-Rowsell, Edmund. *The Wines of Bordeaux*. Allen Lane and Penguin Books, 1979

Pepin, Jacques. *La Technique*. Simon and Schuster, 1976

——. *La Méthode*. Times Books, 1979

Peterson, James. *Splendid Soups*. Bantam, 1993

Pichon, Jérôme, ed. *Le Ménagier de Paris. . . .* 2 volumes. Paris, 1846

——, and Georges Vicaire, eds. *Le Viandier de Guillaume Tirel, dit Taillevent*. Paris, 1892. Reprint, Edgar Soete, n.d.

Planche, Jean, Jacques Sylvestre, and Jean-Paul Champenier. *Les "Nouvelles" Bases de la Cuisine*. Lanore, 1988

Platina, Barolomeo. *Platine en françoys tresutile et necessaire pour le corps humain qui tract de hôneste volupté. . . .* Translated by Didier Christol. Lyons, 1505

Poulain, René. *Vignes et Vins de France*. Flammarion, 1960

Poultry. Time-Life Books, 1979

Read, Jan. *The Wines of Spain*. Faber and Faber, 1982

Reboul, J. B. *La Cuisinière Provençale*. Tacussel, 1988

Revel, Jean-François. *Un Festin en Paroles*. Pauvert, 1979

Reynière, Grimod de. *Manuel des Amphitryons*. Paris, 1801

Richie, Donald. *A Taste of Japan*. Kodansha International, 1982

Riley, Gilian. *Painters and Food: Renaissance Recipes*. Pomegranate Artbooks, 1993

Robertson, George. *Port*. Faber and Faber, 1978

Robinson, Jancis. *Vines, Grapes, and Wines*. Knopf, 1986

Robuchon, Joël. *Ma Cuisine Pour Vous*. Robert Laffon, 1986

Roden, Claudia. "Early Arab Cooking and Cookery Manuscripts." *Petits Propos Culinaires 6*, 1980

Rojas-Lombardi, Felipe. *The Art of South American Cooking*. Harper Collins, 1991

Root, Waverley. *The Food of France*. Knopf, 1958

——. *Food*. Simon and Schuster, 1980

——. *The Food of Italy*. Random House, 1972

Rouff, Marcel. *La Vie et la Passion de Dodin-Bouffant, Gourmet*. Librairie Stock, 1925

Routier, Nicole. *The Foods of Vietnnam*. Stewart, Tabori and Chang, 1989

Roux, Michel. *Sauces*. Rizzoli, 1996

Sahni, Julie. *Classic Indian Cooking*. William Morrow, 1980

——. *Moghul Microwave: Cooking Indian Food the Modern Way*. William Morrow, 1990

——. *Classic Indian Vegetarian and Grain Cooking*. William Morrow, 1985

Sailland, Maurice Edmond (Curnonsky). *Cuisines et Vins de France*. Larousse, 1974

Saint-Ange, E. *La Cuisine de Madame Saint-Ange*. Editions Chaix, Grenoble

Salads. Time-Life Books, 1980

Sauces. Time-Life Books, 1983

Sanchez, Jose. *Molecular Gastronomy*. Wiley, 2016

Schmitz, Paungkram C., and Michael J. Worman. *Pracitcal Thai Cooking*. Kodansha International, 1985

Scott, Jeff, and Blake Beshore. *Notes from a Kitchen*. 2 volumes. Tatroux, 2011

Seed, Diane. *The Top One Hundred Pasta Sauces*. Ten Speed Press, 1987

Sichel, Peter. *The Wines of Germany*. Hastings House, 1956

Simeti, Mary Taylor. *Pomp and Sustenance*. Knopf, 1989

Simon, Andre L. *The History of Champagne*. Octopus Books, 1971

Sodsook, Victor. *True Thai: The Modern Art of Thai Cooking*. William Morrow, 1995

Sokolov, Raymond. *The Saucier's Apprentice*. Knopf, 1987

Spoerlian, Margeurite. *La Cuisinière de Haut-Rhin*. Mulhouse, 1842. Reprint, Daniel Morcrette, n.d.

Steinberg, Rafael. *The Cooking of Japan*. Time-Life Internationa. 1970

Tannahill, Reay. *Food in History*. Stein and Day, 1973

Tendret, Lucien. *La Table au Pays de Brillat-Savarin*. Librairie Dardel, 1934

This, Hervé. *Molecular Gastronomy*. Columbia, 2006

Tower, Jeremiah. *New American Classics*. Harper and Row, 1986

Trama, Michel. *La Cuisine en Liberté*. Olivier Orban, 1987

Tridi, Vanna. *Cucina Regionale*. Demetra, 1993

Troigros, Jean and Pierre. *Cuisiniers à Roanne*. Robert Laffont, 1977

Troisgros, Pierre and Michel. *Les Petits Plats des Troisgras*. Robert Laffont, 1985

Tropp, Barbara. *The Modern Art of Chinese Cooking*. William Morrow, 1982

——. *China Moon Cookbook*. Workman, 1992

Tsuji, Kaichi. Kaiseki: *Zen Tastes in Japanese Cooking*. Kodansha International, 1972

Tsuji, Shizuo. *Japanese Cooking: A Simple Art*. Kodansha International, 1980

Vence, Céline. *Les Recettes du Terroir*. Robert Laffont, 1984

Vergé, Roger. *Ma Cuisine de Soleil*. Robert Laffont, 1977

Viazzi, Alfredo. *Cucina e Nostalgia*. Random House, 1979

Vicaire, George. *Bibliographie Gastronomique*. Paris, 1890. Reprint, Slatkine Reprints, 1983

Walden, Hilaire. *French Provincial Cooking*. HP Books, 1995

Wheaton, Barbara Ketcham. *Savoring the Past*. University of Pennsylvania Press, 1983

——. *L'office et la bouche*. Translated by Béatrice Vierne. Calmann-Lévy, 1984

Willan, Anne. *French Regional Cooking*. William Morrow, 1981

Wilson, C. Anne. "The French Connection: Part I." *Petits Propos Culinaires 2*, 1979

——. "The French Connection: Part II." *Petits Propos Culinaires 4*, 1980

——. "The Saracen Connection: Part I." *Petits Propos Culinaires 7*, 1981

——. "The Saracen Connection: Part II." *Petits Propos Culinaires 8*, 1981

Wolfert, Paula. *Couscous and Other Good Foods from Morocco*. Harper and Row, 1973

——. *Mediterranean Cooking*. Ecco Press, 1977

——. *The Cooking of South-West France*. Dial Press, 1983

——. *The World of Food*. Harper and Row, 1988

Young, Wandee, and Byron Ayanoglu. *The Young Thailand Cookbook*. Random House of Canada, 1995

Zaslavsky, Nancy. *A Cook's Tour of Mexico*. St. Martin's Press, 1999

INDEX

A

Absolute, 72
Acid, adding to heavy cream, 105
Acidity in brown sauce, 204
Adrià, Ferran, 18, 73
Agar, 74, 129, 235, 360, 390, 520
Aiguille à piquer, 31, 267
Aïoli sauce, 417, 418–419
à la cuillère, 259
à la ficelle, 256
à la nage, 54, 95
Albuféra sauce, 156–157
Albumin, 451
Algérienne garniture, 263
Alginates, 75, 451, 452
Allemande sauce, 16, 131, 140, 142, 143, 154–156, 217, 257
Allspice, 61
Almond(s), 59, 530–531
    bitter, 530, 621
    in crème anglaise, 621
    in curry sauces, 530
    -garlic purée, 530–531
    gold-plated chicken with ginger, saffron, and, 6–8
    in Indian curry, 605
    peeling, 527
    puréed, 12
    tomato-thickened, sauce, 511
Almond butter, 6, 59, 442
Almond extract, 59
Almond milk, 9, 59, 135
Alsacienne garniture, 263
Aluminum cookware, 22, 26
Amaretto in crème anglaise, 620
Américaine sauce, 334–338, 340, 344, 345, 351, 352
Ancho chile oil, 470–471
Anchoïade, 535, 537–539
Anchois sauce, 221
Ancho chiles, 61
Anchovy(ies), 70
    anchoïade, 537
    anchois sauce, 221
    butter, 442
    chicken with, olives, capers, orange juice and, 14–15
    and crustacean sauce for fish, 401
    in 18th century cooking, 14
    in pasta, 550
    in seafood sauces, 558
    in 17th century cooking, 11
    in vinaigrette, 481
Andalouse garniture, 263
Andalouse sauce, 419

Anguille au vert, 316
Anise seeds, 62–63
Anisette in crème anglaise, 620
Apicius, Marcus Gavius, 3
Apple-horseradish mayonnaise, 421
Aquavit in crustacean sauces, 354
Archestrate, 2
Armagnac, 66
    in braised fish sauces, 306
    in brown sauce, 205
    in crème anglaise, 620
    in crustacean sauces, 351, 354
Aromatic vegetables, 51, 260, 261, 352, 472, 504
Arrowroot, 104, 106, 109, 165
Art de bien traiter, L' (L.S.R.), 11
Artichokes in pasta sauces, 562, 563–564
Asafetida, 3, 42
Asian ingredients, 40–44, 572–615
Asparagus in pasta sauces, 562
Aspic, 359, 639
Assiettes creuses, 214
Aurore sauce, 148–149, 221, 229
Avocado oil, 46, 47, 467

B

Bacon, 60
Bain-maries, 17, 24, 33, 167–168
Ba jiao, 65
Baked garlic purée, 515
Baking dishes, 25
Balloon whisks, 33
Balsamic vinegar, 48, 602
Balzac, Honoré de, 2
Barbecue sauces, 195–196
Bard, 639
Barding fat, 639
Basil, 52, 53, 64
    in bouquet garni, 260
    in infused oils, 468
    in pasta with butter or olive oil, 550
    in 17th century cooking, 10
    in Southeast Asian sauces, 588
    in tomato concassée, 506
Basil oil, 469
Bass fillets
    braised, of wild striped, with cockles and Norman butter, 303–304
    steamed, with yogurt curry sauce, 313–314
Basting, purpose of, 244
Bavarian sauce, 344
Bavaroise sauce, 222
Bay leaves, 3, 51, 53
Beakers, 25, 28

Beans
    black
        in Chinese-style chile oil, 471
        fermented, 44, 599
    cranberry, 540
    fava, 540–541
    lima, 540
    white or flageolet purée, 543
Béarnaise sauce, 104, 389, 393–401, 414
    for crustaceans, 355
    making, 391–392
    with meat glaze, 400
    oil-based, 401
    with tomato, 399
Béchamel sauce, 14, 15, 16, 17, 131–139, 338, 463, 504, 519
Beef
    boeuf bourguignon, 273
    brown, stock, 89–90
    cold braised, 379–380
    daube, 262
    red wine, stew, 273–274
    steaks
        filets of, with Périgueux sauce, 201
        with green peppercorn sauce, 241
        porterhouse, with improvised red wine and mushroom sauce, 207–208
        teriyaki-glazed, 580–581
Bengali five-spice mixture, 608
Benriner cutter, 31
Bercy butter, 442–443
Bercy sauce, 221
Berrichonne garniture, 263
Berries. *See also specific berries*
    in crème anglaise, 620
    in gelée, 634
    in Roman cooking, 3
Beurre blanc, 70, 114, 504, 636
    for crustaceans, 355
    holding and saving, 436
    lemon, 437
    stabilizing, 436–437
    variations, 437
Beurre citron, 437
Beurre fondu, 437, 487, 504
Beurre maître d'hôtel, 442, 444
Beurre manié, 108, 639
Beurre nantais, 434–435
Beurre noir, 440–441
Beurre noisette, 44, 400, 438, 441, 460, 628
    chicken jus with, 246–247
    emulsion, 400
Bigarade sauce, 194–195

649

H

M

Macadamia nuts, 597
Macaroni, with baked tomato sauce, 570–571
Maccheroni con pomidori al forno, 570–571
Mace, 63
Macédoine garniture, 263
Mackerel, 93
Madeira, 58
    in Américaine sauce, 334, 336
    in Crustacean sauces, 351
Madeira sauce, 68, 192
Magnonaise, 16
Maillard reaction, 642
Maître d' butter, 444
Major Grey's chutney, 494
Makrut lime leaves/fruit, 43
    in Southeast Asian sauces, 587–588
Malaga, Moscovite sauce and, 199
Malmsey, 68
Maltaise sauce, 399–400
Mandolines, 31, 58, 622
Mango(es)
    with Crustaceans, 354
    in Indian curry, 606
Marc, 66–67
Marchand de vin butter, 444
Marinades, 63, 642
    for poivrade sauces, 196–197
    for stews and braises, 260
Marjoram, 54, 95
    in bouquet garni, 260
    freshly chopped, 262
    as garnish, 441
    in gelées, 371
    in hot emulsified sauces, 408
    in infused oils, 467, 468
    in infused vinegars, 474
    in vinaigrettes, 477
Marrow, 73
Massailot, 14
Matelotes
    á la canotière, 317
    Alsacienne, 316
    blanche sauce, 221
    Normande, 317
    red wine, 318–319
Matignon, 161, 642
Mayonnaise, 16, 463
    apple-horseradish, 421
    bottled, 411
    caper and herb, 421
    cilantro and hot pepper, 423
    combining poaching liquids with, 297
    contaminated, 412
    defined, 411
    emergency "homemade," 417

flavoring with vegetables, 231
fresh, 411
garlic, 418–419
green, 418
with hard-boiled egg yolks, 421–422
hazelnut, 423
lightening, 414–417
lobster coral, 428
modern description of, 16
morel, 423
mustard-flavored, 420
nage bound with, 427–428
preparing, 411, 413–414
repairing broken, 413
sabayon-based, 414, 416, 426
stabilized, 417
storing, 412
thinning with liquids, 424–425
tomato and sweet red pepper, 419
variations, oils in, 422–425
with whipped cream, 420
Mayonnaise-based sauces, 410–431
    classic, 417–422
    improvising, 429–430
    meat sauces, 429
    seafood, 425–428
    tips for restaurant chef, 431
Mayonnaise-finished sauces
    chantilly sauce, 420
    for crustaceans, 355
    gribiche sauce, 422
    hard-boiled egg yolks in, 421–422
    mustard-based, 420
    rémoulade sauce, 421
    suédoise sauce, 421
    tartar sauce, 422
Measuring cups/spoons, 28, 31
Meat(s)
    integral sauces for sautéed, 234–242
        chicken with fines herbes, 238–239
        pan-deglazed sauces
            light-textured, 235
            making, 237
            model for, 236
            thickened, 235
            unbound version, 235
        pork chops with onion purée–thickened sauce, 242
        poulet sauté à la marengo, 240
        steak with green peppercorn sauce, 241
    trimmings in improving flavor of brown sauce, 203
    using crustacean flavors with, 349–351
    yakitori, 582
Meat gelée
    clarification for, 364
    classic, 362–363

    natural, 360–364
    red wine, 368–369
Meat glaze, 97, 106
Meat jus, 99
Meat sauces
    mayonnaise-based, 429
    pasta, 567–570
Ménagère, 268–269
Ménagier de Paris, Le (Taillevent), 4
Menon, 14
Méres sauce, 16
Meringue, 452
Methylcellulose, 78, 387, 451
Meurette sauce, 189–192, 317, 525
Middle Ages, sauce making in, 4–8, 11, 283
Milk(s)
    coconut, 43–44, 135
    nut, 59–60
Milk frother, 31
Minestra, 547, 567, 642
Mint, 54
    chicken with verjuice, saffron, medieval spices, and, 283–284
    and cilantro yogurt sauce, 466
    in crème anglaise, 621
    in herb-scented cream, 464
    Indian, pesto, 537
    in Middle Ages, 6
    in pasta with butter or olive oil, 550
    sauce, for lamb, 486–487
    in 17th century cooking, 10
    in Southeast Asian sauces, 588
    in vinaigrettes, 480
Mint chutney, 499
Mirabelle (plum brandy), 66, 620
Mirepoix, 63, 99, 508, 567, 574, 642
Mirin, 41, 351, 577, 578
Miroton, 82
Miso, 40, 41, 577, 584
    grilled swordfish with clams and broth-like, sauce, 579–580
The Modern Art of Chinese Cooking (Tropp), 603
Modernist cuisine, 1, 642
Modified starch, 642
Moghul garam masala, 607
Moistening liquids
    in improvising crustacean sauces, 351–352
    for stews and braises, 260
Molds, coating with gelées, 376
Mole, chicken, 281–282
Mollusks, 357
Monkfish, bourride sètois made with, 427
Monter au beurre, 114–115, 434, 642
Montpellier butter, 442, 444, 447, 483
Moong dal, in Indian vegetarian stews, 609

658

Turmeric, 64
    in Indian curry, 606
Turnips, puréed, 526
Twentieth century, sauce making in,
    16–18
Twenty-first century, sauce making in,
    18–19
Twoenjang, 40, 42, 586

U

Ubbelhode viscometers, 37
Ultra-Sperse 3, 79, 110, 129, 158, 163, 216,
    231, 257, 298, 463, 510
Ultra-Tex 3 or 8, 79, 110, 129, 136

V

Vacuum, 644
    concentrating coulis and fruit juices
        in a, 633
Vacuum aspirator, 36
Vacuum chambers, foams made in, 452
Vacuum filtration, 30
Vacuum pump, 30, 36
Vacuum sealer, 35
Varenne, Le, 12
Vatapá fish stew, 317, 532
Veal
    brown sauce, 92
    estragon sauce for, 175
    long brown-braised, shoulder clod,
        266–269
    Orloff, 520
    stock, 17
    white sauce, 91–92
Vegetable oils, 47
Vegetables. *See also specific vegetables*
    aromatic, 51, 260, 261, 504
        in crustacean sauces, 352
        in infused oils, 472
    chutneys, 498–499
    essences, 101
    in fish sauces, 231
    herb, 499
    -infused oils, 472–473
    lamb curry with garam masala and
        mixed, 614–615
    mirepoix, 508
    pasta sauces, 562–566
        fettuccine with peas, 565–566
        orecchiette with cooked green
            leafy vegetables, 564–565
        spaghetti with artichokes, garlic,
            and parsley, 563–564
    root, 526–527
    yakitori, 582
Vegetable stock, 95–96
Velouté sauce, 14, 16, 17, 131, 140–144,
    504

derivatives, 142–143, 148–153, 221
    modernist, 142, 143
Verbena, in crème anglaise, 621
Verdelho, 68
Verjuice, 4, 11, 47, 483
    chicken with, saffron, medieval
        spices, and mint, 283–284
Vermont cheddar, 137
Véron, 15
Versawhip, 79
Verte sauce, 418
Viandier, Le (Taillevent), 4, 5, 6, 11, 126,
    127–128, 162
Vietnamese sauces. *See* Thai and
    Vietnamese sauces
Vietnamese spicy fish sauce, 589
Villageoise sauce, 155–156
Vinaigrettes, 476–490
    -and court-bouillon–based chive
        sauce, 230
    basil, for roast lamb, 489–490
    Chinese ginger- and garlic-flavored,
        602
    cold, 481
    creamy, for salads, 480
    -finished sauces for crustaceans, 355
    finish integral sauces as, 489–490
    flavoring stabilized with essential
        oils, 483
    for green salads, 477–478
    honey-mustard, 480–481
    hot, 486–487
    hot hazelnut and parsley, 490
    hot tomato, 487–488
    neroli, petitgrain, and orange
        blossom, 482–483
    stable, 479
    tomato-based, 229
    warm sweet red pepper and garlic,
        488–489
Vin blanc sauce, 221–222, 404
Vinegar(s), 47–48
    balsamic, 48, 602
    citrus, 475
    fruit, 474
    infused, 48, 474–476
    in the Middle Ages, 4
    in Roman cooking, 3
    in 17th century cooking, 11
    in Southeast Asian sauces, 588
    in stir-fries, 602
    in tomato sauce, 510
    wine, 47–48
Viscometer, 36–37, 636
Viscosity, 636, 637–638
Vitamix, 34
Vodka, 67
    in diluting natural oils, 451

W

Walnut(s), 534–535
    in cream-based pasta sauces, 554
    and Parmesan cheese sauce for pasta,
        534–535
    peeling, 527
    tortellini or tagliatelle with, sauce,
        555–556
    wild mushroom and, oil salad, 481
Watercress, 522–523
    and mushroom sauce for fish, 544
    purée, 522–523
Waterzooï, 317
Wheaton, Barbara, 10
Whipped butters, 433, 448–449
Whipped cream
    adding to hot emulsified egg yolk
        sauce, 403
    hollandaise sauce with, 400
    mayonnaise with, 420
    and truffle-finished game sauce,
        198–199
Whipping siphon, 32–33, 452, 464
Whisk(s), 33, 452
Whiskey, 67
    in crème anglaise, 620
    in crustacean sauces, 351, 354
    deglazing pan with, 309
White beans, 542–543
White chocolate, 626
White cumin, 62
White peppercorns, 64
White sauces, 130–159
    allemande, 140, 142, 143, 154–156
    béchamel, 132–139
    butter-enriched, 144–157
    classic French, 132
    improvising, 157–159
    suprême, 140, 142, 156–157
    velouté, 140–144, 148–153
White stock, 82, 644
    chicken, 88
    veal, 91–92
White wine, 64, 70
    in fish sauces, 295
    fish stews, 321–322
    foams, 455
    and gherkin sauce, 179
    –mustard sauce, 178–179
    pork shoulder chops with prunes
        and, 271–273
    sauce with three liaisons, 113
Wide bowls, 37
Wine, 67–70. *See also* Red wine; Rhine
    wine; White wine
    in fish sauces, 295
    in flavoring gelées, 367–371